A Reading/Language Arts Program

Macmillan/McGraw-Hill

Contributors

Time Magazine, Accelerated Reader

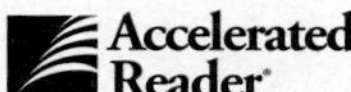

Students with print disabilities may be eligible to obtain an accessible, audio version of the pupil edition of this textbook. Please call Recording for the Blind & Dyslexic at 1-800-221-4792 for complete information.

A

The McGraw-Hill Companies

Macmillan/McGraw-Hill

Published by Macmillan/McGraw-Hill, of McGraw-Hill Education, a division of The McGraw-Hill Companies, Inc., Two Penn Plaza, New York, New York 10121.

Printed in the United States of America

1 2 3 4 5 6 7 8 9 073/055 13 12 11 10 09

A Reading/Language Arts Program

Program Authors

Dr. Diane August
Senior Research Scientist, Center for Applied Linguistics
Washington, D.C.

Dr. Donald R. Bear
University of Nevada, Reno
Reno, Nevada

Dr. Janice A. Dole
University of Utah
Salt Lake City, Utah

Dr. Jana Echevarria
California State University, Long Beach
Long Beach, California

Dr. Douglas Fisher
San Diego State University
San Diego, California

Dr. David J. Francis
University of Houston
Houston, Texas

Dr. Vicki L. Gibson
Educational Consultant, Gibson Hasbrouck and Associates, Massachusetts

Dr. Jan E. Hasbrouck
Educational Consultant – J.H. Consulting
Los Angeles, California

Dr. Scott G. Paris
Center for Research and Practice, National Institute of Education
Singapore

Dr. Timothy Shanahan
University of Illinois at Chicago
Chicago, Illinois

Dr. Josefina V. Tinajero
University of Texas at El Paso
El Paso, Texas

Mc Graw Hill Macmillan/McGraw-Hill

Program Authors

Dr. Diane August

Center for Applied Linguistics, Washington, D.C.

- Principal Investigator, Developing Literacy in Second-Language Learners: Report of the National Literacy Panel on Language-Minority Children and Youth
- Member of the New Standards Literacy Project, Grades 4–5

Dr. Donald R. Bear

University of Nevada, Reno

- Author of *Words Their Way* and *Words Their Way with English Learners*
- Director, E.L. Cord Foundation Center for Learning and Literacy

Dr. Janice A. Dole

University of Utah

- Investigator, IES Study on Reading Interventions
- National Academy of Sciences, Committee Member: Teacher Preparation Programs, 2005–2007

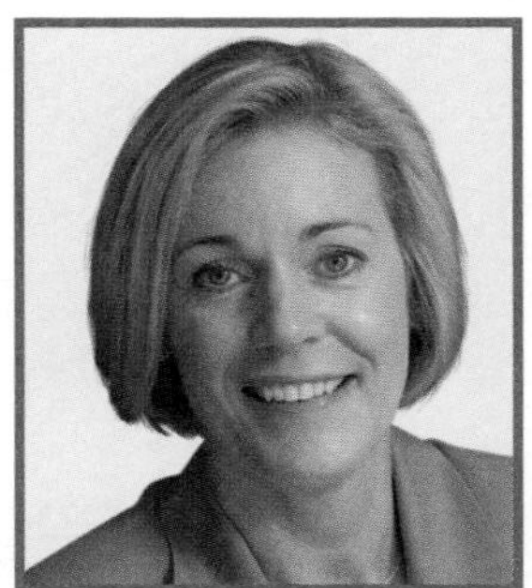

Dr. Jana Echevarria

California State University, Long Beach

- Author of *Making Content Comprehensible for English Learners: The SIOP Model*
- Principal Researcher, Center for Research on the Educational Achievement and Teaching of English Language Learners

Dr. Douglas Fisher

San Diego State University

- Co-Director, Center for the Advancement of Reading, California State University
- Author of *Language Arts Workshop: Purposeful Reading and Writing Instruction* and *Reading for Information in Elementary School*

Dr. David J. Francis

University of Houston

- Director of the Center for Research on Educational Achievement and Teaching of English Language Learners (CREATE)
- Director, Texas Institute for Measurement, Evaluation, and Statistics

Dr. Vicki Gibson

Educational Consultant Gibson Hasbrouck and Associates, Massachusetts

- Author of *Differentiated Instruction: Grouping for Success*

Dr. Jan E. Hasbrouck

Educational Consultant
JH Consulting, Los Angeles

- Developed Oral Reading Fluency Norms for Grades 1–8
- Author of *The Reading Coach: A How-to Manual for Success*

Dr. Scott G. Paris

Center for Research and Practice, National Institute of Education, Singapore

- Principal Investigator, CIERA, 1997–2004

Dr. Timothy Shanahan

University of Illinois at Chicago

- Member, National Reading Panel
- President, International Reading Association, 2006
- Chair, National Literacy Panel and National Early Literacy Panel

Dr. Josefina V. Tinajero

University of Texas at El Paso

- Past President, NABE and TABE
- Co-Editor of *Teaching All the Children: Strategies for Developing Literacy in an Urban Setting* and *Literacy Assessment of Second Language Learners*

Consulting and Contributing Authors

Dr. Adria F. Klein
Professor Emeritus, California State University, San Bernardino

- President, California Reading Association, 1995
- Co-Author of *Interactive Writing* and *Interactive Editing*

Dolores B. Malcolm
St. Louis Public Schools
St. Louis, MO

- Past President, International Reading Association
- Member, IRA Urban Diversity Initiatives Commission
- Member, RIF Advisory Board

Dr. Doris Walker-Dalhouse
Minnesota State University, Moorhead

- Author of articles on multicultural literature and reading instruction in urban schools
- Co-Chair of the Ethnicity, Race, and Multilingualism Committee, NRC

Dinah Zike
Educational Consultant

- Dinah-Might Activities, Inc. San Antonio, TX

Program Consultants

Kathy R. Bumgardner
Language Arts Instructional Specialist
Gaston County Schools, NC

Elizabeth Jimenez
CEO, GEMAS Consulting
Pomona, CA

Dr. Sharon F. O'Neal
Associate Professor
College of Education
Texas State University
San Marcos, TX

Program Reviewers

Mable Alfred
Reading/Language Arts Administrator
Chicago Public Schools, IL

Suzie Bean
Teacher, Kindergarten
Mary W. French Academy
Decatur, IL

Linda Burch
Teacher, Kindergarten
Public School 184
Brooklyn, NY

Robert J. Dandorph
Principal
John F. Kennedy Elementary School
North Bergen, NJ

Suzanne Delacruz
Principal, Washington Elementary
Evanston, IL

Carol Dockery
Teacher, Grade 3
Mulberry Elementary
Milford, OH

Karryl Ellis
Teacher, Grade 1
Durfee School, Decatur, IL

Christina Fong
Teacher, Grade 3
William Moore Elementary School
Las Vegas, NV

Lenore Furman
Teacher, Kindergarten
Abington Avenue School
Newark, NJ

Sister Miriam Kaeser
Assistant Superintendent
Archdiocese of Cincinnati
Cincinnati, OH

LaVonne Lee
Principal, Rozet Elementary School
Gillette, WY

SuEllen Mackey
Teacher, Grade 5
Washington Elementary School
Decatur, IL

Jan Mayes
Curriculum Coordinator
Kent School District
Kent, WA

Bonnie Nelson
Teacher, Grade 1
Solano School, Phoenix, AZ

Cyndi Nichols
Teacher, Grade K/1
North Ridge Elementary School
Commack, NY

Sharron Norman
Curriculum Director
Lansing School District
Lansing, MI

Renee Ottinger
Literacy Leader, Grades K–5
Coronado Hills Elementary School
Denver, CO

Michael Pragman
Principal, Woodland Elementary School
Lee's Summit, MO

Carol Rose
Teacher, Grade 2
Churchill Elementary School
Muskegon, MI

Laura R. Schmidt-Watson
Director of Academic Services
Parma City School District, OH

Dianne L. Skoy
Literacy Coordinator, Grades K–5
Minneapolis Public Schools
Minneapolis, MN

Charles Staszewski
ESL Teacher, Grades 3–5
John H. William School, No. 5
Rochester, NY

Patricia Synan
New York City Department of Education

Stephanie Yearian
Teacher, Grade 2
W. J. Zahnow Elementary
Waterloo, IL

Unit 4 The Big Question

How is working together better than working alone?

Enduring Understanding and Essential Questions

In this unit, children will listen, read, and write about working together. As they progress through the unit, they will also develop and apply key comprehension skills that good readers use as they read.

Big Idea	Enduring Understanding	Essential Questions
Theme: Better Together	Jobs can be easier and done faster when we work with other people.	How is working together better than working alone?

Comprehension	Enduring Understanding	Essential Questions
Cause and Effect Week 1	Good readers know that cause-and-effect relationships make up the events in a story.	Retell the events in a story's beginning, middle, and end. What was the problem and how was it solved?
Use Illustrations Week 2	Good readers use the illustrations to help them describe the characters' traits, motivations, and feelings.	What do the illustrations tell you about the characters and how they think, feel, and act?
Sequence of Events Week 3 Week 4	Good readers describe the order of ideas or events in a selection.	How do signal words such as *first, then,* and *next* to help you, retell the events or ideas presented?
Fantasy and Reality Week 5	Good readers determine whether a story is true or a fantasy, and can explain why.	Is this story true, realistic, or a fantasy? How do you know?

Theme: Better Together

Planning the Unit

Using the Student Book

Wrapping Up the Unit

Additional Resources

Unit Opener

Main Selections

Unit Assessment

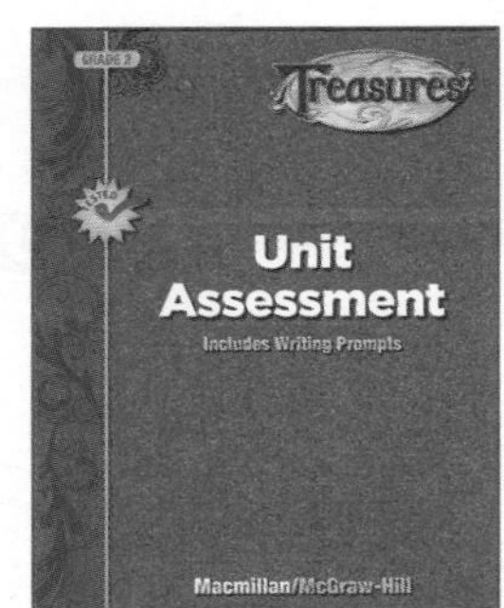

Theme: Better Together

Theme Opener

pp. 10/11–34/35

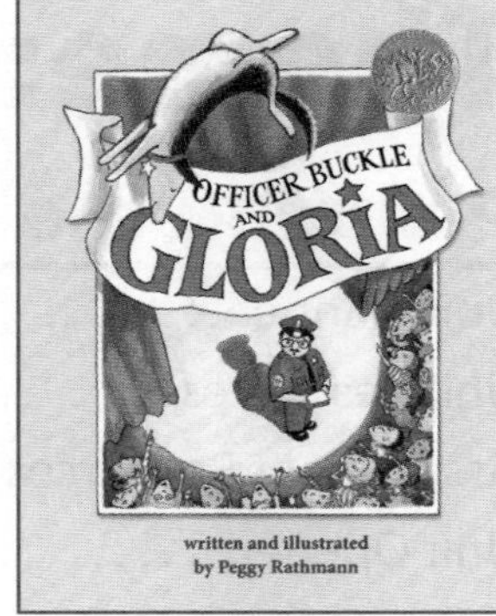

pp. 46/47–68/69

	WEEK 1	WEEK 2
ORAL LANGUAGE		
• Oral Vocabulary	**Theme** Getting the Job Done	**Theme** Special Teams
• Phonemic Awareness	**Phonemic Awareness** Listen for Diphthong *ou*, *ow*	**Phonemic Awareness** Listen for Diphthong *oi*, *oy*
WORD STUDY		
• Phonics	**Phonics** Diphthong *ou*, *ow*	**Phonics** Diphthong *oi*, *oy*
• Spelling	**Spelling** Words with Diphthong *ou*, *ow*	**Spelling** Words with Diphthong *oi*, *oy*
• Vocabulary	**Vocabulary Words** *attached, delicious, frantically, gasped, swung*	**Vocabulary Words** *accident, attention, buddy, enormous, obeys, tip*
READING		
• Comprehension	**Comprehension** **Strategy:** Monitor Comprehension/Reread **Skill:** Cause and Effect	**Comprehension** **Strategy:** Monitor Comprehension/Read Ahead **Skill:** Use Illustrations
• Fluency	**Fluency** Build Fluency: Word Automaticity Echo-Read	**Fluency** Build Fluency: Word Automaticity Echo-Read
• Leveled Readers	Approaching *Wasted Wishes* On Level *Three Wishes From a Fish* Beyond *Three Dog Wishes* ELL *Three Wishes*	Approaching *Road Safety* On Level *Road Safety* Beyond *Road Safety* ELL *Street Safety*
LANGUAGE ARTS		
• Grammar	**Grammar** Linking Verbs	**Grammar** Helping Verbs
• Writing	**Writing** Personal Narrative	**Writing** Expository: Persuasive Essay

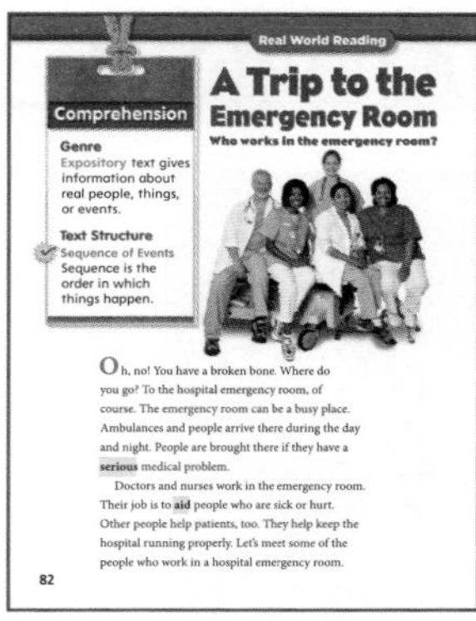

pp. 82/83–84/85

pp. 94/95–112/113

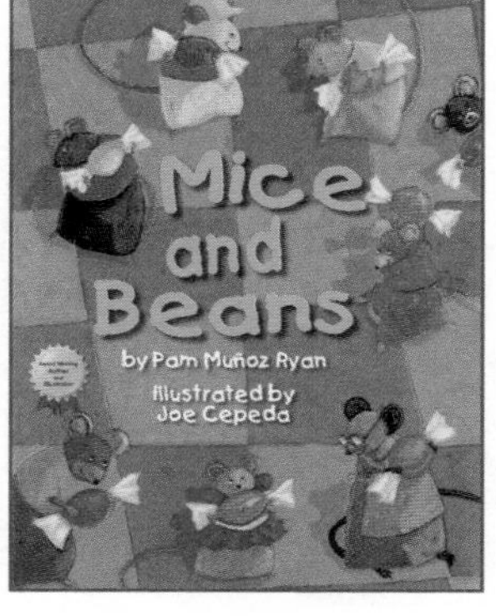

pp. 124/125–152/153

Review and Assess

WEEK 3

Theme
Worker Teams

Phonemic Awareness
Listen for Vowel Digraph *oo, ui, ew, ue, u, ou, oe*

Phonics
Vowel Digraph *oo, ui, ew, ue, u, ou, oe*

Spelling
Words with Vowel Digraph *oo, ui, ew, ue, oe*

Vocabulary Words
aid, heal, informs, personal, serious

Comprehension
Strategy: Analyze Text Structure
Skill: Sequence of Events

Fluency
Build Fluency: Word Automaticity
Echo-Read

Approaching
People at Work

On Level
People at Work

Beyond
People at Work

ELL
People Work

Grammar
Irregular Verbs

Writing
Expository: Nonfiction Article

WEEK 4

Theme
Community Teams

Phonemic Awareness
Listen for Vowel Digraph *oo, ou*

Phonics
Vowel Digraph *oo, ou*

Spelling
Words with Vowel Digraph *oo, ou*

Vocabulary Words
examines, hunger, mammal, normal, rescued, young

Comprehension
Strategy: Analyze Text Structure
Skill: Sequence of Events

Fluency
Build Fluency: Word Automaticity
Echo-Read

Approaching
Bald Eagle Alert

On Level
Bald Eagle Alert

Beyond
Bald Eagle Alert

ELL
Bald Eagles

Grammar
Irregular Verbs

Writing
Expository: Friendly Letter

WEEK 5

Theme
Surprising Teamwork

Phonemic Awareness
Listen for Vowel Digraph *au, aw, a*

Phonics
Vowel Digraph *au, aw, a*

Spelling
Words with Vowel Digraph *au, aw, a*

Vocabulary Words
assembled, devoured, fetch, menu, simmered

Comprehension
Strategy: Analyze Story Structure
Skill: Distinguish Between Fantasy and Reality

Fluency
Build Fluency: Word Automaticity
Echo-Read

Approaching
Saving Sofia

On Level
A Party and a Half

Beyond
A Lucky New Year

ELL
The Summer Party

Grammar
Contractions

Writing
Expository: Descriptive Flyer

WEEK 6

Show What You Know
Spiral Review
Cause and Effect; Sequence of Events; Fantasy and Reality; Character; Setting; Synonyms

Writing
Expository: Composition

Unit 4 Assessment, 167M–167N

Comprehension
Monitor Comprehension/ Reread and Read Ahead; Cause and Effect; Use Illustrations; Analyze Text and Structure; Sequence of Events; Fantasy/Reality

Phonemic Awareness/ Phonics
Diphthong *ou, ow, oi, oy*; Vowel Digraph *oo, ui, ew, ue, u, ou, oe, au, aw, a*

Text Features/Study Skills
Drop-Down Menu, Floor Plan (Diagram), Written Directions; Using the Internet

Grammar
Verbs (linking, helping, irregular), Contractions

Fluency Assessment

Diagnose and Prescribe
Interpret Assessment

Theme: Better Together

Literature

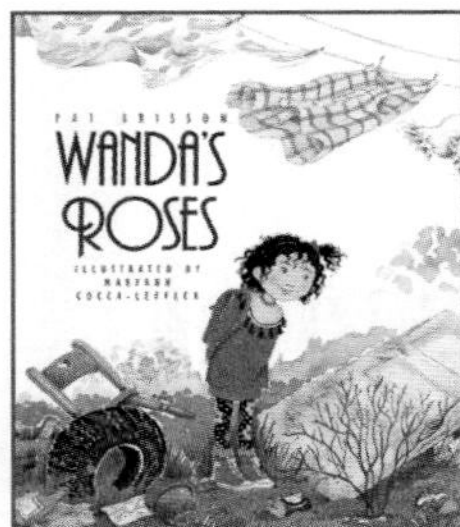
Literature Big Books (6)

Student Book (2)

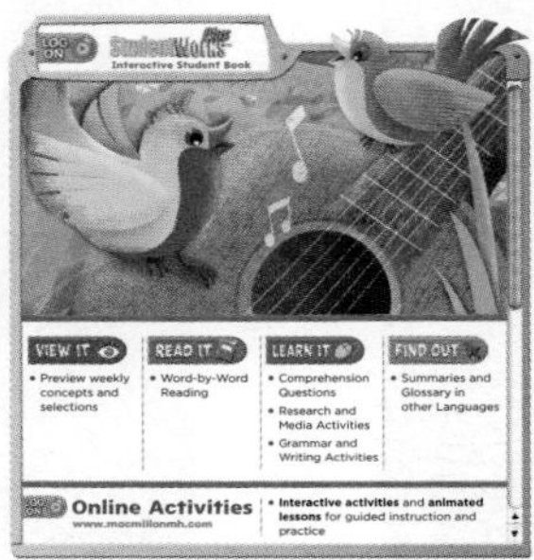
StudentWorks Plus
Online and CD-ROM

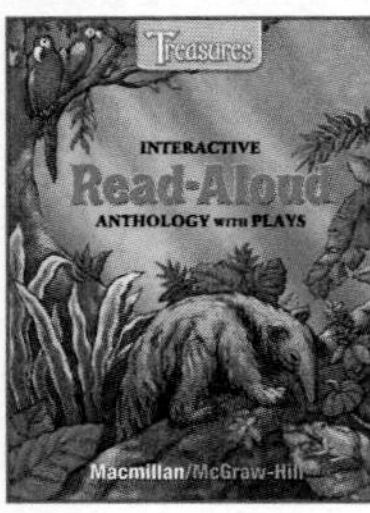
Read-Aloud Anthology
Includes Plays for Readers Theater

Decodable Reader Library (6)

Approaching Level

On Level

Beyond Level

ELL

Leveled Readers

Retelling Cards
(30 sets)

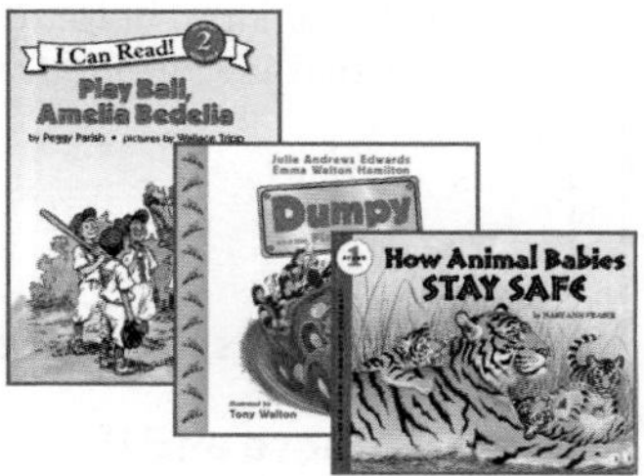
Leveled Classroom Library Books (18)

Oral Vocabulary Cards (30 sets)

Teaching Support

Teacher's Edition

Teacher's Resource Book

Vocabulary Cards

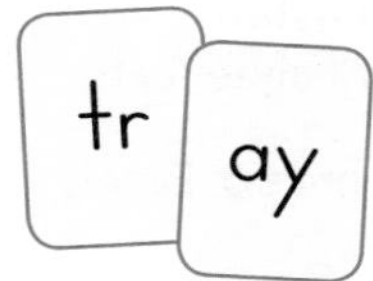

Word-Building Cards

High-Frequency Word Cards

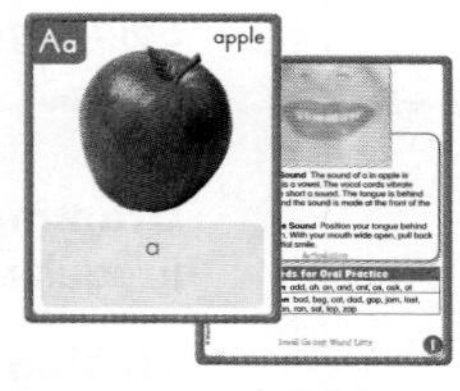
Sound-Spelling Cards

Photo Cards

Unit 4 Resources

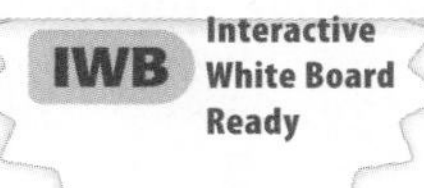

Transparencies
Online and CD-ROM

IWB Interactive White Board Ready

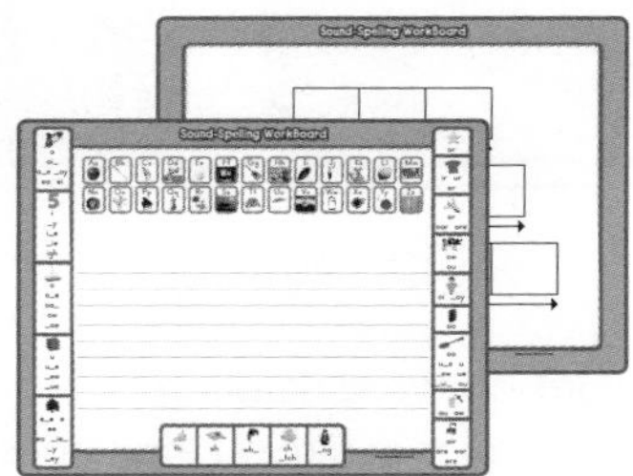

Sound-Spelling WorkBoards

Student Practice

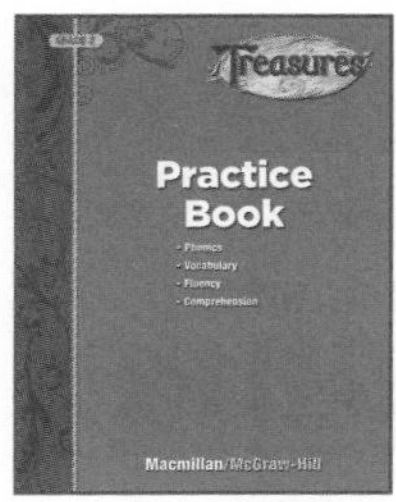

Practice Book

Additional Reproducibles: Approaching Beyond

Phonics/Spelling Practice Book

Grammar Practice Book

Home-School Connection

Handwriting
- Cursive

Dinah Zike's Foldables®

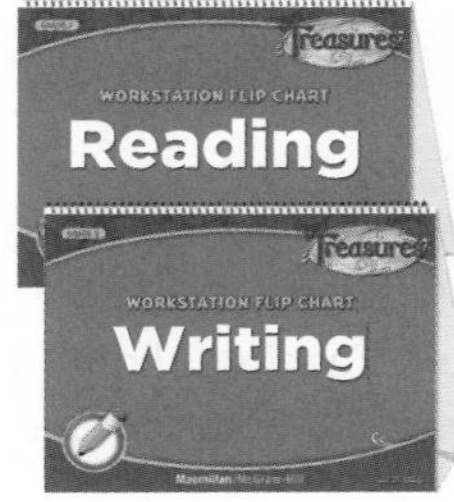

Literacy Workstation Flip Charts

Class Management Tools

How-to Guide

Rotation Chart

Green	
Jack	Eliza
Vincent	Dean
Isabella	Maria

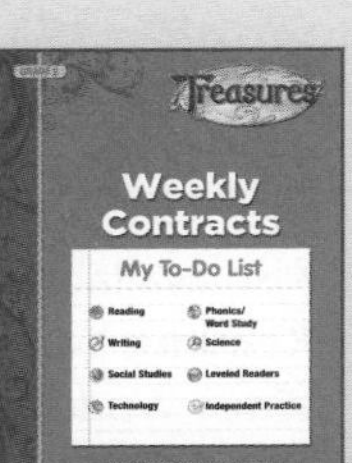

Weekly Contracts

Differentiated Resources

English Language Learners

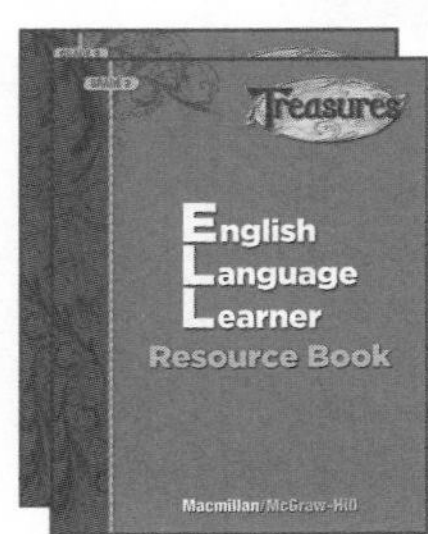

ELL Resource and Practice Books

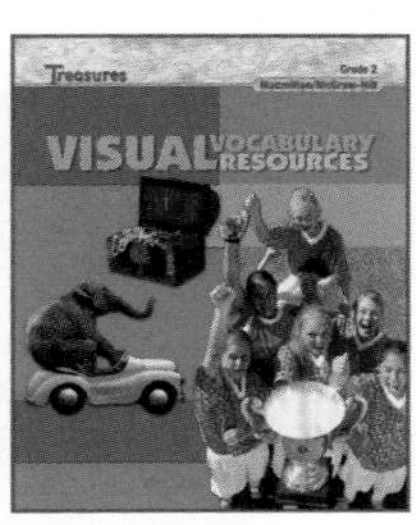

Visual Vocabulary Resources

Response to Intervention

Tier 2 Tier 3

- Phonemic Awareness
- Phonics
- Vocabulary
- Comprehension
- Fluency

Assessment

Time For Kids
- TFK Teacher's Manual
- Apply Answering Questions Strategies

Diagnostic Assessment

Weekly Assessment

Unit Assessment

Benchmark Assessment

Digital Solutions

Go to  http://connected.mcgraw-hill.com
Online Center

Prepare/Plan

ONLINE www.macmillanmh.com

Teacher's Edition Online

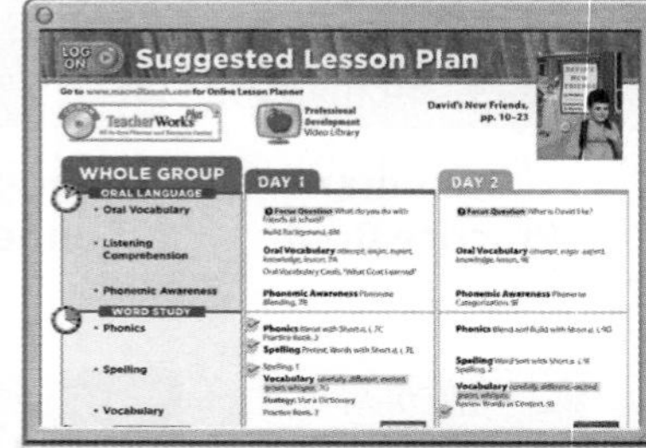

TeacherWorks Plus
All-In-One Planner and Resource Center

Available on CD-ROM

- Interactive Teacher's Edition
- Printable Weekly Resources

Implementation Modules

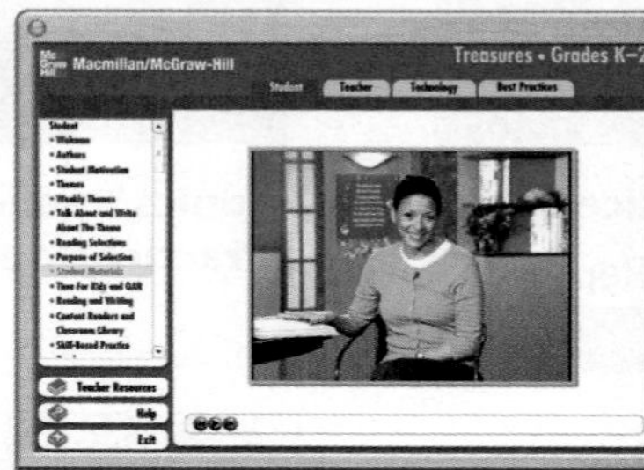

- Support on how to implement the reading program

Balanced Literacy Planner

Balanced Literacy Lesson Plan
- Oral Language Development
- Word Work
- Focus Lesson
  - Shared Reading
  - Read Aloud
- Guided Reading
  - Literacy Centers
- Writing Workshop

- Create customized weekly balanced literacy planners

ELL Strategies

- Teaching strategies for English Language Learners

Reading Video Library

- Video clips of instructional routines

Leadership Handbook

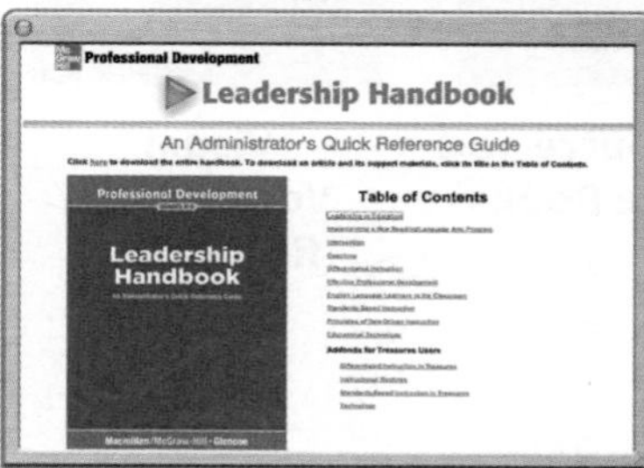

- Professional development for school principals

Teach/Learn

ONLINE www.macmillanmh.com

Interactive Student Book

Interactive Student Book

- Word-by-Word Reading
- Summaries in Other Languages
- Media Literacy and Research

Animated Activities

- Animated comprehension activities

Theme Videos

- Build background and concept vocabulary

Additional Professional Development

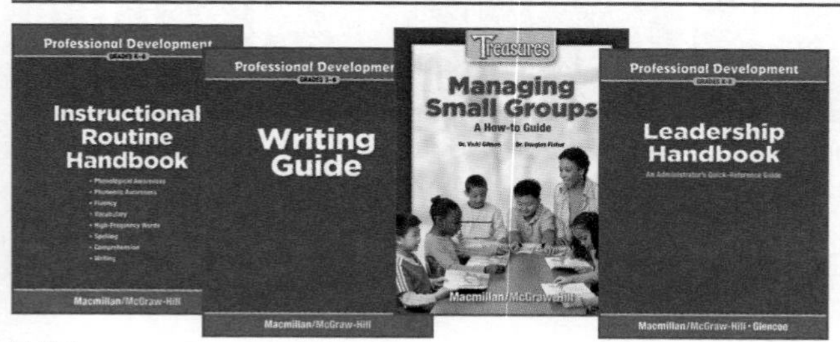

- **Instructional Routine Handbook**
- **Writing Professional Development Guide**
- **Managing Small Groups**
- **Leadership Handbook:** *An Administrator's Quick Reference Guide*

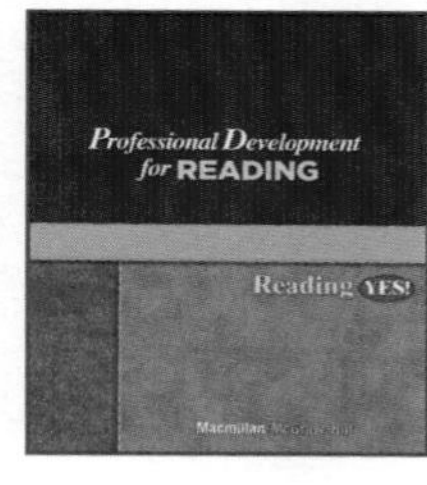

Also available **Reading Yes!** Video Workshops on CD-ROM

LOG ON VIEW IT READ IT LEARN IT FIND OUT

Classroom Presentation Toolkit

- Weekly transparencies, graphic organizers, and guided instruction and practice

Weekly Activities

- Oral Language
- Research Roadmap
- Research and Inquiry
- Vocabulary and Spelling
- Author and Illustrator

Leveled Reader Database

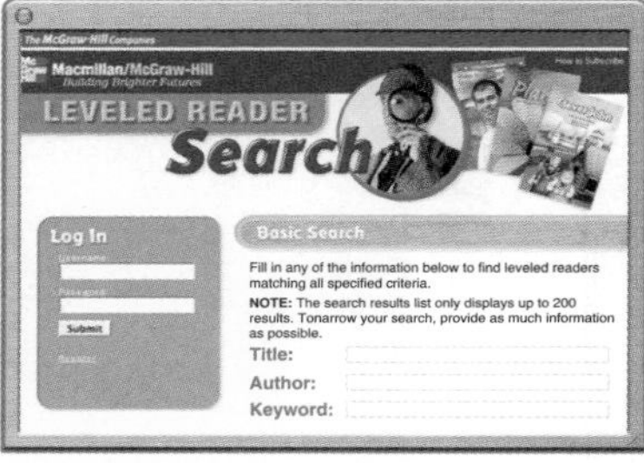

- Search and print Leveled Reader titles

Online and CD-ROM materials are **Interactive White Board Ready!**

IWB

Assess

ONLINE www.macmillanmh.com

Formative Assessment

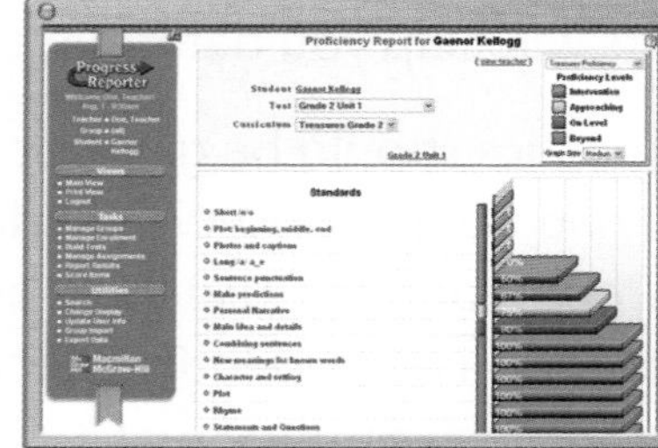

- Prescriptions for Reteaching
- Student Profile System

- Weekly and Unit Tests

Available on CD

- **Listening Library**
- **Fluency Solutions**
- **Sound Pronunciation**

Interactive Student Book

- **New Adventures with Buggles and Beezy**
- **Vocabulary PuzzleMaker**

- Accelerated Reader Quizzes

Diagnostic Assessment

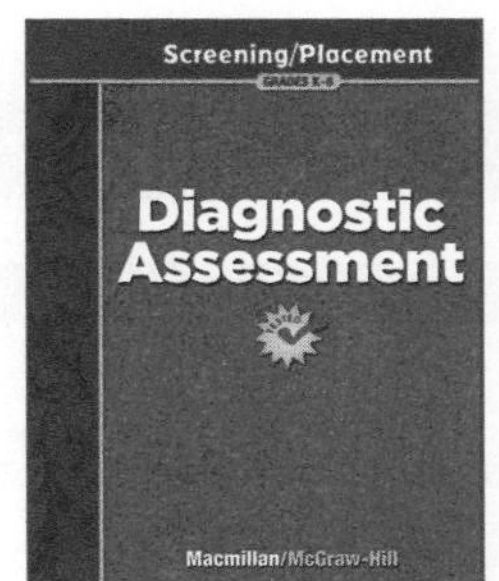

Screening, Diagnosis, and Placement

Use your state or district screener to identify children at risk. In addition, see tests in the **Diagnostic Assessment** book for information on determining the proficiency of children according to specific skills. The results will help you determine where to place children in the program.

Diagnostics should be given at the beginning of the year after you have had time to observe children and they become familiar with classroom routines. Use the diagnostics to determine children in need of intervention or to identify specific prerequisite skill deficiencies that you need to teach during Small Group differentiated instruction time.

Progress Monitoring Assessment

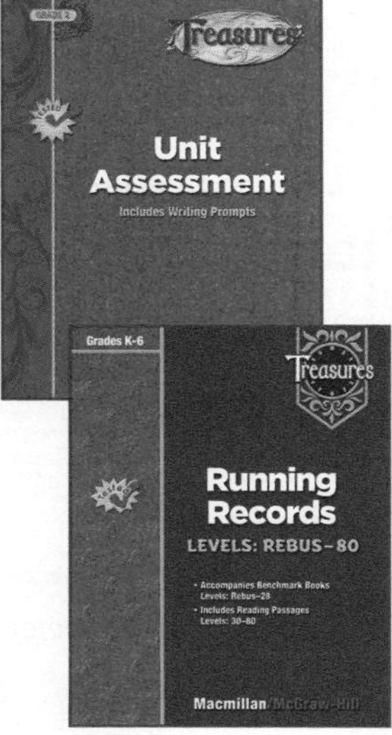

Meeting Grade-Level Expectations

Use weekly and unit tests (every 6–8 weeks). Multiple questions and next-steps information are provided.

Ongoing Informal Assessments

- Daily Quick Check Observations
- Weekly Tests/Selection Tests; Comprehension Check Questions (Student Book)
- Weekly Fluency Practice Book Passages

Formal Assessments

- Unit Assessments
- Fluency Assessments
- Running Records

Benchmark Assessment

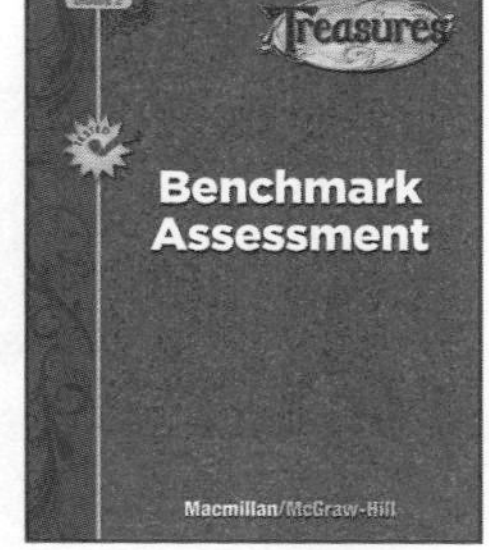

Links to the State Test

Use the **Benchmark Assessment**. Give every trimester, midyear, or at the end of the year to determine whether children have mastered the grade-level content standards and to document long-term academic growth.

Digital Assessment

Assessment Online

- Administer the **Weekly** and **Unit Assessment** electronically
- Score all tests electronically
- Prescriptions for Reteaching
- Student Profile System

Test Generator

- Available on CD-ROM
- **Weekly** and **Unit Assessments**

Test Alignment

GRADE 2 UNIT 4 ASSESSED SKILLS	TerraNova/ CAT 6	SAT 10	ITBS	NAEP
COMPREHENSION STRATEGIES AND SKILLS				
• Strategies: Monitor Comprehension: Reread, Read Ahead; Analyze Text and Story Structure	◆	◆	◆	◆
• Skills: Cause and Effect; Use Illustrations; Identify Sequence of Events; Distinguish Between Fantasy and Reality	◆	◆	◆	◆
VOCABULARY STRATEGIES				
• Context Clues: Synonyms and Antonyms	◆	◆	◆	◆
• Dictionary: Homophones	◆	◆	◆	◆
• Word Parts: Inflectional Endings	◆	◆	◆	◆
PHONEMIC AWARENESS				
• Identify syllables				
• Generate rhyme				
• Phoneme identity				
• Phoneme blending				
• Phoneme categorization				
• Phoneme segmentation				
• Phoneme substitution				
PHONICS				
• Diphthongs *ou, ow; oi, oy*	◆	◆	◆	◆
• Vowel Diagraphs *oo, ui, ew, ue, u, ou, oe; au, aw, a*	◆	◆	◆	◆
TEXT FEATURES AND STUDY SKILLS				
• Drop-down menu				
• Floor plans				
• Written directions				
• Using the Internet	◆	◆	◆	◆
GRAMMAR, MECHANICS, USAGE				
• Verbs (linking, helping, irregular)	◆	◆	◆	◆
• Quotation marks, letter punctuation, Apostrophes	◆	◆	◆	◆
• Book titles, capitalization	◆	◆	◆	◆
• Contractions	◆	◆	◆	◆

KEY

TerraNova/CAT 6	TerraNova, The Second Edition	**ITBS**	Iowa Tests of Basic Skills
SAT 10	Stanford Early Achievement Test	**NAEP**	National Assessment of Educational Progress

Theme Project

Introduce the Theme

Write the theme statement on the board: *Some jobs are too big for one person. Jobs can be easier and done faster when we work with other people.*

Name some people who work together to do big jobs. Have children discuss how working on a team is different than working alone. Remind them to focus on the topic and listen to others.

Help children get ready for their theme project by helping them choose an example of teamwork about which they would like to learn more.

Research and Inquiry

Self-Selected Theme Project

Planning a Project

What do I want to learn about teamwork?

- Have children formulate open-ended questions about working as part of a team.
- Help them decide which sources of information will help them answer their questions.
- Have children record information using notes, charts, pictures, and diagrams.

Doing the Project

- Guide children to use information from text sources found at the library to write a play about teamwork.

Document and Evaluate the Research

How can I share what I have learned?

- Present a play to share your findings about teamwork.
- Share ideas about teamwork, speaking clearly and audibly.

See the Unit Closer on pages 167K and 167L.

Research Strategies

Use the Library

- Create a list of questions.
- Decide which questions may be answered in books, magazines, or on the Internet.
- Begin to use text features, such as the table of contents, index, and glossary.
- Not all information from the Internet is reliable. Find out which Web sites will give you correct information.
- Ask a library media specialist for help in locating information.

Minilesson

Creating a Dramatization

Explain A **dramatization** is a story that is acted out by characters. It can take the form of a skit, play, or other performance. The **plot** of a dramatization can be real or make believe. The **characters** in dramatizations are called actors. They move around the stage, use different voices, and dress in costumes to make their characters more believable. Characters in a dramatization use **dialogue** to speak to one another. Dramatizations should also include a **setting** so that the audience knows where the action is taking place.

Discuss Ask: *What is the function of dialogue in a dramatization?* (Dialogue is the way that actors speak to one another.) *What other elements should you include in a dramatization?* (Dramas include characters, a plot, and a setting)

Apply Arrange children in small groups. Provide each group with a prop, such as a baseball cap, map, or pair of sunglasses. Instruct children to create a short skit using the assigned prop and to include the elements of dramatization.

Minilesson

Speaking Slowly and Clearly

Explain It is important to speak slowly and clearly so that people can understand what you are saying. It is especially important to speak clearly when you are giving an oral presentation or dramatic performance. When you speak clearly, you speak loudly enough for everyone to hear you and slowly enough for everyone to understand the words you are using. It may be helpful to practice speaking in front of your parents or a friend before you will be speaking in front of a larger group of people.

Discuss Ask: *Why so you think it is important to speak clearly?* (When you speak clearly, people will be able to understand the information your are giving them.)

Apply Arrange children in pairs. Have each pair experiment with their volume and speed of speech at different distances in the classroom. Pose different scenarios to children, such as whispering in the library or calling to a friend across the playground, and ask children to determine which volume and speed of speech is appropriate for each.

LISTENING AND SPEAKING

WORKING IN GROUPS

Remind children to:

- Listen attentively to speakers
- Respectfully ask relevant questions to obtain or clarify information
- Use formal and informal language to respond to others' ideas and share information with others in an appropriate way

See Listening and Speaking Checklists in StudentWorks Plus.

Unit 4
Better Together

The Big Question

How is working together better than working alone?

LOG ON VIEW IT Theme Launcher Video
Better Together
www.macmillanmh.com

2

3

Introduce Theme Project

BETTER TOGETHER

Review with children what they have learned so far about teamwork and examples of teamwork they have found in their community.

- Help children identify different types of teamwork, such as athletes working together on a team, construction workers building a large structure, or volunteers working together to clean up a playground. Have partners discuss why it is necessary for people to work together to complete some very big jobs.
- Read and discuss the Research Activity on page 4 of the **Student Book**. Help children brainstorm about the type of teamwork they would like to choose as the focus of their theme project.

Connect to Content

Better Together

Explain to children that being able to work as part of a team is important for being a good citizen. We are good citizens when we work with the other members of our communities to solve problems and to make the world a better place. We are good citizens when we practice teamwork to raise money for charities, fix up schools and playgrounds, and help others.

How is working together better than working alone?

Some jobs are too big for one person to do. Jobs are easier and done faster when we work with other people. Cleaning up the classroom takes a short time when everyone helps. Construction workers work in teams to build bridges, buildings, and roads. In this unit you will learn different ways people work together to complete big tasks. Learning about teamwork will help you work together with other people to get big projects done quickly.

Research Activities

Throughout the unit you will gather information about different places where teamwork happens. As a class we will make a list of topics and create open-ended questions. Then we will research one example from the list.

Keep Track of Ideas

Keep track of what you learn in the **Layered Book Foldable**. On the top flap, write "Better Together." On remaining flaps, write "Teamwork at home," "Teamwork at school," and "Teamwork at play." Write facts you learn about where teamwork happens.

Digital Learning

LOG ON FIND OUT www.macmillanmh.com

StudentWorks Plus
Interactive Student Book

- **Research Roadmap** Follow a step-by-step guide to complete your research project.

Online Resources

- Topic Finder and Other Research Tools
- Videos and Virtual Field Trips
- Photos and Drawings for Presentations
- Related Articles and Web Resources
- Web Site Links

People and Places

The United States Capitol is located in Washington, D.C. It is called a symbol of democracy and home to the legislative branch of government.

KEEP TRACK OF IDEAS

Go to page 22 of the **Foldables™** for instruction on how to create the Layered Book study organizer for this unit. Give children time to create the organizer and their labels.

Read "Keep Track of Ideas" on page 5 of the **Student Book**. Model how children will be using their organizers to keep track of ideas as they read through the stories and selections in the unit. Explain to children that keeping track of the ideas that they read about will help them with ideas for their own theme project.

RESEARCH TOOLS

Tell children that as they read the selections in this unit, they will learn about people working together. Children will be able to use the Research Tools to help them learn more about ways that people can help each other by working together.

LOG ON

Interactive Student Book

Plan, Organize, and Synthesize Activities that will assist children in research planning, organization, and presentation.

Listening and Speaking Resources that will help children apply listening and speaking techniques.

Week 1 ★ At a Glance

Priority Skills and Concepts

Comprehension

- **Genre:** Folktale
- **Strategy:** Reread
- **Skill:** Cause and Effect

- **Draw Conclusions**

High-Frequency Words

- ***family, four, hear***

Oral Vocabulary

- **Build Robust Vocabulary:** ***accomplish, arduous, labor, rejoice, succeed***

Vocabulary

- ***gasped, attached, frantically, swung, delicious***
- **Strategy:** Context Clues

Fluency

- **Expression**

Phonemic Awareness

- **Phoneme Identity**

Phonics/Spelling

- **Vowel Diphthong *ou, ow*: *clown, growl, howl, brown, crown, ground, shout, cloud, house, sound, shark, chair, family, four, hear***

Grammar/Mechanics

- **Linking Verbs**
- **Capitalization**

Writing

- **Personal Narrative**
- **A Strong Paragraph**
- **Trait:** Organization

Key

 Tested in program

 Review Skill

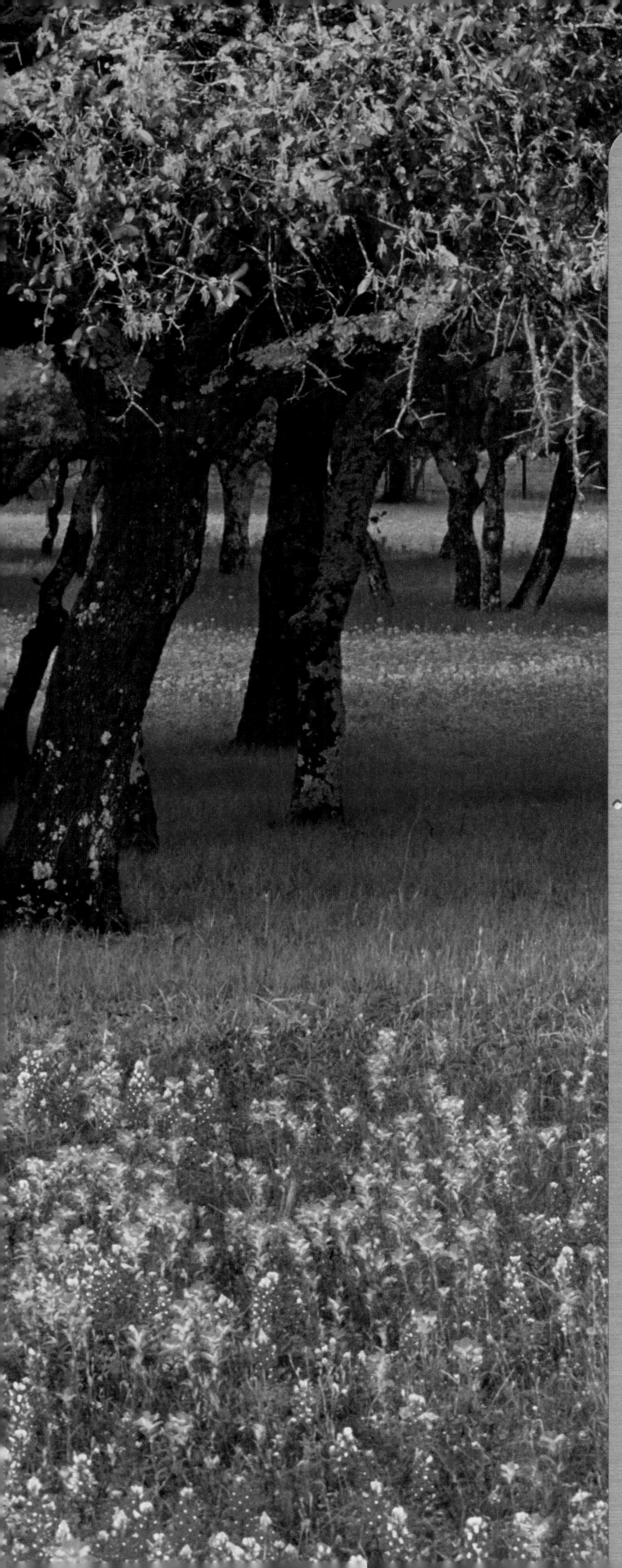

Digital Learning

Digital solutions to help plan and implement instruction.

Teacher Resources

ONLINE www.macmillanmh.com

- **Teacher's Edition**
  - Lesson Planner and Resources also on CD-ROM
- **Formative Assessment**
  - ExamView® on CD-ROM also available
- **Instructional Resources**
  - Unit Videos
  - Classroom Presentation Toolkit
- **Professional Development**
  - Video Library

Student Resources

ONLINE www.macmillanmh.com

- **Interactive Student Book**
- **Leveled Reader Database**
- **Activities**
  - Research Toolkit
  - Oral Language Activities
  - Vocabulary/Spelling Activities

Listening Library

- Recordings of Student Books and Leveled Readers

Fluency Solutions

- Fluency Modeling and Practice

Weekly Literature

Theme: Getting the Job Done

Student Book

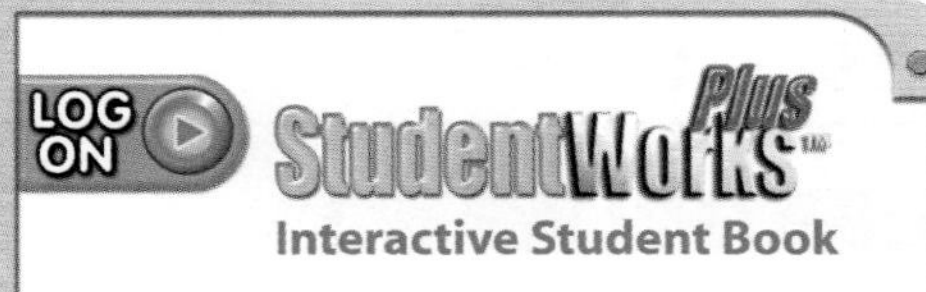

Interactive Student Book

- Word-by-Word Reading
- Summaries in Multiple Languages
- Comprehension Questions

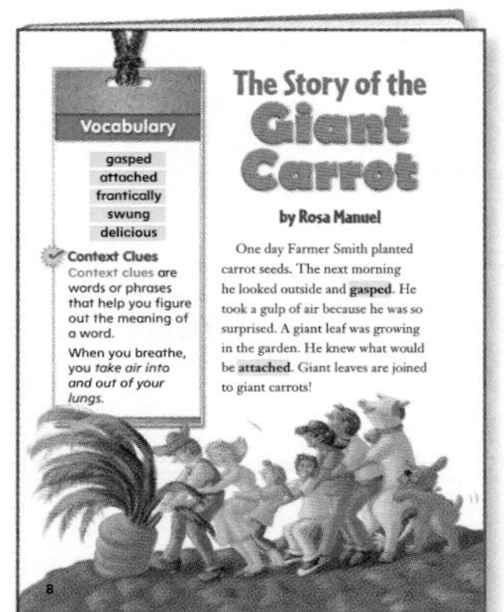

Preteach Vocabulary and Comprehension

Genre Folktale

Main Selection

Genre Folktale

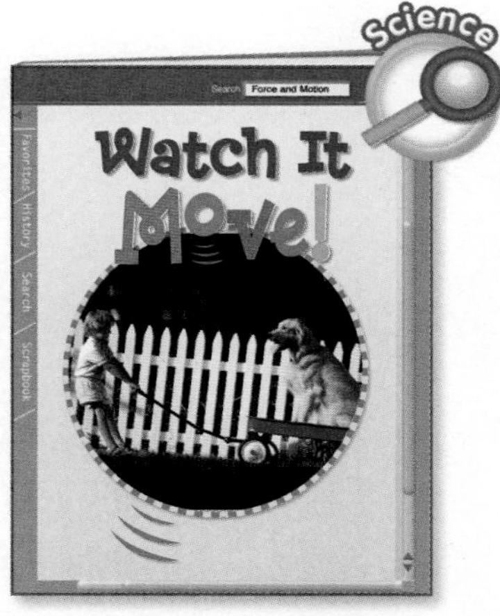

Paired Selection

Genre Expository

Support Literature

Decodable Reader Library

- One decodable read each week

Oral Vocabulary Cards

- Listening Comprehension
- Build Robust Vocabulary

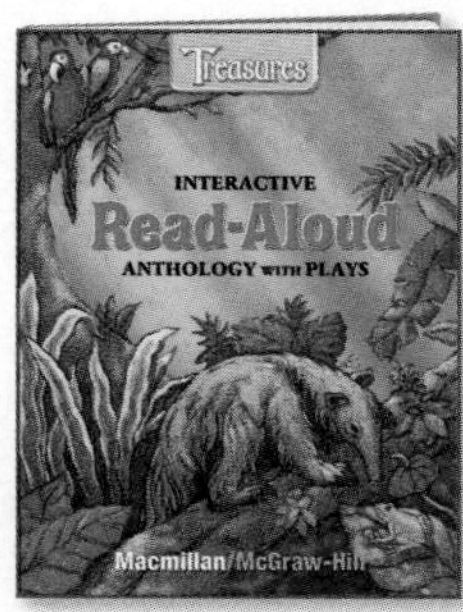

Interactive Read-Aloud Anthology

- Listening Comprehension
- Readers Theater Plays for Fluency

Resources for Differentiated Instruction

Leveled Readers

GR Levels H-O

Genre	Fiction

- Same Theme
- Same Vocabulary
- Same Comprehension Skills

Approaching Level

On Level

Beyond Level

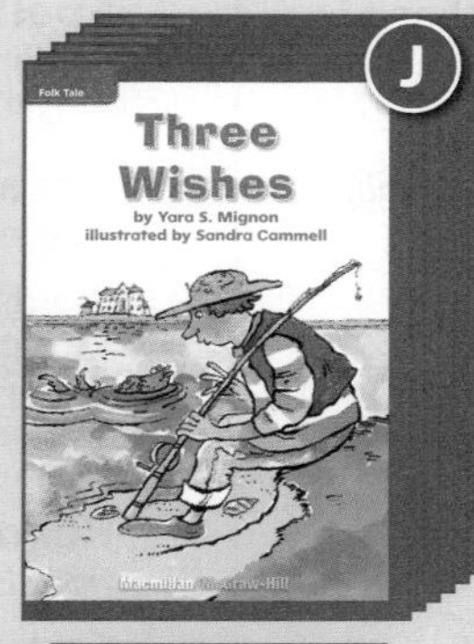

ELL

Leveled Reader Database
Go to **www.macmillanmh.com**.

Leveled Practice

AUDIO CD

Approaching

On Level

Beyond

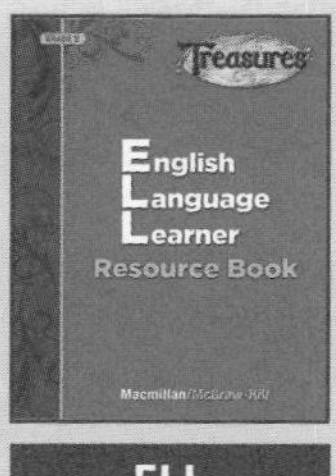

ELL

Leveled Classroom Library

Approaching

On Level

Beyond

Response to Intervention

- Phonemic Awareness
- Phonics
- Vocabulary
- Comprehension
- Fluency

Assessment

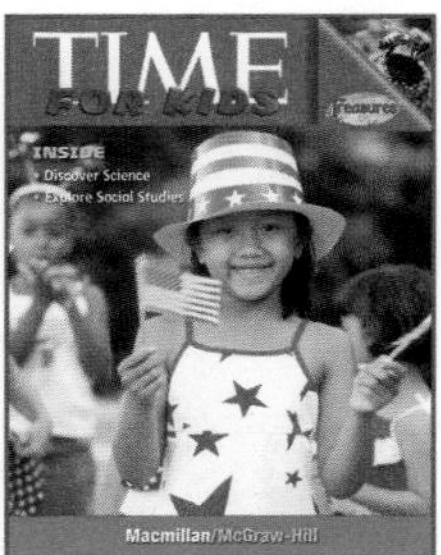

Time For Kids
- Teacher's Edition
- Apply Answering Questions Strategies

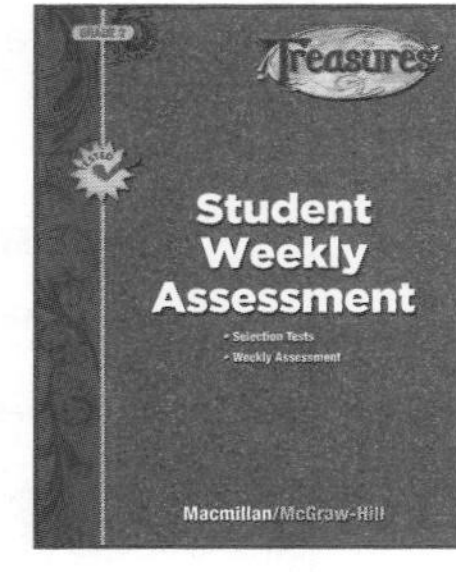

Weekly Assessment

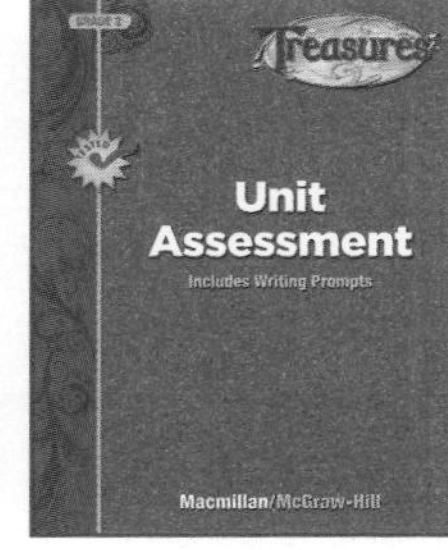

Unit Assessment

Benchmark Assessment

HOME-SCHOOL CONNECTION

- Family letters in English and Spanish
- Take-home stories and activities

LOG ON Suggested Lesson Plan

Go to www.macmillanmh.com for Online Lesson Planner

Head, Body, Legs: A Story from Liberia, pp. 10–35

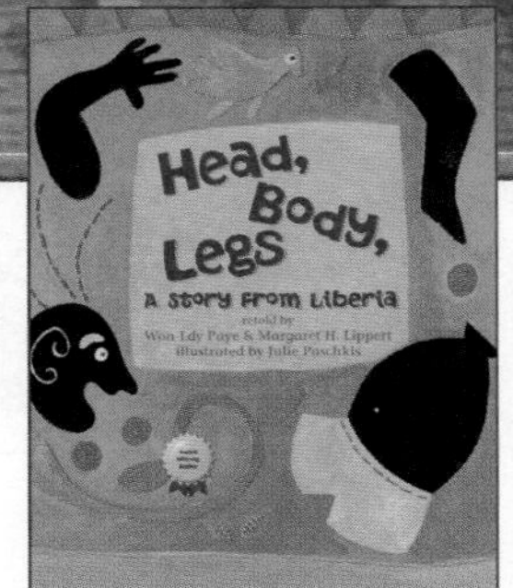

WHOLE GROUP	DAY 1	DAY 2
ORAL LANGUAGE		
• Oral Vocabulary • Listening Comprehension	**Focus Question** Why is it helpful to work together to finish a project? Build Background, 6M **Oral Vocabulary** *accomplish, arduous, labor, rejoice, succeed*, 7A Oral Vocabulary Cards, *The Enormous Yucca*	**Focus Question** What causes the body parts to try to work together? **Oral Vocabulary** *accomplish, arduous, labor, rejoice, succeed*, 9E
• Phonemic Awareness	**Phonemic Awareness** Phoneme Identity, 7B	**Phonemic Awareness** Phoneme Categorization, 9F
WORD STUDY		
• Phonics	**Phonics** Introduce Diphthong *ou, ow*, 7C Practice Book, 178	**Phonics** Blend and Build with Diphthong *ou, ow*, 9G
• Spelling	**Spelling Pretest:** Words with Diphthong *ou, ow*, 7E Spelling, 61	**Spelling** Word Sort with Diphthong *ou, ow*, 9H Spelling, 62
• High-Frequency Words	**Vocabulary** *attached, delicious, frantically, gasped, swung*, 7G **Strategy:** Context Clues Practice Book, 179	**Vocabulary** *attached, delicious, frantically, gasped, swung* Words in Context, 9I
READING		
• Comprehension	**Read** Decodable Reader, *The Missing String Beans*, 7F Decodable Reader **Comprehension**, 9A–9B "The Story of the Giant Carrot," 8/9 **Strategy:** Monitor Comprehension: Reread **Skill:** Identify Cause and Effect	**Read** *Head, Body, Legs: A Story from Liberia*, 10/11–34/35 Student Book **Comprehension**, 9J–37A **Strategy:** Monitor Comprehension: Reread **Skill:** Identify Cause and Effect Practice Book 176–177
• Fluency	**Fluency** Build Fluency, 7C	**Fluency** Build Fluency, 9G
LANGUAGE ARTS		
• Writing	**Writing** **Daily Writing Prompt** Look at the picture. Write about what you see, 6M Personal Narrative, 9D	**Writing** **Daily Writing Prompt** Write a new ending to *The Enormous Yucca* describing the arduous task of getting the yucca out of the ground, 9E Prewrite a Personal Narrative, 37C
• Grammar	**Grammar** Linking Verbs, 9C Grammar, 76	**Grammar** Past-Tense Forms of Be, 37B Grammar, 77
ASSESSMENT		
• Informal/Formal	**Quick Check** Phonics, 7D Vocabulary, 8/9	**Quick Check** Comprehension, 34/35

SMALL GROUP Lesson Plan — **Differentiated Instruction 6G–6H**

Priority Skills

Phonics
Diphthong /ou/*ou, ow*

Vocabulary
Words: *gasped, attached, frantically, swung, delicious*
Strategy: Context Clues

Comprehension
Strategy: Monitor Comprehension: Reread
Skill: Identify Cause and Effect

Writing
Personal Narrative

Science

DAY 3

Focus Question How did the illustrations help show that the story was made up?
Read Aloud: "The Storytelling Stone," 37D

Oral Vocabulary *accomplish, arduous, labor, rejoice, succeed,* 37K
Phonemic Awareness Phoneme Blending, 37E

Phonics Blend and Build with Diphthong *ou, ow,* 37F
Inflectional Endings *-s, -es,* 37G
Practice Book, 178
Spelling Word Sort, 37H
Spelling, 63
Vocabulary *attached, delicious, frantically, gasped, swung*
Strategy: Context Clues, 37J
Practice Book, 179

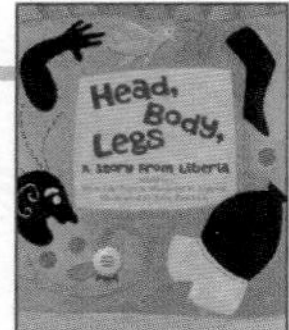
Student Book

Read *Head, Body, Legs: A Story from Liberia,* 10/11–34/35
Comprehension, 37N
Review Skill: Draw Conclusions
Fluency Repeated Reading: Prosody/ Expression, 37L
Practice Book, 180

Writing
Daily Writing Prompt Respond to the Read-Aloud by writing about how the great stone affected the boy and his family. 37D
Writing Trait: Organization, 37Q
A Strong Paragraph, 37P
Draft a Personal Narrative, 37Q
Grammar **Mechanics:** Capitalization of Proper Nouns, 37O
Grammar, 78

Quick Check Fluency, 37M

DAY 4

Focus Question In *Head, Body, Legs,* what kind of force do the arms and legs use to paddle across the river?

Oral Vocabulary *accomplish, arduous, labor, rejoice, succeed,* 37R
Phonemic Awareness Phoneme Categorization, 37S

Phonics Blend and Build Words with Diphthong *ou, ow,* 37T
Spelling Practice Words with Diphthong *ou, ow,* 37U
Spelling, 64
Vocabulary *attached, delicious, frantically, gasped, swung*
Words in Context, 37V

Student Book

Read "Watch It Move," 38/39
Comprehension, 37W–39A
Text Feature: Drop-Down Menu, 37W
Content Vocabulary: *force, friction, gravity*, 37W
Practice Book, 181
Fluency Build Fluency, 37T

Writing
Daily Writing Prompt Write a story about how the parts of a plant or something else in nature come together to accomplish something. 37R
Revise and Proofread a Personal Narrative, 39D
Grammar Linking Verbs, 39B
Grammar, 79

Quick Check Spelling, 37U

DAY 5
Review and Assess

Focus Question How will rereading help you understand another selection?

Oral Vocabulary *accomplish, arduous, labor, rejoice, succeed,* 41A
Phonemic Awareness Phoneme Blending, 41C

Phonics Blend with Diphthong *ou, ow,* 41C
Spelling Posttest, 41E
Vocabulary *attached, delicious, frantically, gasped, swung*, 41F

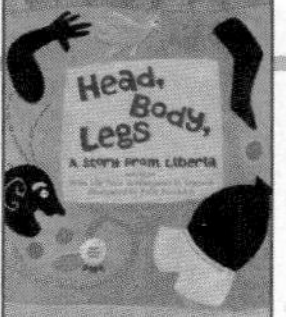
Student Book

Read Self-Selected Reading, 6K
Comprehension, 41G
Strategy: Monitor Comprehension: Reread
Skill: Identify Cause and Effect
Fluency Repeated Reading: Prosody/ Expression, 41B

Writing
Daily Writing Prompt Write about how to get your friends to help you with an arduous job, 41F
Publish and Present a Personal Narrative, 41I
Speaking, Listening, and Viewing, 41J
Grammar Capitalization of Proper Nouns; Linking Verbs, 41H
Grammar, 80

Weekly Assessment, 41KK–41LL

Differentiated Instruction

What do I do in small groups?

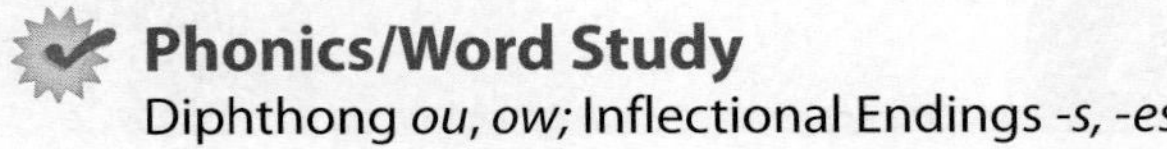

IF... students need additional instruction, practice, or extension based on your Quick Check observations for the following priority skills

Phonics/Word Study
Diphthong *ou, ow;* Inflectional Endings *-s, -es*

Vocabulary Words
attached, delicious, frantically, gasped, swung
Strategy: Context Clues

Comprehension
Strategy: Monitor Comprehension/Reread
Skill: Identify Cause and Effect

Fluency
Phonics, High-Frequency Words, Expression

THEN...

Approaching	Preteach and
English Learners	Reteach Skills
On Level	Practice
Beyond	Enrich and Accelerate Learning

LOG ON Suggested Small Group Lesson Plan

	DAY 1	DAY 2
Approaching Level • **Preteach/Reteach** Tier 2 **Tier 2 Instruction**	• Phonemic Awareness, 41K • Phonics, 41K ELL • High-Frequency/Vocabulary, 41L • Decodable Reader, *The Missing String Beans*, 41L	• Phonemic Awareness, 41Q • Phonics, 41Q ELL • High-Frequency/Vocabulary, 41R • Leveled Reader Lesson 1, 41R
On Level • **Practice**	• Phonics, 41M • Fluency, 41M ELL	• Leveled Reader Lesson 1, 41S ELL
Beyond Level • **Extend/Accelerate** Gifted Talented **Gifted and Talented**	• Phonics, 41N ELL • Vocabulary, 41N	• Leveled Reader Lesson 1, 41T • Analyze, 41T
ELL • **Build English Language Proficiency** • **See ELL in other levels.**	• Prepare to Read, 41O • Academic Language, 41O • Preteach Vocabulary, 41P	• Preteach Main Selection, 41U • Grammar, 41V

Focus on Leveled Readers

Levels H–O

Approaching

On Level

Beyond

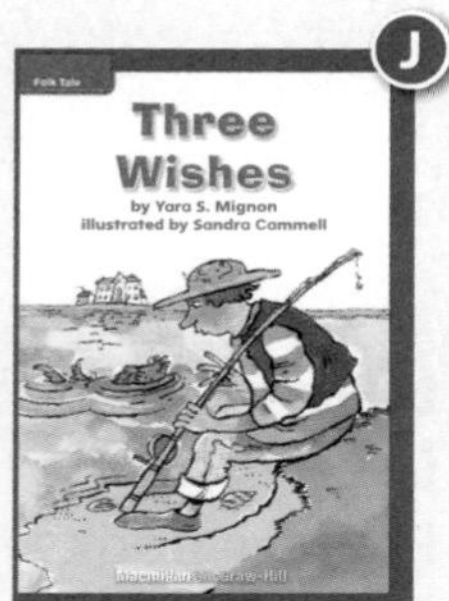

ELL

Additional Leveled Readers

Leveled Reader Database
www.macmillanmh.com

Search by

- Comprehension Skill
- Content Area
- Genre
- Text Feature
- Guided Reading Level
- Reading Recovery Level
- Lexile Score
- Benchmark Level

Subscription also available.

Manipulatives

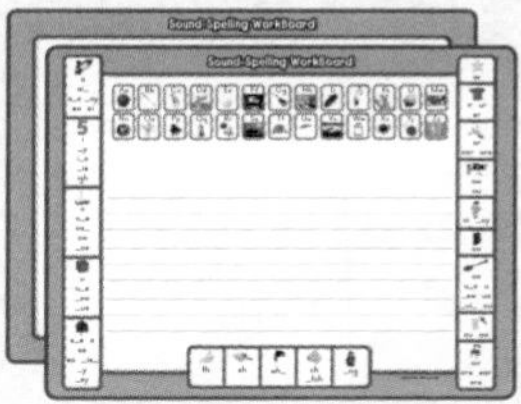

Sound-Spelling WorkBoards

Sound-Spelling Cards

Photo Cards

High-Frequency Word Cards

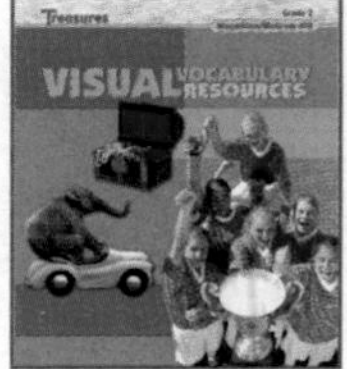

Visual Vocabulary Resources

DAY 3	DAY 4	DAY 5
• Phonemic Awareness, 41W • Phonics, 41W ELL • High-Frequency/Vocabulary, 41X • Leveled Reader Lesson 2, 41X • Book Talk, 41X	• Phonemic Awareness, 41CC • Phonics, 41CC ELL • High-Frequency/Vocabulary, 41DD • Fluency, 41DD • Review Leveled Readers, 41DD	• Oral Language, 41GG ELL • Fluency, 41HH • Self-Selected Indepedent Reading, 41HH
• Leveled Reader Lesson 2, 41Y • Fluency, 41Y • Book Talk, 41Y	• Fluency, 41EE	• Self-Selected Intependent Reading, 41II ELL
• Leveled Reader Lesson 2, 41Z • Synthesize and Evaluate, 41Z • Fluency, 41Z • Book Talk, 41Z	• Fluency, 41EE	• Self-Selected Independent Reading, 41II • Evaluate, 41II
• Leveled Reader Lesson 1, 41AA • Writing/Spelling, 41BB	• Preteach Paired Selection, 41FF • Leveled Reader Lesson 2, 41FF	• Fluency, 41JJ • Self-Selected Independent Reading, 41JJ

Managing the Class

What do I do with the rest of my class?

- Literacy Workstations
- Leveled Reader Activities
- Practice Book and Reproducibles
- Online Activities
- English Language Learner Practice Book

Classroom Management Tools

Weekly Contract

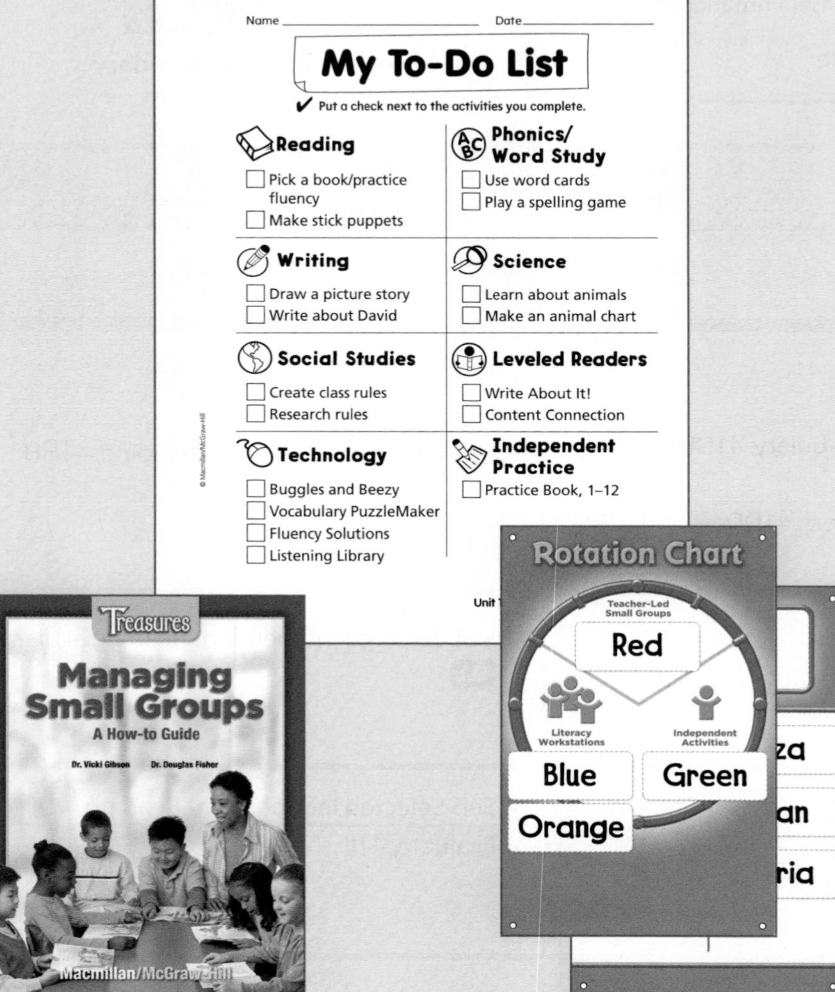

Name ____________ Date ____________

My To-Do List

✔ Put a check next to the activities you complete.

Reading	**Phonics/ Word Study**
☐ Pick a book/practice fluency	☐ Use word cards
☐ Make stick puppets	☐ Play a spelling game
Writing	**Science**
☐ Draw a picture story	☐ Learn about animals
☐ Write about David	☐ Make an animal chart
Social Studies	**Leveled Readers**
☐ Create class rules	☐ Write About It!
☐ Research rules	☐ Content Connection
Technology	**Independent Practice**
☐ Buggles and Beezy	☐ Practice Book, 1–12
☐ Vocabulary PuzzleMaker	
☐ Fluency Solutions	
☐ Listening Library	

How-to Guide

Rotation Chart

Digital Learning

StudentWorks Plus

- Summaries in Multiple Languages
- Word-by-Word Reading
- Comprehension Questions

Meet the Author/Illustrator

Joe Cepeda

- Joe remembers having bruises from trying to get the candy that fell out of piñatas at childhood birthday parties.
- Joe has illustrated several books.
- He lives in Southern California with his family.

Other books illustrated by Joe Cepeda

- Herron, Carolivia. *Nappy Hair.* New York: Bantam Doubleday Dell Books for Young Readers, 1999.
- Lester, Julius. *What a Truly Cool World.* New York: Scholastic, Inc., 1999.

- Read Other Books by the Author or Illustrator

Leveled Practice

On Level

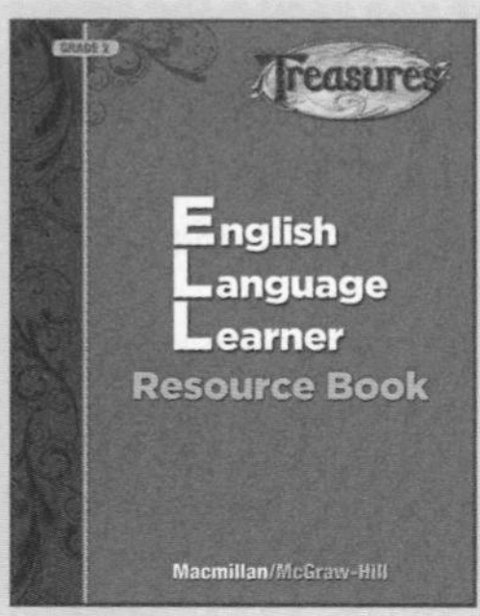

ELL

Also Available:

Approaching Reproducible

Beyond Reproducible

Independent Activities

ONLINE INSTRUCTION www.macmillanmh.com

Oral Language Activities

- Focus on Vocabulary and Concepts
- English Language Learner Support

Leveled Reader Database

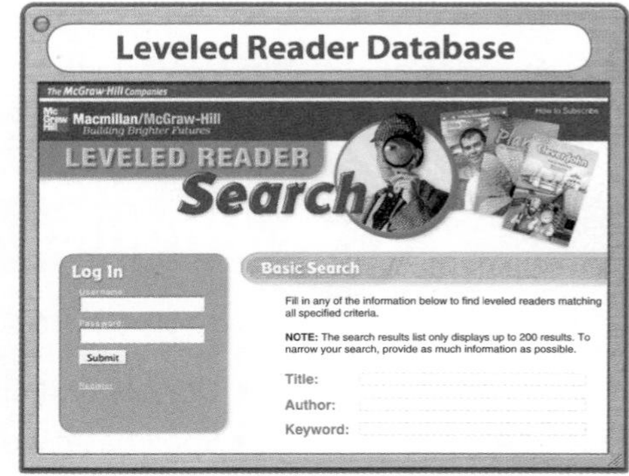

- Leveled Reader Database
- Search titles by level, skill, content area and more

Vocabulary/Spelling Activities

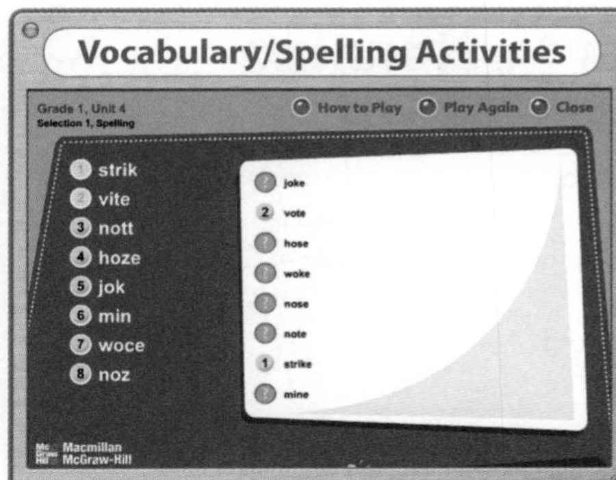

- Differentiated Lists and Activities

Research Toolkit

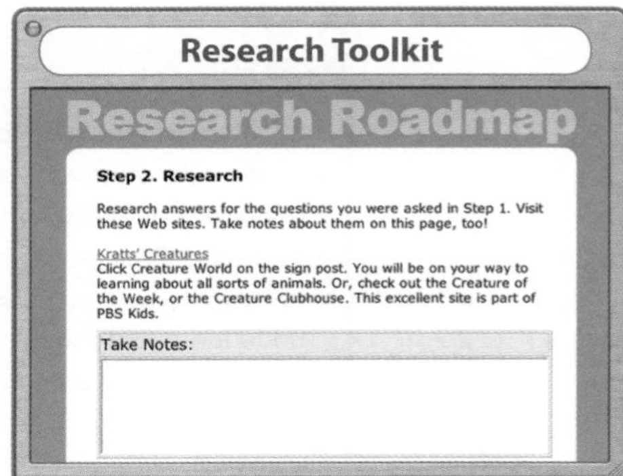

- Research Roadmap
- Research and Presentation Tools
- Theme Launcher Video
- Links to Science and Social Studies

Available on CD

LISTENING LIBRARY
Recordings of selections
- Main Selections
- Paired Selections
- Leveled Readers
- ELL Readers

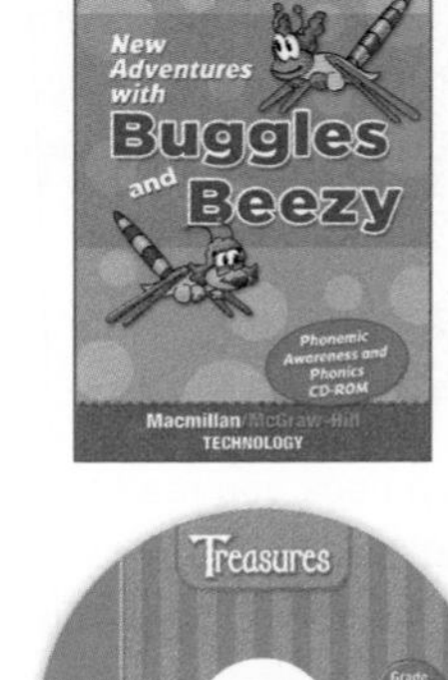

NEW ADVENTURES WITH BUGGLES AND BEEZY
Phonemic awareness and phonics activities

FLUENCY SOLUTIONS
Recorded passages at two speeds for modeling and practicing fluency

Leveled Reader Activities

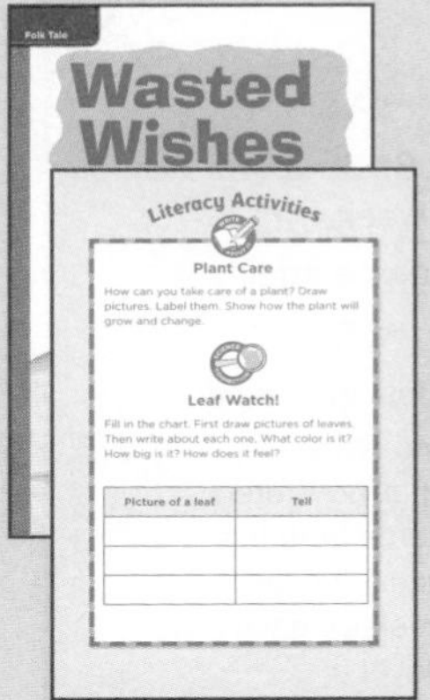

Approaching

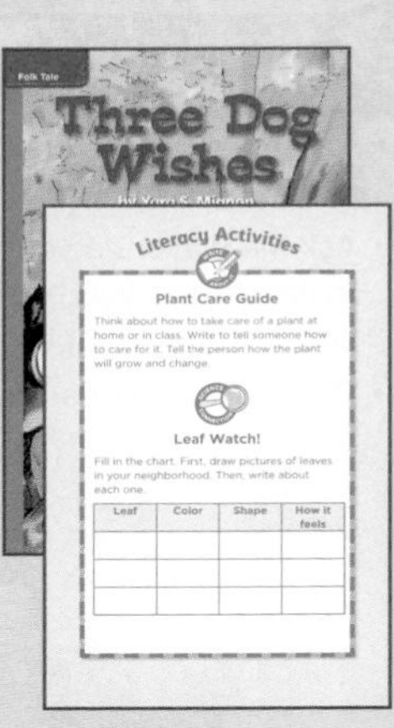

On Level

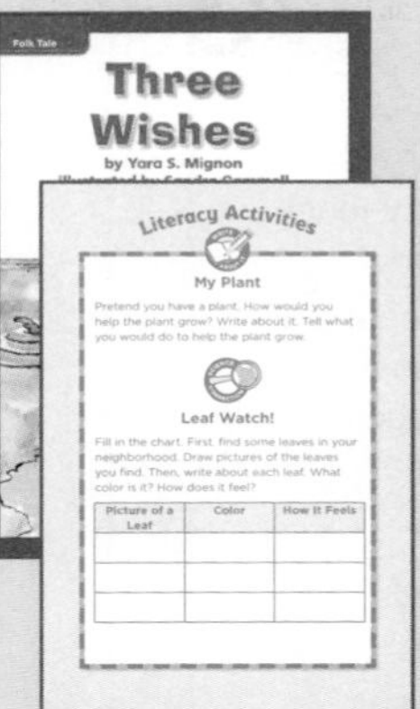

Beyond

ELL

See inside cover for all Leveled Readers.

Literacy Workstations

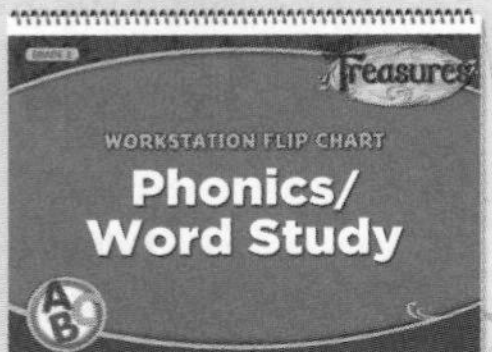

See lessons on pages 6K–6L

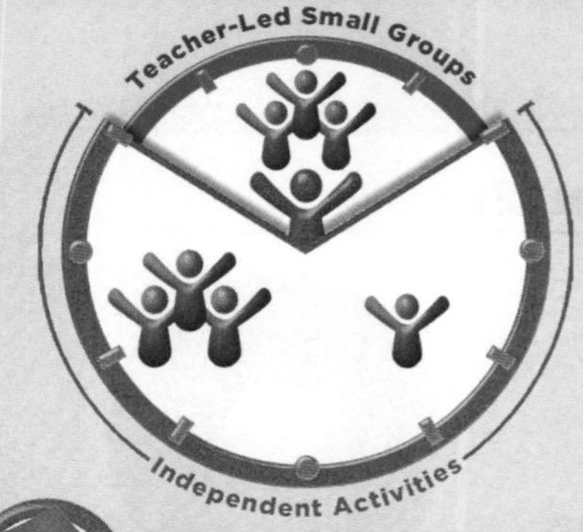

What do I do with the rest of my class?

Reading

Objectives

- Read independently for a sustained period of time and record information in the Reading Log, Practice Book p. 172
- Retell a story including characters, setting, and plot. Identify the moral lessons of the story

Phonics/Word Study

Objectives

- Use context clues to understand word meanings
- Spell basic words correctly

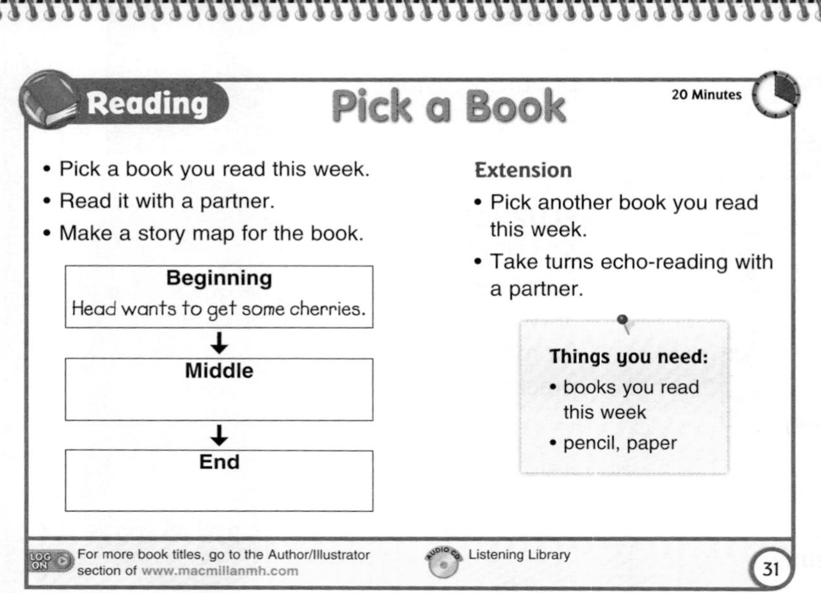

Reading — **Pick a Book** — 20 Minutes

- Pick a book you read this week.
- Read it with a partner.
- Make a story map for the book.

Beginning
Head wants to get some cherries.
↓
Middle
↓
End

Extension

- Pick another book you read this week.
- Take turns echo-reading with a partner.

Things you need:

- books you read this week
- pencil, paper

LOG ON For more book titles, go to the Author/Illustrator section of www.macmillanmh.com

Listening Library

31

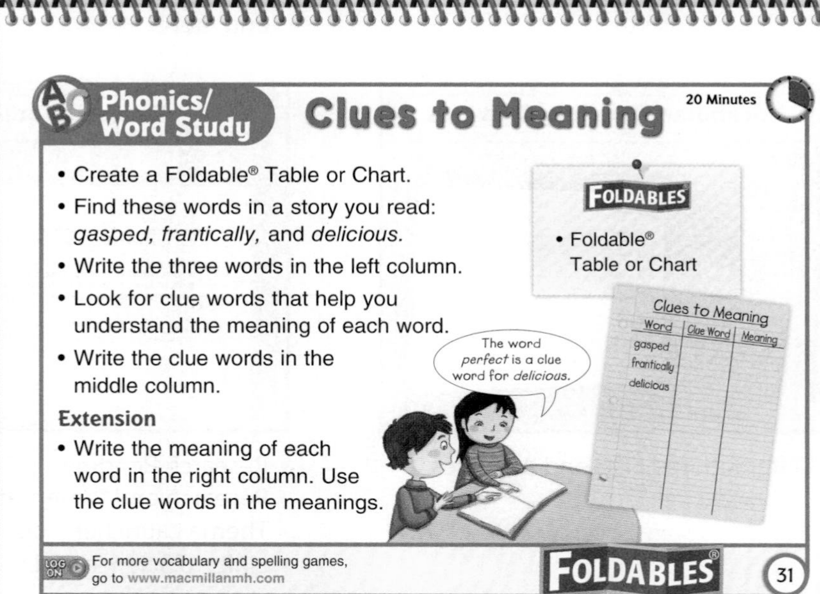

Phonics/Word Study — **Clues to Meaning** — 20 Minutes

- Create a Foldable® Table or Chart.
- Find these words in a story you read: *gasped*, *frantically*, and *delicious*.
- Write the three words in the left column.
- Look for clue words that help you understand the meaning of each word.
- Write the clue words in the middle column.

Extension

- Write the meaning of each word in the right column. Use the clue words in the meanings.

FOLDABLES

- Foldable® Table or Chart

LOG ON For more vocabulary and spelling games, go to www.macmillanmh.com

FOLDABLES®

31

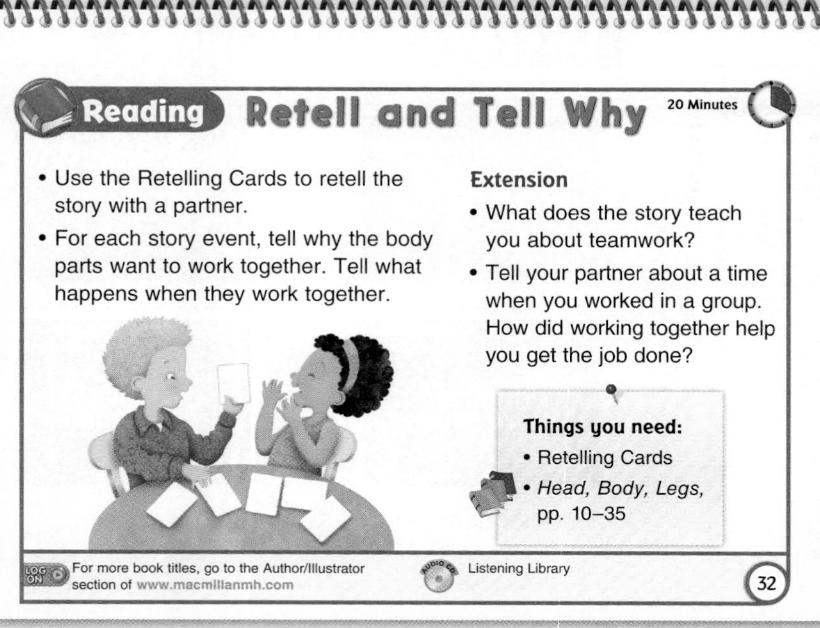

Reading — **Retell and Tell Why** — 20 Minutes

- Use the Retelling Cards to retell the story with a partner.
- For each story event, tell why the body parts want to work together. Tell what happens when they work together.

Extension

- What does the story teach you about teamwork?
- Tell your partner about a time when you worked in a group. How did working together help you get the job done?

Things you need:

- Retelling Cards
- *Head, Body, Legs*, pp. 10–35

LOG ON For more book titles, go to the Author/Illustrator section of www.macmillanmh.com

Listening Library

32

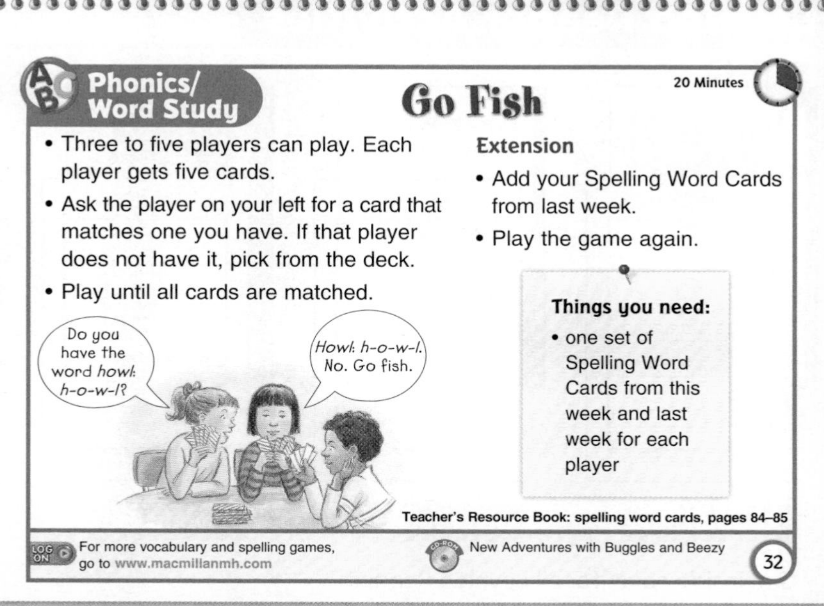

Phonics/Word Study — **Go Fish** — 20 Minutes

- Three to five players can play. Each player gets five cards.
- Ask the player on your left for a card that matches one you have. If that player does not have it, pick from the deck.
- Play until all cards are matched.

Extension

- Add your Spelling Word Cards from last week.
- Play the game again.

Things you need:

- one set of Spelling Word Cards from this week and last week for each player

Teacher's Resource Book: spelling word cards, pages 84–85

LOG ON For more vocabulary and spelling games, go to www.macmillanmh.com

New Adventures with Buggles and Beezy

32

Literacy Workstations

Literacy Workstation Flip Charts

Writing

Objectives

- Write a poster to convince people to follow a safety rule
- Write persuasively maintaining a consistent focus
- Write a composition about a time you worked with others

Content Literacy

Objectives

- Demonstrate map skills by locating various countries
- Research and write about how an animal meets its needs

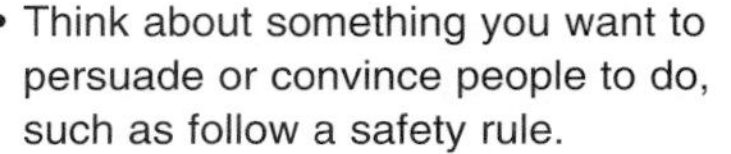

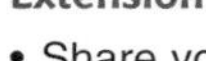

Writing — Persuade with a Poster (20 Minutes)

- Think about something you want to persuade or convince people to do, such as follow a safety rule.
- Create a poster that will convince people to do it. Use action words to tell about it.
- Explain why it is important to do it. Draw a picture.

Extension

- Share your poster with a partner. Point out the action words you used.
- With your partner, talk about each poster. Did your poster convince your partner to do what it says?

Things you need:
- poster paper
- crayons or markers

31

Social Studies — Folk Tales Around the World (20 Minutes)

- Share a favorite folk tale with a partner.
- Find out the country the folk tale comes from. Look for the country on a map.

Anansi the Spider comes from Ghana, which is in Africa.

Extension

- Use the Internet or other sources to research a country in Africa. Find out how people there live.

Things you need:
- world map
- pencil, paper
- Internet or other sources

LOG ON Internet Research and Inquiry Activity www.macmillanmh.com

31

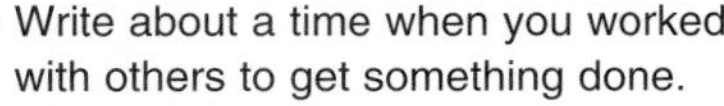

Writing — Let's Work Together (20 Minutes)

- Write about a time when you worked with others to get something done.
- What job did you do? What jobs did others do? Was it helpful to work as a group?

Extension

- Proofread your writing. Make sure each sentence has the correct punctuation.
-  You may wish to add this writing to your portfolio.

Things you need:
- pencil, paper

32

Science — Body Parts Help Animals Eat (20 Minutes)

- Pick a wild animal you like. Draw its picture.
- Think about how your animal gets its food. Does it use its teeth? Does it use its legs to run after food?
- Label the body parts. Tell how they help the animal get its food.

A long neck helps the giraffe reach leaves at the top of the tree.

Extension

- Use the Internet or other sources. Find out more about how your animal gets food.
- Write about it in your journal.

Things you need:
- drawing paper
- crayons
- Internet or other sources
- response journal

32

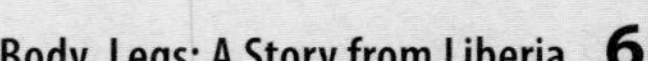

Day 1
At a Glance

WHOLE GROUP

Oral Language
- Build Background
- Oral Vocabulary

Phonemic Awareness
- Phoneme Identity

Phonics
- Diphthong *ou*, *ow*
- Build Fluency
- Spelling: Pretest: *ou*, *ow*
- Read *The Missing String Beans*

Vocabulary
- Teach Words in Context
- Use Context Clues
- Read "The Story of the Giant Carrot"

Comprehension
- Strategy: Monitor Comprehension: Reread
- Skill: Cause and Effect

Language Arts
- Grammar: Linking Verbs
- Writing: Personal Narrative

SMALL GROUP

- Differentiated Instruction, pages 41K–41JJ

Oral Vocabulary

Week 1

accomplish, arduous, labor, rejoice, succeed

Oral Language

Build Background

ACCESS PRIOR KNOWLEDGE
Discuss with children ways people work together to make an **arduous**, or hard, job easier. Ask children to describe a time when they worked together on a job. Write their responses on the board.

SING ABOUT WORKING TOGETHER
Sing the song "The Wee Falorie Man" and have children add verses and act out ways people can work together to do a job.

The Wee Falorie Man

I am the wee Falorie man,
A rattlin' rovin' Irishman,
I can do all that ever you can,
For I am the wee Falorie man.

I am a good old workin' man,
Each day I carry my wee tin can,
A large penny bap and a clipe of ham,
I am a good old workin' man.

FOCUS QUESTION Ask children to chorally read the "Talk About It" question on **Student Book** page 7. Have them describe what is happening in the photograph. Point out how sharing the **labor**, or work, helps people **accomplish**, or finish, a job easily.

Use the Picture Prompt

BUILD WRITING FLUENCY
Ask children to respond to the picture by writing for five minutes in their Writer's Notebooks about a time when they worked with others to do a job. Meet with children during individual Writing Conference time to provide feedback.

ELL ENGLISH LANGUAGE LEARNERS

Beginning	Intermediate	Advanced
Respond Tell children about the photograph. *The woman and the girl are in a garden. The woman and girl are working together. They are taking care of plants.* Then ask children to tell you about the photograph.	**Discuss** Ask children to describe the photograph. *Where are the woman and girl? What are they doing? Do you think they are working together?* Elicit details to support children's responses.	**Expand** Ask children to elaborate on the concept. *What are the woman and girl doing? Why do you think they are working together in the garden? When have you worked with someone?* Elicit details to support children's responses.

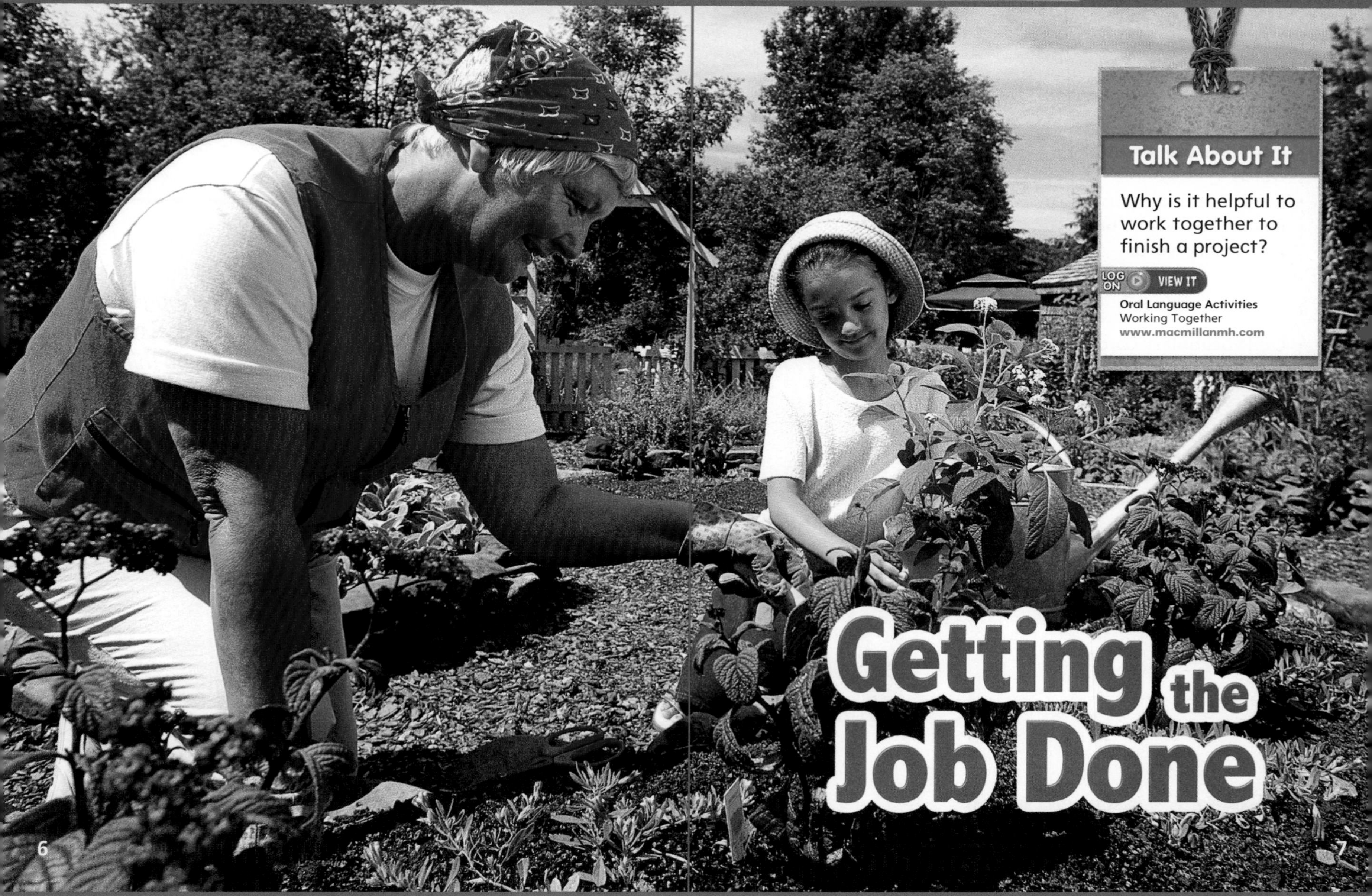
Talk About It
Why is it helpful to work together to finish a project?
LOG ON VIEW IT
Oral Language Activities
Working Together
www.macmillanmh.com
Getting the Job Done
6
7

Connect to the Unit Theme

When we work together, we can get more done.

CONNECT TO THEME
Ask children what they know about how important it is to work together to get a job done.

USE THEME FOLDABLE
Read aloud the **Big Idea** statement. Write the word **accomplish** on the board. Remind children that *accomplish* means "to finish a job." Read it aloud and have children repeat. Ask children to add it to their Unit Theme Foldable. Tell children that they will add pictures of different ways people work together to accomplish jobs.

Dinah Zike's FOLDABLES® Study Organizer

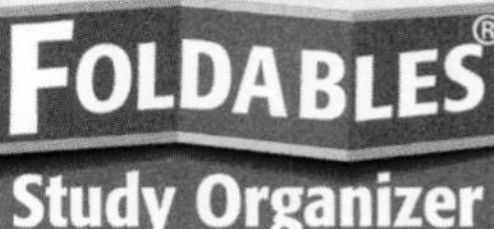

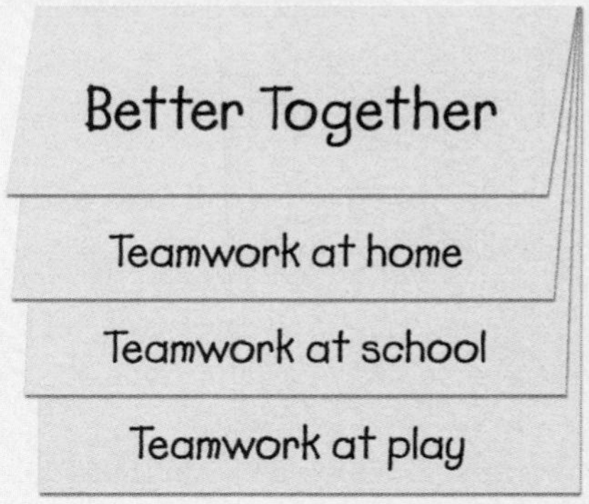
Better Together
Teamwork at home
Teamwork at school
Teamwork at play

Unit 4 Theme Foldable

Objectives

- Introduce oral vocabulary words
- Read "The Enormous Yucca"
- Review last week's oral vocabulary words

Materials

- Oral Vocabulary Cards: "The Enormous Yucca"

Oral Language

Build Robust Vocabulary

BUILD BACKGROUND Display "The Enormous Yucca" **Oral Vocabulary Card** 1 and read the title aloud. *We are going to read a folktale today about a man named Fernando who grew a huge yucca, or vegetable, in his garden.* Remind children that a folktale is a made-up story based on the customs of a people or region. *Do you think this story is fiction or nonfiction? Why?*

- Read the story on the back of the cards aloud. During the first reading, check children's listening comprehension using the Retell prompts. Review the story vocabulary words using the routine below.

Oral Vocabulary Cards

Additional Vocabulary

To provide 15–20 minutes of additional vocabulary instruction, see **Oral Vocabulary Cards** 5-Day Plan. The pre- and post-tests for this week can be found on **Teacher's Resource Book** pages 245–263.

Vocabulary Routine

Use the routine below to discuss the meaning of each story word.

Define: To **accomplish** means "to finish or complete."
Example: *We accomplish many things at school each day.*
Ask: What did you accomplish today? DESCRIPTION

- If something is **arduous**, it is difficult or hard. *Painting a room is an arduous job.* What is the most arduous job you have done lately? EXAMPLE
- **Labor** is hard work. *The construction workers were hungry after a day of labor.* Which is a kind of labor: building a brick wall or playing catch? EXAMPLE
- To **rejoice** is to show or feel great joy. *I will rejoice if I win the race.* Who will rejoice when summer vacation ends? PRIOR KNOWLEDGE
- To **succeed** means "to do something well." *After three tries, Maria finally succeeded at solving the puzzle.* What do you have to do to succeed at school? EXAMPLE

Use the routine to review last week's words: *coincidence*, *contemplate*, *explain*, *scheme*, and *worthy*.

Phonemic Awareness

Phoneme Identity

Explain/Model

Show children how to identify the same diphthong /ou/ sound in different words.

Listen as I say the sounds in a word: /h/ /ou/ /s/, *house*. The sound in the middle of *house* is /ou/. Now listen as I say the sounds in two more words: /l/ /ou/ /d/, *loud*, and /p/ /i/ /t/, *pit*. The words *house* and *loud* have the same /ou/ vowel sound in the middle. The word *pit* does not have /ou/ in the middle.

Repeat with *howl*, *pout*, *spin*; *round*, *pool*, *crown*; *ripe*, *brown*, *sound*; and *cow*, *rope*, *cloud*.

Guided Practice/Practice

Have children practice identifying the diphthong /ou/ sound in words. Guide practice with the first two sets.

Let's do some together. I will say the sounds in three words. Listen to the sounds in each word and identify which ones have the /ou/ sound.

foul, town, tan

rest, ground, clown

pounce, pull, now

spout, mouse, moat

grouch, moth, mouth

Objective

- Identify phoneme /ou/

ELL

Minimal Contrasts Focus on articulation. Make the /ou/ sound and point out your mouth position. Have children repeat. Use the articulation photos on the small Sound-Spelling Cards. Repeat for the /ō/ sound. Then have children say each sound together, noticing the slight differences in mouth position. Continue the articulation by having children read minimal contrast word pairs, such as *howl/hole*, *couch/coach*, *town/tone*.

Objectives

- Identify letter-sound correspondence for diphthong /ou/*ou*, *ow*
- Blend words with *ou*, *ow*
- Review previously taught phonics skills

Materials

- Sound-Spelling Card: *Cow*
- Word-Building Cards; Teacher's Resource Book, p. 66
- chart paper
- Practice Book, p. 173

Skills Trace

Diphthong *ou*, *ow*

Introduce	7C-D
Practice/ Apply	7F, 9G, 37F–G, 37I, 37T; Practice Book: p. 173; Decodable Reader: *The Missing String Beans*
Reteach/ Review	41C-D; 41K-N, 41Q, 41W, 41CC
Assess	Weekly Test; Unit 4 Test
Maintain	Build Fluency: Sound/Spellings

ELL

Speak Provide extra practice with the diphthong /ou/ by having children closely observe the shape of your mouth as you pronounce /ou/. Have them emulate. Provide a mirror that children can use to observe their own mouths as they say /ou/. Point out how your mouth glides, or moves, as the sound is made.

Sound Pronunciation

See **Sound Pronunciation CD** for a model of the /ou/ sound. Play this for children needing additional models.

Phonics

Diphthong *ou*, *ow*

Model

Teach the sound /ou/ spelled *ou*. Show the *Cow* **Sound-Spelling Card**. Model writing *ou*. Use the handwriting models provided.

This is the *Cow* Sound-Spelling Card. The sound is /ou/. The /ou/ sound can be spelled with the letters *ou* or *ow*. Say it with me: /ou/. Watch as I write the letters *ow*. I will say the sound /ou/ as I write the letters several times.

Guided Practice/Practice

Have children practice connecting letters and sound through writing. Repeat with *ow*.

Now do it with me. Say /ou/ as I write the letters *ou*.

This time, write the letters *ou* five times as you say the /ou/ sound.

Build Fluency: Sound/Spellings

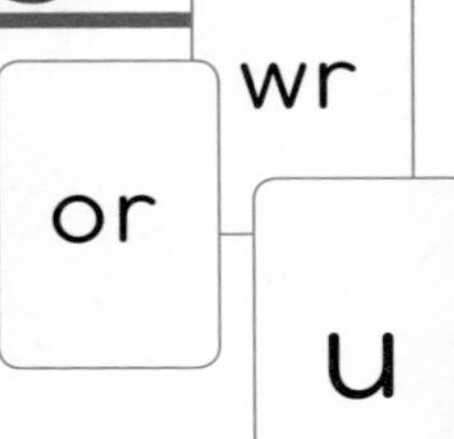

Display the following **Word-Building Cards:** *ou, ow, are, air, ear, ere, or, ore, oar, ar, gn, kn, wr, mb, eer, ere, ear, er, ir, ur, u, u_e, ew, ue*. Have children chorally say each sound. Repeat and vary the pace.

Blend Words with *ou*, *ow*

Model

Display Word-Building Cards *l, o, u, d*. Model blending sounds as you run your finger under each letter.

Continue by modeling the words *town*, *around*, *out*, *clown*, and *cloudy*.

This is the letter *l*. It stands for /l/. These are the letters *ou*. They stand for /ou/. Listen as I blend these sounds together: /lou/. This is the letter *d*. It stands for /d/. Listen as I blend all three sounds together: /loud/, *loud*. Say it with me.

Guided Practice/Practice

Write the words below on chart paper. Read each one in the first row, blending the sounds. For example: /d/ /ou/ /n/, /doun/. The word is *down*. Have children blend the sounds in each word with you. Then use the appropriate blending level to complete the remaining lines chorally. See **Sound-by-Sound Blending Routine** in the **Instructional Routine Handbook** for support. Save the chart paper for use in tomorrow's lesson.

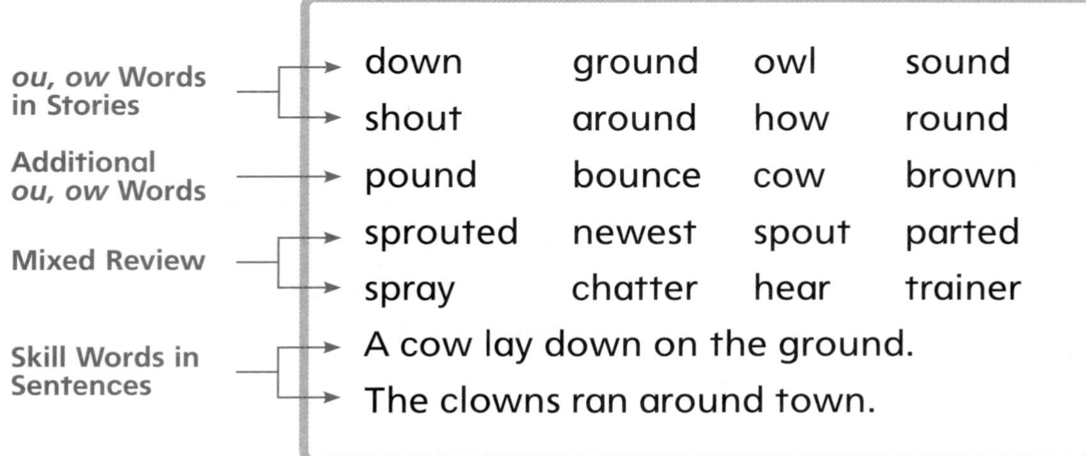

Corrective Feedback

Blending: Sound Error Model the sound that the children missed, then have them repeat the sound. Say: *My turn.* Tap under the letters and say: *Sound? /ou/. What's the sound?* Then return to the beginning of the word. Say: *Let's start over.* Blend the sounds in the word with children again.

Quick Check

Can children blend the sounds in words with diphthong *ou, ow*?

During **Small Group Instruction**

Tier 2

If No → **Approaching Level** Repeat blending using the chart above. Explicitly correct the error and provide more "with me" type practice. Use a lower level of blending to provide support.

If Yes → **On Level** Consolidate the learning by having children read additional words with diphthong *ou, ow*. See page 41M.

Beyond Level Extend the learning by having children read harder words containing diphthong *ou, ow*. See page 41N.

Daily Handwriting

Teach children how to form the uppercase letters *A, O, C, E*. See **Handwriting** pages 50, 52–53, and 104–112 for daily practice and additional information on ball-and-stick or slant models.

ON YOUR OWN

Practice Book, page 173

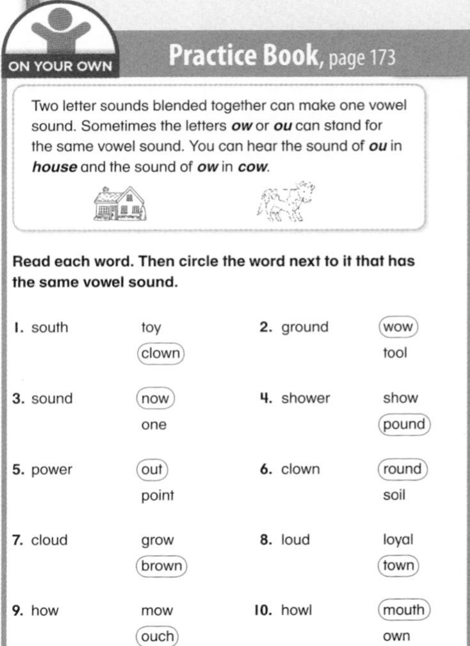

Two letter sounds blended together can make one vowel sound. Sometimes the letters ***ow*** or ***ou*** can stand for the same vowel sound. You can hear the sound of ***ou*** in ***house*** and the sound of ***ow*** in ***cow***.

Read each word. Then circle the word next to it that has the same vowel sound.

1. south — toy, (clown)
2. ground — (wow), tool
3. sound — (now), one
4. shower — show, (pound)
5. power — (out), point
6. clown — (round), soil
7. cloud — grow, (brown)
8. loud — loyal, (town)
9. how — mow, (ouch)
10. howl — (mouth), own

Approaching Reproducible, page 173

Beyond Reproducible, page 173

Objectives

- Spell words with diphthong *ou, ow*
- Spell high-frequency words
- Identify spelling patterns

Materials

- Phonics/Spelling Practice Book, p. 61
- paper and pencils

5-Day Spelling	
DAY 1	Dictation; Pretest
DAY 2	Teacher-Modeled Word Sort
DAY 3	Student Word Sort
DAY 4	Test Practice
DAY 5	Posttest

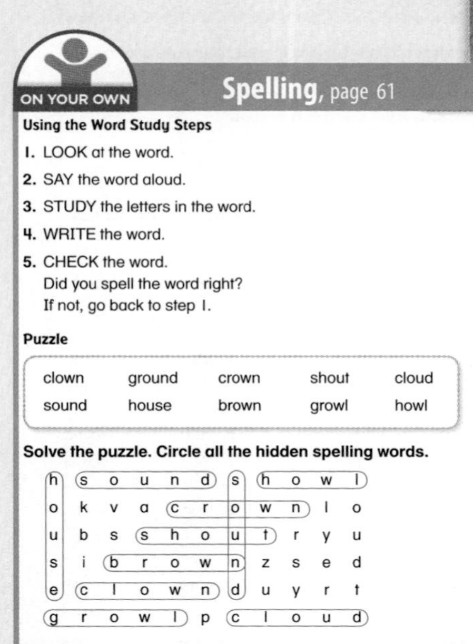
ON YOUR OWN

Spelling, page 61

Using the Word Study Steps

1. LOOK at the word.
2. SAY the word aloud.
3. STUDY the letters in the word.
4. WRITE the word.
5. CHECK the word.
Did you spell the word right?
If not, go back to step 1.

Puzzle

clown	ground	crown	shout	cloud
sound	house	brown	growl	howl

Solve the puzzle. Circle all the hidden spelling words.

h	s	o	u	n	d	s	h	o	w	l
o	k	v	a	c	r	o	w	n	l	o
u	b	s	s	h	o	u	t	r	y	u
s	i	b	r	o	w	n	z	s	e	d
e	c	l	o	w	n	d	u	y	r	t
g	r	o	w	l	p	c	l	o	u	d

Phonics/Spelling

Words with Diphthong *ou, ow*

DICTATION

Use dictation to help children transfer their growing knowledge of sound-spellings to writing. Follow the **Dictation Routine** below with each spelling word.

DICTATION ROUTINE

- Pronounce one word at a time. Have children clearly state the word. Then repeat the word for children and use it in a sentence.
- Ask children to orally segment the word to think about the individual sounds in the word, then have them write the word. Prompt children to use the **Sound-Spelling Card** spellings as they write. Provide **WorkBoards** for children who need support.

PRETEST

Pronounce each spelling word. Read the sentence and pronounce the word again. Ask children to say each word softly, stretching the sounds, before writing it. After the pretest, write each word on the board as you say the letter names. Have children check their words.

Spelling Words

Approaching	On Level	Beyond
cow	clown	scowling
clown	growl	growling
howl	howl	howling
brown	brown	gown
pound	crown	crown
round	ground	bounced
loud	shout	around
cloud	cloud	pouches
house	house	crowds
sound	sound	underground
star	shark	rare
chair	chair	area
family	family	family
four	four	four
hear	hear	hear

1. **clown:** The clown has a red nose.
2. **growl:** Bears growl in the woods.
3. **howl:** The coyotes howl at night.
4. **brown:** The dirty sand is brown.
5. **crown:** The king wears a crown.
6. **ground:** The tent is on the ground.
7. **shout:** Shout if you need help.
8. **cloud:** The dark cloud brought rain.
9. **house:** Our house is gray brick.
10. **sound:** The frog made a soft sound.
11. **shark:** We saw a shark at the zoo.
12. **chair:** We put a chair at the table.
13. **family:** My family has six members.
14. **four:** There are four kites in the air.
15. **hear:** "Can you hear me?" asked Mom.

Decodable Reader

- **Review High-Frequency Words** Write **believe**, **built**, and **material** on the board. Review the words with children using the **Read/Spell/Write** routine.

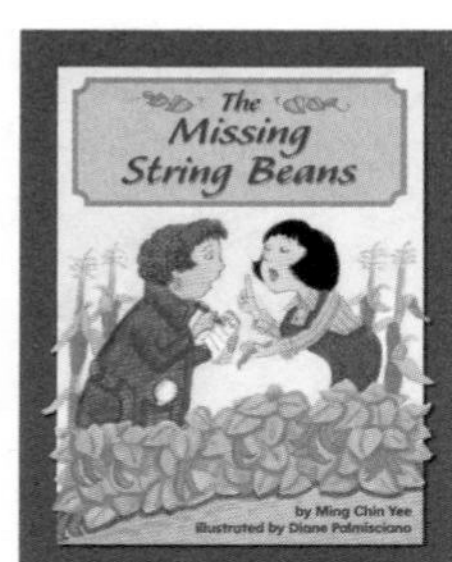

The Missing String Beans

- **Preview and Predict** Point to the book's title and have children sound out each word as you run your finger under it. Then ask:
  - *Where are the people in the picture?*
  - *What are they doing?*
  - *What do you think the story will be about?*

- **First Read** Turn to page 2. Have children point to each word, sounding out decodable words and saying the high-frequency words quickly. Children should chorally read the story the first time through. If children have difficulty, provide corrective feedback page by page as needed. See the **Decodable Text Routine** in the **Instructional Routine Handbook** for correction models.

- **Check Comprehension** Ask the following:
  - *What was Susie Sprout's problem?*
  - *Why do you think she called Detective Strong?*
  - *Explain what happened to Susie's string beans.*
  - *Turn to a partner and retell the story.*

- **Second Read** Reread the story with children.
  - Approaching Level If children struggle sounding out words, provide "with you" blending models. Then review blending using the words on the Word List at the end of the story during Small Group time. Conclude by guiding children through a rereading of the book.
  - Beyond Level If children can sound out the words, then have them quietly read the text with a partner.

Objectives

- Decode words with *ou*, *ow* in connected text
- Identify and read last week's high-frequency words *believe*, *built*, and *material*

Materials

- Decodable Reader Library: *The Missing String Beans*

High-Frequency Words

Use the **Read/Spell/Write** routine to teach each high-frequency word.

- **Read** Read the word. Have children repeat.
- **Spell** Chorally spell the word.
- **Write** Have children write the word as they spell it aloud. Then ask each child to write a sentence using each word.

SMALL GROUP OPTION

You may wish to read the Decodable Reader during **Small Group** time.

See pages 41K–41JJ

Objectives

- Introduce the meanings of vocabulary words
- Use context clues to teach words
- Review last week's vocabulary words

Materials

- Student Book: "The Story of the Giant Carrot"
- Practice Book, p. 174

Vocabulary

attached delicious
frantically gasped
swung

ELL

Preteach Vocabulary
See page 41P to preteach the vocabulary words to ELL and Approaching Level children. Use the **Visual Vocabulary Resources** to demonstrate and discuss each word.

Vocabulary

TEACH WORDS
Introduce each word using the **Define/Example/Ask** routine. Model reading each word.

Vocabulary Routine

Use the routine below to discuss the meaning of each word.

Define: When something is **attached**, it is stuck to something else.
Example: *Your hair is attached to your head.*
Ask: Tell about something else that is attached to your body. PRIOR KNOWLEDGE

- Food that is **delicious** tastes very good. *I think pears are delicious.* Name a word that has the same meaning as *delicious*. SYNONYM
- When you do something **frantically**, you are in a hurry and also worried. *I frantically dialed 911 when I saw the fire.* Name a word that means the opposite of *frantically*. ANTONYM
- If you **gasped**, you took a fast and loud breath from being scared or surprised. *I gasped when the loud fire bell rang suddenly*. Tell about a time when you gasped. DESCRIPTION
- Something that **swung** moved back and forth. *Jenny swung her book bag back and forth.* What is something that swung back and forth the last time you were at the playground? EXAMPLE

Word Wall Add these words to the Word Wall. Remove words from the wall as children master them.

Use the vocabulary routine to review last week's words *creating, familiar, glamorous, imagination, memories*, and *occasions*.

STRATEGY Use Context Clues

- Tell children that context clues are hints that suggest the meaning of an unfamiliar word. *When you come to an unfamiliar word, look at the words and sentences around it. Ask yourself what meaning of the unfamiliar word would fit.* Tell children to then try the meaning out. If they're still unsure, remind them they can use a dictionary.

Have children find the word *gasped* in "The Story of the Giant Carrot" on page 8 and read the sentence with the word.

Think Aloud I'm not sure what *gasped* means. I see that the sentence following it has the words "took a gulp of air." This tells me that when people gasp, they take air in very quickly.

Vocabulary

- gasped
- attached
- frantically
- swung
- delicious

Context Clues
Context clues are words or phrases that help you figure out the meaning of a word.

When you breathe, you *take air into and out of your lungs.*

The Story of the Giant Carrot

by Rosa Manuel

One day Farmer Smith planted carrot seeds. The next morning he looked outside and **gasped**. He took a gulp of air because he was so surprised. A giant leaf was growing in the garden. He knew what would be **attached**. Giant leaves are joined to giant carrots!

Farmer Smith ran outside **frantically**. He was very, very excited. He jumped up and grabbed the leaf. It was so high, he **swung** from it! His body waved from side to side. Once his feet were back on the ground, he pulled on the leaf. The giant carrot would not come out.

First he called to his family for help. The family pulled, but the carrot was too big. Then he asked his neighbors to help. They pulled so hard that they had to stop to catch their breath. Finally he called to the dog and cow for help. They all pulled, and at last the carrot popped out!

The Smith family fed the whole town with the **delicious** carrot. Everyone said it was the best-tasting carrot they had ever eaten!

Reread for Comprehension

Reread

Cause and Effect A cause is why something happened. An effect is what happens. Rereading parts of a story can help you figure out the cause and effect in a story. Use the Cause and Effect chart to fill out information as you read.

Cause → Effect

LOG ON LEARN IT Comprehension www.macmillanmh.com

Read "The Story of the Giant Carrot"

Read "The Story of the Giant Carrot" with children. Stop at each **highlighted** word. Ask children to identify clues to the meanings of the highlighted words. Tell children that they will read these words again in *Head, Body, Legs: A Story from Liberia*. Then have children compare this story with "The Enormous Yucca." Ask them to identify what is similar about the plot, setting, or characters.

Quick Check

Do children understand word meanings?

During **Small Group Instruction**

If No → **Approaching Level** Vocabulary pages: 41L, 41R, 41X, 41DD

If Yes → **On Level** Reread Vocabulary Selection

Beyond Level Reread Vocabulary Selection

ON YOUR OWN

Practice Book, page 174

Use what you know about the words in the clues to choose a word from the box that makes sense for each question. Then write the answers in the puzzle.

swung gasped delicious frantically attached

Across
3. A baseball player _____ the bat to hit the ball.
4. Your head is _____ to your neck.
5. People who love pizza think it tastes _____.

Down
1. Kendra _____ searched for her lost dog.
2. The tired runner _____ when she won the race.

Puzzle answers: 1 frantically, 2 gasped, 3 swung, 4 attached, 5 delicious

Approaching Reproducible, page 174

Beyond Reproducible, page 174

Objectives

- Monitor comprehension by rereading
- Identify cause and effect
- Use academic language

Materials

- Transparencies 7, 16a, 16b
- Student Book: "The Story of the Giant Carrot"

Skills Trace

Cause and Effect	
Introduce	U2: 199A–B
Practice/ Apply	U2: 199J–231A; Practice Book: 73–74
Reteach/ Review	U2: 235G, 235R–T, 235X-Z; U3: 403A–B, 403K–429A, 435G, 435R–T, 435X-Z; Practice Book: 151–152
Assess	Weekly Tests; Units 2, 3, 4, 6 Tests
Maintain	U2: 243N; U3: 457N; U4: 9A–9B, 9J–37A, 41G, 41R–T, 41X–Z, 71N; U6: 409A–B, 409J–433A, 437G, 437R–T, 437X–Z, 457N; Practice Book: 176–177, 322–323

ELL

Academic Language Preteach the following academic language words to ELL and Approaching Level children during Small Group time: *monitor comprehension, reread, cause and effect.* See page 41O.

Comprehension

STRATEGY Monitor Comprehension: Reread

EXPLAIN

What Is It? Explain to children that when they **monitor** their **comprehension** they make sure they understand what they are reading. Remind children that if something they are reading does not make sense, they may have missed an important detail. They should make a correction by going back and **rereading** the passage silently or aloud to make adjustments to their understanding.

Why Is It Important? Tell children that rereading a part of a story when it does not make sense will help them better understand it.

SKILL Cause and Effect

EXPLAIN

What Is It? A **cause** is an event that makes something happen. An **effect** is what happens because of an action or event. An effect may have more than one cause and a cause may have more than one effect. *Causes and effects help make up the events in a story. Identifying them can help readers place events in sequence and retell the story.*

Why Is It Important? Identifying causes and their effects can help readers understand what happens in a story's plot and why it happens.

Transparency 16a

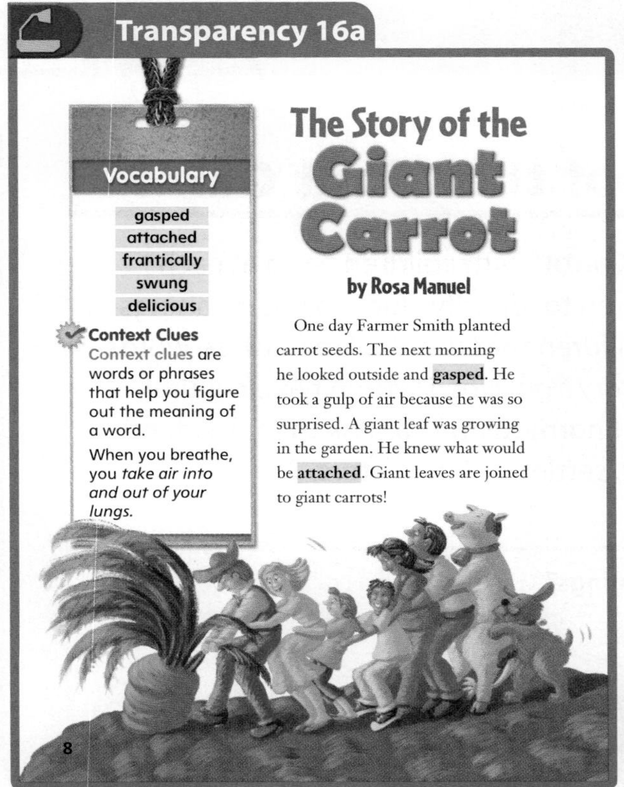

Vocabulary

gasped
attached
frantically
swung
delicious

Context Clues
Context clues are words or phrases that help you figure out the meaning of a word.

When you breathe, you *take air into and out of your lungs.*

The Story of the Giant Carrot

by Rosa Manuel

One day Farmer Smith planted carrot seeds. The next morning he looked outside and **gasped**. He took a gulp of air because he was so surprised. A giant leaf was growing in the garden. He knew what would be **attached**. Giant leaves are joined to giant carrots!

8

Transparency 16b

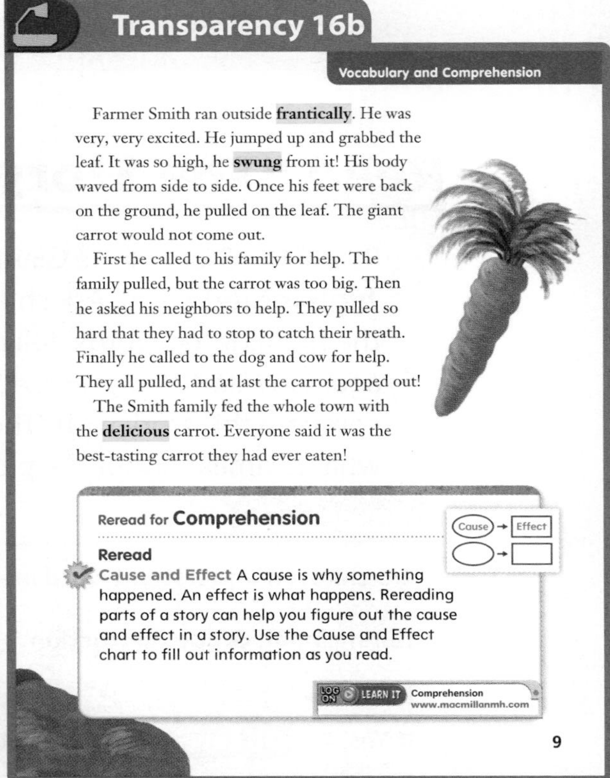

Vocabulary and Comprehension

Farmer Smith ran outside **frantically**. He was very, very excited. He jumped up and grabbed the leaf. It was so high, he **swung** from it! His body waved from side to side. Once his feet were back on the ground, he pulled on the leaf. The giant carrot would not come out.

First he called to his family for help. The family pulled, but the carrot was too big. Then he asked his neighbors to help. They pulled so hard that they had to stop to catch their breath. Finally he called to the dog and cow for help. They all pulled, and at last the carrot popped out!

The Smith family fed the whole town with the **delicious** carrot. Everyone said it was the best-tasting carrot they had ever eaten!

Reread for Comprehension

Reread
Cause and Effect A cause is why something happened. An effect is what happens. Rereading parts of a story can help you figure out the cause and effect in a story. Use the Cause and Effect chart to fill out information as you read.

LOG ON LEARN IT Comprehension www.macmillanmh.com

9

Student Book pages 8–9 are available on Comprehension Transparencies 16a and 16b.

- Words such as *because*, *so*, and *since* are clues that the author is describing a cause and its effect.
- Sometimes a cause and its effect does not contain a clue word. Tell children they can ask *What happened?* to find the effect, and *Why?* to find the cause. They can also use the logical sequence of events to find cause and effect relationships in a story. This can help them retell a story's beginning, middle, and end. It can also help them describe the plot, as the problem and solution in a story may be identified in a cause and effect relationship.

MODEL

How Do I Use It? Read the first paragraph of "The Story of the Giant Carrot" on **Student Book** page 8. Model for children how to identify cause-and-effect relationship in the story.

Think Aloud I read that Farmer Smith gasped. I ask myself, *Why did he gasp?* The answer to that question will be the cause. I reread the first part of the story and see that he was surprised to find a giant leaf growing in his garden. So, seeing a giant leaf in his garden and being surprised is the cause. The effect is Farmer Smith gasping. I also see the clue word because in the sentence *He took a gulp of air because he was so surprised.* The first part of that sentence is the effect, and the part after *because* is the cause.

Display the Cause and Effect Chart on **Transparency 7**. *What happened?* For Effect, write: *Farmer Smith gasped.* Ask: *Why did Farmer Smith gasp?* (He gasped because he was surprised.) For Cause, write: *Farmer Smith was surprised.*

GUIDED PRACTICE

- Have children reread the first paragraph and tell all of the events that happened. Then ask them to explain why these things happened in sequence. Fill in the next row of the Chart.
- Continue helping children identify important plot events and why they happened. Remind them that the effect is something that happened and the cause is why it happened. Causes come before effects in the sequence of events.

PRACTICE

Have children reread the remainder of "The Story of the Giant Carrot" and complete the Cause and Effect Chart. Then ask children to explain how they decided what caused each effect.

Ask children to use the chart to identify the causes and effects as they retell the story to a partner.

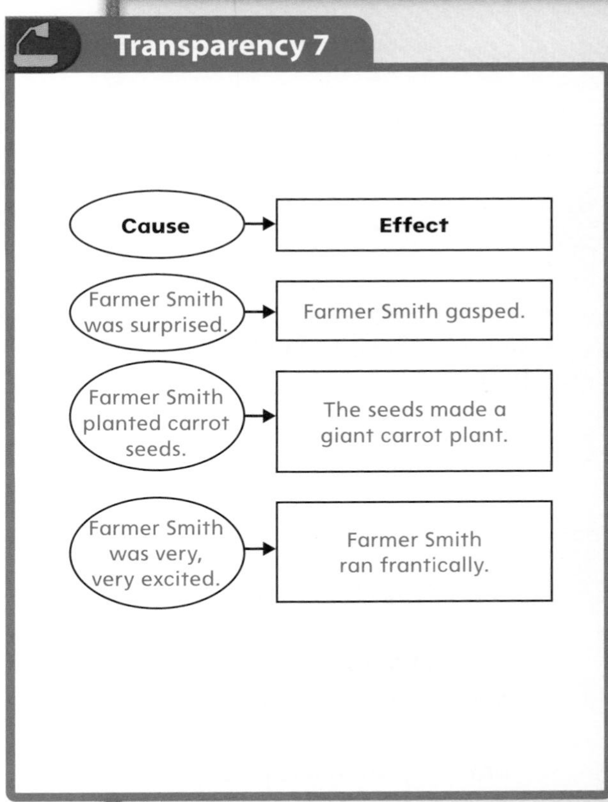

Graphic Organizer Transparency

Objectives

- Form present-tense of *be*
- Understand and use linking verbs

Materials

- Transparency 76
- Grammar Practice Book, p. 76

5-Day Grammar	
Linking Verbs	
DAY 1	Linking Verbs: Present-Tense Forms of *Be*
DAY 2	Past-Tense Forms of *Be*
DAY 3	Mechanics: Capitalization
DAY 4	Past-Tense Forms of *Be* Proofread
DAY 5	Review and Assess Capitalization Linking Verbs

ON YOUR OWN **Grammar**, page 76

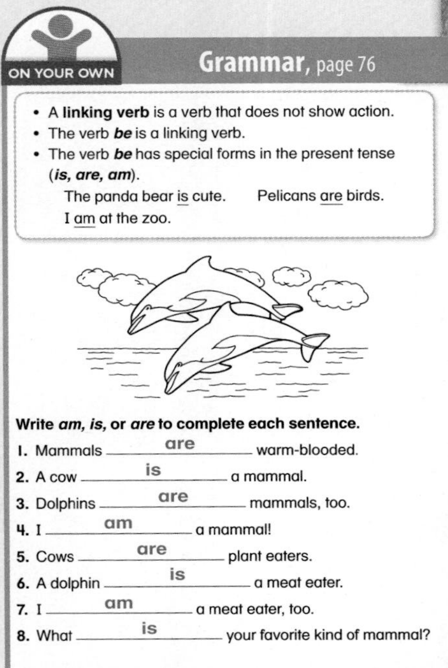

- A **linking verb** is a verb that does not show action.
- The verb ***be*** is a linking verb.
- The verb ***be*** has special forms in the present tense (***is, are, am***).

The panda bear is cute. Pelicans are birds.
I am at the zoo.

Write *am, is,* or *are* to complete each sentence.

1. Mammals are warm-blooded.
2. A cow is a mammal.
3. Dolphins are mammals, too.
4. I am a mammal!
5. Cows are plant eaters.
6. A dolphin is a meat eater.
7. I am a meat eater, too.
8. What is your favorite kind of mammal?

Grammar

Linking Verbs

EXPLAIN/MODEL

- Tell children that a **linking verb** is a verb that does not show action. The verb *be* is a linking verb. (e.g., When will you *be* six?)
- Tell them the verb *be* has special forms in the present tense. If the subject is *I*, use *am*. (e.g., I *am* on the baseball team.)
- Explain that if the subject is singular (such as *he* or *she*), use *is*. (e.g., She *is* in our car. He *is* at summer camp.)
- Tell children if the subject is *you*, *we*, or *they*, use *are*. (e.g., We *are* sad to leave. You *are* my favorite author. They *are* at the zoo.)

Write *is*, *are*, and *am* on the board. Model using each linking verb in a sentence. Write the sentences on the board. Have children chorally read each sentence and pick out the linking verb.

Use item 1 on **Grammar Transparency 76** to model for children how to complete sentences with linking verbs *is*, *are*, or *am*. Explain that each linking verb links the subject with the rest of the sentence.

Transparency 76

Linking Verbs

1. Ms. Okobi is the coach of our swim team.
2. I am the fastest swimmer in our school.
3. The team is at the pool to raise money.
4. The swimmers are in the water.
5. We are part of a project to clean the park.

Grammar Transparency

GUIDED PRACTICE/PRACTICE

Work with children to complete each sentence on the transparency with *is*, *are*, or *am*.

Writing

Personal Narrative

DISCUSS THE MODEL

- Explain to children that a **personal narrative** is written in the first person about the writer's real experiences, using words such as *I* and *my*. A personal narrative tells events in a logical sequence, or time order. The writer shares how he or she feels about a topic.

Present and discuss the features of a personal narrative using the model and callouts on **Writing Transparency 91**.

Transparency 91

Cooking for a Crowd

Last month, my parents hosted a family reunion. Aunts, uncles, cousins, and grandparents came from all over the country to spend the weekend together. Our biggest challenge was the barbecue. We had to cook mountains of food for all our relatives. On Friday, my cousins and I made tons of potato salad. On Saturday, my father and his brothers took turns making burgers at the grill. My mom and grandmother spent two whole days making desserts. I am proud that all our hard work made the barbecue on Saturday night a big success!

The narrative starts with a clear topic sentence.

The author uses first-person words, such as we and our.

Events are told in logical sequence.

The writer expresses feelings.

Writing Transparency

FOCUS AND PLAN

Identify Purpose and Audience The purposes of writing a personal narrative are to entertain and inform. The audience may be your classmates, your teacher, your friends, or your family.

Develop a Topic This week you will write a personal narrative about a time when you worked with a group of people to complete a task. (See **Student Book** page 40.) Brainstorm a list of topics in your Writer's Notebook.

Teacher Think Aloud Think about times when you worked with a group of people to do a job or solve a problem. What did you do? Were the people you worked with friends, family members, or classmates? Did you do your work inside or outside? What about the job made it too difficult for one person to do alone? Write down what you did and organize it into a logical sequence.

Objectives

- Introduce the features of a personal narrative
- Generate ideas for a topic for a personal narrative

Materials

- Transparency 91

5-Day Writing

Personal Narrative	
DAY 1	Focus and Plan
DAY 2	Prewrite
DAY 3	Skill: A Strong Paragraph; Draft
DAY 4	Revise; Edit/Proofread
DAY 5	Publish and Present

ELL

Describe To help children brainstorm a topic, provide them with sentence frames. Say each of the following sentence frames aloud and have children complete them orally: *At school, I work in a group when ________. I feel ________. The other people in the group help me ________. Group work is helpful because ________.* Give children ample time to respond.

Day 2 At a Glance

WHOLE GROUP

Oral Language
- Build Robust Vocabulary

Phonemic Awareness
- Phoneme Categorization

Phonics
- Diphthong *ou, ow*
- Build Fluency
- Reread *The Missing String Beans*
- Spelling: Sort Words with *ou, ow*

Vocabulary
- Review Words in Context

Comprehension
- Strategy: Monitor Comprehension: Reread
- Skill: Cause and Effect
- Read *Head, Body, Legs: A Story from Liberia*

Language Arts
- Grammar: Linking Verbs
- Writing: Personal Narrative

SMALL GROUP

- Differentiated Instruction, pages 41K–41JJ

Oral Language

Build Robust Vocabulary

Reread the **Oral Vocabulary Cards** to review this week's vocabulary words. Ask questions to check children's comprehension of the folktale. *Why was Fernando excited to see the results of his labor? What did he accomplish and why did it make him feel proud? Do you think pulling an enormous yucca out of the ground is an arduous thing to do? What helped Fernando succeed? How did everyone rejoice after they were successful?*

Oral Vocabulary Cards

REVIEW WORDS

Ask the following probing questions to generate discussion and use the words in oral speech.

- Name something that you can **accomplish** in an afternoon with the help of a friend.
- Which is an example of an **arduous** thing to do: moving a pile of bricks from one place to another or taking a nap?
- Why is it important to **labor** until a job is done?
- How would you **rejoice** if your baseball team won a game?
- What is the opposite of **succeed**? Name something you would like to be successful at.

- Review last week's words *coincidence*, *contemplate*, *explain*, *scheme*, and *worthy* using similar questions.

Write About It

Think about the oral vocabulary story "The Enormous Yucca." Write a new ending about the arduous task of getting the giant yucca out of the ground.

Phonemic Awareness

Phoneme Categorization

Model

Show children how to listen for the medial /ou/ in words.

Repeat the routine with *town*, *fowl*, *mouth*, *house*, and *pouch*.

Listen as I say each sound in the word *shout*. I hear /sh/ at the beginning of *shout*. I hear /ou/ in the middle of *shout*. I hear /t/ at the end of *shout*. Listen: /shout/, *shout*.

Now I am going to say three words. Two of them have the vowel sound /ou/ in the middle and one does not: *found*, *fast*, *drown*. The word *fast* does not have /ou/ in the middle.

Guided Practice/Practice

Have children practice with these examples.

Guide practice with the first row.

I am going to say more groups of words. Listen carefully. Tell me which word has a different vowel sound in the middle.

sound, couch, math	pounce, part, clown
grass, frown, pound	blouse, brag, loud
sprout, proud, free	slip, scowl, crowd
how, hop, hound	mouse, low, town
skate, scout, count	south, ground, fun

Objectives

- Categorize words with /ou/
- Review folktale

Materials

- Practice Book for folktale, p. 175

Objectives

- Substitute initial and final sounds
- Blend sounds in words with diphthong *ou, ow*
- Review words with variant vowel *au, aw*
- Read multisyllabic words

Materials

- Word-Building Cards; Teacher's Resource Book, p. 66
- pocket chart
- word chart from Day 1

Skills Trace

Diphthong *ou, ow*	
Introduce	7C-D
Practice/ Apply	7F, 9G, 37F-G, 37I, 37T; Practice Book: p. 173; Decodable Reader: *The Missing String Beans*
Reteach/ Review	41C-D; 41K-N, 41Q, 41W, 41CC
Assess	Weekly Test; Unit 4 Test
Maintain	Build Fluency: Sound/Spellings

Build Fluency

Connected Text

Have children independently reread *The Missing String Beans* from the **Decodable Reader Library**.

Phonics

Blend Words with *ou, ow*

Model

Place **Word-Building Cards** *h, o, w, l* in the pocket chart to form *howl*. Model how to generate and blend the sounds to say the word.

The letter *h* stands for /h/. The letters *ow* stand for /ou/. The letter *l* stands for /l/. Now listen as I blend all three sounds: /houl/. Now you say it. Let's read the word together.

Repeat with *round*, *mouse*, *town*, *proud*, and *sprout*.

Guided Practice/Practice

Repeat with additional words. Have children blend the sounds in the words with you.

chow	found	crown	sour
ground	house	growl	pounce
crowd	slouch	trout	south

Build Words with *ou, ow*

Model

Place Word-Building Cards *r, o, u, n, d* in the pocket chart. Blend the phonemes.

Let's blend all the sounds together and read the word: /round/, *round*.

Change *r* to *f* and repeat with *found*.

Let's blend all the sounds together and read the word: /found/, *found*.

Change *nd* to *l* and repeat with *foul*.

Let's blend all the sounds together and read the word: /foul/, *foul*.

Guided Practice/Practice

Continue building with other sets of words. Blend sounds together and read the words.

couch, pouch, pounce, bounce, bounces
spout, pout, pouch, grouch, grouchy
cow, how, howl, hound, hounded
crowd, crown, crouch, slouch, slouches

Phonics/Spelling

Word Sort with *ou, ow*

- Display the pocket chart. Place index cards with the key words *town* and *found* to form two columns in the pocket chart. Generate sentences for the key words *town* and *found*.
- Say each key word and pronounce the sounds: /t/ /ou/ /n/; /f/ /ou/ /n/ /d/. Pronounce each word again, emphasizing the /ou/ sound. Ask children to chorally spell each word.
- Hold up the word *clown*. Pronounce each sound clearly: /k/ /l/ /ou/ /n/. Blend the sounds: /kloun/. Repeat with the card for *ground*. Place words below the correct key word label so there is one example of each. Have children read each word, listening for the /ou/ sound. Ask children to chorally spell each word.
- Have children place remaining cards under the correct key label.
- Hold up the cards for *family*, *four*, and *hear*. As you say and spell them with children, point out that these words do not contain the /ou/ sound. Place these cards in a separate column in the pocket chart. Make sure children recognize that the spelling pattern *ou* in the word *four* does not have the /ou/ sound.
- **Build Fluency: Word Automaticity** Have children chorally read the words several times for fluency.

Analyze Errors — Articulation Support

- Use children's pretest errors to analyze spelling problems and provide corrective feedback. For example, children may have difficulties with the final *-nd* in *sound* and *round*.
- Clearly pronounce the word, emphasizing the /nd/ sounds at the end. Have children repeat. Use **Sound-Spelling Workboards** to help children segment the word sound by sound to emphasize these two final sounds. Then have children write the word in the Sound-Spelling Workboards before writing it on their papers.

Objectives

- Spell and sort words with diphthong *ou*, *ow*
- Build Fluency: Word Automaticity

Materials

- pocket chart
- large index cards with spelling words
- Sound-Spelling Workboard; Teacher's Resource Book, p. 143
- markers
- Phonics/Spelling Practice Book, p. 62

5-Day Spelling

DAY 1	Dictation; Pretest
DAY 2	Teacher-Modeled Word Sort
DAY 3	Student Word Sort
DAY 4	Test Practice
DAY 5	Posttest

ON YOUR OWN — Spelling, page 62

clown	ground	crown	shout	cloud
sound	house	brown	growl	howl

A. Word Sort

Look at the spelling words in the box. Fill in the blanks below with spelling words that match each spelling pattern.

ow	*ou*
1. clown	6. ground
2. crown	7. shout
3. brown	8. cloud
4. growl	9. sound
5. howl	10. house

B. Rhyme Time

Write the spelling words that rhyme with each of these words.

11. pound — ground, sound
12. mouse — house
13. owl — growl, howl

Objectives

- Apply knowledge of word meanings and context clues
- Review last week's vocabulary words

Materials

- Transparency 31

Vocabulary

Words in Context

REVIEW

Review the meanings of the vocabulary words. Display **Transparency 31**. Model how to use word meanings and context clues to fill in the first missing word.

Think Aloud In the first paragraph, I read that the fruit is *attached* to a tree, but I'm not sure what *attached* means. In the next sentence, it says the fruit was stuck to a tree. *Attached* must mean almost the same thing as *stuck*.

Transparency 31

delicious attached gasped frantically swung

Once upon a time, there was only one fruit in the world. It was (1) attached to a tree high above Earth. It had been stuck there forever. One day, the animals decided to try to get the fruit. They got in a circle and threw Monkey up into the tree. Monkey (2) swung from branch to branch using his long arms. When he got close, he kicked his legs (3) frantically. He knocked off the fruit!

All the animals (4) gasped as Monkey and the fruit fell from the tree. Hippo caught Monkey and the fruit hit the ground. They could all breathe again.

Then they ate the fruit. It was (5) delicious. It was the best thing they had ever tasted. As they ate, the seeds sprinkled. Soon there were fruit all over Earth.

Vocabulary Transparency

GUIDED PRACTICE/PRACTICE

- Have children use context clues to write missing words 2–5 on their papers. Then ask partners to check each other's answers and explain which context clues they used. Have children chorally reread the paragraphs on the transparency to build fluency.
- During independent work time, have children write sentences in their Writer's Notebooks using their vocabulary words.

Review last week's words *creating*, *familiar*, *glamorous*, *imagination*, *memories*, and *occasions* in context.

Comprehension

STRATEGY Monitor Comprehension: Reread

Remind children that monitoring comprehension means stopping and checking to see if they understand what they are reading. Tell them that if something does not make sense, they can make a correction and **reread** the passage. *As we read, we'll stop and make sure we understand everything that has happened so far. If we don't, we'll go back and reread a section, either aloud or silently, and make adjustments. That way we will better understand what we read.*

Main Selection

SKILL Cause and Effect

Review with children that an **effect** is what happens in a story and a **cause** is why something happens. The plot in a story is often a series of cause-and-effect relationships. *As you read the story, ask yourself, What happened? Why did it happen? This will help you identify causes and effects. Doing so will help you better understand the story's events.*

Prepare to Read

PREVIEW AND PREDICT

- Ask children to use ideas such as the title and illustrations to help make predictions about *Head, Body, Legs: A Story from Liberia. What does the story seem to be about? What kinds of pictures does the story have? Does the story look like it could happen in real life? Explain.*
- **Genre** Have a child read the definition of a folktale on **Student Book** page 10. *A folktale is a made-up story based on the customs and traditions of a people or region. The events in the story may not happen in real life, but they may teach a lesson or explain how things came to be.*

SET A PURPOSE FOR READING

- **Focus Question** Discuss the "Read to Find Out" question on page 10. Remind children to look for the answer as they read.
- Point out the Cause and Effect Chart in the Student Book and have children turn to the chart on **Practice Book** page 176. Remind them that they will use the chart to record causes and effects in the story.
- Ask children to set their own purposes for reading.

Objectives

- **Monitor comprehension: Reread**
- **Identify cause and effect**
- **Use a graphic organizer**
- **Use academic language: *cause, effect***

Materials

- **Student Book: *Head, Body, Legs: A Story from Liberia*, pp. 10–35**
- **Practice Book, p. 176**

Skills Trace

Cause and Effect	
Introduce	U2: 199A–B
Practice/ Apply	U2: 199J–231A; Practice Book: 73–74
Reteach/ Review	U2: 235G, 235R–T, 235X-Z; U3: 403A–B, 403K–429A, 435G, 435R–T, 435X-Z; Practice Book: 151–152
Assess	Weekly Tests; Units 2, 3, 4, 6 Tests
Maintain	U2: 243N; U3: 457N; U4: 9A–9B, 9J–37A, 41G, 41R–T, 41X–Z, 71N; U6: 409A–B, 409J–433A, 437G, 437R–T, 437X–Z, 457N; Practice Book: 176–177, 322–323

Digital Learning

Story available on **Listening Library Audio CD** and **StudentWorks Plus**, the Interactive eBook.

Interactive Student Book

www.macmillanmh.com

Comprehension

Genre
A Folktale is usually a made-up story that takes place long ago.

Reread
Cause and Effect
As you read, use your Cause and Effect Chart.

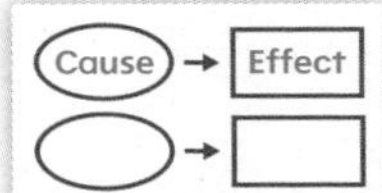

Read to Find Out
What causes the body parts to work together?

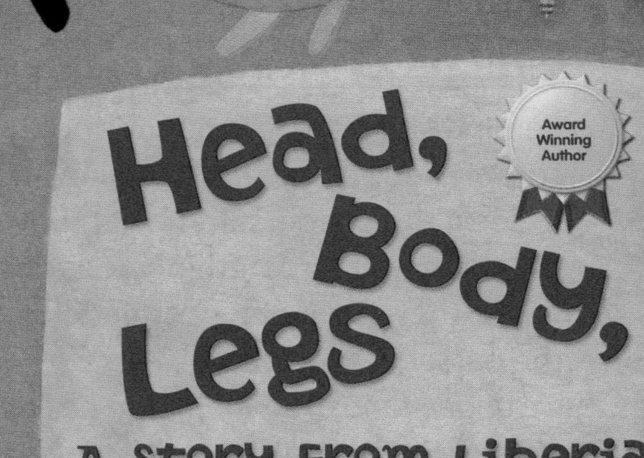

10 11

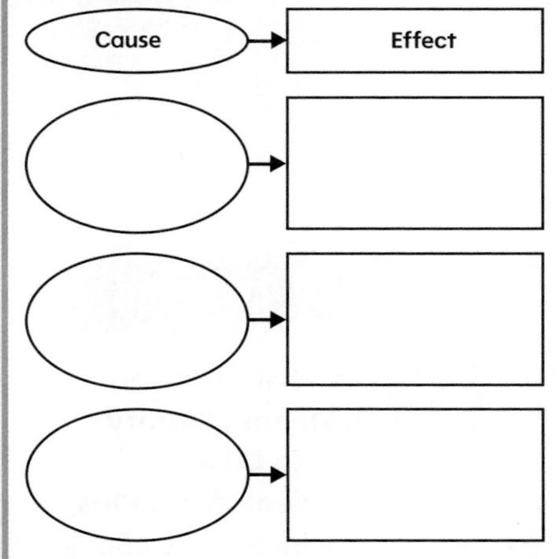

ON YOUR OWN **Practice Book**, page 176

As you read *Head, Body, Legs: A Story from Liberia*, fill in the Cause and Effect Chart.

Cause	Effect

How does the information you wrote in this Cause and Effect Chart help you to better understand the sequence of events in *Head, Body, Legs: A Story from Liberia*?

Approaching Reproducible, page 176

Beyond Reproducible, page 176

Read Main Selection

PURPOSE FOR READING
Ask children to read the "Read to Find Out Question." Remind them to pay attention to how the body parts tried to work together.

PARTNERS

Preteach	Read Together
Have Approaching Level children in English Language Learners listen to the story on **StudentWorks Plus**, the Interactive eBook before reading with the class.	Use the prompts to guide comprehension and model how to complete the graphic organizer. Have children use **Think/Pair/Share** as they respond to the prompts.

LOG ON StudentWorks Plus Interactive Student Book

Long ago, Head was all by himself.

He had no legs, no arms, no body. He rolled everywhere. All he could eat were things on the ground that he could reach with his tongue. 1

At night he rolled under a cherry tree. He fell asleep and dreamed of sweet cherries.

12 13

Develop Comprehension

1 SKILL Cause and Effect

In the story, Head must roll everywhere he goes. Why must head do this? Find the **cause** that makes this happen. (Head has no legs, arms, or body to move himself with, so he can only get from one place to another by rolling.) The cause behind this effect has another effect. What else must Head do besides roll everywhere? (Without body parts, Head can't get off the ground. So he has to eat what he can pick up off the ground with his tongue.)

Think/Pair/Share Discuss these cause-and-effect relationships with a partner and then add them to your Cause and Effect charts.

ELL

Preview Text Have children use **StudentWorks Plus**, the interactive eBook, to preview the text. This eBook contains summaries in multiple languages, word-by-word reading support, bilingual glossary, and comprehension questions with corrective feedback. Use the Interactive Questions Response Guide on pages 210–223 of the ELL Resource Book to preteach the content in "Head, Body, Legs: A Story from Liberia" and develop meaning.

One morning Head woke up and thought, "I'm tired of grass and mushrooms. I wish I could reach those cherries."

He rolled himself up a little hill. "Maybe if I get a good head start I can hit the trunk hard enough to knock some cherries off," he thought. He shoved with his ears and began to roll down the hill. "Here I go!" he shouted.

Faster and faster he rolled.

CRASH!

"OWWWW!" he cried. 2

"Who's there?" someone asked.

14 15

Develop Comprehension

2 STRATEGY Monitor Comprehension: Reread

If you do not understand why Head is rolling down the hill, what can you do to monitor your comprehension and make adjustments?

Teacher Think Aloud To understand this section better, I went back and reread it. This is a correction I made when my understanding broke down. On page 13 I reread that Head dreamed of sweet cherries. He says on page 14 that he is tired of grass and mushrooms. I think that Head wants those cherries very much. He rolls down the hill very quickly so he can smash into the cherry tree, thinking that the cherries might be knocked loose and fall on the ground. So, he risks hurting himself to try to knock some cherries to the ground, where he can reach them.

Decoding

Apply Phonics Skills While reading, point out words with the sound/spelling patterns children have recently learned. You may focus on words with *ou*, *ow*, such as *shouted*, *down*, *ground*, and *bounced*.

Model blending each word sound by sound. Then have children repeat.

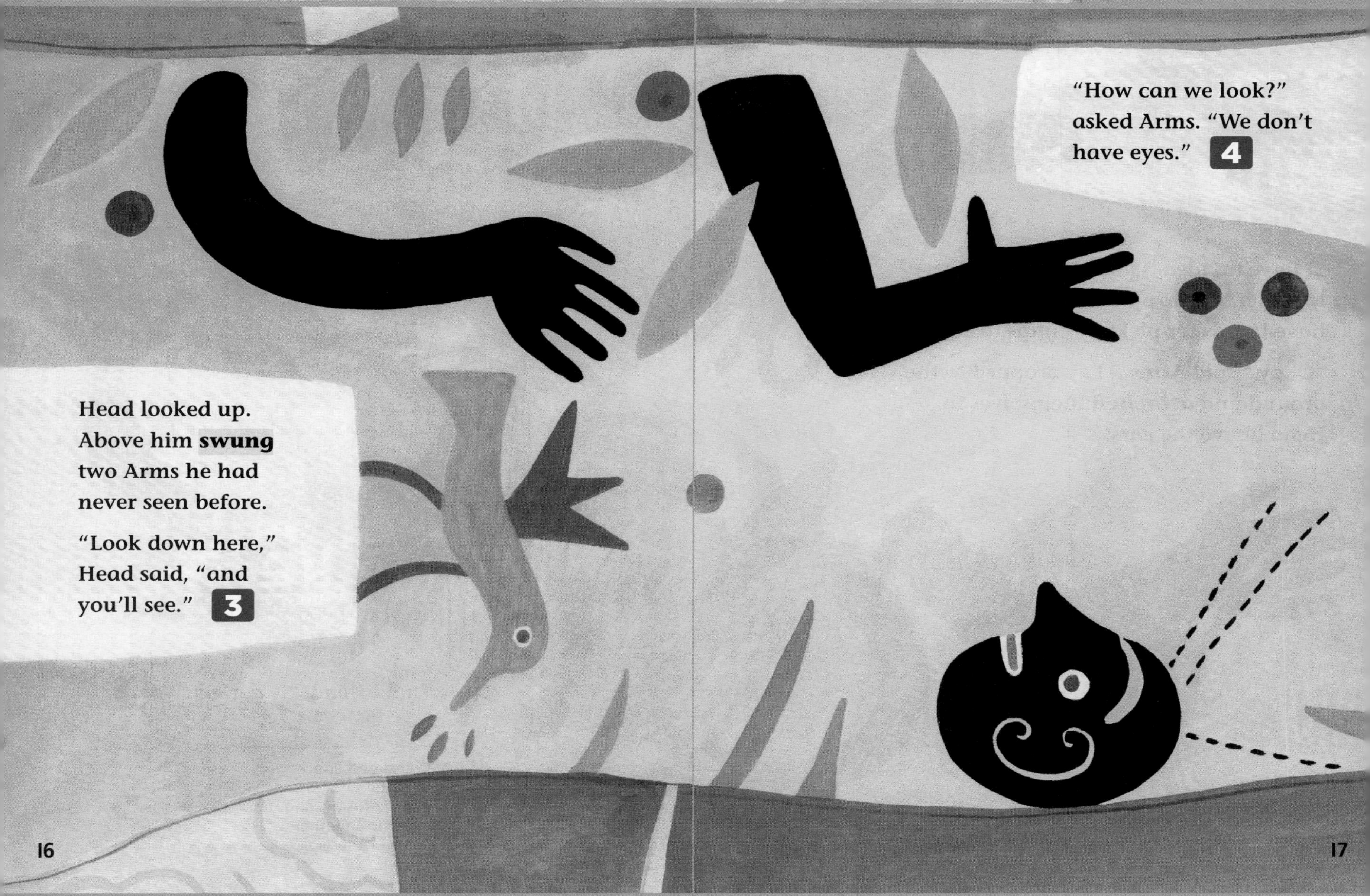

Head looked up. Above him **swung** two Arms he had never seen before.

"Look down here," Head said, "and you'll see." **3**

"How can we look?" asked Arms. "We don't have eyes." **4**

16

17

3 **SKILL** **Cause and Effect**

Why does Head roll down the hill and hit the tree? (He can only move by rolling and he wanted to knock the cherries from the tree so he could eat them off the ground.) What causes Arms to notice Head? (Arms heard Head crash into the tree and yell "OWWWW!")

Think/Pair/Share Working with a partner, add these cause-and-effect relationships to your Cause and Effect Charts.

4 **GENRE: FOLKTALE**

Remind children that a **folktale** is usually a made-up story that takes place long ago. How do you know that this story is a folktale? (Folktales are fiction. I know this story is made up because heads and arms aren't separate in real life. I read on page 12 that the events in the story happened long ago.)

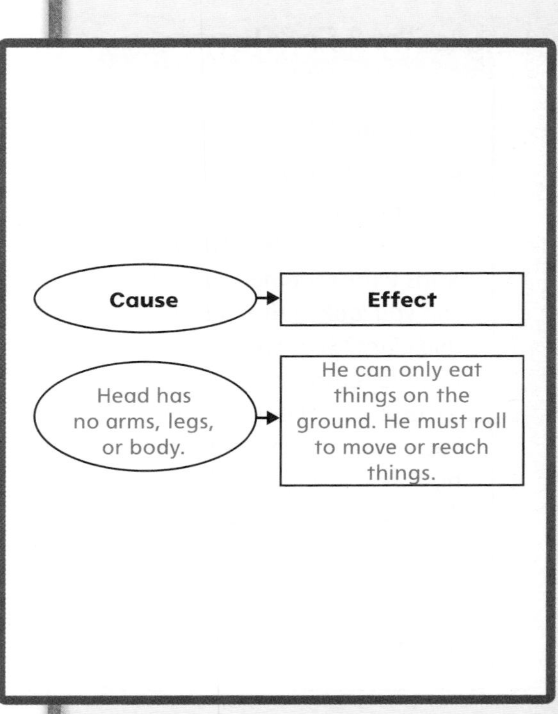

Text Evidence

Cause and Effect

Have students reread Question 6. Then ask, *What could happen if Head and Arms work together? Where can you look in the text to find clues?* Students would want to return to page 12 to recall that Head can only eat things he can reach with his tongue. On page 17 the Arms admit that they have no eyes to see. As Head points out on page 18, if they join together they will both be able to see and pick food.

Develop Comprehension

5 FLUENCY: EXPRESSION

Point out the quotation marks on pages 18 and 19. Tell children that the words in between the quotation marks are the words that the characters speak. This is called *dialogue*. When you read dialogue, it should sound like the way you imagine the character speaks. Let's read the pages together, using lots of expression. Remember that Head is probably excited because he has a good idea, so we should sound excited as we read his dialogue.

6 SKILL Cause and Effect

Describe one possible effect of Arms and Head working together. (They will be able to reach more things to eat.)

Hands picked cherries, and Head ate every single one.

"It's time for a nap," said Head, yawning. Soon he was fast asleep.

While Head slept, Body bounced along and landed on top of him.

"Help!" **gasped** Head. "I can't breathe!" **7** Arms pushed Body off.

"Hey," said Body. "Stop pushing me. Who are you?"

"It's us, Head and Arms," said Head. "You almost squashed us. Watch where you're going!" **8**

"How can I?" asked Body. "I can't see."

7 **MONITOR AND CLARIFY: READ AHEAD**

What new problem do Head and Arms have? (Body rolls on top on Head and Arms because he can't see.) I'm not sure what will happen next. Will Head and Arms help Body see? To find more information, we can read ahead to make an adjustment. (I read ahead and find that they solve the new problem.)

8 **STRATEGY** **Monitor Comprehension: Reread**

Teacher Think Aloud Body and Arms share the same problem. Neither can see. Why is this more of a problem for Body?

Tell children to apply the strategy in the Think Aloud to make corrections and adjustments to their reading.

Student Think Aloud Body was bouncing along. He landed on top of Head. Head crashed into the tree where Arms lived.

Extra Support

Summarize Supply children with events from the story. Ask them to summarize what's happened so far. For example: *Head wanted cherries, but was not able to reach them. What happened next?*

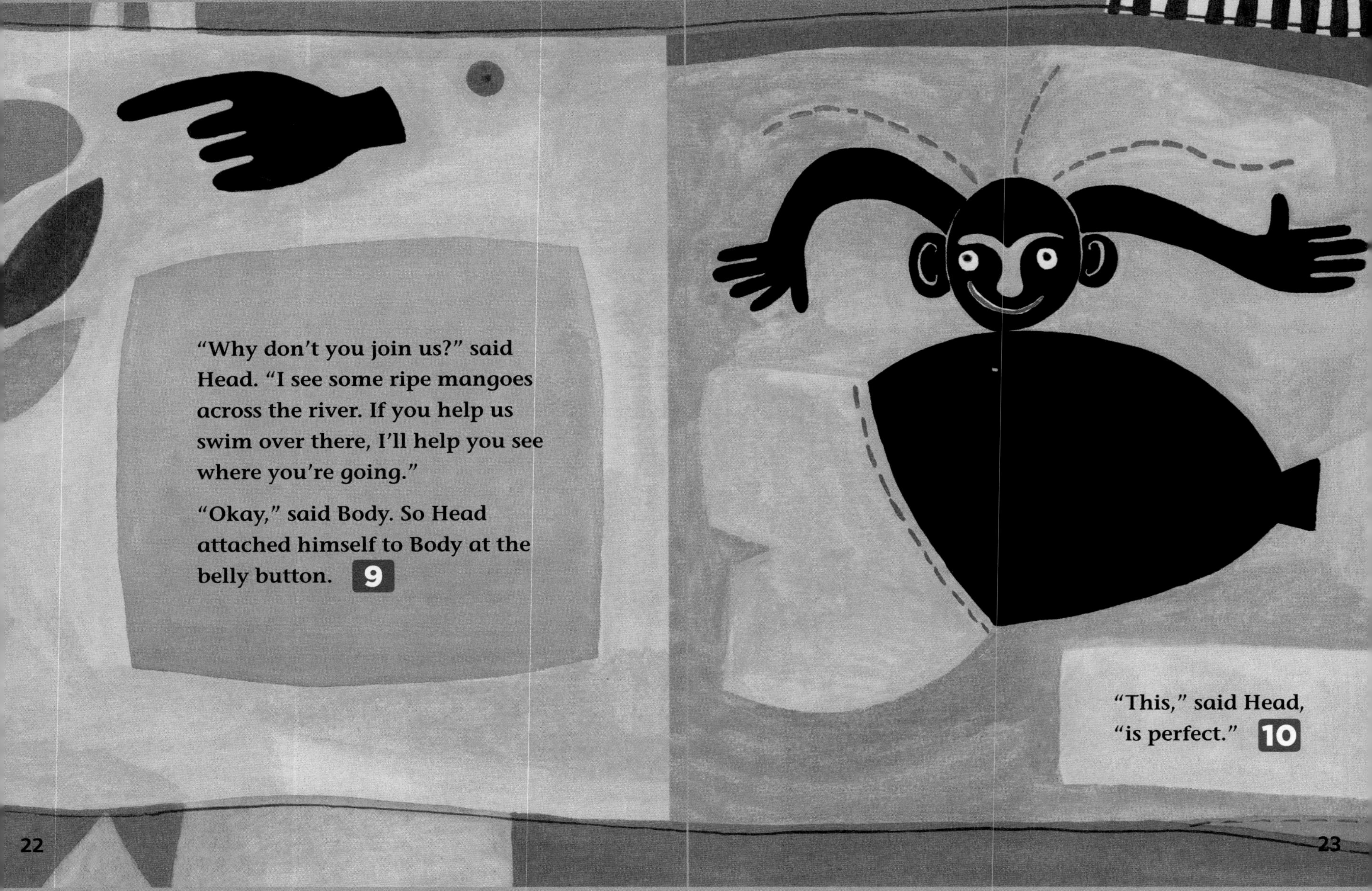

"Why don't you join us?" said Head. "I see some ripe mangoes across the river. If you help us swim over there, I'll help you see where you're going."

"Okay," said Body. So Head attached himself to Body at the belly button. **9**

"This," said Head, "is perfect." **10**

22 23

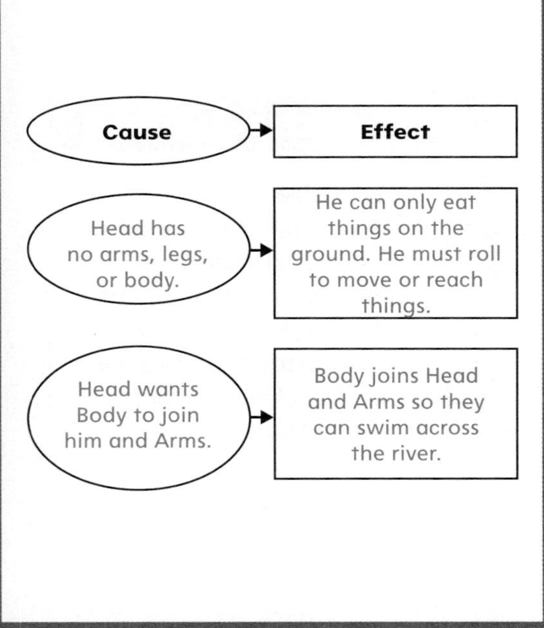

Develop Comprehension

9 SKILL Cause and Effect

What does Head want Body to do? (Head wants Body to attach to himself and Arms.) What effect will this have? (This will help Head swim across the river to get some ripe mangoes to eat.) Let's add this information to our Cause and Effect Chart.

Think/Pair/Share Retell the cause-and-effect relationships that you have identified so far to a partner. Make sure you retell the events in sequence.

10 SELF-SELECTED STRATEGY USE

What strategies did you use to make sense of what you read? Where did you use them? How did they help?

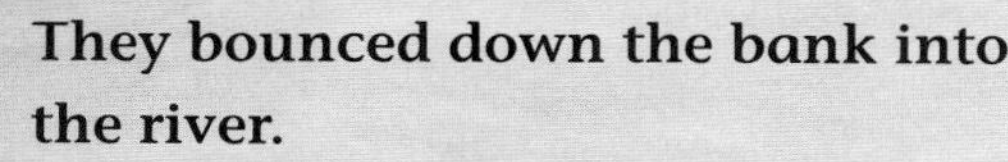

They bounced down the bank into the river.

"Pull right . . . pull left," Head shouted to Arms, who paddled **frantically** against the current. 11

24 25

11 VOCABULARY: CONTEXT CLUES

There is an alligator in the water. How do you think Head, Arms, and Body felt when they saw the alligator? (I think they felt very scared.) How should they swim to get away from the alligator? (They should swim very fast!) What do you think the word *frantically* means? (I think it means acting quickly with fear and panic.) How can you use context clues to find the meanings of words, like you did for *frantically*? (I can look at the words and sentences around them for clues. I can also look at the illustrations. Seeing the alligator on page 24 made me think that Head, Arms, and Body were afraid and needed to swim fast.)

Soon they reached the far bank and bounced up to the mango tree.

"Pick some," Head ordered. Arms stretched as high as they could, but they couldn't quite reach. Head looked around for a stick. Standing near the tree were two crossed Legs with feet on the ends.

"Get those," Head said to Arms. 12

26 27

Connect to Content

Head, Body, Legs is a traditional story from Liberia. Folktales are often part of the heritage, or tradition, of a community. What stories can you think of from your local community's or culture's tradition? For example, the story of George Washington and the cherry tree is part of the heritage of the United States.

Develop Comprehension

12 REVIEW Draw Conclusions

How do you think Head, Arms, and Body feel once they are together? (I think that they probably feel happy. Head is happy because with the help of Arms and Body, he can swim across the river to get mangoes to eat. Arms and Body can see now.) What conclusion can you draw about the theme or moral lesson of the story so far? Use clues from the text and your own experiences in your answer. (So far in the story the body parts are working together to try and figure out how to help each other. I know that working together can sometimes be a better way to get things done. I can make the conclusion that a theme in this story is that working together helps you accomplish things.)

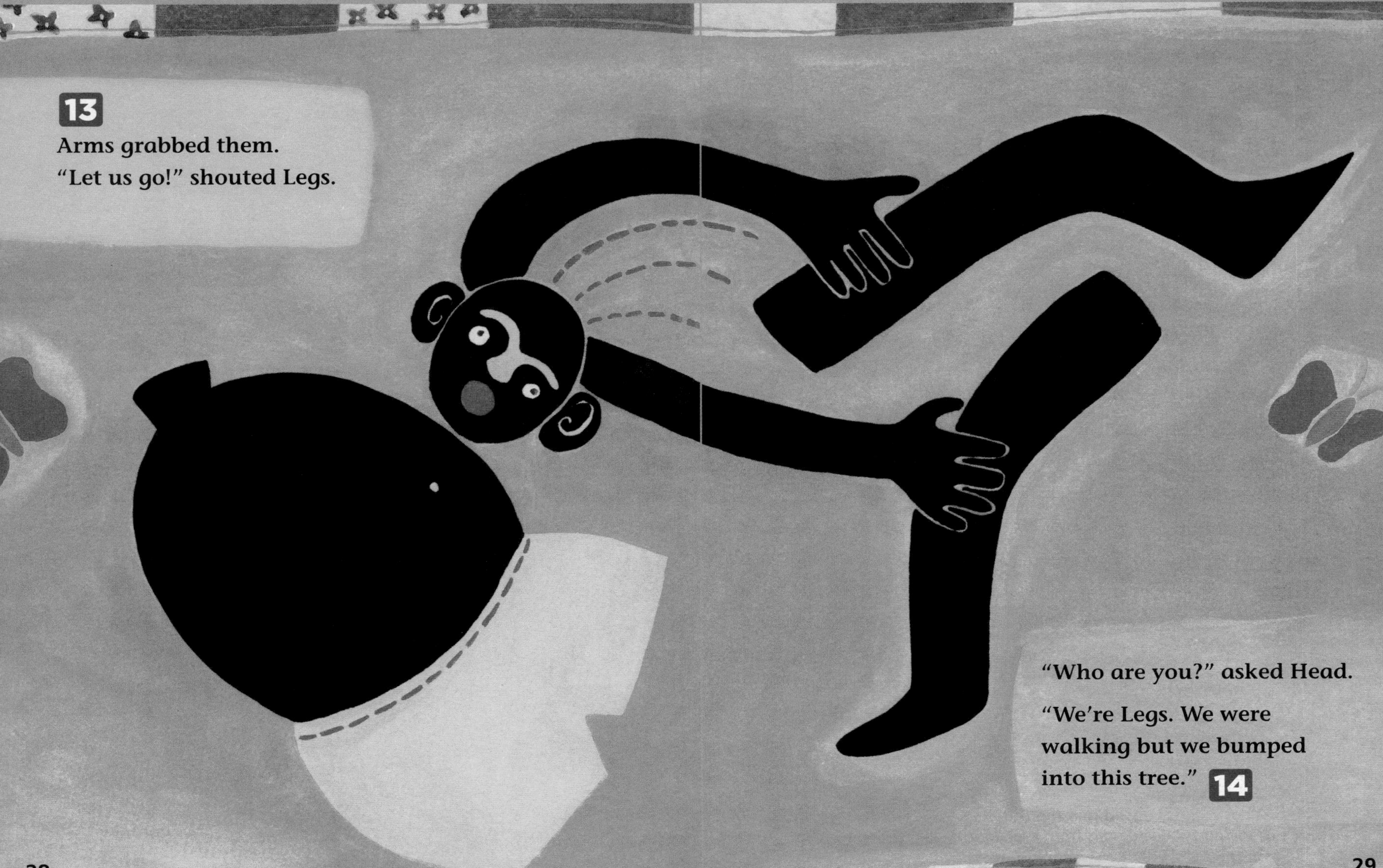

13 FLUENCY: EXPRESSION

Remind children that the words in between the quotation marks are called dialogue. They are the words that the characters speak. Good readers use punctuation to help them read with expression and use their voices to read dialogue the way they think the characters speak. Chorally read pages 28 and 29 together. Tell children to use lots of expression.

14 REVIEW Draw Conclusions

Legs tells Head they were walking along when they bumped into a tree. What problem do you think Legs shares with Arms and Body based on this text evidence? (Legs, like Arms and Body, does not have eyes to see like Head.)

"Join us," said Head. "I have eyes. I can show you where to go, and you can help us reach those mangoes."

"Okay," said Legs. So Legs attached themselves to the hands.

15 **Cause and Effect**
What causes Legs to join the other body parts? Use details from the story.

"Not there," said Arms. "The hands need to be free to pick mangoes."

"I should be in the middle," said Body, "because I'm the biggest." 16

30 31

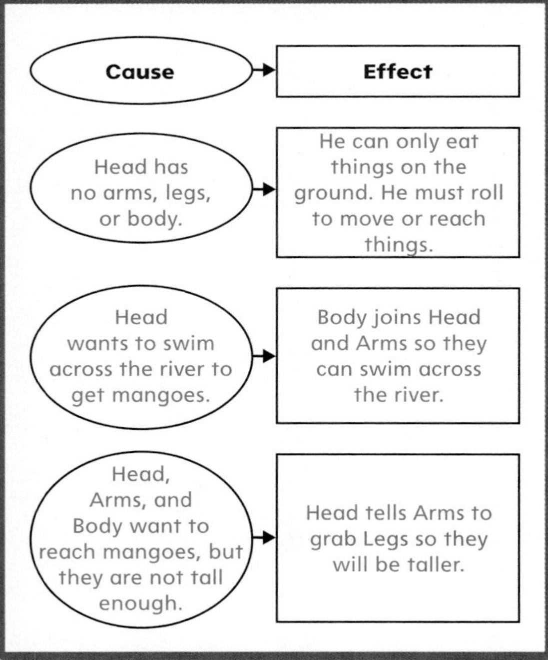

Cause	Effect
Head has no arms, legs, or body.	He can only eat things on the ground. He must roll to move or reach things.
Head wants to swim across the river to get mangoes.	Body joins Head and Arms so they can swim across the river.
Head, Arms, and Body want to reach mangoes, but they are not tall enough.	Head tells Arms to grab Legs so they will be taller.

Develop Comprehension

15 SKILL Cause and Effect

Why can't Head, Arms, and Body reach the mangoes? (They are not tall enough.) What **causes** Legs to join the other body parts? (Head tells Legs that he has eyes to see and can show them where to go; with Legs they will also then be tall enough to reach the mangoes.) Let's add this information to the Cause and Effect Chart.

16 THEME

What is the theme, or moral lesson, of this story? Use text evidence and details from the story to support your answer. (In the story, the body parts are working together to try and help one another. Head asks Legs, Arms and Body to join him because he can see. They can help him reach different kinds of food. The theme or message is: working together can be a better way to get things done.)

"That's right," said Head. "You should be at the bottom, Legs. I'll swing around on top of Body so I can see everything. And Arms, you move to the shoulders." **17**

32 33

17 SKILL **Cause and Effect**

How has looking for cause and effect helped you place events in sequence, and retell the story?

Student Think Aloud As I read the story, I could ask myself *Why?* to find a cause, and *What happened?* to find an effect. Cause and effect relationships make up the events of the story. Recognizing them can help me put the events of the story in sequence and retell it. First, Head wants to eat some cherries up in a tree. This causes him to roll down a hill to hit a tree and knock some cherries off of it. As a result, he meets Arms. Then, when Head and Arms wanted to get some mangoes, they met Body. Finally, they meet Legs and everyone slid into place.

SELF-SELECTED STRATEGY USE

What stategies did you use to make sense of what you read?

ELL

Question 17 IDENTIFY CAUSE AND EFFECT

Use questioning techniques to help children identify why Head wants to add Legs (the cause) and what effect adding Legs will have. *What do Head, Arms, and Body want to do? Why can't they pick the mangoes? Where are the mangoes? What do they need to do to reach the mangoes? What body part would make them taller?*

Everyone slid into place. Legs stood on tiptoe. Body straightened out. Arms stretched up and the hands picked a mango. Head took a bite.

34

"Mmm, **delicious**," Head said. "Now THIS is perfect!"

35

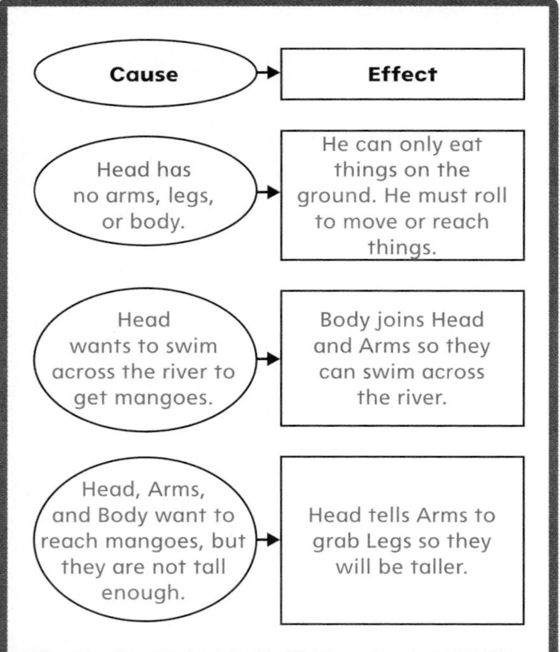

Cause	Effect
Head has no arms, legs, or body.	He can only eat things on the ground. He must roll to move or reach things.
Head wants to swim across the river to get mangoes.	Body joins Head and Arms so they can swim across the river.
Head, Arms, and Body want to reach mangoes, but they are not tall enough.	Head tells Arms to grab Legs so they will be taller.

Develop Comprehension

COMPLETE THE CAUSE AND EFFECT CHART

Review the information on the Cause and Effect Chart. Ask children to add any additional details they wish.

RETURN TO PREDICTIONS AND PURPOSES

Review children's predictions and purposes and the Focus Question. Have children use ideas to confirm their predictions.

Quick Check

Can children reread to clarify meaning? Can they identify cause and effect?

During **Small Group Instruction**

If No → **Approaching Level** Apply the skill to simpler text, 41R and 41X.

If Yes → **On Level** Apply the skill to another text, 41S and 41Y.

Beyond Level Apply the skill to a harder text, 41T and 41Z.

Telling stories with the Authors and Illustrator

Won-Ldy Paye came to this country from Liberia, which is in Africa. He is a storyteller as well as a writer. To write *Head, Body, Legs,* Won-Ldy worked with children's writer **Margaret Lippert**. Margaret travels all over the world learning folk stories. She shares her stories by writing children's books.

Artist **Julie Paschkis** is also a storyteller. She says she tells stories through her art. Julie has illustrated many children's books.

Another book by Won-Ldy Paye, Margaret Lippert, and Julia Paschkis

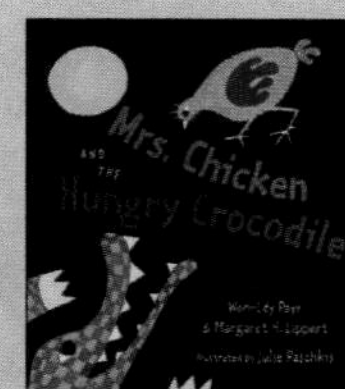

LOG ON FIND OUT
Authors Won-Ldy Paye and Margaret Lippert
Illustrator Julie Paschkis
www.macmillanmh.com

Author's Purpose
Won-Ldy Paye and Margaret Lippert worked together to tell a story. Think about a time you worked with others to do something. What did you do? Write about the experience.

36

Meet the Authors/Illustrator

Read aloud page 36 with children. Discuss the lives of the authors and illustrator. Talk about where Won-Ldy Paye came from and how he wrote the story. Have children tell how the authors used personification. Then have children compose questions that they might ask the authors.

Author's Purpose

Won-Ldy Paye uses African folktales to create and write his stories. He hopes that readers enjoy learning about the traditions of his country. Tell children to think about work they enjoy doing with others. Do they each have special jobs? Help children focus on one time they worked together. Have them write about the experience.

Author's Craft

Personification

- A folktale is a made-up story from long ago that often includes things that do not happen in real life. Folktales sometimes have nonhuman characters, such as animals or objects, that act, talk, or have feelings like real people. This story starts with a character called Head who talks and thinks like a human, even though he is only one body part.
- *What is another example of a body part acting like a human in* Head, Body, Legs?

Genre

Folktale

Many folktales share a theme, or an overall message about life, with the reader. Students can identify the theme by thinking about what the characters say and do and what happens in the story as a result of their actions. Help students identify the theme of cooperation in *Head, Body, Legs*. Ask, *What happened when all the body parts worked together?* (They were able to enjoy delicious mangoes.) *What might the author want us to learn from this effect?* (By working together, all of the body parts got to enjoy something. Working together is a good idea and benefits, or helps, everyone.

Objectives

- Retell a story to show understanding
- Answer comprehension questions

Materials

- Student Book: *Head, Body, Legs: A Story From Liberia,* pp. 10–35
- Retelling Cards for *Head, Body, Legs: A Story from Liberia*
- chart paper
- Practice Book, p. 177

Retelling Rubric

4 Excellent

Retells the selection without prompting, in sequence, and using supporting details. Clearly describes the setting, main characters, and the complete plot. Describes the problem and its solution.

3 Good

Retells the selection with little guidance, in sequence, and using some details. Generally describes the setting, main characters, and the plot. Recognizes either a problem or a solution.

2 Fair

Retells the selection with some guidance, mostly in sequence, and using limited details. Partially describes the setting, main characters, and plot. Cannot state the problem or solution.

1 Unsatisfactory

Retells the selection only when prompted, out of sequence, and using limited details. Does not describe the main characters or plot.

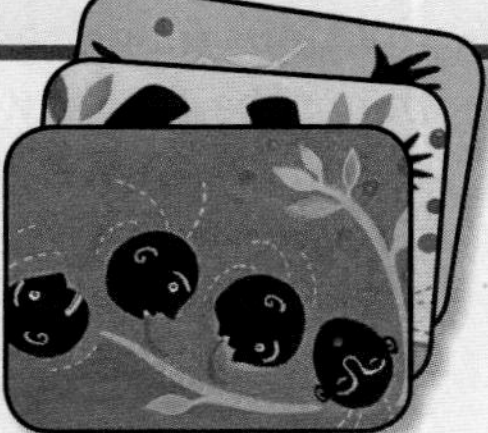

Retelling Cards

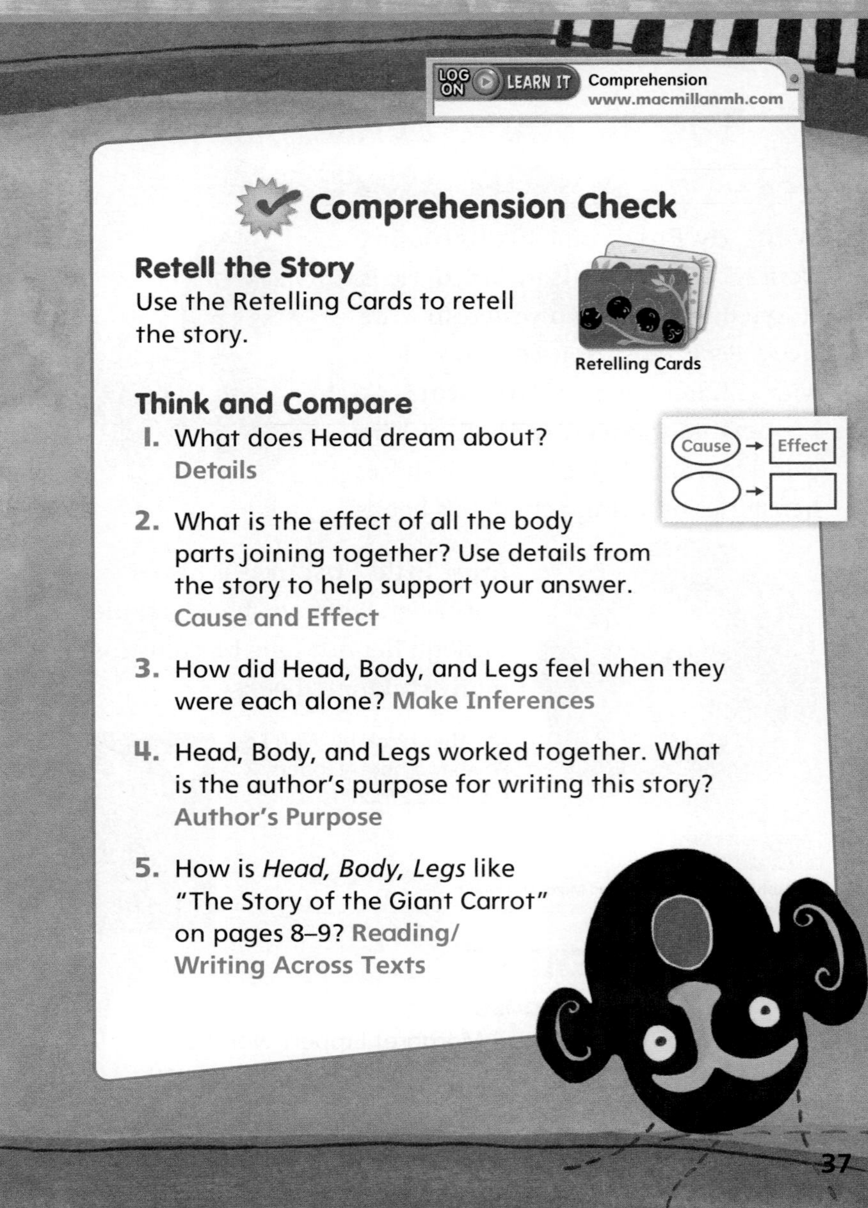

LOG ON LEARN IT Comprehension www.macmillanmh.com

Comprehension Check

Retell the Story
Use the Retelling Cards to retell the story.

Retelling Cards

Think and Compare

1. What does Head dream about? Details
2. What is the effect of all the body parts joining together? Use details from the story to help support your answer. Cause and Effect
3. How did Head, Body, and Legs feel when they were each alone? Make Inferences
4. Head, Body, and Legs worked together. What is the author's purpose for writing this story? Author's Purpose
5. How is *Head, Body, Legs* like "The Story of the Giant Carrot" on pages 8–9? Reading/Writing Across Texts

37

Retell the Story

RETELL *HEAD, BODY, LEGS: A STORY FROM LIBERIA*

- Remind children that as they read *Head, Body, Legs: A Story from Liberia*, they identified causes and effects in the story. Now they will use this information to summarize and retell the story in logical order. (You can record children's retelling on chart paper.)
- **Model Retelling** Use the prompts provided on the backs of **Retelling Cards** 1 and 2 to model retelling the story.
- ELL **Guide Retelling** Use the leveled language acquisition prompts provided to guide children's retelling.
- **Discuss Retelling** *Why does Head need Arms? How does Body help Head? What causes the body parts to work together?*

Phonemic Awareness

Phoneme Blending

Objective

- **Blend phonemes**

Model

Show children how to blend phonemes in words.

Listen carefully as I say the sounds in a word. Then I will blend the sounds to form the word.

Continue with the words *found, bounce, count, flour, howl, now, gown, clout, bound,* and *loud*.

Listen to the sounds: /s/ /ou/ /n/ /d/. This word has four sounds: /s/ /ou/ /n/ /d/. Listen as I blend the sounds to form the word: /sound/. The word is *sound*.

Guided Practice/Practice

Have children practice with these examples. Do the first two together.

Let's do some together. I will say one sound at a time. Then we will blend the sounds to say the word.

/k/ /l/ /ou/ /d/   /b/ /r/ /ou/

Now it's your turn. Listen carefully.

/sh/ /ou/ /t/   /s/ /p/ /ou/ /t/
/k/ /ou/   /ou/ /t/
/m/ /ou/ /th/   /w/ /ou/ /n/ /d/
/g/ /ou/ /n/   /h/ /ou/
/s/ /k/ /ou/ /l/   /k/ /ou/ /ch/

Objectives

- Identify letter-sound correspondence for diphthong /ou/*ou*, *ow*
- Blend sounds in words with *ou*, *ow*
- Review previously taught phonics skills
- Read multisyllabic words

Materials

- Sound-Spelling Card: *Cow*
- Word-Building Cards; Teacher's Resource Book, p. 66
- chart paper
- Practice Book, p. 178

Skills Trace

Diphthong *ou*, *ow*	
Introduce	7C–D
Practice/ Apply	7F, 9G, 37F-G, 37I, 37T; Practice Book: p. 173; Decodable Reader: *The Missing String Beans*
Reteach/ Review	41C-D; 41K-N, 41Q, 41W, 41CC
Assess	Weekly Test; Unit 4 Test
Maintain	Build Fluency: Sound/Spellings

Phonics

Review Words with *ou*, *ow*

Model

Review the sound /ou/ spelled *ow*. Show the *Cow* **Sound-Spelling Card**.

Then review the sound /ou/ spelled *ou*. Use the word *mouth*.

This is the *Cow* Sound-Spelling Card. The sound is /ou/. One way the /ou/ sound is spelled is with the letters *ow*. Say it with me: /ou/. This is the sound at the end of the word *cow*. Listen: /k/ /ou/, *cow*. We've been reading words with the /ou/ sound all week. Today we will read more.

Guided Practice/Practice

Have children practice connecting the letters and sound.

(Point to the letters *ou* and *ow*.) What are these letters? What sound do they stand for?

Build Fluency: Sound/Spellings

Display the following **Word-Building Cards** one at a time: *ou, ow, are, air, ear, ere, or, ore, oar, ar, gn, kn, wr, mb, eer, ere, ear, er, ir, ur, u, u_e, ew, ue*. Have children chorally say each sound. Repeat and vary the pace.

ow ou are

Blend Words with *ou*, *ow*

Model

Display Word-Building Cards *m*, *o*, *u*, *t*, *h*. Model how to blend the sounds together as you run your finger under each letter.

Continue by modeling the words *mound*, *fowl*, *house*, *hound*, *recount*, *scowling*, *clown*, *trout*, and *sprouted*.

(Point to *m*.) This is the letter *m*. It stands for /m/. (Point to *ou*.) These are the letters *ou*. They stand for /ou/. Listen as I blend these sounds together: /mou/.

(Point to *th*.) These are the letters *th*. They stand for /th/. Listen as I blend all three sounds together: /mouth/, *mouth*. Say it with me.

Guided Practice/Practice
Write the words below on chart paper. Read the first line with children. Then have children chorally read the words on the chart. Use the appropriate blending level.

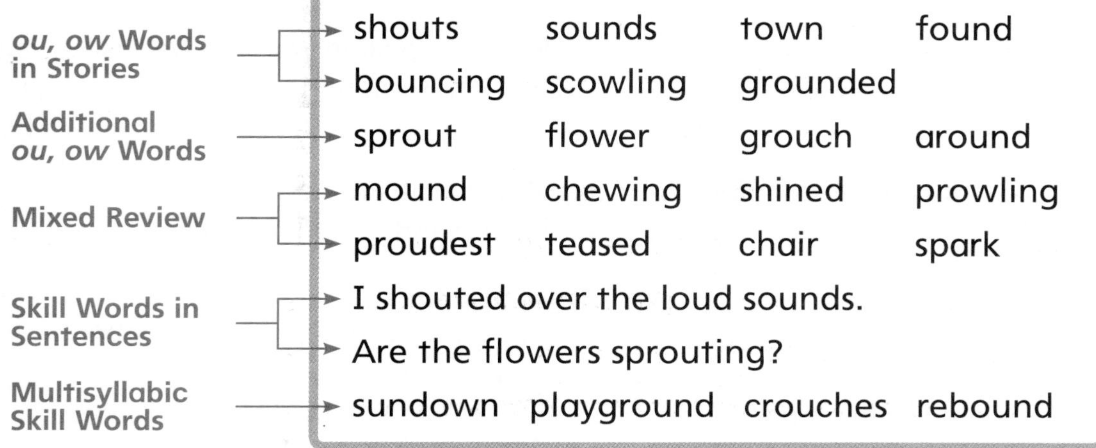

ou, ow Words in Stories	shouts	sounds	town	found
	bouncing	scowling	grounded	
Additional *ou, ow* Words	sprout	flower	grouch	around
Mixed Review	mound	chewing	shined	prowling
	proudest	teased	chair	spark
Skill Words in Sentences	I shouted over the loud sounds.			
	Are the flowers sprouting?			
Multisyllabic Skill Words	sundown	playground	crouches	rebound

Corrective Feedback

Blending Error Say: *My turn*. Model blending using the appropriate signaling procedures. Then lead children in blending the sounds. Say: *Do it with me*. You will respond with children to offer support. Then say: *Your turn. Blend*. Have children chorally blend. Return to the beginning of the word. Say: *Let's start over*.

Inflectional Endings *-s, -es*

Teach

- Write the words *cow* and *cows* on the board. Underline the letter *-s* at the end of *cows*.
- Tell children that the letter *-s* at the end of *cows* means there is more than one *cow*. It is a plural.
- Write the words *couch* and *couches* on the board. Underline the *-es* in *couches*. Explain that when a word ends in *s, sh, ch,* or *x*, we add *-es* to make it plural.

Practice/Apply

- Help children blend the sounds in the following words: *plow, plows; cloud, clouds; clown, clowns; pouch, pouches; hound, hounds; town, towns; ounce, ounces.*
- Ask children to look for words that end in *-s* and *-es* as they read this week's stories. Keep a running list.

ON YOUR OWN

Practice Book, page 178

Use **-s** or **-es** to make some words mean more than one. For words that end with a consonant and **y**, change the **y** to **i** and add **-es**.

story – y + i + es = stories

Complete each sentence by changing the underlined word to mean more than one.

1. Max and his friend Ben wanted some cherry. cherries
2. There are no cherry trees in city. cities
3. Cherry trees grow on farm. farms
4. Max and Ben went to a farm with their father fathers and baby sister sisters.
5. The boy boys needed help picking.
6. Baby Babies can't pick, so the sisters cannot help.
7. Max and Ben carried two large basket baskets.
8. Soon everyone was eating the red, ripe berry. berries

Approaching Reproducible, page 178

Beyond Reproducible, page 178

DAY 3
WHOLE GROUP

Objectives

- Sort words with *ou*, *ow* and high-frequency words
- Practice spelling words
- Build Fluency: Word Automaticity

Materials

- index cards from Day 2
- pocket chart
- Spelling Word Cards BLM; Teacher's Resource Book, p. 70
- Phonics/Spelling Practice Book, p. 63

5-Day Spelling	
DAY 1	Dictation; Pretest
DAY 2	Teacher-Modeled Word Sort
DAY 3	Student Word Sort
DAY 4	Test Practice
DAY 5	Posttest

ON YOUR OWN **Spelling,** page 63

clown	ground	crown	shout	cloud
sound	house	brown	growl	howl

A. Match-Ups

Draw a line from each spelling word to its meaning.

1. clown — the earth under your feet
2. brown — a person who makes you laugh
3. ground — a color
4. crown — a building to live in
5. shout — something worn by a king or queen
6. house — yell

B. Sentences to Complete

Write a spelling word on the line to complete each sentence.

7. Will the dog __growl__ at a stranger?
8. The __cloud__ in the sky was fluffy and white.
9. There was a loud __sound__ when the alarm went off.
10. I think I heard a coyote __howl__.

Phonics/Spelling

Word Sort with *ou*, *ow*

WORD SORT

- Use index cards from Day 2 for each spelling word, as well as for *ou* and *ow*. Place *ou* and *ow* cards to form two columns in a pocket chart. Blend sounds with children.
- Hold up the *cloud* card. Say and spell it. Pronounce each sound clearly: /k/ /l/ /ou/ /d/. Blend the sounds: /kloud/. Place the word below the *ou* label.
- Repeat this step with *howl*. Place the word below the *ow* label. Have children read each word. *What do you notice about these spelling words?* (They have the /ou/ sound.) Repeat the process with the rest of the spelling words.
- Display the words *family*, *four*, and *hear*. Read and spell the words together with children. Point out that these spelling words do not contain the /ou/ sound. Note especially for children that although the word *four* has the *ou* spelling pattern, it does not contain the /ou/ sound.
- **Build Fluency: Word Automaticity** Conclude by asking children to chorally read the words to build fluency. Then ask them to orally generate additional words that rhyme with each word.

High-Frequency Words

- **Teach High-Frequency Words** Write the new high-frequency words for the week **family**, **four**, and **hear** on the board. Teach the words using the **Read/Spell/Write** routine below.
  - **Read** Read the word. Have children repeat.
  - **Spell** Chorally spell the word.
  - **Write** Have children write the word as they spell it aloud. Then ask children to write a sentence using each word.
- **Practice** Write sample cloze sentences for each word on the board.

  My __________ went on a car trip to visit my grandma.
  Horses have __________ legs.
  I like to __________ music performed.
- Have children read the sentences and write the missing word for each one.
- **Additional High-Frequency Words** Introduce an additional six words (Additional Words #201–206: **bring**, **today**, **place**, **all**, **water**, **or**) for more practice. Have children use the **Read/Spell/Write** routine to learn the words. Finish with a speed drill of all the words taught for the day. Display each High-Frequency Word Card quickly and have children identify and read the word aloud. Repeat with any words children have difficulty with.

Decodable Reader

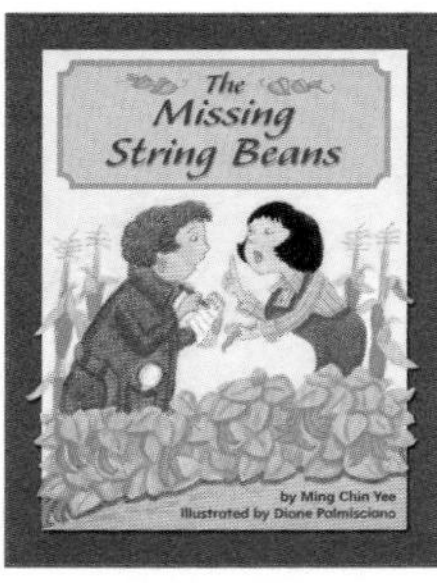

Decodable Reader

- **Review High-Frequency Words** Review the high-frequency words that appear in the book: **believe**, **built**, and **material**. Have children read each aloud and provide a sentence for each.
- PARTNERS **Reread Decodable Reader** Have children quietly reread *The Missing String Beans* to a partner.
- **Check Comprehension** Have children retell the Decodable Reader to their partner. Direct them to page through the book and say in their own words what they learned on each page about the story. Reinforce high-frequency words and key vocabulary that they struggle with.
- **Reteach** If children have difficulty, provide corrective feedback page by page as needed. See the **Decodable Text Routine** in the Instructional Routine Handbook for correction models.

Objectives

- Decode words with *ou*, *ow* in connected text
- Read high-frequency words *family*, *four*, *hear*
- Review last week's high-frequency words

Materials

- Decodable Reader Library: *The Missing String Beans*

SMALL GROUP OPTION

You may wish to read the Decodable Reader during **Small Group** time.

See pages 41K–41JJ

Objectives

- Use context clues to determine word meanings
- Review this week's and last week's vocabulary words

Materials

- Transparency 32
- Practice Book, p. 179

Vocabulary

STRATEGY Use Context Clues

EXPLAIN

- Tell children that they can figure out the meaning of an unfamiliar word by finding clues in the surrounding sentences.

MODEL

Read aloud the first paragraph on the transparency. Model how to use context clues to figure out the meaning of the word **gasped**.

Think Aloud I don't know the meaning of the word **gasped**. I will read the sentences around it for clues. I see that to gasp, we must suck air quickly through our mouths and fill the lungs with air. I think that **gasped** means "to gulp air into our lungs."

Transparency 32

Henry told us a story at lunch. It was about our bodies and how they work. He said that when we run around and get out of breath, sometimes we need to suck more air into our lungs in a quick way. Someone who gasped might have *gulped* lots of air after playing soccer for awhile. Our bodies need air to continue to run and play.

Then Henry told us about our hearts. Our hearts pump blood through our bodies. They push the blood from one part of our bodies to another. **The heart** squeezes hard to push the blood. **Henry said that our hearts and lungs** work together. **They are partners. The hearts pump blood and the lungs breathe air.** Each does its own part for our body.

Vocabulary Transparency

GUIDED PRACTICE/PRACTICE

Read the second paragraph chorally with children. Help them use context clues to find the meaning of *pump* and *partners* in the second paragraph.

REVIEW WORDS

Review the definition of each vocabulary word and write a sentence using the word on the board.

Practice Ask children questions relating each word to their own experience, such as: *What foods do you think are* delicious?

Repeat using last week's words *creating*, *familiar*, *glamorous*, *imagination*, *memories*, and *occasions*.

Vocabulary

attached	delicious
frantically	gasped
swung	

Practice Book, page 179

Sometimes the other words in a sentence can help you figure out the meaning of a new word. These words are **context clues** and can come before or after an unknown word.

Read each sentence. Then circle the meaning of the word in dark type that makes sense.

1. The teacher let Lorna and me work on the project **together**, so each of us completed half of the work.
   (with another person) alone
2. The **coach** helps us learn to throw and hit balls.
   (person who trains a team) a type of ball
3. Each camper completed a **task** to help the camp.
   camp (job)
4. Everyone got along and **cooperated** to get the job done.
   (worked together) worked separately
5. Megan used a screwdriver to **assemble** the toy house.
   play with (build)
6. All of us **participated** in the reading program by reading five books each.
   (took part) ate

Approaching Reproducible, page 179
Beyond Reproducible, page 179

Oral Vocabulary

REVIEW WORDS
Remind children of the week's oral vocabulary words.

Say the word **accomplish**. Remind children that to accomplish something means to finish or complete it. *I have a lot of things to accomplish today.*

Something that is **arduous** is difficult or hard. *Building the fence is an arduous job.*

Labor means hard work. *My brother does a lot of labor around the house.*

People **rejoice** when they have something to celebrate. *Will you rejoice with me if we win the game?*

The word **succeed** means "to do something well." *Michael will succeed if he tries hard enough.*

Use the following sentences and questions to help reinforce the meanings of the words:

- *What would be a good reason to rejoice?*
- *Describe three arduous jobs.*
- *What are some things you need to know to succeed at riding a bicycle?*
- *Name two things you can accomplish at the same time.*
- *Think of one kind of labor you like to do around the house.*
- Then have a child say what each word means and use it in a sentence.

- Use similar activities to review last week's words: *coincidence*, *contemplate*, *explain*, *scheme*, and *worthy*.

Objectives

- Practice repeated oral reading
- 62–82 WCPM
- Practice fluency prosody

Materials

- Transparency 16
- Fluency Solutions Audio CD
- Practice Book, p. 180

Fluency

Repeated Reading: Prosody

EXPLAIN/MODEL

- **Punctuation** Explain that the punctuation in a text helps readers know when to pause or stop. In dialogue, quotation marks help readers to see the words the speaker says.

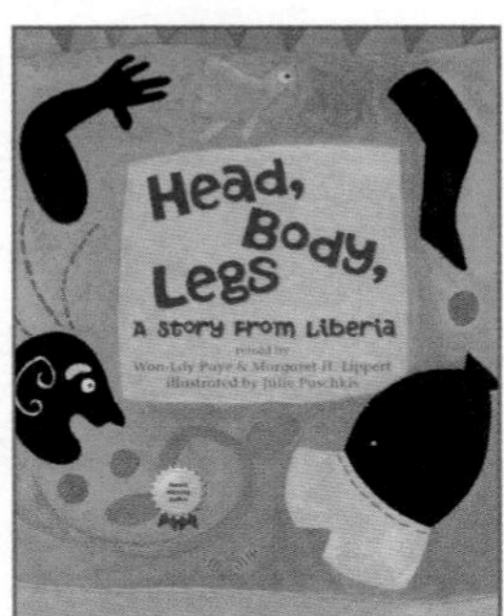

Main Selection

Write this sentence on the board and read it aloud with children: *"Where are you going?" asked James*. Point out the quotation marks and question mark. Model reading the sentence with and without expression. *Which way is easier to understand? In dialogue, punctuation marks help us read the words the way the speaker would have said them.*

- **Phrasing** Display **Transparency 16** and point out the single and double slashes. Explain that the single slashes show pauses and the double slashes show stops.

Point out that when the words between slashes are read together, they help us form a mental picture of the text. *If we struggle with any word, we should decode it or ask for help, then go back to the beginning of the slash and reread that section of the text.* Model reading aloud the section on Transparency 16. *When did I pause when I read? When did I stop longer?*

Transparency 16

While Head slept, / Body bounced along and landed on top of him. // "Help!" / gasped Head. // "I can't breathe!" // Arms pushed Body off. //

"Hey," / said Body. // "Stop pushing me. // Who are you?" //

"It's us, / Head and Arms," / said Head. // "You almost squashed us. // Watch where you're going!" //

"How can I?" / said Body. // "I can't see." //

—from *Head, Body, Legs* (page 21)

Fluency Transparency

ELL

Read with Prosody Ask children to think about how they would feel if they bumped into someone. Model reading with prosody. Have children read aloud the passage in a way that shows how the characters feel. Correct for pronunciation as needed.

- **Expression** Discuss how your intonation changes depending on what activity is being described in each sentence.

Demonstrate how you adjust your reading rate based on the style of the writing. *When the author is describing exciting actions, you adjust your reading rate by reading more quickly.* Model reading the passage with natural expression.

Point out that you read the text the way the speaker would have said the words, expressing the same emotion and using the same expression.

- **Pronunciation** Model reading the passage. Have children note your pronunciation of *bounced* and *squashed*. Point out that good readers slow down their reading rate when reading longer or unfamiliar words to make sure that they pronounce them correctly.

PRACTICE

- Have children reread the passage chorally, using the slashes to think about their phrasing. Remind them to read as if the character is speaking.

Repeat the reading to give children even more practice with natural phrasing, speed, and prosody.

- **Daily Fluency** Children will practice fluency by reading **Practice Book** page 180 aloud, then paraphrasing what they have read. Students may also practice by listening to the **Fluency Solutions Audio CD**. The passage is recorded at a slow, practice speed, and a faster, fluent speed.

Quick Check

Can children read the passage fluently and with prosody?

During **Small Group Instruction**

If No → **Approaching Level** See pages: 41DD, 41HH

If Yes → **On Level** See Fluency 41EE

Beyond Level See Fluency 41EE

ON YOUR OWN

Practice Book, page 180

As I read, I will pay attention to my expression.

A fisherman lived with his wife in a little house.
10 Every morning he went to the sea. He tried to catch
21 fish to eat.
24 One day the fisherman caught nothing. Then he
32 felt a strong tug on his fishing line. The fishing rod
43 swung from side to side. The fisherman fought
51 **frantically** to hold on to it.
57 The fisherman reeled in the line. There
64 was a golden fish **attached** to his hook.
72 "Please let me go!" it cried. "I cannot breathe out
82 of water!"
84 The fish was beautiful. But it was too small to
94 eat, so the fisherman let it go. 101

Comprehension Check

1. What made the fisherman's fishing rod swing from side to side?
   Draw Conclusions A fish caused the rod to swing from side to side.
2. Why did the fisherman go down to the sea every morning?
   Cause and Effect The fisherman went to the sea every morning to catch fish to eat.

	Words Read	–	Number of Errors	=	Words Correct Score
First Read		–		=	
Second Read		–		=	

Approaching Reproducible, page 180

Beyond Reproducible, page 180

Objectives

- Draw conclusions about plot and theme
- Express personal responses to literature
- Discuss genre characteristics

Materials

- Student Book: *Head, Body, Legs: A Story from Liberia*, pp. 10–35

Comprehension

MAINTAIN **Draw Conclusions**

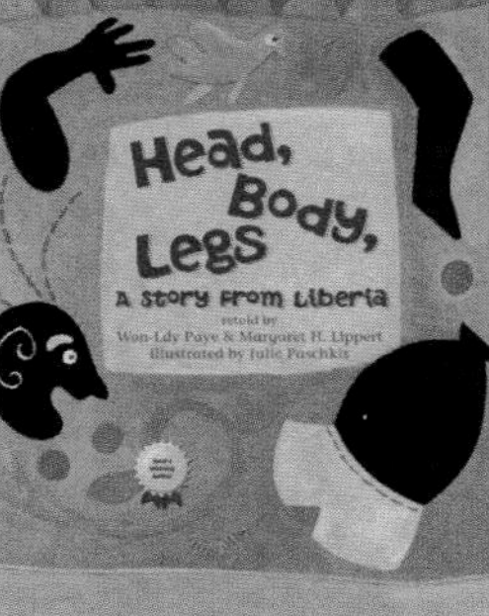

Main Selection

EXPLAIN/MODEL

- Tell children that good readers draw conclusions about what they read. To draw conclusions, they should

1. Think about two or more pieces of information in a selection.
2. Combine that textual evidence with what they already know about the subject or story elements, such as the characters, in the selection.

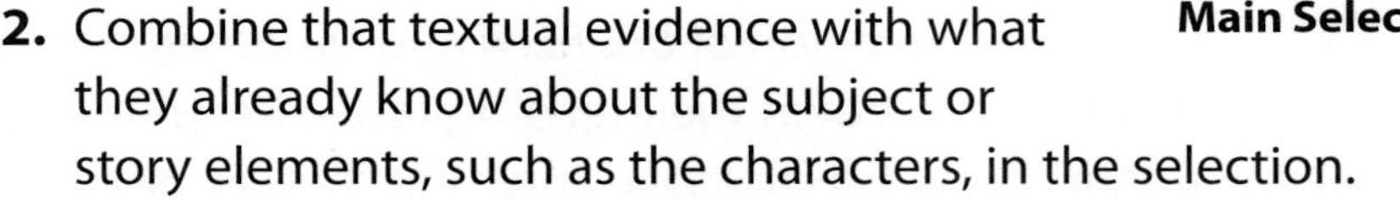

3. Analyze all the information to reach a new understanding, or conclusion, about an event or character in the text. This will help them understand the characters and events better and identify themes in the story.

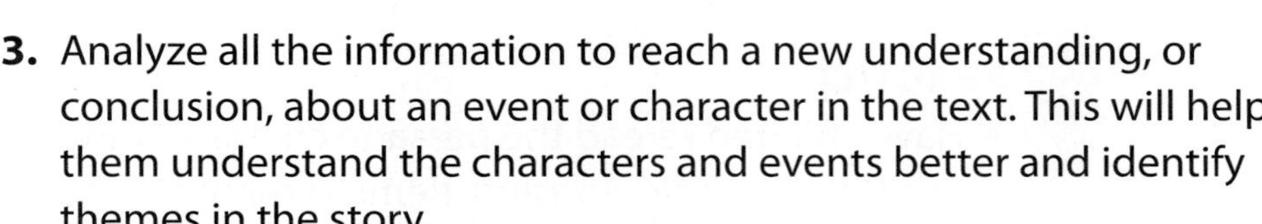

PRACTICE

Ask children to draw a conclusion about *Head, Body, Legs. Do you think Head is happy he found and joined with the other body parts? Use details from the story and what you know from real life to support your answer.*

Skills Trace

Draw Conclusions

Introduce	U3: 439A–B
Practice/ Apply	U3: 439K–457A; Practice Book: 163–164
Reteach/ Review	U3: 461G, 461R–T, 461X–Z; U5: 175A–B, 175K–201A, 205G, 205R–T, 205X–Z; Practice Book: 232–233
Assess	Weekly Tests; Units 3, 5 Tests
Maintain	U4: 37N; U5: 233N, 247N

Respond to Literature

Personal Response Discuss children's responses to *Head, Body, Legs.* Have children pose *how, why,* or *what-if* clarifying questions that they can answer in their Writer's Notebooks.

- *When you began the story, how did you think Head would solve his problem? Why? How was your prediction different from what happened? How was it the same?*
- *Think about one thing that happened in the story and describe its effect.*
- *Describe the setting in* Head, Body, Legs, *using details from the story.*

Focus Question: Folktale Remind children that a folktale is a made-up story that takes place long ago.

- *Did you ever have a problem like one of the characters in the story? What was it? How did you solve it?*
- *How did the illustrations help show that the story was made up?*
- Retell *Head, Body, Legs,* making sure to describe some causes and their effects.

Grammar

Capitalization of Proper Nouns

EXPLAIN/MODEL

- Remind children that proper nouns name special people, places, and times. (e.g., Bob, Mr. Lopez, San Diego, Presidents' Day)
- Tell children that proper nouns name days of the week, months, and holidays. A proper noun begins with a capital letter. (e.g., Tuesday, April)

Write the following sentence on the board: *On tuesday, mr. fox's class is going to a museum in new york city*. Point out the proper nouns in the sentence. Then rewrite it, modeling how to capitalize proper nouns.

Transparency 78

Capitalization

1. In august my friends and I will paint a mural.
(In August my friends and I will paint a mural.)
2. It should be finished by labor day.
(It should be finished by Labor Day.)
3. The mural will show abraham lincoln.
(The mural will show Abraham Lincoln.)
4. The president came to northboro one september.
(The president came to Northboro one September.)
5. We will remember lincoln's visit on the second monday of the month.
(We will remember Lincoln's visit on the second Monday of the month.)

Grammar Transparency

GUIDED PRACTICE/PRACTICE

Read the first sentence on **Grammar Transparency 78** to model identifying and capitalizing proper nouns. Work with children to identify the proper noun in each sentence on the transparency and correct the capitalization.

Objectives

- Use capital letters to begin proper nouns
- Use capital letters for months and days of the week

Materials

- Transparency 78
- Grammar Practice Book, p. 78

5-Day Grammar

Linking Verbs	
DAY 1	Linking Verbs: Present-Tense Forms of *Be*
DAY 2	Past-Tense Forms of *Be*
DAY 3	Mechanics: Capitalization
DAY 4	Past-Tense Forms of *Be* Proofread
DAY 5	Review and Assess Capitalization Linking Verbs

ON YOUR OWN

Grammar, page 78

- A proper noun begins with a capital letter.
- The name of a day, month, or holiday begins with a capital letter.

My dog Ralph had puppies in June.

Find capitalization mistakes in the sentences. Write the corrected sentences on the lines below.

1. memorial day was last monday.
Memorial Day was last Monday.
2. molly jones went fishing with her family.
Molly Jones went fishing with her family.
3. The month of may is a nice time to go fishing.
The month of May is a nice time to go fishing.
4. Molly's brother ted caught a bass.
Molly's brother Ted caught a bass.
5. Mr. jones fried the fish for lunch on tuesday.
Mr. Jones fried the fish for lunch on Tuesday.

Writing

A Strong Paragraph

Objectives

- Write strong paragraphs with ideas in a logical sequence
- Revise by adding and deleting
- Draft a personal narrative

Materials

- Transparencies 93, 94

REVIEW

Remind children that a paragraph is a group of sentences that tells about one idea. Good writers tell readers about this main idea in the topic sentence, which is the first sentence of a paragraph. The other sentences in a paragraph, arranged in a logical order, give details about the main idea.

Display **Writing Transparency 93**. Read the paragraph with children. *What is the main idea of this paragraph? Which sentence tells you the main idea?*

Teacher Think Aloud As I read this paragraph, I think about how all the sentences fit together. All the sentences give details about how the girl and her mother build a birdhouse. This main idea is clearly stated in the very first sentence, which makes it easier for readers to understand what's happening in this piece of writing.

Transparency 93

(1) My mom and I built a beautiful birdhouse. (2) On Saturday morning, my mom and I went to the hardware store to buy some wood. (3) When we got home, she taught me how to trace shapes onto the wood. (4) We had cheese sandwiches for lunch. (5) Next, my mom cut out the shapes I had drawn on the wood. (6) Mom and I worked together to nail together the pieces. (7) The last step was painting the birdhouse a bright shade of blue. (8) My favorite color is green. (9) The birdhouse looks great hanging in our backyard.

Responses: The main idea is in sentence 1. Sentences 4 and 8 do not support the main idea and should be deleted.

WRITING PROMPT: Think about a time you and your friends worked together to build something. Write a paragraph to describe that experience. Be sure to write a paragraph with a clear topic sentence and many supporting details.

Writing Transparency

GUIDED PRACTICE/PRACTICE

Help children identify all the sentences that give information about the main idea. Instruct children to identify the sentences that do not belong in this paragraph because they are off-topic. Direct children to respond to the writing prompt at the bottom of the transparency for further practice writing strong paragraphs.

5-Day Writing

Personal Narrative	
DAY 1	Focus and Plan
DAY 2	Prewrite
DAY 3	Skill: A Strong Paragraph; Draft
DAY 4	Revise; Edit/Proofread
DAY 5	Publish and Present

Personal Narrative

DISCUSS THE MODEL

Display **Writing Transparency 94**. Read Jewel's draft with children. Help them to see how this draft includes features of a personal narrative. Discuss the following points as you reread the model:

- Jewel describes a real experience that she had. Her personal narrative describes a series events in a logical order.
- Not all of the sentences in Jewel's paragraph give more information about the topic. She did not include many supporting details that tell more about the main idea.

WRITE THE DRAFT

Have children draft their own personal narratives about real-life experiences. Direct them to review their Sequence Charts to organize their ideas into a logical order. As they draft, remind them to think about their purpose and audience.

ORGANIZATION AND FOCUS

- As children draft, remind them to include first-person words, such as *I*, *my*, *we*, and *our*.
- Remind children to group together related ideas in their writing and maintain a consistent focus on their topics. Tell children to stay focused by only including details that tell about the main idea.

Writing Trait: Organization

EXPLAIN/MODEL

Good writers plan how they will order the ideas and details in their writing. It is important for writing to be organized so that it is easy for readers to follow. A personal narrative is usually organized so that events are told in the correct time order. This means that the writer describes events in the order that they happened. The writer can also use time-order transition words, such as *then* or *next*, to show the order of events or ideas. Display Writing Transparency 94 and read the draft aloud with children. Ask children to identify each event in the narrative. *Are these events written in an order that makes sense? Is it easy or difficult to understand what the children did to clean the park?*

GUIDED PRACTICE/PRACTICE

Write the following sentences on the board and then ask children to organize them properly: *At the end of the day, we were tired but happy. Magda and I cleaned the whole house today. Then, we cleaned the bathroom. First, we washed the kitchen floor.*

ELL

Beginning

Draw Have children draw comic strips showing the series of events in their narratives. Help children to write labels that describe the events.

Intermediate

Draw Have children draw comic strips showing the series of events in their narratives. Help them by writing sentence frames for captions as needed.

Advanced

Write Have children write short paragraphs about their experiences. Ask them to circle first-person words to make sure they have been included and make sense. Give children sentence frames as needed.

DAY 4 At a Glance

WHOLE GROUP

Oral Language
- Build Robust Vocabulary
- Review Oral Vocabulary Words

Phonemic Awareness
- Phoneme Categorization

Phonics
- Diphthong *ou, ow*
- Spelling: Test Practice

Vocabulary
- Review Words in Context

Informational Text
- Genre: Internet Article
- Text Feature: Drop-Down Menu
- Read "Watch It Move!"

Language Arts
- Grammar: Linking Verbs
- Writing: Personal Narrative

SMALL GROUP

- Differentiated Instruction, pages 41K–41JJ

Oral Language

Build Robust Vocabulary

REVIEW WORDS

Lead a class discussion using as many of the oral vocabulary words as possible. Make sure to connect the discussion to the weekly Big Idea.

- *Name one job that you can* **accomplish** *more quickly with the help of your friends? Why do you think that is the case?*
- *Describe an* **arduous** *job. What about the task makes it so arduous?*
- *What kind of* **labor** *would you like to do when you get older? Why?*
- *Describe how your family likes to* **rejoice** when things go well.
- *Which of the following do you need to know in order to* **succeed** *at growing a garden: how to pull weeds, how to water plants, how to pour milk into a cup, how to plant seeds, how to mow the grass?*
- Have children say what each word means and use it in a sentence.

- Review last week's words: *coincidence*, *contemplate*, *explain*, *scheme*, and *worthy*.

Write About It

The story *Head, Body, Legs: A Story from Liberia* tells about how the parts of the body came together. Write a similar story about how the parts of a plant, or something else in nature, came together to accomplish something.

Phonemic Awareness

Phoneme Categorization

Objective

- Categorize words with diphthong /ou/

Model

Show children how to listen for the medial /ou/ in words.

Listen as I say each sound in the word *mouse*. I hear /m/ at the beginning of *mouse*. I hear /ou/ in the middle of *mouse*. I hear /s/ at the end of *mouse*. Listen: /mous/, *mouse*.

Repeat the routine with *sounds*, *clock*, and *houses*.

Now I am going to say three words. Two of them have the vowel sound /ou/ in the middle and one does not: *pounce*, *park*, *sprout*. The word *park* does not have /ou/ in the middle.

Guided Practice/Practice

Have children practice with these examples.

Guide practice with the first row.

I am going to say more groups of words. Listen carefully. Tell me which word has a different vowel sound in the middle.

shout, what, sound	mouse, howl, boy
ground, grown, loud	torch, trout, down
mouth, drown, hunt	dirt, south, snout
bounce, cloud, hair	spray, sprout, out
grouch, hills, proud	house, soil, couch

Objectives

- Substitute initial and final sounds
- Blend and build words with diphthong *ou*, *ow*
- Read multisyllabic words

Materials

- Word-Building Cards; Teacher's Resource Book, p. 66
- pocket chart

Skills Trace	
Diphthong *ou*, *ow*	
Introduce	7C–D
Practice/ Apply	7F, 9G, 37F-G, 37I, 37T; Practice Book: p. 173; Decodable Reader: *The Missing String Beans*
Reteach/ Review	41C-D; 41K-N, 41Q, 41W, 41CC
Assess	Weekly Test; Unit 4 Test
Maintain	Build Fluency: Sound/Spellings

Phonics

Blend Words with *ou*, *ow*

Model

Place **Word-Building Cards** *t*, *o*, *w*, *n* in the pocket chart to form *town*. Model how to generate and blend the sounds to say the word.

The letter *t* stands for /t/. The letters *ow* stand for /ou/. The letter *n* stands for /n/. Now listen as I blend all three sounds: /toun/. Your turn. Let's read the word together: *town*.

Repeat the routine with *sound*.

Guided Practice/Practice

Repeat with additional words. Have children blend the sounds in the words "with you."

hound	mouth	drown	sounds
plow	fowl	south	crowd
houses	cows	founded	proud

Build Words with *ou*, *ow*

Model

Place Word-Building Cards *l*, *o*, *u*, *d* in the pocket chart. Blend the phonemes.

Let's blend all the sounds together and read the word: /loud/, *loud*.

Add *c* and repeat with *cloud*.

Let's blend all the sounds together and read the word: /kloud/, *cloud*.

Change *oud* to *own* and repeat with *clown*.

Let's blend all the sounds together and read the word: /kloun/, *clown*.

Guided Practice/Practice

Continue by building additional words.

Do the first set together.

sound, mound, mouth
how, howl, hound, house
spouse, spout, pout, pound
couch, couches, pouches
bouncing, rebound, roundest
brownie, drowning, frowns, frowned

Phonics/Spelling

Words with *ou, ow*

PARTNERS

- Provide pairs of children with individual copies of the **Spelling Word Cards**.
- While one partner reads the words one at a time, the other partner should orally segment the word (e.g., /b/ /r/ /ou/ /n/) and then write the word. Have **WorkBoards** available for children who need hands-on support in segmenting the word and attaching one spelling to each sound.
- After reading all the words, partners should switch roles.
- When both partners have spelled all the words, children should correct their own papers.

Quick Check

Can children spell words with diphthong *ou, ow*?

During **Small Group Instruction**

If No → **Approaching Level** Repeat blending using the weekly spelling words. Explicitly correct the error, and provide more "with me" type practice. Use a lower level of blending to provide support.

If Yes → **On Level** Consolidate the learning by having children spell additional words with diphthong *ou, ow*. See page 41M.

Beyond Level Extend the learning by having children spell harder words containing diphthong *ou, ow*. See page 41N.

Objective

- Spell words with diphthong *ou, ow*

Materials

- Spelling Word Cards BLM; Teacher's Resource Book, p. 70
- paper and pencils
- Phonics/Spelling Practice Book, p. 64

5-Day Spelling	
DAY 1	Dictation; Pretest
DAY 2	Teacher-Modeled Word Sort
DAY 3	Student Word Sort
DAY 4	Test Practice
DAY 5	Posttest

ON YOUR OWN

Spelling, page 64

A. There are six spelling mistakes in the report below. Circle the misspelled words. Write the words correctly on the lines below.

A desert is a hot, dry place. It may look broun because few green plants can survive there. Some animals can and do live in the desert. You may hear a lowd soond at night. What is it? It might be the houl of a coyote. Or it might be the groowl of a dingo. Dingoes are like dogs. Some dangerous animals live in the desert, too. If you see one of them, go back into your howse.

1. brown
2. loud
3. sound
4. howl
5. growl
6. house

B. Writing

Write a short report about animals that live in the desert. Use four of the spelling words in your report.

Answers will vary.

Objectives

- Use this week's and last week's vocabulary words context
- Build Fluency: Word Automaticity

Vocabulary

Words in Context

REVIEW VOCABULARY

Review this week's vocabulary words (**attached**, **delicious**, **frantically**, **gasped**, **swung**) using the sentence stems below. Have children orally complete each one.

- Our hands are __________ to our arms.
- After being underwater, the boy came to the surface and __________ for air.
- The mother searched __________ for her car keys.
- The four trapeze artists __________ in the big circus tent.
- I ate a bowl of __________ strawberries after dinner.
- Then have children use each word in a sentence.

- Repeat the activity with last week's vocabulary words: *creating*, *familiar*, *glamorous*, *imagination*, *memories*, and *occasions*.

Science Informational Text

Genre

INTERNET ARTICLE

Tell children that the next selection they will read focuses on force and motion. It is an **Internet article**. Internet articles can both inform and entertain readers. Discuss text and graphic features that children might find in an Internet article (for example, drop-down menu, photos).

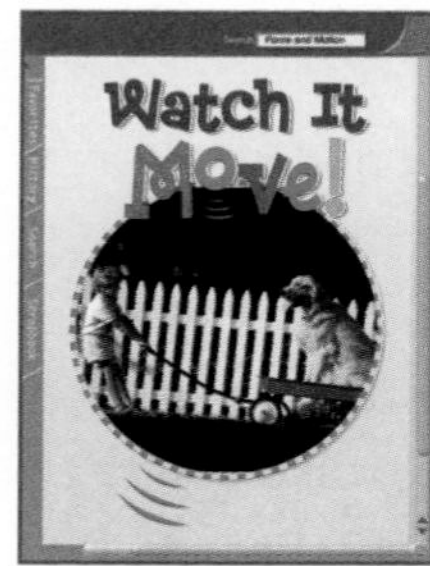

Paired Section

PREVIEW AND PREDICT

- Turn to page 38 in the **Student Book** and read the title. *How do things move? What do you think this article is going to be about? What do you notice about the way the text is presented?*

Text Feature: Drop-Down Menu

EXPLAIN/MODEL

Point out the drop-down menu on Student Book page 39. Explain that a drop-down menu is a feature in an Internet article. It lists links to other related information on the Web site.

Think Aloud The drop-down menu lists Web sites that have information about the topic of this article. This is helpful because I can go to those Web sites on the Internet to read more about how things move. The titles of the Web sites give me an idea of what the articles are about. That helps me because I don't have to go to every Web site if I am looking for specific information.

Science Content Vocabulary

"WATCH IT MOVE!"

Discuss the content vocabulary: *force*, *friction*, *gravity*.

- Write the words *force*, *friction*, and *gravity* on the board. Have children tell what each word means and to use it in a sentence.
- Tell children that they will see these words in the next selection.

SCIENCE WORDS

Define the content words using child-friendly definitions and selection visuals.

Objectives

- Read informational text
- Use text feature: drop-down menu
- Recognize the purposes of internet articles

Materials

- Student Book: "Watch It Move!" pp. 38–39

ELL

Paired Reading Prepare children to read the story prior to the whole-class reading. Use the Interactive Question-Response Guide Technique in the English Language Learners Resource Book, pages 224–225, to preteach the story content, build language, and develop meaning.

Content Vocabulary

Science Words

Define the content words using child-friendly definitions and selection visuals.

force (p. 38): something that changes the motion of an object

friction (p. 39): something that slows movement between two surfaces moving against each other

gravity (p. 39): force that pulls things toward the center of Earth

Search Force and Motion

Science

Science

Genre
Expository An Internet article gives facts about a topic and is found on the World Wide Web.

Text Feature
The Drop-Down Menu in an Internet article has links to related information on the Web site.

Content Vocabulary
force
friction
gravity

Watch It Move!

1 Rolling a ball and pulling a wagon are both examples of **force**. Force changes the way an object moves. Force can be a push, like when you roll a ball to a friend. Force can also be a pull, like when you drag a wagon.

2 Another force is called **friction**. Friction is when two things rub against each other. A ball slows down because of friction with the floor.

Gravity is a force, too. Hold a ball over your head and let it go. The ball will fall because Earth's **gravity** pulls it down. 3

Force and Motion Links

For more information about force and motion, check out:

- Experiments in Force and Motion
- The Force of Gravity
- Understanding Friction

Connect and Compare

1. What other information about force can you link to in this article? **Drop-Down Menus**
2. Think about this article and *Head, Body, Legs: A Story from Liberia*. What kind of force do the arms use to paddle across the river? **Reading/Writing Across Texts**

Science Activity

Research force and motion activities online. Choose an activity and show it to the class. Explain why you chose this activity. Remember to speak at an appropriate pace.

Science Force and motion
www.macmillanmh.com

ON YOUR OWN

Practice Book, page 181

A home page on the Internet is the starting place for getting information. It has links to other related information on the Web site. A **drop-down menu** will help you find more links.

Look at the home page below. Then follow the directions and answer the question.

1. What is the title of this Web page?
   Stories Galore
2. What are two links under Products?
   Possible responses provided: DVDs and Posters
3. Where would you find the link Summer Camp?
   under Programs
4. What would you click on to contact the president of Stories Galore?
   in the drop-down menu Contact Us at the bottom of the page

Approaching Reproducible, page 181
Beyond Reproducible, page 181

Read Informational Text

1 MONITOR AND CLARIFY: READ AHEAD
How could you find out more about force? (I could read ahead to see if the writer gives examples of force. I could also use the drop-down menu to get information to make an adjustment to my reading.)

2 USE TEXT FEATURE: DROP-DOWN MENUS
Identify where the drop-down menu is. What do you think you will learn from each site? (The first will tell about force and motion experiments; the next about gravity; and the last about friction.)

3 STRATEGY Monitor Comprehension: Reread

Teacher Think Aloud Web sites have a lot of information in different formats, which can be confusing. If you do not understand something you read on a Web site, try rereading that section or other parts of the site to make an adjustment.

Connect and Compare

SUGGESTED ANSWERS

1. In this article I can find links to Web sites about force and motion experiments and more information about friction and gravity.

TEXT FEATURE: DROP-DOWN MENU

2. Focus Question: Possible response: I think that Arms used pulling and Legs used pushing to move through the water. When I swim I pull water with my hands and push it when I kick with my feet.

READING/WRITING ACROSS TEXTS

Connect to Content

Science Activity

- Have children work in small groups to compare how different surfaces can change the force on an object. Distribute a small object, such as a block or toy car, to each group. Have children place the object on a variety of surfaces, such as a smooth tabletop, a carpet, a plastic surface, and then sandpaper. On each surface, tell children to give the object a gentle tap. Have them use a ruler to measure how far the object travels. Record children's findings on a class chart. Guide them to understand the object travels farther on the smoother surfaces and that the friction on the rougher surfaces slows down the object and prevents it from traveling as far.

Research and Inquiry

RESEARCH: FORCE AND MOTION Guide small groups of children in choosing one type of force and researching it using the Internet. Tell children to generate research questions using key words, such as *force* or *gravity*. Invite an engineer or scientist to come in and demonstrate how simple machines make use of different forces. Have children write simple observations of the demonstration, using some of their research. Tell each group to illustrate their report and present their findings to the class. Remind children to ask questions to clarify their understanding of the topics.

Objectives

- Use text feature: drop-down menu
- Connect reading across texts
- Research force and motion on the Internet

Materials

- Student Book: "Watch It Move!" pp. 38–39
- Practice Book, p. 181

Test Practice

Answering Questions

To apply **answering questions strategies** to content-area reading, see pages 5–10 in the *Time for Kids Test Practice Edition.*

Digital Learning

Story available on **Listening Library Audio CD** and **StudentWorks Plus**, the Interactive eBook.

www.macmillanmh.com

Objectives

- Proofread for capitalization, punctuation, and correct use of linking verbs
- Use linking verbs in reading, writing, and speaking

Materials

- paper and pencils
- Proofreading Marks BLM; Teacher's Resource Book, p. 191
- Transparency 79
- Grammar Practice Book, p. 79

5-Day Grammar	
Linking Verbs	
DAY 1	Linking Verbs: Present-Tense Forms of *Be*
DAY 2	Past-Tense Forms of *Be*
DAY 3	Mechanics: Capitalization
DAY 4	Proofread
DAY 5	Review and Assess Capitalization Linking Verbs

Grammar

Linking Verbs

REVIEW

- Remind children that a **linking verb** does not show action. The linking verb *be* has special forms.
- Tell them that a **proper noun** begins with a capital letter. (e.g., Tomorrow is Tuesday. We are going to New Mexico in June. My teacher's name is Mr. Hobbs.)

PRACTICE

- Have children work in pairs to write sentences about a time when they worked with other people to get a job done. One partner should write two sentences using linking verbs with *I*, *he*, or *she* in their sentences. The other partner should write two sentences using linking verbs with *you*, *we*, and *they*. Tell them to include proper nouns. Example sentences are:
  - I am baking cookies, and he is helping me mix ingredients. She is reading us Grandma's recipe.
  - You are making a sign for the lemonade stand that we are having. They are the customers who will help us raise money.

- Have partners exchange papers and rewrite the sentences using the linking verbs and subjects they used. Then exchange back and have each child check for correct linking verb usage and capitalization of proper nouns. Then children should read their sentences aloud to their partners.

ELL ENGLISH LANGUAGE LEARNERS

Beginning

Practice Draw a happy face. Say and write *She is happy.* Draw another happy face next to the first. Say and write *They are happy.* Give other sentences showing examples of the single and plural usage of "be." Then write frames such as *We are* ___________. *She is* ___________. Have partners work together to complete the frames.

Intermediate

Practice Write sentence frames that partners can complete by filling in the correct correct form of the verb "be." Sample sentence frame: *They* ___________ *hungry.* Read the sentence aloud. After children are finished copying and completing the sentences, ask them to read them aloud. Correct for grammar as needed.

Advanced

Edit Write the following types of sentences and have partners decide if they are correct or incorrect. Have partners rewrite incorrect sentences. *We was working. I am tired. They is helping me.*

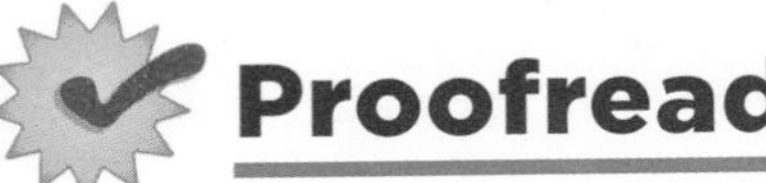

Proofread

EXPLAIN/MODEL

Explain that good writers always proofread their work. This means they reread their writing to check that the grammar, punctuation, and spelling are correct. They will edit their writing to correct any mistakes they find or to make improvements.

Model how to use special marks. Write the following sentence on the board: *my neighbor, mrs. jacobs, walks every morning.*

Think Aloud Writers use special marks to show changes that need to be made to make their writing correct. One mark shows where to put a capital letter and one shows where to add a period. Let's read the sentence. I see that the first word in the sentence is not capitalized. I also see that the title abbreviation for *mrs* is not capitalized. To correct these mistakes, I will make three small lines under the *m* in *my* and the *m* in *mrs*.

Transparency 79

Proofread

This coming independence day was going to be the best ever? The whole town of buzzville are ready to work together. there is a meeting last saturday to think of ideas! My father and mother is leaders of a group to plan a Parade. we will be as busy as bees the whole month of june.

Grammar Transparency

GUIDED PRACTICE/PRACTICE

Display **Grammar Transparency 79**. Read the first sentence with children. Point out that the words *independence day* should be capitalized and that the sentence should have an exclamation mark at the end instead of a question mark. Rewrite the sentence on the board.

Use the transparency to guide children's practice. Continue proofreading the sentences, but give children the chance to suggest corrections.

Proofreading Marks

≡	Make a capital letter.
/	Make a small letter.
⊙	Add a period.
sp	Check spelling.
∧	Add.
ℊ	Take out.
¶	New paragraph.

Available on **Teacher's Resource Book** page 191

ON YOUR OWN

Grammar, page 79

- The words ***is***, ***are***, ***am***, ***was***, and ***were*** can be linking verbs.

Read the paragraph and find the mistakes. Rewrite the passage correctly on the lines below.

Brown bears is one of the largest types of bears. A female brown bear are about half the size of a male. These bears has thick fur that are usually brown. Some bears is lighter, and others is almost black. Brown bear cubs are born between january and march.

Brown bears are one of the largest types of bears. A female brown bear is about half the size of a male. These bears have thick fur that is usually brown. Some bears are lighter, and others are almost black. Brown bear cubs are born between January and March.

Objectives

- Revise a personal narrative by adding and deleting
- Proofread and edit a personal narrative
- Participate in peer review

Materials

- Student Book, pp. 40–41
- Transparencies 94–96
- Proofreading Marks BLM; Teacher's Resource Book, p. 191

5-Day Writing

Personal Narrative	
DAY 1	Focus and Plan
DAY 2	Prewrite
DAY 3	Skill: A Strong Paragraph; Draft
DAY 4	Revise; Edit/Proofread
DAY 5	Publish and Present

ELL

Retell Have partners read each other's personal narratives. Then ask each child to retell the main idea of each paragraph of the partner's personal narrative and what details they thought supported the main ideas.

Writing

Personal Narrative

REVISE DRAFTS

Have children read the writing box at the top of **Student Book** page 40. Point out that good writers create strong paragraphs in their writing. Read aloud the model and callouts with children.

READING AND WRITING CONNECTION

Tell children to look at Student Book pages 38 and 39. Read aloud the paragraphs with children. Direct children to notice the organization of the sentences within each paragraph. *Where is the main idea of each paragraph? What details support each main idea?*

Teacher Think Aloud The author of this selection uses strong paragraphs. Each paragraph starts with a topic sentence that states the main idea. The other sentences in each paragraph give more information about the main idea.

STUDY THE MODEL

- Display the model of a draft of a personal narrative on **Writing Transparency 94**. Remind children that a narrative tells about a real event in a writer's life. *Let's reread this draft as if we were editors. How can we improve this personal narrative? What could we add or delete?* Ask children to share ideas about how it could be revised.

- Now display the revised model on **Writing Transparency 95**. Help children notice how the writer revised the text by adding important details that give more information about the main idea. Direct children to look for similar ways to revise their own writing. Have children revise their personal narratives.

PROOFREAD

Explain/Model After children revise their work, explain that good writers proofread their work to correct grammar, spelling, and punctuation errors. Display **Writing Transparency 96**. Discuss the corrections on the model. Have children proofread their own writing.

PRACTICE/APPLY

Peer Review Have partners review each other's writing using the Writer's Checklist on Student Book page 41. Use the peer conferencing tips on the following page to facilitate the peer review.

Independent Review Have children review their partners' suggestions and evaluate their own work using the Writer's Checklist. They should then finish revising and proofreading their work.

Writing

A Strong Paragraph

A strong paragraph has a topic sentence and details that support it.

Reading and Writing Connection

This is the topic sentence of my paragraph.

I include details that give more information about my topic.

Teamwork in the Park

Last month my whole class worked together to clean up the town playground. It was a big job. Pieces of paper and empty cans covered the ground. All 15 students worked as a team to throw away the garbage. It took more than four hours to get the job done. I am glad there were so many people to sweep and put trash in bags. Thanks to teamwork, the playground is now a clean and fun place for kids to play!

Personal Narrative

Your Writing Prompt

Some jobs are too big for one person to do alone.

Think about a time when you worked in a group or on a team to get something done.

Now write a personal narrative about that event.

Writer's Checklist

- ☑ My writing clearly tells about a time when I worked in a group.
- ☑ My writing has a strong paragraph with a topic sentence and supporting details.
- ☐ The details in my writing give more information about the topic.
- ☑ I put capital letters and punctuation in the right places. I use linking verbs correctly.

Peer Conferencing Tips

Peer Conferencing Have children read each other's personal narratives. Tell them to point out parts that work well and point out parts that are not as successful. Children can ask the following questions as they conference:

- Does the personal narrative tell about a real event from the writer's life?
- Does the writer include strong paragraphs? Does each paragraph tell about one main idea? Do the other sentences support the main idea?
- Is the writing organized in a way that is easy for the reader to follow?
- Does the writer use linking verbs correctly?

DAY 5 At a Glance

WHOLE GROUP

Oral Language
- Build Robust Vocabulary

Fluency
- Expression

Phonemic Awareness
- Phoneme Blending

Phonics
- Diphthong *ou, ow*
- Build Fluency
- Spelling: Posttest

Vocabulary
- Words in Context
- Spiral Review

Comprehension
- Strategy: Monitor Comprehension: Reread
- Skill: Cause and Effect

Language Arts
- Grammar: Linking Verbs
- Writing: Personal Narrative

SMALL GROUP

- Differentiated Instruction, pages 41K–41JJ

Review and Assess

Oral Language

Build Robust Vocabulary

ASSESS WORD KNOWLEDGE

To review the week's vocabulary words, ask children to think about working together to finish a project. Ask them what kinds of things people can do to make an **arduous** job easier. Have them describe ways to **accomplish** a job by working together. *What are some things you can do to* **succeed**? *How can you split up the* **labor** *so that everyone is doing a fair amount of the work?* Tell children to think of things they can do to **rejoice** at completion of a project.

Read aloud the oral vocabulary words. Have children say a sentence using each word. Provide the following sentence starters:

- Weeding the garden is an **arduous** task because ________.
- One way to **accomplish** a difficult job is to ________.
- My favorite **labor** is ________ because ________.
- My friends will **rejoice** together when we finish the project by ________.
- When people work together, they can **succeed** because ________.
- Reread the **Oral Vocabulary Cards** to teach additional vocabulary.

ELL ENGLISH LANGUAGE LEARNERS

Beginning

Express Explain the meaning of vocabulary words using gestures, examples, and pictures. Then use the vocabulary words to make statements and ask children questions, for example, *I think painting a house is arduous. What job do you think is arduous?* Have children work together to come up with answers. Allow children ample time to respond.

Intermediate

Demonstrate Understanding Read the first sentence starter and give an example of completed sentence. Clarify and discuss meaning as needed. Then have pairs work together to discuss and complete the sentence starter with their own answers. Do the same for all the sentence starters. Help with correct pronunciation if necessary.

Advanced

Speak Pair children of different proficiency levels. and have partners work together to complete the sentences. Help by giving give sample answers as needed.

Review and Assess
Fluency

Expression

MODEL FLUENT READING

- Read aloud a few pages of *Head, Body, Legs: A Story from Liberia*. Model reading with good expression. Have children echo each sentence you read. Point out how you read dialogue the way you think the characters in the story would say the words.

Main Selection

- Have partners reread the selection aloud, working on how they read dialogue. Circulate, listen in, and provide corrective feedback. Note children who need additional work with decoding and reading high-frequency words. Work with these children during Small Group time.

REPEATED READINGS

- Have children select a story from the **Student Book** or a book that they have previously read. Tell children that by rereading these books, they can become better readers. *The more practice we have sounding out words and seeing those important high-frequency words in text, the easier it will be for us to read new stories.*
- Provide 15–20 minutes for children to enjoy independent reading. Then have students paraphrase what they have read. You may read with children or use this time to assess individuals using the Fluency Assessment in the **Diagnostic Assessment Handbook**.

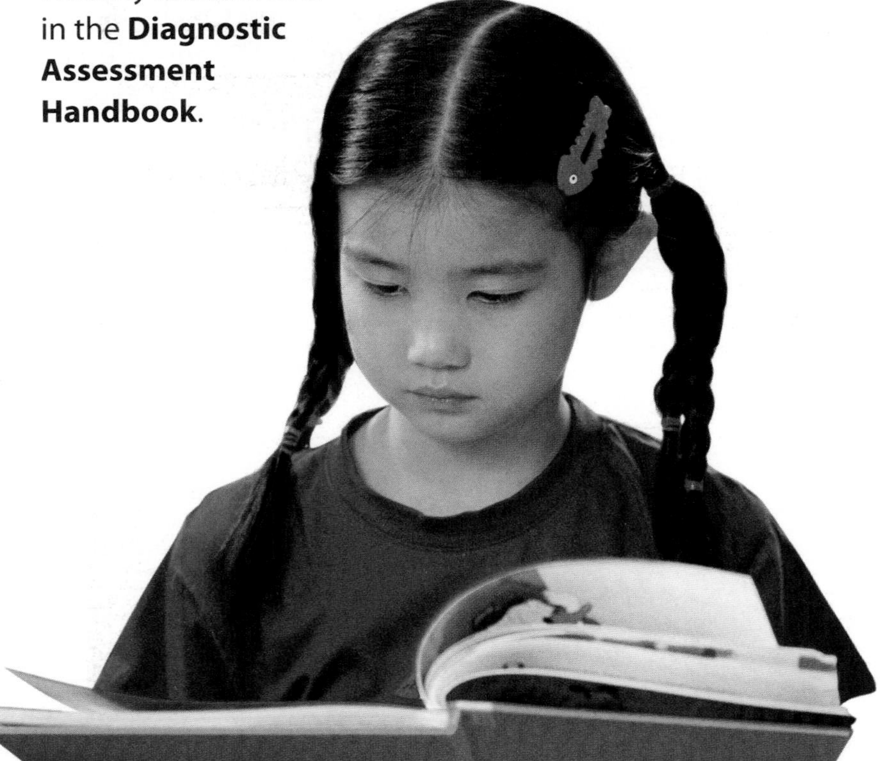

Objectives

- Review and assess vocabulary
- Build fluency

Materials

- Student Book

Readers Theater

BUILDING LISTENING AND SPEAKING SKILLS
Distribute copies of "A Whale of a Story" from **Read-Aloud Anthology** pages 179–191. Have children practice reading the play throughout the unit. Assign parts and have children present the play or perform it as a dramatic reading at the end of the unit.

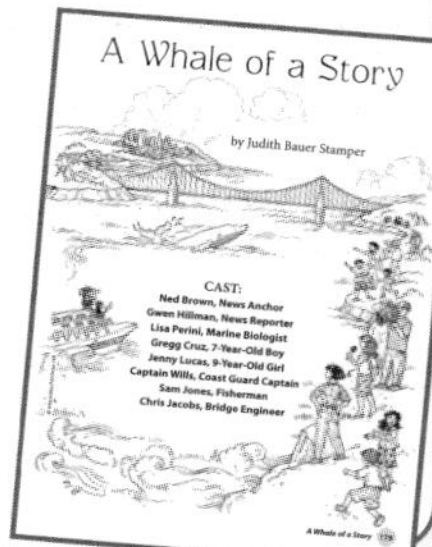

Objectives

- Blend phonemes
- Blend sounds in words with diphthong *ou, ow*
- Read multisyllabic words
- Review phonics decoding strategy

Materials

- Word-Building Cards BLM; Teacher's Resource Book, p. 66
- pocket chart
- word charts from Days 1, 3
- Decodable Reader Library: *The Missing String Beans*
- Practice Book for phonics decoding strategy, p. 182

Skills Trace

Diphthong *ou, ow*	
Introduce	7C–D
Practice/ Apply	7F, 9G, 37F-G, 37I, 37T; Practice Book: p. 173; Decodable Reader: *The Missing String Beans*
Reteach/ Review	41C-D; 41K-N, 41Q, 41W, 41CC
Assess	Weekly Test; Unit 4 Test
Maintain	Build Fluency: Sound/Spellings

Review and Assess

Phonemic Awareness

Phoneme Blending

Guided Practice/Practice

Have children practice blending sounds to make words with /ou/. Guide practice with the first word.

I am going to say a word sound by sound. I want you to blend the sounds to form the word. Let me try first. The sounds are /s/ /ou/ /th/. Listen as I blend the sounds: /south/, *south*. The word is *south*.

Your turn.

/p/ /ou/ /t/	/r/ /ou/ /n/ /d/
/m/ /ou/ /th/	/h/ /ou/ /s/
/h/ /ou/ /l/	/p/ /l/ /ou/
/ou/ /t/	/g/ /ou/ /n/
/k/ /l/ /ou/ /d/	/p/ /r/ /ou/ /d/

Review and Assess

Phonics

Build Fluency: Sound/Spellings

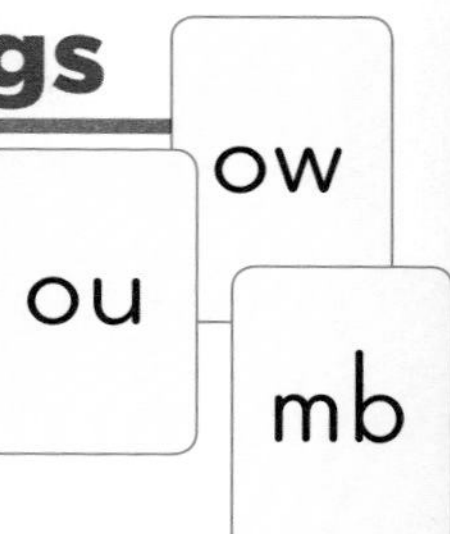

Display the following **Word-Building Cards** one at a time: *ou, ow, are, air, ear, ere, or, ore, oar, ar, gn, kn, wr, mb, eer, ere, ear, er, ir, ur, u, u_e, ew, ue*. Have children chorally say each sound. Mix, repeat, and vary the pace.

Blend Words with *ou, ow*

Guided Practice

Display **Word-Building Cards** *m, o, u, n, t.* Blend.

What sounds do each of these letters stand for? Help me blend the sounds together: /mount/. Let's read the word together: *mount.*

Repeat using *crown, loud, town, proud,* and *cow.*

Practice

Have children practice generating and blending sounds. Write the words on the board. Have children practice with nonsense words.

hound	pound	how	fowl
south	mound	house	clown
proudest	drowning	recount	crowded
drow	shound	fowt	flound

Build Fluency: Word Automaticity

Use word charts from Days 1 and 3. Point to each word as children chorally read it. Model blending the sounds in any words children miss. Then point to words in random order at varying speeds for children to chorally read.

down	ground	owl	sound
shout	around	how	round
pound	bounce	cow	brown
sprouted	newest	spout	parted
spray	chatter	hear	trainer

A cow lay down on the ground.
The clowns ran around town.

shouts	sounds	town	found
bouncing	scowling	grounded	
sprout	flower	grouch	around
mound	chewing	shined	prowling
proudest	teased	chair	spark

I shouted over the loud sounds.
Are the flowers sprouting?

sundown	playground	crouches	rebound

Build Fluency: Connected Text

- Have children reread with a partner *The Missing String Beans* from the **Decodable Reader Library**. Circulate and listen in, providing corrective feedback as needed.
- Comment on children's **speed**, **accuracy**, and **intonation**. Model each as needed. For example, model how your voice rises at the end of a question.

The Missing String Beans

Inflectional Endings *-s, -es*

Teach

- Write the words *cow* and *cows* on the board. Underline the letter *-s* at the end of *cows.*
- Tell children that the letter *-s* at the end of *cows* means there is more than one *cow.* It is a plural.
- Write the words *couch* and *couches* on the board. Underline the *-es* in *couches.* Explain that when a word ends in *s, sh, ch,* or *x,* we add *-es* to make it plural.

Practice/Apply

- Help children blend the sounds in the following words: *plow, plows; cloud, clouds; clown, clowns; pouch, pouches; hound, hounds; town, towns; ounce, ounces.*
- Ask children to look for words that end in *-s* and *-es* as they read this week's stories. Keep a running list on chart paper.

Corrective Feedback

For children needing additional practice reading *ou, ow* words, use the one syllable and multisyllabic Speed Drills in the **Intervention Kit (Fluency)**.

Objectives

- Spell words with diphthong *ou, ow*
- Spell high-frequency words
- Use the Word Wall to find spellings

Materials

- paper and pencils

5-Day Spelling	
DAY 1	Dictation; Pretest
DAY 2	Teacher-Modeled Word Sort
DAY 3	Student Word Sort
DAY 4	Test Practice
DAY 5	Posttest

Review and Assess

Phonics/Spelling

Words with Diphthong *ou, ow*

POSTTEST

Use the following procedure to assess children's spelling of the weekly spelling words.

- Say a spelling word and use it in the sentence provided below.
- Have children write the word on a piece of paper. Then continue with the next word.
- When children have finished, collect their papers and analyze their spellings of misspelled words.
- Have children create personal word lists in their Writer's Notebooks that include words they need to continue practicing.

1. **clown:** The clown made me laugh.
2. **growl:** The dogs growl at strangers.
3. **howl:** The wolves howl in the desert.
4. **brown:** The soil in my yard is brown.
5. **crown:** The queen wears a crown.
6. **ground:** I planted flowers in the ground.
7. **shout:** We are not allowed to shout in school.
8. **cloud:** I saw a dark cloud in the sky.
9. **house:** The door to my house is red.
10. **sound:** The mouse made a tiny sound.
11. **shark:** The gray shark at the zoo is named Skipper.
12. **chair:** The boy gave his chair to his grandmother.
13. **family:** The family that lives next door is big.
14. **four:** Chris has four pairs of pants.
15. **hear:** I can hear the wind blow during the storm.

Word Wall Use a Word Wall to group words by spelling patterns. Also use it to review previous weeks' spelling words. Remove words from the Word Wall when children have mastered them.

Review and Assess
Vocabulary

Words in Context

REVIEW

Tell children that some words in each sentence mean about the same thing as a vocabulary word. Have children tell which vocabulary word fits into each sentence and reread the sentence substituting the correct vocabulary word for the words in bold.

- After running a long way, I stopped and **breathed in quickly and loudly**. (gasped)
- The octopus **stuck itself** to the side of the boat. (attached)
- My lunch is **tasting very good** today. (delicious)
- The swing **moved back and forth in the air**. (swung)
- The man moved **quickly and with worry** when he couldn't find his wallet. (frantically)
- Then have children use each word in a sentence.

Spiral Vocabulary Review

Divide the class into two groups for an activity. Make sets of word cards using this week's vocabulary words and those from last week: *creating, familiar, glamorous, imagination, memories, occasions*.

Give each group four cards. Have teams develop three clues for each word, and write them on a piece of paper. Clues can include number of syllables, part of speech, or meaning. Groups then trade cards.

Group 1: One child reads a clue aloud.

Group 2: Children try to match the clue to one of the cards. If they identify it correctly, it is placed faceup to the side. If not, they ask for another clue.

Groups continue providing clues until all the words are identified.

Write About It

Write about what it might be like to try to get your friends to help you with an arduous job. How can you convince them to help you complete it? Try to use at least one vocabulary word.

Objectives

- Use context clues to determine the meaning of unfamiliar words
- Use vocabulary words in context
- Review this week's and last week's vocabulary words

Materials

- index cards

Objectives

- Determine when they might need to monitor comprehension again
- Identify cause and effect
- Make comparisons across texts
- Review seeking clarification about stories and using supporting evidence from the text

Materials

- Practice Book for seeking clarification about stories and using supporting evidence from the text, p. 183

Skills Trace

Cause and Effect	
Introduce	U2: 199A–B
Practice/ Apply	U2: 199J–231A; Practice Book: 73–74
Reteach/ Review	U2: 235G, 235R–T, 235X-Z; U3: 403A–B, 403K–429A, 435G, 435R–T, 435X-Z; Practice Book: 151–152
Assess	Weekly Tests; Units 2, 3, 4, 6 Tests
Review	U2: 243N; U3: 457N; U4: 9A–9B, 9J–37A, 41G, 41R–T, 41X–Z, 71N; U6: 409A–B, 409J–433A, 437G, 437R–T, 437X–Z, 457N; Practice Book: 176–177, 322–323

Review and Assess

Comprehension

STRATEGY Monitor Comprehension: Reread

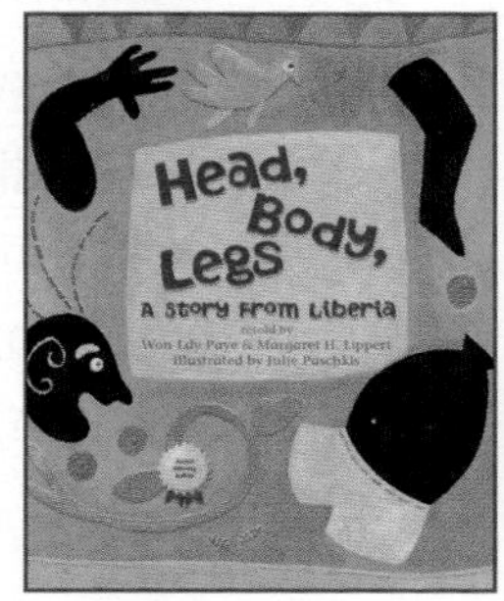

Main Selection

TRANSFER THE STRATEGY Remind children that they made corrections and reread sections of *Head, Body, Legs: A Story from Liberia* when they were confused or if something didn't make sense. Model how using this strategy helped you make adjustments to your reading.

Think Aloud When I read *Head, Body, Legs,* I stopped and corrected my reading. I reread a passage when something didn't make sense. For example, I didn't understand why Head was tired of eating grass and mushrooms. I stopped and reread that part of the story. I saw that the author wrote that Head can only eat things on the ground because he couldn't reach anything else. Knowing that helped me understand his actions in the story.

Focus Question Ask children to describe how the strategy helped them monitor their comprehension. Offer the following sentence starters:

I reread a part of the story when ________.

Rereading sections helped me ________.

How might this strategy help you when you read another selection?

SKILL Cause and Effect

READING ACROSS TEXTS Model making a connection between the cause-and-effect relationships you identified in "The Story of the Giant Carrot" and *Head, Body, Legs: A Story from Liberia*.

Think Aloud I made a connection between the causes and effects I identified in the two stories. Characters in both stories want to get food. In *Head, Body Legs*, the characters wanted to get cherries and mangoes. In "The Story of the Giant Carrot," Farmer Smith wants to pull out the giant carrot. These are both causes. In both stories, the effect is that characters to work together with others to get the food they want.

Provide a sentence starter to help children make their own connections between stories:

I made a connection between ________.

Review and Assess
Grammar

Capitalization of Proper Nouns

REVIEW

- Remind children that **proper nouns** name special people, places, and times. Some proper nouns name days of the week, months, and holidays.
- Remind them that proper nouns begin with a capital letter.
- Have chidren write sample sentences using proper nouns.

Linking Verbs

REVIEW

- Remind children that **linking verbs** do not show action. The verb *be* is a linking verb. The verb *be* has special forms in the past and present tenses.

GUIDED PRACTICE/PRACTICE

Use the first sentence on **Grammar Transparency 80** to help children practice what they have learned about linking verbs and proper nouns. Work with them and tell them to rewrite the sentence on paper. Then have children correct the remaining errors in capitalization on the transparency. Have them underline the linking verbs and proper nouns in each sentence.

Transparency 80

Proper Nouns and Linking Verbs

1. **Our neighbors, felix and miranda, was sad when their barn burned down.**
   Our neighbors, Felix and Miranda, were sad when their barn burned down.
2. **The fire is the biggest event of last september.**
   The fire was the biggest event of last September.
3. **Our baseball team are ready to help build a new barn.**
   Our baseball team was ready to help build a new barn.
4. **We is sure we could finish by thanksgiving.**
   We were sure we could finish by Thanksgiving.
5. **Our neighbors was so happy with the new barn.**
   Our neighbors were so happy with the new barn.

Grammar Transparency

Objectives

- Review capitalization of proper nouns
- Proofread sentences for proper use of the linking verb *be*

Materials

- Transparency 80
- Grammar Practice Book, p. 80

5-Day Grammar	
Linking Verbs	
DAY 1	Linking Verbs; Present-Tense Forms of *Be*
DAY 2	Past-Tense Forms of *Be*
DAY 3	Mechanics: Capitalization
DAY 4	Linking Verbs Proofread
DAY 5	Review and Assess Capitalization Linking Verbs

ON YOUR OWN

Grammar, page 80

Circle the present form of the verb *be* in each sentence. Rewrite the sentence. Change the verb to past tense.

1. I (am) at the kitchen window.
   I was at the kitchen window.
2. The leaves of the maple tree (are) bright red.
   The leaves of the maple tree were bright red.
3. A chipmunk (is) in the grass.
   A chipmunk was in the grass.
4. Its nest (is) under the ground.
   Its nest was under the ground.
5. Some nuts and seeds (are) on the grass.
   Some nuts and seeds were on the grass.
6. The chipmunk's cheeks (are) full.
   The chipmunk's cheeks were full.

Objective

- Publish and share a personal narrative

5-Day Writing

Personal Narrative	
DAY 1	Focus and Plan
DAY 2	Prewrite
DAY 3	Skill: A Strong Paragraph; Draft
DAY 4	Revise; Edit/Proofread
DAY 5	Publish and Present

Handwriting

Have children self-check their writing to make sure the circular characters are closed and the letters rest on the line. For ball-and-stick and slant models, see pages 104–112 in **Handwriting**.

Review and Assess

Writing

Personal Narrative

PUBLISH

- Tell children that to publish their writing, they should make neat final copies. Have children use their neatest, most legible handwriting or a computer. Children should use the narrative on **Student Book** page 40 as a model.
- Tell children to read their final published writing one more time to make sure they have not left anything out. Instruct children to add their personal narratives to their Writing Portfolios.

EVALUATE

To evaluate children's writing, use the 4-point Scoring Rubric. Consider children's efforts, possibly adding a plus (+) for excellent organization.

4-POINT SCORING RUBRIC

4 Excellent	3 Good	2 Fair	1 Unsatisfactory
Focus and Coherence Gives interesting and detailed information about a central topic.	**Focus and Coherence** Gives information about a central topic.	**Focus and Coherence** Gives information about a topic, but may stray from focus.	**Focus and Coherence** Does not give information about a central topic.
Organization Presents a main idea that is supported by clear, factual details.	**Organization** Presents a main idea and supports it with details.	**Organization** Omits a main idea or offers few supporting details.	**Organization** Does not present a main idea supported by details.
Development of Ideas/ Word Choice Thoroughly develops ideas. Uses precise word choice to enhance quality of content.	**Development of Ideas/ Word Choice** Attempts to develop ideas. Uses word choice to suit the purpose.	**Development of Ideas/ Word Choice** Attempts to develop ideas, but may be inconsistent. Chooses words that are often ill-suited for the purpose.	**Development of Ideas/ Word Choice** Provides little or no development of ideas. Omits or fails to use chosen words correctly.
Voice Uses a personal voice that adds an inviting, unique tone to the writing.	**Voice** Uses a personal voice that generally expresses an inviting, unique tone.	**Voice** Writer has difficulty expressing an inviting, unique tone.	**Voice** Writer does not express a personal voice.
Conventions/Sentence Fluency Writing is almost entirely free of mechanical, grammatical, and spelling errors. Sentences flow from one to the other.	**Conventions/Sentence Fluency** Spelling, capitalization, punctuation, and usage are mostly correct. Sentences lead naturally to those that follow.	**Conventions/Sentence Fluency** Makes mistakes that can interfere with the reading of the writing. Sentences flow in a somewhat fluid manner.	**Conventions/Sentence Fluency** Makes frequent errors in grammar, spelling, mechanics, and usage. Sentences run together or are confusing.

Speaking, Listening, and Viewing

SPEAKING STRATEGIES

Share the following strategies for presenting information about writing a personal narrative.

- Take some time to plan your presentation. Organize your presentation to maintain a clear focus. Stay focused by only talking about information that relates to the topic of your writing.
- Practice your presentation beforehand.
- Tell the audience what your narrative is about. Recount experiences in a logical sequence, or order. Retell the narrative, including details about the characters, setting, and plot.
- Make eye contact with the audience.
- Speak clearly and at an appropriate pace for this type of communication.

LISTENING STRATEGIES

Share the following strategies for listening to a personal narrative.

- Look at the speaker and give him or her your full attention.
- Determine the purpose of listening to the presentation. Figure out whether you are listening to obtain information, to solve problems, or for enjoyment. For example, if you are listening for enjoyment, you will want to think about how the speaker's experiences are like ones from your own life.
- Sit quietly and listen politely to the speaker.
- Paraphrase information that has been shared orally by the speaker to make sure you understand it.
- After the speaker has finished, ask relevant questions to clarify information and ideas that you did not understand.

PRESENT AND EVALUATE

When children are ready, have them make their presentations about their personal narratives.

- Evaluate the speakers: Do they speak loudly and clearly? Do they make eye contact with the audience? Do they use expression in their voices? Do they speak with proper phrasing? Do they speak in complete sentences and correctly use nouns and verbs?
- Evaluate the listeners: Did they look at and listen to the speaker? Did they ask questions to clarify their understanding? Can they paraphrase the information from the oral presentation?

ELL

Use Visuals Review the names of the objects displayed in the **Reproducible**. Have English Language Learners practice naming the objects.

Approaching Level

Phonemic Awareness

Objective Identify the middle sound in words

Materials • none

PHONEME IDENTITY

- Say: *Listen carefully to these words:* house, */h/ /ou/ /s/;* shout */sh/ /ou/ /t/. The middle sound is the same in both words: /ou/.* Then say three words: *loud, whale, log*. Have children identify the word with the /ou/ sound in the middle. Repeat with *shirt, gown, loan*.
- Say these word sets, having children name the word with /ou/: *feel, sew, clown; loud, lie, lone; hear, hair, how; pride, proud, float.*

Phonics

Objective Decode words with vowel diphthong /ou/*ou, ow*

Materials
- **Sound-Spelling Cards**
- **Approaching Reproducible**, p. 173
- **Sound-Spelling WorkBoards**
- **Word-Building Cards**

SOUND-SPELLING REVIEW

Tier 2

- Display **Word-Building Cards** for the following: *ou, ow, are, air, ear, ere, or, ore, oar, ar, gn, kn, wr, mb, eer, ere, ear, er, ir, ur, u, u_e, ew, ue*. Have children chorally say each sound. Repeat and vary the pace. Then say a sound. Have children find the corresponding letter(s) on the **WorkBoard** and write the letter(s).

VOWEL DIPHTHONG *ou, ow*

- Display the *Cow* **Sound-Spelling Card**. Say: *This is the* Cow *Sound-Spelling Card. The sound is /ou/. The /ou/ sound is spelled with the letters* ou *and* ow. *Say it with me: /ou/. Repeat: /ou/. This is the sound at the end of the word* cow. *What are the letters?* (ow) *What is the sound?* (/ou/) *This is also the sound in the middle of the word* loud. *What are the letters?* (ou) *What is the sound?* (/ou/)
- **Articulation** Show the back of the small Sound-Spelling Card and discuss how the /ou/ sound is formed. Model correct mouth position, and have children repeat. Compare the /ou/ sound to the /ō/ sound. Point out how different each sound feels.
- **Model Blending** Write words and sentences from the chart on page 7D on the board. Model how to blend the sounds in each word using the **Blending Routine**. Have children repeat. Then have children read the words multiple times.

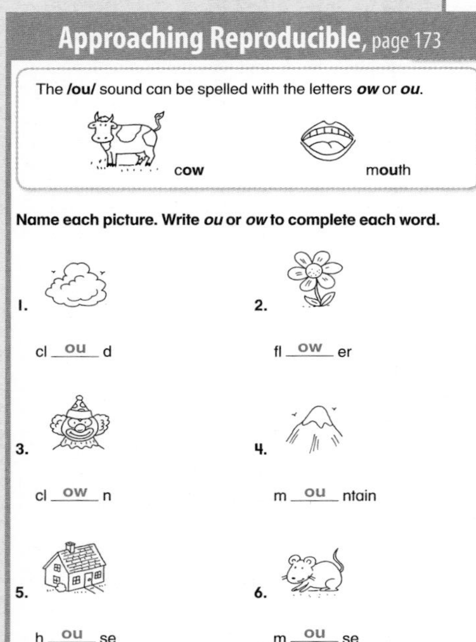

Approaching Reproducible, page 173

The **/ou/** sound can be spelled with the letters ***ow*** or ***ou***.

cow mouth

Name each picture. Write *ou* or *ow* to complete each word.

1. cl ou d
2. fl ow er
3. cl ow n
4. m ou ntain
5. h ou se
6. m ou se

Approaching Level

High-Frequency/Vocabulary

Objective Identify high-frequency words and selection vocabulary

Materials
- **High-Frequency Word Cards**
- **Sound-Spelling WorkBoards**
- **Visual Vocabulary Resources**
- **Vocabulary Cards**
- **Approaching Reproducible**, p. 174

PRETEACH WORDS

- **Introduce High-Frequency Words** Preteach the high-frequency words **family**, **four**, and **hear** using the **Read/Spell/Write** routine. Display the **High-Frequency Word Cards** and have children write each word on their **WorkBoards**.
- **Introduce Vocabulary Words** Use the **Visual Vocabulary Resources** to preteach the words **attached**, **delicious**, **gasped**, **frantically**, and **swung**. Refer to the routine on the cards.
- Have children write each word on their WorkBoards. Use the context sentences on **Approaching Reproducible** page 174.

CUMULATIVE REVIEW

Tier 2

Display the High-Frequency Word Cards for **family**, **four**, and **hear**. Display one card at a time as children chorally say the word. Then repeat this procedure using the High-Frequency Word Cards from the previous four to six weeks. Note words needing review.

Then display the **Vocabulary Cards** from the previous four weeks. Say the meaning of each word and have children identify it. Then point to words randomly for children to provide definitions.

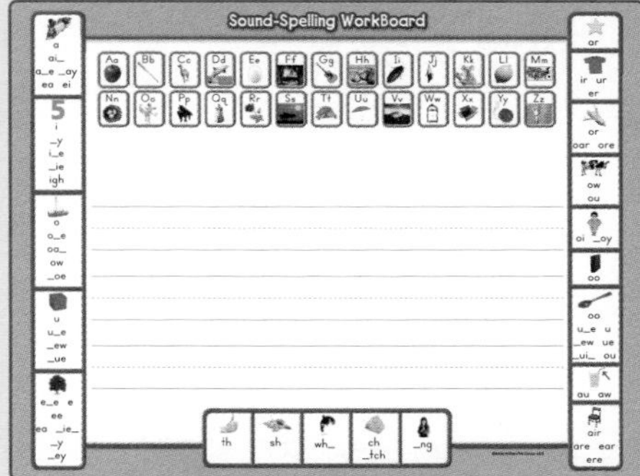

Sound-Spelling WorkBoard

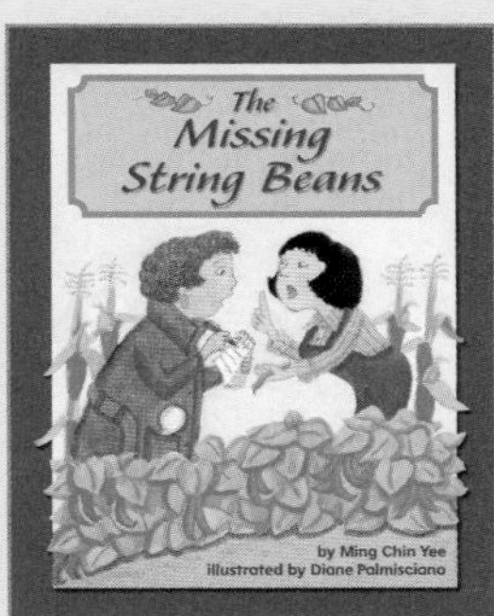

Decodable Reader

Decodable Reader

Objective Read and decode words with vowel diphthong *ou, ow* in connected text

Materials
- **Decodable Reader:** *The Missing String Beans*

READ THE TEXT

- **Preview and Predict** Point to the book's title and have children sound out each word as you point to it. *I see a woman showing a string bean to another woman.* Ask: *What do you think is going on?*
- **Read the Book** Turn to page 2. Have children point to each word, sounding out decodable words and saying the high-frequency words quickly. If children struggle sounding out words, provide "with you" blending models.
- **Check Comprehension** Ask the following:
  - *What happened to the string beans?*
  - *Why did Detective Split walk to the stream?*

Interactive Student Book

If you wish to preteach the main selection, use StudentWorks Plus for:
- Vocabulary preteaching
- Word-by-word highlighting
- Think Aloud prompts

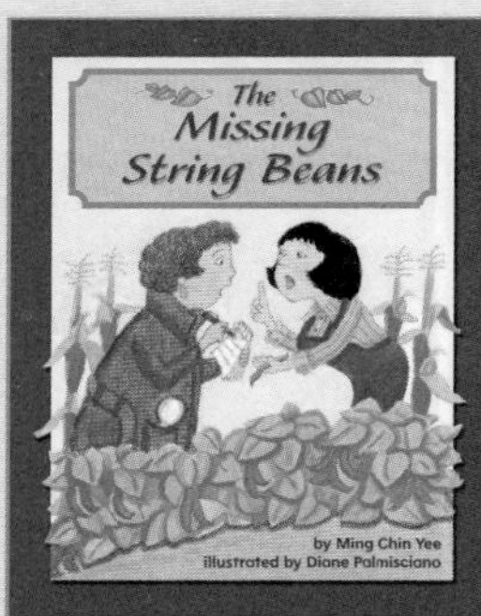

Decodable Reader

On Level

Phonics

Objective Decode words with vowel diphthong *ou, ow*

Materials
- **Sound-Spelling Cards**
- **Word-Building Cards**
- **Decodable Reader**

REVIEW VOWEL DIPHTHONG *ou, ow*

- **Review Vowel Diphthong *ou, ow*** Display the *Cow* **Sound-Spelling Card**. Remind children that the sound /ou/ can be spelled with the letters *ou* or *ow*.
- **Blend Words** Write words and sentences from the chart on pages 7D and 37G on the board. Quickly have children chorally read the words. Repeat by pointing to the words in random order. Model blending the sounds in any words children have difficulty reading. Continue with the words below to help children apply their skills to new words. Write each on the board for children to read.

cow	frowns	town	crown	shouted
ground	round	cloud	down	sounds
how	howling	house	mouse	brown

- **Build Words** Display **Word-Building Cards** for the following: *ou, ow, e, a, i, o, u, e_e, a_e, o_e, i_e, u_e, er, or, air, ear, ck, g, h, j, p, v, w, x, y,* and *z*. Have partners make as many words as they can. Suggest that they sort their words in lists based on spelling patterns. For example, they could sort all the words that have *ou* in one list and the words that have *ow* in another list. Provide time for children to share their lists.

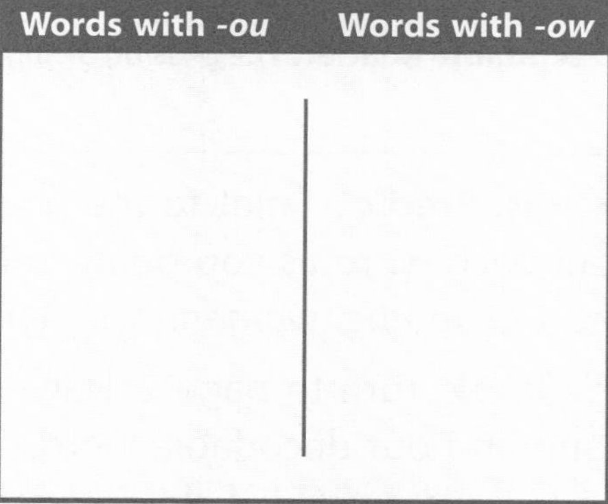

REREAD FOR FLUENCY

- Have partners reread *The Missing String Beans*. Work with children to read at the appropriate rate and expression. Model fluent reading as needed.

ELL

Reread for Fluency Use the Interactive Question-Response Guide Technique to help English Language Learners understand the content of *The Missing String Beans*. As you read the text, make the meaning clear by pointing to the pictures, demonstrating word meaning, paraphrasing text, and asking children questions.

Beyond Level

Phonics

Objective Decode words with vowel diphthong *ou, ow*

Materials • none

EXTEND/ACCELERATE

- **Vowel Team Syllables** Tell children that when they see a vowel team in a long word, such as *ou* or *ow*, the letters that make up the team must remain together in the same syllable. This can help them decide how to chunk an unfamiliar word to figure out how to pronounce it. Help children read the words below.

shouted	bounced	pronounce	frowning
downward	playground	crowded	around
knockout	roughhouse	powwow	crackdown

- **Find Words in Books** Have children go on a word hunt for words with diphthong *ou* or *ow* in books they've read this week. Ask children to state each word found, read aloud the sentence, and record these words in their Writer's Notebooks. Challenge them to search other classroom books for *ou* and *ow* words.

Vocabulary

Objective Identify and use words that are opposite in meaning

EXPAND ORAL VOCABULARY

- Review the meanings of oral vocabulary words *accomplish* and *labor* with children. Then explain that an antonym is a word that means almost the same thing as another word.
  - Say: *An antonym for the word accomplish is abandon. When you abandon something, you give it up. I abandoned cleaning my room when my mother called me to dinner.*
  - Say: *An antonym for the word labor is recreation. Recreation is playing sports, games or doing something of special interest to you. For recreation, she took tennis and basketball lessons.*

  - Have children take turns using the new words *abandon* and *recreation* in sentences. Then tell children that they will work with a partner to come up with a sentence using the new words.
  - Have partners share their sentences with the group.

ELL

Minimal Contrasts Focus on articulation. Make the /ou/ sound and point out your mouth position. Have children repeat. Use the articulation photos on the small Sound-Spelling Cards. Repeat for the /ō/ sound. Then have children say each sound together, noticing the slight differences in mouth position. Continue the articulation by having children read minimal-contrast word pairs, such as *howl/hole, couch/coach, town/tone.*

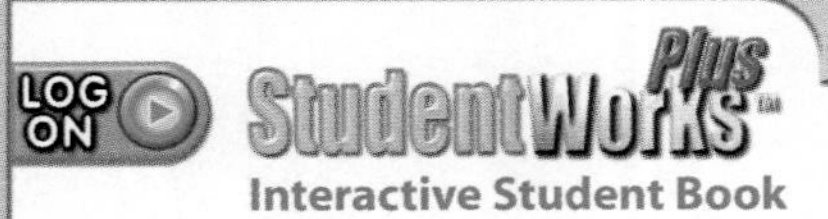

Interactive Student Book

If you wish to preteach the main selection, use StudentWorks Plus for:

- Vocabulary preteaching
- Word-by-word highlighting
- Think Aloud prompts

Cognates

Help children identify similarities and differences in pronunciation and spelling between English words and Spanish cognates.

Cognates

arduous *arduo*

delicious *delicioso*

cause *causa*

effect *effecto*

verb *verbo*

ELL ENGLISH LANGUAGE LEARNERS

Prepare to Read

Content Objective Read a folk tale that tells how our body parts came together.

Language Objective Use key words to retell an African folktale about how our body parts came together.

Materials • **StudentWorks Plus** (interactive eBook)

BUILD BACKGROUND

All Language Levels

- This version of the **Student Book** contains oral summaries in multiple languages, on-line multilingual glossaries, word-by-word highlighting, and questions that assess and build comprehension.
- Children can build fluency by reading along as the text is read or by listening during the first reading and, at the end of each paragraph, returning to the beginning and reading along.
- Children can build their comprehension by reviewing the definitions of key words in the on-line glossary and by answering the comprehension questions. When appropriate, the text required to answer the question is highlighted to provide children with additional support and scaffolding.
- Following the reading, ask children to respond in writing to a question that links the story to their personal experiences, such as *Do you know a folk tale from another country? What is it about?*

Academic Language

Language Objective Use academic language in classroom conversations

All Language Levels

- This week's academic words are **boldfaced** throughout the lesson. Define the word in context and provide a clear example from the selection. Then ask children to generate an example or a word with a similar meaning.

Academic Language Used in Whole Group Instruction

Oral Vocabulary Words	Key Selection Words	Strategy and Skill Words
labor	**gasped**	**cause**
accomplish	**attached**	**effect**
arduous	**frantically**	**reread**
succeed	**swung**	**folk tale**
rejoice	**delicious**	**linking verb**

ENGLISH LANGUAGE LEARNERS

Vocabulary

Language Objective Demonstrate understanding and use of key words by describing how body parts came together based on a folk tale

Materials • **Visual Vocabulary Resources** • **ELL Resource Book**, p. 226

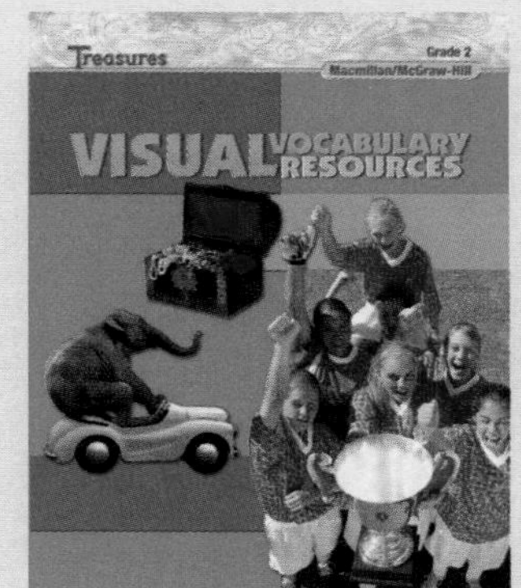

Visual Vocabulary Resources

PRETEACH KEY VOCABULARY

All Language Levels

Use the **Visual Vocabulary Resources** to preteach the key selection words **attached**, **delicious**, **frantically**, **gasped**, and **swung**. Focus on two words per day. Use the following routine that appears in detail on the cards.

- Define the word in English and provide the example given.
- Define the word in Spanish, if appropriate, and indicate if the word is a cognate.
- Display the picture and explain how it illustrates or demonstrates the word. Engage children in structured partner-talk about the image, using the key word.
- Ask children to chorally say the word three times. Point out any known sound-spellings or focus on a key aspect of phonemic awareness related to the word.
- Distribute copies of the Vocabulary Glossary, **ELL Resource Book** page 226.

PRETEACH FUNCTION WORDS AND PHRASES

All Language Levels

Use the Visual Vocabulary Resources to preteach the function words and phrases *on top of*, *middle*, *at the bottom*, and *on tiptoe*. Focus on one word per day. Use the detailed routine on the cards.

- Define the word in English and, if appropriate, in Spanish. Point out if the word is a cognate.
- Refer to the picture and talk with children about the word. Children can partner-talk using sentence frames or listen to sentences and replace a word or phrase with the function word.
- Ask children to chorally repeat the word three times.

TEACH BASIC WORDS

Beginning/Intermediate

Use the Visual Vocabulary Resources to teach the basic words *stretch*, *reach*, *grab*, *stand*, *swim*, and *bounce*. Teach these "things you can do with your body" words using the routine provided on the card.

ELL Resource Book, page 226

Use the word chart to study this week's vocabulary words. Write a sentence using each word in your writer's notebook.

Word	Context Sentence	Illustration
gasped	We gasped when we saw the size of the huge spider.	What has made you gasp?
attached	We wondered if a fish would be attached to the hook.	
frantically	Jack and I looked frantically for his missing cat.	
swung	We watched as the monkey swung from branch to branch.	
delicious	Together, we made a delicious meal.	What would you describe as delicious?

Approaching Level

Phonemic Awareness

Objective Categorize medial phonemes

Materials • none

PHONEME CATEGORIZATION (MEDIAL SOUND)

Tier 2

- Tell children you will say three words. Two of them have the same middle sound, and one does not. Say: *mouse, ground, leg.* Tell children that the words *mouse* and *ground* both have the /ou/ sound. Repeat with the words *crown, fair,* and *cloud.*
- Say the following sets of words, one at a time. Have children tell which words have the same middle sound. Say: *brown, home, clown; proud, town, hair; hear, house, sound; found, cave, shout.*

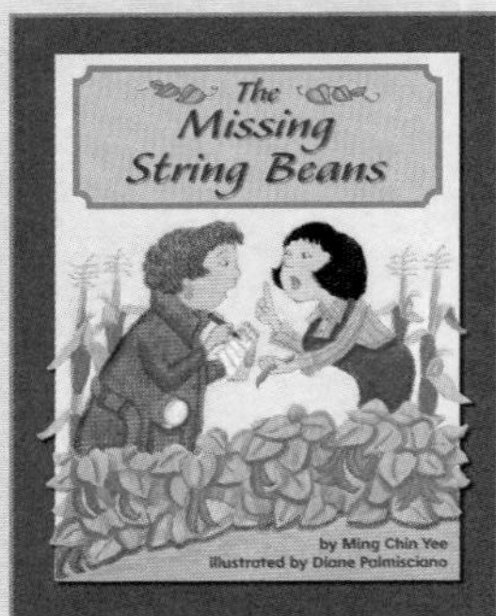

Decodable Reader

Phonics

Objective Decode words with diphthong *ou, ow*

Materials • **Sound-Spelling Cards** • **Word-Building Cards** • pocket chart • **Decodable Reader:** *The Missing String Beans*

SOUND-SPELLING REVIEW

Tier 2

Display **Word-Building Cards** for the following: *ou, ow, are, air, ear, ere, or, ore, oar, ar, gn, kn, wr, mb, eer, ere, ear, er, ir, ur, u, u_e, ew, ue.* Have children chorally say each sound. Repeat.

RETEACH SKILL

- Display the *Cow* **Sound-Spelling Card**. Review that the /ou/ sound can be spelled with the letters *ou* or *ow.*
- **Model Blending** Write words and sentences from the chart on page 7D on the board. Model how to blend the sounds in each word using the **Blending Routine**. Have children repeat. Then have children read each word multiple times.
- **Build Words** Place Word-Building Card *t* in a pocket chart. Ask: *What sound does this stand for?* Place Word-Building Cards *o, w* next to *t.* Ask: *What sound does this stand for?* Blend the sounds: /tou/. Say: *Now you say it.* Then place the Word-Building Card *n* next to *ou.* Ask: *What sound?* Blend the sounds: /toun/. Say: *Now you blend the sounds. What's the word?*

  Repeat with the words *down, clown, cloud, loud, found,* and *ground.*

REREAD FOR FLUENCY

- Reread *The Missing String Beans* with children. Then have them practice rereading the book with the appropriate expression to a partner. Circulate, listen in and provide corrective feedback.

ELL

Reread for Fluency Use the Interactive Question-Response Guide Technique to help English Language Learners understand the content of *The Missing String Beans.* As you read the text, make the meaning clear by pointing to the pictures, demonstrating word meaning, paraphrasing text, and asking children questions.

Approaching Level

High-Frequency/Vocabulary

Objective Identify high-frequency words and vocabulary words

Materials • **High-Frequency Word Cards** • **Vocabulary Cards**

RETEACH WORDS

Tier 2

Display the **High-Frequency Word Cards** for **family**, **four**, and **hear**. Review using the **Read/Spell/Write** routine. Display **Vocabulary Cards** for **attached**, **delicious**, **frantically**, **gasped**, and **swung**. Review each word using the **Define/Example/Ask** routine.

CUMULATIVE REVIEW

Display the High-Frequency and Vocabulary Cards from the past six weeks. Have children chorally read the words. Repeat. Note words needing review.

Leveled Reader Library

Leveled Reader Lesson 1

Objectives Describe the plot; read to apply skills and strategies

Materials
- **Leveled Reader:** *Wasted Wishes*
- **Approaching Reproducible**, p. 176

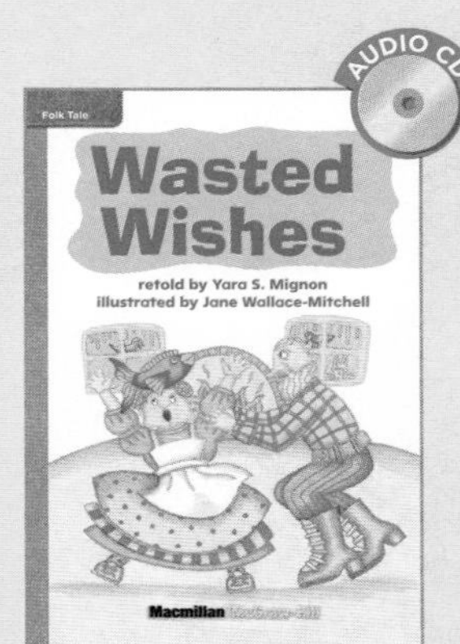

Leveled Reader

BEFORE READING

- **Preview and Predict** Read the title and author name. Have children turn to the title page. Ask: *How can wishes be wasted?*
- **Review Skills** Use the inside front cover to review the phonics skill and vocabulary words.
- **Set a Purpose** Say: *Let's read to find out what happens with the wishes and why it happens.*

DURING READING

- Have children whisper-read each page. Circulate and provide corrective feedback, such as modeling how to blend a word.
- **Cause and Effect** Draw a Cause and Effect Chart like the one shown on the Reproducible. Have children copy it. After children have read a few pages, ask them what has happened in the plot so far and why. Model how to record the information and have children begin to fill in their Cause and Effect Chart. Help children focus on the problem and solution of the story.

AFTER READING

- Discuss words that gave children difficulty and the decoding strategies they used. Reinforce good reading behaviors you saw.

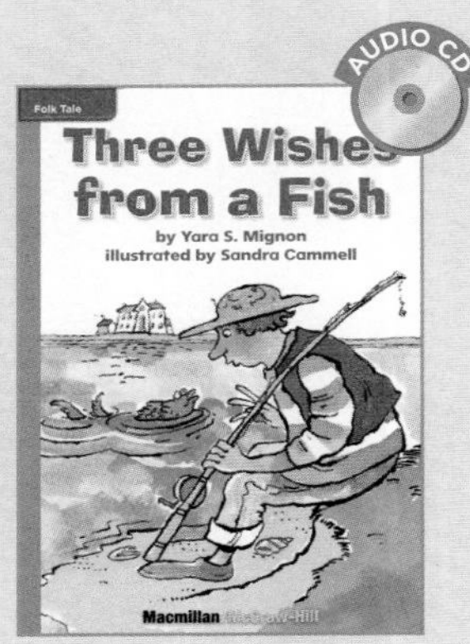

Leveled Reader

On Level

Leveled Reader Lesson 1

Leveled Reader Library

Objectives Describe the plot; read to apply skills and strategies

Materials • **Leveled Reader:** *Three Wishes from a Fish* • **Practice Book**, p. 176

BEFORE READING

Preview and Predict Read the title and the names of the author and illustrator. Ask: *Why do you think a fish would give someone three wishes? What do you think will happen in this book?* Preview the title page and the illustrations.

Review Skills Use the inside front cover to review the phonics skill and teach the new vocabulary words.

Set a Purpose Say: *Let's read to find out what happens with the wishes and why it happens.*

DURING READING

- Have children turn to page 2 and begin by whisper-reading the first two pages.
- Remind children to look for the new vocabulary words. Tell them that you will help them blend the sounds in words with diphthong *ou*, *ow*.
- Monitor children's reading. Stop periodically and ask open-ended questions to facilitate rich discussion, such as *What important events happen in the story? What is the plot?* Build on children's responses to develop deeper understanding of the text.

- **Cause and Effect** Remind children that thinking about what happens in a story (effect) and why it happens (cause) will help them understand the plot. Draw a Cause and Effect Chart like the one shown on the **Practice Book** page. Have children copy it. As children reread, ask them what happens and why it happens. Model how to record the information and have children copy it. Then have them begin to fill in their Cause and Effect Chart.

AFTER READING

- Discuss words that gave children difficulty and the strategies they used to decode them. Reinforce good reading behaviors you noticed.
- **Retell** Have children take turns retelling the selection. Help them make a personal connection (Text-to-Self) by asking, *Would you have let the fish go? Why or why not?*

ELL

Retell Use the Interactive Question-Response Guide Technique to help English Language Learners understand the content of *Three Wishes from a Fish*. As you read the text, make the meaning clear by pointing to the pictures, demonstrating word meaning, paraphrasing text, and asking children questions.

Beyond Level

Leveled Reader Lesson 1

Objectives Describe the plot; read to apply skills and strategies

Materials
- **Leveled Reader:** *Three Dog Wishes*
- self-stick notes
- **Beyond Reproducible**, p. 176

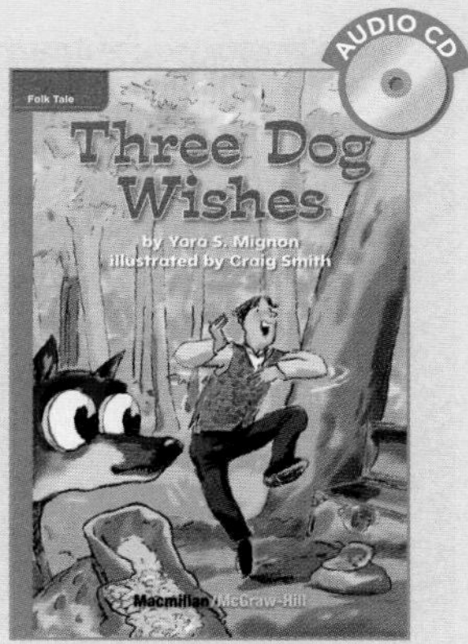

Leveled Reader

BEFORE READING

Preview and Predict Read the title and the names of the author and illustrator. Preview the title page and illustrations. *Who do you think gets the three wishes and what might he or she do with them?*

Review Skills Use the inside front cover to review the phonics skill and new vocabulary words.

Set a Purpose *Let's read to see what happens in this story and why.*

DURING READING

- Have children turn to page 2 and begin by whisper-reading the first two pages. Have them place self-stick notes next to words they have difficulty with.
- Remind children that when they see an unfamiliar word, they can look for familiar spellings and chunks. They should break longer words into smaller chunks, or syllables, to sound out.
- Monitor children's reading. Stop periodically and ask open-ended questions to facilitate rich discussion, such as *What has happened in the plot so far? Who is given three wishes?* Have children support answers with evidence from the text.

- **Cause and Effect** Draw a Cause and Effect Chart like the one shown on the Reproducible. Stop after a few pages and ask children what happened so far in the plot and why it happened. Model how to record the information. Have children complete their Cause and Effect Charts as they read. Ask them to explain strategies they used to problem-solve as they read.

AFTER READING

Gifted Talented

- **Analyze** Review the story with children. *What was the underlying theme of this story? What lesson did the man learn?*

- Have children work in pairs to make a flow chart that shows the important events of the story.
- **Model** Model writing the first event in the flow chart: *The young man was kind to a dog*. Discuss the effect of the man having been kind. Have children complete their flow charts.
- Have children share their flow charts. Then discuss the effects of the events, where applicable.

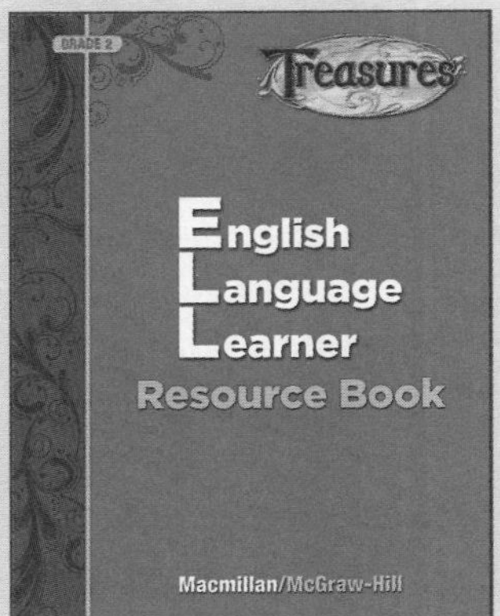
ELL Resource Book

ELL ENGLISH LANGUAGE LEARNERS

Access to Core Content

Content Objective Read grade-level text
Language Objective Discuss text using key words and sentence frames
Materials • **ELL Resource Book**, pp. 210–223

PRETEACH MAIN SELECTION (PAGES 10–35)

All Language Levels

Use the Interactive Question-Response Guide on **ELL Resource Book** pages 210–223 to introduce children to *Head, Body, Legs: A Story from Liberia*. Preteach half of the selection on **Day 2** and half on **Day 3**.

- Use the prompts provided in the guide to develop meaning and vocabulary. Use the Partner-Talk and whole-class responses to engage children and increase student talk.
- When completed, have partners reread the story.

Beginning	Intermediate	Advanced
Use Visuals During the Interactive Reading, select several pictures that show cause and effect. Describe the cause and effect in simple terms. Then ask a simple cause and effect question where a one word answer will suffice.	**Show Comprehension** During the Interactive Reading, select a few lines of text that illustrates a cause and effect. After you read it and explain it, ask a question that children can answer using the cause and effect skill.	**Expand** During the Interactive Reading, select a larger portion of text illustrating cause and effect. After you read it and explain it, ask a question that children can answer using the cause and effect skill.

ELL ENGLISH LANGUAGE LEARNERS

Grammar

Content Objective Identify linking verbs
Language Objective Speak in complete sentences, using sentence frames
Materials • none

LINKING VERBS

Beginning/Intermediate

- Review that a linking verb is a verb that does not show action and that the verb *be* is a linking verb.

All Language Levels

- Review that a linking verb is a verb that does not show action and that the verb *be* is a linking verb.
- Write the following on the board: *Head is tired of eating grass*. Underline the linking verb. (*is*) Tell children that this is the present tense of the verb *be* that is used with a singular (one) subject. The past tense of *is* is *was*. Replace *is* with *was;* reread the new sentence. Repeat with the sentence *Head and Arms are sleepy*. Underline *are*. Explain that this is the present tense of *be,* used with a plural (more than one) subject. The past tense of *are* is *were*. Replace *are* with *were;* reread the new sentence.
- Write sentences on the board, such as those provided below. Have children underline the correct linking verb for each sentence, then read the sentence aloud. Have them say: *The verb ________ is (singular/plural).*

  Head and Body (is, are) happy to be together.
  Head (was, are) awake. *Body (is, were) attached to Head.*

PEER DISCUSSION STARTERS

All Language Levels

- Write the following sentences on the board.

  Legs are ________. A force is ________.
- Pair children and have them complete each sentence frame by providing details from this week's readings. Circulate, listen in, and take note of each child's language use and proficiency.

Beginning

Use Visuals Describe the pictures in *Head, Body, Legs: A Story from Liberia* to children. Use linking verbs in your descriptions. Ask: *What do you see?* Restate children's words or phrases by using linking verbs.

Intermediate

Describe Ask children to describe the same pictures by using linking verbs in their descriptions. Have them use complete sentences.

Advanced

Describe Ask children to describe the pictures, adding more sentences and using both plural and singular forms of linking verbs.

Transfer Skills

Linking Verbs The verb *be* can be omitted with adjectives and prepositional phrases in Cantonese, Hmong, and Vietnamese. Children speaking these languages may therefore say "Head tired of eating," omitting the verb *is*. Model correct usage in additional examples, and have children repeat. Look for opportunities to point out how the verb *be* is used in other parts of the lesson and in the reading selections.

Corrective Feedback

During whole group grammar lessons, follow the routine on the **Grammar Transparencies** to provide children with extra support. This routine includes completing the items with English Language Learners while other children work independently, having children reread the sentences with partners to build fluency, and providing a generative task such as writing a new sentence using the skill.

Approaching Level

Phonemic Awareness

Objective Blend phonemes to form words
Materials • none

PHONEME BLENDING

Tier 2

Have four children stand side by side. Ask the first child to say the sound /f/. Have the next child say the sound /ou/. Have the third child say the sound /n/. Have the last child say the sound /d/. Have children say the sounds in order and blend them: /found/, *found*. Repeat with other sound sets and groups of children.

/f/ /r/ /ou/ /n/	/k/ /l/ /ou/ /d/	/sh/ /ou/ /t/
/h/ /ou/ /l/	/k/ /r/ /ou/ /d/	/g/ /r/ /ou/ /n/ /d/

Phonics

Objective Decode words with vowel diphthong *ou, ow*
Materials • **Sound-Spelling Cards** • **Word-Building Cards** • pocket chart • **Decodable Reader:** *The Missing String Beans*

Decodable Reader

SOUND-SPELLING REVIEW

Tier 2

Display **Word-Building Cards** for the following: *ou, ow, are, air, ear, ere, or, ore, oar, ar, gn, kn, wr, mb, eer, ere, ear, er, ir, ur, u, u_e, ew, ue*. Have children chorally say each sound.

RETEACH SKILL

- Display the *Cow* **Sound-Spelling Card**. Review that the /ou/ sound can be spelled with the letters *ou* or *ow*.
- **Model Blending** Write words and sentences from the chart on page 37G on the board. Model how to blend the sounds in each word using the **Blending Routine**. Have children repeat. Then have children read each word multiple times.
- **Build Words** Build vowel diphthong *ou, ow* words. Place Word-Building Cards *p, o, u, c, h* in a pocket chart. Help children blend the sounds to read the word. Then do the following:

  Change the ch *in pouch to* nd. *What word did you make?*
  Change the p *in pound to* h. *What word did you make?*
  Change the ound *in* hound *to* owl. *What word did you make?*
  Change the h *in* howl *to* gr. *What word did you make?*

  Repeat with the word set *mouse, house, how, plow, clown, down*.
- **Read the Decodable** Reread *The Missing String Beans* with children. Provide blending models. When completed, chorally reread the story.

ELL

Demonstrate Comprehension Use the Interactive Question-Response Guide Technique to help English Language Learners understand the content of *The Missing String Beans.* As you read the text, make the meaning clear by pointing to the pictures, demonstrating word meaning, paraphrasing text, and asking children questions.

Approaching Level

High-Frequency/Vocabulary

Objective Identify high-frequency words and vocabulary words

Materials • **High-Frequency Word Cards** • **Vocabulary Cards**

BUILD WORD AUTOMATICITY

Fluency Display **High-Frequency Word Cards** for **family, four, hear** and **Vocabulary Cards** for **attached**, **delicious**, **frantically**, **gasped**, and **swung**. Point to the words in random order. Have children chorally read them. Repeat at a faster pace.

CUMULATIVE REVIEW

Display High-Frequency Word Cards and Vocabulary Cards from the past four weeks. Display cards as children chorally read words. Repeat. Note words for review.

Leveled Reader Lesson 2

Objectives Describe the plot; read to apply skills and strategies

Materials • **Leveled Reader:** *Wasted Wishes* • **Sound-Spelling WorkBoards** • **Approaching Reproducible**, pp. 176, 177

BEFORE READING

- **Review** Have children retell *Wasted Wishes*. Have them say in their own words what happens on each page of the story. Reinforce new vocabulary by restating children's responses with key words.

DURING READING

- **Cause and Effect** As they reread the book, help children finish adding details on their Cause and Effect Charts. Have them stop periodically and describe the plot. Model how to connect what happens in the story (effect) and why it happens (cause). Afterwards, discuss the problem and solution of the story.

AFTER READING

- **Retell** Have children use their Cause and Effect Charts to orally retell what happens in the fantasy story *Wasted Wishes*.
- **Model Fluency** Read the sentences in the book one at a time. Have children chorally repeat. Point out how you read with expression. Coach children as needed.

Book Talk

Bringing Groups Together Children will work with peers of various language and reading abilities to discuss this week's Leveled Readers. Refer to page 179 in the **Teacher's Resource Book** for how to conduct a Book Talk.

Leveled Reader

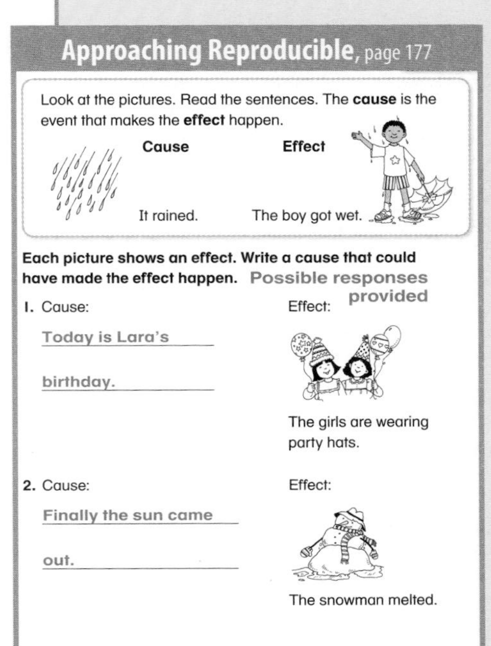
Approaching Reproducible, page 177

Look at the pictures. Read the sentences. The **cause** is the event that makes the **effect** happen.

Cause	Effect
It rained.	The boy got wet.

Each picture shows an effect. Write a cause that could have made the effect happen. Possible responses provided

1. Cause: Today is Lara's birthday. Effect: The girls are wearing party hats.
2. Cause: Finally the sun came out. Effect: The snowman melted.

On Level

Leveled Reader Lesson 2

Objectives Describe the plot; read to apply skills and strategies

Materials
- **Leveled Reader:** *Three Wishes from a Fish*
- **Practice Book**, pp. 176, 180

Leveled Reader

BEFORE READING

- **Review** Have children retell *Three Wishes from a Fish*. If children struggle, have them page through the story and tell what happens on each page and explain why it happens. Reinforce vocabulary by restating children's sentences using more sophisticated language. For example, *The fish could not breathe out of the water. It was probably gasping for air!*

DURING READING

- **Cause and Effect** Explain to children that good readers look for cause-and-effect relationships in a story to help them remember what happens in the plot and understand why. As children reread the book, help them complete their Cause and Effect Charts. Model your thinking as you fill in the chart.

AFTER READING

- Have children use their Cause and Effect Charts to tell what happens in *Three Wishes from a Fish* and explain why.

REREAD FOR FLUENCY

- Read the sentences in the book one at a time. Have children chorally repeat. Point out to children how you use expression to make the reading interesting and how your voice goes up at the end of a question.
- Have children read a portion of *Three Wishes from a Fish* for fluency.
- Have children continue to work on their fluency using **Practice Book** page 180.

Book Talk

Bringing Groups Together Children will work with peers of various language and reading abilities to discuss this week's Leveled Readers. Refer to page 179 in the **Teacher's Resource Book** for how to conduct a Book Talk.

Practice Book, page 180

As I read, I will pay attention to my expression.

A fisherman lived with his wife in a little house.
10 Every morning he went to the sea. He tried to catch
21 fish to eat.
24 One day the fisherman caught nothing. Then he
32 felt a strong tug on his fishing line. The fishing rod
43 swung from side to side. The fisherman fought
51 **frantically** to hold on to it.
57 The fisherman reeled in the line. There
64 was a golden fish **attached** to his hook.
72 "Please let me go!" it cried. "I cannot breathe out
82 of water!"
84 The fish was beautiful. But it was too small to
94 eat, so the fisherman let it go. 101

Comprehension Check

1. What made the fisherman's fishing rod swing from side to side? **Draw Conclusions** A fish caused the rod to swing from side to side.
2. Why did the fisherman go down to the sea every morning? **Cause and Effect** The fisherman went to the sea every morning to catch fish to eat.

	Words Read	–	Number of Errors	=	Words Correct Score
First Read		–		=	
Second Read		–		=	

Beyond Level

Leveled Reader Lesson 2

Objectives Describe the plot; read to apply skills and strategies

Materials
- **Leveled Reader:** *Three Dog Wishes*
- **Beyond Reproducible**, pp. 176, 180

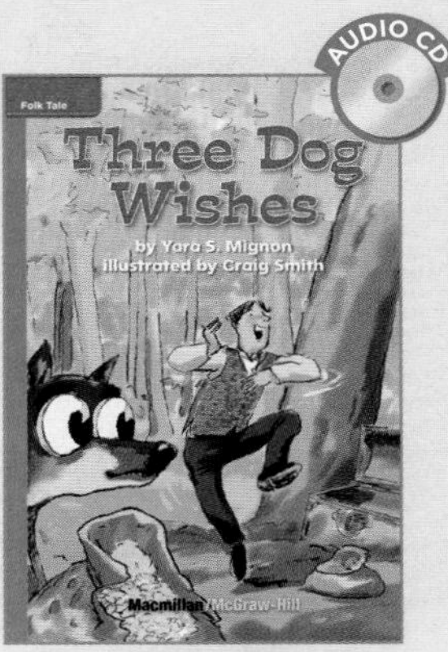

Leveled Reader

BEFORE READING

- **Review** Have children retell *Three Dog Wishes* to a partner. Circulate and listen in. Prompt children to use the new words they learned from the book in their retellings.

DURING READING

- **Cause and Effect** As children reread the book, help them complete their Cause and Effect Charts on their reproducible page. Guide them by asking questions about the plot. Then discuss the problem and solution of the story.

AFTER READING

- **Retell** Have children use their Cause and Effect Charts to write about the important events in *Three Dog Wishes*.

Gifted and Talented

- **Review Flow Charts** Have children review their Flow Charts showing the important events of the story.
- **Synthesize** Tell children that they will write a new ending for the story by having the young man make a different last wish. Ask: *What else might the young man have wished for?* Discuss as a group before children go to work with their partner.
- Have children work in pairs to create their new ending. Encourage children to discuss their ideas with their partner before they write them down.
- **Evaluate** Have each pair present their new ending to the group. Have children respond to each ending by telling why they like it.

REREAD FOR FLUENCY

- Read the sentences in the book one at a time. Have children chorally repeat. Point out to children how you use expression to make the reading interesting and how your voice goes up at the end of a question.

- Have children practice reading the book to a partner. Say: *Read expressively. Use your voice to show expression. When you see a questions read with curiosity by raising your voice at the end.*
- Have children continue to work on their fluency using Practice Book page 180.

Book Talk

Bringing Groups Together Children will work with peers of various language and reading abilities to discuss this week's Leveled Readers. Refer to page 179 in the **Teacher's Resource Book** for how to conduct a Book Talk.

Beyond Reproducible, page 180

As I read, I will pay attention to my expression.

Once upon a time, there was a young man who had no
12 family and no job. He was poor and hungry.
21 One day he took a walk through the woods near his town.
33 He heard noises coming from some bushes.
40 He pushed aside the branches. There he found a little
50 dog that had become attached to some vines. The young
60 man helped set it free. Then he gave the dog a few stale
73 pieces of bread that he had in his pocket.
82 He was very surprised when the dog spoke to him.
92 "You have been kind to me," said the little dog. "In
103 return, I will tell you how to find treasure. Do you see that
116 big oak tree over there? Dig a hole at the base of
128 its trunk." 130

Comprehension Check

1. Why does the dog tell the man how to find treasure? **Cause and Effect** The man set him free from the vines and gave him food.
2. How did the man happen to find the little dog trapped in the vines? **Draw Conclusions** He heard the dog whimpering there.

	Words Read	–	Number of Errors	=	Words Correct Score
First Read		–		=	
Second Read		–		=	

Leveled Reader

Vocabulary

Preteach Vocabulary Use the routine in the **Visual Vocabulary Resources**, pages 411–412 to preteach the ELL Vocabulary listed on the inside front cover of the Leveled Reader.

ELL ENGLISH LANGUAGE LEARNERS

Leveled Reader Library

Leveled Reader Lesson 1

Content Objective Read to apply skills and strategies
Language Objective Retell information using complete sentences
Materials • **Leveled Reader:** *Three Wishes* • **Visual Vocabulary Resources**

BEFORE READING

All Language Levels

- **Preview** Read the title *Three Wishes*. Ask: *What's the title? Say it again.* Repeat with the author's name. Then page through the book. Use simple language to tell about each page. Immediately follow up with questions, such as *Look at the fisherman. What is the fisherman doing? What is the wife doing? Why?*
- **Review Skills** Use the inside front cover to review the phonics skill and vocabulary words.
- **Set a Purpose** Say: *Let's read to find out what happens when a fish grants, or gives, wishes.*

DURING READING

All Language Levels

- Have children read each page aloud using the differentiated suggestions. Provide corrective feedback, such as modeling how to blend a decodable word or clarifying meaning by using techniques from the Interactive Question-Response Guide.
- **Cause and Effect** After every two pages, ask children to tell what caused the events that have happened so far. Help them to complete the Cause and Effect chart. Restate children's comments when they have difficulty using story-specific words. Provide differentiated sentence frames to support children's responses and engage children in partner-talk where appropriate.

Beginning

Echo-Read Have children echo-read after you.

Check Comprehension Point to pictures and ask questions such as *Show me the fisherman. Is he happy or sad? Look at this picture. Point to the fish.*

Intermediate

Choral-Read Have children choral-read with you.

Check Comprehension Ask questions/prompts such as *What did the wife wish for now? What happened? Why did the fish do this?*

Advanced

Choral-Read Have children choral-read.

Check Comprehension Ask: *Did you like the fisherman? his wife? the fish? Why or why not? Did you like the way the story ended? Why or why not?*

ELL ENGLISH LANGUAGE LEARNERS

AFTER READING

Use the chart below and the Think and Compare questions from page 16 of *Three Wishes* to determine children's progress.

Think and Compare	Beginning	Intermediate	Advanced
1 Look at page 5. Why did the fish grant the fisherman's wish?	Possible Responses: Nonverbal response. Fisherman save. Good. Nice.	Possible Responses: Saved his life. Good man. He saved his life.	Possible Responses: The fisherman saved his life.
2 Why do you think the fisherman didn't ask for any wishes?	Possible Responses: Nonverbal response. Doesn't want. Happy.	Possible Responses: Happy man. He was happy at life.	Possible Responses: The fisherman was already happy with his life.
3 What are some things people wish for? Why do people wish for things?	Possible Responses: Nonverbal response. House. Happy. Toy. Want things.	Possible Responses: Big house. New toys. Be rich. Healthy. People want things.	Possible Responses: People wish for toys. People wish to be rich. People want more things.

Writing/Spelling

Content Objective Spell words correctly

Language Objective Write in complete sentences, using sentence frames

All Language Levels

- Write the key vocabulary words on the board: **attached**, **delicious**, **frantically**, **gasped**, and **swung**. Have children copy each word on their **WorkBoards**. Then help them say, then write sentences for, each word.

Beginning/Intermediate

- Help children spell words using their growing knowledge of English sound-spelling relationships. Model how to segment the word children are trying to spell and attach a spelling to each sound (or spellings to each syllable if a multisyllabic word). Use the **Sound-Spelling Cards** to reinforce the spellings for each English sound.

Advanced/Advanced High

- Dictate the following words for children to spell: *mouse, ground, brown, town, house, pouch, owl*. Guide children using the Sound-Spelling Cards as they spell each word.
- When completed, review the meanings of words that can be easily demonstrated or explained. Use actions, gestures, and available pictures.

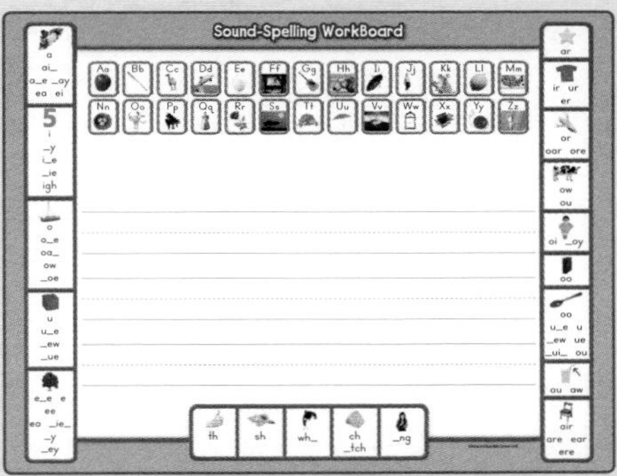

Sound-Spelling WorkBoard

Phonics/Word Study

For English Language Learners who need more practice with this week's phonics/spelling skill, see the Approaching Level lesson on page 41K. Focus on minimal contrasts, articulation, and those sounds that do not transfer from the child's first language to English. For a complete listing of language transfers, see pages T18–T33.

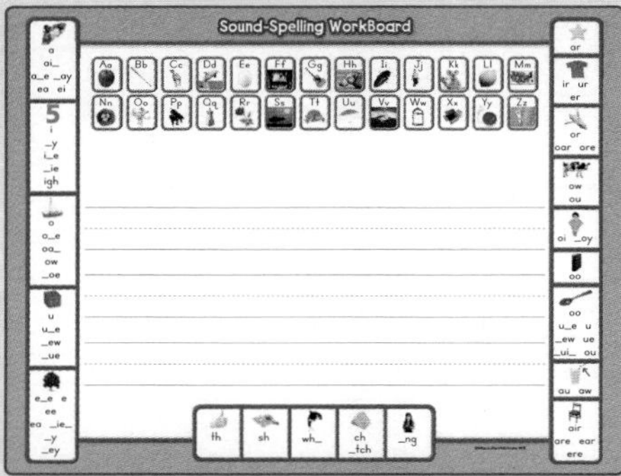
Sound-Spelling WorkBoard

Approaching Level

Phonemic Awareness

Objective Segment words into phonemes

Materials • **Sound-Spelling WorkBoards** • markers

PHONEME SEGMENTATION

Tier 2

- Distribute **WorkBoards** and markers. Say a word, stretching each sound for two seconds. Model for children how to drag one marker onto each box for each sound. Have children repeat and count the number of sounds. Do this for the following words: *how, cow, fowl, found, sound, down, town, clown, bounce*.
- **Link to Spelling** When completed, segment each word again. Then help children replace each marker with a letter or letters that stand(s) for the sound. Help children read the words.

Phonics

Objective Decode words with vowel diphthong *ou, ow*

Materials • **Sound-Spelling Cards** • **Word-Building Cards** • **Decodable Reader:** *The Missing Green Beans*

SOUND-SPELLING REVIEW

Tier 2

Display **Word-Building Cards** for the following: *ou, ow, are, air, ear, ere, or, ore, oar, ar, gn, kn, wr, mb, eer, ere, ear, er, ir, ur, u, u_e, ew, ue*. Have children chorally say each sound.

RETEACH SKILL

- Display the *Cow* **Sound-Spelling Card**. Review that the vowel diphthong /ou/ can be spelled with the letters *ou* or *ow*.
- **Model Blending** Write words and sentences from the chart on page 37G on the board. Model how to blend sounds using the **Blending Routine**. Have children read each word multiple times.
- **Read in Context** Write the sentences below on the board. Have children chorally read the sentences. Help children blend the sounds in decodable words and read vocabulary words.

  The queen is proud of her crown.
  I found a brown horse near the house on the farm.
  We gasped as the plane soared into the clouds.
  The scout swung around when he heard a loud sound.
  The clown does tricks for the crowd over there.

- **Read the Decodable** Reread *The Missing Green Beans* with children. Then have children practice reading the story to a partner. Circulate, listen in, and provide corrective feedback.

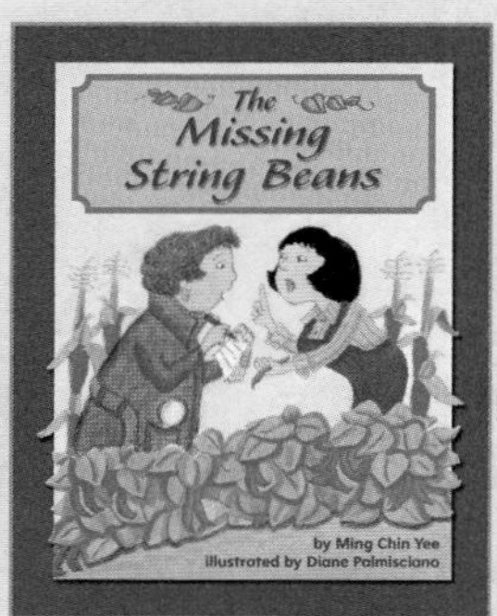
Decodable Reader

ELL

Reread Continue using the Interactive Question-Response Guide Technique to help English Language Learners understand the content of *The Missing String Beans*. As you read the text, make the meaning clear by pointing to the pictures, demonstrating word meaning, paraphrasing text, and asking children questions.

Approaching Level

High-Frequency/Vocabulary Words

Objective Identify high-frequency and vocabulary words

Materials
- **Vocabulary Cards**
- **Sound-Spelling WorkBoards**
- **High-Frequency Word Cards**

REVIEW WORDS

- Display **High-Frequency Word Cards** for **family**, **four**, **hear**, and **Vocabulary Cards** for **attached**, **delicious**, **frantically**, **gasped**, and **swung**. Have children copy each word on their **WorkBoards**. Then help them write sentences for each word. Provide sentence stems or starters, such as *We* gasped *loudly when we saw the* ________ or *I* attached *a* ________ *to my bike.*

CUMULATIVE REVIEW

- Display the High-Frequency Word Cards and Vocabulary Cards from the previous four to six weeks. Display one card at a time as children chorally read the word. Mix and repeat. Note words children need to review.

Fluency

Objective Read aloud with fluency and comprehension

Materials
- **Leveled Reader:** *Wasted Wishes*
- **Approaching Reproducible**, p. 180

READ FOR FLUENCY

- Tell children that they will be doing a final fluent reading of *Wasted Wishes*.
- As they read, note words children struggle to read. Also note their expression. Use this information to determine if additional instruction is needed on this week's phonics skill and vocabulary. Send the book home for independent reading.

REREAD PREVIOUSLY READ BOOKS

Tier 2

- Distribute copies of the past six **Leveled Readers**. Tell children that rereading these books will help them develop their skills. The more times they read the same words, the quicker they will learn these words.
- Circulate and listen in as children read. Stop children periodically and ask them how they are figuring out difficult words or checking their understanding as they read.
- Instruct children to read other previously read Leveled Readers during independent reading time or for homework.

Meet Grade-Level Expectations

As an alternative to this day's lesson, guide children through a reading of the On Level Leveled Reader. See page 41S. Because both books contain the same vocabulary, phonics, and comprehension skills, the scaffolding you provided will help most children gain access to this more challenging text.

Approaching Reproducible, page 180

As I read, I will pay attention to my expression.

A woodcutter and his wife lived in the forest.
9 One day the woodcutter was about to chop down a tree.
20 Then a squeaky voice yelled, "Stop!" The woodcutter
28 did not see anyone.
32 "Look in the tree!" said a little green elf.
41 "This tree is my home," said the elf. "Leave it
51 alone, and I will give you three wishes!" The
60 woodcutter agreed.
62 He ran home to tell his wife the good news. 72

Comprehension Check

1. Why will the elf grant the woodcutter three wishes? **Cause and Effect** The elf will grant him three wishes if he doesn't cut down the tree.
2. Why do you think the elf doesn't want the tree to be cut down? **Draw Conclusions** He doesn't want the tree cut down because the tree is his home.

	Words Read	–	Number of Errors	=	Words Correct Score
First Read		–		=	
Second Read		–		=	

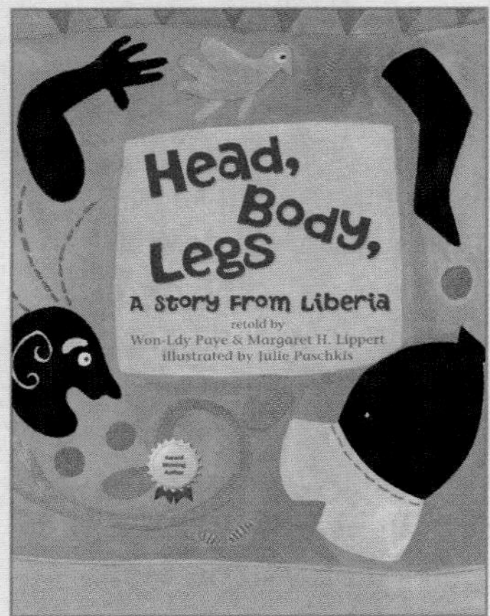

Student Book

On Level

Fluency

Objectives Read aloud with fluency; develop speaking skills

Materials • **Student Book:** *Head, Body, Legs: A Story from Liberia*

REREAD FOR FLUENCY

- Have children reread *Head, Body, Legs: A Story from Liberia*. Work with children to read with accuracy and the appropriate expression. Model fluent reading as needed.
- Provide time for children to read a section of the text to you. Comment on their accuracy, rate, and expression and provide corrective feedback.

DEVELOP SPEAKING/LISTENING SKILLS

- Provide time for children to read aloud a portion of *Head, Body, Legs* to the class. Ask children to name ways the reader read with expression. Challenge children to memorize a few lines of the text, such as the dialogue of the characters each time a new body part is introduced.

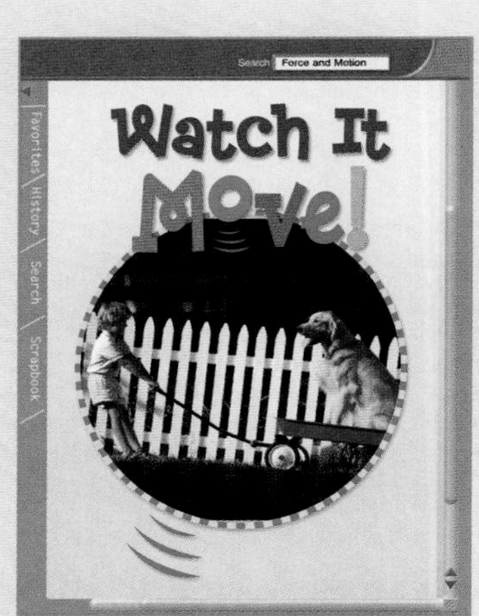

Student Book

Beyond Level

Fluency

Objectives Read aloud with fluency; develop speaking skills

Materials • **Student Book:** *Head, Body, Legs: A Story from Liberia*; "Watch It Move!"

REREAD FOR FLUENCY

- Have children reread *Head, Body, Legs: A Story from Liberia* and "Watch It Move!" Work with children to read with the appropriate rate and expression. Provide time for children to read a section of the text to you. Comment on their accuracy, rate, and expression and provide corrective feedback.

DEVELOP SPEAKING/LISTENING SKILLS

- Provide time for children to read aloud *Head, Body, Legs* or "Watch It Move!" to the class. Ask children to name ways the reader expressed the emotion of the characters with his or her voice or read the nonfiction piece with accuracy.
- Challenge children to memorize their favorite page of the text and recite it for you.

ELL ENGLISH LANGUAGE LEARNERS

Access to Core Content

Content Objective Read grade-level text
Language Objective Discuss text using key words and sentence frames
Materials • **ELL Resource Book**, pp. 224–225

PRETEACH PAIRED SELECTION (PAGES 38–39)

All Language Levels

Use the Interactive Question-Response Guide on **English Learner Resource Book** pages 224–225 to preview the paired selection "Watch It Move!" Preteach the selection on **Day 4**.

ELL Resource Book

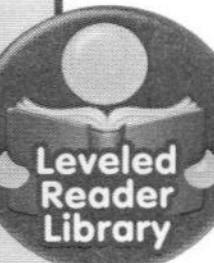

Leveled Reader Lesson 2

Content Objective Read grade-level text
Language Objective Discuss text using key words and sentence frames
Materials • **ELL Resource Book**, p. 227 • **Leveled Reader:** *Three Wishes*

AFTER READING

All Language Levels

Book Talk Talk Distribute copies of ELL Resource Book page 227. Children will work with peers of varying language abilities to discuss them. Help students determine who will be the leader for the discussion.

Develop Listening and Speaking Skills Tell children to remember the following while engaged in the Book Talk:

- Share information in cooperative learning interactions. Remind children to work with their partners to retell the story and complete any activities. Ask: *What happened next in the story?*
- Employ self-corrective techniques and monitor their own and other children's language production. Children should ask themselves: *What parts of this passage were confusing to me? Can my classmates help me clarify a word or sentence that I don't understand?*
- Distinguish between formal and informal English and know when to use each one. Remind children to note whether the selection is written in formal or informal English. Ask: *Why do you think it is written in this way?* Remind children that they may use informal English when speaking with their classmates, but they should use formal language when they talk to teachers or write essays.
- Use high-frequency English words to describe people, places, and objects.

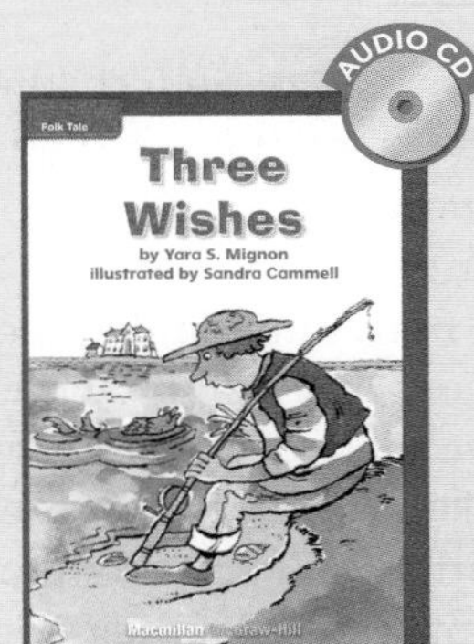

Leveled Reader

Book Talk

Bringing Groups Together
Children will work with peers of varying language abilities to discuss the Book Talk questions. Form groups so that students who read the Beyond Level, On Level, Approaching Level, and English Language Learner readers are in the same group for the activity.

Approaching Level

Oral Language

Objectives Build vocabulary related to body parts; review week's oral vocabulary words

Materials • chart paper

EXPAND VOCABULARY

- Draw a two-column chart on chart paper. Label the columns *Parts of the Body* and *How They Move*. Remind children that this week they read about parts of the body and how they combined to form a person in *Head, Body, Legs: A Story from Liberia*. For example, children learned that the head could talk and eat.
- Write *head* in column 1 of the chart and *talk, eat* in column 2. Point to each word, read it, and have children repeat.

Parts of the Body	How They Move
head (eyes, nose, ears, mouth)	talk, eat, hear, see
arms (hands, elbow, fingers)	swing, pick food, feed the head
body (chest, stomach)	swim, bounce
legs/feet (knees, feet, toes)	walk, run

- Ask children to name other parts of the body. Point to a body part for them to identify, if necessary. Use the diagram in *Head, Body, Legs* to review where these parts are.
- Then write the following body words on the board and read each aloud: *ears, eyes, nose, mouth, hands, elbow, fingers, chest, stomach, feet, knees*, and *toes*. Work with children to determine which part of the body each is on. Add this information in parenthesis next to each body part to complete the chart.

REVIEW VOCABULARY

Tier 2

- Use the **Define/Example/Ask** vocabulary routine in the **Instructional Routine Handbook** to review this week's oral vocabulary words: *accomplish, arduous, labor, rejoice, succeed*.
- Tell children you are going to start a sentence using one of the words and you want them to think of an ending. For example, say: *Let's be happy and* rejoice *that ________!* Repeat for the remaining words.

ELL

Understand Help children understand the meaning of words on the chart by pointing to the parts of the body and miming the actions. If children do not have the oral vocabulary to make suggestions for the chart, encourage them to point to parts of their body and mime or draw actions. Say the body-part name and action and then write it in the chart.

Approaching Level

Fluency

Objectives Read aloud with fluency; review high-frequency and vocabulary words

Materials
- **Student Book:** *Head, Body, Legs: A Story from Liberia*
- **High-Frequency Word Cards**
- **Vocabulary Cards**

REREAD FOR FLUENCY

- Have children reread a portion of *Head, Body, Legs*. Direct them to focus on two to four of their favorite pages from the selection. Work with children to read the pages with accuracy and the appropriate expression. For example, read each sentence and have children echo.
- Provide time to listen as children read their sections of text. Comment on their accuracy and expression and provide corrective feedback by modeling proper fluency.

REVIEW HIGH-FREQUENCY/VOCABULARY WORDS

- Display **High-Frequency Word Cards** for **family**, **four**, **hear**, and **Vocabulary Cards** for **attached**, **delicious**, **gasped**, **frantically**, and **swung**. Model using two or three of the words in a sentence. Then have children come up with their own sentence using two or three of the words.

CUMULATIVE REVIEW

- Display the High-Frequency Word Cards and Vocabulary Cards from the previous four weeks. Display one card at a time as children chorally read the word. Mix and repeat. Note words children need to review.

Self-Selected Reading

Objective Read independently and give examples of cause and effect

Materials
- **Leveled Classroom Library**
- other fiction books

APPLY SKILLS TO INDEPENDENT READING

- Have each child choose a fiction book for independent reading. (See the **Theme Bibliography** on pages T8–T9 for book suggestions.)
- After reading, ask children to use their Cause and Effect Charts to orally retell the books. Provide time for children to comment on their reactions to the books. Ask: *Would you like to read more folktales like this one? Why or why not?*

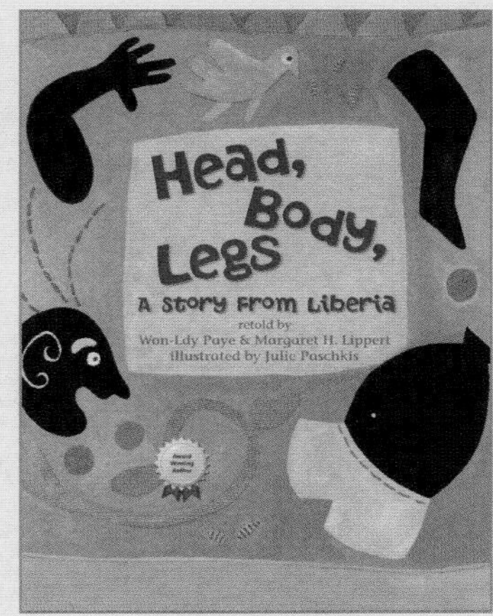

Student Book

Decodable Text

Use the decodable stories in the **Teacher's Resource Book** to help children build fluency with basic decoding patterns.

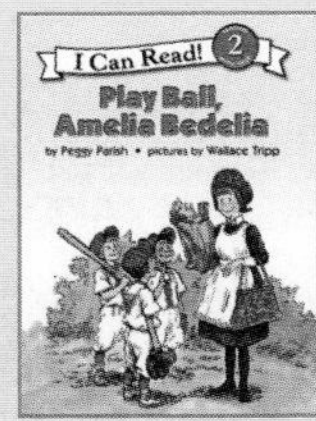

Approaching
Leveled Classroom Library
See Leveled Classroom Library lessons on pages T2–T7.

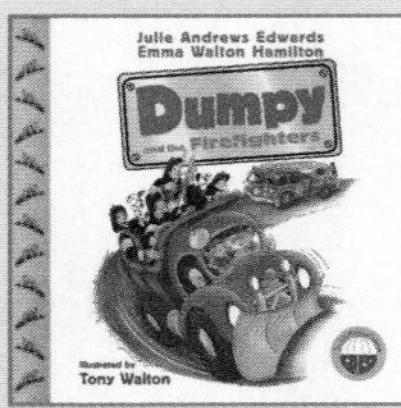

On Level

Leveled Classroom Library

See Leveled Classroom Library lessons on pages T2–T7.

On Level

Self-Selected Reading

Objective Read independently and retell a fiction story

Materials • **Leveled Classroom Library** • other fiction books

APPLY SKILLS TO INDEPENDENT READING

- Have each child choose a fiction book for independent reading. (See the **Theme Bibliography** on pages T8–T9 for book suggestions.)
- After reading, ask children to use their Cause and Effect Charts to orally retell the books. Provide time for children to comment on their reactions to the books. Ask: *What did you like best about this book? Would you recommend this book to a classmate? Why or why not?*

ELL

Share Information Pair English Language Learners with fluent speakers. Have them choose the same book and work together on the Retelling Chart.

Beyond Level

Self-Selected Reading

Objective Read independently and retell information learned

Materials • **Leveled Classroom Library** • other fiction books

APPLY SKILLS TO INDEPENDENT READING

- Have each child choose a fiction book for independent reading. (See the **Theme Bibliography** on pages T8–T9 for book suggestions.)
- After reading, ask children to use their Cause and Effect Charts to write about the most important events, why they happened, and what caused them to happen in their Writer's Notebooks. Provide time for children to comment on their reactions to the books. Ask: *Was this book what you expected? Why or why not?*

EVALUATE

Gifted Talented

- Challenge students to discuss how the self-selected books they have chosen relate to the theme of this unit, Better Together. Ask: *How is it better if we work together? Have children discuss their views.*

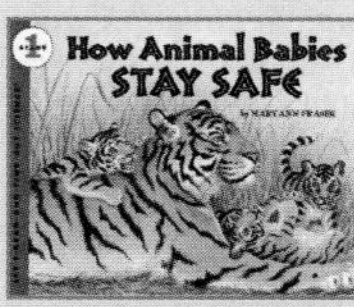

Beyond

Leveled Classroom Library

See Leveled Classroom Library lessons on pages T2–T7.

ELL ENGLISH LANGUAGE LEARNERS

Fluency

Content Objectives Reread selections to develop fluency; develop speaking skills
Language Objective Tell a partner what a selection is about
Materials • **Decodable Reader:** *The Missing String Beans*
• **Student Book:** *Head, Body, Legs: A Story from Liberia*, "Watch It Move!"

REREAD FOR FLUENCY

Beginning

Have children read the Decodable Reader.

Intermediate/Advanced

- Have children reread a portion of *Head, Body, Legs: A Story from Liberia*. Suggest that they focus on two to four of their favorite pages from the selection. Work with children to read the pages with accuracy and the appropriate phrasing. For example, read each sentence of the first paragraph and have children echo. Remind them to pay attention to punctuation as they read, pausing after commas and end punctuation.
- Provide time for children to read their sections of text to you. Comment on their expression and provide corrective feedback by modeling proper fluency.

DEVELOP SPEAKING/LISTENING SKILLS

All Language Levels

- Have children practice reading "Watch It Move." Work with children to read with accuracy and appropriate phrasing.
- Provide time for children to read aloud the article to a partner. Ask children to tell their partner what they learned from the article. Provide the sentence frame *I learned about* ________.

Self-Selected Reading

Content Objective Read independently
Language Objective Orally retell a story read
Materials • **Leveled Classroom Library** • other fiction books

APPLY SKILLS AND STRATEGIES TO INDEPENDENT READING

All Language Levels

- Have each child choose a fiction book for independent reading. (See the **Theme Bibliography** on pages T8–T9 for book suggestions.) After reading, ask children to orally summarize the book. Provide time for children to comment on their reactions to the book and share them with classmates. Ask: *Would you recommend this book to a classmate? Why or why not?*

Student Book

Progress Monitoring

Weekly Assessment

ASSESSED SKILLS

- Phonics: Diphthong *ou*, *ow*; Inflectional Endings *-s*, *-es*
- Selection Vocabulary
- Comprehension: Cause and Effect
- Grammar: Linking Verbs

Selection Test for* Head, Body, Legs: A Story from Liberia *Also Available.

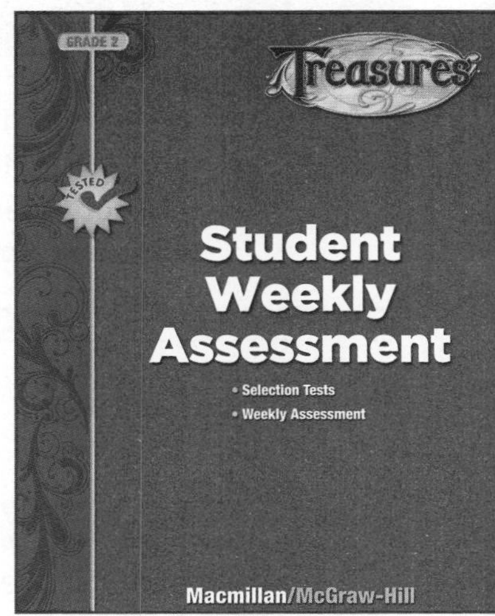

Student Weekly Assessment Unit 4 Week 1

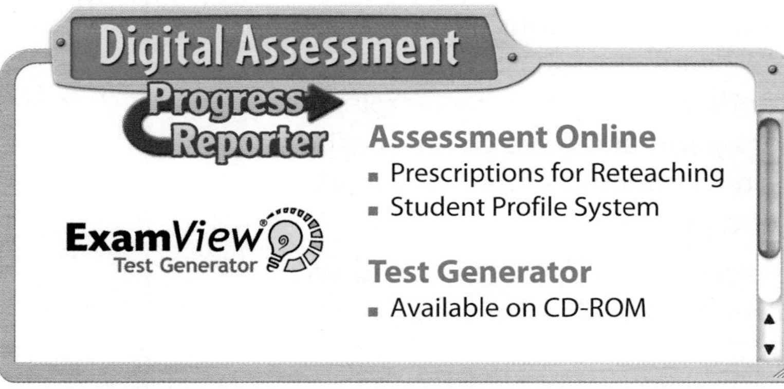

Assessment Online
- Prescriptions for Reteaching
- Student Profile System

Test Generator
- Available on CD-ROM

Fluency Assessment

Assess fluency for one group of students per week. Use the Oral Fluency Record Sheet to track the number of words read correctly. Fluency goals for all students:

62–82 words correct per minute (WCPM)

Approaching Level	Weeks 1, 3, 5
On Level	Weeks 2, 4
Beyond Level	Week 6

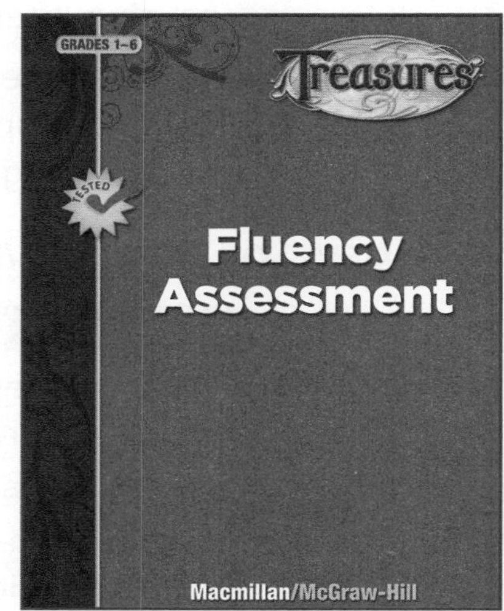

Fluency Assessment

DIBELS LINK

PROGRESS MONITORING

Use your DIBELS results to inform instruction.

IF

DIBELS Oral **R**eading **F**luency (**DORF**) 0–67

THEN

Evaluate for Intervention

TPRI LINK

PROGRESS MONITORING

Use your TPRI scores to inform instruction.

IF

Graphophonemic Knowledge	Still Developing
Reading Fluency/Accuracy	Reading Grade 2, Story 4 Less Than 75 WCPM
Reading Comprehension Questions	0–3 correct

THEN

Evaluate for Intervention

Diagnose		Prescribe
Review the assessment answers with students. Have them correct their errors. Then provide additional instruction as needed.		
	IF...	**THEN...**
PHONICS AND SPELLING Dipthong *ou*, *ow* Inflectional Endings *s*, *-es*	0–1 items correct . . .	LOG ON Online Practice: Go to **www.macmillanmh.com**. See **Phonics Intervention Teacher's Edition.** See Sound-Spelling Fluency and mixed review blending lines in upcoming lessons.
VOCABULARY WORDS **VOCABULARY STRATEGY** Context Clues	0–1 items correct . . .	See **Phonics Intervention Teacher's Edition.** SPIRAL REVIEW See Vocabulary review lessons Unit 4, Week 2.
COMPREHENSION Cause and Effect	0–1 items correct . . .	See **Comprehension Intervention Teacher's Edition.** SPIRAL REVIEW See Cause and Effect lessons Unit 4, Week 2.
GRAMMAR Linking Verbs	0–1 items correct . . .	See the **Grammar and Writing Handbook.**
FLUENCY	53–61 WCPM	AUDIO CD Fluency Solutions Audio CD
	0–52 WCPM	See **Fluency Intervention Teacher's Edition.**

Response to Intervention

To place students in Tier 2 or Tier 3 Intervention use the *Diagnostic Assessment.*

- Phonemic Awareness
- Phonics
- Vocabulary
- Comprehension
- Fluency

Week 2 ★ At a Glance

Priority Skills and Concepts

Comprehension
- **Genre:** Fiction
- **Strategy:** Read Ahead
- **Skill:** Use Illustrations

- **Cause and Effect**

High-Frequency Words
- ***above, color, song***

Oral Vocabulary
- **Build Robust Vocabulary:** ***advice, hesitate, panic, secure, vowed***

Vocabulary
- ***attention, buddy, accident, tip, enormous, obeys***
- **Strategy:** Context Clues: Synonyms

Fluency
- **Intonation**

Phonemic Awareness
- **Phoneme Segmentation**

Phonics/Spelling
- **Vowel Diphthongs *oi, oy*** ***soil, broil, moist, point, boil, oil, toy, joy, avoid, royal, crown, house, above, color, song***

Grammar/Mechanics
- ***Have*** **as a Helping Verb**
- **Quotation Marks**

Writing
- **Persuasive Essay**
- **A Strong Opening**
- **Trait:** Ideas

Key

 Tested in program

 Review Skill

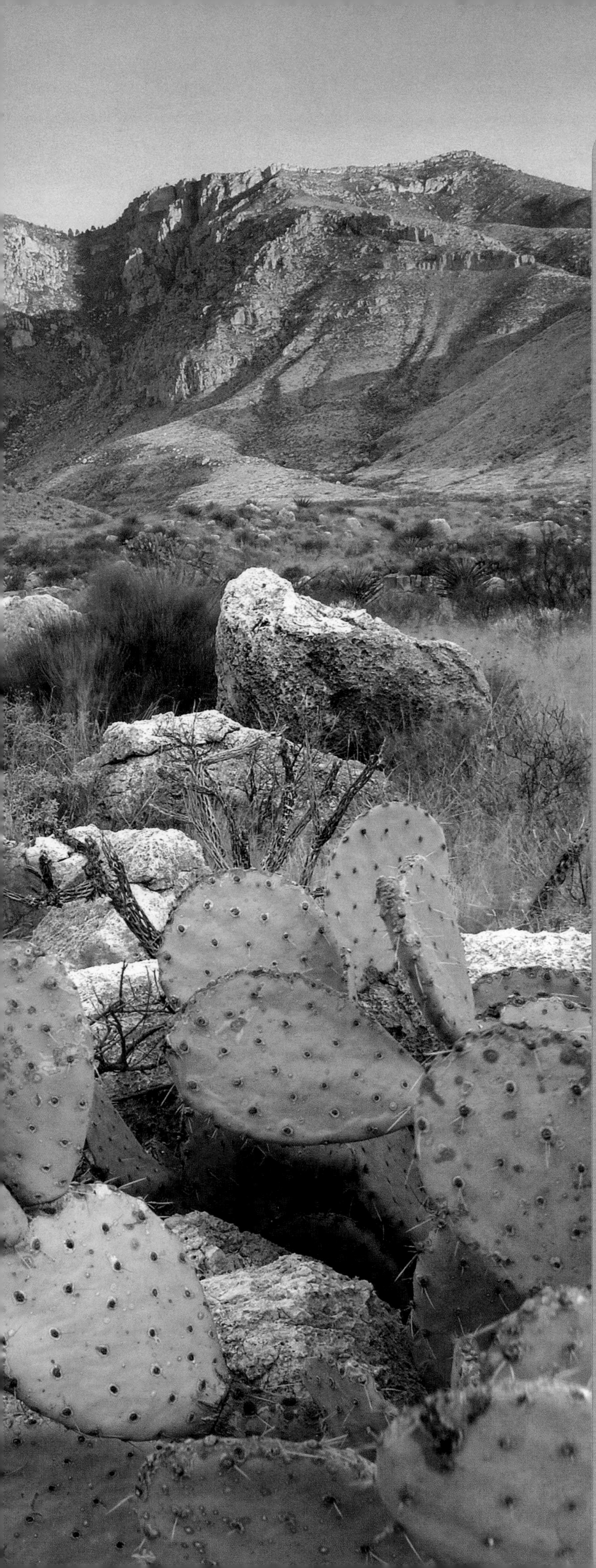

Digital Learning

Digital solutions to help plan and implement instruction.

Teacher Resources

ONLINE
www.macmillanmh.com

- **Teacher's Edition**
  - Lesson Planner and Resources also on CD-ROM

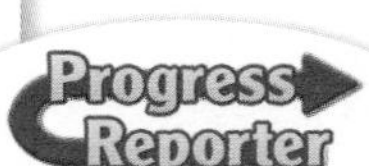

- **Formative Assessment**
  - ExamView® on CD-ROM also available

- **Instructional Resources**
  - Unit Videos
  - Classroom Presentation Toolkit
- **Professional Development**
  - Video Library

Student Resources

ONLINE
www.macmillanmh.com

- **Interactive Student Book**
- **Leveled Reader Database**
- **Activities**
  - Research Toolkit
  - Oral Language Activities
  - Vocabulary/Spelling Activities

Listening Library
- Recordings of Student Books and Leveled Readers

Fluency Solutions
- Fluency Modeling and Practice

Theme: Special Teams

Student Book

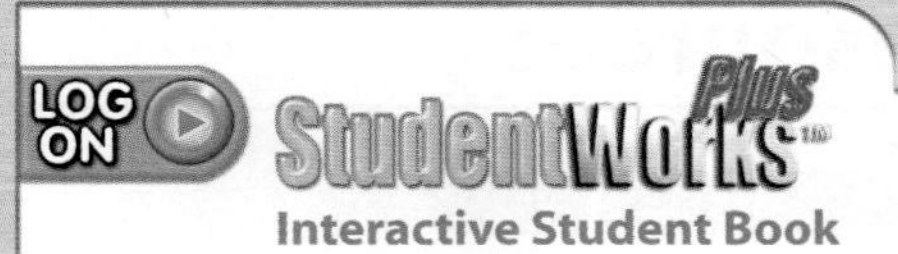

- Word-by-Word Reading
- Summaries in Multiple Languages
- Comprehension Questions

Preteach Vocabulary and Comprehension

Genre Fiction

Main Selection

Genre Fiction

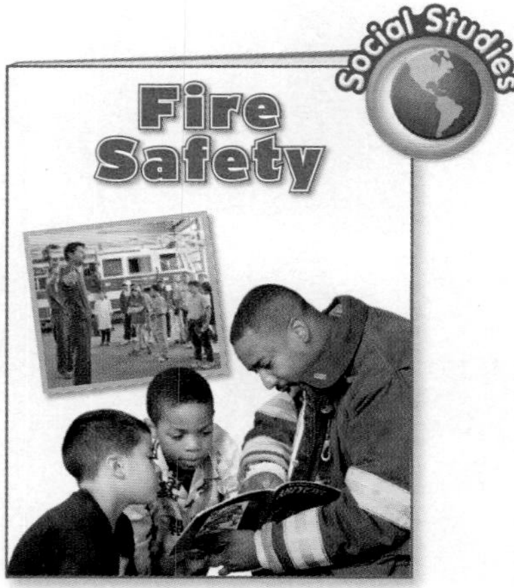

Paired Selection

Genre Expository

Support Literature

Decodable Reader Library
- One decodable read each week

Oral Vocabulary Cards
- Listening Comprehension
- Build Robust Vocabulary

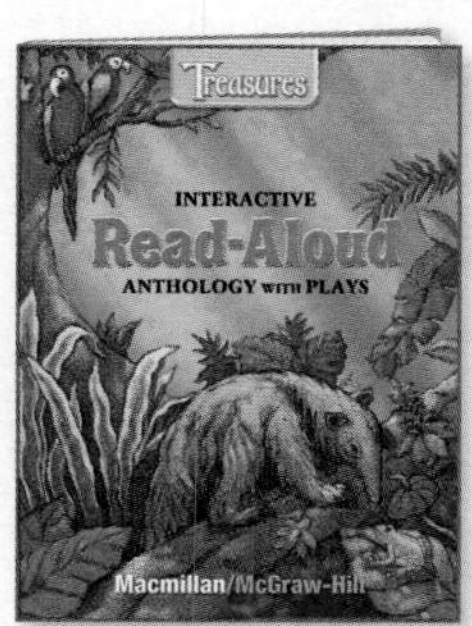

Interactive Read-Aloud Anthology
- Listening Comprehension
- Readers Theater Plays for Fluency

Resources for Differentiated Instruction

Leveled Readers: Social Studies

GR Levels H-O

Genre	Expository

- Same Theme
- Same Vocabulary
- Same Comprehension Skills

Approaching Level

On Level

Beyond Level

ELL

Leveled Reader Database
Go to www.macmillanmh.com.

Leveled Practice

Approaching

On Level

Beyond

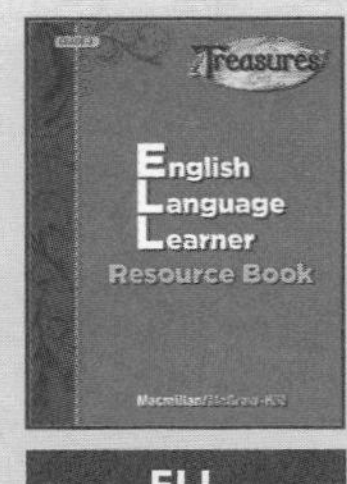

ELL

Leveled Classroom Library

Approaching

On Level

Beyond

Response to Intervention

- Phonemic Awareness
- Phonics
- Vocabulary
- Comprehension
- Fluency

Assessment

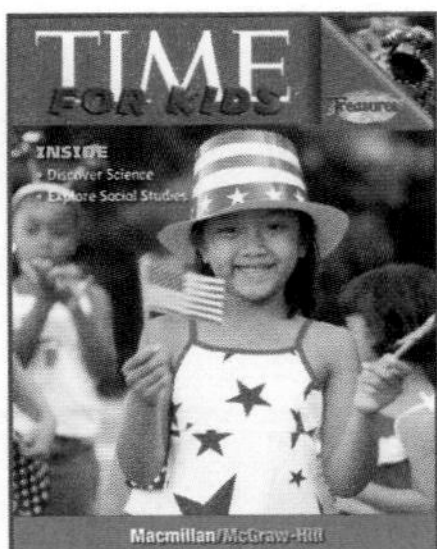

Time For Kids

- Teacher's Edition
- Apply Answering Questions Strategies

Weekly Assessment

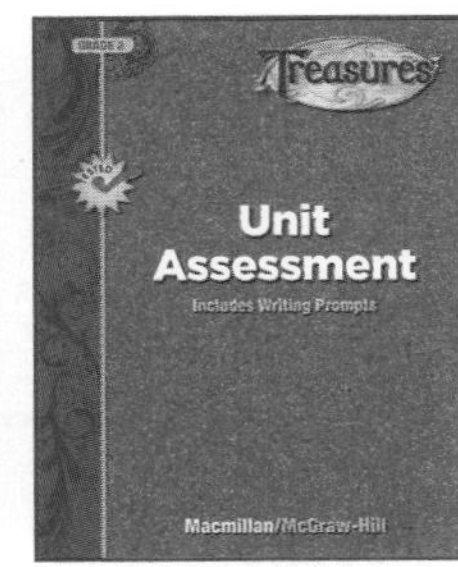

Unit Assessment

Benchmark Assessment

HOME-SCHOOL CONNECTION

- Family letters in English and Spanish
- Take-home stories and activities

LOG ON Suggested Lesson Plan

Go to www.macmillanmh.com for Online Lesson Planner

Officer Buckle and Gloria, pp. 46/47–68/69

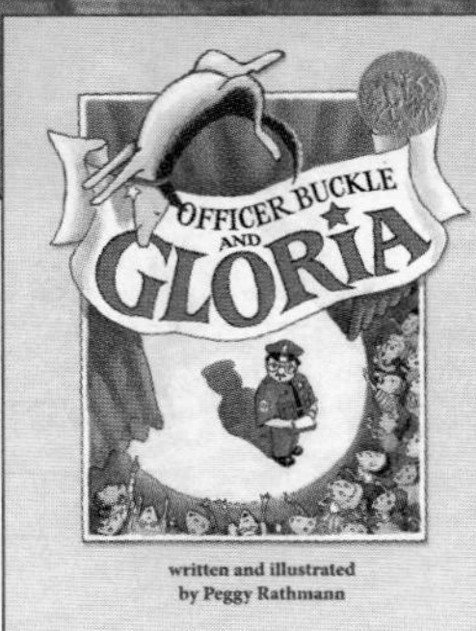

WHOLE GROUP	DAY 1	DAY 2
ORAL LANGUAGE • Oral Vocabulary • Listening Comprehension • Phonemic Awareness	**Focus Question** Describe ways people and animals can work together as a team. Build Background, 42M **Oral Vocabulary** *advice, hesitate, panic, secure, vowed*, 43A Oral Vocabulary Cards, "Tikki Tikki Tembo," 43A **Phonemic Awareness** Phoneme Segmentation, 43B	**Focus Question** How do the illustrations help make the story funny? **Oral Vocabulary** *advice, hesitate, panic, secure, vowed*, 45E **Phonemic Awareness** Phoneme Blending, 45F
WORD STUDY • Phonics • Spelling • High-Frequency Words	**Phonics** Introduce Diphthong *oi, oy*, 43C Practice Book, 184 **Spelling** Pretest: Words with Diphthong *oi, oy*, 43E Spelling, 65 **Vocabulary** *accident, attention, buddy, enormous, obeys, tip*, 43G **Strategy:** Context Clues/Synonyms Practice Book, 185	**Phonics** Blend and Build with Diphthong *oi, oy*, 45G **Spelling** Word Sort with Diphthong *oi, oy*, 45I Spelling, 66 **Vocabulary** *accident, attention, buddy, enormous, obeys, tip* Review Words in Context, 45
READING • Comprehension • Fluency	Decodable Reader: *Let's Join Joy's Show!* **Read** Decodable Reader, *Let's Join Joy's Show!*, 43F **Comprehension**, 45A–45B "Safety at School," 44/45 **Strategy:** Monitor Comprehension/Read Ahead **Skill:** Use Illustrations 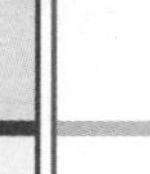 **Fluency** Build Fluency, 43C	 Student Book **Read** *Officer Buckle and Gloria*, 46/47–68/69 **Comprehension**, 45K–71A **Strategy:** Monitor Comprehension/Read Ahead **Skill:** Use Illustrations Practice Book, 187–188 **Fluency** Build Fluency, 45H
LANGUAGE ARTS • Writing • Grammar	 **Writing** **Daily Writing Prompt** Look at the picture. Write about what you see, 42M Brainstorm a Persuasive Essay, 45D  **Grammar** Helping Verbs, 45C Grammar, 81	**Writing** **Daily Writing Prompt** Tell which safety rule is most important when working on a team with an animal and why, 45E Prewrite a Persuasive Essay, 71C  **Grammar** Helping Verbs, 71B Grammar, 82
ASSESSMENT • Informal/Formal 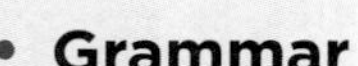	 **Quick Check** Phonics, 43D Vocabulary, 44/45	**Quick Check** Comprehension, 68/69

SMALL GROUP Lesson Plan — **Differentiated Instruction 42G–42H**

Priority Skills

Phonics	Vocabulary	Comprehension	Writing
Diphthong /oi/*oi, oy*	**Words:** *accident, attention, buddy, enormous, obeys, tip* **Strategy:** Context Clues	**Strategy:** Monitor Comprehension: Read Ahead **Skill:** Use Illustrations	Persuasive Essay **Social Studies**

DAY 3

Focus Question Compare and contrast Officer Buckle and Gloria. How are these characters alike? How are they different?

Read Aloud, "Police Patrol," 71R

Oral Vocabulary *advice, hesitate, panic, secure, vowed,* 71K

Phonemic Awareness Phoneme Substitution, 71E

Phonics Blend and Build Words with Diphthong *oi, oy,* 71F; Prefixes *re-, un-, dis-,* 71G
Practice Book, 189

Spelling Word Sort, 71H
Spelling, 67

Vocabulary *accident, attention, buddy, enormous, obeys, tip*
Strategy: Context Clues, 71J
Practice Book, 190

Student Book

Read *Officer Buckle and Gloria,* 46/47–68/69

Comprehension
Review Skill: Cause and Effect

Fluency Repeated Reading: Prosody/Intonation, 71L
Practice Book, 191

Writing

Daily Writing Prompt Respond to the Read Aloud by writing what you learned about police work, 71D

Writing Trait: Ideas, 71Q

A Strong Opening, 71P

Draft a Persuasive Essay, 71Q

Grammar Mechanics: Quotation Marks, 71O
Grammar, 83

Quick Check Fluency, 71M

DAY 4

Focus Question What are some other safety tips that firefighters might try to teach to students and families?

Oral Vocabulary *advice, hesitate, panic, secure, vowed,* 71R

Phonemic Awareness Phoneme Segmentation, 71S

Phonics Build and Blend Words with Diphthong *oi, oy,* 71T

Spelling Practice Words with Diphthong *oi, oy,* 71V
Spelling, 68

Vocabulary *accident, attention, buddy, enormous, obeys, tip*

Review Words in Context, 71W

Fire Safety
Student Book

Read "Fire Safety," 72/73–74/75

Comprehension
Text Feature: Floor Plans 71X

Content Vocabulary:
calm, hazards, route

Practice Book, 192

Fluency Build Fluency, 71U

Writing

Daily Writing Prompt Imagine you could be a part of an animal team. Describe what animal you would be with and what your team would do, 71K

Revise and Proofread a Persuasive Essay, 75D

Grammar Helping Verbs, 75B
Grammar, 84

Quick Check Spelling, 71V

DAY 5
Review and Assess

Focus Question How will reading ahead help you read and understand another selection?

Oral Vocabulary *advice, hesitate, panic, secure, vowed,* 77A

Phonemic Awareness Phoneme Blending, 77C

Phonics Blend with Diphthong *oi, oy,* 77C

Spelling Posttest, 77E

Vocabulary *accident, attention, buddy, enormous, obeys, tip*, 77F

Student Book

Read Self-Selected Reading, 42K

Comprehension, 77G

Strategy: Monitor Comprehension/Read Ahead

Skill: Use Illustrations

Fluency Repeated Reading: Prosody/Intonation, 77B4

Writing

Daily Writing Prompt Think about various animals. Write a list of animals that can work with people on teams and why, 77F

Publish and Present a Persuasive Essay, 77I
Speaking, Listening, Viewing, 77J

Grammar Helping Verbs, Quotation Marks, 77H
Grammar, 85

Weekly Assessment, 77KK–77LL

Differentiated Instruction

What do I do in small groups?

Focus on Skills

IF... **students need additional instruction, practice, or extension based on your Quick Check observations for the following priority skills**

 **Phonics/Word Study**
Diphthong *oi*, *oy*; Prefixes *re-*, *un-*, *dis-*

 **Vocabulary Words**
accident, attention, buddy, enormous, obeys, tip
Strategy: Context Clues: Synonyms

 **Comprehension**
Strategy: Monitor Comprehension/ Read Ahead
Skill: Use Illustrations

 **Fluency**
Phonics, High-Frequency Words, Intonation

THEN...

Approaching	Preteach and
English Learners	Reteach Skills
On Level	Practice
Beyond	Enrich and Accelerate Learning

LOG ON Suggested Small Group Lesson Plan

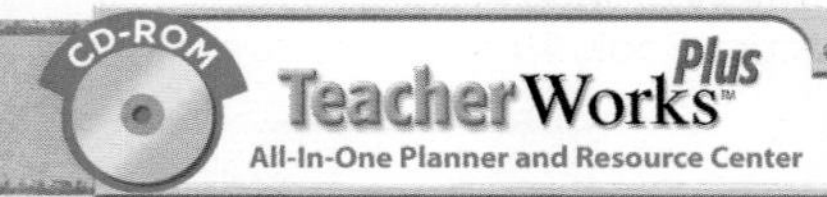

	DAY 1	DAY 2
Approaching Level • **Preteach/Reteach**  Tier 2 **Tier 2 Instruction**	• Phonemic Awareness, 77K • Phonics, 77K ELL • High-Frequency/Vocabulary, 77L • Decodable Reader, *Let's Join Joy's Show*, 77L	• Phonemic Awareness, 77Q • Phonics, 77Q ELL • High-Frequency/Vocabulary, 77R • Leveled Reader Lesson 1, 77R
On Level • **Practice**	• Phonics, 77M • Fluency, 77M ELL	• Leveled Reader Lesson 1, 77S ELL
Beyond Level • **Extend/Accelerate** Gifted Talented **Gifted and Talented**	• Phonics, 77N ELL • Vocabulary, 77N	• Leveled Reader Lesson 1, 77T • Analyze, 77T
ELL • **Build English Language Proficiency** • **See ELL in other levels.**	• Prepare to Read, 77O • Academic Language, 77O • Preteach Vocabulary, 77P	• Preteach Main Selection, 77U • Grammar, 77V

Focus on Leveled Readers

Levels H-O

Approaching

On Level

Beyond

ELL

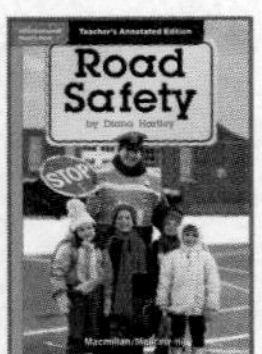

Social Studies

Teacher's Annotated Edition

Describe how governments establish order, provide security and manage conflict; Identify characteristic of good citizenship such as a belief in justice, truth, equality, and responsibility for the common good.

Additional Leveled Readers

Leveled Reader Database

www.macmillanmh.com

Search by

- Comprehension Skill
- Content Area
- Genre
- Text Feature
- Guided Reading Level
- Reading Recovery Level
- Lexile Score
- Benchmark Level

Subscription also available.

Manipulatives

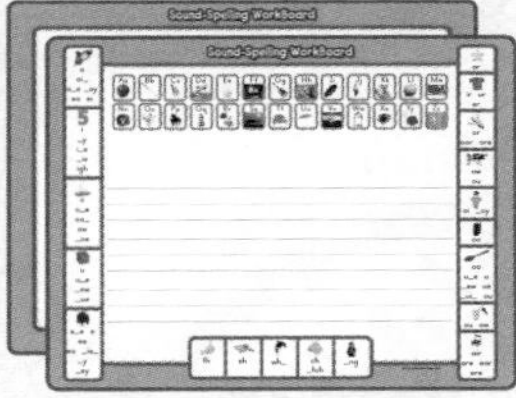

Sound-Spelling WorkBoards

Sound-Spelling Cards

Photo Cards

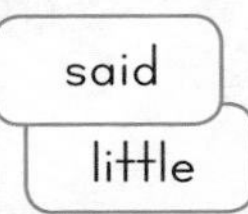

High-Frequency Word Cards

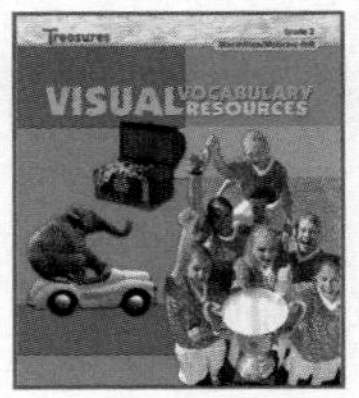

Visual Vocabulary Resources

DAY 3

- Phonemic Awareness, 77W
- Phonics, 77W ELL
- High-Frequency/Vocabulary, 77X
- Leveled Reader Lesson 2, 77X
- Book Talk, 77X

- Leveled Reader Lesson 2, 77Y
- Fluency, 77Y
- Book Talk, 77Y

- Leveled Reader Lesson 2, 77Z
- Synthesize and Evaluate, 77Z
- Fluency, 77Z
- Book Talk, 77Z

- Leveled Reader Lesson 1, 77AA
- Writing/Spelling, 77BB

DAY 4

- Phonemic Awareness, 77CC
- Phonics, 77CC ELL
- High-Frequency/Vocabulary, 77DD
- Fluency, 77DD
- Review Leveled Readers, 77DD

- Fluency, 77EE

- Fluency, 77EE

- Preteach Paired Selection, 77FF
- Leveled Reader Lesson 2, 77FF

DAY 5

- Oral Language, 77GG ELL
- Fluency, 77HH
- Self-Selected Independent Reading, 77HH

- Self-Selected Independent Reading, 77II ELL

- Self-Selected Independent Reading, 77II
- Evaluate, 77II

- Fluency, 77JJ
- Self-Selected Independent Reading, 77JJ

What do I do with the rest of my class?

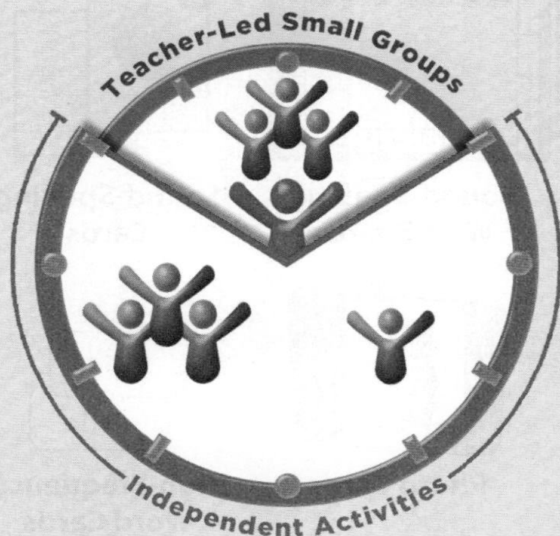

- Literacy Workstations
- Leveled Reader Activities
- Practice Book and Reproducibles
- Online Activities
- English Language Learner Practice Book

Classroom Management Tools

Weekly Contract

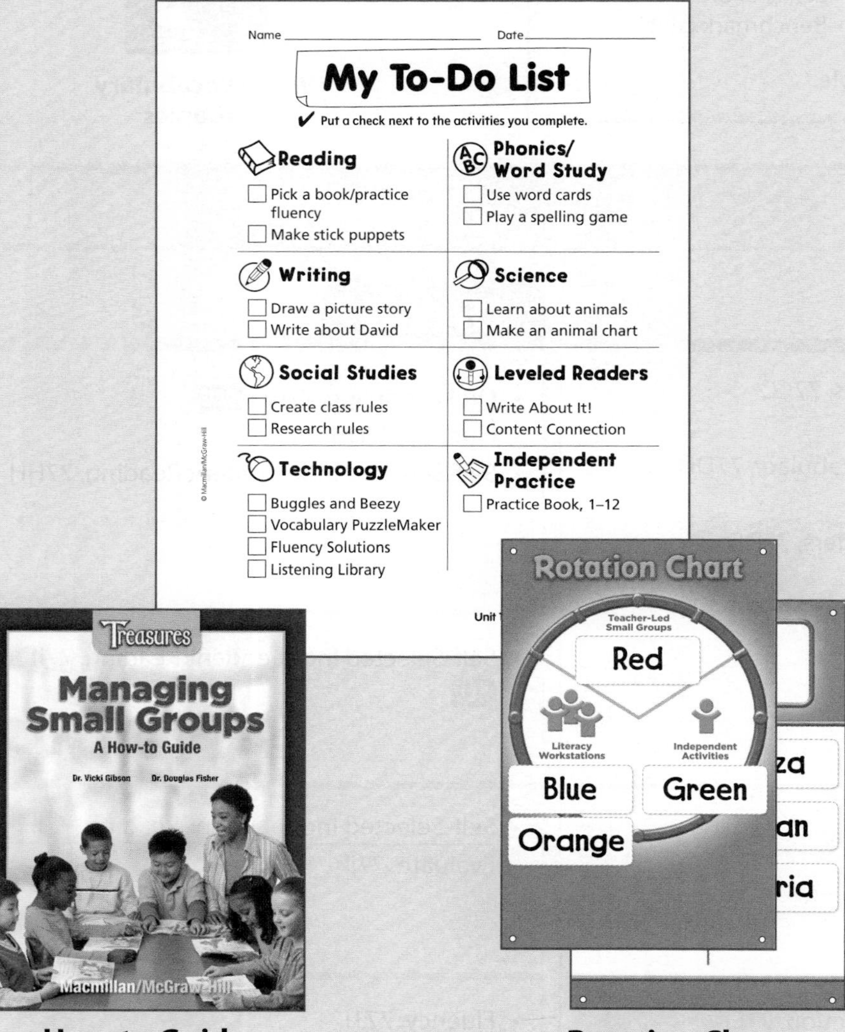
Name ______ Date ______

My To-Do List

✔ Put a check next to the activities you complete.

Reading	Phonics/ Word Study
☐ Pick a book/practice fluency ☐ Make stick puppets	☐ Use word cards ☐ Play a spelling game
Writing	**Science**
☐ Draw a picture story ☐ Write about David	☐ Learn about animals ☐ Make an animal chart
Social Studies	**Leveled Readers**
☐ Create class rules ☐ Research rules	☐ Write About It! ☐ Content Connection
Technology	**Independent Practice**
☐ Buggles and Beezy ☐ Vocabulary PuzzleMaker ☐ Fluency Solutions ☐ Listening Library	☐ Practice Book, 1–12

How-to Guide

Rotation Chart

Digital Learning

StudentWorks Plus

- Summaries in Multiple Languages
- Word-by-Word Reading
- Comprehension Questions

- Read Other Books by the Author or Illustrator

Leveled Practice

On Level

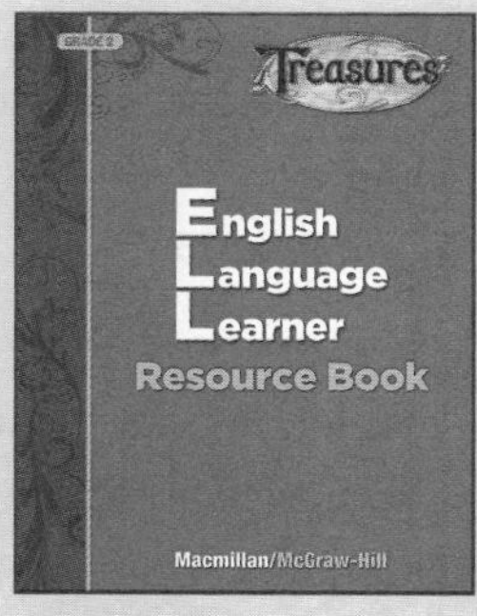

ELL

Also Available:

Approaching Reproducible

Beyond Reproducible

Independent Activities

ONLINE INSTRUCTION www.macmillanmh.com

Oral Language Activities

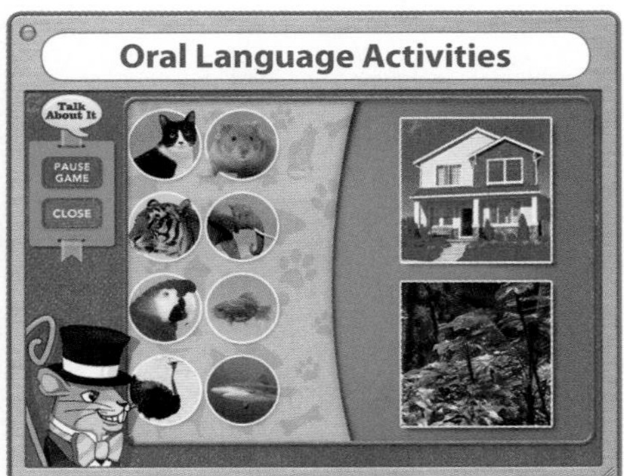

- Focus on Vocabulary and Concepts
- English Language Learner Support

Leveled Reader Database

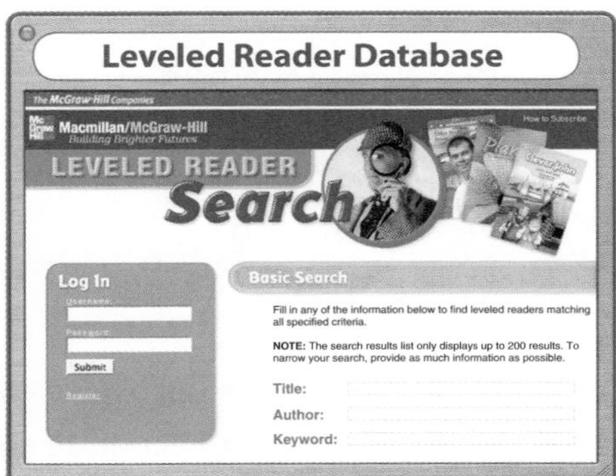

- Leveled Reader Database
- Search titles by level, skill, content area, and more

Vocabulary/Spelling Activities

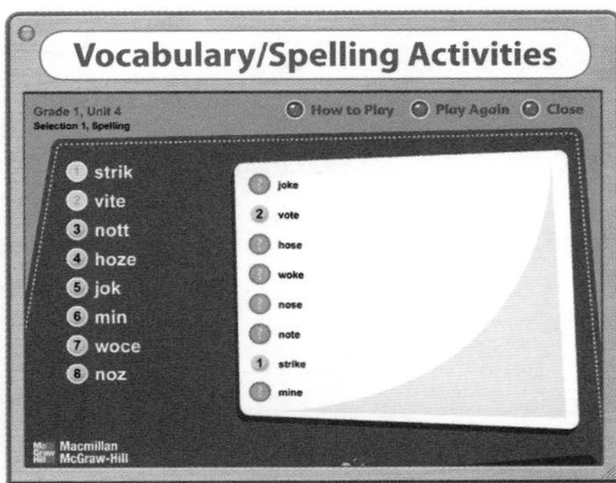

- Differentiated Lists and Activities

Research Toolkit

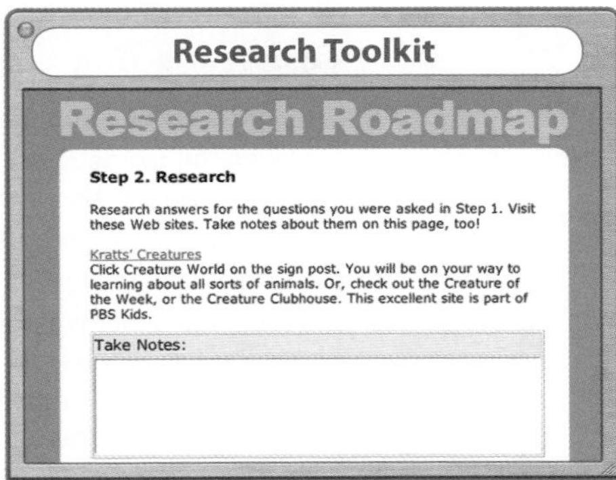

- Research Roadmap
- Research and Presentation Tools
- Theme Launcher Video
- Links to Science and Social Studies

Available on CD

LISTENING LIBRARY
Recordings of selections

- Main Selections
- Paired Selections
- Leveled Readers
- ELL Readers

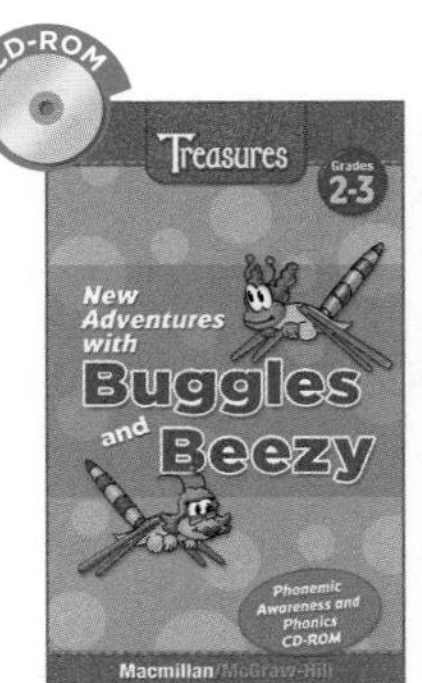

NEW ADVENTURES WITH BUGGLES AND BEEZY
Phonemic awareness and phonics activities

FLUENCY SOLUTIONS
Recorded passages at two speeds for modeling and practicing fluency

Leveled Reader Activities

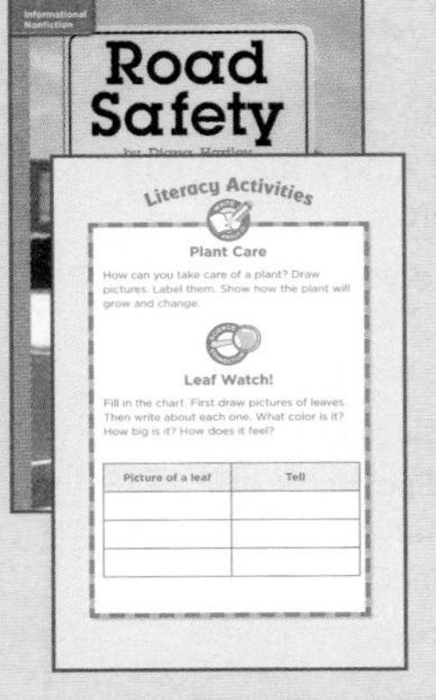

Approaching

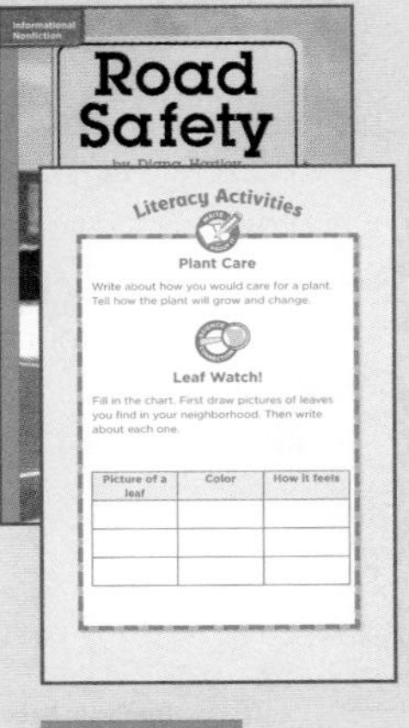

On Level

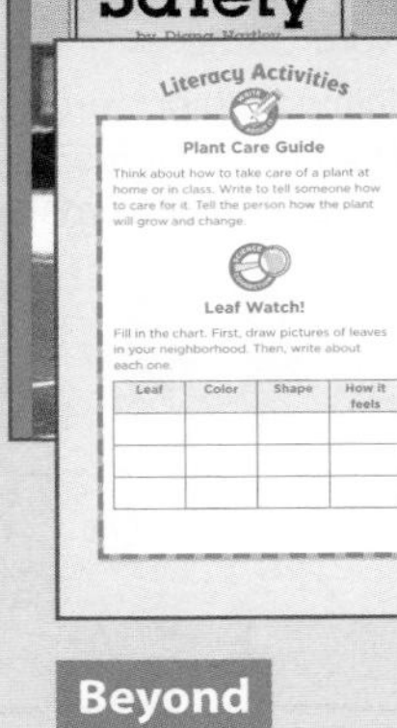

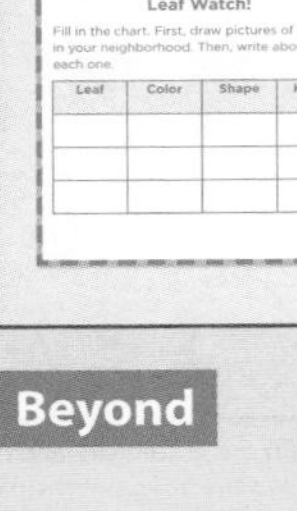

Beyond

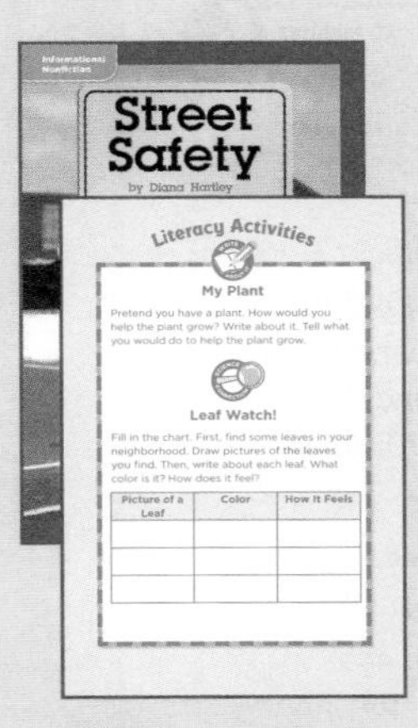

ELL

See inside cover for all Leveled Readers.

Literacy Workstations

See lessons on pages 42K–42L

Managing the Class

What do I do with the rest of my class?

Reading

Objectives

- Read aloud to a partner fluently and with expression
- Write in your journal about safety rules or tips
- Retell stories and support answers with evidence from text

Phonics/Word Study

Objectives

- Recognize and know the meaning of common synonyms
- Recognize and use knowledge of spelling patterns

Reading — **Pick a Book** — 20 Minutes

- Pick a book you read this week.
- Read it with a partner.
- In your journal, make a list of safety rules or tips that you learned.

Extension

- Pick a Practice Reader you read this week. Choose a funny or interesting part.
- Read it to your partner. Use the Fluency Solutions Audio CD.

Things you need:
- books you read
- pencil, paper

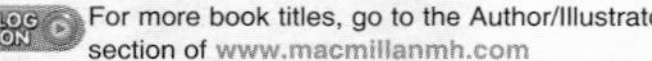

For more book titles, go to the Author/Illustrator section of www.macmillanmh.com

Listening Library Fluency Solutions

33

Phonics/Word Study — **Synonym Search** — 20 Minutes

- Create a Four-Door Foldable®.
- Write the words *rules, smiled, large,* and *friend* on the outside tabs.
- Work with a partner. Look through the story for synonyms for the words.
- Write the synonyms to the four words on the inside tabs.
- Read aloud the sentence that contains the word. Then read the sentence again, using the synonym.

Extension

- Write your own sentences for each synonym pair.

FOLDABLES
- Four-Door Foldable®

rules | smiled | large | friend

For more vocabulary and spelling games, go to www.macmillanmh.com

FOLDABLES®

33

Reading — **Retell and Talk About the Pictures** — 20 Minutes

- Work with a partner. Use the Retelling Cards to retell the story.
- Talk about how the drawings make the story funny. Which one is your favorite?

Extension

- Talk about why Officer Buckle and Gloria are a good team.
- Tell about a time when you worked with a friend. Were you a good team? Explain.

Things you need:
- Retelling Cards
- *Officer Buckle and Gloria,* pp. 46–69

For more book titles, go to the Author/Illustrator section of www.macmillanmh.com

Listening Library

34

Phonics/Word Study — **WORD SORTS** — 20 Minutes

- With a partner, sort your Spelling Word Cards.
- Think of other words with *oi* and *oy.* Write these words on index cards and sort your words again.

Extension

- Think of a new way to sort your words.
- Write your sort in your journal.

Things you need:
- Spelling Word Cards
- index cards
- response journal

Teacher's Resource Book: spelling word cards, page 86

For more vocabulary and spelling games, go to www.macmillanmh.com

New Adventures with Buggles and Beezy

34

Literacy Workstations

Literacy Workstation Flip Charts

Writing

Objectives

- Write a speech that persuades
- Maintain a consistent focus so that your message is clear
- Write and draw about a safety tip

Content Literacy

Objectives

- Use visual materials to convey safety rules and laws
- Use reference materials to research helpful animals

Writing — **Speak Out** — 20 Minutes

- Write a speech about something you would like to see changed in your community to make it safer.
- Be sure that your message is clear, so that you can persuade others that you have a good idea.

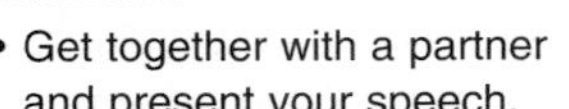

Extension

- Get together with a partner and present your speech.
- Talk about whether your message was clear. How did you persuade your partner?
- 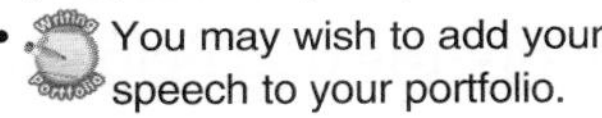 You may wish to add your speech to your portfolio.

Things you need:
- pencil, paper

There are broken bottles in the park. It's not safe.

33

Social Studies — **Safety Signs** — 20 Minutes

- Think about the safety signs you see.
- Draw a picture of one safety sign.
- Under the picture, write the rule or law that the sign is telling people to obey.

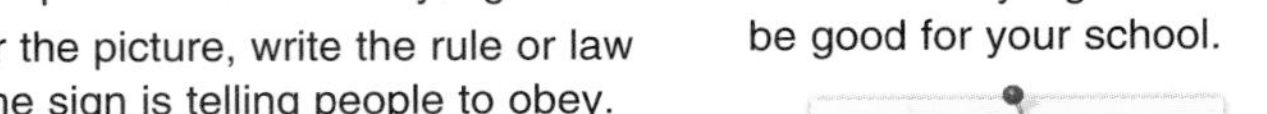

Extension

- Draw a safety sign that would be good for your school.

Things you need:
- drawing paper
- crayons or markers

33

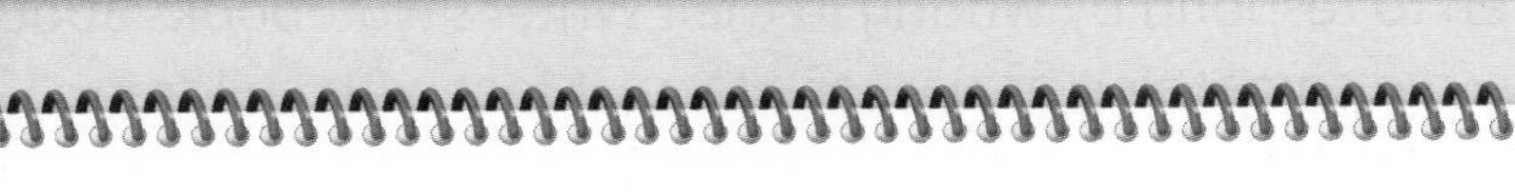

Writing — **More Safety Tips** — 20 Minutes

- Think of a new safety tip that Officer Buckle can share with children.
- Write the safety tip. Draw a picture that shows Officer Buckle and Gloria telling and showing the safety tip.

Extension

- Share your safety tip and picture with a partner.
- Talk about other tips that Officer Buckle might share. Tell how Gloria might act them out.

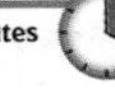

Things you need:
- drawing paper
- pencil or crayons

34

Science — **How Animals Help** — 20 Minutes

- Find out about dogs and other animals that help people. Use the Internet or other sources.
- Share what you found out with a partner.

Helpful Animals
- seeing-eye dogs
- rescue dogs

Extension

- Choose one way an animal can help people.
- Do more research. Find out how people train the animals.
- Write about what you found out.

Things you need:
- Internet or other reference sources
- pencil, paper

LOG ON Internet Research and Inquiry Activity www.macmillanmh.com

34

Day 1 At a Glance

WHOLE GROUP

Oral Language
- Build Background
- Oral Vocabulary

Phonemic Awareness
- Phoneme Segmentation

Phonics
- Diphthong *oi, oy*
- Build Fluency
- Spelling: Pretest: Words with *oi, oy*
- Read *Let's Join Joy's Show!*

Vocabulary
- Teach Words in Context
- Use Context Clues: Synonyms
- Read "Safety at School"

Comprehension
- Strategy: Monitor Comprehension/Read Ahead
- Skill: Use Illustrations

Language Arts
- Grammar: Helping Verbs
- Writing: Expository

SMALL GROUP

- Differentiated Instruction, pages 77K–77JJ

Oral Vocabulary

Week 2

advice	hesitate
panic	secure
vowed	

Oral Language

Build Background

ACCESS PRIOR KNOWLEDGE
Discuss with children that working together as a team to get something done is better than working alone. Animals can be a part of that team with people. *What do you think is unique about working on a team with an animal? What do you think the challenges are?*

SING ABOUT TEAMWORK
Sing the song "Shake the Papaya Down" and have children add verses and act out jobs that can be done with a team.

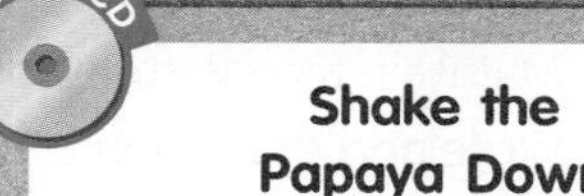

Shake the Papaya Down

Mama says no play,
This is a work day.
Up with the bright sun,
Get all the work done.
If you will help me,
Climb up the tall tree,
Shake the papaya down.

FOCUS QUESTION Have children read the "Talk About It" question on **Student Book** page 43. Describe the photograph, providing academic language. The dog is wearing a vest that shows it is part of a rescue team. A rescue team **vows**, or promises, to help others. How might the dog help someone be **secure**, or safe? What might the dog do when someone feels **panic**, or is very afraid?

Use the Picture Prompt

BUILD WRITING FLUENCY
Ask children to respond by writing in their Writer's Notebooks about a time they did something as part of a team. Meet with children during individual Writing Conference time to provide feedback and revision assignments.

ELL ENGLISH LANGUAGE LEARNERS

Beginning

Describe Tell children about the photograph. *This dog helps people. This dog rescues, or helps, people who are in the water.* Ask children to tell you about the photograph. Accept one-word responses and restate in complete sentences.

Intermediate

Describe Ask children to describe the photograph. *Where is this dog? Who does this dog help? How can a dog be part of a team?* Elicit details to support children's responses.

Advanced

Expand Ask children to elaborate on the concept. Discuss that the dog is part of a team and that team members help each other. Ask, *Have you been part of a team? What kind of team? What did you do?* Elicit details to support children's responses.

Talk About It

Describe how working on a team is better than working alone.

Oral Language Activities
Special Teams
www.macmillanmh.com

42 43

Connect to the Unit Theme

Sometimes working as a team is better than working alone.

CONNECT TO THEME
Ask children what they have learned so far about teamwork.

USE THEME FOLDABLE
Read aloud the **Big Idea** statement. Write the word **advice** on the board. Read it aloud and have children repeat. Tell children that when you give someone advice, you tell what you think the person should or should not do. Ask children to add it to their Unit Theme Foldables. Tell children that they will add pictures of topics they have given advice on or received advice on throughout the week.

Dinah Zike's

Better Together

Teamwork at home

Teamwork at school

Teamwork at play

Unit 4 Theme Foldable

Objectives

- Introduce oral vocabulary words
- Read the myth "Tikki Tikki Tembo"
- Review last week's oral vocabulary words

Materials

- Oral Vocabulary Cards: "Tikki Tikki Tembo"

Oral Language

Build Robust Vocabulary

BUILD BACKGROUND Display "Tikki Tikki Tembo" **Oral Vocabulary Card** 1 and read the title aloud. *We are going to read a myth about two brothers named Tikki and Chen who live in China. The brothers do not follow their mother's rules about staying away from the well. What is a well? Remember that myths are stories used to explain how things came to be. What kind of story might this be, real or make-believe?*

- Read the story on the back of the cards aloud. During the first reading, check children's listening comprehension using the Retell Details prompts on Card 4. Review the story vocabulary words using the routine below.

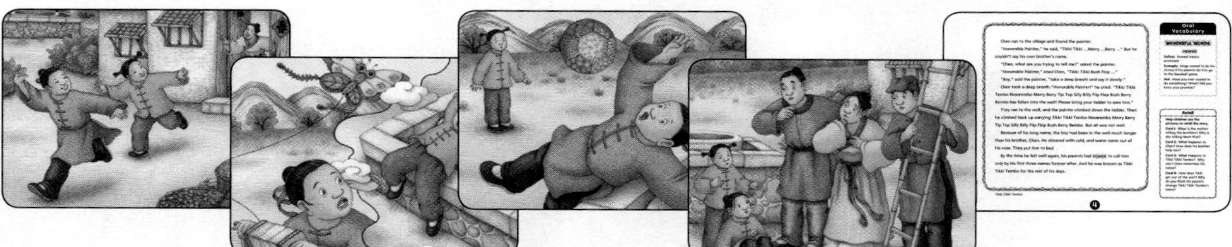

Oral Vocabulary Cards

Additional Vocabulary

To provide 15–20 minutes of additional vocabulary instruction, see **Oral Vocabulary Cards** 5-Day Plan. The pre- and post-tests for this week can be found on **Teacher's Resource Book** pages 245–263.

Vocabulary Routine

Use the routine below to discuss the meaning of each story word.

Define: When you give **advice**, you tell what you think someone should or should not do.
Example: *Sometimes I give my little brother advice about baseball.*
Ask: What advice do you get? What advice do you give? PRIOR KNOWLEDGE

- When I **hesitate**, I stop to think about what I will do. *The students did not hesitate when the alarm went off. They got out of the school.* When do you hesitate? When don't you hesitate? EXAMPLE
- Something that is **secure** is safe. *I made sure the ladder was secure before I climbed up.* Why is it important for a ladder to be secure? EXPLANATION
- If a person feels **panic**, he or she is very frightened or afraid. *Jim was in a panic when his dog was missing.* What might cause someone to be in a panic? EXAMPLE
- **Vowed** means "promised." *Jorge vowed to do his chores before going to play.* Have you ever vowed to do something? What? EXPLANATION

Use the routine to review last week's words: *accomplish*, *arduous*, *labor*, *rejoice*, and *succeed*.

Phonemic Awareness

Phoneme Segmentation

Model

Show children how to segment phonemes in words with diphthong /oi/.

Repeat the routine with the words *oil, toy, boil, coin, join*.

I am going to say a word sound by sound. Listen carefully to all the sounds in the word *boy*. The first sound is /b/. The second sound is /oi/ because the letters *o* and *y* together make the /oi/ sound. Now watch as I say each sound in the word *boy* again and hold up one finger for each sound: /b/ /oi/.

How many sounds does *boy* have? (2) Now say the word with me sound by sound: /b/ /oi/, *boy*.

Guided Practice/Practice

Have children practice with the examples provided. Do the first row with them.

Now I am going to say a word. I want you to say each sound in the word. Let me try first. The word is *soil*. *Soil*, /s/ /oi/ /l/. *Soil* has three sounds.

It's your turn. Listen carefully. How many sounds are in these words?

soy (2)	ploy (3)	coy (2)	noise (3)
point (4)	loin (3)	coil (3)	broil (4)

To extend, ask children to continue segmenting the phonemes in these additional words and tell how many sounds they have.

foil (3)	toil (3)	spoil (4)	groin (4)
joy (2)	hoist (4)	poise (3)	moist (4)

Objective

- Segment phonemes in words with diphthong /oi/

ELL

Minimal Contrasts Focus on articulation. Make the /oi/ sound and point out your mouth position. Have children repeat. Use the articulation photos on the small Sound-Spelling Cards. Repeat for the /ō/ sound. Have children say each sound together, noticing the slight differences in mouth position. Continue by having children read minimal contrast word pairs, such as *join/Joan, boil/bowl, toy/toe*.

Objectives

- Identify letter-sound correspondence for diphthong /oi/*oi*, *oy*
- Blend sounds in *oi*, *oy* words
- Review previously taught phonics skills

Materials

- Sound-Spelling Card: *Boy*
- Word-Building Cards; Teacher's Resource Book, p. 66
- Practice Book, p. 184

Skills Trace

Diphthong *oi*, *oy*	
Introduce	43C–D
Practice/ Apply	43F, 45G-H, 71F-G, 71I, 71T-U; Practice Book: 184; Decodable Reader: *Let's Join Joy's Show!*
Reteach/ Review	77C-D; 77K-N, 77Q, 77W, 77CC
Assess	Weekly Test; Unit 4 Test
Maintain	Build Fluency: Sound/Spellings

ELL

Pronunciation Most languages do not have diphthongs, so this sound may be difficult for some children. Provide practice in saying the diphthong alone and in simple words. Have children watch how lip position changes during pronunciation, and also point out and exaggerate how the tone falls from the first part of the sound to the second.

Sound Pronunciation

See **Sound Pronunciation CD** for a model of the /oi/ sound.

Phonics

Introduce Diphthong *oi*, *oy*

Model

Teach the sound /oi/ spelled *oi* or *oy*. Show the *Boy* **Sound-Spelling Card**.

This is the *Boy* Sound-Spelling Card. The sound is /oi/. The /oi/ sound can be spelled with the letters *oi* or *oy*. Say the sound with me: /oi/.

Model writing the letters several times.

Watch as I write the letters. I will say the sound /oi/ as I write *oi* and *oy*.

Guided Practice/Practice

Have children practice connecting the letters and sound through writing.

Now do it with me. Say /oi/ as I write the letters *oi*. (Repeat with the letters *oy*.)

This time, write *oi* and *oy* five times each as you say the sound /oi/.

Build Fluency: Sound/Spellings

kn ir wr

Display the following **Word-Building Cards:** *oi, oy, ou, ow, are, air, ear, ere, or, ore, oar, ar, gn, kn, wr, mb, eer, ere, ear, er, ir, ur*. Have children chorally say each sound. Repeat and vary the pace.

Blend Words with *oi*, *oy*

Model

Display Word-Building Cards *o*, *i*, *l*. Model how to blend the sounds as you run your finger under each letter.

These are the letters *o, i*. Together they stand for /oi/. This is the letter *l*. It stands for /l/. Listen as I blend these sounds together: /oil/, *oil*. Say it with me: *oil*.

Continue by modeling *foil*, *toys*, *boiling*, *boy*, *joyful*, and *soiled*.

Guided Practice/Practice

Write the words below on chart paper. Read each one in the first row, blending the sounds. For example, /j/ /oi/ /n/. The word is *join*. Have children blend the sounds in each word with you. Then use the appropriate blending level to complete the remaining lines chorally. See the **Sound-by-Sound Blending Routine** in the **Instructional Routine Handbook** for support. Save the chart paper for use in tomorrow's lesson.

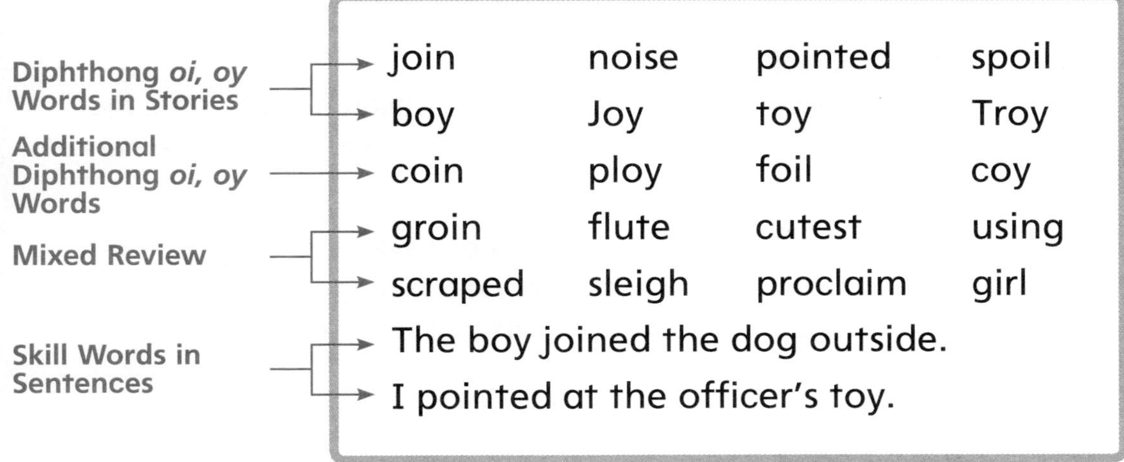

Diphthong *oi, oy* Words in Stories	join	noise	pointed	spoil
	boy	Joy	toy	Troy
Additional Diphthong *oi, oy* Words	coin	ploy	foil	coy
Mixed Review	groin	flute	cutest	using
	scraped	sleigh	proclaim	girl
Skill Words in Sentences	The boy joined the dog outside.			
	I pointed at the officer's toy.			

Corrective Feedback

Blending: Sound Error Model the sound that children missed, then have them repeat the sound. Say: *My turn.* Tap under the letters and say: *Sound? /oi/. What's the sound?* Then return to the beginning of the word. Say: *Let's start over.* Blend the sounds in the word with children again.

Quick Check

Can children blend sounds in words with diphthong *oi, oy*?

During **Small Group Instruction**

Tier 2

If No → **Approaching Level** Repeat blending using the chart above. Explicitly correct the error and provide more "with me" type practice. Use a lower level of blending to provide support.

If Yes → **On Level** Consolidate the learning by having children read additional words with diphthong *oi, oy*. See page 77M.

Beyond Level Extend the learning by having children read harder words containing diphthong *oi, oy*. See page 77N.

Daily Handwriting

Teach children how to form the uppercase letters *L, D, B,* and *R*. See **Handwriting** pages 54–55 and 104–112 for daily practice and additional information on ball-and-stick or slant models.

ON YOUR OWN **Practice Book**, page 184

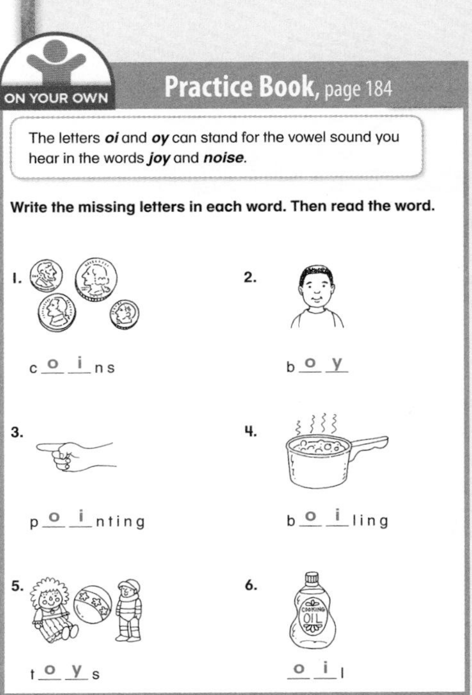

The letters *oi* and *oy* can stand for the vowel sound you hear in the words *joy* and *noise*.

Write the missing letters in each word. Then read the word.

1. c o i ns
2. b o y
3. p o i nting
4. b o i ling
5. t o y s
6. o i l

Approaching Reproducible, page 184

Beyond Reproducible, page 184

Objectives

- Spell words with diphthong *oi, oy*
- Identify spelling patterns
- Spell high-frequency words

Materials

- WorkBoards; Teacher's Resource Book, p. 143
- Phonics/Spelling Practice Book, p. 65

5-Day Spelling	
DAY 1	Dictation; Pretest
DAY 2	Teacher-Modeled Word Sort
DAY 3	Student Word Sort
DAY 4	Test Practice
DAY 5	Posttest

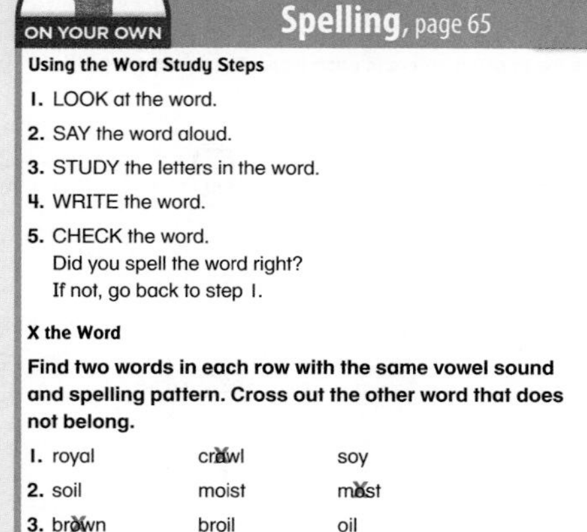

ON YOUR OWN **Spelling**, page 65

Using the Word Study Steps

1. LOOK at the word.
2. SAY the word aloud.
3. STUDY the letters in the word.
4. WRITE the word.
5. CHECK the word.
   Did you spell the word right?
   If not, go back to step 1.

X the Word

Find two words in each row with the same vowel sound and spelling pattern. Cross out the other word that does not belong.

1. royal	crawl	soy
2. soil	moist	moist
3. brown	broil	oil
4. joy	job	toy
5. boil	point	point

Phonics/Spelling

Words with *oi, oy*

DICTATION

Use dictation to help children transfer their growing knowledge of sound-spellings to writing. Follow the **Dictation Routine** below with each spelling word.

DICTATION ROUTINE

- Pronounce one word at a time. Have children clearly state the word. Then repeat the word for children and use it in a sentence.
- Ask children to orally segment the word to think about the individual sounds in the word. Then have them write the word. Prompt children to use the **Sound-Spelling Card** spellings as they write. Provide **WorkBoards** for those who need support.

PRETEST

Pronounce each spelling word. Read the sentence and pronounce the word again. Ask children to say each word softly, stretching the sounds, before writing it. After the pretest, write each word on the board as you say the letter names. Have children check their words.

Spelling Words

Approaching	On Level	Beyond
soil	soil	soil
boil	broil	broiling
choice	moist	moist
point	point	annoyed
broil	boil	coil
oil	oil	choices
toy	toy	foil
joy	joy	coy
soy	avoid	avoid
noise	royal	royal
brown	crown	crown
house	house	crowds
above	above	above
color	color	color
song	song	song

1. **soil:** I will plant seeds in the soil.
2. **broil:** Dad will broil fish for dinner.
3. **moist:** My towel is still moist.
4. **point:** I broke the point on my pencil.
5. **boil:** Ed will boil water to cook pasta.
6. **oil:** The oil in the pan is hot.
7. **toy:** My favorite toy is a puppet.
8. **joy:** I was full of joy with the new baby.
9. **avoid:** Avoid junk food when you can.
10. **royal:** The royal family lives in a castle.
11. **crown:** The prince puts on his crown.
12. **house:** Our house is painted blue.
13. **above:** Look at the bird above you.
14. **color:** My favorite color is green.
15. **song:** That is a lively song.

Decodable Reader

- **Review High-Frequency Words** Write **family**, **four**, and **hear** on the board. Review the words with children using the **Read/Spell/Write** routine.

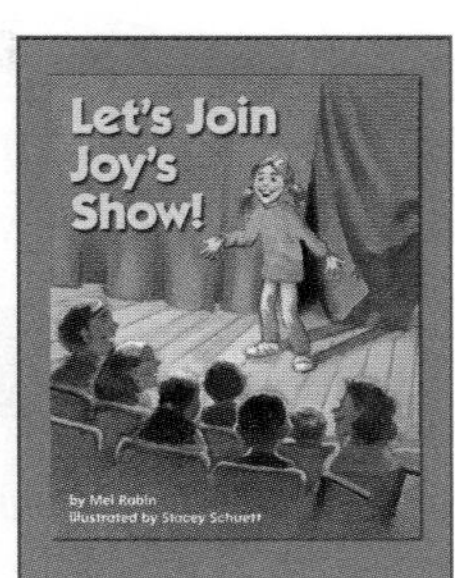

Let's Join Joy's Show!

- **Preview and Predict** Point to the book's title and have children sound out each word as you run your finger under it. Then ask:
  - *Where are the people?*
  - *What kind of show do you think Joy will have?*
  - *Does Joy look happy? How do you know?*
- **First Read** Turn to page 8. Have children point to each word, sounding out decodable words and saying the high-frequency words quickly. Children should chorally read the story the first time through. If children have difficulty, provide corrective feedback page by page as needed. See the **Decodable Text Routine** in the **Instructional Routine Handbook** for correction models.
- **Check Comprehension** Ask the following:
  - *What can Joy do best?*
  - *What idea did Joy have?*
  - *What happened the day of the show?*
  - PARTNERS *Turn to a partner and retell the story.*
- **Second Read** Reread the story with children.
  - **Approaching Level** If children struggle sounding out words, provide "with you" blending models. Then review blending using the words on the Word List at the end of the book during Small Group time. Conclude by guiding children through a rereading of the book.
  - **Beyond Level** If children can sound out the words, have them quietly read the text with a partner.

Objectives

- Decode words with *oi* and *oy* in connected text
- Identify and read high-frequency words
- Review last week's high-frequency words *family*, *four*, and *hear*

Materials

- Decodable Reader Library: *Let's Join Joy's Show!*

High-Frequency Words

Use the **Read/Spell/Write** routine to teach each high-frequency word.

- **Read** Read the word. Have children chorally repeat.
- **Spell** Chorally spell the word.
- **Write** Have children write the word as they spell it aloud. Then ask children to write a sentence using each word.

SMALL GROUP OPTION

You may wish to read the Decodable Reader during **Small Group** time.

See pages 77K–77JJ

Objectives

- Learn the meanings of vocabulary words
- Use context clues to identify and use synonyms
- Review last week's vocabulary words

Materials

- Student Book: "Safety at School"
- Practice Book, p. 185

Vocabulary	
accident	attention
buddy	enormous
obeys	tip

ELL

Preteach Vocabulary
See page 119P to preteach the vocabulary words to ELL and Approaching Level children. Use the **Visual Vocabulary Resources** to demonstrate and discuss each word.

Vocabulary

TEACH WORDS
Introduce each word using the **Define/Example/Ask** routine. Model reading each word.

Vocabulary Routine

Use the routine below to discuss the meaning of each word.

Define: An **accident** happens by chance. People can get hurt in accidents.
Example: *I had an accident when I tripped and fell.*
Ask: Tell how an accident could happen. EXPLANATION

- When you pay **attention**, you watch and listen carefully. *It is important to pay attention when riding a bike.* How can you pay attention in class? DESCRIPTION
- A **buddy** is a good friend. *I walk to school every day with my buddy Sam.* What is another word for *buddy*? SYNONYM
- Something **enormous** is very, very big. *My dog is so enormous.* What word means the opposite of *enormous*? ANTONYM
- When someone **obeys** someone or something, he or she does what he or she is told. *My mother obeys the doctor's orders.* Tell about when the class obeys the teacher. PRIOR KNOWLEDGE
- Pieces of advice someone gives you are **tips**. *The coach gives tips on catching the ball.* Name tips for staying safe in the kitchen. EXAMPLE
- **Word Wall** Add these words to your Word Wall. Remove words from the wall as children master them.

Use the vocabulary routine to review last week's words: *attached, delicious, frantically, gasped,* and *swung*.

STRATEGY Use Context Clues: Synonyms

- Explain that context clues are hints that suggest the meaning of an unfamiliar word. Synonyms are one kind of context clue. They are words that have almost the same meanings. Tell children to try to identify synonyms near unfamiliar words.
- Have children find the word **enormous** in "Safety at School" on page 45 and read the sentence with the word.

Think Aloud I'm not sure what *enormous* means. I see that the sentence following it has the words "so huge." This tells me that *huge* is a synonym for *enormous*. I know that *huge* means "very big," so now I know *enormous* means "very big," too.

Vocabulary

attention
buddy
accident
tip
enormous
obeys

Context Clues
Synonyms are words that have almost the same meaning.
Enormous and *huge* are synonyms.

SAFETY AT SCHOOL

by Brian Sullivan

"We need to talk about the school rules," our teacher, Mr. Wall, said. It was the second day of school. "What do you do when I turn out the lights?"

"Pay **attention** and listen carefully to you," said Pete.

"Good," said Mr. Wall. "What about lining up?"

"Find your line **buddy** and stand in line at the door," said Rosa.

"Right!" said Mr. Wall. "Remember, your line buddy is the friend you line up with. What is another rule, Julia?"

"No running in the halls," Julia said. "No one wants to fall or slip and have an **accident**."

"Good **tip**," said Mr. Wall. "That's helpful information to keep in mind. Also, why should we stay together in the halls?"

"This school is **enormous**. It's so huge it would be easy to get lost," said Liam.

"I know you all will follow the rules," said Mr. Wall. "When everyone **obeys** them, we stay safe."

Reread for **Comprehension**

Read Ahead
Use Illustrations Reading ahead and using illustrations can help you understand story events and give you some ideas about what might happen next. Use the chart to understand what the illustrations tell you about this story.

Illustration	What I Learn From the Picture

Comprehension www.macmillanmh.com

Read "Safety at School"

Read "Safety at School" with children. Stop at each **highlighted** word. Ask children to identify text clues to reveal the meanings of the highlighted words. Model asking relevant questions to seek clarification and check overall comprehension of the passage. Review the meanings of the words to confirm understanding. Tell children that they will read these words again in *Officer Buckle and Gloria*.

Quick Check

Do children understand word meanings?

During **Small Group Instruction**

If No → **Approaching Level** Vocabulary pages: 77L, 77R, 77X, 77DD.

If Yes → **On Level** Reread Vocabulary Selection.

Beyond Level Reread Vocabulary Selection.

ON YOUR OWN

Practice Book, page 185

A. Read the passage. Use what you know about the other words in the story to choose a word from the box that makes the most sense in the blank. Write it on the line.

tips obeys accident buddy enormous attention

Our class took a field trip to the zoo. I couldn't believe how big the zoo was. It was enormous! Each of us had to hold hands with a buddy. We paid attention to our teacher. He told us the rules. He said, "A good student obeys the rules. Following rules can keep you from having an accident. I don't want you to get hurt or lost." Our teacher also gave us good ideas about what to look for at the zoo. His tips helped us have a good time.

B. Use two vocabulary words to write two new sentences.
Possible responses provided

1. My buddy is coming to my party.
2. I couldn't finish the enormous dish of ice cream.

Approaching Reproducible, page 185
Beyond Reproducible, page 185

Objectives

- Monitor comprehension and make corrections by reading ahead
- Use illustrations to describe characters
- Use academic language: *comprehension, illustrations*

Materials

- Transparencies 17a, 17b, 5
- Student Book: "Safety at School," pp. 44–45

Skills Trace

Use Illustrations	
Introduce	U4: 45A–B
Practice/ Apply	U4: 45K–71A; Practice Book: 187–188
Reteach/ Review	U4: 77G, 77R–T, 77X–Z
Assess	Weekly Test; Unit 4 Test
Maintain	U4: 115N

ELL

Academic Language
Preteach the following academic language words to ELL and Approaching Level children during Small Group time: *comprehension, illustrations*. See page 119O.

Comprehension

STRATEGY Monitor Comprehension: Read Ahead

EXPLAIN

What Is It? You **monitor comprehension** when you stop and check to see if you understand what you are reading. If you do not, you can make a correction by **reading ahead**. By doing this you can try to find out more information about the text or answer a question you have about it. Reading ahead can include looking at the illustrations.

Why Is It Important? Reading ahead in the text can help you understand something that might be confusing. When you know what might happen later in the story, it can help you understand what is currently taking place and make an appropriate adjustment.

SKILL Use Illustrations

EXPLAIN

What Is It? An **illustration** is a picture in a selection. Illustrations tell you about characters and story events, too. If you don't understand something in the text, you can monitor your comprehension by looking for clues in an illustration.

Why Is It Important? When you can see what is taking place in the pictures of a story, you can better understand the text. Illustrations can also help you to visualize and describe the characters in a story.

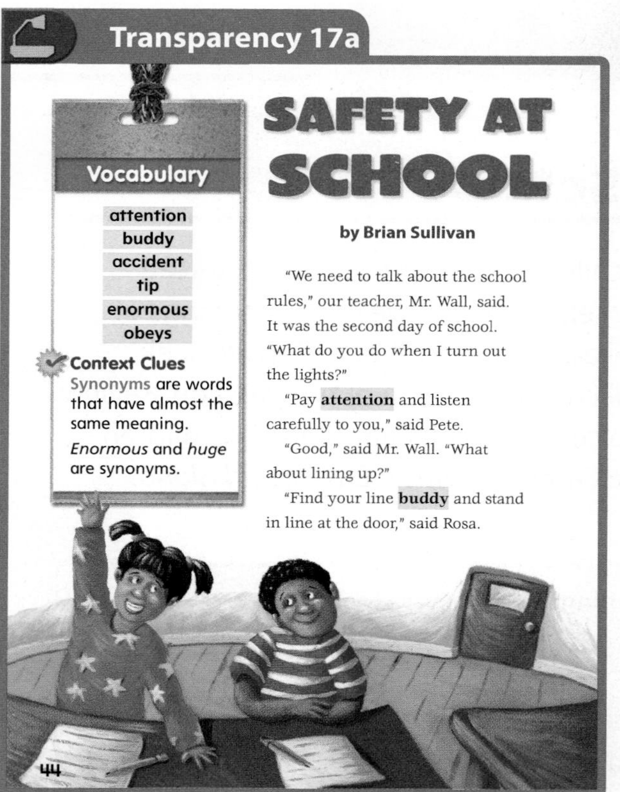

Transparency 17a

Vocabulary
attention
buddy
accident
tip
enormous
obeys

Context Clues
Synonyms are words that have almost the same meaning.
Enormous and *huge* are synonyms.

SAFETY AT SCHOOL

by Brian Sullivan

"We need to talk about the school rules," our teacher, Mr. Wall, said. It was the second day of school. "What do you do when I turn out the lights?"

"Pay **attention** and listen carefully to you," said Pete.

"Good," said Mr. Wall. "What about lining up?"

"Find your line **buddy** and stand in line at the door," said Rosa.

44

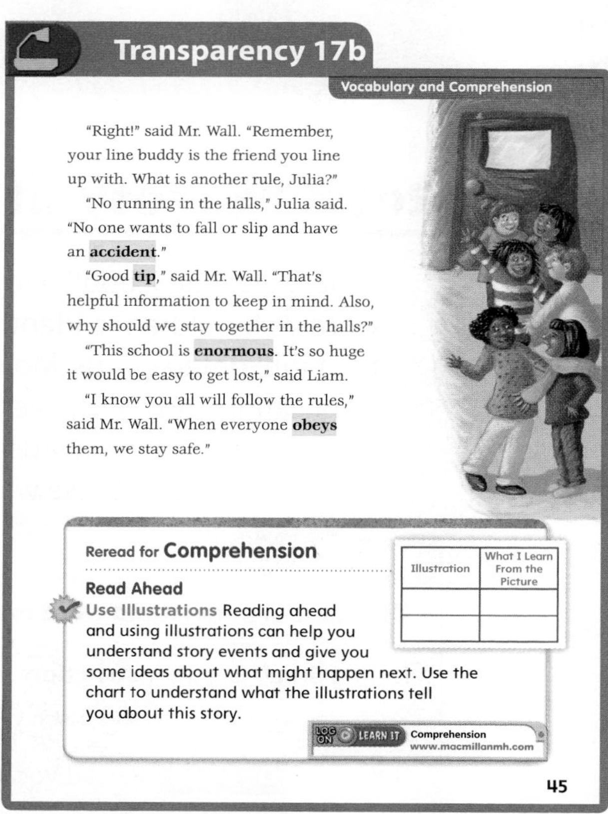

Transparency 17b

Vocabulary and Comprehension

"Right!" said Mr. Wall. "Remember, your line buddy is the friend you line up with. What is another rule, Julia?"

"No running in the halls," Julia said. "No one wants to fall or slip and have an **accident**."

"Good **tip**," said Mr. Wall. "That's helpful information to keep in mind. Also, why should we stay together in the halls?"

"This school is **enormous**. It's so huge it would be easy to get lost," said Liam.

"I know you all will follow the rules," said Mr. Wall. "When everyone **obeys** them, we stay safe."

Reread for Comprehension

Read Ahead
Use Illustrations Reading ahead and using illustrations can help you understand story events and give you some ideas about what might happen next. Use the chart to understand what the illustrations tell you about this story.

Illustration	What I Learn From the Picture

LOG ON LEARN IT Comprehension www.macmillanmh.com

45

Student Book pages 44–45 are available on Comprehension Transparencies 17a and 17b.

MODEL

How Do I Use It? Read the first paragraph of "Safety at School" on **Student Book** page 44.

Think Aloud I know from the title that this story is about safety at school. But after reading the first paragraph, I'm not sure why the teacher, Mr. Wall, needs to talk about school rules. So I will make an adjustment and read ahead for clues. Sometimes the author of a story says directly what is going on or how a character feels. Then I can find the answer in the text. But sometimes that information is found in the pictures. As I read, I will also look at the illustrations for clues about the story's events, settings, and characters. I will use the illustrations to find out more about the characters' traits, motivations, and feelings.

- Display the Illustrations Chart on **Transparency 5**. For Illustration, write: *children raising their hands.*
- Ask children: *What does this picture show about the characters? What do you think these children are doing?* Have children read the first page to confirm their answers. Write in the second column of the chart: *The children are having a class discussion about safety rules.*

Transparency 5

Illustration	What I Learn From the Picture
children raising their hands	The children are having a class discussion about safety rules.
children standing in a straight line	Lining up means standing in a straight line.

Graphic Organizer Transparency

GUIDED PRACTICE

Have children read the third paragraph on page 44 and look closely at the illustration on page 45. Then fill in the first column to describe the picture. *Does the picture tell you what* lining up *means?* Ask children to explain the meaning and fill in the chart. Then discuss Mr. Wall's character traits and motivation.

PRACTICE

Have children reread the remainder of "Safety at School." Add to the Illustrations Chart by asking children to look at the illustrations to help figure out what a "line buddy" is. Then discuss Mr. Wall's character traits and motivation. Ask: *What words would you use to describe Mr. Wall? Why does he want his class to know the school rules?*

After they have completed their charts, ask children to share what they have learned from the illustrations in the selection and to retell the story to a partner.

DAY 1
WHOLE GROUP

Objectives

- Identify helping verbs
- Use subject-verb agreement in sentences

Materials

- Transparency 81
- Grammar Practice Book, p. 81

5-Day Grammar	
Helping Verbs	
DAY 1	*Have* as a Helping Verb
DAY 2	*Be* as a Helping Verb
DAY 3	Mechanics: Quotation Marks
DAY 4	Helping Verbs Proofread
DAY 5	Review and Assess Quotation Marks Helping Verbs

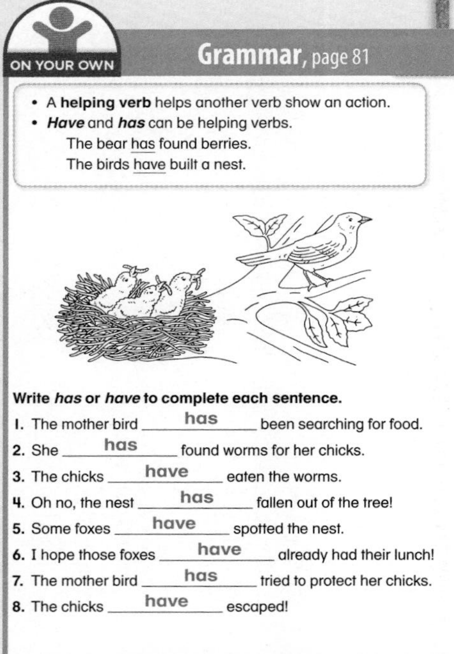

ON YOUR OWN **Grammar**, page 81

- A **helping verb** helps another verb show an action.
- ***Have*** and ***has*** can be helping verbs.
  The bear has found berries.
  The birds have built a nest.

Write *has* or *have* to complete each sentence.

1. The mother bird ___has___ been searching for food.
2. She ___has___ found worms for her chicks.
3. The chicks ___have___ eaten the worms.
4. Oh no, the nest ___has___ fallen out of the tree!
5. Some foxes ___have___ spotted the nest.
6. I hope those foxes ___have___ already had their lunch!
7. The mother bird ___has___ tried to protect her chicks.
8. The chicks ___have___ escaped!

Grammar

Have as a Helping Verb

EXPLAIN/MODEL

- Tell children that a **helping verb** helps another verb to show an action. *Have* and *has* are helping verbs that tell about actions that have already happened. Use *has* when the subject is singular (e.g., My mom has given her a lot of help.) and *have* when the subject is plural or *I* or *you* (e.g., I have given her two dollars.).

Write the following sentences on the board and read them aloud: *He has walked to the library. They have taken a bus to the library.* Point out that in the first sentence the word *has* is a helping verb that tells that the word *walked* happened in the past and is used with the subject *he*, which is singular. Then note that in the second sentence the word *have* is the helping verb and is used because the subject *they* is plural.

Use item 1 on **Grammar Transparency 81** to model how to use helping verbs *has* or *have* with other verbs. Identify the other verb.

Transparency 81

Helping Verbs

1. Anna ________ (packed) four boxes of books for the library sale.
   has
2. She and her mother ________ (tried) to pick them up.
   have
3. They ________ (asked) us to help.
   have
4. We ________ (decided) to use smaller boxes.
   have
5. This ________ (saved) us from getting hurt.
   has

Grammar Transparency

GUIDED PRACTICE/PRACTICE

Guide practice with item 2. Have children complete the remaining sentences with *has* or *have* and then circle the other verbs.

Writing

Expository: Persuasive Essay

DISCUSS THE MODEL

- Explain to children that an **essay** is a first-person expression of a writer's opinion. A writer can write a persuasive essay to persuade readers to act in a certain way or to agree with the writer's point of view about a particular topic.

Present and discuss the features of an essay using the model and callouts on **Writing Transparency 97**.

Transparency 97

Cross the Street Safely

It's important to stay safe when walking. Crossing at crosswalks is one way I stay safe. Crosswalks tell drivers to slow down for people.	*The writer states an opinion.* *Reasons support the opinion.*
I look both ways before crossing, even at crosswalks. Last Tuesday, I walked without looking. A car came around a corner. It had to stop really fast at the crosswalk. Cross safely! Cross at crosswalks! Look both ways!	*The writer uses first-person pronouns.* *The writer asks readers to agree and act.*

Writing Transparency

FOCUS AND PLAN

Identify Purpose and Audience The purpose of a persuasive essay is to convince readers that they should do or believe something. The audience may be your classmates, family members, or anyone you want to act or think in a certain way.

Develop a Topic This week you will write a persuasive essay about safety in your school or community. (See **Student Book** page 76.) In your Writer's Notebook, list some possible topics for your essay. Think about things your friends and family members can do to stay safe.

Teacher Think Aloud When you brainstorm, think about specific actions that people can take to stay safe. What should children do to stay safe on the playground? How can people stay safe when crossing the street? What can your town do to keep all its residents safe?

Objectives

- Introduce the features of an essay
- Brainstorm ideas for a persuasive essay
- Write persuasively about safety

Materials

- Transparency 97

5-Day Writing

Essay	
DAY 1	Focus and Plan
DAY 2	Prewrite
DAY 3	Skill: A Strong Opening; Draft
DAY 4	Revise; Edit/Proofread
DAY 5	Publish and Present

ELL

Explain Work with children to brainstorm topics. Then have children choose the same topic. Discuss why the topic is important and ways that people keep safe. Restate childrens' responses as needed and write their ideas on the board for them to copy into their Writer's Notebook.

Day 2 At a Glance

WHOLE GROUP

Oral Language
- Build Robust Vocabulary

Phonemic Awareness
- Phoneme Blending

Phonics
- Diphthong *oi*, *oy*
- Build Fluency
- Reread *Let's Join Joy's Show!*
- Spelling: Sort Words with *oi*, *oy*

Vocabulary
- Review Words in Context

Comprehension
- Read *Officer Buckle and Gloria*
- Strategy: Monitor Comprehension: Read Ahead
- Skill: Use Illustrations

Language Arts
- Grammar: Helping Verbs
- Writing: Expository

SMALL GROUP

- Differentiated Instruction, pages 77K–77JJ

Oral Language

Build Robust Vocabulary

Reread the **Oral Vocabulary Cards** to review this week's oral vocabulary words. Ask and model clarifying questions to check children's comprehension of the myth. *What advice does Tikki and Chen's mother give them every time they go outside? Why does Tikki not hesitate to run to his mother? Why does Chen panic? What if the ladder they used was not secure? What had Tikki's parents vowed to do forever?*

Oral Vocabulary Cards

REVIEW WORDS

Ask the probing questions below to generate discussion and use of the words in oral speech.

- If your bike is **secure**, is it safely locked up or left on the grass?
- Who gives better **advice**, your friends or your parents? Why?
- What is something you **hesitate** trying to do? Why?
- Explain which would cause you to **panic**, seeing a grizzly bear or a mouse.
- What is something you have **vowed** to do better? How will you do that?

- Review last week's words, *accomplish*, *arduous*, *labor*, *rejoice*, and *succeed*, using similar questions.

Write About It

Tell which safety rule you think is most important when working on a team with an animal. Tell why. You may wish to add this sample to your Writing Portfolio.

Phonemic Awareness

Phoneme Blending

Model

Place markers in the **WorkBoard** to show children how to orally blend phonemes.

Repeat using the words *oil*, *boy*, *foil*, and *join*.

I am going to put one marker in each box as I say each sound. Then I will blend the sounds to form a word.

Listen and watch. /k/ (Place marker in the first box.) /oi/ (Place marker in the second box.) /n/ (Place marker in the third box.)

This word has three sounds: /k/ /oi/ /n/. Listen as I blend the sounds to form the word: /koin/. The word is *coin*.

Guided Practice/Practice

Help children practice blending. Distribute copies of Sound Boxes. Do the first six words together.

Let's do some together. Place a marker for each sound you hear. I will say one sound at a time. Then we will blend the sounds to say the word.

/s/ /oi/ /l/   /k/ /oi/   /j/ /oi/
/p/ /oi/ /z/   /h/ /oi/ /s/ /t/   /p/ /l/ /oi/

Now it's your turn. Listen carefully.

/m/ /oi/ /s/ /t/   /p/ /oi/ /n/ /t/   /s/ /oi/
/b/ /r/ /oi/ /l/   /t/ /oi/   /b/ /oi/ /l/

Objectives

- Blend phonemes in words with diphthong /oi/
- Review myth

Materials

- Sound-Spelling WorkBoard; Teacher's Resource Book, p. 143
- markers
- Practice Book for myth, p. 186

Objectives

- Blend and build words with diphthong *oi* and *oy*
- Review previously taught phonics skills
- Read multisyllabic words

Materials

- Word-Building Cards; Teacher's Resource Book, p. 66
- pocket chart
- word chart from Day 1
- Decodable Reader Library: *Let's Join Joy's Show!*

Skills Trace

Diphthong *oi, oy*	
Introduce	43C–D
Practice/ Apply	43F, 45G-H, 71F-G, 71I, 71T-U; Practice Book: 184; Decodable Reader: *Let's Join Joy's Show!*
Reteach/ Review	77C-D; 77K-N, 77Q, 77W, 77CC
Assess	Weekly Test; Unit 4 Test
Maintain	Build Fluency: Sound/Spellings

Phonics

Build Fluency: Sound/Spellings

Display the following **Word-Building Cards** one at a time: *oi, oy, ou, ow, are, air, ear, ere, or, ore, oar, ar, gn, kn, wr, mb, eer, ere, ear, er, ir, ur*. Have children chorally say each sound. Repeat and vary the pace. Children should work to say each sound within a two-second pause.

Blend Words with *oi, oy*

Model

Place Word-Building Cards *b, o, i*, and *l* in the pocket chart to form *boil*. Model how to generate and blend the sounds to say the word.

Repeat with *ploy*.

The letter *b* stands for /b/. The letters *o* and *i* stand for /oi/. The letter *l* stands for /l/. Now listen as I blend all three sounds: /boil/. Now you say it. Let's read the word together: *boil*.

Guided Practice/Practice

Repeat with additional words. Have children blend the sounds in words with you.

join	oink	broil	cloy
moist	coin	joy	oil
voices	choice	spoil	avoid

Build Words with *oi, oy*

Model

Place **Word-Building Cards** *j, o, y* in the pocket chart. Blend the phonemes. Let's blend all the sounds together and read the word: /joi/, *joy*.

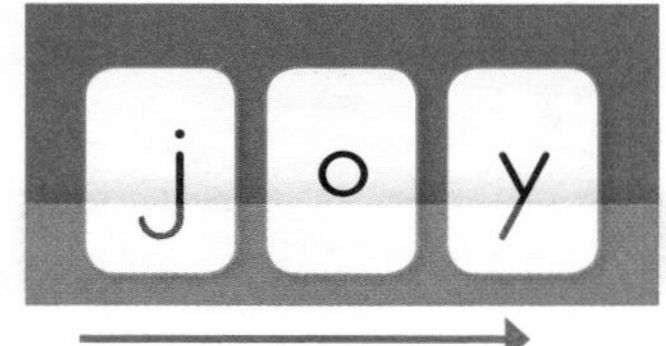

Change *j* to *b* and repeat with *boy*. Let's blend all the sounds together and read the word: /boi/, *boy*.

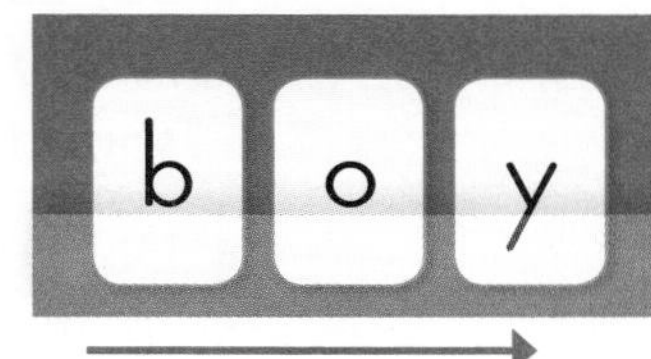

Change *b* to *s* and repeat with *soy*. Let's blend all the sounds together and read the word: /soi/, *soy*.

Guided Practice/Practice

Use these word sets for more building practice.

oil, coil, coin, join, joins, joint, jointed

broil, boil, point, poise, noise, noises

Build Fluency: Word Automaticity

Display the word chart from Day 1. Point to each word as children chorally read it. Aim for one word every two seconds. Model blending sounds in words children miss. Then point to words in random order at varying speeds for children to read.

join	noise	pointed	spoil
boy	Joy	toy	Troy
coin	ploy	foil	coy
groin	flute	cutest	using
scraped	sleigh	proclaim	girl

The boy joined the dog outside.
I pointed at the officer's toy.

Build Fluency: Connected Text

Have children independently reread *Let's Join Joy's Show!* from the **Decodable Reader Library**. Circulate and listen in, providing corrective feedback as needed.

- **Approaching Level** Have children read with a more skilled partner or listen to the text on **Audio CD** and read with the narrator.
- **Beyond Level** While the other children are reading, teach the Accelerate Pacing lesson.

Let's Join Joy's Show!

Transition to Multisyllabic Words

Accelerate Pacing: Vowel Team Syllables

- Remind childen that a syllable has one vowel sound.
- Explain that many vowel sounds are spelled with vowel digraphs; the letters of the vowel digraph, or vowel team, appear in the same syllable.
- The vowels *oi* and *oy* act as a team to stand for the sound /oi/.
- Write these words on the board: *appoint*, *employ*, *exploit*, *viewpoint*, *spoilage*, *poison*, and *turmoil*. Ask children to listen for the vowel sound /oi/ as you say each word.
- Have children draw lines to divide the words into syllables and then underline each /oi/ spelling.

ELL

Build Vocabulary Review the meanings of words on your word chart that can be demonstrated or explained in a concrete way. For example, ask children to *point* to a *boy*, something that makes *noise*, and so on. Model the action for *join*, saying, "I will join the rest of the class," and have children repeat. Provide sentence starters for children to complete, such as *One of my favorite* toys *is* ______.

Objectives

- Spell and sort words with diphthong *oi, oy*
- Build Fluency: Word Automaticity
- Read and identify high-frequency words

Materials

- large index cards with spelling words
- pocket chart
- Phonics/Spelling Practice Book, p. 66

5-Day Spelling	
DAY 1	Dictation; Pretest
DAY 2	Teacher-Modeled Word Sort
DAY 3	Student Word Sort
DAY 4	Test Practice
DAY 5	Posttest

ON YOUR OWN **Spelling,** page 66

boil moist joy toy point
broil soil avoid royal oil

A. Word Sort

Look at the spelling words in the box. Write the spelling words that have the *oi* pattern.

1. boil 2. moist 3. broil
4. soil 5. oil 6. point
7. avoid

Write the spelling words that have the *oy* pattern.

8. joy 9. toy 10. royal

B. Missing Letter

A letter is missing from each spelling word below. Write the missing letter in the box. Then write the spelling word correctly on the line.

11. brol [i] broil
12. roal [y] royal
13. moit [s] moist
14. pont [i] point
15. sil [o] soil

Phonics/Spelling

Word Sort with *oi, oy*

- Display the pocket chart. Place index cards with the key word cards *coin* and *loyal* to form two columns in the pocket chart.
- Say each key word and pronounce the sounds: /k/ /oi/ /n/; /l/ /oi/ /ə/ /l/. Pronounce each word again, emphasizing the /oi/ sound. Ask children to chorally spell each word.
- Hold up the word card *soil*. Pronounce each sound clearly: /s/ /oi/ /l/. Blend the sounds, /soil/. Repeat with each *oi* and *oy* word. Place words below the correct key word labels so there is one example of each. Have children read each word, listening for the /oi/ sound. Ask children to chorally spell each word.

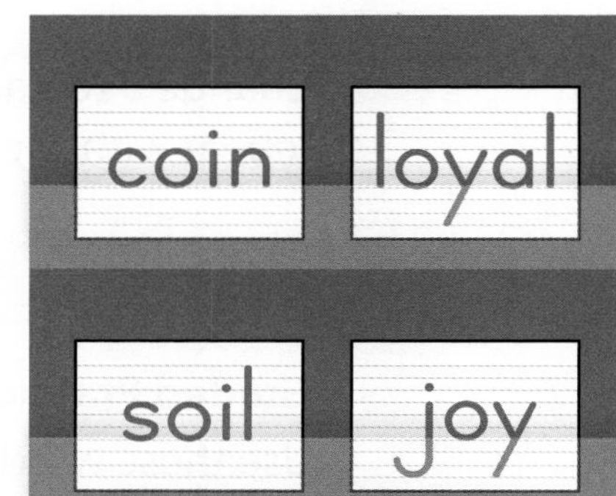

- Have children place remaining cards under the correct key label.
- **Build Fluency: Word Automaticity** Have children chorally read the words several times for fluency.

Analyze Errors — Articulation Support

- Use children's pretest errors to analyze spelling problems and provide corrective feedback. For example, the /oi/ and /ō/ sounds are formed in similar ways. Some children will substitute the letter *o* for the letters *oi* or *oy*.
- Have these children say /oi/, paying attention to how it feels in the mouth. Use hand mirrors, if available. Then have children make the /ō/ sound, noting how the face position changes slightly. Go back and forth between /oi/ and /ō/ to help them feel the difference.
- Then have children orally segment one of the spelling words. When children get to the /oi/ sound, ask: *How does your mouth feel? What letters do we write for that sound?*

Vocabulary

Words in Context

REVIEW

Review the vocabulary words. Display **Transparency 33**. Model how to use word meanings and context clues to fill in the first word.

Think Aloud In the first paragraph, I see the sentence *Our teacher talks about staying safe.* This tells me that the missing word has to do with sharing advice about safety. The missing word is **tips** because tips are pieces of advice someone gives you.

Transparency 33

accident obeys attention enormous buddy tips

Our teacher talks about staying safe. She gives us some (1) tips so no one will get hurt on the playground. The first rule is: One child at a time on the slide.

On the playground, everyone (2) obeys the tips we learned. We take turns one at a time on the slide. When we use the swings, we pay (3) attention so we don't bump people. We watch out for our (4) buddy, and never leave the playground without this friend.

Still, Nat has an (5) accident. He falls down and cuts his knees. No one does anything wrong. The accident just happens. The nurse cleans the cut. She gives Nat an (6) enormous sticker that is the size of a big book.

Vocabulary Transparency

GUIDED PRACTICE/PRACTICE

- Help children with the next word. Then have them use context clues to write missing words 3–6. Ask partners to check each other's answers and to identify context clues they used to fill in the words.
- Have children write sentences using the vocabulary words in their Writer's Notebooks during independent work time.

Review last week's words *gasped*, *attached*, *frantically*, *swung*, and *delicious* in context.

Objectives

- Apply knowledge of word meanings and context clues
- Review last week's vocabulary words

Materials

- Transparency 33

Objectives

- Monitor comprehension by reading ahead
- Use illustrations to describe character, setting, and plot
- Use a graphic organizer
- Use academic language: *illustrations, fiction*

Materials

- Student Book: *Officer Buckle and Gloria*, pp. 46–69
- Practice Book, p. 187

Skills Trace

Use Illustrations	
Introduce	U4: 45A–B
Practice/ Apply	U4: 45K–71A; Practice Book: 187–188
Reteach/ Review	U4: 77G, 77R–T, 77X–Z
Assess	Weekly Test; Unit 4 Test
Maintain	U4: 115N

Story Words

Children may find these words difficult. Provide child-friendly definitions.

police (p. 50): people who make sure laws and rules are followed

department (p. 50): a group or section of an organization or company

Digital Learning

Story available on **Listening Library Audio CD** and **StudentWorks Plus**, the Interactive eBook.

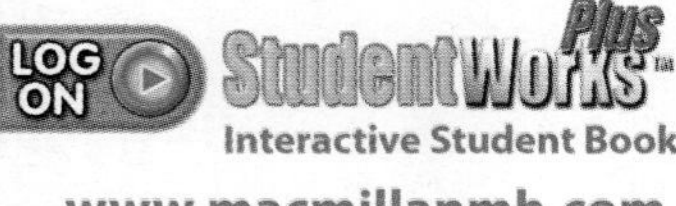

www.macmillanmh.com

Comprehension

STRATEGY Monitor Comprehension: Read Ahead

Main Selection

Remind children that when they **monitor** their **comprehension** they check to make sure that they understand what they are reading. **Reading ahead** in a story, including looking ahead at illustrations, is one way to make a correction if they don't. Point out that these strategies can give them more information about a character or plot event. *As you read, pay special attention to any parts that do not make sense. When this happens, you can make an adjustment to your reading. Look ahead at the illustrations, or read ahead to see if any information will help you understand what is taking place on the page you're reading.*

SKILL Use Illustrations

Review with children that **using illustrations** means looking at the pictures for clues to better understand what is going on in the story. *As we read, pay attention to how the pictures help you understand the characters' traits, motivations, and feelings and where the events in the story are taking place.*

Prepare to Read

PREVIEW AND PREDICT

- Ask children to preview the title and illustrations to find ideas to make predictions about *Officer Buckle and Gloria. What does the story seem to be about? What kinds of pictures does the story have?* Have children write their predictions in their Writer's Notebooks.
- **Genre** Read the definition of fiction on **Student Book** page 46. Share these features: tells about made-up characters and events; has illustrations that show the characters and events.

SET A PURPOSE FOR READING

- **Focus Question** Discuss the "Read to Find Out" question on Student Book page 46. Remind children to look for the answer as they read.
- Point out the Illustration Chart in the Student Book and have children turn to the chart on Practice Book page 187. Tell children they will use the chart to record information from illustrations.

Comprehension

Genre
Fiction is a story with made-up characters and events.

Read Ahead
Use Illustrations
As you read and look at the pictures, use the Illustrations Chart.

Illustration	What I Learn From the Picture

Read to Find Out
How do the illustrations help make the story funny?

46

Main Selection

written and illustrated
by Peggy Rathmann

47

Read Main Selection

PURPOSE FOR READING Ask children to read aloud the "Read to Find Out" question. Remind them to pay attention to the illustrations and how they help make the story funny.

PARTNERS **Preteach**	**Read Together**
Have Approaching Level children in English Language Learners listen to the story on **StudentWorks Plus**, the Interactive eBook before reading with the class.	Use the prompts to guide comprehension and model how to complete the graphic organizer. Have children use **Think/Pair/Share** as they respond to the prompts.

LOG ON StudentWorks Plus Interactive Student Book

ON YOUR OWN **Practice Book**, page 187

As you read *Officer Buckle and Gloria*, fill in the Illustrations Chart.

Illustration	What I Learn

How does the information you wrote in this Illustrations Chart help you to better understand the characters in feelings of the *Officer Buckle and Gloria*?

Approaching Reproducible, page 187
Beyond Reproducible, page 187

Officer Buckle knew more safety **tips** than anyone else in Napville.

Every time he thought of a new one, he thumbtacked it to his bulletin board.

Safety Tip #77
NEVER stand on a SWIVEL CHAIR.

48

Officer Buckle shared his safety tips with the students at Napville School.

Nobody ever listened.

Sometimes, there was snoring.

Afterward, it was business as usual.

Mrs. Toppel, the principal, took down the welcome banner.

"NEVER stand on a SWIVEL CHAIR," said Officer Buckle, but Mrs. Toppel didn't hear him.

49

ELL

Preview Text Have children use **StudentWorks Plus**, the interactive eBook, to preview the text. This eBook contains summaries in multiple languages, word-by-word reading support, bilingual glossary, and comprehension questions with corrective feedback. Use the Interactive Question-Response Guide on pages 228–239 of the ELL Resource book to preteach the content in *Officer Buckle and Gloria* and develop meaning.

Develop Comprehension

1 SKILL Use Illustrations

Illustrations can tell you more about a story's characters, setting, and plot. What can you learn about where Officer Buckle gets ideas for his safety tips from the illustration on page 48? (In the illustration, I see Officer Buckle falling off a swivel chair. Then I see that his new tip is about swivel chairs. His own fall motivated, or caused, him to think of a new tip. So, Officer Buckle gets ideas for new safety tips after he has his own accidents.)

Think/Pair/Share Look at the illustration on page 49. How many accidents can you find in the picture? What safety tips could you come up with for Napville School? Share your new tips with a partner.

Then one day, Napville's police department bought a police dog named Gloria.

When it was time for Officer Buckle to give the safety speech at the school, Gloria went along.

2 "Children, this is Gloria," announced Officer Buckle. "Gloria **obeys** my commands. Gloria, SIT!" And Gloria sat.

Officer Buckle gave Safety Tip Number One:

"KEEP your SHOELACES tied!"

The children sat up and stared.

Officer Buckle checked to see if Gloria was sitting at **attention**. She was.

2 FLUENCY: INTONATION

Read the third paragraph on page 50. Use your voice to signal text in quotation marks and exclamation points. Remind children to read text in quotes the way they think the characters would say the words and to use good expression. Work with children to practice using ending punctuation to read sentences with fluency and correct intonation. Have them chorally read pages 50 and 51.

3 STRATEGY Monitor Comprehension: Read Ahead

What is an adjustment or correction I can make if I am having trouble understanding the story?

Teacher Think Aloud **Reading ahead** can help me understand what is happening on page 51. The illustration shows Gloria doing funny things like pointing her paw, but I don't know why. When I read ahead, I see that Gloria keeps doing funny things during the speeches when Officer Buckle is not watching her.

Decoding

Apply Phonics Skills
While reading, point out words with the sound-spelling patterns children have recently learned.

Model blending each word sound by sound. Then have children repeat.

"Safety Tip Number Two," said Officer Buckle.

"ALWAYS wipe up spills BEFORE someone SLIPS AND FALLS!"

The children's eyes popped.

Officer Buckle checked on Gloria again.

"Good dog," he said.

Officer Buckle thought of a safety tip he had discovered that morning.

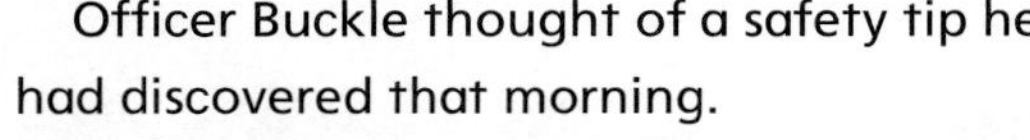

"NEVER leave a THUMBTACK where you might SIT on it!"

The audience roared.

4 **Use Illustrations**
Use the illustration to explain how Gloria makes Officer Buckle's speeches more interesting.

Social Studies

Connect to Content

Say: *Remember that a good citizen helps others in his or her community, such as by keeping people safe.* Talk about how Officer Buckle shows good citizenship. He thinks of important safety tips and shares them with others. Ask students to discuss examples of good citizenship in the story: *Which pictures illustrate Officer Buckle's actions as a good citizen?*

Develop Comprehension

4 STRATEGY Monitor Comprehension: Read Ahead

Teacher Think Aloud I can tell from the pictures that the students seem to be a lot more interested in Officer Buckle's safety speeches since Gloria joined him than they were before. How could you find out if the students are really paying attention to the speeches and not just watching Gloria's tricks?

Tell children to apply the strategy in a Think Aloud.

Student Think Aloud I think that if students listened to Officer Buckle, there would be fewer accidents. I can't tell from this page if this will happen so I will read ahead to check if my understanding is correct. Reading ahead is one way of making an adjustment to be sure I understand what is taking place.

5

Officer Buckle grinned. He said the rest of the tips with *plenty* of expression.

The children clapped their hands and cheered. Some of them laughed until they cried.

Officer Buckle was surprised. He had never noticed how funny safety tips could be.

After *this* safety speech, there wasn't a single **accident**.

6 The next day, an **enormous** envelope arrived at the police station. It was stuffed with thank-you letters from the students at Napville School.

Every letter had a drawing of Gloria on it.

Officer Buckle thought the drawings showed a lot of imagination.

5 SKILL Use Illustrations

How do the **illustrations** show that Gloria is making Officer Buckle's speeches more interesting? (The pictures show Gloria acting out the safety rules that Officer Buckle explains. When he looks at her, she is sitting quietly but when he turns his back she is jumping around.) Let's add this information to our chart.

Think/Pair/Share With a partner, point to each picture that shows Gloria doing something funny while Officer Buckle is not looking.

6 VOCABULARY: CONTEXT CLUES: SYNONYMS

Read the first sentence on page 55. Do you think an *enormous* envelope is large or small? What text and picture clues help you define this word? (The picture shows many letters pouring out of it and the text says that it is "stuffed," or very full.) What are some **synonyms** you can identify for enormous? (*huge, gigantic*)

Illustration	What I Learn from the Picture
It shows Gloria being funny while Officer Buckle is talking to the students with his back turned.	We discover that Officer Buckle does not know Gloria is doing tricks.

His favorite letter was written on a star-shaped piece of paper. It said:

8 Officer Buckle was thumbtacking Claire's letter to his bulletin board when the phones started ringing. Grade schools, high schools, and day-care centers were calling about the safety speech.

"Officer Buckle," they said, "our students want to hear your safety tips! And please, bring along that police dog."

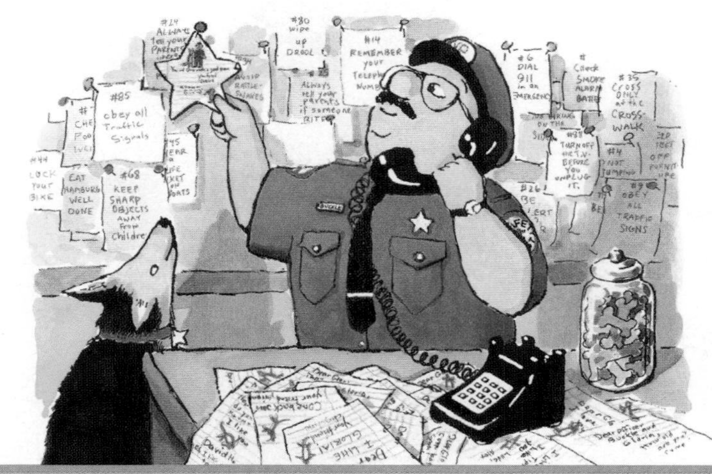

Text Evidence

Use Illustrations

Have students reread Question 9. Ask: *Where can you look in the text to find information to answer the second question? Point to the clues you find.* In addition to pages 58–59, students would return to page 51, where Gloria points her paw, and page 53, where she jumps. Students would recall that on page 52, when Officer Buckle looks back at her, she sits at attention.

Develop Comprehension

7 SELF-SELECTED STRATEGY USE

What strategies have you used so far to help you understand the selection? Where did you use them? Why? How did they help you?

8 MONITOR AND CLARIFY: ADJUST READING RATE

How can you **adjust** your **reading rate** to make sure you understand pages with a lot of text? (I can break up the text into smaller sections and pause between chunks or paragraphs. This can help me think more closely about what I am reading and adjust my comprehension. When I pause, I can make corrections to my reading.)

Officer Buckle told his safety tips to 313 schools. Everywhere he and Gloria went, children sat up and listened.

9

After every speech, Officer Buckle took Gloria out for ice cream.

Officer Buckle loved having a **buddy**. 10

9 SKILL Use Illustrations

What is Gloria doing in the **illustrations** on these pages? (She is doing flips and lying on her back. She is signing autographs for kids.) Do you think Officer Buckle can see her? How can you tell? (No. He is facing the kids, not Gloria, when she does her tricks.)

Think/Pair/Share With a partner, find other pictures where Officer Buckle's back is turned.

10 VOCABULARY: CONTEXT CLUES: SYNONYMS

Which **context clues** in the text and illustrations tell you what the word *buddy* means? What is a **synonym** for *buddy*? (The text says that Officer Buckle and Gloria went to 313 schools, so they have been spending a lot of time together. The picture shows them smiling and sharing ice cream. Synonyms for *buddy* are *friend* and *pal*.)

ELL

Question 9 USE ILLUSTRATIONS

Look at the picture. Act out what Officer Buckle is doing. Act out what Gloria is doing. Do you think Officer Buckle knows what Gloria is doing?

Help children use these sentence frames to describe what they see on the page: *Officer Buckle is _________. Gloria is _________. The kids are cheering because _________. Officer Buckle does not know _________.*

11 Then one day, a television news team videotaped Officer Buckle in the state college auditorium. When he finished Safety Tip Number Ninety-nine,

DO NOT GO SWIMMING DURING ELECTRICAL STORMS!,

the students jumped to their feet and applauded.

12 "Bravo! Bravo!" they cheered. Officer Buckle bowed again and again.

ELL

Use Visual Aids Use visual aids with the text to help children understand difficult words. Point to the word *bravo*. Ask children to infer what this means using the illustration that shows the audience smiling and clapping when the speech is over.

Develop Comprehension

11 GENRE: FICTION

How can you tell that this story's **genre** is fiction? (It is fiction because it has made-up events that could not really happen, like when Gloria acts out safety tips.) Which events in this fiction story are realistic and which are not? (A police officer speaking about safety is realistic. Having a dog that acts out tips is not realistic.)

12 STRATEGY Monitor Comprehension: Read Ahead

I know that Officer Buckle can't see Gloria act out his speeches. I wonder how he would feel about this if he knew.

Teacher Think Aloud Officer Buckle might be upset about Gloria acting out his speeches because he wants people to listen carefully. Or he might like that it makes the audience interested. I will make a correction by reading ahead to see how he feels.

That night, Officer Buckle watched himself on the 10 o'clock news.

13 Use Illustrations
What does Officer Buckle find out about his safety speeches? Use the illustrations to explain your answer.

13 SKILL Use Illustrations

What is Officer Buckle's reaction to the news report about his safety speeches? How can you tell from the illustration? (The illustration shows Officer Buckle watching himself during the report about his safety tips speech. In the mirror's reflection, we can see the TV screen. Gloria is lying on the stage while Officer Buckle bows. He seems very shocked. His face looks surprised and he is spilling his popcorn and knocking over a glass. Gloria looks nervous in the picture, as if she is afraid of what Officer Buckle might do.) Add children's responses to the Illustrations Chart.

Think/Pair/Share Share your description of the illustration on pages 62 and 63 with a partner. Compare the details you both have included in your Illustration Charts.

Illustration	What I Learn from the Picture
It shows Gloria being funny while Officer Buckle is talking to the students with his back turned.	We discover that Officer Buckle does not know Gloria is doing tricks.
It shows Officer Buckle watching his speech on tv and seeing Gloria performing tricks.	Officer Buckle discovers what Gloria has been doing all along.

The next day, the principal of Napville School telephoned the police station.

"Good morning, Officer Buckle! It's time for our safety speech!"

Officer Buckle frowned.

"I'm not giving any more speeches! Nobody looks at me, anyway!"

"Oh," said Mrs. Toppel. "Well! How about Gloria? Could she come?"

14

Someone else from the police station gave Gloria a ride to the school.

Gloria sat onstage looking lonely. Then she fell asleep. So did the audience.

After Gloria left, Napville School had its biggest accident ever....

Illustration	What I Learn from the Picture
It shows Gloria being funny while Officer Buckle is talking to the students with his back turned.	We discover that Officer Buckle does not know Gloria is doing tricks.
It shows Officer Buckle watching his speech on tv and seeing Gloria performing tricks.	Officer Buckle discovers what Gloria has been doing all along.
Officer Buckle looks sad and has written a new safety tip.	Officer Buckle is upset with Gloria. He does not want to work with her anymore.

Develop Comprehension

14 SKILL Use Illustrations

Look at the **illustrations**. What is Officer Buckle's 100th safety tip? (The illustration shows that Officer Buckle's 100th safety tip is "Never turn your back on a strange dog.") What does that tip tell you about how Officer Buckle feels about Gloria doing tricks behind his back? (The look on his face shows us that Officer Buckle feels angry and hurt that Gloria did tricks behind his back. In the next illustration, Gloria appears on stage alone. This tells us that feeling angry and hurt motivated Officer Buckle to stop working with Gloria.) Add what you learned to the Illustration Chart.

Think/Pair/Share Discuss with a partner how the students look in the picture on page 65. What does this tell you? (The students are sleeping. They must be bored without Officer Buckle there, too.)

It started with a puddle of banana pudding....

SPLAT!
SPLATTER!
SPLOOSH!

Everyone slid smack into Mrs. Toppel, who screamed and let go of her hammer.

66

67

15 REVIEW Cause and Effect

What happens at the school? (There is a very big accident.) What caused this accident to happen? (The text says that it all started with a puddle of banana pudding. The illustration shows that someone spilled pudding and didn't clean it up. Then everyone slid into Mrs. Toppel, who should not have been standing on a swivel chair. She let go of her hammer as a result. No one was following Officer Buckle's safety tips.)

SELF-SELECTED STRATEGY USE

What strategies did you use to make sense of what you read? Where? How were these strategies helpful?

Extra Support

Summarize To check comprehension, have children summarize what has happened in the story. Ask them to describe how the events in the story lead Officer Buckle to become so popular. (He gets a dog named Gloria. She does tricks while Officer Buckle gives his safety speech. The students are used to hearing Officer Buckle's boring safety speech. Gloria brings excitement to his safety tips. Everyone finally pays attention to the safety tips.)

The next morning, a pile of letters arrived at the police station.

Every letter had a drawing of the accident.

Officer Buckle was shocked.

At the bottom of the pile was a note written on a paper star.

Officer Buckle smiled.

The note said:

Gloria gave Officer Buckle a big kiss on the nose. Officer Buckle gave Gloria a nice pat on the back. Then, Officer Buckle thought of his best safety tip yet...

Safety Tip #101

"ALWAYS STICK WITH YOUR BUDDY!"

Illustration	What I Learned
It shows Gloria being funny while Officer Buckle is talking to the students with his back turned.	We discover that Officer Buckle does not know Gloria is doing tricks.
It shows Officer Buckle watching his speech on tv and seeing Gloria performing tricks.	Officer Buckle discovers what Gloria has been doing all along.
Officer Buckle looks sad and has written a new safety tip.	Officer Buckle is upset with Gloria. He does not want to work with her anymore.

Develop Comprehension

COMPLETE THE ILLUSTRATION CHART

Review the information recorded on the Illustration Chart.

RETURN TO PREDICTIONS AND PURPOSES

Review children's predictions and purposes and the Focus Question. Then have children use ideas to confirm their predictions.

Quick Check

Can children monitor their comprehension by reading ahead and using illustrations?

During **Small Group Instruction**

If No → **Approaching Level** Apply the skill to simpler texts. See pages 77R and 77X.

If Yes → **On Level** Apply the skill to another text. See page 77S and 77Y.

Beyond Level Apply the skill to a harder text. See page 77T and 77Z.

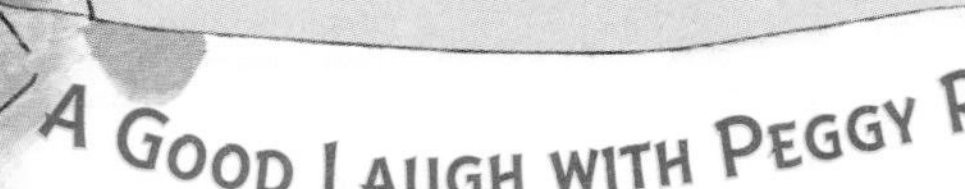

Peggy Rathmann got the idea for *Officer Buckle and Gloria* from a videotape. The tape shows Peggy's mother talking. In the background, their dog licks the eggs that were set out for breakfast.

The next part of the tape, Peggy says, "shows the whole family at the breakfast table, complimenting my mother on the delicious eggs." Of course, no one knew what the dog had done! "The first time we watched that tape we were so shocked, we couldn't stop laughing," Peggy says.

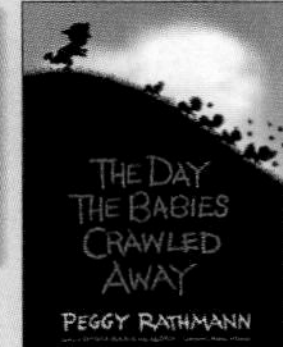

Other books written by Peggy Rathmann

Author Peggy Rathmann
www.macmillanmh.com

Author's Purpose
Peggy Rathmann wrote this story to show what can happen in the background. Have you ever done something behind the scenes without anyone knowing it? What did you do?

70

Author's Craft

Author's Purpose

- Author's purpose is why an author writes a story. An author may try to entertain us or teach us something. Sometimes, an author tries to do both.
- For example, Peggy Rathmann tries to entertain us by showing all the funny things that Gloria does while Officer Buckle is speaking. However, the author also teaches us about being a good friend and about safety rules.
- Discuss places where the author incorporates safety rules into the illustrations. (Possible answers: Never run with scissors. Never stand on a swivel chair. Obey all traffic signs.)

Meet the Author/Illustrator

Read aloud page 70 with children. Ask them where the author got the idea for writing *Officer Buckle and Gloria*. Ask children to look back through the story and share what they think Peggy Rathmann's purpose was in writing the story. Then have them share their thoughts on the illustrations.

Author's Purpose

Peggy Rathmann had two reasons for writing *Officer Buckle and Gloria*: to entertain us and to teach us. *Did she do both of these things? Which do you think was more important?* Help children think about why authors write. Then help them organize their thoughts to write about doing something kind. Instruct them to tell how they felt after doing this.

Genre

Fiction

Some of the events in *Officer Buckle and Gloria* could happen in real life, such as a police officer giving a speech with safety tips. Other events probably would not happen, like a massive banana pudding spill leading to an accident involving the whole school. Ask students to identify which story events could happen in real life and which would not. Point out that the story is fiction because of these made-up events.

Objectives

- Retell a story to show understanding
- Answer comprehension questions

Materials

- Student Book: *Officer Buckle and Gloria*, pp. 46–69
- Retelling Cards for *Officer Buckle and Gloria*
- chart paper
- Practice Book, p. 188

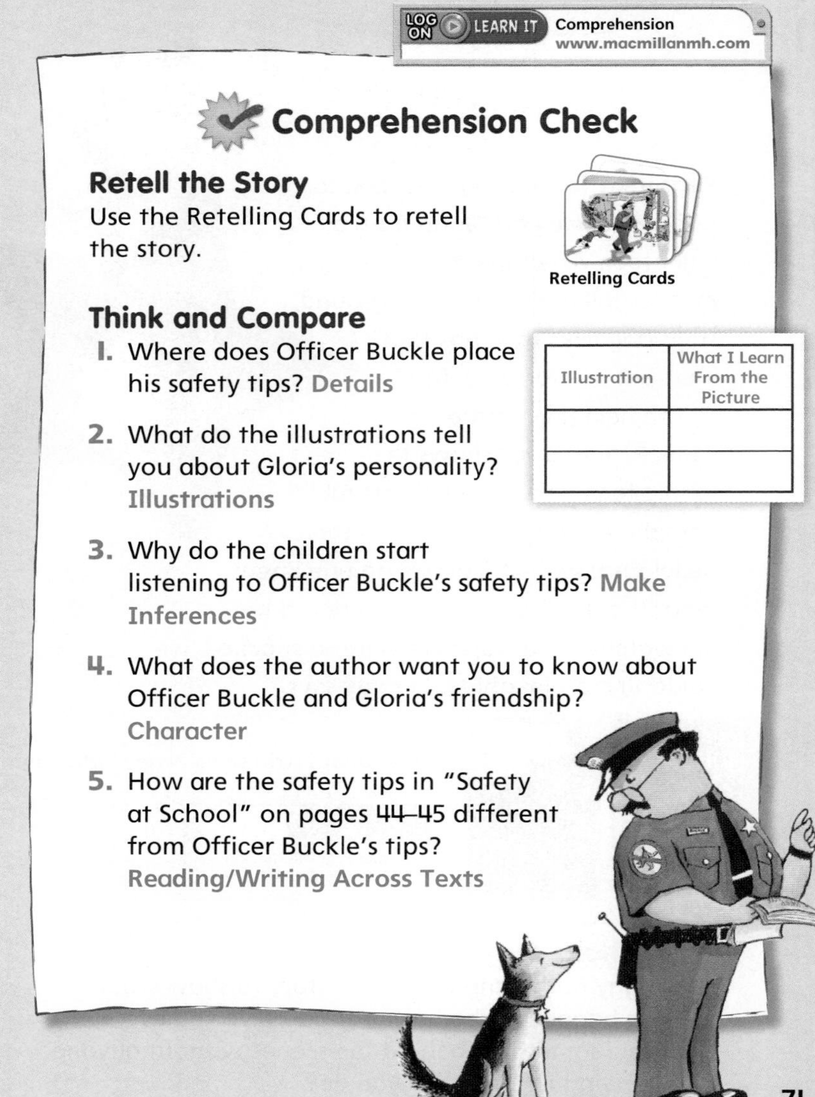

LOG ON LEARN IT Comprehension www.macmillanmh.com

Comprehension Check

Retell the Story
Use the Retelling Cards to retell the story.

Retelling Cards

Think and Compare

1. Where does Officer Buckle place his safety tips? Details
2. What do the illustrations tell you about Gloria's personality? Illustrations
3. Why do the children start listening to Officer Buckle's safety tips? Make Inferences
4. What does the author want you to know about Officer Buckle and Gloria's friendship? Character
5. How are the safety tips in "Safety at School" on pages 44–45 different from Officer Buckle's tips? Reading/Writing Across Texts

Illustration	What I Learn From the Picture

71

Retelling Rubric

4 Excellent

Retells the selection without prompting, in sequence, and using supporting details. Clearly describes the setting, main characters, and the complete plot. Describes the problem and its solution.

3 Good

Retells the selection with little guidance, in sequence, and using some details. Generally describes the setting, main characters, and the plot. Recognizes either a problem or a solution.

**2 Fair**

Retells the selection with some guidance, mostly in sequence, and using limited details. Partially describes the setting, main characters, and plot. Cannot state the problem or solution.

**1 Unsatisfactory**

Retells the selection only when prompted, out of sequence, and using limited details. Does not describe the main characters or plot.

Retelling Cards

Retell the Story

RETELL *OFFICER BUCKLE AND GLORIA*

- Remind children that as they read *Officer Buckle and Gloria*, they used the illustrations to help them understand the story. Now they will use this information to retell the story in logical order. You can record children's retelling on chart paper.
- **Model Retelling** Use the prompts on the back of Retelling Cards to model retelling the story.
- ELL **Guide Retelling** Use the leveled language acquisition prompts provided to guide children's retelling.
- **Discuss the Retelling** *What are some illustrations you remember from the story? How did the illustrations help you understand what was happening in the story?*

Phonemic Awareness

Phoneme Substitution

Model

Show children how to substitute initial sounds.

Repeat the routine with *coil/foil*; *coin/join*; *boy/toy*; *moist/hoist*; *loyal/royal*.

Listen as I say a word. Then listen as I change the beginning sound. The word is *coy*. I'll change the /k/ in *coy* to /s/. The new word is *soy*.

Guided Practice/Practice

Help children use these examples to practice substituting initial sounds to make new words.

Guide practice with the first one.

I am going to say more words. Listen carefully. Change the beginning sound in the word I say to the new sound to create a new word.

cloy	Change /k/ to /p/.
joint	Change /j/ to /p/.
poise	Change /p/ to /n/.
soil	Change /s/ to /k/.
boil	Change /b/ to /s/.

Objective

- Substitute phonemes in words to create new words with *oi*, *oy*

Objectives

- Identify letter-sound correspondence for diphthong /oi/*oi*, *oy*
- Blend sounds in words with *oi*, *oy*
- Review previously taught phonics skills
- Read multisyllabic words

Materials

- Sound-Spelling Card: *Boy*
- Word-Building Cards; Teacher's Resource Book, p. 66
- pocket chart
- chart paper
- Practice Book, p. 189

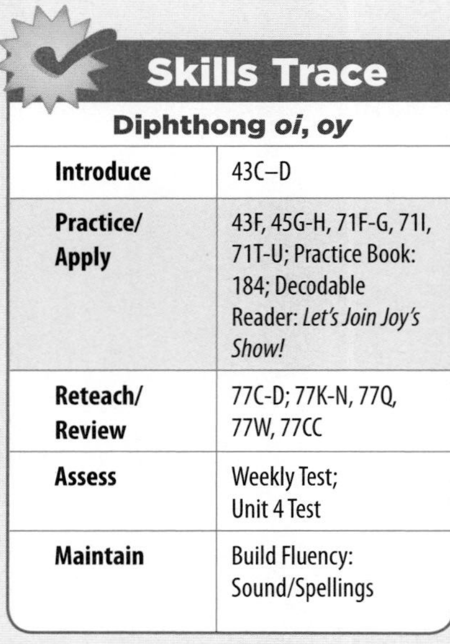

Skills Trace

Diphthong *oi*, *oy*	
Introduce	43C–D
Practice/ Apply	43F, 45G-H, 71F-G, 71I, 71T-U; Practice Book: 184; Decodable Reader: *Let's Join Joy's Show!*
Reteach/ Review	77C-D; 77K-N, 77Q, 77W, 77CC
Assess	Weekly Test; Unit 4 Test
Maintain	Build Fluency: Sound/Spellings

Phonics

Diphthong *oi*, *oy*

Model

Review the sound /oi/ spelled *oi*. Then review the sound /oi/ spelled *oy*. Show the *Boy* **Sound-Spelling Card**.

This is the *Boy* Sound-Spelling Card. The sound is /oi/. This is the sound at the end of *boy*. The /oi/ sound can be spelled with the letters *oi* or *oy*. Say it with me: /oi/.

We've been reading words with the /oi/ sound all week. Today we will read more.

Guided Practice/Practice

Have children practice connecting the letters and sound.

(Point to the Sound-Spelling Card spellings.) What are these letters? What sound do they stand for?

Build Fluency: Sound/Spellings

oy oi er

Display these **Word-Building Cards** one at a time: *oi, oy, ou, ow, are, air, ear, ere, or, ore, oar, ar, gn, kn, wr, mb, eer, ere, ear, er, ir, ur*. Have children chorally say each sound. Repeat, varying the pace.

Blend Words with *oi*, *oy*

Model

Display Word-Building Cards *f, o, i, l*. Model how to blend the sounds together as you run your finger under each letter.

Continue by modeling the words *noise*, *point*, *oil*, *joyful*, and *joined*.

(Point to *f*.) This is the letter *f*. It stands for /f/.

(Point to *oi*.) These are the letters *o* and *i*. They stand for /oi/. Listen as I blend these sounds together: /foi/.

(Point to *l*.) This is the letter *l*. It stands for /l/. Listen as I blend all three sounds together: /foil/, *foil*. Say it with me.

Guided Practice/Practice

Write the words below on chart paper. Read the first line with children. Then have them chorally read the words on the chart. Use the appropriate blending level.

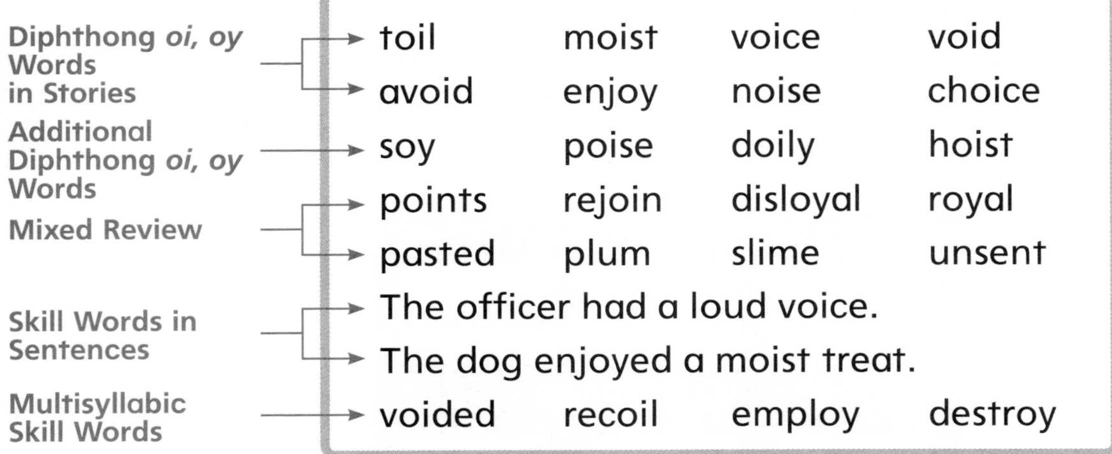

Diphthong *oi, oy* Words in Stories	toil	moist	voice	void
	avoid	enjoy	noise	choice
Additional Diphthong *oi, oy* Words	soy	poise	doily	hoist
Mixed Review	points	rejoin	disloyal	royal
	pasted	plum	slime	unsent
Skill Words in Sentences	The officer had a loud voice.			
	The dog enjoyed a moist treat.			
Multisyllabic Skill Words	voided	recoil	employ	destroy

Corrective Feedback

Speakers of other languages may need additional support for some /oi/ words, such as *void*, *royal*, *poise*, *toil*, and *doily*. Provide more time for practice, since children will need extra help in both decoding and understanding meaning.

Prefixes *re-, un-, dis-*

Teach

- Say the words *replay, unable,* and *dislike*. Ask children to listen closely to the beginning sounds.
- Point out *re-*, *un-*, and *dis-*.
- Write the words on the board and underline the prefixes.
- Explain that the prefix *re-* means "again," *un-* means "not able," and *dis-* means "opposite" or "not."
- Ask children to give the meanings of the words and use them in sentences.

Practice/Apply

- Then help children make new words by adding prefixes to these base words: *make*, *tie*, *agree*, *obey*, *tell*, *read*, *safe*, *own*, and *trust*.
- Ask children to look for words with these prefixes as they read. Keep a running list on chart paper.

Practice Book, page 189

A **prefix** is a word part that can be added to the beginning of a word to change the word's meaning.
re- = "again" *un-* = "not" *dis-* = "opposite of"

Read each sentence. Then write the meaning of the underlined word on the line below.

1. Jed fills in the hole and redigs it.
 digs again
2. The team of workers will fix the unsafe road.
 not safe
3. The team disagreed about the best way to do the job.
 did not agree, opposite of agree
4. Jack's friends wanted him to rejoin the baseball team.
 join again
5. Sara must review the notes she wrote.
 view again, look at again
6. The team was unsure what to do next.
 not sure

Approaching Reproducible, page 189
Beyond Reproducible, page 189

Objectives

- Sort and spell words with diphthong *oi* and *oy*
- Review high-frequency words
- Build Fluency: Word Automaticity

Materials

- index cards from Day 2
- pocket chart
- Spelling Word Cards BLM; Teacher's Resource Book, p. 70
- Phonics/ Spelling Practice Book, p. 67

5-Day Spelling	
DAY 1	Dictation; Pretest
DAY 2	Teacher-Modeled Word Sort
DAY 3	Student Word Sort
DAY 4	Test Practice
DAY 5	Posttest

ON YOUR OWN

Spelling, page 67

boil	moist	joy	toy	point
broil	soil	avoid	royal	oil

A. Sentences to Complete

Write a spelling word on each line to complete the sentence.

1. Mom fried the fish in oil.
2. The new baby brought much joy to her family.
3. I can broil the meat in the oven.
4. Water made the towel feel moist.
5. The royal family sat on their thrones.

B. Definitions

Write the spelling word for each definition.

6. An object that children play with. toy
7. A small mark or dot used in writing. point
8. Dirt that plants grow in. soil
9. To heat water until it bubbles. boil
10. To stay away from. avoid

Phonics/Spelling

Word Sort with Diphthong *oi, oy*

WORD SORT

- Use index cards from Day 2 for each spelling word, as well as for *noise* and *ploy*. Place cards to form two columns in a pocket chart. Blend sounds with children.

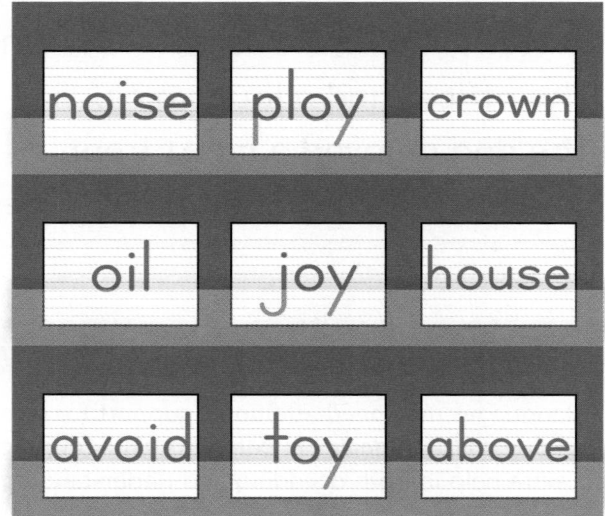

- Hold up the *oil* card. Say and spell it. Pronounce each sound clearly: /oi/ /l/. Blend the sounds: /oil/.
- Repeat this step with *avoid*. Place both words below the *noise* label. Have children read each word. *What do you notice about these spelling words?* (They have the /oi/ sound spelled *oi*.) Repeat the process with the *oy* words.
- Display the words *crown*, *house*, *above*, *color*, and *song* in a separate column. Read and spell the words together with children. Point out that these spelling words do not contain the /oi/ sound.
- Conclude by asking children to orally generate additional words that rhyme with each word.
- **Build Fluency: Word Automaticity** Have children chorally read the words several times for fluency.

High-Frequency Words

- **Teach High-Frequency Words** Write the new high-frequency words for the week, **above**, **color**, and **song**, on the board. Teach the words using the **Read/Spell/Write** routine below.
  - **Read** Read the word. Have children repeat.
  - **Spell** Chorally spell the word.
  - **Write** Have children write the word as they spell it aloud. Then ask children to write a sentence using each word.
- **Practice** Write sample cloze sentences for each word on the board.

  I liked to look at the stars _________ me while at the campfire.
  Megan's favorite _________ is green.
  In music class, we sang a new _________ together.

- Have children read the sentences and write the missing word for each one.
- **Additional High-Frequency Words** Introduce an additional six words (Additional Words #207–212: **poor**, **enough**, **also**, **wish**, **eight**, **people**) for more practice. Have children use the Read/Spell/Write routine to learn the words. Finish with a speed drill of all the words taught for the day. Display each High-Frequency Word Card quickly and have children identify and read the word aloud. Repeat with any words children have difficulty with.

Decodable Reader

- **Review High-Frequency Words** Review the high-frequency words that appear in the book: **family**, **four**, and **hear**. Have children read each one aloud and provide a sentence for each.

Decodable Reader

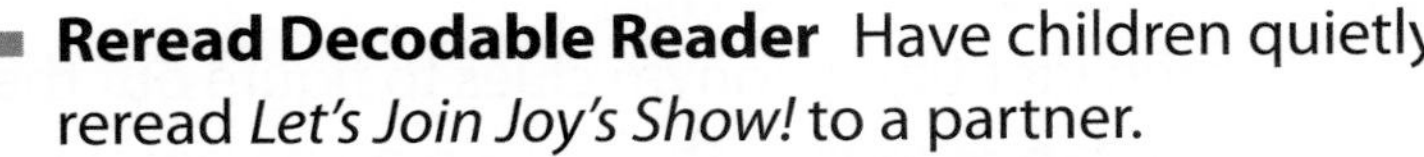
- **Reread Decodable Reader** Have children quietly reread *Let's Join Joy's Show!* to a partner.

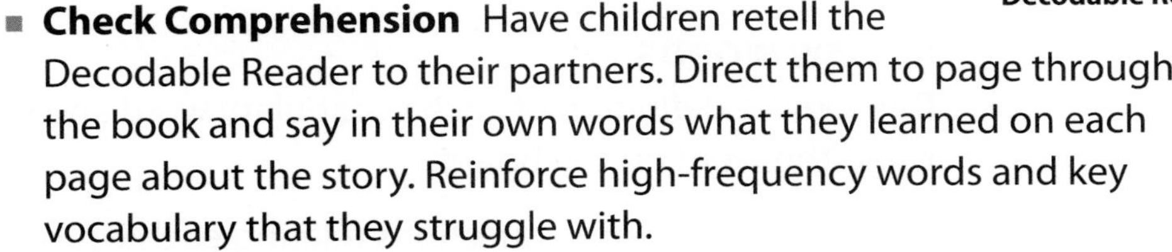
- **Check Comprehension** Have children retell the Decodable Reader to their partners. Direct them to page through the book and say in their own words what they learned on each page about the story. Reinforce high-frequency words and key vocabulary that they struggle with.

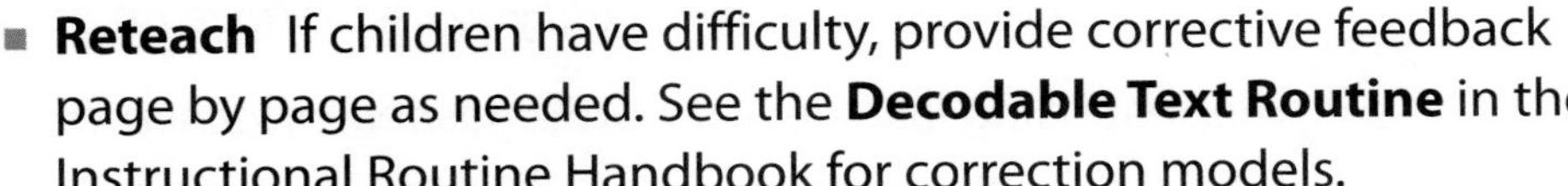
- **Reteach** If children have difficulty, provide corrective feedback page by page as needed. See the **Decodable Text Routine** in the Instructional Routine Handbook for correction models.

Objectives

- Decode words with *oi*, *oy* in connected text
- Introduce high-frequency words *above*, *color*, *song*

Materials

- Decodable Reader Library: *Let's Join Joy's Show!*

SMALL GROUP OPTION

You may wish to read the Decodable Reader during **Small Group** time.

See pages 77K–77JJ

Objectives

- Use context clues and synonyms to determine word meaning
- Review this week's and last week's vocabulary words

Materials

- Transparency 34
- Practice Book, p. 190

Vocabulary

accident	attention
buddy	enormous
obeys	tip

Practice Book, page 190

ON YOUR OWN

Synonyms are words that have the same or almost the same meaning.

Read each pair of sentences. A word in the first sentence and a word in the second sentence are synonyms. Circle the synonyms. Then write them on the lines.

1. It was time for Gina to go.
   She was ready to leave.
   go leave
2. Gina put on her helmet to begin her bike ride.
   She could not wait to start.
   begin start
3. Gina had to ride her mom's big bike.
   The large bike was a little bit hard to ride.
   big large
4. Gina was careful as she rode quickly.
   She wanted to get to her friend's house fast.
   quickly fast

Approaching Reproducible, page 190

Beyond Reproducible, page 190

Vocabulary

STRATEGY Use Context Clues: Synonyms

EXPLAIN

- Tell children that to figure out the meaning of an unfamiliar word, they should find synonym clues in the surrounding sentences.

MODEL

Use the first paragraph on **Transparency 34** to model how to identify and use synonyms to figure out the meaning of **enormous**.

Think Aloud I don't know the meaning of **enormous**. I will read the sentences around it for synonym clues. I see that the ball is "really big" and "so large that it comes to my waist." I think that **enormous** means "really big."

Transparency 34

My mother has an enormous ball. She uses this really big ball to get strong. The ball is so large that it comes to my waist.

When my buddy Shane comes to my house, we play with the ball. Shane has been my friend since we were little. We play together after school all the time.

Mom says we have to be very careful with the ball. It could be dangerous, or unsafe, to play hard with it. Shane and I are very careful and we never get hurt.

Vocabulary Transparency

GUIDED PRACTICE/PRACTICE

Help children identify synonym clues to figure out the meanings of **buddy** and **dangerous** in the remaining paragraphs.

REVIEW WORDS

Review the definition of each vocabulary word and write a sentence using the word on the board.

Practice Ask children questions relating each word to their own experience, such as *Why would you like to have an animal* buddy?

Repeat using last week's words: *gasped*, *attached*, *frantically*, *swung*, and *delicious*.

Oral Vocabulary

REVIEW WORDS

Remind children of the week's oral vocabulary words.

- **Hesitate** means "to stop and think about what you will do." *Tikki does not hesitate to tell his mother that Chen fell into the well.*
- **Panic** means "to feel very frightened or afraid." *Chen begins to panic when he cannot say his brother's name.*
- To give **advice** is to tell someone what you think they should or should not do. *Joe gave Tom advice on how to make a model airplane.*
- When you **secure** something, you make it safe. *You need to secure your baby sister in the car seat.*
- **Vowed** means "promised." *I vowed to study for my test before going to see the tennis match.*

Use the statements and questions below to help reinforce the meanings of the words.

- *Why should you hesitate before crossing the street?*
- *Show us how you would look if you were lost and were in a panic.*
- *Describe the advice you might give someone who is climbing a ladder.*
- *Why is it important to make sure your seat belt is secure?*
- *Which word goes with* promised? *(vowed)*
- Then have a child say what each word means and use it in a sentence.

- Use similar activities to review last week's words: *accomplish, arduous, labor, rejoice,* and *succeed.*

Objectives

- Practice repeated oral reading
- 62–82 WCPM
- Practice fluency prosody

Materials

- Transparency 17
- Fluency Solutions Audio CD
- Practice Book, p. 191

ELL

Prosody Pick another passage and review the meaning of each sentence in it. Then read the passage with inflection. Have children mimic your animated tone.

Fluency

Repeated Reading: Prosody

EXPLAIN/MODEL

- **Punctuation** Explain that the punctuation in a text helps readers know when to pause or stop, or how to read a sentence.
- For example, a comma in the middle of a sentence tells readers to pause slightly. (e.g., This is my best friend, Marie.) *In dialogue, commas help us read the words the way the speaker would have said them.*

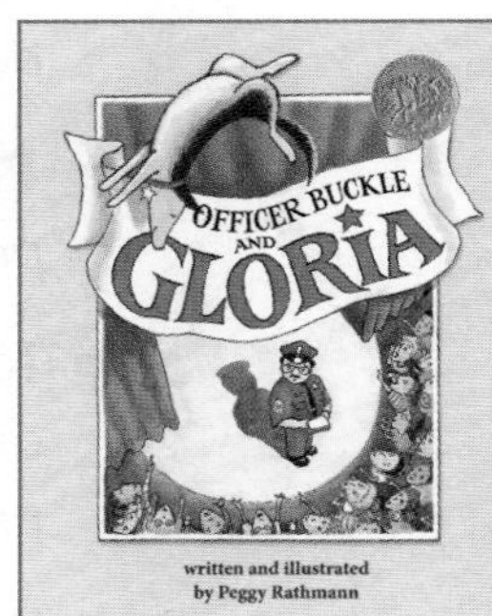

Main Selection

- **Phrasing** Display **Transparency 17** and point out the single and double slashes. Explain that the single slashes show pauses and the double slashes show stops.
- Point out that when the words between slashes are read together, they help us form a mental picture of the text. *If we struggle with any word, we should decode it or ask for help, then go back to the beginning of the slash and reread that section of the text.* Model reading aloud the section on Transparency 17. *When did I pause when I read? When did I stop longer?*

Transparency 17

"Children, / this is Gloria," / announced Officer Buckle. // "Gloria obeys my commands. // Gloria, / SIT!" // And Gloria sat. //

Officer Buckle gave Safety Tip Number One: //

"KEEP your SHOELACES tied!" //

The children sat up and stared. //

Officer Buckle checked to see if Gloria was sitting at attention. // She was. //

—from *Officer Buckle and Gloria* (pages 50–51)

Fluency Transparency

- **Intonation** Discuss how your intonation changes depending on what activity is being described in each sentence.

Demonstrate how you adjust your reading rate based on the style of the writing. *When the author is describing exciting actions, you adjust your reading rate by reading more quickly.* Model reading the passage with natural expression.

Point out that you read the text the way the speaker would have said the words, expressing the same emotion and using the same expression.

- **Pronunciation** Model reading the passage. Have children note your pronunciation of *shoelaces* and *obeys*. Point out that good readers slow down their reading rate when reading difficult words or unfamiliar words to make sure that they pronounce them correctly.

PRACTICE

- Have children reread the passage chorally, using the slashes to think about their phrasing. Remind them to read as if the character is speaking.

Repeat the reading to give children even more practice with natural phrasing, speed, and prosody.

- **Daily Fluency** Children will practice fluency by reading aloud, then paraphrasing, **Practice Book** page 191. Students can also listen to the **Fluency Solutions Audio CD** for practice. The passage is recorded at a slow, practice speed, and a faster, fluent speed.

Quick Check

Can children read the passage fluently and with prosody?

During **Small Group Instruction**

If No → **Approaching Level** See pages: 77DD, 77HH.

If Yes → **On Level** See Fluency 77EE.

Beyond Level See Fluency 77EE.

ON YOUR OWN

Practice Book, page 191

As I read, I will pay attention to my intonation.

Roads can be dangerous places. Pay attention when you
9 are on or near a road. If you are not careful, an accident
22 may happen. Here are some tips to keep you safe.
32 Always walk on the sidewalk. If there is no sidewalk,
42 walk on the side of the road. Face cars coming toward you.
54 You should also be careful when crossing the road.
63 A safe pedestrian obeys these rules.
69 Follow these five steps when you need to cross the road:
80 **Step 1: STOP** at the side of the road.
88 **Step 2: LOOK** for any traffic.
93 **Step 3: LISTEN** for any traffic that might be coming.
102 **Step 4: WAIT** until there is no traffic before you cross.
112 **Step 5: GO** when it is safe to cross. 120

Comprehension Check

1. Why should you pay attention when you are on or near a road? **Main Idea and Details** If you are not careful, an accident may happen.
2. Why do you think it is a good idea to wait until there is no traffic to cross the street? **Make Inferences** Drivers may not see you in time to slow down or stop.

	Words Read	–	Number of Errors	=	Words Correct Score
First Read		–		=	
Second Read		–		=	

Approaching Reproducible, page 191

Beyond Reproducible, page 191

Objectives

- Determine cause and effect
- Describe characters' motivations
- Express personal responses to literature
- Discuss genre characteristics

Materials

- Student Book: *Officer Buckle and Gloria*, pp. 46–69

Comprehension

MAINTAIN Cause and Effect

Main Selection

EXPLAIN

Review with children that identifying **cause and effect** in a selection can help them clarify what happens and why it happens in a text. It can also help them understand the motivations of characters, or what causes them to feel, think, say, or do certain things. Identifying cause-and-effect relationships helps them better understand the information in a selection.

- To identify cause and effect

1. ask yourself what happened in the selection (this is the effect)
2. look for clues that tell why it happened (this is the cause)

PRACTICE

Ask children to discuss the following questions: *What caused Officer Buckle to stop giving speeches with Gloria? What effect did this have on Napville?*

Skills Trace

Cause and Effect	
Introduce	U2: 199A–B
Practice/ Apply	U2: 199J–231A; Practice Book: 73–74
Reteach/ Review	U2: 235G, 235R–T, 235X-Z; U3: 403A–B, 403K–429A, 435G, 435R–T, 435X-Z; Practice Book: 151–152
Assess	Weekly Tests; Units 2, 3, 4, 6 Tests.
Maintain	U2: 243N; U3: 457N; U4: 9A–9B, 9J–37A, 41G, 41R–T, 41X–Z, 71N; U6: 409A–B, 409J–433A, 437G, 437R–T, 437X–Z, 457N; Practice Book: 176–177, 322–323

Respond to Literature

Personal Response Have children pose clarifying questions such as *how*, *why*, or *what-if* questions about *Officer Buckle and Gloria*. They can write their responses in their Writer's Notebooks.

- *What made Officer Buckle's safety speeches so popular with the kids?*
- *How would Officer Buckle's life be different if Gloria had never been a part of his team?*
- *What did you learn about the the theme of teamwork in* Officer Buckle and Gloria*?*
- *In addition to the importance of teamwork, what other themes did you learn in the story?*

Focus Question: Fiction Remind children that fiction is a made-up story about made-up characters and events.

- *Think about the story structure. Describe the problem and solution in* Officer Buckle and Gloria.
- *Compare and contrast Officer Buckle and Gloria. How are these characters alike? How are they different?*

Phonemic Awareness

Phoneme Segmentation

Model

Review with children how to segment phonemes in words.

Repeat the routine with the words *ploy, poison, annoy, enjoy,* and *toilet*.

I am going to say a word sound by sound. Listen carefully to all the sounds in the word *coin*. The first sound is /k/. The second sound is /oi/; the letters *o* and *i* together make the /oi/ sound. The last sound is /n/. Now watch as I say each sound in the word *coin* again and hold up one finger for each sound: /k/ /oi/ /n/.

How many sounds does *coin* have? (3) Now say the word with me sound by sound: /k/ /oi/ /n/, *coin*.

Guided Practice/Practice

Have children practice with the examples provided. Do the first row with them.

Now I am going to say a word. I want you to say each sound in the word. Let me try first. The word is *coil*. *Coil*, /k/ /oi/ /l/. *Coil* has three sounds.

It's your turn. Listen carefully. How many sounds are in these words?

avoid (4)	point (4)	joins (4)	moist (4)
alloy (3)	choice (3)	voyage (4)	broil (4)

For additional practice, have children use the **WorkBoard** to orally segment two syllable words. Then have them clap to show the syllables in a word. Do the first example for children.

Use the following words *enjoy*, *royal*, *employ*, *loyal*, *boiling*.

I am going to put one marker in each box as I say each sound, then I will blend the sounds to form a word. Listen and watch. /e/ (Place marker in the first box.) /n/ (Place marker in the second box.) /j/ (Place marker in the third box.) /oi/ (Place marker in the fourth box.) This word has four sounds: /e/ /n/ /j/ /oi/. Listen as I blend the sounds to form the word: /enjoy/. The word is *enjoy*. How many sounds does the word have? Now let's clap when we hear a syllable or a word part with a vowel sound. Listen as I say the syllables in the word /en/ clap, /joy/ clap. I clapped twice because this word has two vowel sounds or two syllables.

Objective

- Segment phonemes in words with /oi/

Objectives

- Blend and build words with diphthong *oi, oy*
- Review previously taught phonics skills
- Read multisyllabic words

Materials

- Word-Building Cards; Teacher's Resource Book, p. 66
- pocket chart
- word chart from Day 3

Phonics

Build Fluency: Sound/Spellings

Display the following **Word-Building Cards** one at a time: *oi, oy, ou, ow, are, air, ear, ere, or, ore, oar, ar, gn, kn, wr, mb, eer, ere, ear, er, ir, ur.* Have children chorally say each sound. Repeat and vary the pace. Children should work to say each sound within a two-second pause.

Blend Words with Diphthong *oi, oy*

Model

Place Word-Building Cards *s, o, i, l* in the pocket chart to form *soil*. Model how to generate and blend the sounds to say the word.

The letter *s* stands for /s/. The letters *o* and *i* together stand for /oi/. The letter *l* stands for /l/. Now listen as I blend all three sounds: /soil/. Your turn. Let's read the word together: *soil.*

Repeat the routine with *royal, boil, joint, joys,* and *avoid.*

Guided Practice/Practice

Repeat with additional words.

Have children blend the sounds in the words with you.

oink	coy	Troy	enjoy
toil	noise	hoist	broil
oil	disloyal	point	choice
spoiled	pointer	deploy	tomboy
toiling	oinked	employ	appoint

Skills Trace

Diphthong *oi, oy*	
Introduce	43C–D
Practice/ Apply	43F, 45G-H, 71F-G, 71I, 71T-U; Practice Book: 184; Decodable Reader: *Let's Join Joy's Show!*
Reteach/ Review	77C-D; 77K-N, 77Q, 77W, 77CC
Assess	Weekly Test; Unit 4 Test
Maintain	Build Fluency: Sound/Spellings

Build Words with Diphthong *oi, oy*

Model

Place **Word-Building Cards** *j, o, i, n* in the pocket chart. Blend the phonemes.

Let's blend all the sounds together and read the word: /join/, *join*.

Add *s* after *n* and repeat with *joins*.

Let's blend all the sounds together and read the word: /joinz/, *joins*.

Change *j* to *c* and repeat with *coins*.

Let's blend all the sounds together and read the word: /koinz/, *coins*.

Guided Practice/ Practice

Continue with the words *toil*, *moist*, *poise*, *avoid*, and *void*.

Build Fluency: Word Automaticity

Display the word chart from Day 3. Point to each word as children chorally read it. Aim for one word every two seconds. Model blending the sounds in any words children miss. Then point to words in random order at varying speeds for children to read.

toil	moist	voice	void
avoid	enjoy	noise	choice
soy	poise	doily	hoist
points	rejoin	disloyal	royal
pasted	plum	slime	unsent

The officer had a loud voice.
The dog enjoyed a moist treat
voided recoil employ destroy

Transition to Multisyllabic Words

Teach

- Say the words *replay, unable,* and *dislike*. Ask children to listen closely to the beginning sounds.
- Point out the prefixes *re-*, *un-*, and *dis-*.
- Write the words on the board and underline the prefixes.
- Explain that the prefix *re-* means "again," *un-* means "not able," and *dis-* means "opposite" or "not."
- Ask children to give the meanings of the words and use them in sentences.

Practice/Apply

- Then help children make new words by adding prefixes to these base words: *make*, *tie*, *agree*, *obey*, *tell*, *read*, *safe*, *own*, and *trust*.
- Ask children to look for words with these prefixes as they read this week's stories. Keep a running list on chart paper.

ELL

Build Vocabulary Review the meanings of words on your word chart that can be explained or demonstrated in a concrete way. For example, ask children to act out something they *enjoy* doing. Have children raise their *voices*. Provide sentence starters for children to complete, such as *I try to* avoid __________.

Objectives

- Practice spelling test
- Build Fluency: Word Automaticity

Materials

- Spelling Word Cards BLM; Teacher's Resource Book, p. 70
- paper and pencils
- Sound-Spelling WorkBoard; Teacher's Resource Book, p. 66
- Phonics/Spelling Practice Book, p. 68

5-Day Spelling	
DAY 1	Dictation; Pretest
DAY 2	Teacher-Modeled Word Sort
DAY 3	Student Word Sort
DAY 4	Test Practice
DAY 5	Posttest

ON YOUR OWN **Spelling,** page 68

A. There are six spelling mistakes in the paragraph below. Circle the misspelled words. Write the words correctly on the lines below.

Once I was in a play about a king and queen. The stage was a rouyal castle. The queen wanted to avoyid cooking. She had her servant boel water for her tea. The king was very funny. He put soy sauce on everything he ate! I played the king and queen's child. I brought them great joiy. My favorite toiy in the castle was a nutcracker. The nutcracker squeaked when I used it. I learned how to oel it so it did not make any noise. The play was fun!

1. royal 2. avoid 3. boil
4. joy 5. toy 6. oil

B. Writing

Write about acting in a play. Use four or five of your spelling words. Circle the spelling words you use.

Answers will vary.

Phonics/Spelling

Words with Diphthong *oi, oy*

PRACTICE

- Provide pairs of children with individual copies of the **Spelling Word Cards**.
- While one partner reads the words one at a time, the other partner should orally segment the word (e.g., /p/ /oi/ /n/ /t/) and then write the word. Have **WorkBoards** available for children who need hands-on support in segmenting the word and attaching one spelling to each sound.
- After reading all the words, partners should switch roles.
- When both partners have spelled all the words, children should correct their own papers.
- **Build Fluency: Word Automaticity** Have children chorally read the words several times for fluency.

Quick Check

Can children spell words with diphthong *oi, oy*?

During **Small Group Instruction**

If No → Approaching Level Repeat blending using the weekly spelling words. Explicitly correct the error, and provide more "with me" type practice. Use a lower level of blending to provide support.

If Yes → On Level Consolidate the learning by having children spell additional words with diphthong *oi, oy*. See page 77M.

Beyond Level Extend the learning by having children spell harder words containing diphthong *oi, oy*. See page 77N.

Vocabulary

Words in Context

REVIEW

Review this week's vocabulary words (**attention**, **buddy**, **accident**, **tip**, **enormous**, **obeys**) using the sentence stems below. Have children orally complete each one.

- Pay __________ when I am speaking to you.
- He __________ his parents and treats them with respect.
- I had an __________ and fell down the steps.
- My __________ and I go to the park every day.
- The teacher gave me a __________ on how to solve the math problem.
- The girl lived in an __________ house with a huge backyard.
- Then have children use each word in a sentence.

- Repeat the activity with last week's vocabulary words: *gasped*, *attached*, *frantically*, *swung*, and *delicious*.

Objective

- Use this week's and last week's vocabulary words in context

Objectives

- Read an expository article
- Use text features to interpret: diagram: floor plans
- Follow multi-step directions

Materials

- Student Book: "Fire Safety," pp. 72–75
- chart paper

ELL

Mimic Write the word *calm* on the board. Sit back in your chair and assume a relaxed look. Say: *I am calm.* Have children act out the word *calm* by relaxing in their seats. Have them say: *I am calm.*

Content Vocabulary

Social Studies Words

Define the content words using child-friendly definitions and select visuals.

hazards (p. 72): sources of danger

route (p. 74): a regular or chosen course of travel

calm (p. 74): a peaceful, unworried feeling

Social Studies
Informational Text

Genre

EXPOSITORY

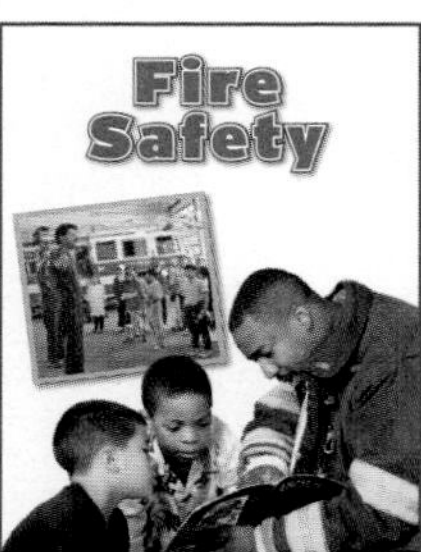

Paired Selection

Remind children that **expository** articles tell facts about real people, things, or events. Tell children that the next selection they will read is a an expository article that gives fire-safety information and directions. Discuss the text and the graphic features that children might find in a nonfiction article, such as lists, multi-step directions, photos, and floor plans.

PREVIEW AND PREDICT

Have children turn to **Student Book** page 72. Ask children to identify the subheadings on pages 72–75 and use them to make predictions about what they will read in the article. *What information might you learn in this article? What do you notice about the way the text is presented?*

Text Feature: Diagram: Floor Plans

EXPLAIN/MODEL

Point out the floor plan on page 74. *A floor plan is a map that shows where all the rooms in a building are. It usually has labels to identify the rooms and other important places in or near a building.*

Think Aloud The floor plan is like a map. I can tell which room is which because each one is labeled. The arrows show me the way that a person could escape from each room in the house.

Content Vocabulary

SAFETY FIRST

Discuss the content vocabulary: *hazards*, *route*, and *calm*.

- Remind children of their discussion during oral language about how to stay safe in different situations.
- Write the words *hazards*, *route*, and *calm* on chart paper. Prompt children to help you tell what each word means and to use it in a sentence. Explain that children will see these words in the next

Social Studies

Genre
Expository text gives information about real people, things, or events.

Text Features
Floor Plans are maps that show where all the rooms in a building are.

Content Vocabulary
hazards
route
calm

Fire Safety

Firefighters want everyone to be safe. They teach families how to avoid fire **hazards**,which are dangerous items or situations. You can help prevent fires by following fire safety rules. You can also stay safe by knowing what to do if a fire starts nearby.

Social Studies

How to Stay Safe from Fire

1
- Never play with matches or lighters.
- Do not touch lit candles.
- Do not cook unless an adult is with you.
- Be careful around irons, stoves, fireplaces, and grills.
- Never touch electric cords, plugs, or outlets.

Stop! Drop! Roll!

If your clothes catch fire, do these three things right away.

2

1 **Stop!** Running and walking can make fire worse.

2 **Drop!** Get down on the ground. Cover your face and eyes.

3 **Roll!** Roll over and over until the flames are out.

Read Informational Text

1 MONITOR AND CLARIFY: ADJUST READING RATE
There is a lot of information in the article. How can you **adjust** your **reading rate** to help yourself understand it better? (I can read more slowly to make sure I understand all of the text and make corrections. I can take time to look at the pictures and floor plans.)

2 RETELL EVENTS IN ORDER
What should you do if your clothes catch on fire? (The first step is to Stop. The second step is to Drop. The last step is to Roll.)

STRATEGY Monitor Comprehension: Read Ahead

These directions only show how to prevent fires and what to do if clothes catch fire. If you do not understand where to go in a fire, you can make an adjustment and read ahead to find out.

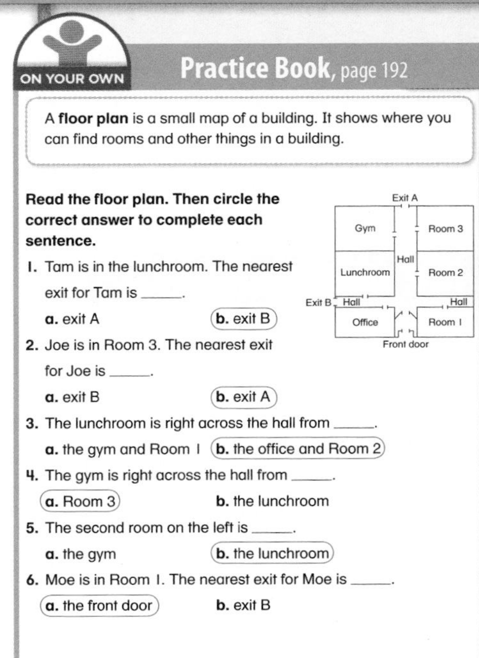

ON YOUR OWN **Practice Book**, page 192

A **floor plan** is a small map of a building. It shows where you can find rooms and other things in a building.

Read the floor plan. Then circle the correct answer to complete each sentence.

1. Tam is in the lunchroom. The nearest exit for Tam is ____.
   a. exit A b. exit B
2. Joe is in Room 3. The nearest exit for Joe is ____.
   a. exit B b. exit A
3. The lunchroom is right across the hall from ____.
   a. the gym and Room 1 b. the office and Room 2
4. The gym is right across the hall from ____.
   a. Room 3 b. the lunchroom
5. The second room on the left is ____.
   a. the gym b. the lunchroom
6. Moe is in Room 1. The nearest exit for Moe is ____.
   a. the front door b. exit B

Approaching Reproducible, page 192
Beyond Reproducible, page 192

Make a Plan!

You and your family can learn how to stay safe if there is a fire in your home. Make a floor plan of your home. Mark the best ways to get out of the house. Make sure your plan has more than one **route** in case one path gets blocked. Pick a safe place to meet outside. Have fire drills to practice your plan. Practicing will help you stay **calm** and find a safe path to the outside.

Fire Safety Floor Plan

3

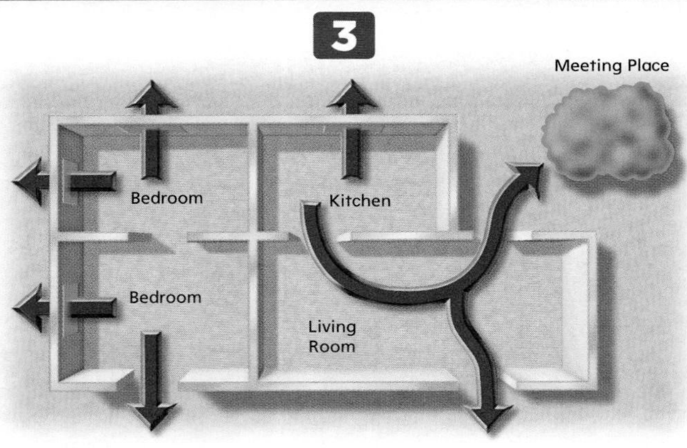

This floor plan shows several ways to get out of a home in case a fire starts.

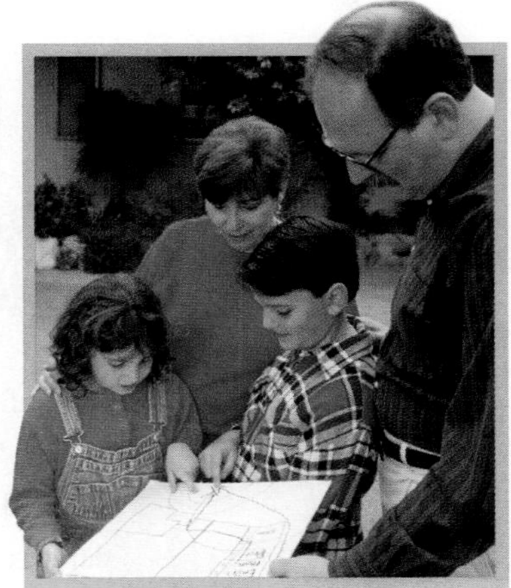

After you are safely out of the house, call 9-1-1 for help. Wait for the firefighters to arrive. Never go back into the house for anything! 4

Connect and Compare

1. What two escape routes from each bedroom does the floor plan show? **Floor Plan**
2. Think about this article and *Officer Buckle and Gloria*. What are some other safety tips that firefighters might try to teach to students and families? **Reading/Writing Across Texts**

Social Studies

Draw a floor plan of your home. Show at least two escape routes and your outside meeting place. Give a copy to your family.

Vocabulary

Reinforce the content words during reading using the context sentences and photos. Have children record these sentences, with illustrations, in their Writer's Notebooks.

3 USE TEXT FEATURES: DIAGRAM: FLOOR PLANS

How many different ways are there to escape from the house shown in the **floor plan**? (There are seven exits.) How do the labels help you? (They help identify each room in the floor plan and also the meeting place outside.)

4 AUTHOR'S PURPOSE

What is the **author's purpose** for writing this selection? (This selection is filled with facts and information about real-life events. The author wrote this to inform readers about how to stay safe in case there is a fire. The multi-step directions show readers exactly what to do in the event of a fire emergency.)

Connect and Compare

SUGGESTED ANSWERS

1. The floor plan shows leaving one bedroom through a door or a window and leaving the other bedroom through one of two windows. TEXT FEATURE: FLOOR PLAN

2. Focus Question Firefighters might teach students and families to check the batteries in their smoke alarms to make sure they are working. They might also teach people to make sure they turn off ovens and stoves before leaving their homes. READING/WRITING ACROSS TEXTS

Connect to Content

Social Studies Activity

- Suggest that children talk to their families to get input before they create their floor plans and escape routes. Ask children to share their plans with the class. Have them display their plans and discuss the escape routes.
- Extend the activity by having children draw a simple map of their neighborhood as well.

Research and Inquiry

RESEARCH: FIRE SAFETY Ask individuals and partners to research how to stay safe from fire. Help them select and use a variety of sources to gather information (e.g., videos, books, pamphlets, and the Internet) and determine which sources are relevant and appropriate. Tell children to keep a list of all their sources, including the title and author.

For each source, guide children to take notes and organize them using graphic organizers or outlines. Ask children to list all the ideas they find in their research. Then they can each pick one and use it to make a fire safety poster. Tell children to use appropriate technology to enhance their poster and communicate their ideas.

When children's posters are complete, have each child or pair share them with the class. You may also invite the local fire department to have a representative speak to the class about fire safety.

Objectives

- Analyze text feature: diagram: floor plans
- Connect reading across texts
- Research the theme of fire safety

Materials

- Student Book: "Fire Safety," pp. 72–75
- Practice Book, p. 192

Test Practice

Answering Questions

To apply **answering questions strategies** to content-area reading, see pages 11–16 in the *Time for Kids Test Practice Edition.*

Digital Learning

Story available on **Listening Library Audio CD** and **StudentWorks Plus,** the Interactive eBook.

www.macmillanmh.com

Objectives

- Proofread for capitalization, correct use of helping verbs, and quotation marks
- Use helping verbs in reading, writing, and speaking

Materials

- Transparency 84
- Proofreading Marks BLM; Teacher's Resource Book, p. 191
- Grammar Practice Book, p. 84

5-Day Grammar	
Helping Verbs	
DAY 1	*Have* as a Helping Verb
DAY 2	*Be* as a Helping Verb
DAY 3	Mechanics: Quotation Marks
DAY 4	Helping Verbs Proofread
DAY 5	Review and Assess Quotation Marks Helping Verbs

Grammar

Helping Verbs

REVIEW

- Remind children that *is*, *are*, and *am* are present-tense helping verbs. (e.g., We are eating oranges.)
- Tell them that *have*, *has*, *was*, and *were* are past-tense helping verbs. (e.g., Mom was eating an orange.)
- Remind children to use quotation marks at the beginning and at the end of a speaker's exact words. (e.g., Tina said, "I love going out to dinner!") Review that a proper noun begins with a capital letter. (e.g., Andy was not happy.)

PRACTICE

- Have children work in pairs to write a conversation between two people who just saw a mounted police officer. They should use at least one helping verb in their sentences and make sure quotation marks are placed correctly. Have partners proofread each other's sentences. Then partners should practice reading the sentences aloud to each other. A sample conversation:
- "The horse was so big and beautiful and the officer looked so proud," said Susan.
- Juan said, "Yes, they made a great team and were working very hard."

ELL ENGLISH LANGUAGE LEARNERS

Beginning

Practice Have a child hold up a book. Say and write *(child's name) is holding a book.* Give other examples of present-tense helping verbs by using simple sentences. Use images from the book to create sentence frames and then guide children to complete them with an action verb. *Officer Buckle is* ________. *The children are* ________.

Intermediate

Recognize Write *have, had, was,* and *were* on the board. Write sentence frames that children can complete with the correct verbs. Sample sentence frame: *The horses* ________ *running.* Read the sentences aloud. Have children work in pairs to copy the frames and complete them with the correct verbs. Have children read their sentences aloud, and correct for grammar as needed.

Advanced

Edit Write the following types of sentences and have partners work together to decide which sentences are incorrect and then rewrite the incorrect sentences. *They were watching a police officer on a horse. She said, "That horse were looking at me."*

Review and Assess
Fluency

Intonation

MODEL FLUENT READING

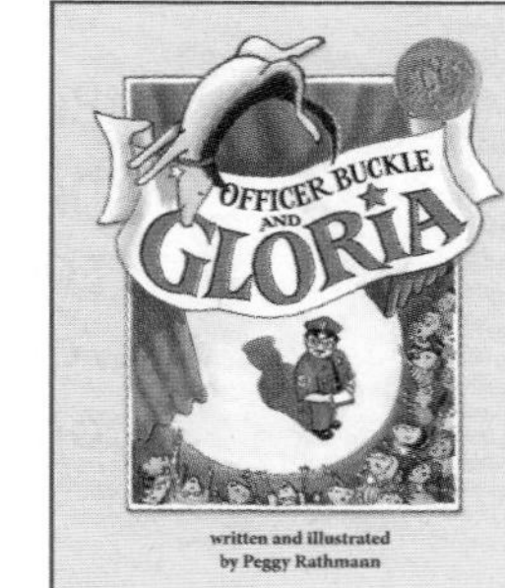

Main Selection

- Read aloud a few pages of *Officer Buckle and Gloria*. Model reading with appropriate intonation and good expression. Have children echo each sentence you read. Point out how you raise your voice at the end of questions.

- Have partners reread the selection aloud, working on how they read the questions. Circulate, listen in, and provide corrective feedback. Note children who need additional work during Small Group time with decoding and reading high-frequency words.

REPEATED READINGS

- Have children select a story from the **Student Book** or a book that they have previously read. Tell children: *The more practice we have sounding out words and seeing those important high-frequency words in text, the easier it will be for us to read new stories.*
- Provide 15–20 minutes for children to enjoy independent reading. Then ask students to paraphrase what they have read. You may read with children or use this time to use the Fluency Assessment in the **Diagnostic Assessment Handbook**.

Objectives

- Review and assess vocabulary
- Build fluency
- Read independently and paraphrase, maintaining meaning

Materials

- Student Book

Readers Theater

BUILDING LISTENING AND SPEAKING SKILLS
Distribute copies of "A Whale of a Story" from **Read-Aloud Anthology** pages 179–191. Have children practice reading the play throughout the unit. Assign parts and have children present the play or perform it as a dramatic reading at the end of the unit.

Objectives

- Blend phonemes
- Blend sounds in words with diphthong *oi, oy*
- Read multisyllabic words
- Review diphthong *oi, oy*

Materials

- Word-Building Cards; Teacher's Resource Book, p. 66
- pocket chart
- word charts from Days 1, 3
- Decodable Reader Library: *Let's Join Joy's Show!*
- Practice Book for diphthong *oi, oy*, p. 193

Skills Trace

Diphthong *oi, oy*	
Introduce	43C–D
Practice/ Apply	43F, 45G-H, 71F-G, 71I, 71T-U; Practice Book: 184; Decodable Reader: *Let's Join Joy's Show!*
Reteach/ Review	77C-D; 77K-N, 77Q, 77W, 77CC
Assess	Weekly Test; Unit 4 Test
Maintain	Build Fluency: Sound/Spellings

Review and Assess

Phonemic Awareness

Phoneme Blending

Guided Practice/Practice

Review with children how to orally blend the sounds in words with /oi/. Model the first one.

I am going to say a word sound by sound. I want you to blend the sounds to form the word. The sounds are /m/ /oi/ /s/ /t/. Listen as I blend the sounds: /moist/, *moist*. The word is *moist*. Your turn.

point	poison	join	coy	employ
annoy	coin	foil	royal	soy

Review and Assess

Phonics

Build Fluency: Sound/Spellings

Display the following **Word-Building Cards** one at a time: *oi, oy, ou, ow, are, air, ear, ere, or, ore, oar, ar, gn, kn, wr, mb, eer, ere, ear, er, ir, ur*. Have children chorally say each sound. Mix, repeat, and vary the pace.

Blend Words with *oi, oy*

Guided Practice

Display **Word-Building Cards** *p, o, i, n, t*. Blend.

What sounds do these letters stand for? Let's blend the sounds and read the word: *point*.

Practice

Have children practice generating and blending sounds to form words and nonsense words. Use the examples provided. Write each word on the board.

broil	oink	toil	toy	enjoy
spoil	choice	oily	foil	loyal
Troy	noisy	hoist	moist	soy
annoy	broiled	royal	decoy	spoiling
zoily	zoyal	unvoim	goiting	woit

Build Fluency: Word Automaticity

Use word charts from Days 1 and 3. Point to each word as children chorally read it. Model blending the sounds in any words children miss. Then point to words in random order at varying speeds for children to chorally read.

join	noise	pointed	spoil
boy	Joy	toy	Troy
coin	ploy	foil	coy
groin	flute	cutest	using
scraped	sleigh	proclaim	girl

The boy joined the dog outside.
I pointed at the officer's toy.

toil	moist	voice	void
avoid	enjoy	noise	choice
soy	poise	doily	hoist
points	rejoin	disloyal	royal
pasted	plum	slime	unsent

The officer had a loud voice.
The dog enjoyed a moist treat.

voided	recoil	employ	destroy

Build Fluency: Connected Text

- Have children reread with a partner *Let's Join Joy's Show!* from the **Decodable Reader Library**. Circulate and listen in, providing corrective feedback as needed.
- Comment on children's **speed**, **accuracy**, and **intonation**. Model each as needed. For example, model how your voice rises at the end of a question.

Let's Join Joy's Show!

Corrective Feedback

For children needing additional practice reading words with *oi* and *oy*, use the one-syllable and multisyllabic Speed Drills in the **Intervention Kit** (**Fluency**).

Objectives

- Spell and assess words with diphthong *oi, oy*
- Spell high-frequency words
- Use the Word Wall to find spellings

Materials

- paper and pencils

5-Day Spelling	
DAY 1	Dictation; Pretest
DAY 2	Teacher-Modeled Word Sort
DAY 3	Student Word Sort
DAY 4	Test Practice
DAY 5	Posttest

Review and Assess

Phonics/Spelling

Words with *oi, oy*

POSTTEST

Use the following procedure to assess children's spelling of the weekly spelling words.

- Pronounce each spelling word and use it in the sentence provided below. Say the word again.
- Have children softly repeat each word before they write it.
- Tell children to write the word on a sheet of paper.
- Prompt children to write words they know in their Writer's Notebooks for use in their writing.
- Have children write misspelled words as homework.

1. **soil:** We planted the seeds in the soil.
2. **broil:** Mom will broil the meat in the oven.
3. **moist:** I cleaned my face with a moist cloth.
4. **point:** Her hat had a point on top of it.
5. **boil:** Dad will boil the water on the stove.
6. **oil:** I put oil on the chain of my bike.
7. **toy:** The train set is my favorite toy.
8. **joy:** I will jump for joy if we win this game!
9. **avoid:** Do not avoid doing your homework.
10. **royal:** The king is part of the royal family.
11. **crown:** The king would like to wear his crown.
12. **house:** The house is near the pond.
13. **above:** Draw a cloud above the trees.
14. **color:** Color with the crayons or markers.
15. **song:** Sing the song with me.

Word Wall Use a Word Wall to group words by spelling patterns. Also use it to review previous weeks' spelling words. Remove words from the Word Wall when children have mastered them.

Review and Assess

Vocabulary

Words in Context

REVIEW

Ask these questions that use a synonym or similar words for each vocabulary word. Have children tell what vocabulary word fits into each sentence and reread the sentence using the word.

- Did you listen to the **rules** for staying safe? (tips)
- Who **follows** the rules? (obeys)
- Did you give your **most careful thought** to what the teacher said? (attention)
- Did you get hurt from your bicycle by **mistake**? (accident)
- Which is **huge**, an elephant or a chicken? (enormous)
- Do you play often with your **friend**? (buddy)
- Then have children use each word in a sentence.

Spiral Vocabulary Review

Tell the class that everyone will work together to create a story. The goal will be to write a story on the board that uses the vocabulary words from this week and last week (*swung*, *attached*, *gasped*, *frantically*, and *delicious*).

- Read the words aloud. Have children tell what each word means. Discuss ways the words may connect, and brainstorm possible story lines.
- Have children sit in a circle. Choose a child to start telling the story. You might offer a first sentence, such as *My buddy Mara got hurt yesterday*.
- Have each child add one sentence that includes a vocabulary word. Continue around the circle until each child has contributed. All vocabulary words must be used, but they can be used more than once.

Write About It

Think about various animals. Write a list of animals that can work with people on teams and explain why. Try to use the vocabulary words in your writing.

Objectives

- Use vocabulary in context
- Review this week's and last week's vocabulary words

Objectives

- Determine when children might need to monitor comprehension and read ahead again
- Use illustrations to better understand text
- Make comparisons across texts
- Review Using Strategies (use ideas to make and confirm predictions)

Materials

- Practice Book for Using Strategies, p. 194

Skills Trace

Use Illustrations	
Introduce	U4: 45A–B
Practice/ Apply	U4: 45K–71A; Practice Book: 187–188
Reteach/ Review	U4: 77G, 77R–T, 77X–Z
Assess	Weekly Test; Unit 4 Test
Maintain	U4: 115N

Review and Assess

Comprehension

STRATEGY Monitor Comprehension: Read Ahead

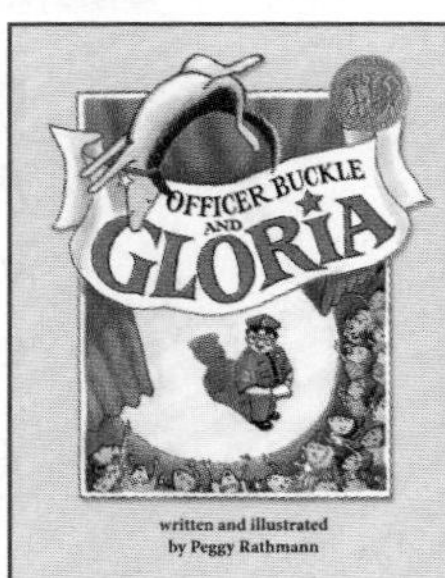

Main Selection

TRANSFER THE STRATEGY Remind children that as they read *Officer Buckle and Gloria* they tried to monitor their comprehension by making a correction and reading ahead if they didn't understand something. Model how using this strategy helped you make adjustments when your understanding broke down.

Think Aloud Sometimes things that I don't understand become clearer to me when I find out what is happening on the next page. When I didn't understand that Gloria had become very popular, I read ahead and found out that grade schools, high schools, and day care centers all wanted her to go along with Officer Buckle. Reading ahead helped me monitor my comprehension and better understand the story.

Focus Question *How did the strategy help you? When might you use the strategy again?* Offer these sentence starters:

I read ahead to find out _________.

Reading ahead helped me _________.

SKILL Use Illustrations

READING ACROSS TEXTS Model making a connection between the illustrations for "Safety at School" and *Officer Buckle and Gloria.*

Think Aloud I made a connection between the illustrations in these two stories. Both of the stories showed characters, kids in school, learning about safety. In both stories, the illustrations helped me to understand what was happening in the story. The pictures sometimes show a character's traits, motivations, or feelings that the words do not tell about. They also can show actions or events that the words do not describe.

Provide a sentence starter to help children make their own connections between selections:

The pictures in "Safety at School" and Officer Buckle and Gloria *helped me* _________.

Approaching Level

High-Frequency/Vocabulary

Objective Identify high-frequency words and selection vocabulary

Materials
- **High-Frequency Word Cards**
- **Sound-Spelling WorkBoards**
- **Visual Vocabulary Resources**
- **Vocabulary Cards**
- **Approaching Reproducible**, p. 185

PRETEACH WORDS

- **Introduce High-Frequency Words** Preteach the high-frequency words **above**, **color**, and **song** using the **Read/Spell/Write** routine. Display the **High-Frequency Word Cards** and have children write each word on their **WorkBoards**.
- **Introduce Vocabulary Words** Use the **Visual Vocabulary Resources** to preteach the words **accident**, **attention**, **buddy**, **enormous**, **obeys**, and **tip**. Refer to the routine on the cards.
- Introduce words using the **Define/Example/Ask** routine. Use the context sentences on **Approaching Reproducible** page 185.

CUMULATIVE REVIEW

Tier 2

Display the High-Frequency Word Cards for **above**, **color**, and **song**. Display one card at a time as children chorally say the word. Then repeat this procedure using the High-Frequency Word Cards from the previous four to six weeks. Note words needing review.

Then display the **Vocabulary Cards** from the previous four weeks. Say the meaning of each word and have children identify it. Then point to words randomly for children to provide definitions.

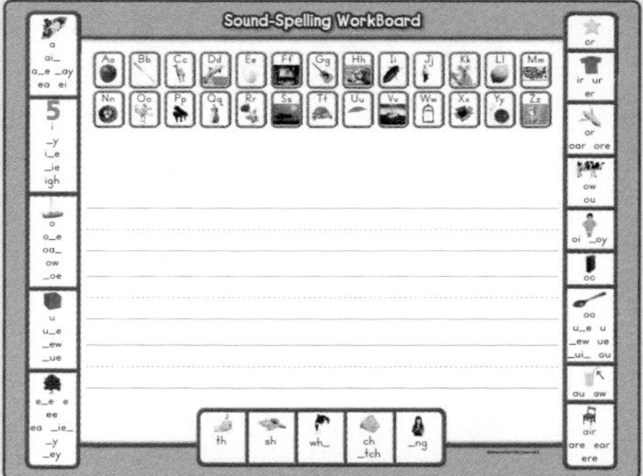

Sound-Spelling WorkBoard

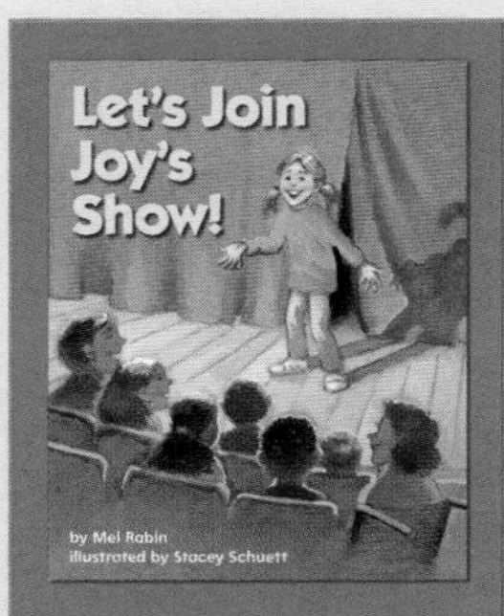

Decodable Reader

Decodable Reader

Objective Read and decode words with vowel diphthong *oi, oy* in connected text

Materials
- **Decodable Reader:** *Let's Join Joy's Show!*

READ THE TEXT

- **Preview and Predict** Point to the book's title and have children sound out each word as you run your finger under it. *I see a girl on stage.* Ask: *What do you think she will perform?*
- **Read the Book** Turn to page 8. Have children point to each word, sounding out decodable words and saying the high-frequency words quickly. If children struggle sounding out words, provide "with you" blending models.
- **Check Comprehension** Ask the following:
  - *What was special about Joy?*
  - *Why did Joy want to put on a show?*

Interactive Student Book

If you wish to preteach the main selection, use StudentWorks Plus for:
- Vocabulary preteaching
- Word-by-word highlighting
- Think Aloud prompts

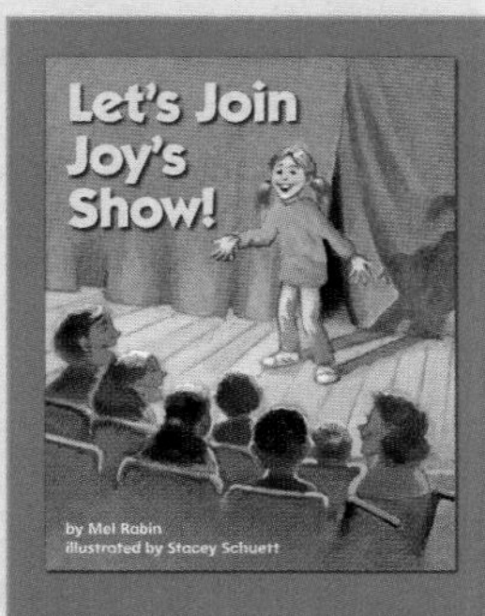

Decodable Reader

On Level

Phonics

Objective Decode words with vowel diphthong *oi, oy*

Materials
- **Sound-Spelling Cards**
- **Word-Building Cards**
- **Decodable Reader:** *Let's Join Joy's Show!*

REVIEW VOWEL DIPHTHONG *oi, oy*

- **Review Diphthong *oi, oy*** Display the *Boy* **Sound-Spelling Card**. Remind children that the vowel diphthong /oi/ can be spelled with the letters *oi* or *oy*.
- **Blend Words** Write words and sentences from the charts on pages 43D and 71G on the board. Quickly have children chorally read the words. Repeat by pointing to the words in random order. Model blending the sounds in any words children have difficulty reading. Continue with the words below to help children apply their skills to new words. Write each word on the board for children to read.

coins	joined	loyal	royal	coy
toy	uncoil	boys	foil	toiling
soil	oiled	boiling	soy	joyful

- **Build Words** Display **Word-Building Cards** *o, i, y, a, b, c, f, g, j, l, n, r, s,* and *t*. Have partners make as many words as they can. Direct them to write their words in lists based on spelling patterns. For example, words that end in *-oy* go in one list, words that end in *-oil* go in another list, and so on. Provide time for children to share their lists.

Words with *-oil*	Words with *-oin*	Words with *-oint*	Words with *-oy*

REREAD FOR FLUENCY

- Have partners reread *Let's Join Joy's Show!* Work with children to read at the appropriate rate and intonation. Model fluent reading as needed.

ELL

Reread for Fluency Use the Interactive Question-Response Guide Technique to help English Language Learners understand the content of *Let's Join Joy's Show!* As you read the text, make the meaning clear by pointing to the pictures, demonstrating word meaning, paraphrasing text, and asking children questions.

Beyond Level

Phonics

Objective Use syllabication patterns to decode words with diphthong *oi, oy*
Materials • none

EXTEND/ACCELERATE

- **Review Vowel Diphthong *oi, oy*** Guide children into reading more complex words with *oi, oy*. Say: *You will be able to decode longer words if you divide the word into word parts. Read each part, then put them together.* Remind children to look for prefixes to help them read the words. Write each sample word on the board and draw a line or lines to divide the words into word parts.
- **Blend Words** Help children read longer *oi* and *oy* words. Write each word below on the board. Model blending as needed.

ointment	oyster	overjoyed
voyage	rejoice	disloyal
avoid	destroy	sirloin

- Have children search *Road Safety* for diphthong *oi* and *oy* words. Ask children to state the word found and read aloud the sentence. Have children record these words in their Writer's Notebooks. Challenge them to search classroom books for words with diphthong *oi* to add to the list.

Vocabulary

Objective Use context to determine word meaning

EXPAND ORAL VOCABULARY

Gifted Talented

- Review the meanings of oral vocabulary words *advice, hesitate, secure, panic, vowed* with children. Write the words on the board.
  - Explain that you will now use two of the words in a sentence. Have children listen as you say the following sentence: *My* advice *to you is to not* panic.
  - Then write the sentence on the board and underline the words *advice* and *panic*. Discuss the meaning of the underlined words with children.

  - Have children work with a partner to come up with another sentence that uses two or three of the oral vocabulary words.
  - Have partners share their sentences with the group.

ELL

Minimal Contrasts Focus on articulation. Make the /oi/ sound and point out your mouth position. Have children repeat. Use the articulation photos on the small Sound-Spelling Cards. Repeat for the /ō/ sound. Then have children say each sound together, noticing the slight differences in mouth position. Continue by having children read minimal-contrast word pairs, such as *join/Joan, boil/bowl, toy/toe*.

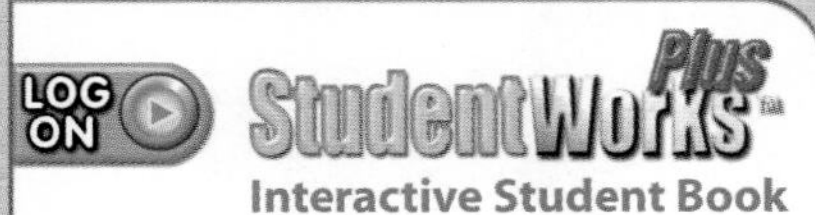

Interactive Student Book

If you wish to preteach the main selection, use StudentWorks Plus for:

- Vocabulary preteaching
- Word-by-word highlighting
- Think Aloud prompts

Cognates

Help children identify similarities and differences in pronunciation and spelling between English words and Spanish cognates.

Cognates

panic *pánico*

attention *attentión*

accident *accidente*

enormous *enorme*

obey *obedecer*

illustration *ilustración*

comprehension *comprensión*

verb *verbo*

ELL ENGLISH LANGUAGE LEARNERS

Prepare to Read

Content Objective Use humor to show the importance of teamwork

Language Objective Use key words to tell about Officer Buckle and his buddy giving safety tips

Materials • **StudentWorks Plus** (interactive eBook)

BUILD BACKGROUND

All Language Levels

- This version of the Student Book contains oral summaries in multiple languages, on-line multilingual glossaries, word-by-word highlighting, and questions that assess and build comprehension.
- Children can build their word-reading fluency by reading along as the text is read or by listening during the first reading and, at the end of each paragraph, returning to the beginning of the paragraph and reading along.
- Children can build their comprehension by reviewing the definitions of key words in the on-line glossary and by answering the comprehension questions. When appropriate, the text required to answer the question is highlighted to provide children with additional support and scaffolding.
- Following the reading, ask children to respond in writing to a question that links the story to their personal experiences, such as *What's the funniest thing you ever saw an animal do?*

Academic Language

Language Objective Use academic language in classroom conversations

All Language Levels

- This week's academic words are **boldfaced** throughout the lesson. Define the word in context and provide a clear example from the selection. Then ask children to generate an example or a word with a similar meaning.

Academic Language Used in Whole Group Instruction

Oral Vocabulary Words	Key Selection Words	Strategy and Skill Words
advice	**attention**	**illustrations**
hesitate	**buddy**	**monitor**
panic	**accident**	**comprehension**
secure	**tip**	**read ahead**
vowed	**enormous**	**helping verb**
	obeys	

ENGLISH LANGUAGE LEARNERS

Vocabulary

Language Objective Demonstrate understanding and use of key words to tell how Officer Buckle and Gloria work together to give safety tips

Materials • **Visual Vocabulary Resources** • **ELL Resource Book**, p. 242

PRETEACH KEY VOCABULARY

All Language Levels

Use the **Visual Vocabulary Resources** to preteach the key selection words **accident**, **attention**, **buddy**, **enormous**, **obeys**, and **tip**. Focus on two words per day. Use the following routine, which appears in detail on the cards.

- Define the word in English and, if appropriate, Spanish. Indicate if the word is a cognate, and provide the example given.
- Display the picture and explain how it illustrates or demonstrates the word. Engage children in structured partner-talk about the image, using the key word.
- Ask children to chorally say the word three times.
- Point out any known sound-spellings or focus on a key aspect of phonemic awareness related to the word.
- Distribute copies of the Vocabulary Glossary, **ELL Resource Book** page 242.

PRETEACH FUNCTION WORDS AND PHRASES

All Language Levels

Use the Visual Vocabulary Resources to preteach the function words and phrases *always*, *never*, *again and again*, and *as usual*. Focus on one word per day. Use the detailed routine on the cards.

- Define the word in English and, if appropriate, in Spanish. Point out if the word is a cognate.
- Refer to the picture and engage children in talk about the word. For example, children will partner-talk using sentence frames or they will listen to sentences and replace a word or phrase with the new function word.
- Ask children to chorally repeat the word three times.

TEACH BASIC WORDS

Beginning/Intermediate

Use the Visual Vocabulary Resources to teach the basic words *swivel chair*, *shoelace*, *electrical storm*, *spills* (noun), *thumbtack*, and *hammer*. Teach these “things to be careful with” using the routine provided on the card.

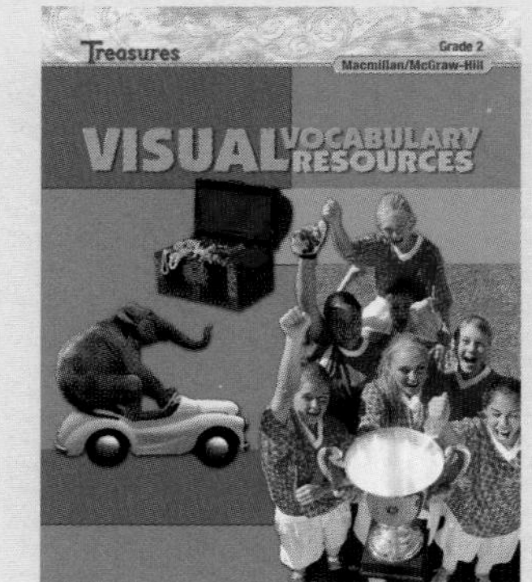

Visual Vocabulary Resources

ELL Resource Book, page 242

Use the word chart to study this week's vocabulary words.
Write a sentence using each word in your writer's notebook.

Word	Context Sentence	Illustration
attention	Sam was not paying attention to where he was going.	
buddy	I walk to school with my buddy Jack.	
accident	Tie your shoelaces so you don't trip and have an accident.	
tip	Washing your hands before you eat is a good tip for staying healthy.	
enormous	I felt small next to the enormous tree.	What is a another word for *enormous*?
obeys	My dog obeys me when I tell him to sit.	

Approaching Level

Phonemic Awareness

Objective Blend phonemes to form words

Materials
- none

PHONEME BLENDING

Tier 2

- Model for children how to blend phonemes to say words. Say: *Listen as I say these sounds: /oi/ /l/.* Blend the sounds together, drawing them out, and then say the word naturally: /oil/, *oil*.
- Have children practice with these words. Do the first one together. /b/ /oi/ /l/ (boil); /t/ /oi/ (toy); /k/ /oi/ (coy); /s/ /p/ /oi/ /l/ (spoil); /j/ /oi/ /n/ /t/ (joint).

Phonics

Objective Decode words with vowel diphthong *oi, oy*

Materials
- **Sound-Spelling Cards**
- **Word-Building Cards**
- pocket chart
- **Decodable Reader:** *Let's Join Joy's Show!*

SOUND-SPELLING REVIEW

Tier 2

Display the **Word-Building Cards** for the following, one at a time: *oi, oy, ou, ow, are, air, ear, ere, or, ore, oar, ar, gn, kn, wr, mb, eer, ere, ear, er, ir, ur.* Have children chorally say each sound. Repeat and vary the pace.

RETEACH SKILL

- Display the *Boy* **Sound-Spelling Card** for vowel diphthong *oi, oy*. Review that the /oi/ sound can be spelled with the letters *oi* or *oy*.
- **Model Blending** Write words and sentences from the chart on page 43D on the board. Model how to blend the sounds in each word using the **Blending Routine**. Have children repeat. Then have children read each word multiple times.
- **Build Words** Place Word-Building Cards *o* and *i* in a pocket chart. Ask: *What sound do these letters stand for?* Place *l* next to *oi*. Ask: *What sound does this stand for?* Blend the sounds: /oil/. Say: *Now you say it. You blend the sounds. What's the word?*

  Repeat with the words *toil*, *boil*, *toy*, *boy*, and *join*.

REREAD FOR FLUENCY

- Reread *Let's Join Joy's Show!* with children. Then have them practice rereading the book using the appropriate rate and intonation to a partner. Circulate, listen in, and provide feedback.

Decodable Reader

ELL

Reread for Fluency Use the Interactive Question-Response Guide Technique to help English Language Learners understand the content of *Let's Join Joy's Show!* As you read the text, make the meaning clear by pointing to the pictures, demonstrating word meaning, paraphrasing text, and asking children questions.

Approaching Level

High-Frequency/Vocabulary

Objective Identify high-frequency words and vocabulary words

Materials • **High-Frequency Word Cards** • **Vocabulary Cards**

RETEACH WORDS

Tier 2

Display **High-Frequency Word Cards** for **above**, **color**, and **song**. Review using the **Read/Spell/Write** routine. Display **Vocabulary Cards** for **accident**, **attention**, **buddy**, **enormous**, **obeys**, and **tip**. Review using the **Define/Example/Ask** routine.

CUMULATIVE REVIEW

Display the High-Frequency and Vocabulary Cards from the previous four to six weeks. Display one card at a time as children chorally read the word. Note words children need to review.

Leveled Reader Library

Leveled Reader Lesson 1

Objectives Use graphic features to interpret text; read to apply skills and strategies

Materials • **Leveled Reader:** *Road Safety* • **Approaching Reproducible**, p. 187

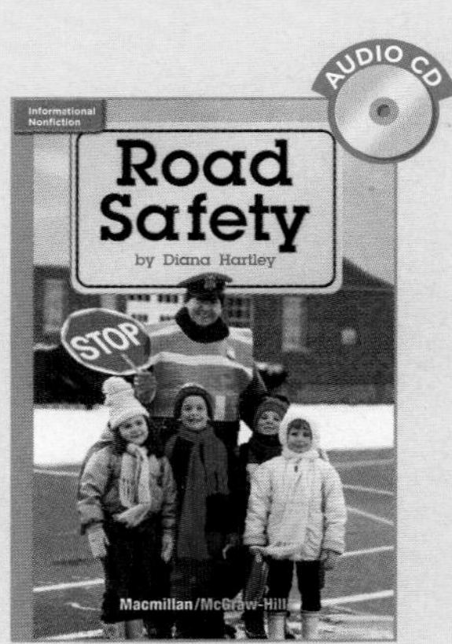

Leveled Reader

BEFORE READING

- **Preview and Predict** Read the title and author name. Ask: *What do you think we will learn about in this book?*
- **Review Skills** Use the inside front cover to review the phonics skill and vocabulary words.
- **Set a Purpose** Say: *Let's read to find out how to be safe on the road.*

DURING READING

- Have children whisper-read each page. Listen in and provide corrective feedback, such as modeling how to blend a word.
- **Use Illustrations/Photographs** Remind children that authors use photographs to help us learn information. Draw an Illustrations/Photographs Chart like the one on the Reproducible. Have children copy it. After children have read a few pages, ask them to tell what they learned from one picture. Model how to record the information. Have children copy it and start to fill in their own charts.

AFTER READING

- Discuss words that gave children difficulty and the strategies they used to decode them. Reinforce good reading behaviors.
- **Retell** Have children take turns retelling the selection.

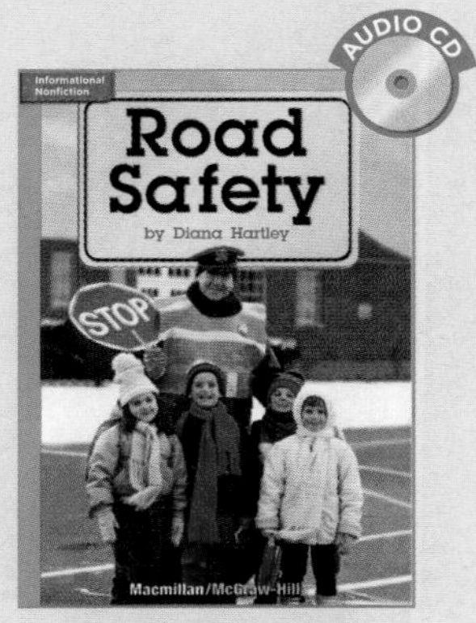

Leveled Reader

On Level

Leveled Reader Lesson 1

Objectives Use graphic features to interpret text; read to apply skills and strategies

Materials • **Leveled Reader:** *Road Safety* • **Practice Book**, p. 187

BEFORE READING

Preview and Predict Read the title and the name of the author. Ask: *What do you think this book will be about? How can you tell?* Preview the title page and the pictures.

Review Skills Use the inside front cover to review the phonics skill and teach the new vocabulary words.

Set a Purpose Say: *Let's read to find out how to be safe on the road.*

DURING READING

- Have children turn to page 2 and begin by whisper-reading the first two pages.
- Remind children to look for the new vocabulary words. Tell them that you will help them blend sounds in words with *oi* and *oy*.
- Monitor children's reading. Stop periodically and ask open-ended questions to facilitate rich discussion, such as *What is the author telling us about rules? What does the author want us to know about all safety rules?* Build on children's responses to develop deeper understanding of the text.

- **Use Illustrations** Remind children that photographs can help you get additional information from a selection. Draw an Illustrations/Photographs Chart like the one on the **Practice Book** page. Have children copy it. As children reread, ask them to tell what they have learned about one illustration or photograph. Model how to record the information and have children copy it. Then have them begin to fill in their Illustrations/Photographs Chart.

AFTER READING

- Discuss words that gave children difficulty and the strategies they used to decode them. Reinforce good reading behaviors you noticed.
- **Retell** Have children take turns retelling the selection. Help them make a personal connection (Text-to-Self) by asking, *What kinds of safety rules do we have in our school? Can you think of other rules that might be needed? What are some examples?*

ELL

Retell Use the Interactive Question-Response Guide Technique to help English Language Learners understand the content of *Road Safety*. As you read the text, make the meaning clear by pointing to the pictures, demonstrating word meaning, paraphrasing text, and asking children questions.

Beyond Level

Leveled Reader Lesson 1

Objectives Use graphic features to interpret text; read to apply skills and strategies

Materials
- **Leveled Reader:** *Road Safety*
- **Beyond Reproducible**, p. 187
- self-stick notes

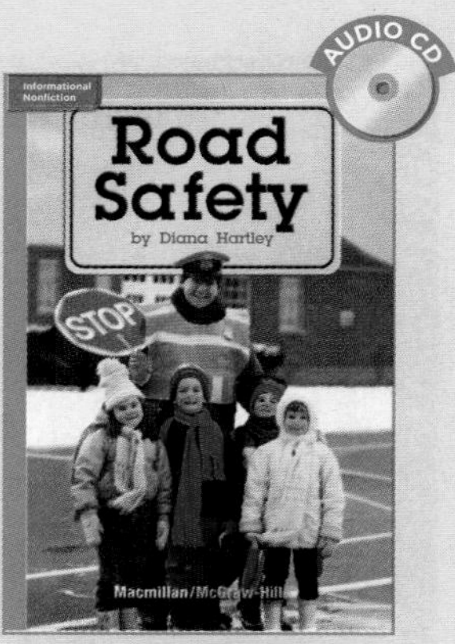

Leveled Reader

BEFORE READING

Preview and Predict Read the title and the name of the author. Preview the title page and the pictures.

Review Skills Use the inside front cover to review the phonics skill and vocabulary words.

Set a Purpose Say: *Let's read to find out about road safety.*

DURING READING

- Have children turn to page 2 and begin by whisper-reading the first two pages. Direct them to place self-stick notes next to words they have difficulty with.
- Remind children that when they come to an unfamiliar word, they can look for familiar spellings and chunks. For longer words, they will need to break the word into smaller chunks, or syllables, and sound out each part.
- Monitor children's reading. Stop periodically and ask open-ended questions to facilitate rich discussion, such as *What is the author telling us about safety rules? What does the author want us to know about why safety rules are important?* Have children support answers with evidence from the text.

- **Use Photographs** Draw an Illustrations/Photographs Chart like the one on the Reproducible. Discuss how photographs can help us get information from a selection. Model how to record information about a photograph. Have children complete their charts as they read. Ask them to explain strategies they used to problem-solve as they read.

AFTER READING

Gifted Talented

- **Analyze** Review the selection with children. *What is the main idea of this book? Why is it important?*

- Tell children they will work with a partner to write another chapter for this book called "Riding in a Car Safely." Ask a volunteer to name a rule for riding in a car.
- Have children work together to come up with some rules for riding in a car. Have them write their rules in a list.
- Then have children share their lists with the group.

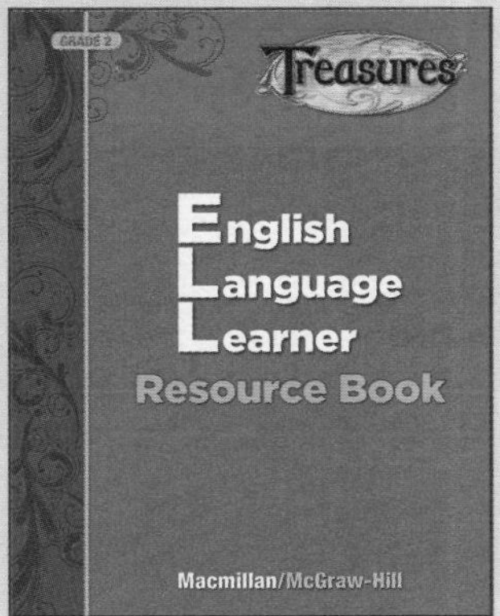

ELL Resource Book

ELL ENGLISH LANGUAGE LEARNERS

Access to Core Content

Content Objective Read grade-level text
Language Objective Discuss text using key words and sentence frames
Materials • **ELL Resource Book**, pp. 228–239

PRETEACH MAIN SELECTION (PAGES 46–71)

All Language Levels

Use the Interactive Question-Response Guide on **ELL Resource Book** pages 228–239 to introduce children to *Officer Buckle and Gloria*. Preteach half of the selection on **Day 2** and half on **Day 3**.

- Use the prompts provided in the guide to develop meaning and vocabulary. Use the partner-talk and whole-class responses to engage children and increase student talk.
- When completed, have partners reread the story.

Beginning

Use Visuals During the Interactive Reading, select several pictures. Describe them and have children summarize what you said.

Intermediate

Use Visuals During the Interactive Reading, select a few lines of text. After you read and explain them, give children time to study the corresponding illustration. Have children tell you what additional information they find in the illustration.

Advanced

Expand During the Interactive Reading, select a larger portion of text. After you read and explain it, give children time to study the corresponding illustration. Have children tell you what additional information they find in the illustration.

ENGLISH LANGUAGE LEARNERS

Grammar

Content Objective Identify helping verbs
Language Objective Speak in complete sentences, using sentence frames

HELPING VERBS

Beginning/Intermediate

- Review that a helping verb helps another verb to show action and that the verb *have* is a helping verb.

All Language Levels

- Review that a helping verb helps another verb to show action and that the verb *have* is a helping verb.
- Write this sentence on the board: *The firefighters have helped many families.* Underline the helping verb (*have*). Tell children: Have *and* has *are helping verbs that tell about actions in the past. Use* has *with singular subjects and* have *with plurals.* Point out the plural subject *firefighters.* Repeat with the sentence *The boy is showing us how to roll.* Underline the helping verb *is*. Say: Am, are, *and* is *are helping verbs in the present tense.* Were *and* was *are in the past.*
- Write sentences on the board, such at those provided below. Have children circle the correct helping verb and then read the sentence aloud. Have them say: *The helping verb _________ is (singular/plural).*

  Officer Buckle (is, are) talking. The children (has, have) seen the show.

PEER DISCUSSION STARTERS

All Language Levels

- Write the following sentences on the board.

  Fire safety tips are taught _________.
  Officer Buckle and Gloria have shown _________.
- Pair children and have them complete each sentence frame by providing details from this week's readings. Take note of each child's language use and proficiency.

Beginning	Intermediate	Advanced
Use Visuals Use helping verbs as you describe the illustration in *Office Buckle and Gloria* to children. Ask: *What do you see?* Help children use helping verbs in their answers.	**Describe** Ask children to describe the same illustrations, adding more helping verbs to their descriptions. Have them use complete sentences.	**Narrate** Ask children to describe the photographs, adding new helping verbs to their descriptions.

Transfer Skills

Verbs In Hmong and Khmer, nouns do not change form to show the plural. Therefore, children speaking these languages may not easily distinguish the plural forms of nouns from the singular forms. Make sure children understand that there is a difference between one and more than one thing. Display and name classroom people and objects (*boy/boys, desk/desks*) to illustrate the singular and plural forms of regular nouns. Point out that identifying the subject in each of the sentences in this activity as singular or plural is necessary to decide which form of the helping verb is correct.

Corrective Feedback

During Whole Group grammar lessons, follow the routine on the **Grammar Transparencies** to provide children with extra support. This routine includes completing the items with English Learners while other children work independently, having children reread the sentences with partners to build fluency, and providing a generative task such as writing a new sentence using the skill.

Approaching Level

Phonemic Awareness

Objective Recognize when a phoneme is changed in a word

Materials • none

PHONEME SUBSTITUTION

Tier 2

- Model how to substitute phonemes. Say: *Listen as I say this word:* boy. *I will change the /b/ in* boy *to /j/ to make a new word:* joy.
- Give children the examples below for practice. Change the first sound to make a new word. Do the first one together.

toil	*Change /t/ to /f/.* (foil)	loyal	*Change /l/ to /r/.* (royal)
coin	*Change /k/ to /j/.* (join)	joint	*Change /j/ to /p/.* (point)

Phonics

Objective Decode words with vowel diphthong *oi, oy*

Materials • **Sound-Spelling Cards** • **Word-Building Cards** • pocket chart • **Decodable Reader:** *Let's Join Joy's Show!*

SOUND-SPELLING REVIEW

Tier 2

Display the **Word-Building Cards** for the following, one at a time: *oi, oy, ou, ow, are, air, ear, ere, or, ore, oar, ar, gn, kn, wr, mb, eer, ere, ear, er, ir, ur.* Have children chorally say each sound.

RETEACH SKILL

- Display the *Boy* **Sound-Spelling Card** for vowel diphthong *oi, oy.* Review that the /oi/ sound can be spelled with the letters *oi* or *oy.*
- **Model Blending** Write words and sentences from the chart on page 71G on the board. Model how to blend the sounds in each word using the **Blending Routine**. Have children repeat.
- **Build Words** Place Word-Building Cards *b, o, y* in a pocket chart. Help children blend the sounds to read the word. Then:

  Change the b *in* boy *to* j. *What word did you make?*
  Change the y *in* joy *to* i *and add an* n. *What word did you make?*
  Change the j *in* join *to* c. *What word did you make?*
  Change the n *in* coin *to* l. *What word did you make?*

  Repeat with the word set *toil, toy, soy, soil, boil,* and *broil.*
- **Read the Decodable** Reread *Let's Join Joy's Show* with children. Provide blending models. When completed, have children chorally reread the story.

Decodable Reader

ELL

Demonstrate Comprehension Use the Interactive Question-Response Guide Technique to help English Language Learners understand the content of *Let's Join Joy's Show!* As you read the text, make the meaning clear by pointing to the pictures, demonstrating word meaning, paraphrasing text, and asking children questions.

Approaching Level

High-Frequency/Vocabulary

Objective Identify high-frequency words and vocabulary words
Materials • **High-Frequency Word Cards** • **Vocabulary Cards**

BUILD WORD AUTOMATICITY

Fluency Display **High-Frequency Word Cards** for **family**, **four**, **hear** and **Vocabulary Cards** for **accident**, **attention**, **buddy**, **enormous**, **obeys**, and **tip**. Point to the words in random order. Have children chorally identify them. Repeat at a faster pace.

CUMULATIVE REVIEW

Display the High-Frequency and Vocabulary Cards from the previous six weeks. Display one card at a time as children chorally read the word. Mix and repeat. Note words needing review.

Leveled Reader Lesson 2

Objectives Use graphic features to interpret text; read to apply skills and strategies
Materials • **Leveled Reader:** *Road Safety*
• **Approaching Reproducible**, pp. 187, 188

BEFORE READING

Review Have children retell *Road Safety*. Ask them to page through the book and say in their own words what they learned about road safety rules. Reinforce key vocabulary words by restating children's responses with the key words.

DURING READING

Use Photographs As children reread the book, help them finish adding information to their Illustrations/Photographs Charts. Explain that an author can also use photographs to present information that is not in the text.

AFTER READING

- **Retell** Have children use their Illustrations/Photographs Charts to orally retell the important facts learned in *Road Safety*.
- **Model Fluency** Read the sentences in the book one at a time. Have children chorally repeat. Point out to children how you adjust your reading rate to read more fluently.

Book Talk

Bringing Groups Together Children will work with peers of various language and reading abilities to discuss this week's Leveled Readers. Refer to page 179 in the **Teacher's Resource Book** for how to conduct a Book Talk.

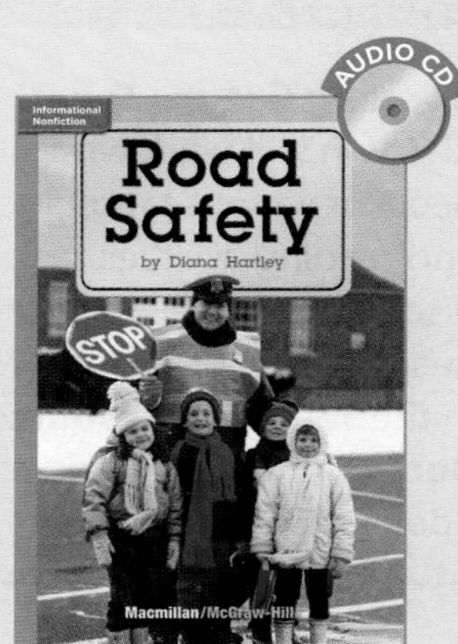

Leveled Reader

Approaching Reproducible, page 188

Illustrations are pictures. They can help you understand the motivations of the characters you are reading about.

The firefighter tells us how to stay safe.
She shows us her truck.

Circle the picture that helps you understand the sentence.

1. The children ran into the house because a thunderstorm was coming.
2. People could not swim because the pool had no lifeguard.

3. He wore his helmet while he rode his bike.

4. She wore her life jacket when she was on the boat.

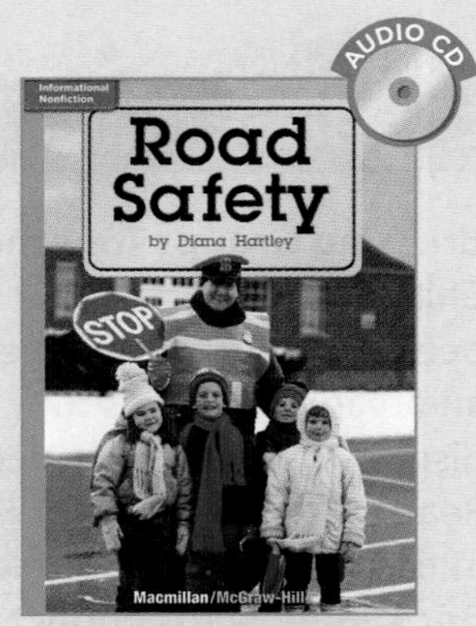

Leveled Reader

On Level

Leveled Reader Lesson 2

Objectives Use graphic features to interpret text; read to apply skills and strategies

Materials
- **Leveled Reader:** *Road Safety*
- **Practice Book**, pp. 187, 191

BEFORE READING

- **Review** Have children retell *Road Safety*. If children struggle, have them page through the selection and say what they learned about rules on each page. Reinforce vocabulary by restating children's sentences using more sophisticated language.

DURING READING

- **Use Photographs** Explain to children that good readers can use illustrations or photographs to help them retell a selection. *The photographs help you remember details as you summarize what you read.* As children reread the book, help them add information to complete their Illustrations/Photographs Charts. Model your thinking as needed as you work through the selection and add information.

AFTER READING

- Have children use their Illustrations/Photographs Charts to orally retell what happened in *Road Safety*.

REREAD FOR FLUENCY

- Read the sentences in the book one at a time. Have children chorally repeat. Point out to children how you use intonation to make the reading interesting and how your voice goes up at the end of a question.
- Have children read a portion of *Road Safety* for fluency.
- Have children continue to work on their fluency using **Practice Book** page 191.

Book Talk

Bringing Groups Together Children will work with peers of various language and reading abilities to discuss this week's Leveled Readers. Refer to page 179 in the **Teacher's Resource Book** for how to conduct a Book Talk.

Practice Book, page 191

As I read, I will pay attention to my intonation.

Roads can be dangerous places. Pay attention when you
9 are on or near a road. If you are not careful, an accident
22 may happen. Here are some tips to keep you safe.
32 Always walk on the sidewalk. If there is no sidewalk,
42 walk on the side of the road. Face cars coming toward you.
54 You should also be careful when crossing the road.
63 A safe pedestrian obeys these rules.
69 Follow these five steps when you need to cross the road:
80 **Step 1: STOP** at the side of the road.
88 **Step 2: LOOK** for any traffic.
93 **Step 3: LISTEN** for any traffic that might be coming.
102 **Step 4: WAIT** until there is no traffic before you cross.
112 **Step 5: GO** when it is safe to cross. 120

Comprehension Check

1. Why should you pay attention when you are on or near a road? **Main Idea and Details** If you are not careful, an accident may happen.
2. Why do you think it is a good idea to wait until there is no traffic to cross the street? **Make Inferences** Drivers may not see you in time to slow down or stop.

	Words Read	–	Number of Errors	=	Words Correct Score
First Read		–		=	
Second Read		–		=	

Beyond Level

Leveled Reader Lesson 2

Objectives Use graphic features to interpret text; read to apply skills and strategies

Materials • **Leveled Reader:** *Road Safety* • **Beyond Reproducible**, pp. 187, 191

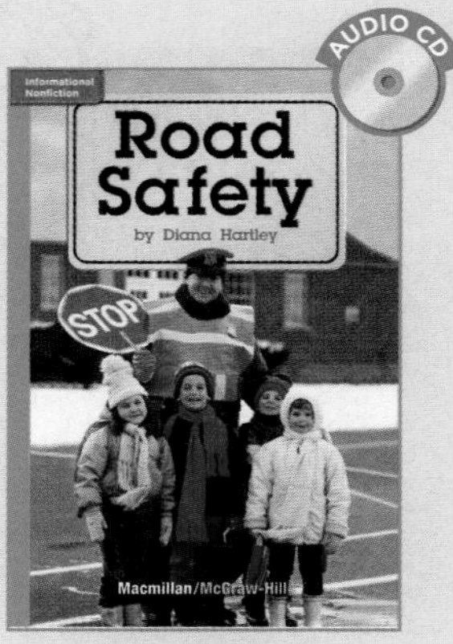

Leveled Reader

BEFORE READING

- **Review** Have children retell *Road Safety* to a partner. Circulate and listen in. Prompt children to use the new words they learned from the book in their retellings.

DURING READING

- **Use Photographs** As children reread the book, model how the author used photographs to help them understand the information in the text. Then help children add more information to their Illustrations/Photographs Charts.

AFTER READING

- **Retell** Have children use their Illustrations/Photographs Charts to write a list of safety rules learned in *Road Safety*.

Gifted and Talented

- **Review Lists** Have children review their lists showing the rules for riding in a car safely.
- **Synthesize** Tell children that they will plan a Safety Week Fair. Children will work in pairs and pick one of the following topics: Bus, Car, Skateboard, or Bike Safety. Tell them they should plan activities to have in a booth at a fair.
- Have children work in pairs to create their booth. Explain that they can create a poster and demonstrations about safety. Have children write down their ideas for their booth.
- **Evaluate** Have each pair present their plan to the group. Have children respond to each pair's plan by telling what they liked about it.

REREAD FOR FLUENCY

- Read the sentences in the book one at a time. Have children chorally repeat. Point out to children how you use intonation to make the reading interesting and how your voice goes up at the end of a question.

- Have children practice reading the book to a partner. Say: *Use your voice to show expression. When you see a question, read with curiosity by raising your voice at the end.*
- Have children continue to work on their fluency using **Practice Book** page 191.

Book Talk

Bringing Groups Together Children will work with peers of various language and reading abilities to discuss this week's Leveled Readers. Refer to page 179 in the **Teacher's Resource Book** for how to conduct a Book Talk.

Beyond Reproducible, page 191

As I read, I will pay attention to my intonation.

Boat rides are a great way to be near the water without getting
13 wet. Follow these rules to stay safe while boating.
22 **Safe Boating Tips**
25 • Never go on a boat without an adult.
33 • Check the weather before you leave. Don't get in a boat if a
46 storm is coming.
49 • Always wear a life jacket.
54 • Be careful when you get in and out of a boat. It's easy to slip
69 and fall in the water.
74 • Don't jump around on a boat. The boat can tip over.
85 • Don't jump or dive from a boat before asking an adult. There
97 could be a rock or other sharp objects under the water.
108 People who have problems with their boats at sea can get help
120 from the U.S. Coast Guard. The Coast Guard watches over the
131 coastline and the seas. 135

Comprehension Check

1. What is the Coast Guard mainly responsible for? **Character and Setting** It watches over the coastline and the seas.
2. Why is it a good idea to wear a life jacket on a boat ride? **Make Inferences** It will help you float and keep your head above water if you fall off the boat.

	Words Read	–	Number of Errors	=	Words Correct Score
First Read		–		=	
Second Read		–		=	

Leveled Reader

Vocabulary

Preteach Vocabulary Use the routine in the **Visual Vocabulary Resources**, pages 414–415, to preteach the ELL Vocabulary listed on the inside front cover of the Leveled Reader.

ELL ENGLISH LANGUAGE LEARNERS

Leveled Reader Library

Leveled Reader Lesson 1

Content Objective Read to apply skills and strategies
Language Objective Retell information using complete sentences
Materials • **Leveled Reader:** *Street Safety* • **Visual Vocabulary Resources**

BEFORE READING

All Language Levels

- **Preview** Read the title *Street Safety*. Ask: *What's the title? Say it again.* Repeat with the author's name. Then page through the book. Use simple language to tell about each page. Immediately follow up with questions, such as *Look at this photo. What safety tip does it show?*
- **Review Skills** Use the inside front cover to review the phonics skill and the vocabulary words.
- **Set a Purpose** Say: *Let's read to find out about how to stay safe on the street.*

DURING READING

All Language Levels

- Have children read each page aloud using the differentiated suggestions. Provide corrective feedback, such as modeling how to blend a decodable word or clarifying meaning by using techniques from the Interactive Question-Response Guide.
- **Use Photographs** After every two pages, ask children to state the main ideas they have learned so far. Remind them that looking at photographs can help them remember information. Help children complete the Illustrations/Photographs Charts. Restate children's comments when they have difficulty using story-specific words. Provide differentiated sentence frames to support children's responses and engage them in partner-talk where appropriate.

Beginning

Echo-Read Have children echo-read.

Check Comprehension Point to pictures and ask: *Do you see the crossing guard? Point to him. Look at the photo. Are the children wearing helmets? Point to the helmets.*

Intermediate

Choral-Read Have children choral-read with you.

Check Comprehension Ask: *What do you need to stay safe when you skateboard? What does the author want you to know about walking safely?*

Advanced

Choral-Read Have children choral-read.

Check Comprehension Ask: *What new tips did you learn about staying safe? What should you do before crossing the street?*

ELL ENGLISH LANGUAGE LEARNERS

AFTER READING

Use the chart below and the Think and Compare questions from page 16 of *Street Safety* to determine children's progress.

Think and Compare	Beginning	Intermediate	Advanced
1 Look at page 3. What color is the traffic light when you cross the street? How does the picture show this?	Possible responses: Nonverbal response. Green. Boy walking.	Possible responses: Green light. It's green. The boy is walking.	Possible responses: It's green. The boy in the picture is walking across the street.
2 Where are the safest places to bike or skateboard. Why?	Possible responses: Nonverbal response. Park.	Possible responses: In the park. It's safe in the park.	Possible responses: Parks are the safest places to bike or skateboard. There aren't any cars.
3 Why should everyone use street safety rules?	Possible responses: Nonverbal response. Be safe.	Possible responses: Protect us. Rules protect us.	Possible response: Everyone should use street saftey rules to protect themselves.

Writing/Spelling

Content Objective Spell words correctly

Language Objective Write in complete sentences, using sentence frames

All Language Levels

- Write the key vocabulary words on the board: **accident**, **attention**, **buddy**, **enormous**, **obeys**, and **tip**. Have children copy each word on their **WorkBoards**. Then help them say, then write sentences for, each word.

Beginning/Intermediate

- Help children spell words using their growing knowledge of English sound-spelling relationships. Model how to segment the word children are trying to spell and attach a spelling to each sound (or spellings to each syllable if a multisyllabic word). Use the **Sound-Spelling Cards** to reinforce the spellings for each English sound.

Advanced/Advanced High

- Dictate the following words for children to spell: *boy, toy, joy, coin, boil, join*. Guide children using the Sound-Spelling Cards as they spell each word. When completed, review the meanings of words that can be easily demonstrated or explained. Use actions, gestures, and available pictures.

Sound-Spelling WorkBoard

Phonics/Word Study

For English Learners who need more practice with this week's phonics/spelling skill, see the Approaching Level lesson on page 77K. Focus on minimal contrasts, articulation, and those sounds that do not transfer from the child's first language to English. For a complete listing of language transfers, see pages T18–T33.

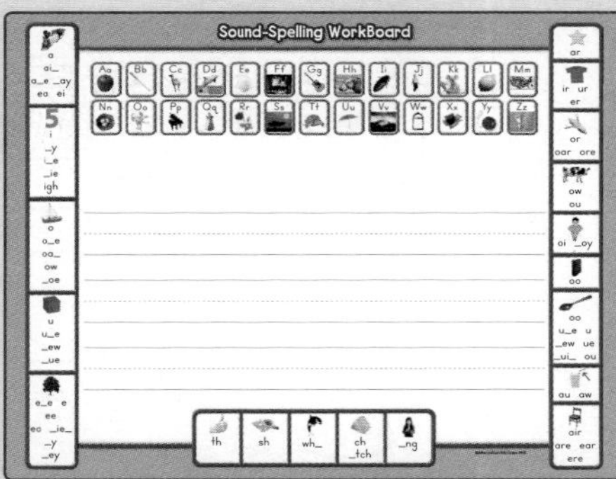

Sound-Spelling WorkBoard

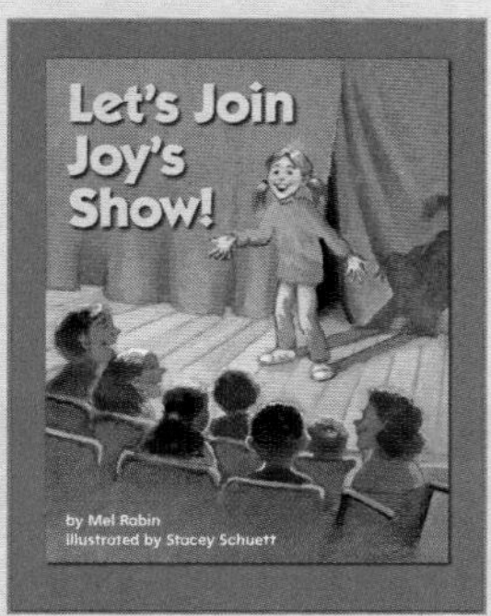

Decodable Reader

ELL

Reread Continue using the Interactive Question-Response Guide Technique to help English Language Learners understand the content of *Let's Join Joy's Show!* As you read the text, make the meaning clear by pointing to the pictures, demonstrating word meaning, paraphrasing text, and asking children questions.

Approaching Level

Phonemic Awareness

Objective Segment words into phonemes

Materials
- **Sound Boxes**
- **WorkBoard Sound Boxes**
- markers
- **Teacher's Resource Book**, p. 143

PHONEME SEGMENTATION

Tier 2

- Distribute copies of the **WorkBoards** and markers. Say a word, stretching each vowel sound for $1\frac{1}{2}$ seconds. Model for children how to drag one marker onto each box for each sound. Then have children repeat and count the number of sounds. Do this for the following words: *boy, coin, toil, joint, joy, choice*.
- **Link to Spelling** When completed, segment words again. Then help children replace each marker with a letter or letters that stand for the sound. Help children read the completed words.

Phonics

Objective Decode words with vowel diphthong *oi, oy*

Materials
- **Sound-Spelling Cards**
- **Word-Building Cards**
- **Decodable Reader:** *Let's Join Joy's Show!*

SOUND-SPELLING REVIEW

Tier 2

Display the **Word-Building Cards** for the following, one at a time: *oi, oy, ou, ow, are, air, ear, ere, or, ore, oar, ar, gn, kn, wr, mb, eer, ere, ear, er, ir, ur.* Have children chorally say each sound.

RETEACH SKILL

- Display the *Boy* **Sound-Spelling Card**. Review that the vowel diphthong /oi/ sound can be spelled with the letters *oi* or *oy*.
- **Model Blending** Write words and sentences from the chart on page 71G on the board. Model blending using the **Blending Routine**. Have children blend and read the words multiple times.
- **Read in Context** Write the sentences below on the board. Have children chorally read the sentences. Help children blend sounds in decodable words and read vocabulary words.

  The top of the soil is wet.
  What color is the toy?
  Point to the chart.
  Her voice is loud.
  I hear an enormous noise outside.
  Can we join the game?
  Joyce pays attention to the accident.
  The royal crown is gold.

- **Read the Decodable** Reread *Let's Join Joy's Show* with children. Then have children practice reading the story to a partner. Circulate, listen in, and provide corrective feedback.

Approaching Level

High-Frequency/Vocabulary Words

Objective Read high-frequency and vocabulary words

Materials
- **Vocabulary Cards**
- **Sound-Spelling WorkBoards**
- **High-Frequency Word Cards**

REVIEW WORDS

- Display **High-Frequency Word Cards** for **family**, **four**, and **hear** and **Vocabulary Cards** for **accident**, **attention**, **buddy**, **enormous**, **obeys**, and **tip**. Have children copy each word on their **WorkBoards**. Then help them write sentences for each word. Provide sentence stems or starters, such as *You should always pay* attention *to* ________.

CUMULATIVE REVIEW

- Display the High-Frequency and Vocabulary Cards from the previous six weeks. Display one card at a time as children chorally read the word. Mix and repeat.

Fluency

Objective Read aloud with fluency and comprehension

Materials
- **Leveled Reader:** *Road Safety*
- **Approaching Reproducible**, p. 191

READ FOR FLUENCY

- Tell children that they will be doing a final fluent reading of *Road Safety*. Remind them to pay particular attention to their expression and intonation.
- As they read, note words children mispronounce or struggle to read. Also note their overall reading rate. Use this information to determine if additional instruction is needed on this week's phonics skill and vocabulary words. Send the book home for independent reading.

REREAD PREVIOUSLY READ BOOKS

Tier 2

- Distribute copies of the past six **Leveled Readers**. Tell children that rereading these books will help them develop their skills. The more times they read the same words, the quicker they will learn these words.
- Circulate and listen in as children read. Stop children periodically and ask them how they are figuring out difficult words or checking their understanding as they read.
- Instruct children to read other previously read Leveled Readers during independent reading time or for homework.

Meet Grade-Level Expectations

As an alternative to this day's lesson, guide children through a reading of the On Level Leveled Reader. See page 77S. Because both books contain the same vocabulary, phonics, and comprehension skills, the scaffolding you provided will help most children gain access to this more challenging text.

Approaching Reproducible, page 191

As I read, I will pay attention to my intonation.

Stay safe outside while working in the garden
8 or playing.
10 Here are some garden rules.
15 **Garden Safety Rules:**
18 Work with an adult.
22 Use tools carefully. Many tools are sharp.
29 Do not leave tools out.
34 Be careful when you play in the sun. Wear a hat
45 on hot days. Wear sunblock, too. Drink a lot of
55 water. Do not run too much.
61 You can be someone's safety buddy. Tell them
69 about the tips in this book. 75

Comprehension Check

1. Why is it important to put tools away after you have finished using them? **Make Inferences** Someone could get hurt or you could lose them.
2. Why is it a good idea to drink a lot of water when you are playing in the sun? **Make Inferences** Heat makes your body sweat. Drinking water will replace the water that is lost.

	Words Read	–	Number of Errors	=	Words Correct Score
First Read		–		=	
Second Read		–		=	

Student Book

On Level

Fluency

Objectives Read aloud with fluency; develop speaking skills
Materials • **Student Book:** *Officer Buckle and Gloria*

REREAD FOR FLUENCY

- Have children reread *Officer Buckle and Gloria*. Work with children to read with accuracy and the appropriate intonation. Model fluent reading as needed.
- Provide time for children to read a section of the text to you. Comment on their accuracy, rate, and intonation, and provide corrective feedback.

DEVELOP SPEAKING/LISTENING SKILLS

- Provide time for children to read aloud a portion of *Officer Buckle and Gloria* to the class. Ask children to name ways the reader showed excitement during the reading.
- Challenge children to memorize a few lines of the text, such as a portion of Officer Buckle's dialogue, and recite it for you.

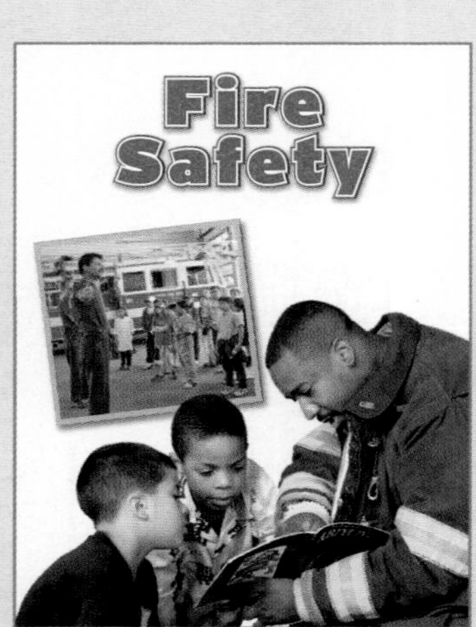

Student Book

Beyond Level

Fluency

Objectives Read aloud with fluency; develop speaking skills
Materials • **Student Book:** *Officer Buckle and Gloria*; "Fire Safety"

REREAD FOR FLUENCY

- Have children reread *Officer Buckle and Gloria* and "Fire Safety." Work with children to read with accuracy and the appropriate intonation.
- Provide time for children to read a section of the text to you. Comment on their accuracy, rate, and intonation, and provide corrective feedback.

DEVELOP SPEAKING/LISTENING SKILLS

- Provide time for children to read aloud *Officer Buckle and Gloria* or "Fire Safety" to the class. Ask children to name ways the reader read with intonation during the selection.
- Challenge children to memorize their favorite page or two of one of the texts and recite it for you.

ELL ENGLISH LANGUAGE LEARNERS

Access to Core Content

Content Objective Read grade-level text
Language Objective Discuss text using key words and sentence frames
Materials • **ELL Resource Book**, pp. 240–241

PRETEACH PAIRED SELECTION (PAGES 72–75)

All Language Levels

Use the Interactive Question-Response Guide on **ELL Resource Book** pages 240–241 to preview the paired selection "Fire Safety." Preteach the selection on **Day 4**.

ELL Resource Book

Leveled Reader Lesson 2

Content Objective Apply skills and strategies
Language Objective Retell information using complete sentences
Materials • **ELL Resource Book**, p. 243 • **Leveled Reader:** *Street Safety*

AFTER READING

All Language Levels

Book Talk Distribute copies of ELL Resource Book page 243. Children will work with peers of varying language abilities to discuss them. Help students determine who will be the leader for the discussion.

Develop Listening and Speaking Skills Tell children to remember the following while engaged in the Book Talk:

- Share information in cooperative learning interactions. Remind children to work with their partners to retell the story and complete any activities. Ask: *What happened next in the story?*
- Employ self-corrective techniques and monitor their own and other children's language production. Children should ask themselves: *What parts of this passage confused me? Can my classmates help me clarify a word or sentence I don't understand?*
- Distinguish between formal and informal English and know when to use each one. Remind children to note whether the selection is written in formal or informal English. Ask: *Why do you think it is written in this way?* Remind children that they may use informal English with their classmates, but they should use formal language when they talk to teachers or write essays.
- Use high-frequency English words to describe people, places, and objects.

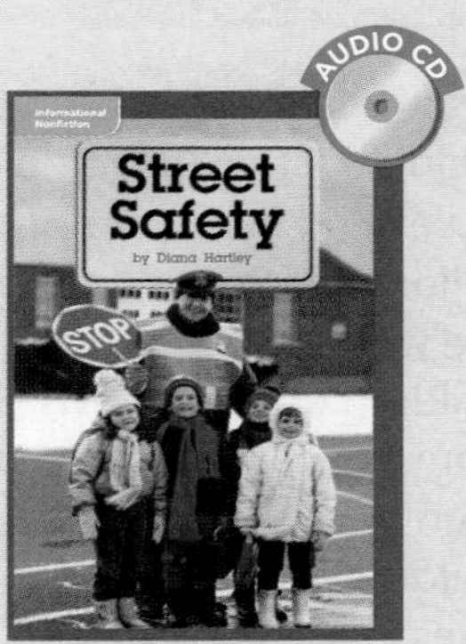

Leveled Reader

Book Talk

Bringing Groups Together
Children will work with peers of varying language abilities to discuss the Book Talk questions. Form groups so that students who read the Beyond Level, On Level, Approaching Level, and English Language Learner readers are in the same group for the activity.

Approaching Level

Oral Language

Objectives Build safety-related vocabulary; review week's oral vocabulary words

Materials • chart paper

EXPAND VOCABULARY

- Begin a two-column chart on chart paper. Label the left column *Safety at Home*. Label the right column *Safety at School*. Remind children that this week they learned about rules that keep us safe. For example, in *Road Safety*, they learned rules that keep us safe on the street.
- Begin the list by writing the words *fire drill* in each column. Point to the words, read them, and have children repeat. Discuss the fire drill routine at school.

Safety at Home	Safety at School
fire drill	fire drill
fire extinguisher	playground rules
emergencies	safe behavior

- Guide children in brainstorming safety words that they should know for home and for school. Remind them of rules they have already learned.
- Then write the following safety words on the board and read each one aloud: *fire extinguisher, emergencies, playground rules, safe behavior*. Work with children to determine when they must keep in mind each safety word. Add the information to the chart. Have children add other safety words they know.

REVIEW VOCABULARY

Tier 2

- Use the **Define/Example/Ask** vocabulary routine in the **Instructional Routine Handbook** to review this week's oral vocabulary words: *advice*, *hestitate*, *panic*, *secure*, and *vowed*.
- Explain to children you are going to start a sentence using one of the words and you want them to think of an ending. For example, say: *One of the most valuable pieces of* advice *I ever heard was* ________. Repeat for the remaining words.

ELL

Draw Use images from the main selection, paired piece, or Leveled Reader to help children better understand the words in the chart. Have children use the words from the chart to draw and then label pictures showing children obeying safety rules.

Approaching Level

Fluency

Objectives Read aloud with fluency; review high-frequency and vocabulary words

Materials
- **Student Book:** *Officer Buckle and Gloria*
- **High-Frequency Word Cards**
- **Vocabulary Cards**

REREAD FOR FLUENCY

- Have children reread a portion of *Officer Buckle and Gloria.* Ask them to focus on two to four of their favorite pages from the selection. Work with children to read the pages with accuracy and the appropriate intonation. For example, read each sentence and have children echo. Remind them to read the text at an appropriate rate.
- Provide time to listen as children read their sections of text. Comment on their reading rate, and provide corrective feedback by modeling proper fluency.

REVIEW HIGH-FREQUENCY/VOCABULARY WORDS

- Display **High-Frequency Word Cards** for **family**, **four**, and **hear** and **Vocabulary Cards** for **accident**, **attention**, **buddy**, **enormous**, **obeys**, and **tip**. Model using two or three of the words in a sentence. Then have children come up with their own sentence using two or three of the words.

CUMULATIVE REVIEW

- Display the High-Frequency Word Cards and Vocabulary Cards from the previous four weeks. Display one card at a time as children chorally read the word. Mix and repeat. Note words needing review.

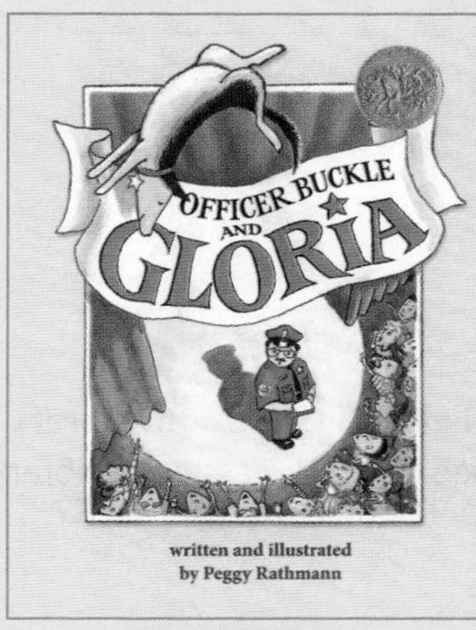

Student Book

Decodable Text

Use the decodable stories in the **Teacher's Resource Book** to help children build fluency with basic decoding patterns.

Self-Selected Reading

Objective Read independently and retell a story read

Materials
- **Leveled Classroom Library**
- other fiction books

APPLY SKILLS TO INDEPENDENT READING

- Have each child choose a fiction book for independent reading. (See the **Theme Bibliography** on pages T8–T9 for book suggestions.)
- After reading, ask children to use their Illustrations/Photographs Charts to orally retell the books. Provide time for children to share their reactions to the books. Ask: *How did the illustrations affect your reading of this story? How does the plot of this story compare with those of other stories you have read?*

Approaching

Leveled Classroom Library

See Leveled Classroom Library lessons on pages T2–T7.

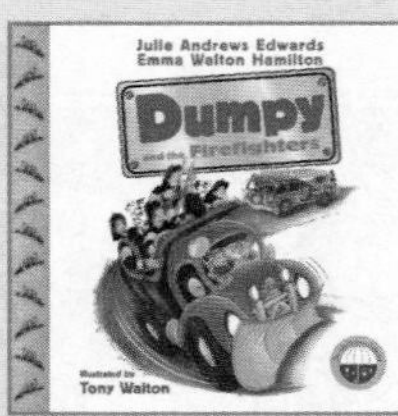

On Level

Leveled Classroom Library

See Leveled Classroom Library lessons on pages T2–T7.

On Level

Self-Selected Reading

Objective Read independently and retell a fiction story

Materials • **Leveled Classroom Library** • other fiction books

APPLY SKILLS TO INDEPENDENT READING

- Have each child choose a fiction book for independent reading. (See the **Theme Bibliography** on pages T8–T9 for book suggestions.)
- After reading, ask children to use their Illustrations/Photographs Charts to orally retell the books. Provide time for children to share their reactions to the books. Ask: *What would you tell a friend about this story? What character was your favorite?*

ELL

Share Information Pair English Language Learners with fluent speakers. Have them choose the same book and work together on the Retelling Chart.

Beyond Level

Self-Selected Reading

Objective Read independently and retell a story read

Materials • **Leveled Classroom Library** • other fiction books

APPLY SKILLS TO INDEPENDENT READING

- Have each child choose a fiction book for independent reading. (See the **Theme Bibliography** on pages T8–T9 for book suggestions.)
- After reading, ask children to use their Illustrations/Photographs Charts to write a retelling of the books in their Writer's Notebooks. Provide time for children to share their reactions to the books. Ask: *What was your favorite part of this story? Why did you like it?*

EVALUATE

Gifted Talented

- Challenge students to discuss how the self-selected books they have read relate to the theme of this unit, Better Together. Ask: *How is working as a team better than working alone?* Have children debate to discuss their views.

Beyond

Leveled Classroom Library

See Leveled Classroom Library lessons on pages T2–T7.

ELL ENGLISH LANGUAGE LEARNERS

Fluency

Content Objectives Reread selections to develop fluency; develop speaking skills
Language Objective Tell a partner what a selection is about
Materials
- **Student Book:** *Office Buckle and Gloria,* "Fire Safety"
- **Decodable Reader:** *Let's Join Joy's Show!*

REREAD FOR FLUENCY

Beginning

Have children reread the Decodable Reader.

Intermediate/Advanced

- Have children reread a portion of *Officer Buckle and Gloria*. Ask children to focus on two to four of their favorite pages from the selection. Work with children to read the pages with accuracy and the appropriate pace. For example, read each sentence of the first two pages and have children echo. Remind them to pay attention to their reading rate.
- Provide time for children to read their sections of text to you. Comment on their expression, and provide corrective feedback by modeling proper fluency.

DEVELOP SPEAKING/LISTENING SKILLS

All Language Levels

- Have children practice reading "Fire Safety." Work with children to read with accuracy and appropriate pacing.
- Provide time for children to read aloud the article to a partner. Ask them to tell what they learned about fire safety. Provide the sentence frame *From this article I learned that* ________.

Self-Selected Reading

Content Objective Read independently
Language Objective Orally retell a story read.
Materials
- **Leveled Classroom Library**
- other fiction books

APPLY SKILLS AND STRATEGIES TO INDEPENDENT READING

All Language Levels

- Have children choose a fiction book for independent reading. (See the **Theme Bibliography** on pages T8–T9.)
- After reading, ask children to orally summarize the book. Provide time for children to comment on their reactions to the book and share them with classmates. Ask: *Would you recommend this book to a classmate? Why or why not?*

Student Book

End-of-Week Assessment

Progress Monitoring

Weekly Assessment

ASSESSED SKILLS

- Phonics: Diphthong *oi*, *oy*; Prefixes *re-*, *un-*, *dis-*
- Selection Vocabulary
- Comprehension: Use Illustrations
- Grammar: Helping Verbs

Selection Test for* Officer Buckle and Gloria *Also Available.

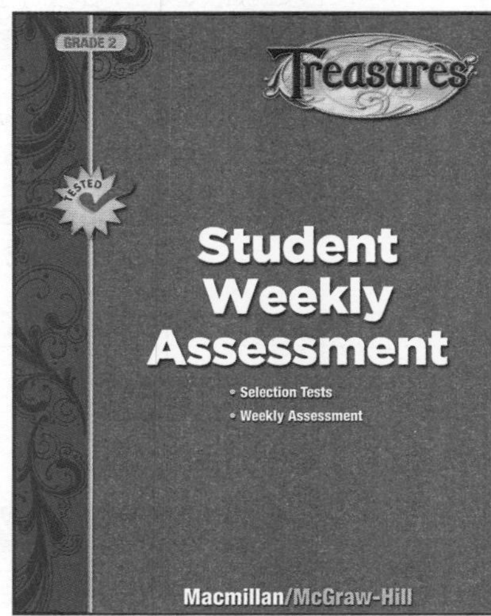

Student Weekly Assessment Unit 4 Week 2

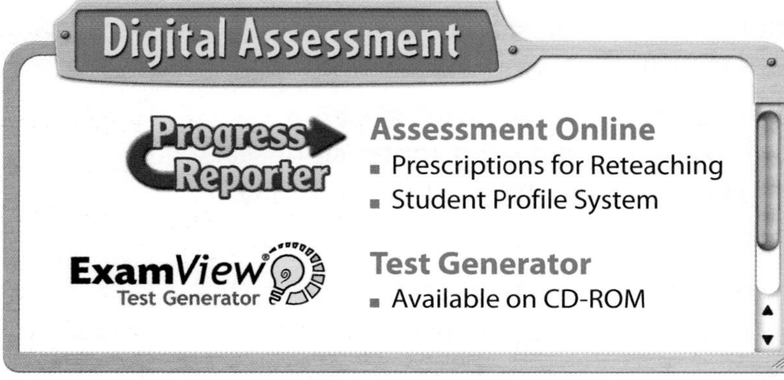

Fluency Assessment

Assess fluency for one group of students per week. Use the Oral Fluency Record Sheet to track the number of words read correctly. Fluency goals for all students:

62–82 words correct per minute (WCPM)

Approaching Level	Weeks 1, 3, 5
On Level	Weeks 2, 4
Beyond Level	Week 6

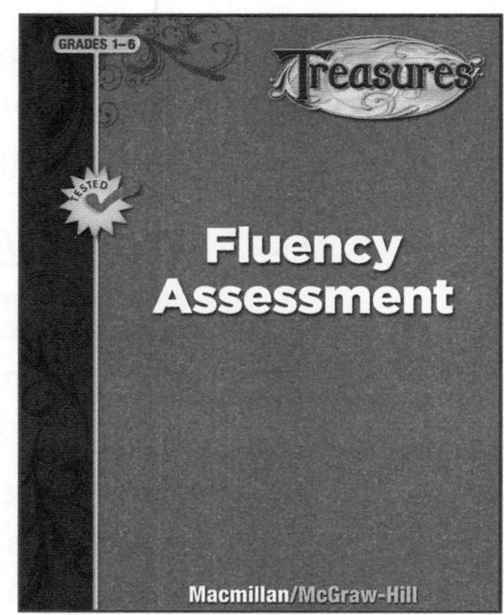

Fluency Assessment

DIBELS LINK

PROGRESS MONITORING

Use your DIBELS results to inform instruction.

IF

DIBELS Oral **R**eading **F**luency (**DORF**) 0–67

THEN

Evaluate for Intervention

TPRI LINK

PROGRESS MONITORING

Use your TPRI scores to inform instruction.

IF

Graphophonemic Knowledge	Still Developing
Reading Fluency/Accuracy	Reading Grade 2, Story 4 Less Than 75 WCPM
Reading Comprehension Questions	0–3 correct

THEN

Evaluate for Intervention

Diagnose		Prescribe
Review the assessment answers with students. Have them correct their errors. Then provide additional instruction as needed.		
	IF...	**THEN...**
PHONICS AND SPELLING Diphthong *oi, oy* Prefixes *re-, un-, dis-*	0–1 items correct . . .	LOG ON Online Practice: Go to **www.macmillanmh.com**. See **Phonics Intervention Teacher's Edition.** See Sound-Spelling Fluency and mixed review blending lines in upcoming lessons.
VOCABULARY WORDS **VOCABULARY STRATEGY** Context Clues: Synonyms	0–1 items correct . . .	See **Phonics Intervention Teacher's Edition.** SPIRAL REVIEW See Vocabulary review lessons Unit 4, Week 3.
COMPREHENSION Use Illustrations	0–1 items correct . . .	See **Comprehension Intervention Teacher's Edition.** SPIRAL REVIEW See Use Illustrations lessons Unit 4, Week 4.
GRAMMAR Helping Verbs	0–1 items correct . . .	See the **Grammar and Writing Handbook.**
FLUENCY	53–61 WCPM	AUDIO CD Fluency Solutions Audio CD
	0–52 WCPM	See **Fluency Intervention Teacher's Edition.**

Response to Intervention

To place students in Tier 2 or Tier 3 Intervention use the *Diagnostic Assessment.*

- Phonemic Awareness
- Phonics
- Vocabulary
- Comprehension
- Fluency

Week 3 ★ At a Glance

Priority Skills and Concepts

Comprehension
- **Genre:** Expository
- **Strategy:** Analyze Text Structure
- **Skill:** Sequence of Events

- **Fiction vs. Nonfiction**

High-Frequency Words
- ***follow, near, paper***

Oral Vocabulary
- **Build Robust Vocabulary:** ***clever, comfort, recuperate, sympathy, urgent***

Vocabulary
- ***serious, personal, informs, heal, aid***
- **Strategy:** Dictionary/Homophones

Fluency
- **Pronunciation**

Phonemic Awareness
- **Generate Rhyme**

Phonics/Spelling
- **Vowel Diagraph *oo, ui, ew, ue, u, ou, oe*:** ***room, tool, suit, fruit, clue, glue, flew, new, shoe, canoe, point, royal, follow, near, paper***

Grammar/Mechanics
- **Irregular Verbs**
- **Book Titles**

Writing
- **Expository Composition**
- **Time-Order Words**
- **Trait:** Organization

Key

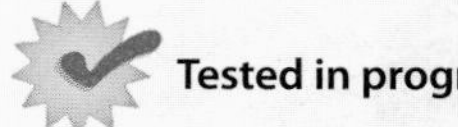

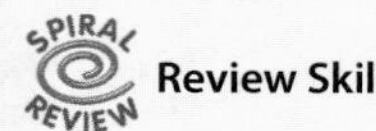

Digital Learning

Digital solutions to help plan and implement instruction.

Teacher Resources

ONLINE www.macmillanmh.com

- **Teacher's Edition**
  - Lesson Planner and Resources also on CD-ROM
- **Formative Assessment**
  - ExamView® on CD-ROM also available
- **Instructional Resources**
  - Unit Videos
  - Classroom Presentation Toolkit
- **Professional Development**
  - Video Library

TeacherWorks Plus

Progress Reporter

VIDEO

Student Resources

ONLINE www.macmillanmh.com

- **Interactive Student Book**
- **Leveled Reader Database**
- **Activities**
  - Research Toolkit
  - Oral Language Activities
  - Vocabulary/Spelling Activities

StudentWorks Plus

Listening Library

- Recordings of Student Books and Leveled Readers

Fluency Solutions

- Fluency Modeling and Practice

Theme: Worker Teams

Student Book

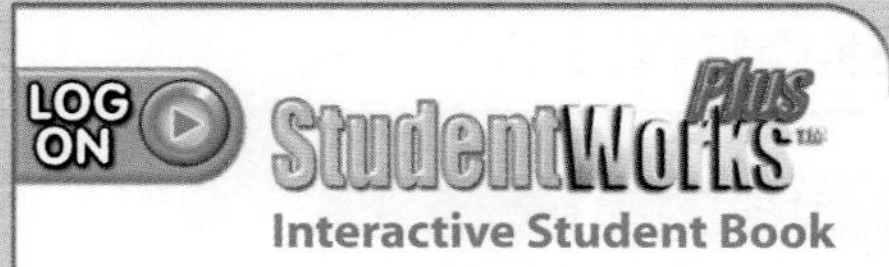

Interactive Student Book

- Word-by-Word Reading
- Summaries in Multiple Languages
- Comprehension Question

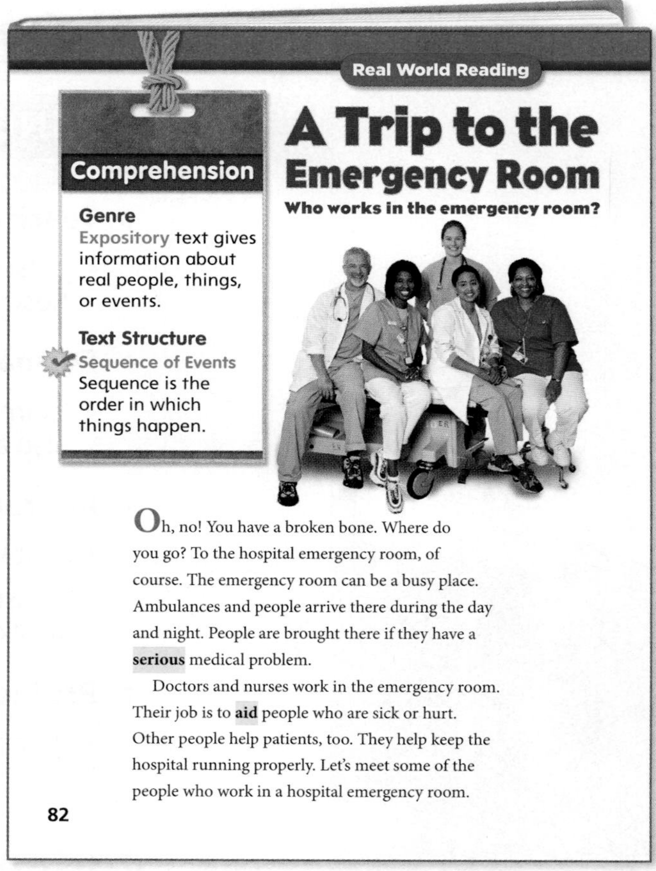

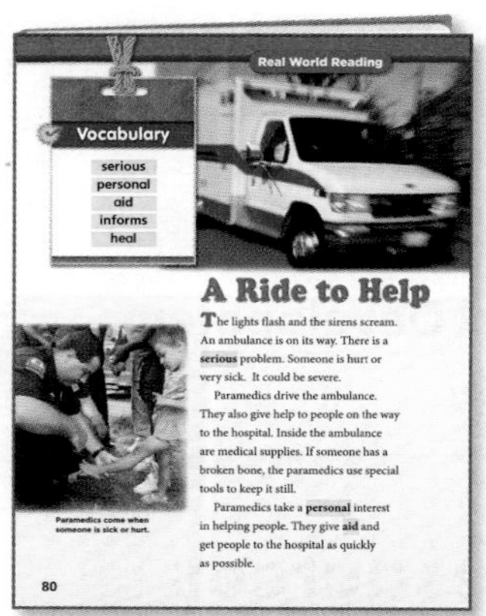

Preteach Vocabulary and Comprehension

Genre Expository

Main Selection

Genre Expository

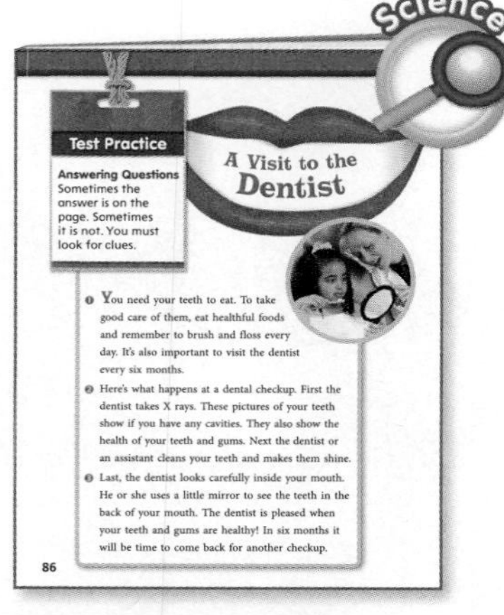

Test Practice

Genre Expository

Support Literature

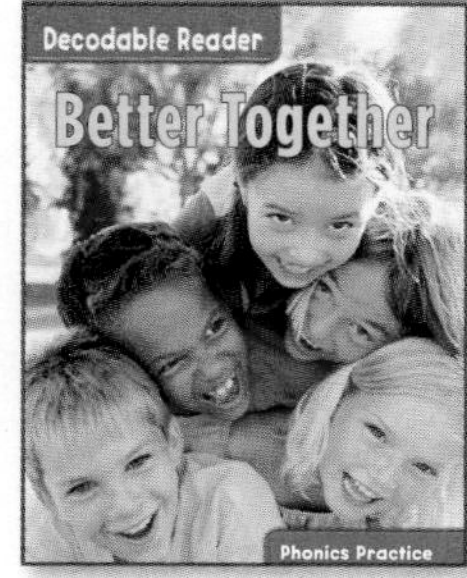

Decodable Reader Library

- One decodable read each week

Oral Vocabulary Cards

- Listening Comprehension
- Build Robust Vocabulary

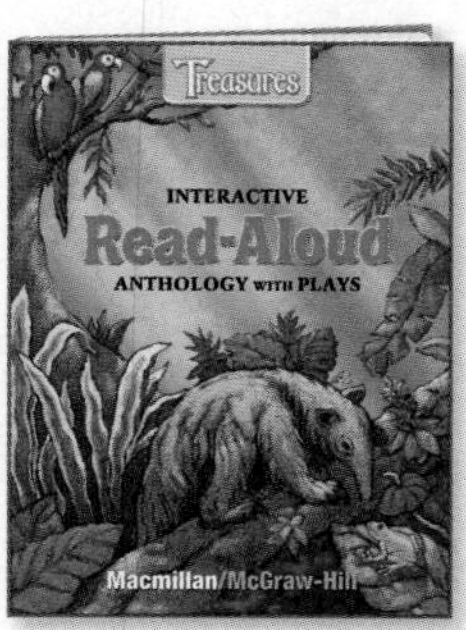

Interactive Read-Aloud Anthology

- Listening Comprehension
- Readers Theater Plays for Fluency

Resources for Differentiated Instruction

Leveled Readers: Social Studies

GR Levels H-O

Genre	Expository

- Same Theme
- Same Vocabulary
- Same Comprehension Skills

Approaching Level

On Level

Beyond Level

ELL

Leveled Reader Database
Go to www.macmillanmh.com.

Leveled Practice

Approaching

On Level

Beyond

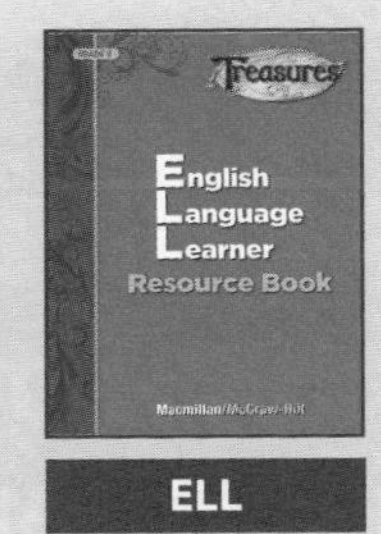

ELL

Leveled Classroom Library

Approaching

On Level

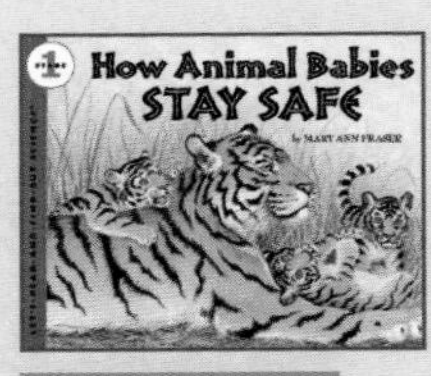

Beyond

Response to Intervention

- Phonemic Awareness
- Phonics
- Vocabulary
- Comprehension
- Fluency

Assessment

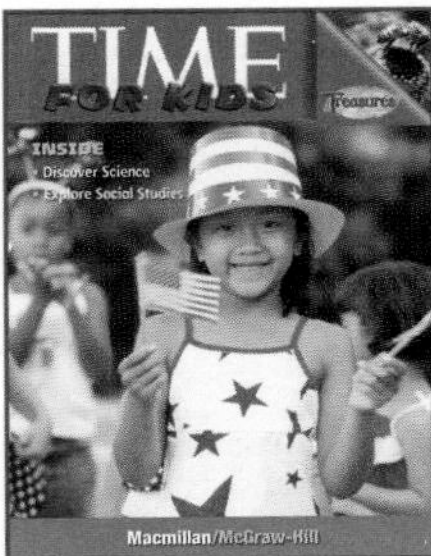

Time For Kids
- Teacher's Edition
- Apply Answering Questions Strategies

Weekly Assessment

Unit Assessment

Benchmark Assessment

HOME-SCHOOL CONNECTION

- Family letters in English and Spanish
- Take-home stories and activities

Online Homework
www.macmillanmh.com

Suggested Lesson Plan

Go to www.macmillanmh.com for Online Lesson Planner

A Trip to the Emergency Room, pp. 82/83–84/85

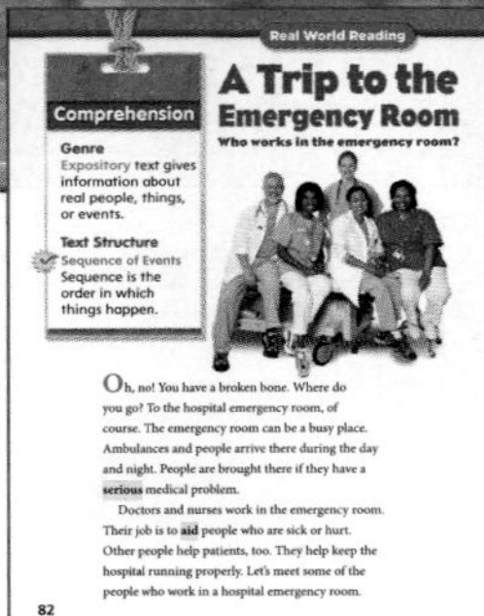

WHOLE GROUP	DAY 1	DAY 2
ORAL LANGUAGE • Oral Vocabulary • Listening Comprehension	**Focus Question** Describe some jobs that require adults to work together. Build Background, 78M **Oral Vocabulary** *clever, comfort, recuperate, sympathy, urgent,* 79A **Oral Vocabulary Cards,** "Little Red Riding Hood"	**Focus Question** Who works in the emergency room? **Oral Vocabulary** *clever, comfort, recuperate, sympathy, urgent,* 81E
• Phonemic Awareness	**Phonemic Awareness** Generate Rhyme, 79B	**Phonemic Awareness** Initial Sound Substitution, 81F
WORD STUDY • Phonics • Spelling • Vocabulary	**Phonics** Introduce Vowel Digraph *oo, ui, ew, ue, u, ou, oe,* 79C Practice Book, 195 **Spelling** Pretest: Words with Variant Vowel *oo, ui, ew, ue, u, ou, oe,* 79E Spelling, 69 **Vocabulary** *aid, heal, informs, personal, serious*, 79G **Strategy:** Dictionary/Homophones Practice Book, 196	**Phonics** Blend and Build with Variant Vowel *oo, ui, ew, ue, u, ou, oe,* 81G–81H **Spelling** Word Sort with *oo, ui, ew, ue, u, ou, oe,* 81I Spelling, 70 **Vocabulary** *aid, heal, informs, personal, serious* Words in Context, 81J
READING • Comprehension	**Read** Decodable Reader, *Soon the North Wind Blew,* 79F Decodable Reader **Comprehension,** 81A–81B "A Ride to Help," "Time for an X Ray," 80/81 **Strategy:** Analyze Text Structure **Skill:** Identify Sequence of Events	**Read** "A Trip to the Emergency Room," 82/83–84/85 Student Book **Comprehension,** 81K–85A **Strategy:** Analyze Text Structure **Skill:** Sequence of Events Practice Book, 198–199
• Fluency	**Fluency** Build Fluency, 79C	**Fluency** Build Fluency, 81H
LANGUAGE ARTS • Writing	**Writing** **Daily Writing Prompt** Look at the picture. Write about what you see, 78M Expository: Composition, 81D	**Writing** **Daily Writing Prompt** Imagine that you were the forest ranger. How would you help Little Red Riding Hood and her grandmother with the emergency? 81E Prewrite a Composition, 85C
• Grammar	**Grammar** Irregular Verbs, 81C Grammar, 86	**Grammar** Irregular Verbs, 85B Grammar, 87
ASSESSMENT • Informal/Formal	**Quick Check** Phonics, 79D Vocabulary, 80/81	**Quick Check** Comprehension, 84/85

SMALL GROUP Lesson Plan — **Differentiated Instruction 78G–78H**

Priority Skills

Phonics
Variant Vowel *oo, ui, ew, ue, u, ou, oe*

Vocabulary
Words: *aid, heal, informs, personal, serious*
Strategy: Dictionary/Homophones

Comprehension
Strategy: Analyze Text Structure
Skill: Identify Sequence of Events

Writing
Composition

DAY 3

Focus Question Who are some of the emergency room workers you learned about in the article? What is one way that each worker helps people?

Read Aloud: "A Special Trade," 85D

Oral Vocabulary *clever, comfort, recuperate, sympathy, urgent,* 85K

Phonemic Awareness Phoneme Blending, 85E

Phonics Blend and Build with Variant Vowel *oo, ui, ew, ue, u, ou, oe,* 85F
Suffixes *-ful, -less,* 85G
Practice Book, 200

Spelling Word Sort, 85H
Spelling, 71

Vocabulary *aid, heal, informs, personal, serious*
Strategy: Dictionary/Homophones, 85J
Practice Book, 201

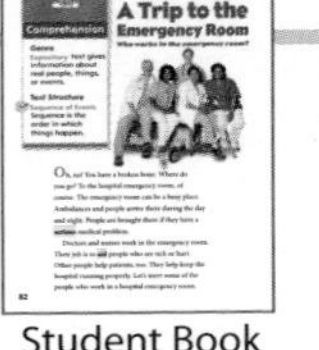
Student Book

Read "A Trip to the Emergency Room," 82/83–84/85

Comprehension, Nonfiction vs. Fiction, 85N

Research and Study Skills: Using the Internet, 85O

Fluency Repeated Reading: Prosody/Pronunciation, 85L
Practice Book, 202

Writing
Daily Writing Prompt Respond to the Read Aloud by writing a fictional narrative about a special relationship, 85D
Writing Trait: Organization, 85S
Time-Order Words, 85R
Draft a Composition, 85S

Grammar **Mechanics:** Book Titles, 85P
Grammar, 88

Quick Check Fluency, 85M

DAY 4

Focus Question What can a dentist teach you?

Oral Vocabulary *clever, comfort, recuperate, sympathy, urgent,* 85T

Phonemic Awareness Initial Sound Substitution, 85U

Phonics Blend and Build Words with Variant Vowel *oo, ui, ew, ue, u, ou, oe,* 85V

Spelling Practice Words with Variant Vowel *oo, ui, ew, ue, u, ou, oe,* 85X
Spelling, 72

Vocabulary *aid, heal, informs, personal, serious*
Words in Context, 85Y

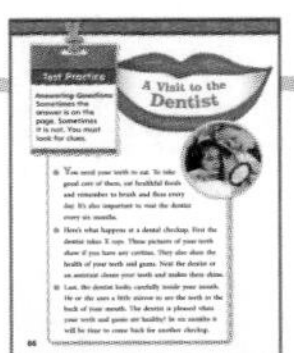
Student Book

Read "A Visit to the Dentist," 86/87

Comprehension,
Test Strategy: Answering Questions, 85Z

Write to a Prompt: Personal Narrative, 87A
Practice Book, 203

Fluency Build Fluency, 85V

Writing

Daily Writing Prompt Describe what you think it would be like to be a paramedic, 85T
Revise and Proofread a Composition, 89C

Grammar Irregular Verbs, 89A
Grammar, 89

Quick Check Spelling, 85X

DAY 5 Review and Assess

Focus Question How will analyzing text structure help you read and understand another selection?

Oral Vocabulary *clever, comfort, recuperate, sympathy, urgent,* 89E

Phonemic Awareness Phoneme Blending, 89G

Phonics Blend with Variant Vowel *oo, ui, ew, ue, u, ou, oe,* 89G

Spelling Posttest, 89I

Vocabulary *aid, heal, informs, personal, serious*

Student Book

Read Self-Selected Reading, 78I

Comprehension, 89K
Strategy: Analyze Text Structure
Skill: Identify Sequence of Events, 89K

Fluency Repeated Reading: Prosody/Pronunciation, 89F

Writing
Daily Writing Prompt Which hospital or emergency worker do you think is most interesting? Write about what this person does and explain why you want to do this job, 89E
Publish and Present, 89M

Grammar Book Title; Irregular Verbs, 89L
Grammar, 90

Weekly Assessment, 89OO–89PP

Differentiated Instruction

What do I do in small groups?

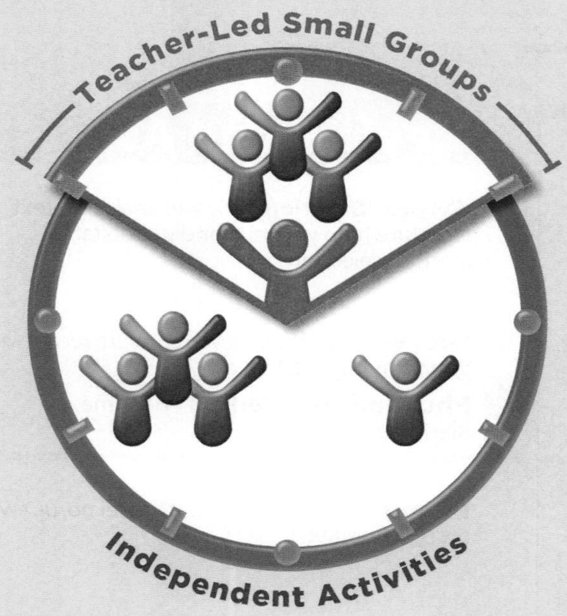

Focus on Skills

IF... students need additional instruction, practice, or extension based on your  **observations for the following priority skills**

 **Phonics/Word Study**
Variant Vowel *oo, ui, ew, ue, u, ou, oe*; Suffixes *-ful, -less*

 **Vocabulary Words**
aid, heal, informs, personal, serious
Strategy: Dictionary: Homophones

 **Comprehension**
Strategy: Analyze Text Structure
Skill: Identify Sequence of Events

Fluency
Phonics, High-Frequency Words, Pronunciation

THEN...

Approaching	Preteach and
English Learners	Reteach Skills
On Level	Practice
Beyond	Enrich and Accelerate Learning

LOG ON Suggested Small Group Lesson Plan

	DAY 1	DAY 2
Approaching Level • **Preteach/Reteach**  **Tier 2 Instruction**	• Phonemic Awareness, 89O • Phonics, 89O ELL • High-Frequency/Vocabulary, 89P • Decodable Reader, *Soon the North Wind Blew*, 89P	• Phonemic Awareness, 89U • Phonics, 89U ELL • High-Frequency/Vocabulary, 89V • Leveled Reader Lesson 1, 89V
On Level • **Practice**	• Phonics, 89Q ELL • Fluency, 89Q ELL	• Leveled Reader Lesson 1, 89W ELL
Beyond Level • **Extend/Accelerate** **Gifted and Talented**	• Phonics, 89R ELL • Vocabulary, 89R	• Leveled Reader Lesson 1, 89X • Analyze, 89X
ELL • **Build English Language Proficiency** • **See ELL in other levels.**	• Prepare to Read, 89S • Academic Language, 89S • Preteach Vocabulary, 89T	• Preteach Main Selection, 89Y • Grammar, 89Z

Focus on Leveled Readers

Levels H-O

Approaching

On Level

Beyond

ELL

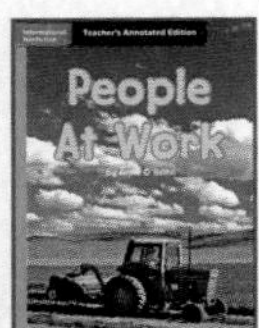

Social Studies

Teacher's Annotated Edition

Explain how work provides income to purchase goods and services; explain choices people can make abouut earning, spending, and saving money.

Additional Leveled Readers

Leveled Reader Database
www.macmillanmh.com

Search by

- Comprehension Skill
- Content Area
- Genre
- Text Feature
- Guided Reading Level
- Reading Recovery Level
- Lexile Score
- Benchmark Level

Subscription also available.

Manipulatives

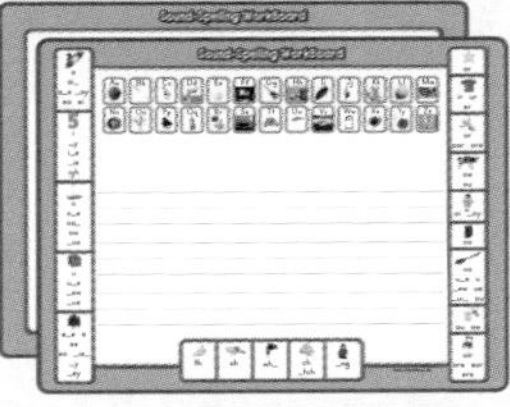

Sound-Spelling WorkBoards

Sound-Spelling Cards

Photo Cards

High-Frequency Word Cards

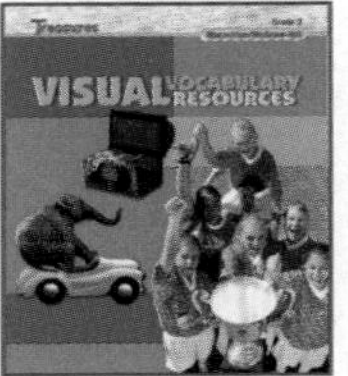

Visual Vocabulary Resources

DAY 3	DAY 4	DAY 5
• Phonemic Awareness, 89AA • Phonics, 89AA ELL • High-Frequency/Vocabulary, 89BB • Leveled Reader Lesson 2, 89BB • Book Talk, 89BB	• Phonemic Awareness, 89GG • Phonics, 89GG ELL • High-Frequency/Vocabulary, 89HH • Fluency, 89HH • Review Leveled Readers, 89HH	• Oral Language, 89KK ELL • Fluency, 89LL • Self-Selected Independent Reading, 89LL
• Leveled Reader Lesson 2, 89CC • Fluency, 89CC • Book Talk, 89CC	• Fluency, 89II	• Self-Selected Independent Reading, 89MM ELL
• Leveled Reader Lesson 2, 89DD • Synthesize and Evaluate, 89DD • Fluency, 89DD • Book Talk, 89DD	• Fluency, 89II	• Self-Selected Independent Reading, 89MM • Evaluate, 89MM
• Leveled Reader Lesson 1, 89EE • Writing/Spelling, 89FF	• Preteach Paired Selection, 89JJ • Leveled Reader Lesson 2, 89JJ	• Fluency, 89NN • Self-Selected Independent Reading, 89NN

What do I do with the rest of my class?

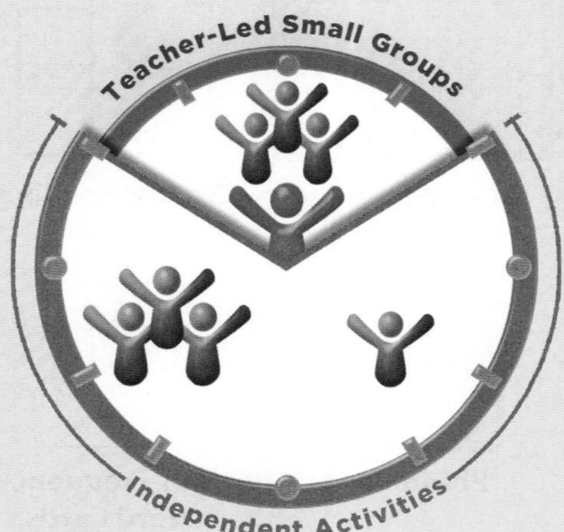

- Literacy Workstations
- Leveled Reader Activities
- Practice Book and Reproducibles
- Online Activities
- English Language Learner Practice Book

Classroom Management Tools

Weekly Contract

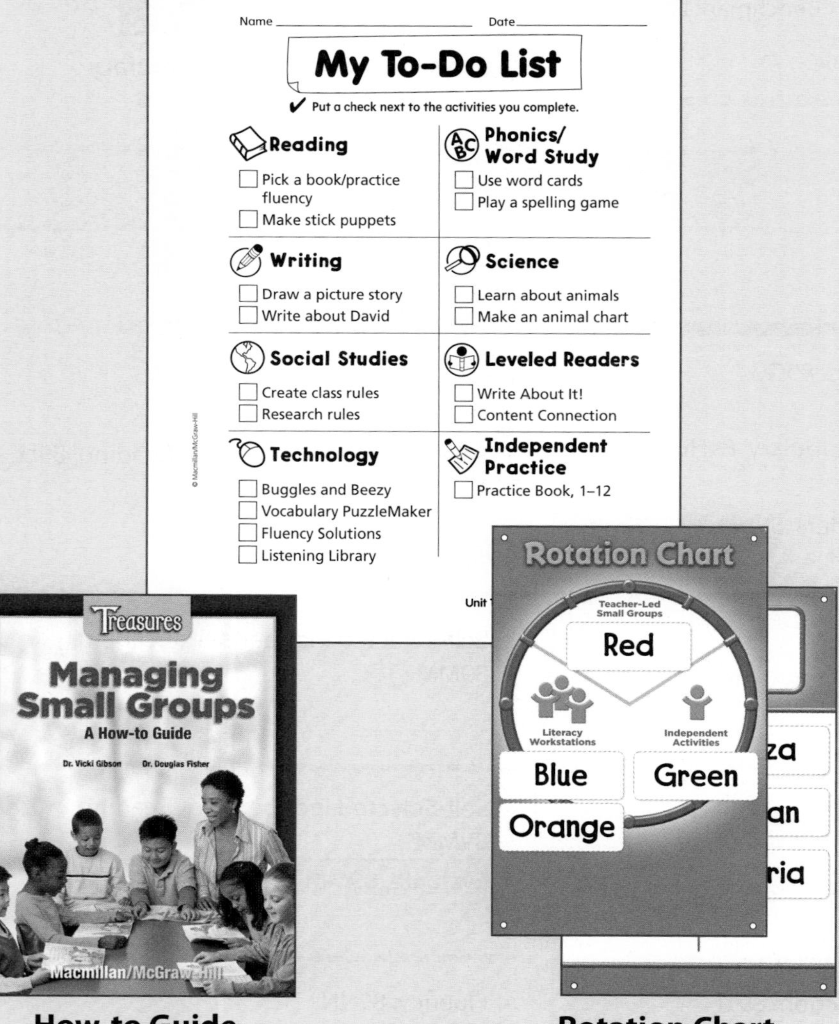
Name ______________ Date ______________

My To-Do List

✔ Put a check next to the activities you complete.

Reading
- ☐ Pick a book/practice fluency
- ☐ Make stick puppets

Phonics/ Word Study
- ☐ Use word cards
- ☐ Play a spelling game

Writing
- ☐ Draw a picture story
- ☐ Write about David

Science
- ☐ Learn about animals
- ☐ Make an animal chart

Social Studies
- ☐ Create class rules
- ☐ Research rules

Leveled Readers
- ☐ Write About It!
- ☐ Content Connection

Technology
- ☐ Buggles and Beezy
- ☐ Vocabulary PuzzleMaker
- ☐ Fluency Solutions
- ☐ Listening Library

Independent Practice
- ☐ Practice Book, 1–12

How-to Guide

Rotation Chart

Digital Learning

StudentWorks Plus
- Summaries in Multiple Languages
- Word-by-Word Reading
- Comprehension Questions

Meet the Author/Illustrator

Joe Cepeda

- Joe remembers having bruises from trying to get the candy that fell out of piñatas at childhood birthday parties.
- Joe has illustrated several books.
- He lives in Southern California with his family.

Other books illustrated by Joe Cepeda
- Herron, Carolivia. *Nappy Hair.* New York: Bantam Doubleday Dell Books for Young Readers, 1999.
- Lester, Julius. *What a Truly Cool World.* New York: Scholastic, Inc., 1999.

- Read Other Books by the Author or Illustrator

Leveled Practice

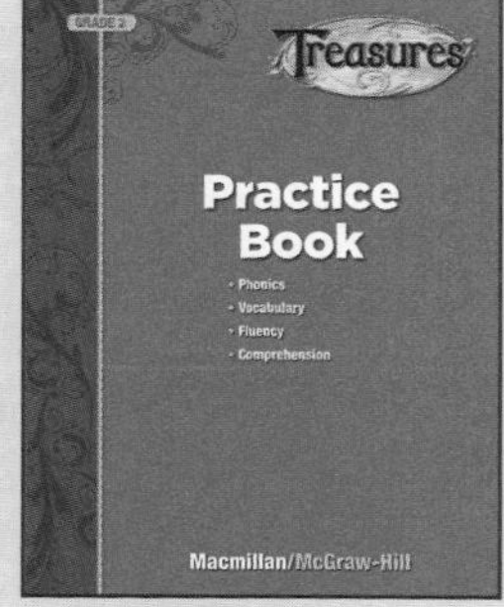

On Level

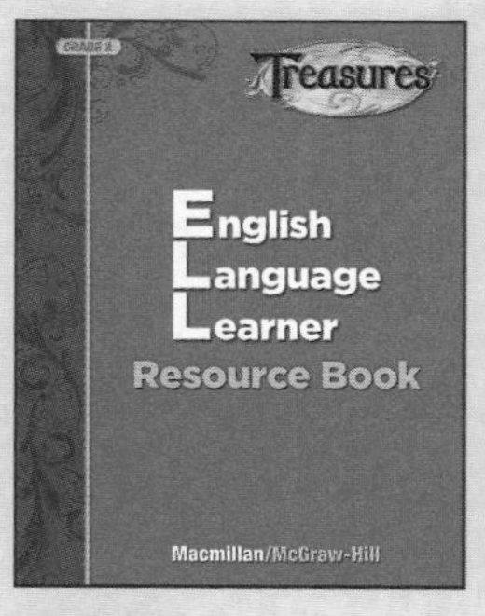

ELL

Also Available:

Approaching Reproducible

Beyond Reproducible

Independent Activities

ONLINE INSTRUCTION www.macmillanmh.com

Oral Language Activities

- Focus on Vocabulary and Concepts
- English Language Learner Support

Leveled Reader Database

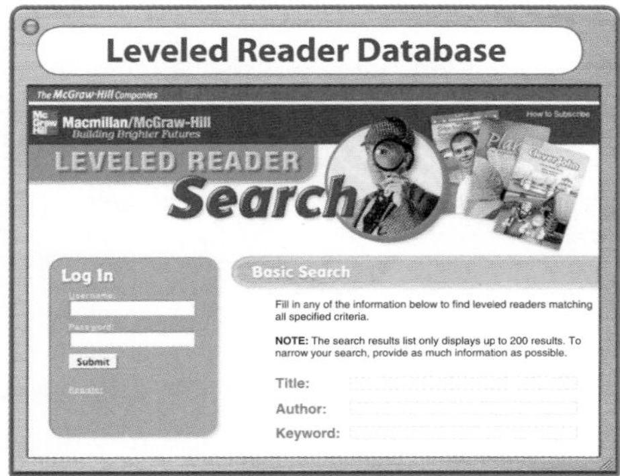

- Leveled Reader Database
- Search titles by level, skill, content area and more

Vocabulary/Spelling Activities

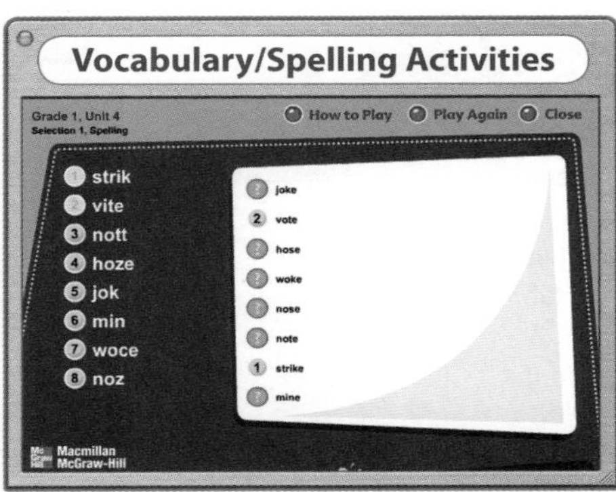

- Differentiated Lists and Activities

Research Toolkit

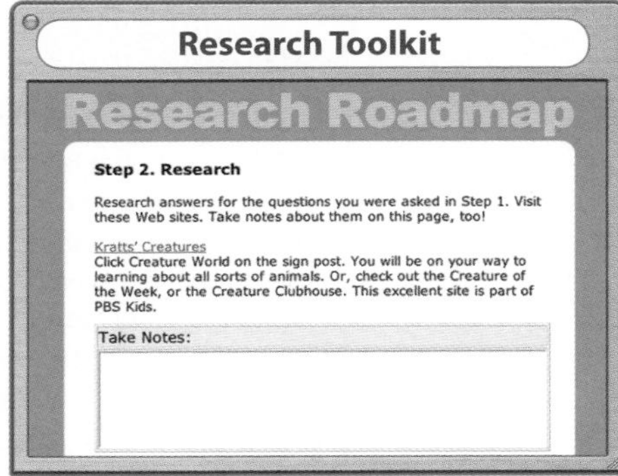

- Research Roadmap
- Research and Presentation Tools
- Theme Launcher Video
- Links to Science and Social Studies

Available on CD

LISTENING LIBRARY
Recordings of selections
- Main Selections
- Paired Selections
- Leveled Readers
- ELL Readers

NEW ADVENTURES WITH BUGGLES AND BEEZY
Phonemic awareness and phonics activities

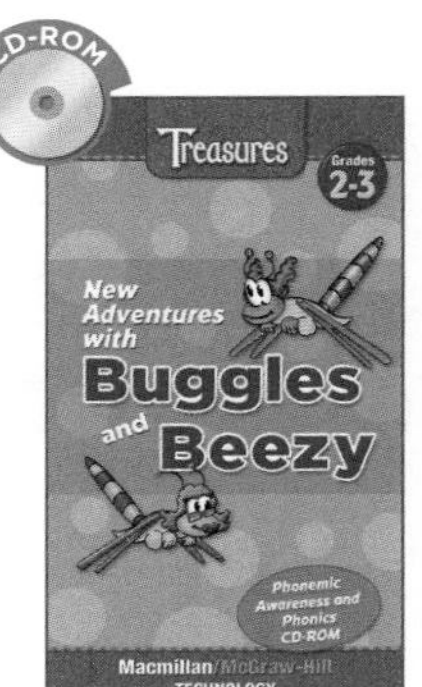

FLUENCY SOLUTIONS
Recorded passages at two speeds for modeling and practicing fluency

Leveled Reader Activities

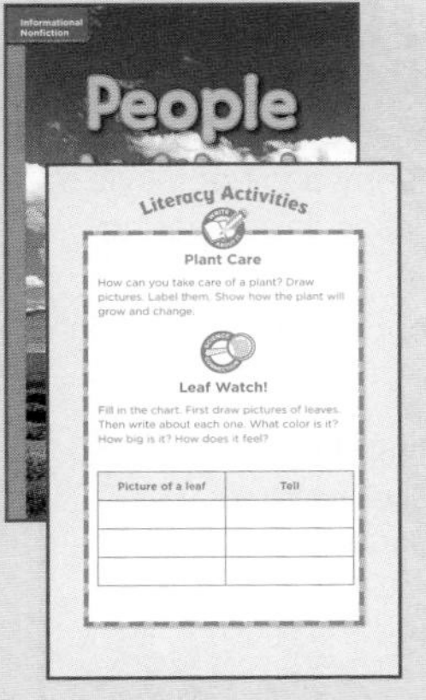

Approaching

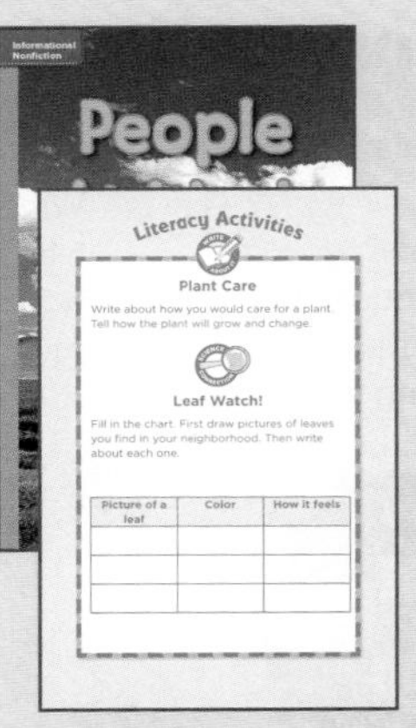

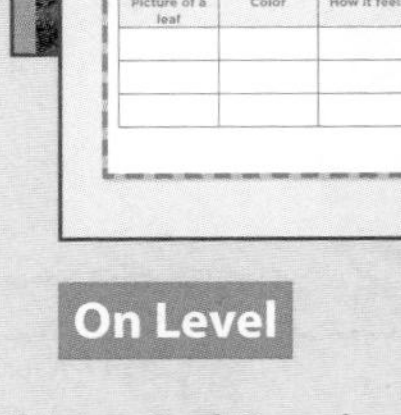

On Level

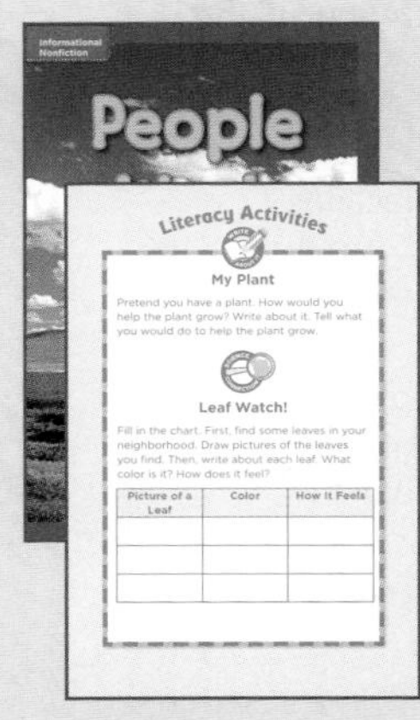

Beyond

ELL

See inside cover for all Leveled Readers.

Literacy Workstations

See lessons on pages 78K–78L

What do I do with the rest of my class?

Reading

Objectives

- Summarize a selection, identify the main idea and details
- Read aloud fluently and accurately
- Make a chart to show how a selection is organized

Phonics/Word Study

Objectives

- Identify and understand homophones
- Identify and use spelling words of the week
- Spell basic word patterns correctly

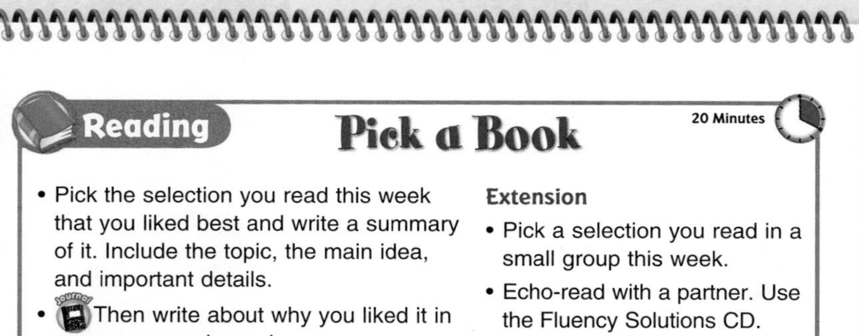

Reading — **Pick a Book** — 20 Minutes

- Pick the selection you read this week that you liked best and write a summary of it. Include the topic, the main idea, and important details.
- Then write about why you liked it in your response journal.

"A Ride to Help" is about ambulances and the paramedics who work on them. I liked it because I think paramedics have exciting jobs.

Extension

- Pick a selection you read in a small group this week.
- Echo-read with a partner. Use the Fluency Solutions CD.

Things you need:

- books you read this week
- pencil
- response journal
- Fluency Solutions CD

For more book titles, go to the Author/Illustrator section of www.macmillanmh.com

Listening Library Fluency Solutions

35

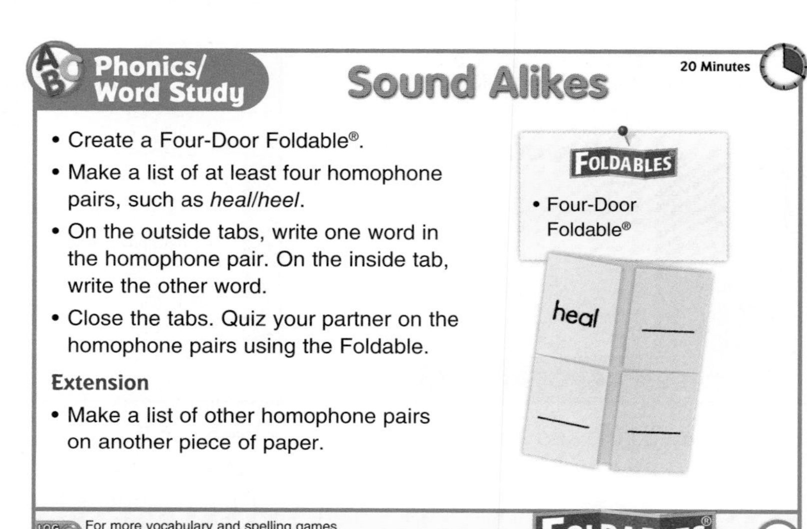

Phonics/Word Study — **Sound Alikes** — 20 Minutes

- Create a Four-Door Foldable®.
- Make a list of at least four homophone pairs, such as *heal/heel*.
- On the outside tabs, write one word in the homophone pair. On the inside tab, write the other word.
- Close the tabs. Quiz your partner on the homophone pairs using the Foldable.

Extension

- Make a list of other homophone pairs on another piece of paper.

FOLDABLES

- Four-Door Foldable®

heal

For more vocabulary and spelling games, go to www.macmillanmh.com

FOLDABLES®

35

Reading — **Read More About It** — 20 Minutes

- Pick a book about hospitals and health care workers.
- Read it alone or with a partner.

The article "A Race to the Hospital" has a beginning, middle, and end. I can tell because the article tells a true story about a boy who has an accident in the beginning.

Extension

- Think about the selections you read this week. Are they organized the same way? Why or why not?
- Make a chart to show how they are organized in the same way or in different ways.

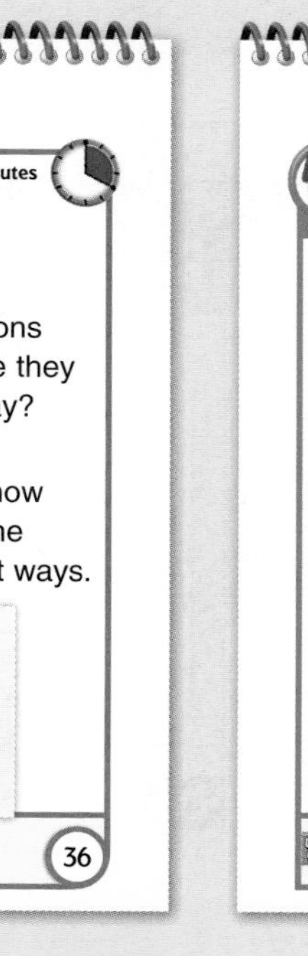

Things you need:

- books about hospital workers
- paper, pencil

For more book titles, go to the Author/Illustrator section of www.macmillanmh.com

Listening Library

36

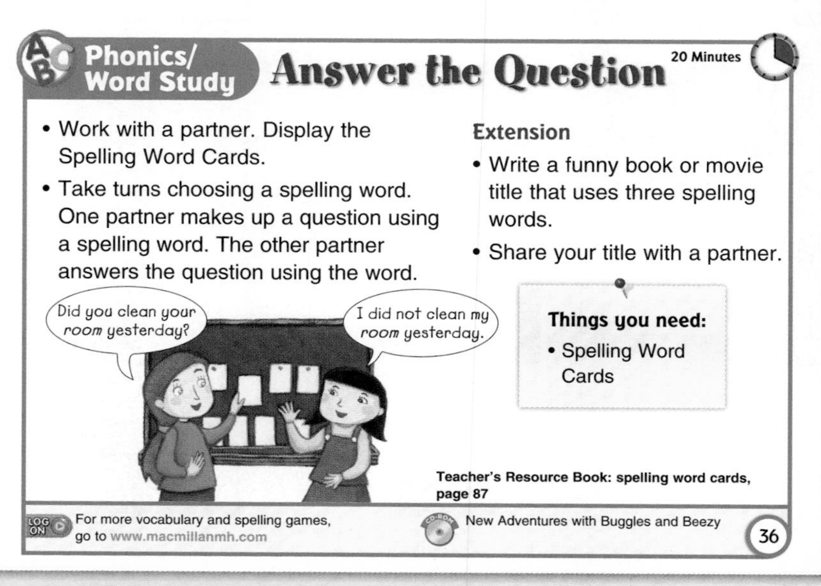

Phonics/Word Study — **Answer the Question** — 20 Minutes

- Work with a partner. Display the Spelling Word Cards.
- Take turns choosing a spelling word. One partner makes up a question using a spelling word. The other partner answers the question using the word.

Extension

- Write a funny book or movie title that uses three spelling words.
- Share your title with a partner.

Things you need:

- Spelling Word Cards

Teacher's Resource Book: spelling word cards, page 87

For more vocabulary and spelling games, go to www.macmillanmh.com

New Adventures with Buggles and Beezy

36

Literacy Workstation Flip Charts

Writing

Objectives

- Write a narrative story about a visit to the hospital
- Include a beginning, middle, and end
- Draft a list of health and safety tips

Content Literacy

Objectives

- Understand and write about the role of health care
- Discuss the choices people can make about where to work
- Create a chart to list and describe parts of the body

Writing — A Hospital Story

20 Minutes

- Think of a story about a visit to the hospital. Use a sequence chart to plan your story.
- Follow your sequence chart to write your story.
- You may add this story to your portfolio.

Extension

- Proofread your story. Check for correct capitalization and punctuation. Rewrite your story in your best handwriting.
- Draw pictures that show the beginning, middle, and end of your story.

Beginning	Middle	End
I fell off my bike and hurt my ankle.	I had an X-ray at the hospital.	My ankle was broken.

Things you need:
- pencil, paper

35

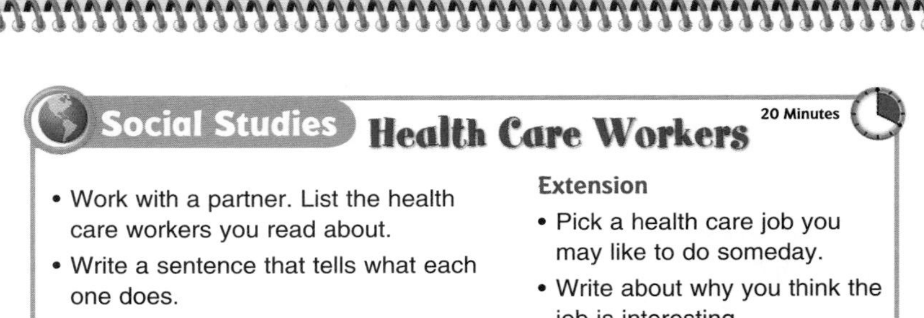

Social Studies — Health Care Workers

20 Minutes

- Work with a partner. List the health care workers you read about.
- Write a sentence that tells what each one does.
- Draw a picture for each sentence.

The paramedic rides in the ambulance and helps sick or hurt people.

Extension

- Pick a health care job you may like to do someday.
- Write about why you think the job is interesting.
- Discuss the following question with a partner. Do you think it is good when people are able to choose where to live and what job to have?

Things you need:
- pencil, paper
- crayons

LOG ON Internet Research and Inquiry Activity
www.macmillanmh.com

35

Writing — Health and Safety Tips

20 Minutes

- Think about ways to stay healthy and keep safe.
- Look in books to find out more.
- List as many health and safety tips as you can.

Extension

- Pick one tip from your list.
- Make a poster that shows this tip. Tell why following this tip is important.

- Cover your mouth when you cough or sneeze.
- Wash your hands often.
- Stay away from people who are sick.

Things you need:
- books about health and safety
- pencil, paper
- crayons

36

Science — Body Parts Help You

20 Minutes

- Body parts work together to help you live. With a partner, make a chart like the one shown below.
- List what you think each part does to help you live. Use the Internet or books to help you.

bones	brain	lungs	heart	stomach
make up skeleton				

Extension

- Choose one body part from the chart and learn more about it.
- Draw and label a picture of that body part.

Things you need:
- paper, pencil
- crayons, markers
- Internet or books

LOG ON Internet Research and Inquiry Activity
www.macmillanmh.com

36

Day 1 At a Glance

WHOLE GROUP

Oral Language
- Build Background
- Oral Vocabulary

Phonological Awareness
- Generate Rhyme

Phonics
- Vowel Digraphs *oo, ui, ew, ue, u, ou, oe*
- Build Fluency
- Spelling: Pretest: Words with Vowel Digraphs *oo, ui, ew, ue, oe*
- Read *Soon the North Wind Blew*

Vocabulary
- Teach Words in Context
- Use a Dictionary: Homophones
- Read "A Ride to Help" and "Time for an X-Ray"

Comprehension
- Strategy: Analyze Text Structure
- Skill: Sequence of Events

Language Arts
- Grammar: Irregular Verbs
- Writing: Expository

SMALL GROUP

- Differentiated Instruction, pages 89O–89NN

Oral Vocabulary

Week 3

clever	comfort
recuperate	sympathy
urgent	

Oral Language

Build Background

ACCESS PRIOR KNOWLEDGE
Discuss with children that many people work together to help children in need. Tell them that doctors and nurses often work together as a team to help children that are injured or sick. Ask children to think of some other worker teams that help people in need.

SING ABOUT WORKER TEAMS
Sing the song "Willum" and have children add verses and act out things that different worker teams do.

AUDIO CD

Willum

Willum he had seven sons,
seven sons, seven sons.
Willum he had seven sons
and this is what they did.

Number one was chopping wood, chopping wood, chopping wood. Number one was chopping wood and this is what he did...

FOCUS QUESTION Discuss the Focus Question under "Talk About It" on **Student Book** page 78. Describe the photograph providing academic language. *How do doctors help people* **recuperate***, or get well again?*

Use the Picture Prompt

BUILD WRITING FLUENCY
Ask children to respond to the picture by writing a paragraph in their Writer's Notebooks about how worker teams have helped them. Tell children to write as much as they can as well as they can. Children should write for eight minutes. Meet with children during individual Writing Conference time to provide feedback and revision assignments.

ELL ENGLISH LANGUAGE LEARNERS

Beginning	Intermediate	Advanced
Discuss Tell children about the photograph. *The doctor will help the boy get better. The mother will also help. They are a team.* Then ask children to tell you about the photograph. Restate responses in complete sentences.	**Describe** Ask children to describe the photograph. *Where is the boy? Who else is in the picture? Are doctors part of a team?* Elicit details to support children's responses.	**Expand** Ask children to elaborate on the concept. Discuss that the doctor is part of a team that helps people recuperate. Ask children to tell who else might be on the team and how they might help.

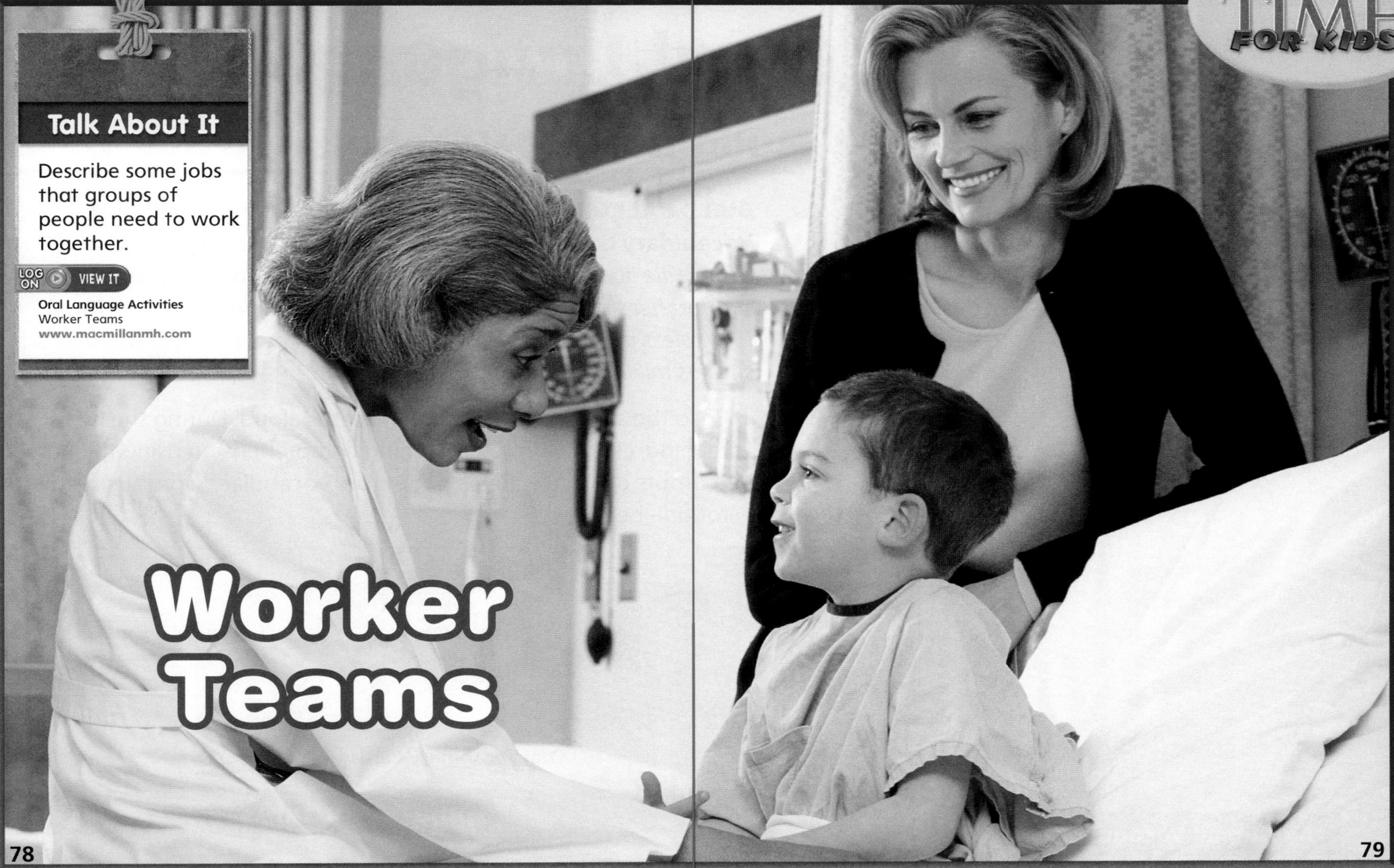
TIME FOR KIDS
Talk About It
Describe some jobs that groups of people need to work together.
LOG ON VIEW IT
Oral Language Activities
Worker Teams
www.macmillanmh.com
Worker Teams
78
79

Connect to the Unit Theme

People work together to help children in need, such as when they are injured or sick.

CONNECT TO THEME
Ask children what they have learned so far about teamwork.

USE THEME FOLDABLE
Read aloud the **Big Idea** statement. Write the word **urgent** on the board. Read it aloud and have children repeat. Remind children that *urgent* means "important or demanding." Ask children to add it to their Unit Theme Foldables. Tell children that they will add pictures of how worker teams help people when they are in urgent situations.

Dinah Zike's FOLDABLES® Study Organizer

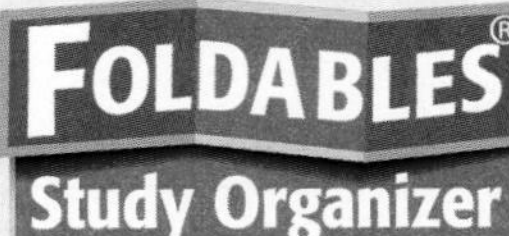

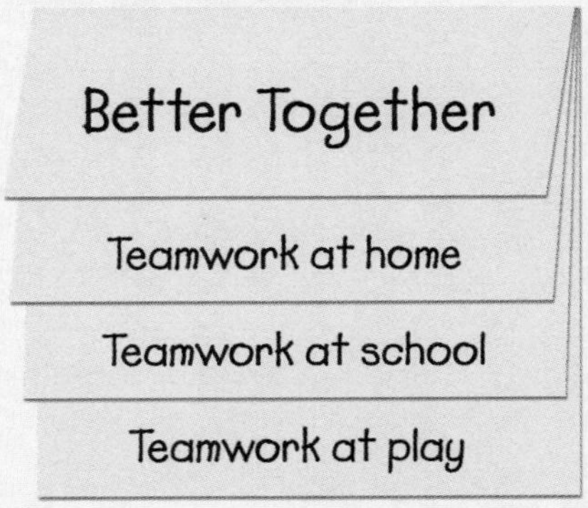
Better Together
Teamwork at home
Teamwork at school
Teamwork at play

Unit 4 Theme Foldable

Objectives

- Introduce oral vocabulary words
- Listen attentively to "Little Red Riding Hood"

Materials

- Oral Vocabulary Cards: "Little Red Riding Hood"

Oral Language

Build Robust Vocabulary

BUILD BACKGROUND Display "Little Red Riding Hood" **Oral Vocabulary Card** 1 and read the title aloud. *We are going to read a fairy tale about a girl named Little Red Riding Hood. She wants to comfort her sick grandmother but a clever wolf plays a trick on her. A fairy tale is a story about both good and bad make-believe characters such as talking animals.*

- Read the story on the back of the cards aloud. During the first reading, check children's listening comprehension using the Retell prompts on Card 4. Review the story vocabulary words using the routine below.

Oral Vocabulary Cards

Vocabulary Routine

Use the routine below to discuss the meaning of each story word.

<u>**Define:**</u> **Clever** means "easily able to understand things or do things."
<u>**Example:**</u> *My clever brother had the idea of tying a bell to the cat so it wouldn't eat mice.*
<u>**Ask:**</u> What clever characters do you know? How do they act clever? EXAMPLE

- When you **comfort** someone, you try to make him or her feel better. *Mothers often rock their babies to comfort them.* How would you comfort a lost kitten? EXPLANATION
- When you **recuperate** from being sick, you get well again. *A person needs plenty of rest to recuperate from the flu.* What helps you recuperate from an illness? PRIOR KNOWLEDGE
- **Sympathy** is the feeling you have when you feel sorry for someone, or when you share someone's sorrow or trouble. *I felt sympathy for my brother when he broke his leg.* When have you felt sympathy for a friend? PRIOR KNOWLEDGE
- If a situation is **urgent**, help is needed immediately. *When our bathtub overflowed, we told the plumber it was urgent.* What kind of situation would you consider to be urgent? EXAMPLE

Use the routine to review last week's words *advice*, *hesitate*, *panic*, *secure*, and *vowed*.

Additional Vocabulary

To provide 15–20 minutes of additional vocabulary instruction, see **Oral Vocabulary Cards** 5-Day Plan. The pre- and post-tests for this week can be found on **Teacher's Resource Book** pages 255–257.

Phonological Awareness

Generate Rhyme

Objective

- Generate a series of original rhyming words

Model

Explain that rhyming words have the same ending vowel and consonant sounds. Model for children how to generate rhyming words.

Repeat the model using the words *shoe, grew; soon, tune; booth, tooth.*

Listen carefully as I say these words: *room, boom*. Both words end with the same sounds, /ü/ /m/. Listen: /r/ /üm/, /b/ /üm/. The words *room* and *boom* rhyme.

What other words rhyme with *room* and *boom*? To figure that out, I need to think of words that end in the sounds /üm/. I know one. *Bloom*, /b/ /l/ /üm/. The word *bloom* ends in /üm/, so it rhymes with *room* and *boom*.

Guided Practice/Practice

Have children generate rhyming words. Do the first two together.

Now let's try it together. Listen to the words I say. Let's name words that rhyme.

soup (hoop, loop, troop, droop, group)
suit (boot, cute, shoot, fruit, pollute)
June (moon, prune, noon, spoon, balloon)
blew (who, flu, blue, too, drew, shoe, you)
truth (booth, tooth, Ruth)
food (mood, rude, feud, include, chewed)
goose (juice, loose, moose, use, reduce)
roof (goof, proof)
fool (school, rule, pool, tool, stool)
news (choose, shoes, refuse, lose, confuse)

Objectives

- Identify letter-sound correspondence for vowel digraphs /ü/*oo*, *ui*, *ew*, *ue*, *u*, *ou*, *oe*
- Blend sounds in words with vowel digraphs /ü/
- Review previously taught phonics skills

Materials

- Sound-Spelling Card: *Spoon*
- Word-Building Cards; Teacher's Resource Book, p. 66
- pocket chart
- chart paper
- Practice Book, p. 195

Skills Trace

Vowel Digraphs *oo*, *ui*, *ew*, *ue*, *u*, *ou*, *oe*

Introduce	79C–D
Practice/ Apply	79F, 81G–H, 85F–G, 85I, 85V–W; Practice Book: 195; Decodable Reader: *Soon the North Wind Blew*
Reteach/ Review	89G–H, 89O–R, 89U, 89AA, 89GG
Assess	Weekly Test; Unit 4 Test
Maintain	Build Fluency: Sound/Spellings

ELL

Variations in Languages In some languages, including Vietnamese and Cantonese, the transfer for the variant vowel /ü/ sound is only approximate. Use the Approaching Level Phonics lessons for pronunciation and decoding practice.

Sound Pronunciation

See **Sound Pronunciation CD** for a model of the /ü/ sound. Play this for children needing additional models.

Phonics

Vowel Digraphs /ü/

Model

Teach the sound /ü/ spelled with vowel digraphs *oo*, *ui*, *ew*, *ue*, *u*, *ou*, *oe*. Show *Spoon* **Sound-Spelling Card**.

Model writing the letters. Use handwriting models provided.

This is the *Spoon* Sound-Spelling Card. The sound is /ü/. The /ü/ sound can be spelled with the letters *oo*. Say it with me: /ü/. Watch as I write the letters *oo*. I will say the sound /ü/ as I write the letters several times. (Repeat with the sound-spellings *ui*, *ew*, *ue*, *u*, *ou*, and *oe*.)

Guided Practice/Practice

Have children practice connecting letters and sound through writing.

Now do it with me. Say /ü/ as I write the letters *oo*. This time, write the letters *oo* five times as you say the /ü/ sound.

Build Fluency: Sound/Spellings

Display the following **Word-Building Cards:** *oo*, *ui*, *ew*, *ue*, *u*, *ou*, *oe*, *oi*, *oy*, *ou*, *ow*, *are*, *air*, *ear*, *ere*, *or*, *ore*, *oar*, *ar*, *gn*, *kn*, *wr*, *mb*, *eer*, *ere*, *ear*. Have children chorally say each sound. Repeat and vary the pace.

ui oe wr

Blend Words with /ü/

Model

Display Word-Building Cards *z*, *o*, *o*. Model how to blend sounds as you run your finger under each letter.

Repeat with *new*, *soup*, *shoe*, *suit*, and *too*.

This is the letter *z*. It stands for /z/.

This is the letter *o*. The letters *oo* together can stand for /ü/. Listen as I blend the two sounds together /zü/, *zoo*. Say it with me.

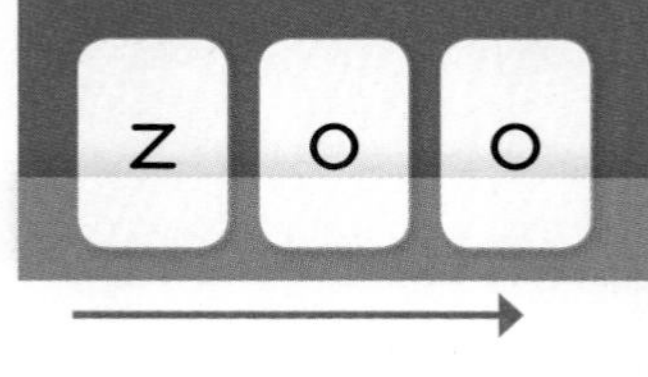

Guided Practice/Practice

Write the words below on chart paper. Read each one in the first row, blending the sounds, for example, /r/ /ü/ /m/, /rüm/. The word is *room*. Have children blend the sounds in each word with you. Then use the appropriate blending level to complete the remaining lines chorally. See **Sound-by-Sound Blending Routine** in the **Instructional Routine Handbook** for support. Save the chart paper for use in tomorrow's lesson.

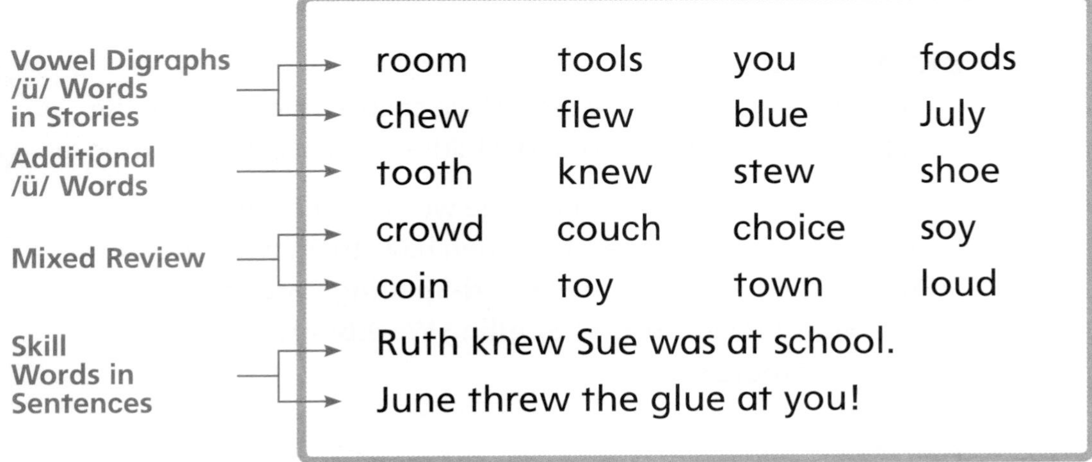

Vowel Digraphs /ü/ Words in Stories	room	tools	you	foods
	chew	flew	blue	July
Additional /ü/ Words	tooth	knew	stew	shoe
Mixed Review	crowd	couch	choice	soy
	coin	toy	town	loud
Skill Words in Sentences	Ruth knew Sue was at school.			
	June threw the glue at you!			

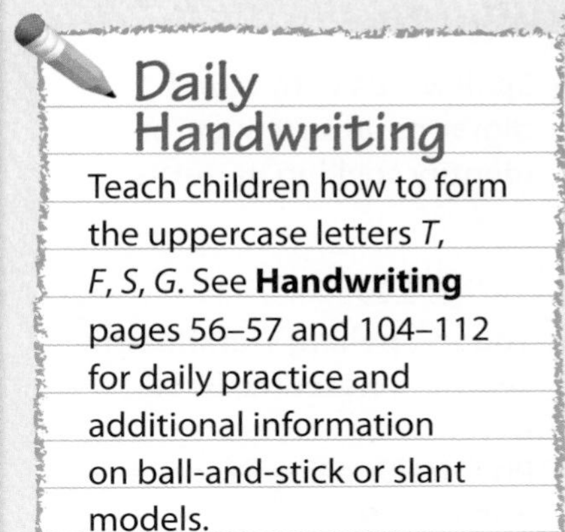

Daily Handwriting

Teach children how to form the uppercase letters *T*, *F*, *S*, *G*. See **Handwriting** pages 56–57 and 104–112 for daily practice and additional information on ball-and-stick or slant models.

Corrective Feedback

Blending: Sound Error Model the sound that children missed. Then have them repeat the sound. Say: *My turn.* Tap under the letters and say: *Sound? /ü/. What's the sound?* Then return to the beginning of the word. Say: *Let's start over.* Blend the sounds in the word with children again.

Quick Check

Can children blend the sounds in words with variant vowel /ü/?

During **Small Group Instruction**

Tier 2

If No → **Approaching Level** Repeat blending using the chart above. Explicitly correct the error and provide more "with me" type practice. Use a lower level of blending to provide support.

If Yes → **On Level** Consolidate the learning by having children read additional words with *oo, ui, ew, ue, u, ou, oe*. See page 89Q.

Beyond Level Extend the learning by having children read harder words containing *oo, ui, ew, ue, u, ou, oe*. See page 89R.

ON YOUR OWN

Practice Book, page 195

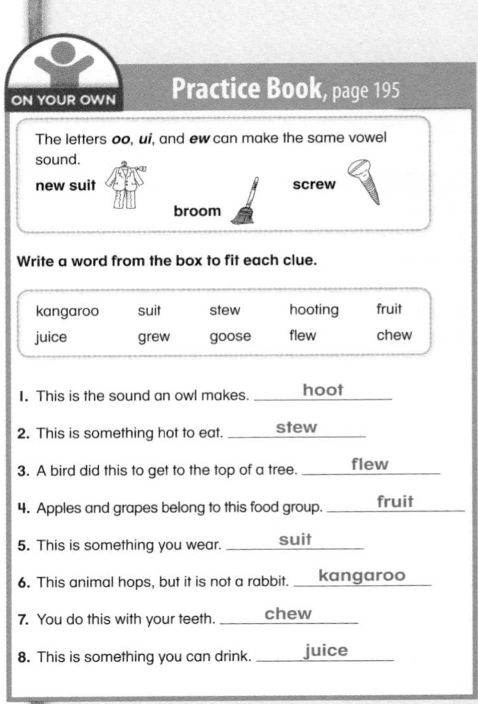

The letters ***oo***, ***ui***, and ***ew*** can make the same vowel sound.

new suit — broom — screw

Write a word from the box to fit each clue.

kangaroo	suit	stew	hooting	fruit
juice	grew	goose	flew	chew

1. This is the sound an owl makes. hoot
2. This is something hot to eat. stew
3. A bird did this to get to the top of a tree. flew
4. Apples and grapes belong to this food group. fruit
5. This is something you wear. suit
6. This animal hops, but it is not a rabbit. kangaroo
7. You do this with your teeth. chew
8. This is something you can drink. juice

Approaching Reproducible, page 195

Beyond Reproducible, page 195

Objectives

- Spell words with vowel digraphs *oo, ui, ew, ue, oe*
- Identify spelling patterns

Materials

- Sound-Spelling WorkBoard; Teacher's Resource Book, p. 143
- Phonics/Spelling Practice Book, p. 69

5-Day Spelling	
DAY 1	Dictation; Pretest
DAY 2	Teacher-Modeled Word Sort
DAY 3	Student Word Sort
DAY 4	Test Practice
DAY 5	Posttest

ON YOUR OWN **Spelling**, page 69

Using the Word Study Steps
1. LOOK at the word.
2. SAY the word aloud.
3. STUDY the letters in the word.
4. WRITE the word.
5. CHECK the word.
Did you spell the word right?
If not, go back to step 1.

Find and Circle

suit	shoe	room	clue	fruit
glue	flew	canoe	new	tool

Circle the ten hidden spelling words.

t	r	o	o	m	k	n	e	w	q
o	p	c	a	n	o	e	l	j	s
o	g	l	f	r	u	i	t	o	u
l	w	u	s	h	g	l	u	e	i
f	l	e	w	g	s	h	o	e	t

Phonics/Spelling

Words with *oo, ui, ew, ue, oe*

DICTATION

Use dictation to help children transfer their growing knowledge of sound-spellings to writing. Follow the **Dictation Routine** below with each spelling word.

DICTATION ROUTINE

- Pronounce one word at a time. Have children clearly state the word. Then repeat the word for children and use it in a sentence.
- Ask children to orally segment the word to think about the individual sounds in the word. Then have them write the word. Prompt children to use the **Sound-Spelling Card** spellings as they write. Provide **Sound-Spelling Workboards** for children who need more support.

PRETEST

Pronounce each spelling word. Read the sentence and pronounce the word again. Ask children to say each word softly, stretching the sounds, before writing it. After the pretest, write each word on the board as you say the letter names. Have children check their words.

Spelling Words

Approaching	On Level	Beyond
too	room	school
room	tool	moody
zoo	suit	bruise
suit	fruit	fruitcake
fruit	clue	clues
clue	glue	glued
glue	flew	flew
dew	new	chewed
new	shoe	shoelace
shoe	canoe	canoe
point	point	moist
joy	royal	royal
follow	follow	follow
near	near	near
paper	paper	paper

1. **room:** Please clean up your room.
2. **tool:** A rake is a garden tool.
3. **suit:** Carla wore a pink suit.
4. **fruit:** Apples are a kind of fruit.
5. **clue:** I need another clue.
6. **glue:** Bill used glue to fix the toy.
7. **flew:** The birds flew away.
8. **new:** I got a new skateboard.
9. **shoe:** This shoe is too small.
10. **canoe:** We took the canoe on the lake.
11. **point:** The pencil point is broken.
12. **royal:** A prince is a part of a royal family.
13. **follow:** The dogs follow me home.
14. **near:** Our house is near the zoo.
15. **paper:** Jeremiah got an A on his paper.

Decodable Reader

- **Review High-Frequency Words** Write **above**, **color**, and **song** on the board. Review the words with children using the **Read/Spell/Write** routine.

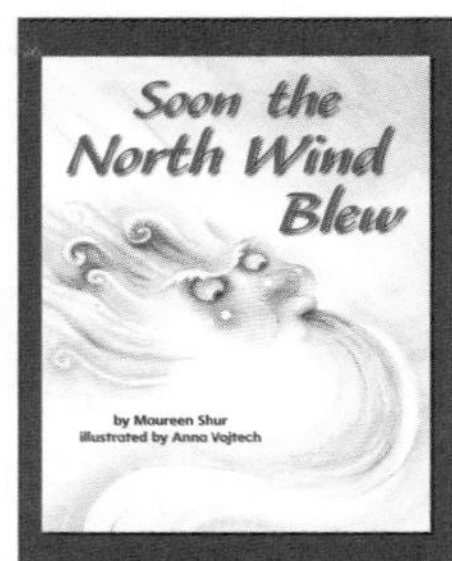

Soon the North Wind Blew

- **Preview and Predict** Point to the book's title and have children sound out each word as you run your finger under it. Discuss the cover illustration. Ask:
  - *What do you see in this picture?*
  - *Based on the title and illustrations, what do you think this story will be about?*
- **First Read** Turn to page 14. Have children point to each word, sounding out decodable words and saying the high-frequency words quickly. Children should chorally read the story the first time through. If children have difficulty, provide corrective feedback page by page as needed. See the **Decodable Text Routine** in the **Instructional Routine Handbook** for correction models.
- **Check Comprehension** Ask the following:
  - *What did the wind and the sun argue about?*
  - *What was the moon's plan?*
  - *What caused the man to take off his coat?*
  - *Turn to your partner and retell the story.*

- **Second Read** Reread the story with children.
  - Beyond Level If children can sound out the words, then have them quietly read the text with a partner.
  - Approaching Level If children struggle sounding out words, provide "with you" blending models. Then review blending using the words on the Word List at the end of the book during Small Group time. Conclude by guiding children through a rereading of the book.

Objectives

- **Decode multisyllabic words in context**
- **Identify and read high-frequency words *above, color, song***

Materials

- **Decodable Reader Library: *Soon the North Wind Blew***

High-Frequency Words

Use the **Read/Spell/Write** routine to teach each high-frequency word.

- **Read** Read the word and have children chorally repeat.
- **Spell** Chorally spell the word.
- **Write** Have children write the word as they spell it aloud. Then ask children to write a sentence using each word.

SMALL GROUP OPTION

You may wish to read the Decodable Reader during **Small Group** time.

See pages 89O–89NN

Objectives

- Learn the meaning of vocabulary words in context
- Use a dictionary to find the meanings of homophones
- Review vocabulary words from last week

Materials

- dictionary
- Student Book, pp. 80–81
- Practice Book, p. 196

Vocabulary	
aid	heal
informs	personal
serious	

ELL

Preteach Vocabulary
See page 89T to preteach the vocabulary words to ELL and Approaching Level children. Use the Visual Vocabulary Resources to demonstrate and discuss each word.

Vocabulary

TEACH WORDS
Introduce each word using the **Define/Example/Ask** routine. Model reading each word.

Vocabulary Routine

Use the routine below to discuss the meaning of each word.

Define: **Aid** means "help or support."
Example: *My friend came to my aid when I fell off my bike.*
Ask: Can you name a time when someone came to your aid? EXAMPLE

- Over time, a broken bone will **heal**, or get better. *The doctor said my broken bone would heal in about six weeks.* What other word sounds like *heal*? What is the definition of the word? HOMOPHONES
- When someone **informs** you, he or she tells you something. *The doctor informs me that I have a broken arm.* Who informs you about the rules you must follow in school? EXAMPLE
- Something that is **personal** has to do with you. *Amy's personal things belong only to her.* What personal school supplies do you keep in your desk? EXAMPLE
- Something that is **serious** is dangerous or important. *A large cut is a serious injury.* Can you name another serious injury? EXAMPLE
- **Word Wall** Add these words to the Word Wall. Remove words from the wall as children master them.

- **Review** Use the routine to review last week's vocabulary words: *attention, buddy, accident, tip, enormous, obeys*.

STRATEGY Use a Dictionary: Homophones

- Homophones are words that sound the same, but have different spellings and different meanings. You can use a dictionary to find the correct meaning for a homophone if you are unsure which word is being used.
- When you come to a homophone, such as *heal*, ask yourself which meaning fits best in the sentence. Then check your thinking by using a dictionary to find the meaning of the word.

Think Aloud The doctor tells the patient that the broken bone will **heal**. I know that *heel*, spelled *h-e-e-l*, is what we call the back part of the foot. I think *heal*, spelled *h-e-a-l* is a different word. I will look in the dictionary to find the correct meaning for this spelling. It says *heal* means "to get better." This is correct.

Real World Reading

Vocabulary

serious
personal
aid
informs
heal

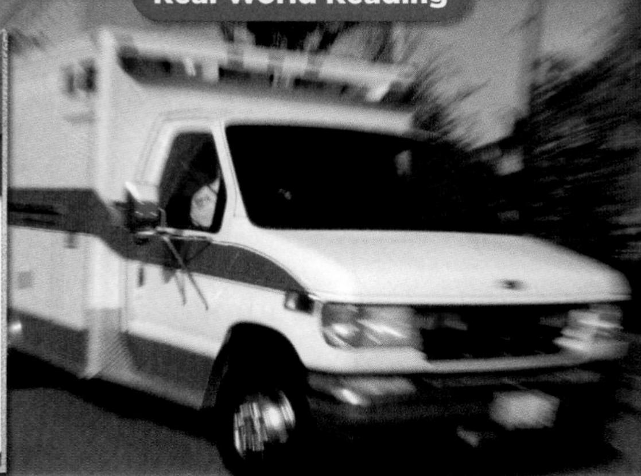

A Ride to Help

The lights flash and the sirens scream. An ambulance is on its way. There is a **serious** problem. Someone is hurt or very sick. It could be severe.

Paramedics drive the ambulance. They also give help to people on the way to the hospital. Inside the ambulance are medical supplies. If someone has a broken bone, the paramedics use special tools to keep it still.

Paramedics take a **personal** interest in helping people. They give **aid** and get people to the hospital as quickly as possible.

Paramedics come when someone is sick or hurt.

TIME FOR KIDS

Time for an X-Ray

Who needs an X-ray? People who have broken a bone will usually get an X-ray taken at the hospital. An X-ray is a special kind of photograph that shows bones and other parts inside the body.

What happens when you get an X-ray? First an X-ray worker takes the picture. Then a doctor looks at the X-ray to find out if a bone is broken. Finally the doctor **informs** the patient about how the bone will **heal**. She may tell the patient that he or she needs a cast. The doctor also explains that the bone will mend over time.

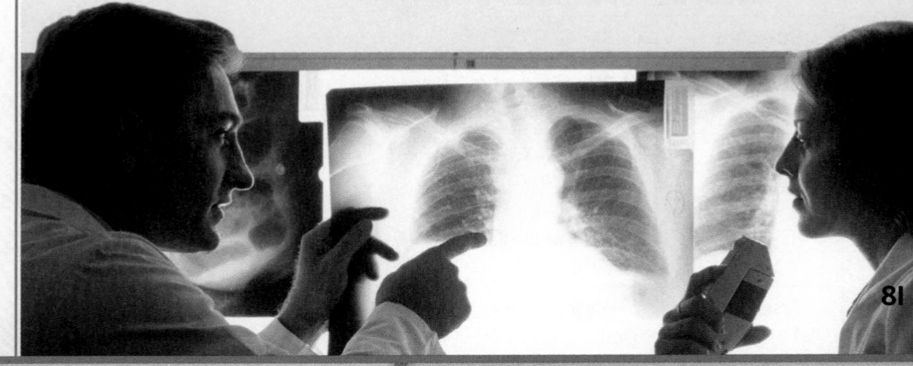

Read "A Ride to Help" and "Time for an X-Ray"

Read "A Ride to Help" and "Time for an X-Ray" with children. Stop at each **highlighted** word. Ask children to identify text clues that reveal the meanings of the highlighted words. Have children ask clarifying questions to check overall comprehension. Tell children that they will read these words again in "A Trip to the Emergency Room."

Quick Check

Do children understand word meanings?

During **Small Group Instruction**

If No → **Approaching Level** Vocabulary pages: 89P, 89V, 89BB, 89JJ.

If Yes → **On Level** Reread Vocabulary Selection.

Beyond Level Reread Vocabulary Selection.

ON YOUR OWN

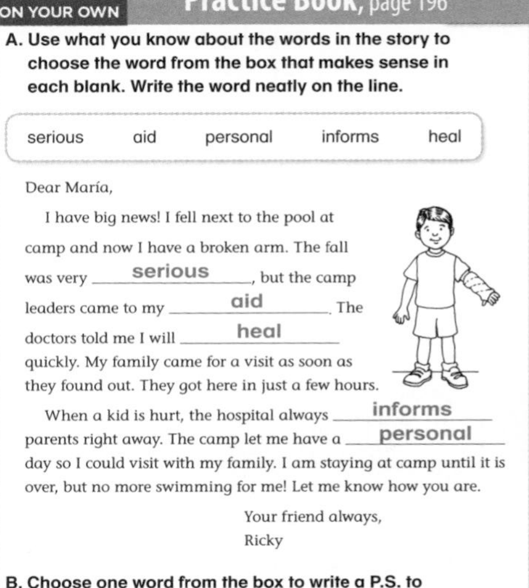

Practice Book, page 196

A. Use what you know about the words in the story to choose the word from the box that makes sense in each blank. Write the word neatly on the line.

serious aid personal informs heal

Dear Maria,

I have big news! I fell next to the pool at camp and now I have a broken arm. The fall was very serious, but the camp leaders came to my aid. The doctors told me I will heal quickly. My family came for a visit as soon as they found out. They got here in just a few hours.

When a kid is hurt, the hospital always informs parents right away. The camp let me have a personal day so I could visit with my family. I am staying at camp until it is over, but no more swimming for me! Let me know how you are.

Your friend always,
Ricky

B. Choose one word from the box to write a P.S. to the letter. Possible response provided

P.S.: Have you ever had a serious fall?

Approaching Reproducible, page 196

Beyond Reproducible, page 196

Objectives

- Analyze text structure in a nonfiction article
- Describe the order of events or ideas in a text
- Use academic language: *text structure, sequence of events*

Materials

- Transparencies 11, 18
- Student Book, p. 81

Skills Trace

Sequence of Events	
Introduce	U4: 81A–B
Practice/ Apply	U4: 81K–85A; Practice Book: 198–199
Reteach/ Review	U4: 89K, 89V–X, 89BB–DD, 93A–B, 93K–115A, 119G, 119R–T, 119X–Z; Practice Book: 209–210
Assess	Weekly Tests; Unit 4, 5 Tests
Maintain	U4: 155N; U5: 201N, 209J–233A, 239G, 239R–T, 239X–Z, 311N; Practice Book: 243–244

ELL

Academic Language
Preteach the following academic language words to ELL and Approaching Level children during Small Group time: *text structure, sequence of events*. See page 89S.

Comprehension

STRATEGY Analyze Text Structure

EXPLAIN

What Is It? Explain that an author of nonfiction can present information in various ways. **Text structure** is a pattern writers use to organize information in nonfiction. Different kinds of text structures include sequence, cause and effect, problem and solution, compare and contrast, and description. Special signal words often help the reader recognize the kind of text structure an author is using.

Why Is It Important? Point out that recognizing the text structure can help readers remember and understand the ideas and events in an expository text.

SKILL Sequence of Events

EXPLAIN

What Is It? Explain that **sequence** is the order of events or ideas in a text. Writers often describe events or ideas in sequence, or in the time order that they happen. Writers may use signal words such as *first*, *next*, *then*, and *last* to help the reader follow the order of events.

Why Is It Important? Understanding and describing the order of events helps readers to identify and remember key events and ideas.

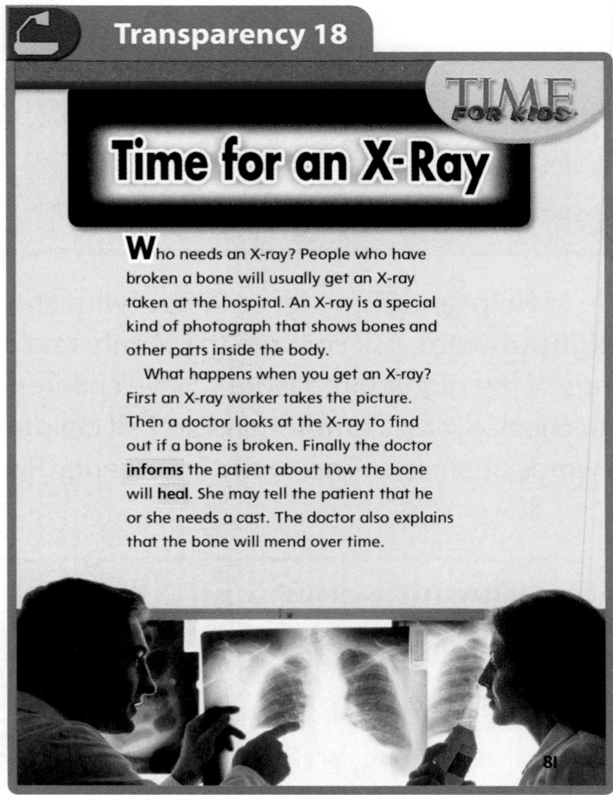
Transparency 18

TIME FOR KIDS

Time for an X-Ray

Who needs an X-ray? People who have broken a bone will usually get an X-ray taken at the hospital. An X-ray is a special kind of photograph that shows bones and other parts inside the body.

What happens when you get an X-ray? First an X-ray worker takes the picture. Then a doctor looks at the X-ray to find out if a bone is broken. Finally the doctor **informs** the patient about how the bone will **heal**. She may tell the patient that he or she needs a cast. The doctor also explains that the bone will mend over time.

81

Student Book page 81 is available on Comprehension Transparency 18.

- To identify when an author is using a sequence text structure, tell children to ask themselves *When is this event taking place?* as they read.
- Have them pay attention to words that signal time order, such as *first*, *next*, *then*, *last*, and *finally*, as well as time phrases, dates, or steps in a process.

MODEL

How Do I Use It? Read aloud "Time for an X-Ray" on **Student Book** page 81. Model for children how to describe the sequence of events.

Think Aloud I see that the second paragraph tells about getting an X-ray. As I read, I will pay attention to the order in which things happen. I see that the second sentence has the signal word *first*. In other sentences, I see the words *then* and *last*. These words will help me understand the order of events.

- Display the Sequence Chart on **Transparency 11**. Ask children: *What happens first when someone goes for an X-ray? What signal word did you use to find that information?* Record their contributions in the chart.

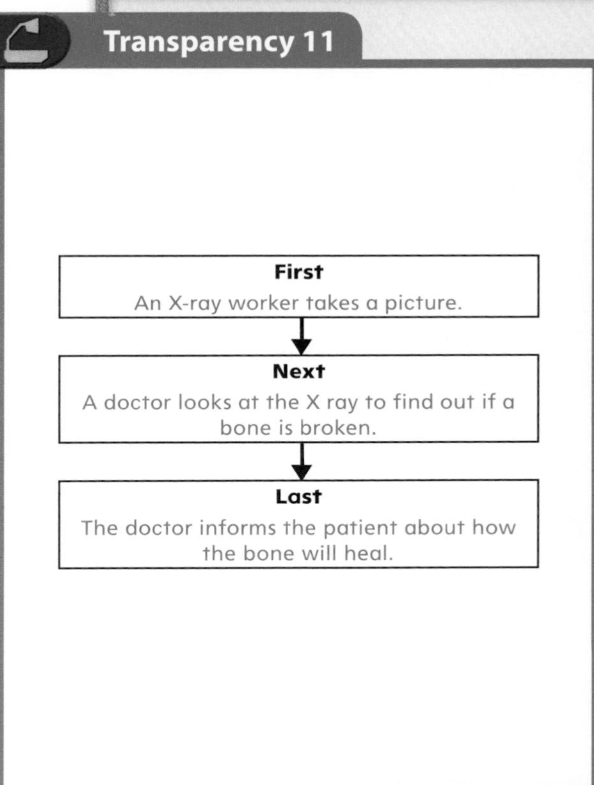

Graphic Organizer Transparency

GUIDED PRACTICE

- Reread the second paragraph of "Time for an X-Ray." Ask children what happens after the x-ray worker takes a picture. Record children's responses in the chart.
- Continue helping children identify the sequence of events by reading the second paragraph with them. Remind children that the sequence of events is the order in which things happen and to look for words that signal time, such as *first*, *then*, *next*, and *last*.

APPLY

- Have children reread the passage and fill in the remainder of the Sequence Chart. Ask questions such as: *What clue words do you see that help you understand the order? What is the first thing to happen when someone gets an X-ray? What is the last thing to happen?*

- Ask children to use the chart to retell the article to a partner.

DAY 1
WHOLE GROUP

Objectives

- Understand and use verbs
- Select appropriate irregular past-tense verbs

Materials

- Transparency 86
- Grammar Practice Book, p. 86

5-Day Grammar	
Irregular Verbs	
DAY 1	Irregular Verbs
DAY 2	More Irregular Verbs
DAY 3	Mechanics: Book Titles
DAY 4	Irregular Verbs Proofread
DAY 5	Review and Assess Book Titles Irregular Verbs

ON YOUR OWN

Grammar, page 86

- Some verbs do not add *-ed* to form the past tense.
- The verbs ***go*** and ***do*** have special forms in the past tense.

I, we, you, they	go	went
I, we, you, they	do	did

Choose the correct verb in ( ). Then write the complete sentence below.

1. Our class (go, went) to the library to learn about pollution.
   Our class went to the library to learn about pollution.
2. We can (do, did) a lot to stop pollution.
   We can do a lot to stop pollution.
3. Toxic wastes should not (go, went) into the ocean.
   Toxic wastes should not go into the ocean.
4. What are you going to (do, did) to stop pollution?
   What are you going to do to stop pollution?
5. Last summer we (go, went) to clean-up day at the beach.
   Last summer we went to clean-up day at the beach.
6. Everyone (do, did) a lot of work picking up trash.
   Everyone did a lot of work picking up trash.

Grammar

Irregular Verbs

EXPLAIN/MODEL

- Some verbs are **irregular**. That means you do not add *-ed* to form the past tense. (e.g., fell, gave, had, sent, went)
- The verbs *go* and *do* have special forms in the past tense. The past tense of *go* is *went*. The past tense of *do* is *did*.

Write the following sentence on the board: *Tiffany went to her grandmother's house yesterday.* Help children to identify the verb in the sentence. Ask whether it is a present-tense or past-tense verb. Point out that the verb *went* is a past-tense verb; it shows action that happened in the past.

Use item 1 on **Grammar Transparency 86** to model how to select the correct tense of each irregular verb.

Transparency 86

Irregular Verbs

1. Last week I (go, went) to the health fair at our school.
2. Some doctors (does, did) a short skit on eating well.
3. My parents (go, went) to the family health talk.
4. A group of the nurses (does, did) house visits last summer.
5. My family (goes, went) for a check-up last month.

Grammar Transparency

GUIDED PRACTICE/PRACTICE

Guide practice with item 2. Have children complete items 3–5 on their own by selecting the correct tense of each irregular verb.

Writing

Expository: Composition

DISCUSS THE TOPIC

- An **expository composition** gives information and facts about real people, places, or events. Explain that this week they will be researching hospitals in order to write an expository composition.

Transparency 103

What I Know	What I Want to Know	What I Learned
Many different people work in a hospital.	What happens when you go to the hospital for an operation? Which workers do you see?	

Writing Transparency

Research and Inquiry

GENERATE QUESTIONS

Display **Writing Transparency 103**. Ask children what they already know about hospitals and what questions they have about hospitals. Record their responses on the KWL chart on the transparency. Direct children to write their own research questions in their Writer's Notebooks. Tell children that they will do research later in the week to answer their questions about hospitals.

DETERMINE REFERENCE SOURCES

Help children brainstorm a list of resources they could use to find the answers to their research questions. Discuss whether each source would be helpful.

Objectives

- Determine a topic for expository writing
- Generate questions and determine sources to research and write an expository composition

Materials

- Transparency 103

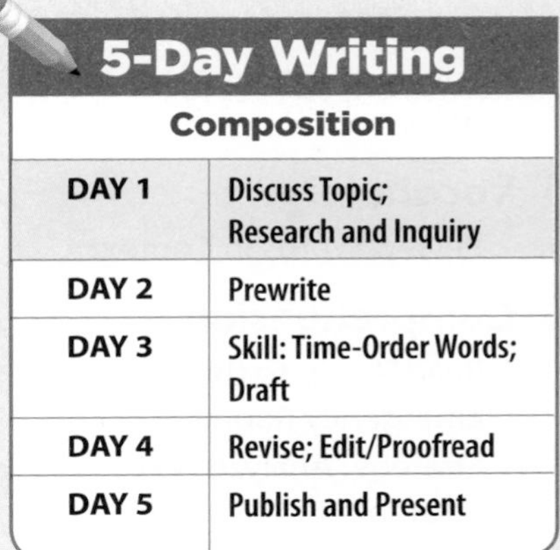

5-Day Writing

Composition	
DAY 1	Discuss Topic; Research and Inquiry
DAY 2	Prewrite
DAY 3	Skill: Time-Order Words; Draft
DAY 4	Revise; Edit/Proofread
DAY 5	Publish and Present

ELL

Share information
Before children share their questions with the whole class, have children work with more English-proficient partners to help them generate questions. Have partners ask each other questions about hospitals. Have the more proficient partner write a list of questions. Then have the ELL child repeat the questions to the whole group.

Day 2 At a Glance

WHOLE GROUP

Oral Language
- Build Robust Vocabulary

Phonemic Awareness
- Initial Sound Substitution

Phonics
- Build Fluency
- Vowel Digraphs /ü/
- Reread *Soon the North Wind Blew*
- Spelling: Sort Words with *oo, ui, ew, ue, oe*

Vocabulary
- Review Words in Context

Comprehension
- Read "A Trip to the Emergency Room"
- Strategy: Analyze Text Structure
- Skill: Sequence of Events

Language Arts
- Grammar: Irregular Verbs
- Writing: Expository

SMALL GROUP
- Differentiated Instruction, pages 89O–89NN

Oral Language

Build Robust Vocabulary

Reread the **Oral Vocabulary Cards** to review this week's oral vocabulary words. Ask and model clarifying questions to check children's comprehension. *Why did Little Red Riding Hood go to comfort her grandmother? What was she taking with her to help Grandmother recuperate? How did the clever wolf trick Little Red Riding Hood? What did the hunter do when there was an urgent situation?*

Oral Vocabulary Cards

REVIEW

Ask the probing questions below to generate discussion and use of the words in oral speech.

- Can you describe a time when you were **clever** while playing a game? What did you do?
- Can you describe an **urgent** situation you were in? Why was it urgent?
- Can you describe a time when you had **sympathy** for a friend? What happened?
- Can you describe a time when you had to **recuperate** from a cold? What did you do to recuperate?
- Can you describe a time when you had to **comfort** someone close to you? What did you do?

- Review last week's words *advice, hesitate, panic, secure,* and *vowed* using similar questions.

Write About It

Imagine that you were the forest ranger. How would you help Little Red Riding Hood and her grandmother with the emergency? Describe what you would do and what happens. You can add this writing sample to your Writer's Notebook.

Phonemic Awareness

Initial Sound Substitution

Model

Show children how to substitute initial phonemes to make new words.

Listen as I say the sounds in the word *cue*: /k/ /ü/. I am going to change the beginning sound /k/ to /d/ to make a new word. The new word is *due*.

Repeat the routine with *zoo, too; mood, food; blue, clue; cool, pool; booth, tooth.*

Guided Practice/Practice

Help children practice with the examples provided. Do the first one together.

I will say a word. Then we will change the beginning sound to make a new word.

hoot   Let's change /h/ to /sh/.

Now it's your turn.

noon   Now change /n/ to /m/.
booth   Next change /b/ to /t/.
soup   Now change /s/ to /gr/.
fruit   Now change /fr/ to /t/.
shoe   Now change /sh/ to /tr/.

Objectives

- Substitute initial phonemes to make new words
- Recognize the change in spoken words when a phoneme is changed

Objectives

- Blend and build words with vowel digraphs /ü/
- Review previously taught phonics skills
- Read multisyllabic words

Materials

- Word-Building Cards; Teacher's Resource Book, p. 66
- pocket chart
- chart paper
- word chart from Day 1
- Decodable Reader Library: *Soon the North Wind Blew*

Skills Trace

Vowel Digraphs *oo, ui, ew, ue, u, ou, oe*	
Introduce	79C–D
Practice/ Apply	79F, 81G–H, 85F–G, 85I, 85V–W; Practice Book: 195; Decodable Reader: *Soon the North Wind Blew*
Reteach/ Review	89G–H, 89O–R, 89U, 89AA, 89GG
Assess	Weekly Test; Unit 4 Test
Maintain	Build Fluency: Sound/Spellings

Phonics

Build Fluency: Sound/Spellings

Display the following **Word-Building Cards** one at a time: *oo, ui, ew, ue, u, ou, oe, oi, oy, ou, ow, are, air, ear, ere, or, ore, oar, ar, gn, kn, wr, mb, eer, ere, ear*. Have children chorally say each sound. Repeat and vary the pace. Children should work to say each sound within a two-second pause.

Blend with Vowel Digraphs /ü/

Model

Place Word-Building Cards *m, o, o, d* in the pocket chart to form *mood*. Model how to generate and blend the sounds to say the word.

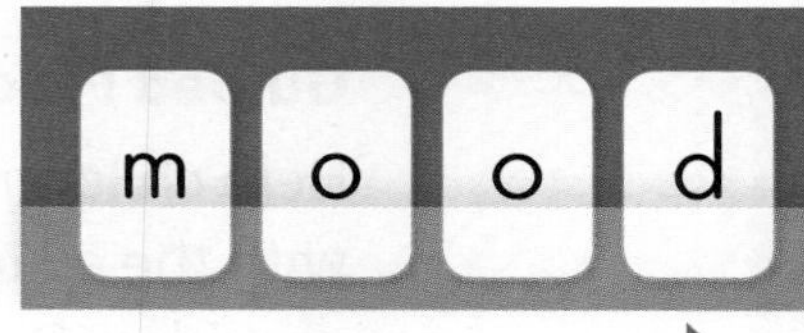

The letter *m* stands for /m/. The letters *oo* together stand for /ü/. The letter *d* stands for /d/. Now listen as I blend all three sounds: /müd/. Now you say it. Let's read the word together.

Repeat with *shoe, suit, flew, soup, cue*.

Guided Practice/Practice

Repeat with additional words. Have children blend the sounds in words "with you."

booth	truth	ooze	spoon
broom	stool	proof	blew
group	fruit	root	due
raccoon	renew	duty	untrue

Build with Vowel Digraphs /ü/

Model

Place **Word-Building Cards** *f*, *e*, *w* in the pocket chart. Blend the phonemes.	Let's blend all the sounds together and read the word: /fü/, *few*.	
Change *f* to *d* and repeat with *dew*.	Let's blend all the sounds together and read the word: /dü/, *dew*.	
Change *d* to *n* and repeat with *new*	Let's blend all the sounds together and read the word: /nü/, *new*.	

Guided Practice/Practice

Give more building practice with these word sets.

cool, pool, tool, drool, room, broom

cue, blue, clue, glue, flu, flew

fruit, suit, soup, group, grew, knew

Build Fluency: Word Automaticity

Display the word chart from Day 1. Point to each word as children chorally read it. Aim for one word every two seconds. Model blending the sounds in words children miss. Then point to words in random order at varying speeds for children to read.

room	tools	you	foods
chew	flew	blue	July
tooth	knew	stew	shoe
crowd	couch	choice	soy
coin	toy	town	loud

Ruth knew Sue was at school.
June threw the glue at you!

Build Fluency: Connected Text

Have children independently reread *Soon the North Wind Blew* from the **Decodable Reader Library**. Circulate and listen in, providing corrective feedback as needed.

- **Beyond Level** While the other children are reading, teach the Accelerate Pacing lesson.
- **Approaching Level** Have children read with a more-skilled partner or listen to the text on **Audio CD** and read with the narrator.

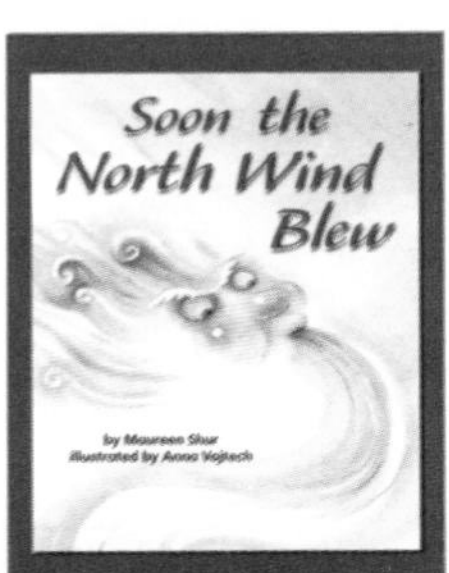

Soon the North Wind Blew

Transition to Multisyllabic Words

Vowel Team Syllables

- Say the words *soup*, *cool*, *juice*, *shoe*, and *true*. Ask children to listen for the vowel digraphs sound /ü/ .
- Write *soup*, *cool*, *juice*, *shoe*, and *true* on the board. Underline the vowel digraph spelling /ü/ in each word.
- Explain that the vowels *ou*, *oo*, *ui*, *oe*, and *ue* act as teams and can stand for the vowel sound /ü/. These vowel digraphs appear in the same syllable.
- Write these words on the board: *cocoon, balloon, honeymoon, raccoon, snowsuit, untrue, unglued, shoelace, grouping*. Help children divide the words into syllables and find each variant vowel /ü/ spellings.

ELL

Build Vocabulary Review the meanings of words on your word chart that can be explained or demonstrated in a concrete way. For example, ask children to point to their *shoe*, their *tooth*, and something *blue*. Model the action for *chew*, say: *I* chew *my food*, and have children repeat. Provide sentence starters for children to complete, such as *The bird* ___________.

DAY 2
WHOLE GROUP

Objectives

- Spell and sort words with vowel digraphs *oo, ui, ew, ue, oe*
- Build Fluency: Word Automaticity

Materials

- large index cards with spelling words
- pocket chart
- Phonics/Spelling Practice Book, p. 70

5-Day Spelling	
DAY 1	Dictation; Pretest
DAY 2	Teacher-Modeled Word Sort
DAY 3	Student Word Sort
DAY 4	Test Practice
DAY 5	Posttest

ON YOUR OWN

Spelling, page 70

suit	shoe	room	clue	fruit
glue	flew	canoe	new	tool

A. Word Sort

Look at the spelling words in the box. Write the spelling words that match each spelling pattern.

oo
1. room
2. tool

ue
3. clue
4. glue

ui
5. suit
6. fruit

ew
7. flew
8. new

oe
9. shoe
10. canoe

B. Rhyme Around

Write the spelling word that completes each rhyme.

11. Dad has a funny suit. The pattern on it is made of fruit.
12. The toy plane flew because it was brand new.
13. We were riding in the canoe when I lost my right shoe.
14. I will give you a clue. This sticky stuff smells like glue.
15. I will get a pan and broom to clean up my messy room.

Phonics/Spelling

Word Sort with *oo, ui, ew, ue, oe*

- Display the pocket chart. Place index cards with the key word cards *moon, juice, grew,* and *blue* to form four columns in the pocket chart. Generate sentences for the key words *moon, juice, grew,* and *blue.*
- Say each key word and pronounce the sounds: /m/ /ü/ /n/; /j/ /ü/ /s/; /g/ /r/ /ü/; /b/ /l/ /ü/. Pronounce each word again, stretching the /ü/ sound. Ask children to chorally spell each word.
- Hold up the word card *room*. Pronounce each sound clearly: /r/ /ü/ /m/. Blend the sounds: /rüm/. Repeat with each *oo, ui, ew,* and *ue* word. Place words below the correct key word labels so there is one example of each. Have children read each word, listening for the /ü/ sound. Ask children to chorally spell each word.
- Have children place the remaining cards under the correct key label. Display the words *shoe* and *canoe* in a separate column. Read and spell the words together with children. Point out that these spelling words have the /ü/ sound spelled *oe.*
- **Build Fluency: Word Automaticity** Have children chorally read the words several times for fluency.

Analyze Errors — Articulation Support

- Use children's pretest errors to analyze spelling problems and provide corrective feedback; for example, the /ü/ and /u/ sounds are formed in similar ways.
- Have these children say /ü/ paying attention to how it feels in the mouth. Use hand mirrors, if available. Then have children make the /u/ sound, noting how the face position changes slightly. Go back and forth between /ü/ and /u/ to help them feel the difference.
- Then have children orally segment one of the spelling words. When children get to the /ü/ sound, ask: *How does your mouth feel? What letters do we write for that sound?*

Vocabulary

Words in Context

REVIEW

Review the meanings of the vocabulary words. Display **Transparency 35**. Model how to use word meanings and context clues to fill in the first missing word.

Think Aloud In the second paragraph, I see that after Taylor crashes his bicycle, his arm hurts. Because Taylor's mom rushed over to him, I think the missing word is **aid**.

Transparency 35

heal   personal   aid   informs   serious

Taylor is pedaling his bicycle as fast as he can to get home for dinner. He doesn't see the rock. Crash! Taylor hits the ground hard and now his arm really hurts. He thinks the bone may be broken.

Taylor's mom quickly rushed to his (1) aid. She carefully touches his arm. "Ouch! That hurts!" he exclaims.

Taylor's mom thinks he may have a (2) serious injury. She tells Taylor that a doctor must look at his arm. At the hospital, a nurse writes down Taylor's (3) personal information. Dr. Parker examines Taylor's arm and (4) informs him that it is broken.

"Don't worry, Taylor," says Dr. Parker. "We'll put a cast on your arm. The bone will (5) heal in about six weeks."

Vocabulary Transparency

GUIDED PRACTICE/PRACTICE

- Help children with the next paragraph.
- Have children use context clues to write missing words 2–5 on their papers. Then ask partners to check each other's answers and to identify which context clues they used to find the missing words.
- Have them write sentences using their vocabulary words from this week and last week.

Review last week's words *attention*, *buddy*, *accident*, *tip*, *enormous*, and *obeys* in context.

Objective

- Apply knowledge of word meanings and context clues

Materials

- Transparency 35

Objectives

- Analyze text structure in a nonfiction article
- Describe sequence of events
- Use academic language: *text structure, sequence of events*

Materials

- Student Book: "A Trip to the Emergency Room"
- Practice Book, p. 198

Skills Trace

Sequence of Events

Introduce	U4: 81A–B
Practice/ Apply	U4: 81K–85A; Practice Book: 198–199
Reteach/ Review	U4: 89K, 89V–X, 89BB–DD, 93A–B, 93K–115A, 119G, 119R–T, 119X–Z; Practice Book: 209–210
Assess	Weekly Tests; Unit 4, 5 Tests
Maintain	U4: 155N; U5: 201N, 209J–233A, 239G, 239R–T, 239X–Z, 311N; Practice Book: 243–244

Story Words

Provide child-friendly definitions when you encounter these words.

ambulances (p. 82): vehicles used to take injured people to the hospital

properly (p. 82): in the right way

patients (p. 83): people who are staying at the hospital

examine (p. 85): to check carefully

Comprehension

STRATEGY Analyze Text Structure

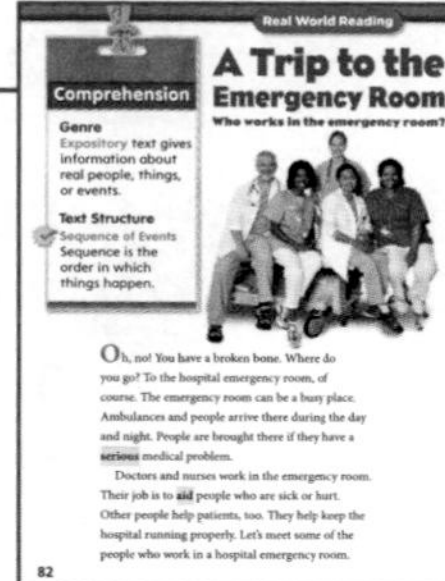

Main Selection

Review that **text structure** is the way writers organize information in nonfiction. The different kinds of text structures include: sequence, cause and effect, problem and solution, compare and contrast, and description. *Readers who can recognize nonfiction text structures will better understand and remember what they read.*

SKILL Sequence of Events

Remind children that writers often describe events or ideas in **sequence**, or the time order in which they happen. Writers may use signal words, such as *first*, *next*, *then*, and *last*, to show the time order of events. *As we read, let's think about the order of events.*

Prepare to Read

PREVIEW AND PREDICT

- Ask children to identify the title and preview the pictures to make predictions about "A Trip to the Emergency Room." *What do you think this selection is going to be about? Who do you think the people in this picture might be?* Have children write in their journals about their predictions and whatever else they want to know about the story.
- **Genre** Have children read the definition of expository on **Student Book** page 82. Share these features: expository explains or describes things using facts; all the facts are true and no part of the selection is made-up; real people, things, or events. *How will knowing this selection is expository help you as you read it?*
- **Text Features** Draw attention to the subheads throughout the selection. Point out that they all name people who work in an emergency room.

SET A PURPOSE FOR READING

- **Focus Question** Discuss the "Read to Find Out" question on page 82. Remind children to look for the answer as they read.
- Have children turn to the Sequence Chart on **Practice Book** page 198. Tell them that they will use it to find information about the people who work in the emergency room at the hospital.
- Prompt children to set their own purpose for reading.

Real World Reading

TIME FOR KIDS

Comprehension

Genre
Expository text gives information about real people, things, or events.

Text Structure
Sequence of Events
Sequence is the order in which things happen.

A Trip to the Emergency Room

Who works in the emergency room?

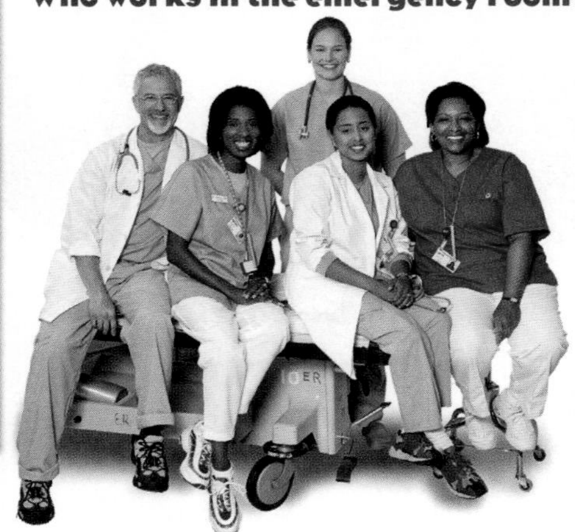

1 Oh, no! You have a broken bone. Where do you go? To the hospital emergency room, of course. The emergency room can be a busy place. Ambulances and people arrive there during the day and night. People are brought there if they have a **serious** medical problem.

2 Doctors and nurses work in the emergency room. Their job is to **aid** people who are sick or hurt. Other people help patients, too. They help keep the hospital running properly. Let's meet some of the people who work in a hospital emergency room.

H Admissions Worker

The first person you see in the emergency room is an admissions worker. The hospital needs to keep track of the patients coming into the emergency room. The admissions person checks you in. The adult who is with you will fill out hospital forms. The forms ask for your **personal** information and why you came to the hospital.

Read Main Selection

1 STRATEGY Analyze Text Structure

What clue on page 83 helps you to figure out the text structure the author is using in this selection? (The phrase *The first person you see* is a clue that the author is using a sequence text structure. The events are presented in time order.)

2 MONITOR AND CLARIFY: PARAPHRASE

If you don't understand something, you can retell it in your own words to better understand the text. Try to **paraphrase** the text on page 82 by retelling it in your own words. Be sure to maintain the meaning of the text. (A hospital emergency room is a busy place. People are go there if they have a medical problem. Doctors and nurses help patients. Other workers keep the hospital running.)

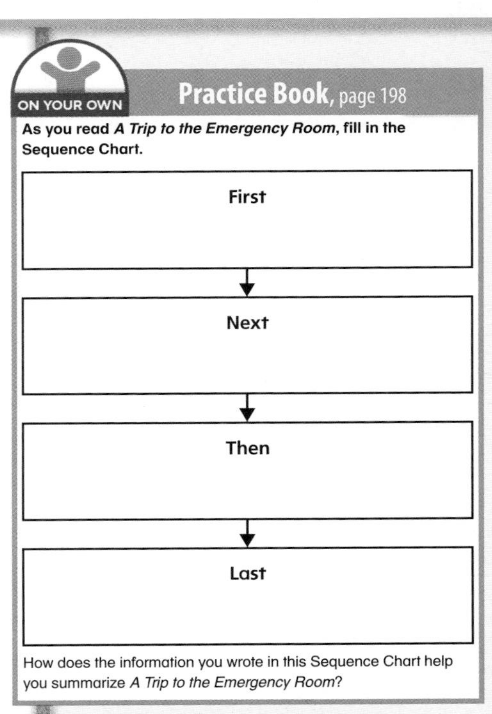

Approaching Reproducible, page 198

Beyond Reproducible, page 198

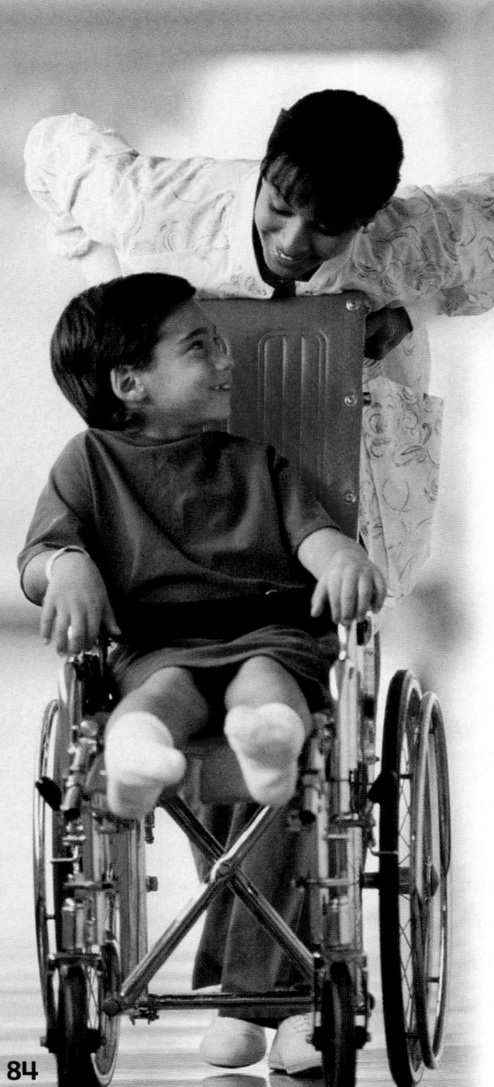

Nurses and Aides

Next a nurse will help you. A nurse's job is to find out about your injury and ask you questions about your health. The nurse will take your temperature and blood pressure and record this information on a chart. The nurse **informs** other people in the hospital about your problem.

Then you will meet an orderly, or nurse's aide. That person will help you get around in the hospital. She will take you to the correct department if you need to get tests done. She may use a wheelchair to take you from one area to another.

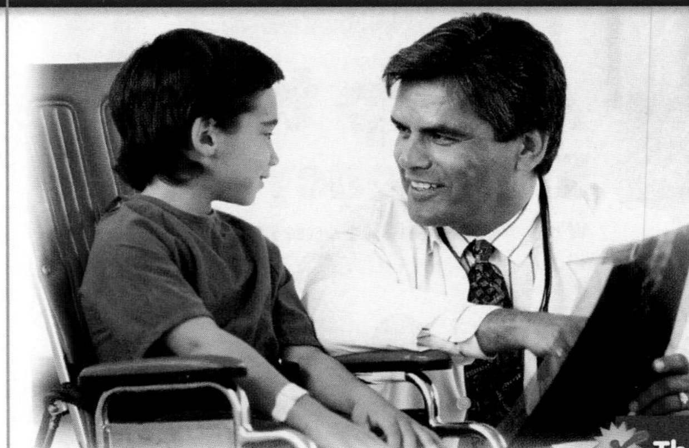

Doctor

3 Last, it's time for the doctor to examine you. The doctor checks your injury. He also looks at your chart. He arranges for you to get an X ray if you need one. The doctor knows how to fix your broken bone. He will probably put on a cast so the bone will **heal**. The doctor also decides whether you need to stay in the hospital or if you can go home right away.

So don't worry if you need to go to the emergency room. Now you know about the people who work there and how they will help you feel better.

Think and Compare

1. When do you go to the emergency room?
2. Describe the people you see in an emergency room in the order you meet them.
3. What would happen if the emergency room did not have an admissions worker?
4. How are paramedics similar to doctors? How are they different?

First
Admissions worker checks you in.

Next
Nurse asks about your injury and health.

Then
Orderly takes you to get tests.

Last
Doctor examines you.

Develop Comprehension

3 SKILL Sequence of Events

What happens when a person visits the emergency room? Describe the order of events. (The first person you see is the admissions worker. Next, you see a nurse, and then an orderly. Last, you see a doctor.) Let's add this to our Sequence Chart.

Quick Check

Can children identify the sequence of events in the text?

During **Small Group Instruction**

If No → Approaching Level Apply the skill to a simpler text. See page 89V.

If Yes → On Level Apply the skill to another text. See page 89W.

Beyond Level Apply the skill to a harder text. See page 89X.

Phonemic Awareness

Phoneme Blending

Model

Show children how to orally blend phonemes.

I am going to put one marker in each box as I say each sound. Then I will blend the sounds to form a word.

Listen and watch. /r/ (Place marker in the first box.) /ü/ (Place marker in the second box.) /m/ (Place marker in the third box.)

This word has three sounds: /r/ /ü/ /m/. Listen as I blend the sounds to form the word: /rüm/. The word is *room*.

Guided Practice/Practice

Help children practice blending. Do the first six words together.

Let's do some together. Place a marker for each sound you hear. I will say one sound at a time. Then we will blend the sounds to say the word.

/k/ /ü/ /l/ /p/ /r/ /ü/ /f/ /b/ /ü/ /t/
/g/ /l/ /ü/ /sh/ /ü/ /t/ /sh/ /ü/

Now it's your turn. Listen carefully.

/p/ /ü/ /l/ /g/ /r/ /ü/ /m/
/d/ /r/ /ü/ /t/ /r/ /ü/ /p/
/n/ /ü/ /s/ /s/ /k/ /r/ /ü/
/d/ /ü/ /s/ /m/ /ü/ /th/
/b/ /l/ /ü/ /i/ /g/ /l/ /ü/

Objective

- Blend spoken phonemes to form one-syllable words

Materials

- Sound-Spelling WorkBoards; Teacher's Resource Book p. 143
- markers

Objectives

- Identify letter-sound correspondence for vowel digraphs /ü/ *oo, ui, ew, ue, u, ou, oe*
- Blend sounds in words with vowel digraphs /ü/
- Review previously taught phonics skills
- Read multisyllabic words

Materials

- Sound-Spelling Card: *Spoon*
- Word-Building Cards; Teacher's Resource Book, p. 66
- chart paper
- Practice Book, p. 200

Skills Trace

Vowel Digraphs *oo, ui, ew, ue, u, ou, oe*	
Introduce	79C-D
Practice/ Apply	79F, 81G–H, 85F–G, 85I, 85V–W; Practice Book: 195; Decodable Reader *Soon the North Wind Blew*
Reteach/ Review	89G–H, 89O–R, 89U, 89AA, 89GG
Assess	Weekly Test; Unit 4 Test
Maintain	Build Fluency: Sound/Spellings

Phonics

Review Vowel Digraphs /ü/

Model

Review the vowel digraphs *oo, ui, ew, ue, u, ou, oe*. Show the *Spoon* **Sound-Spelling Card**.

This is the *Spoon* Sound-Spelling Card. The sound is /ü/. The /ü/ sound can be spelled with the letters *oo, ui, ew, ue, u, ou,* or *oe*. Say it with me: /ü/.

We've been reading words with the /ü/ sound all week. Today we will read more.

Guided Practice/Practice

Have children practice connecting the letters and sound.

(Point to the Sound-Spelling Card.) What are these letters? What sound do they stand for?

Build Fluency: Sound/Spellings

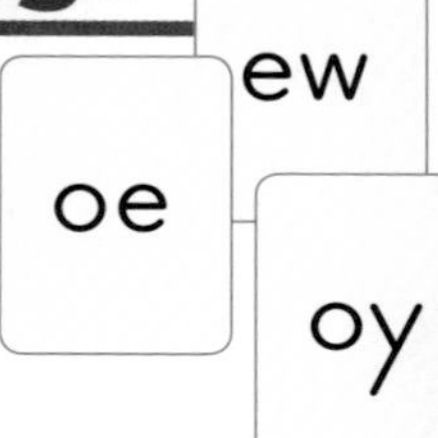

Display the following **Word-Building Cards** one at a time: *oo, ui, ew, ue, u, ou, oe, oi, oy, ou, ow, are, air, ear, ere, or, ore, oar, ar, gn, kn, wr, mb, eer, ere, ear*. Have children chorally say each sound. Repeat and vary the pace.

Blend with Vowel Digraphs /ü/

Model

Display Word-Building Cards *s, u, i, t*. Model how to blend the sounds together as you run your finger under each letter.

Continue by modeling the words *stew, shoe, flu, clue, renew,* and *taboo*.

(Point to *s*.) This is the letter *s*. It stands for /s/.

(Point to *ui*.) These are the letters *u* and *i*. Together they stand for /ü/. Listen as I blend these sounds together: /sü/.

(Point to *t*.) This is the letter *t*. It stands for /t/. Listen as I blend all three sounds together: /süt/, *suit*. Say it with me.

Guided Practice/Practice
Write the words below on chart paper. Read the first line with children. Then have children chorally read the words on the chart. Use the appropriate blending level.

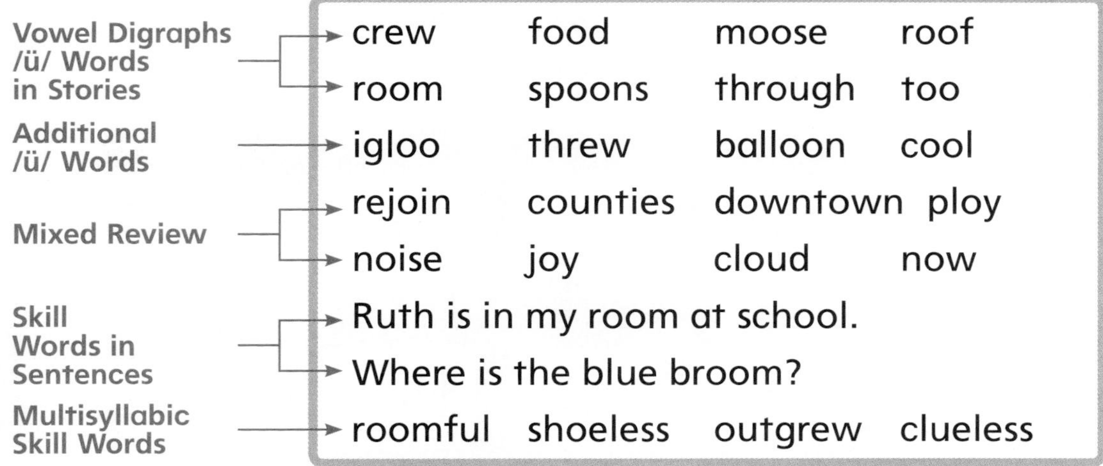

Vowel Digraphs /ü/ Words in Stories	crew	food	moose	roof
	room	spoons	through	too
Additional /ü/ Words	igloo	threw	balloon	cool
Mixed Review	rejoin	counties	downtown	ploy
	noise	joy	cloud	now
Skill Words in Sentences	Ruth is in my room at school.			
	Where is the blue broom?			
Multisyllabic Skill Words	roomful	shoeless	outgrew	clueless

Corrective Feedback

Blending Error: Say: *My Turn.* Model blending using the appropriate signaling procedures. Then lead children in blending the sounds. Say: *Do it with me.* You will respond with children to offer support. Then say: *Your turn. Blend.* Have children chorally blend. Return to the beginning of the word. Say: *Let's start over.*

Suffixes

Teach
- Say the words *fruit*, *fruitful*, and *fruitless*. Ask children to listen closely to hear what is different.
- Point out the *-ful* and *-less* at the end of *fruitful* and *fruitless*.
- Write the words *fruit*, *fruitful*, and *fruitless* on the board. Underline the suffixes *-ful* and *-less*.
- Tell children that to make an adjective that means "full of" something, we can add the suffix *-ful* to the end of many nouns. To make an adjective that means "without," we can add the suffix *-less*.

Practice/Apply
- Have children tell the meaning and think of sentences for the following words: *moonless, clueless, truthful, toothless, youthful, tuneless, roomful, rootless.*

ON YOUR OWN

Practice Book, page 200

A word part that is added to the end of a word to change its meaning is called a **suffix**.
The suffix ***-less*** means "**without**."
The suffix ***-ful*** means "**full of**."
When you add ***-ful*** or ***-less*** to a word that ends with ***y***, you drop the ***y*** and add ***i*** before adding the suffix.
mercy + ful = merciful

Write a word that means the same as the group of words. Your new word will end in *-less* or *-ful*.

1. full of beauty — beautiful
2. full of health — healthful
3. without pain — painless
4. full of cheer — cheerful
5. without a clue — clueless
6. full of taste — tasteful
7. without harm — harmless
8. full of fancy — fanciful

Approaching Reproducible, page 200
Beyond Reproducible, page 200

Objectives

- Sort high-frequency words and words with *oo*, *ui*, *ew*, *ue*, *oe*
- Spelling words with vowel digraphs
- Build Fluency: Word Automaticity

Materials

- Spelling Word Cards BLM; Teacher's Resource Book, p. 87
- index cards from Day 2
- pocket chart
- Phonics/Spelling Practice Book, p. 71

5-Day Spelling	
DAY 1	Dictation; Pretest
DAY 2	Teacher-Modeled Word Sort
DAY 3	Student Word Sort
DAY 4	Test Practice
DAY 5	Posttest

ON YOUR OWN **Spelling,** page 71

canoe	tool	fruit	glue	new
room	shoe	clue	suit	flew

A. Match-Ups

Draw a line from each spelling word to its meaning.

1. room — to make stick
2. glue — a space in a house
3. clue — a set of clothes
4. new — a small boat
5. canoe — recently grown or made
6. suit — a hint

B. Sentences to Complete

Write a spelling word on each line to complete the sentence.

7. He used a ___tool___ to fix the lock.
8. I ate a piece of ___fruit___ for lunch.
9. Which ___shoe___ needs a new lace?
10. Mom ___flew___ to Texas to see her brother.

Phonics/Spelling

Word Sort with *oo, ui, ew, ue, oe*

WORD SORT

- Use index cards from Day 2 for each spelling word including the words *moon*, *juice*, *grew*, and *blue*. Place the key word cards *moon*, *juice*, *grew*, and *blue* to form four columns in the pocket chart. Blend sounds with children.

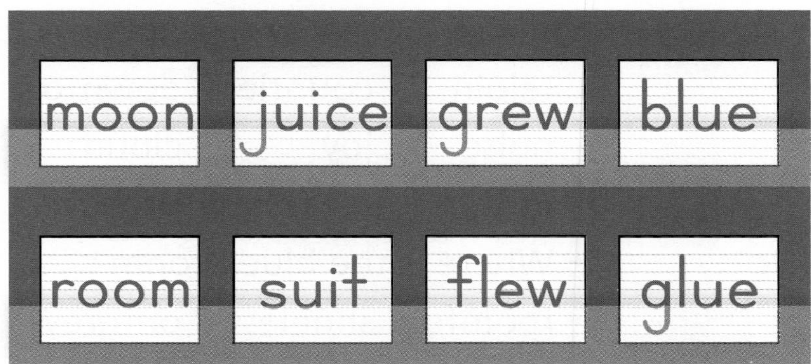

- Hold up the word card for *moon*. Say and spell it. Pronounce each sound clearly: /m/ /ü/ /n/. Blend the sounds: /mün/.
- Repeat this step with *room*. Place the word in the column below the key word *moon*. Have children read each word. *What do you notice about these words?* (They have the /ü/ sound spelled *oo*.) Repeat the process with the *ui*, *ew*, and *ue* words.
- Display the word cards for *shoe* and *canoe*. Place them in a separate column. Read and spell the words together with children. Point out that these spelling words have the /ü/ sound spelled *oe*.
- Display the words *follow*, *near*, and *paper* in a separate column. Read and spell the words together with children. Point out that these spelling words do not contain the /ü/ sound.
- **Build Fluency: Word Automaticity** Conclude by asking children to chorally read the words to build fluency. Ask children to orally generate words that have the same sounds.

High-Frequency Words

- **Teach High-Frequency Words** Write the new high-frequency words for the week **follow**, **near**, and **paper** on the board. Teach the words using the **Read/Spell/Write** routine below.
  - **Read** Read the word. Have children repeat.
  - **Spell** Chorally spell the word.
  - **Write** Have children write the word as they spell it aloud. Then ask children to write a sentence using each word.
- **Practice** Write sample cloze sentences for each word on the board.

  I wrote my name on a sheet of ________.
  My dog will ________ me where ever I go.
  My school is ________ my house.

- Have children read the sentences and write the missing word for each one.
- **Additional High-Frequency Words** Introduce an additional six words (Additional Words #213–218: **sound**, **with**, **air**, **far**, **along**, **eyes**) for more practice. Have children use the **Read/Spell/Write** routine to learn the words. Finish with a speed drill of all the words taught for the day. Display each High-Frequency Word Card quickly and have children identify and read the word aloud. Repeat with any words children have difficulty with.

Decodable Reader

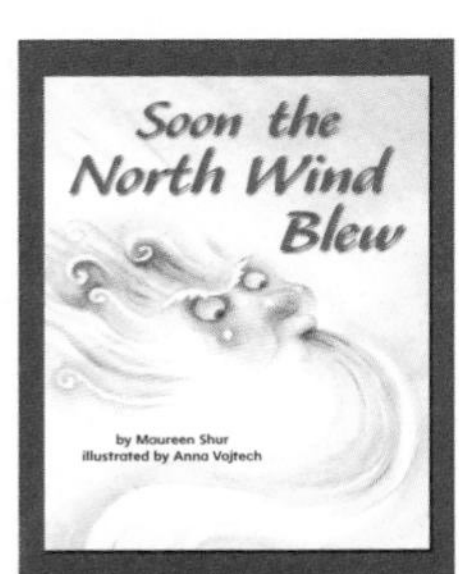

Decodable Reader

- **Review High-Frequency Words** Review the high-frequency words that appear in the book: **above**, **color**, and **song**. Have children read each aloud and provide a sentence for each.

PARTNERS

- **Reread Decodable Reader** Have children quietly reread *Soon the North Wind Blew* to a partner.
- **Check Comprehension** Have children retell the Decodable Reader to their partner. Direct them to page through the book and say in their own words what they learned on each page about the story. Reinforce high-frequency words and key vocabulary that they struggle with.
- **Reteach** If children have difficulty, provide corrective feedback page by page as needed. See the **Decodable Text Routine** in the Instructional Routine Handbook for correction models.

Objectives

- Identify and read high-frequency words *follow, near, paper*
- Review last week's high-frequency words
- Decode multisyllabic words in context

Materials

- Decodable Reader Library: *Soon the North Wind Blew*

SMALL GROUP OPTION

You may wish to read the Decodable Reader during **Small Group** time.

See pages 89O–89NN

Objectives

- Use a dictionary or other sources to find meanings of homophones
- Use resources to find correct spellings
- Review this week's and last week's vocabulary words

Materials

- Transparency 36
- dictionary
- Practice Book, p. 201

Vocabulary	
aid	heal
informs	personal
serious	

Practice Book, page 201

Homophones are words that sound the same but have different meanings and different spellings. When you come to a new word that sounds the same as another word you know, you can use a dictionary to look up the word's meaning.

Study the dictionary entries. Then write a new sentence for each homophone. Possible responses provided

knows *verb* is aware of or understands something. *Alex knows that summer begins in June.*

nose *noun* the part of the face we breathe and smell with. *The boy covered his nose before he sneezed.*

1. My dog knows when I am at the door.
2. My nose was clogged when I had a cold.

weak *adjective* not strong. *Grandma was weak during her illness.*

week *noun* a period of seven days in a row. *We went on vacation for a week.*

3. My baby brother is weak, but I am strong.
4. I had to take medicine for a week.

Approaching Reproducible, page 201

Beyond Reproducible, page 201

Vocabulary

STRATEGY Use a Dictionary: Homophones

EXPLAIN

- A dictionary lists the different meanings words can have and may include sentences that show how they can be used.

MODEL

Read aloud the following sentence from **Student Book** page 85: *He will probably put on a cast so the bone will* **heal**. Use **Transparency 36** to model finding homophones.

Transparency 36

Use a Dictionary

heal *verb* **1.** to fix or get better: *I put a bandage over the cut on my finger to help it heal faster.*

heel *noun* **1.** the back part of your foot: *The skin on your heel is thick and tough.* **2.** the raised part on the bottom of a shoe: *I've worn these shoes for so long that the heels are worn down.*

1. The (heal heel) of my shoe broke off when I tripped.
2. A broken bone needs time to (heal heel).

Vocabulary Transparency

Think Aloud Homophones are words that sound the same but have different spellings and meanings, for example **heal** and *heel*. I look up the spelling *h-e-a-l* in the dictionary and see that it means "to get better." **Heal**, *h-e-a-l*, best fits the sentence.

GUIDED PRACTICE/PRACTICE

Have children identify homophones in the **Practice Book**.

REVIEW WORDS

Review the definition of each vocabulary word and write a sentence using the word on the board.

Practice Ask children questions relating each word on their own experience, such as: *When was a time you needed to heal?*

Repeat using last week's words: *attention, buddy, accident, tip, enormous, obeys*.

Oral Vocabulary

REVIEW WORDS

- Remind children of the week's oral vocabulary words.

Clever means "smart or easily able to understand things or do things." *The clever cat found a way to open the door.*

Comfort means "to soothe a person and make him or her feel better." *My mother gives me soup to comfort me when I am sick.*

When you **recuperate** from being sick, you get well again. *I needed a day to recuperate from my sore throat.*

Urgent means "important or needing attention right away." *It was urgent that my brother use the bathroom right away.*

Sympathy is the feeling you have when you feel sorry for someone, or when you share someone's sorrow or trouble. *I felt sympathy for my cousin when he broke his arm.*

Use the statements and questions below to help reinforce the meanings of the words.

- *If there was an urgent situation on a baseball field, what might have happened?*
- *How might you comfort a friend who is hurt?*
- *Which word goes with "feel sorry for"?* (sympathy)
- *Which word goes with "get well"?* (recuperate)
- *Describe a clever idea you have had.*
- Then have a child say what each word means and use it in a sentence.

- Use similar activities to review last week's words: *advice*, *hesitate*, *panic*, *secure*, and *vowed*.

Objectives

- Read aloud text with fluency and comprehension
- 62–82 WCPM

Materials

- Transparency 18
- Fluency Solutions Audio CD
- Practice Book, p. 202

Fluency

Repeated Reading: Prosody

EXPLAIN/MODEL

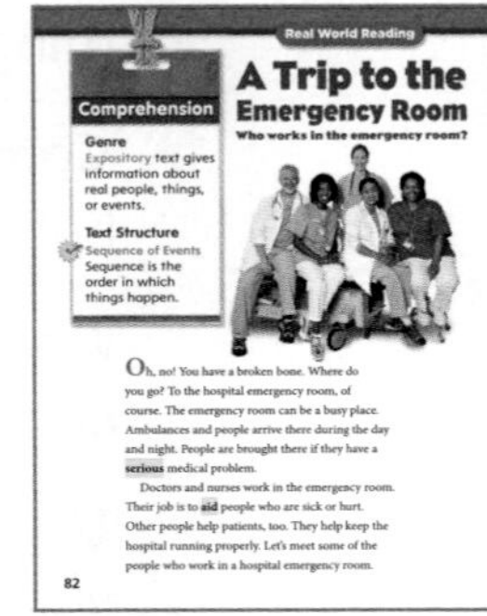

Main Selection

- **Punctuation** Explain that the punctuation in a text helps readers know when to pause or stop, or how to read a sentence.

  Write this sentence on the board and read it aloud with children: *After a visit to the doctor, I always feel better.* Point out that a comma in the middle of a sentence tells us to pause slightly.

- **Phrasing** Display **Transparency 18** and point out the single and double slashes. Explain that the single slashes show pauses and the double slashes show stops.

  Point out that when the words between slashes are read together, they help us form a mental picture of the text. *If we struggle with any word, we should decode it or ask for help, then go back to the beginning of the slash and reread that section of the text.* Model reading aloud the section on Transparency 18. *When did I pause when I read? When did I stop longer?*

Transparency 18

Fluency

Oh, / no! // You have a broken bone. // Where do you go? // To the hospital emergency room, / of course. // The emergency room can be a busy place. // Ambulances and people arrive there during the day and night. // People are brought there if they have a serious medical problem. //

—from "A Trip to the Emergency Room" (page 82)

Fluency Transparency

ELL

Read with Expression
Read the passage and explain what it means. Then have children work in pairs and alternate reading the sentences aloud. Remind children to read with the correct expression.

- **Intonation** Discuss how your intonation changes depending on what activity is being described in each sentence.

  Demonstrate how you adjust your reading rate based on the style of the writing. *When the author is describing exciting actions, you adjust your reading rate by reading more quickly.*

  Model reading the passage with natural expression. Point out that you read the text the way the speaker would have said the words, expressing the same emotion and using the same expression.

PRACTICE

- Have children reread the passage chorally, using the slashes to think about their phrasing.
- Then have children reread the passage aloud to a partner and paraphrase it. The second child should pick another passage to read aloud. Remind children to maintain the meaning of the text as they paraphrase.
- **Daily Fluency** Children will practice fluency reading **Practice Book** page 202 aloud or the **Fluency Solutions Audio CD**. The passage is recorded at a slow, practice speed, and a faster, fluent speed.

Quick Check

Can children read the passage fluently and with prosody?

During **Small Group Instruction**

If No → **Approaching Level** See pages: 89HH, 89LL.

If Yes → **On Level** See Fluency 89II.

Beyond Level See Fluency 89II.

ON YOUR OWN

Practice Book, page 202

As I read, I will pay attention to the pronunciation of vocabulary words.

Your body is working even when you are just
9 sitting still. You can see, hear, smell, taste, and feel.
19 Your body knows when it is cold or hot. It can
30 even **heal** itself when a part is broken or you feel
41 sick.
42 Sometimes a doctor can help your body get well.
51 A doctor can also give you a **personal** checkup
60 once a year to be sure you stay healthy.
69 Let's take a look at the human body. Then
78 we will see how a doctor can help you keep it
89 healthy. 90

Comprehension Check

1. Summarize what the author says in the second paragraph. **Sequence of Events** Answers will vary.
2. How do you know that your body is working even when you are still? **Make and Confirm Predictions** You know your body is working because you see, hear, smell, taste, and feel.

	Words Read	–	Number of Errors	=	Words Correct Score
First Read		–		=	
Second Read		–		=	

Approaching Reproducible, page 202

Beyond Reproducible, page 202

Objectives

- Distinguish between fiction and nonfiction
- Express personal responses to a nonfiction text
- Discuss genre characteristics
- Ask relevant questions about texts

Materials

- Student Book: "A Trip to the Emergency Room," pp. 82–85

Comprehension

Nonfiction vs. Fiction

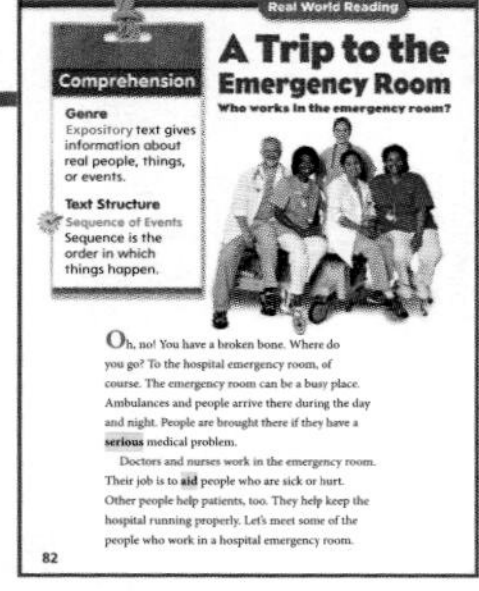

Main Selection

EXPLAIN/MODEL

Remind children of the features of **fiction**. A fiction story has characters, settings, and a plot, or actions that happen during the beginning, middle, and end of the story. Many stories have illustrations or artwork.

In **nonfiction**, the selection is about real people, places, or events. The people and the events in the selection are true. There is usually a main idea of a nonfiction selection and details that give more information about the topic.

- To understand nonfiction

  1. look for true information about a person, place, or an event.
  2. try to figure out the main idea of the selection and look for details about the main idea. Often titles and section headings provide the main ideas.

PRACTICE

Ask children to use the text to answer the following questions about A Trip to the Emergency Room*: What is an emergency room? Is it a real place? What happens on a visit to the emergency room? What clues in the text tell you that this is a nonfiction selection?*

Skills Trace

Text Structure: Nonfiction/Fiction

Introduce	U1: 73N
Practice/ Apply	U1: 103N
Reteach/ Review	U4: 115N

Respond to Literature

Personal Response Have children pose relevant *how*, *why*, or *what-if* questions about "A Trip to the Emergency Room." Ask children to discuss the text evidence they used to support their answers. They can write responses in their Writer's Notebooks.

- *Why do you think we need hospitals? What do the worker teams do in a hospital? What was the most interesting piece of information you learned from this article?*

Focus Question: Nonfiction Article Remind children that a nonfiction article gives information about real people, things, or events.

- *Who are some of the emergency room workers you learned about in the article? What is one way that each worker helps people?*
- *Do you think the photographs make the article more interesting?*

Research
Study Skills

Using the Internet

EXPLAIN

Tell children that they can use the Internet to do research. Discuss how to use the Internet. Display **Transparency 4**.

- A **URL** is the address of a Web site. *You can type a URL in the bar at the top of your browser; it will bring you to the Web site.*
- A **search engine** is a program on the Internet that helps people find information on the World Wide Web. *To find information, type key words related to the subject you want to learn about. The search engine will give you the addresses of Internet sites.*
- A **home page** is the main page of a Web site. The home page may have a **menu**. A menu is like a table of contents. *You can click on a link in the menu to find the information you are looking for.*

MODEL

Think Aloud I want to research worker teams such as paramedics so I type those words into a search engine. The search engine provides me with a list of Web sites that have those words in it.

Transparency 4

SEARCH: paramedic worker teams

Hard-working Teams: A Day with Paramedics
Spend a day with a paramedic team to learn about what they do on the job. http://www.library.example.com

Paramedics: Hospital Teams on the Go
How are paramedics different from doctors? Find out about their work in an ambulance. http://www.paramedics.example.com

Worker Teams: What Does a Paramedic Team Do?
From an accident scene to the hospital, learn about how paramedics work together. http://paramedic.com

Study Skills Transparency

GUIDED PRACTICE/PRACTICE

Help children use the Internet to find facts about what paramedics do and how they work as a team.

Objectives

- Children will use the Internet to research a topic
- Recognize different purposes of media

Materials

- Transparency 4
- Practice Book, p. 203

ON YOUR OWN

Practice Book, page 203

You can use the **Internet** to do research. A **search engine** is a program on the Internet that helps you find information on the World Wide Web. A **URL** is the address of a Web site. A **home page** is the main page of a Web site.

Carl used the Internet to research broken arms. Use his search results to answer the questions below.

Search Engine **Kidlookup**

How do I know if my arm is broken? Learn about what to look to know if an injured arm might be broken. http://www.firstaid.com/broken_arm	Treatments for broken arms: Types of casts Learn about the different kinds of casts doctors use to treat broken arms. http://www.healthcare.com/casts	Bike Safety: How to prevent injuries This site tells about important bike safety tips to protect riders from common injuries. http://ridesafely.com

1. What is the name of the search engine Carl used?
   Kidlookup
2. What is the URL of the site that tells about types of casts?
   http://www.healthcare.com/casts
3. Which Web site would be best to use if you hurt your arm and wanted to find out if it might be broken?
   http://www.firstaid.com/broken_arm
4. Which Web site would not help Carl learn about broken arms and how to treat them?
   http://ridesafely.com

Approaching Reproducible, page 203
Beyond Reproducible, page 203

Objective

- Correctly capitalize and underline words in book titles

Materials

- Transparency 88
- Grammar Practice Book, p. 88

5-Day Grammar	
Irregular Verbs	
DAY 1	Irregular Verbs
DAY 2	More Irregular Verbs
DAY 3	Mechanics: Book Titles
DAY 4	Irregular Verbs Proofread
DAY 5	Review and Assess Book Titles Irregular Verbs

Grammar

Book Titles

EXPLAIN/MODEL

- Remind children to begin the first and last words and each important word in a **book title** with a capital letter. Underline all the words in the title. (e.g., I read Heroes of the World.)

  Write the following sentence on the board: *The teacher told us to read a day at the doctor's over the weekend. Nursing Nell is my favorite book.* Rewrite the sentences, modeling how to identify and correctly capitalize and underline a book title. (e.g. *A Day at the Hospital; Nursing Nell.*)

  Point out in the first example that the words *at* and *the* are not capitalized because they are not the first or last words of the book title; they are not important words.

Have partners work together to write sentences about people who help or worker teams that include book titles. Have the partners write one sentence together. Then have each partner write one sentence individually. Have each partner read the other's sentence and tell whether it is punctuated correctly.

Community Heroes is a book about people who help others.

I read the book People Who Care to my little brother.

The library had a funny book called Laughing with Doctor Linda.

EXTEND

- Explain to children that when indicating the title of a short story, song, or poem, they should use quotation marks around the title. (e.g., "The Singing Cat" "Color Poem" "Song of Joy") Children should note that the first and last words and each important word in the title of a short story, song, and poem begin with a capital letter. Have children write sentences including the titles of their favorite book, short story, song, and poem.

Phonemic Awareness

Initial Sound Substitution

Model

Show children how to substitute initial phonemes to make new words.

Listen as I say the sounds in the word *few*: /f/ /ü/. I am going to change the beginning sound /f/ to /ch/ to make a new word. The new word is *chew*.

Repeat the routine with *clue*, *blue*; *bloom*, *gloom*; *booth*, *tooth*; *new*, *dew*; *cue*, *Sue*.

Guided Practice/Practice

Help children practice with the examples provided. Do the first two together

I will say a word. Then we will change the beginning sound to make a new word.

boot Let's change /b/ to /h/.

crew Now change /k/ to /d/.

Now it's your turn.

mood Next change /m/ to /f/.

soon Next change /s/ to /n/.

too Next change /t/ to /z/.

group Next change /gr/ to /s/.

Objectives

- Substitute initial sounds to make new words
- Recognize the change in a spoken word when a phoneme is changed.

Objectives

- Blend and build words with vowel digraphs *oo, ui, ew, ue, u, ou, oe*
- Use common syllabication patterns to decode words with vowel digraphs
- Review previously taught phonics skills

Materials

- Word-Building Cards; Teacher's Resource Book, p. 66
- pocket chart
- word chart from Day 3

Skills Trace

Vowel Digraphs *oo, ui, ew, ue, u, ou, oe*

Introduce	79C-D
Practice/ Apply	79F, 81G–H, 85F–G, 85I, 85V–W; Practice Book: 195; Decodable Reader: *Soon the North Wind Blew*
Reteach/ Review	89G–H, 89O–R, 89U, 89AA, 89GG
Assess	Weekly Test; Unit 4 Test
Maintain	Build Fluency: Sound/Spellings

Phonics

Build Fluency: Sound/Spellings

Display the following **Word-Building Cards** one at a time: *oo, ui, ew, ue, u, ou, oe, oi, oy, ou, ow, are, air, ear, ere, or, ore, oar, ar, gn, kn, wr, mb, eer, ere, ear*. Have children chorally say each sound. Repeat and vary the pace. Children should work to say each sound within a two-second pause.

Blend with Vowel Digraphs /ü/

Model

Place Word-Building Cards *s, o, u,* and *p* in the pocket chart to form *soup*. Model how to generate and blend the sounds to say the word.

The letter *s* stands for /s/. The letters *ou* stand for /ü/. The letter *p* stands for /p/. Now listen as I blend all three sounds: /süp/. Your turn. Let's read the word together.

Repeat routine for *cool, blew, due, Ruth,* and *shoe*.

Guided Practice/Practice

Repeat with additional words. Have children blend the sounds in words "with you."

spoon	truth	tooth	booth
grew	knew	screw	threw
too	boo	roof	true
cartoon	cashew	duty	suited

Build with Vowel Digraphs /ü/

Model

Place **Word-Building Cards** *b, o, o, m* in the pocket chart. Blend the phonemes.

Let's blend all the sounds together and read the word: /büm/, *boom*.

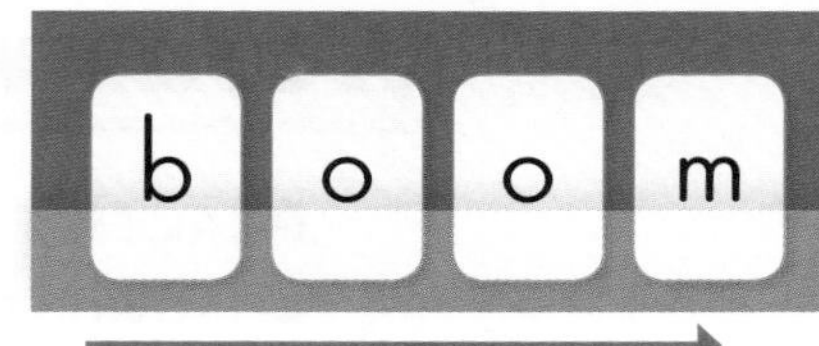

Change *b* to *d* and repeat with *doom*.

Let's blend all the sounds together and read the word: /düm/, *doom*.

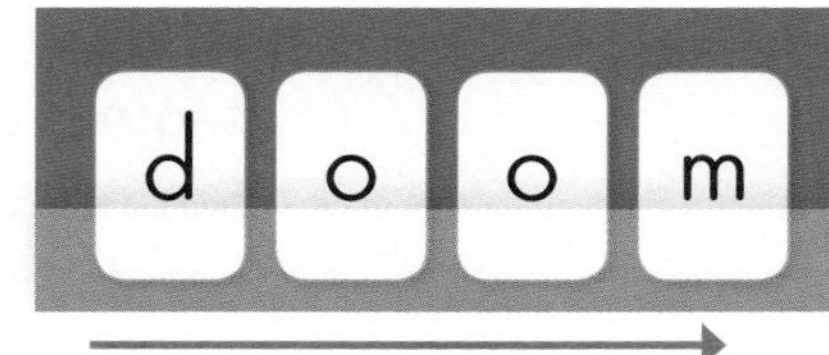

Change *d* to *z* and repeat with *zoom*.

Let's blend all the sounds together and read the word: /züm/, *zoom*.

Guided Practice/Practice

Build with the additional word set *cool, pool, school, schooner.*

Build Fluency: Word Automaticity

Use the word chart from Day 3. Point to each word as children chorally read it. Aim for one word every two seconds. Model blending the sounds in any words children miss. Then point to words in random order at varying speeds for children to read.

crew	food	moose	roof
room	spoons	through	too
igloo	threw	balloon	cool
rejoin	counties	downtown	ploy
noise	joy	cloud	now
Ruth is in my room at school.			
Where is the blue broom?			
roomful	shoeless	outgrew	clueless

Suffixes

Teach

- Write the words *truthful*, and *toothless* on the board. Underline the suffixes *-ful* and *-less.*
- Tell children that to make an adjective that means "full of" something, we can add the suffix *-ful* to the end of many nouns. To make an adjective that means "without," we can add the suffix *-less.*

Practice/Apply

- Have children tell the meaning and think of sentences for the following words: *joyful, clueless, powerless, roomful, foodless, youthful, countless, rootless, fruitful, cloudless.*

ELL

Build Vocabulary Review the meanings of words on your word chart that can be explained or demonstrated in a concrete way. For example, ask children to act out putting on a *shoe*. Model the action for *threw*. Ask children to point to something *blue*. Provide sentence starters for children to complete, such as *One* food *I enjoy eating is* ___________.

Objectives

- Practice for spelling test
- Build Fluency: Word Automaticity

Materials

- Teacher's Resource Book, p. 87
- paper and pencils
- Phonics/Spelling Practice Book, p. 72

5-Day Spelling	
DAY 1	Dictation; Pretest
DAY 2	Teacher-Modeled Word Sort
DAY 3	Student Word Sort
DAY 4	Test Practice
DAY 5	Posttest

ON YOUR OWN **Spelling**, page 72

A. There are five spelling mistakes in the paragraph below. Circle the misspelled words. Write the words correctly on the lines below.

Dave was in his rewm when he saw the weather report. A nue cold front was on its way. There was going to be a big winter storm. The big gray clouds were one clew that snow would start falling soon. Dave rushed to the airport. Somehow the pilot floo the plane and landed it before the storm began. Dave saw his friend get off the plane in a sute. Dave gave him a heavy winter coat and gloves for his cold visit to Chicago.

1. room 2. new 3. clue
4. flew 5. suit

B. Writing

Write about a big storm.
Use five words from your spelling list.
Answers will vary.

Phonics/Spelling

Words with *oo, ui, ew, ue, oe*

PRACTICE

- Provide pairs of children with individual copies of **Spelling Word Cards**.
- While one partner reads the words, the other partner should orally segment the word (e.g., /n/ /ü/) and then write the word. Have **Sound-Spelling WorkBoards** available for children who need hands-on support in segmenting the word and attaching one spelling to each sound.
- After reading all the words, partners should switch roles.
- When both partners have spelled all the words, children should correct their own papers.
- **Build Fluency: Word Automaticity** Partners can practice reading the spelling words aloud to each other to develop fluency.

Quick Check

Can children spell words with vowel digraphs /ü/?

During **Small Group Instruction**

If No → **Approaching Level** Repeat blending using the weekly spelling words. Explicitly correct the error, and provide more "with me" type practice. Use a lower level of blending to provide support.

If Yes → **On Level** Consolidate the learning by having children spell additional words with vowel digraphs /ü/. See page 89Q.

Beyond Level Extend the learning by having children spell harder words containing vowel digraphs /ü/. See page 89R.

Vocabulary

Words in Context

REVIEW: VOCABULARY

Review this week's vocabulary words (**aid**, **heal**, **informs**, **personal**, **serious**) using the sentence stems below. Have children orally complete each one.

- It takes a few weeks for a broken arm to ________.
- The security guard came to my ________ when I lost my glasses.
- Chris had a ________ toothache and had to go to the dentist.
- The nurse always ________ me of my next doctor's appointment.
- The paramedic took a ________ interest in helping me feel better.
- Then have children use each word in a sentence.

- Repeat the activity with last week's vocabulary words: *attention*, *buddy*, *accident*, *tip*, *enormous*, and *obeys*.

Objectives

- Use context to determine the meaning of unfamiliar words
- Review vocabulary words from this week and last week in context

Materials

- Vocabulary Word Cards BLM; Teacher's Resource Book, p. 117

Objective

- Use text evidence to find and answer test questions

Materials

- Student Book: "A Visit to the Dentist," pp. 86–87

Test Practice

Steps for Answering Questions

Teach/Model Tell children to use these steps when answering a question.

1. **Read the story.**
2. **Read** the **question** and all the **answers**.
3. **Restate** the question. Put it in your own words to make sure you understand it.
4. **Reread** the story to find the answer.
5. Sometimes the answer is right there, or **stated**, in the story. You can find, or **locate,** where the answer is stated. You can **combine** parts of the story to find the stated answer.
6. Sometimes the answer is **not stated**. To figure out the answer, you can **find clues** and **evidence** from the story. (**connect** and **analyze**)
7. Choose the best answer to the question. Check your answer by looking back at the story.

Practice/Apply Guide children through these steps as they answer the questions for "A Visit to the Dentist."

Test Practice

Answering Questions

EXPLAIN

Point out the bookmark on **Student Book** page 86. Explain to children that good test takers are good readers who know how to answer questions about the stories they read.

MODEL

Explain that the answers to some questions are stated in the text, but cannot be found in a single sentence. The reader must ***combine***, or put together, information from different parts of the selection to find the answer.

Read the story. Then read the question carefully. What is the question asking? Reread quickly to find where the answer to the question is stated.

Question 1 Read "A Visit to the Dentist" with children. Use the Think Aloud to model how to answer the question.

Think Aloud This question is asking which information from paragraph 1 belongs in the empty oval in the web. I can **combine** the information in the web with information from the article to find the answer. The web is about *Ways to keep your teeth healthy*. The two details that are filled in are *Brush everyday* and *Visit the dentist every six months*. So, I need to find another detail about how to keep teeth healthy. Paragraph 1 says that one way to take care of your teeth is to eat healthful foods. That is the **stated** answer. The best answer is B. THINK AND SEARCH

GUIDED PRACTICE

Have children practice combining information to find the answer to Question 2. Guide practice using the prompts as necessary.

- *Remember to read the question and all of the answer choices. What is this question asking?* (why you should visit the dentist)
- *What information from the text helps you to find the **stated** answer?* (Paragraph 1 says that you should visit the dentist every six months. Paragraph 2 says that the dentist takes X rays to show if you have any cavities.)
- *When you **combine** this information, what is the answer?* (You should go to the dentist every six months to check for cavities.)
- *Look at all of the answer choices. Which answer best fits this information?* (To check for cavities) *The best answer is C.* THINK AND SEARCH

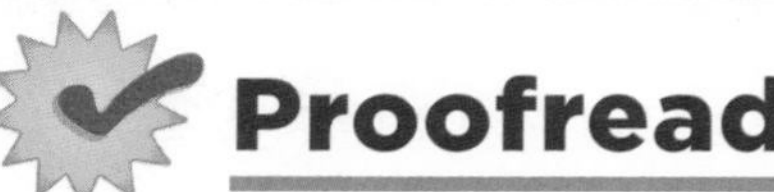

Proofread

EXPLAIN/MODEL

Explain that good writers always proofread their work. This means they check their writing to see that the grammar, spelling, and punctuation are correct. Copy and distribute the Proofreading Marks for all children. Review the Proofreading Marks with children.

Display **Grammar Transparency 89** and model proofreading.

Think Aloud Let's read the first sentence on the transparency. I see that the verb in this sentence is *goed*. I know that the past-tense form of *go* is not made by adding *-ed*. I will cross out *goed*. The verb should be *went*.

Transparency 89

Proofread

My family goed to the doctor last Friday. He sawed my sister first. then he sayed I could go in! He give me the book stay healthy for your whole life. I doed what the book say to do?

(Corrections marked: went, said, gave, did, said)

Grammar Transparency

GUIDED PRACTICE/PRACTICE

Use the second sentence on the transparency to guide children's practice. Continue proofreading the transparency, but give children the chance to suggest the remaining corrections.

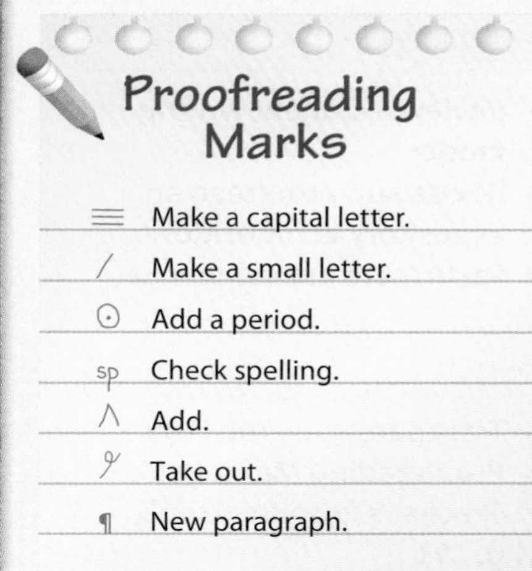

Available on **Teacher's Resource Book** page 191

Grammar, page 89

- The verbs ***come***, ***run***, ***give***, and ***sing*** have special forms in the past tense.
- Begin the first word and each important word in a book title with a capital letter.
- Underline all the words in the title of a book.

Read the paragraph and find the mistakes. Rewrite the passage correctly on the lines below.

Only two friends comed to my party because of the blizzard. We runned around in the snow and had fun. One friend give me a book called blizzards and ice storms. What a perfect present, I said. Then they singed Happy Birthday to me, and we ate cake.

Only two friends came to my party because of the blizzard. We ran around in the snow and had fun. One friend gave me a book called <u>Blizzards and Ice Storms</u>. "What a perfect present," I said. Then they sang Happy Birthday to me, and we ate cake.

Objectives

- Review a student writing model
- Revise and proofread an expository composition
- Participate in peer review

Materials

- Transparencies 106–108
- Proofreading Marks BLM; Teacher's Resource Book, p. 191

5-Day Writing

Expository: Composition

DAY 1	Discuss Topic; Research and Inquiry
DAY 2	Prewrite
DAY 3	Skill: Time-Order Words; Draft
DAY 4	Revise; Edit/Proofread
DAY 5	Publish and Present

ELL

Language Support Use the writing skill lesson from Day 3 to review time-order words. Then work with children to brainstorm a list of time-order and transition words. Prompt them with questions such as *What are some words that tell a reader when something happens? What words can we use to join sentences together?* Write words such as *first, second, next, then, last, so,* and *finally*. Read aloud each word and discuss what it means. Give children simple examples of usage. Leave the list posted so children can refer to it as they revise their writing.

Writing

Expository: Composition

REVISE DRAFTS

Remind children that an expository composition gives information about real people and events. Good writers use time-order words to help readers understand the correct order of events in their writing.

READING AND WRITING CONNECTION

Tell children to look at **Student Book** page 84. Read aloud the text with children. Ask children to identify any time-order words that the author includes in this selection. *What time-order words do you see on this page? Why do you think the author uses these words? Why do readers find these words helpful?*

Teacher Think Aloud The author of this selection uses time-order words, such as *next* and *then,* to help the reader understand the order in which patients see different people in the emergency room. On this page, the time-order words help readers understand that patients will meet the orderly after they meet the nurse. As you revise your drafts today, make sure you use time-order words to help your readers understand what you are describing.

STUDY THE MODEL

Now display the draft of an expository composition on **Writing Transparency 106**. Ask children what they notice about this expository composition. Instruct them to share their ideas about how it could be revised and made better. *How can we improve the details in this composition? Do all the details support the main idea? Does the writer use time-order words to make the order of events clear?*

Display the revised composition on **Writing Transparency 107**. Help children notice how the writer organized the sentences in a logical order and added time-order words to help the reader understand the sequence. Point out how the writer crossed out a sentence that did not fit the main topic of the composition. Remind children that they can look for similar ways to improve their writing as they revise their own compositions. Have children revise their compositions.

EDIT/PROOFREAD

Explain/Model After children revise their compositions, remind them that good writers always proofread their work. Tell children this means they reread their writing to be sure their spelling and grammar are correct. Display **Writing Transparency 108**. Discuss the proofreading corrections that the writer made to the model. Direct children to proofread their own writing.

PRACTICE/APPLY

Peer Review Have partners review each other's compositions. Use the peer conferencing tips below to facilitate the peer review.

Independent Review Have children review their partners' suggestions and evaluate their own work. Have them complete revising and proofreading their compositions.

Peer Conferencing Tips

Peer Conferencing Have children read each other's compositions. Tell them to point out parts that work well and point out parts that are not so successful. Children can ask the following questions as they conference:

- Does the composition have time-order words to organize the information?
- Does the composition use information and facts from the writer's research about hospitals?
- Does the writer capitalize words correctly and use appropriate punctuation marks?

Day 5 At a Glance

WHOLE GROUP

Oral Language
- Build Robust Vocabulary

Fluency
- Pronunciation

Phonemic Awareness
- Phoneme Blending

Phonics
- Vowel Digraphs /ü/
- Build Fluency
- Spelling: Posttest

Vocabulary
- Words in Context
- Spiral Review

Comprehension
- Strategy: Analyze Text Structure
- Skill: Sequence of Events
- Read Across Texts

Language Arts
- Grammar: Book Titles; Irregular Verbs
- Writing: Expository

SMALL GROUP

- Differentiated Instruction, pages 89O–89NN

Review and Assess

Oral Language

Build Robust Vocabulary

ASSESS WORD KNOWLEDGE

Review this week's oral vocabulary words to assess children's depth of knowledge for each word.

Ask children to talk about how hospital or emergency teams help in an **urgent** situation. Then guide children to discuss the importance of hospital workers feeling **sympathy** for and **comforting** people who are sick or hurt. *What could you do to help out in an* **urgent** *situation? What* **clever** *things could you do? How would you help sick or hurt people* **recuperate**?

- Read aloud the oral vocabulary words one at a time. Have children say a sentence using each word. Provide the following sentence starters:
  - I sometimes **comfort** ________ because ________.
  - I had to stay home to **recuperate** from ________ because ________.
  - I have **sympathy** for ________ because ________.
  - It was **urgent** when ________ because ________.
  - A **clever** thing I did was ________ because ________.

- Review last week's words: *advice*, *hesitate*, *panic*, *secure*, and *vowed*.
- Reread **Oral Vocabulary Cards** to teach additional vocabulary.

ELL ENGLISH LANGUAGE LEARNERS

Beginning

Express Help children understand meaning by using the vocabulary words in statements and questions, such as *When I am sick, it is comforting to drink hot soup. What comforts you when you are sick?* Restate children's answers in complete sentences as needed.

Intermediate

Express Read the first sentence starter and give an example of a completed sentence. Clarify and discuss meaning as needed. Then have children take turns completing the sentence starter with their own answers. Do the same for all the sentence starters. Help with correct pronunciation.

Advanced

Comprehend If children are having problems completing the sentences, provide them with sample completed sentences and then have them use their own answers.

Review and Assess
Fluency

Pronunciation

MODEL FLUENT READING

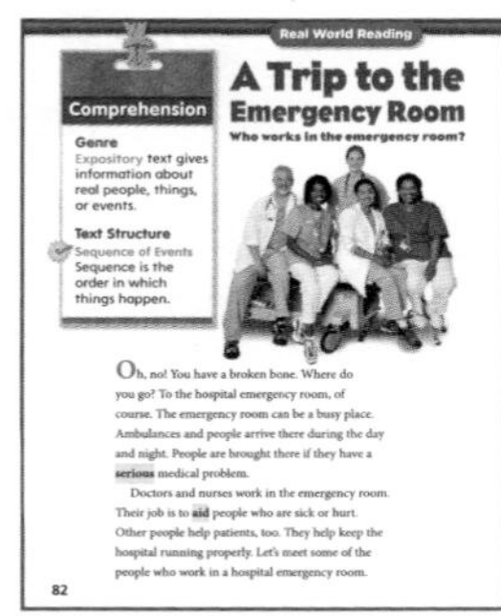
Main Selection

- Read aloud a few pages of *A Trip to the Emergency Room*. Remind children that when reading a nonfiction selection, they may have to pay special attention to their reading rate. Good readers slow down to make sure they pronounce unfamiliar words correctly. Have children echo each sentence you read. Point out how you slowed down when you came to longer words that were more difficult.

- Have partners reread the selection, working on pronouncing words. Circulate, listen in, and provide corrective feedback. Note children who need additional work with decoding and reading high-frequency words. Work with these children during Small Group time.

REPEATED READINGS

- Have children select a story from the **Student Book** or a book that they have previously read. Tell children that by rereading these books, they can become better readers. *The more practice we have sounding out words and seeing those important high-frequency words in text, the easier it will be for us to read new stories.*
- Provide 15–20 minutes for children to enjoy independent reading. Read with children or use this time to assess individuals using the Fluency Assessment in the **Diagnostic Assessment Handbook**.

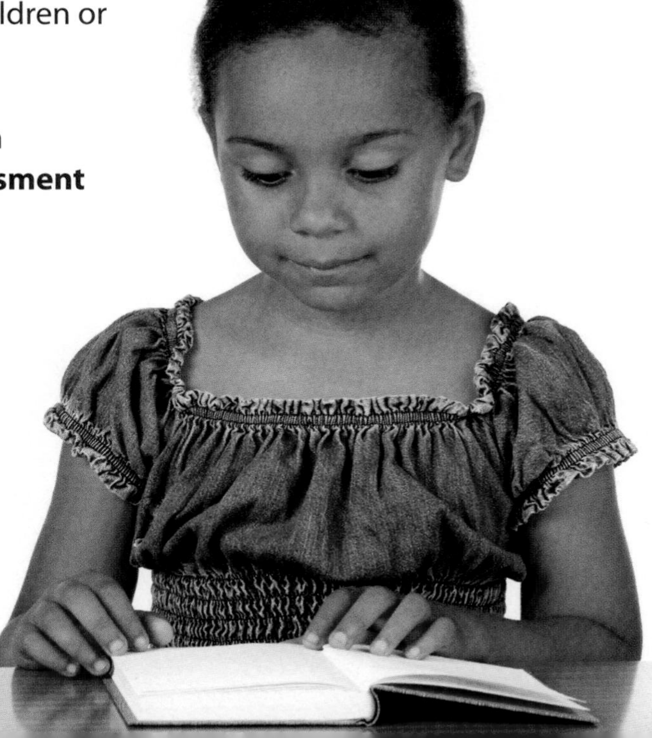

Objectives

- Review and assess vocabulary
- Read aloud grade-level text with fluency and comprehension
- Read independently for a sustained period of time and paraphrase reading

Materials

- Student Book
- Read-Aloud Anthology, "A Whale of a Story," 179–191

Readers Theater

BUILDING LISTENING AND SPEAKING SKILLS

Distribute copies of "A Whale of a Story" from **Read-Aloud Anthology** pages 179–191. Have children practice reading the play throughout the unit. Assign parts and have children present the play or perform it as a dramatic reading at the end of the unit.

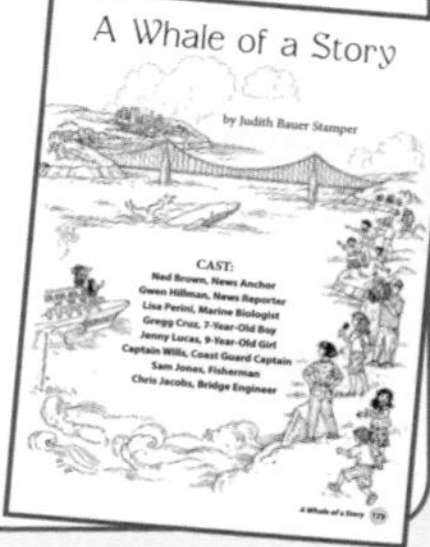

Objectives

- Blend spoken phonemes to form one-syllable words
- Blend with vowel digraphs *oo, ui, ew, ue, u, ou, oe*

Materials

- Word-Building Cards; Teacher's Resource Book, p. 66
- pocket chart
- word charts from Days 1 and 3
- Decodable Reader Library

Skills Trace

Vowel Digraphs *oo, ui, ew, ue, u, ou, oe*	
Introduce	79C–D
Practice/ Apply	79F, 81G–H, 85F–G, 85I, 85V–W; Practice Book: 195; Decodable Reader: *Soon the North Wind Blew*
Reteach/ Review	89G–H, 89O–R, 89U, 89AA, 89GG
Assess	Weekly Test; Unit 4 Test
Maintain	Build Fluency: Sound/Spellings

Review and Assess

Phonemic Awareness

Phoneme Blending

Guided Practice/Practice

Review with children how to orally blend words with vowel digraphs /ü/. Model the first one.

I'm going to say a word sound by sound. I want you to blend the sounds to form the word. The sounds are /b/ /ü/ /th/. Listen as I blend the sounds: /büth/, *booth*. The word is *booth*. Your turn.

/sh/ /ü/ /t/	/s/ /t/ /ü/ /p/	/b/ /l/ /ü/
/k/ /ü/ /l/	/s/ /k/ /ü/ /l/	/b/ /r/ /ü/ /m/
/t/ /ü/ /th/	/g/ /r/ /ü/ /p/	/s/ /ü/ /t/
/t/ /r/ /ü/	/g/ /l/ /ü/	/h/ /ü/ /t/

Review and Assess

Phonics

Build Fluency: Sound/Spellings

Display the following **Word-Building Cards** one at a time: *oo, ui, ew, ue, u, ou, oe, oi, oy, ou, ow, are, air, ear, ere, or, ore, oar, ar, gn, kn, wr, mb, eer, ere, ear*. Have children chorally say each sound. Mix, repeat, and vary the pace.

Blend with Vowel Digraphs /ü/

Guided Practice

Display **Word-Building Cards** *c*, *l*, *u*, *e*. Blend.

Repeat using *zoo*, *glue*, *soup*, *grew*, *blew*, *truth*, *suit*, *spoon*, *scoot*, and *shoe*.

What sounds do each of these letters stand for? Help me blend the sounds together: /klü/. Let's read the word together: *clue*.

Practice

Have children practice reading real words and nonsense words. Use these examples. Write each word on the board.

food	mood	blue	true	Sue
few	knew	chew	crew	threw
fruitless	cashew	trooper	canoe	duty
tood	fru	roup	prue	splew

Build Fluency: Word Automaticity

Use word charts from Days 1 and 3. Point to each word as children chorally read it. Model blending the sounds in any words children miss. Then point to words randomly at varying speeds for children to chorally read.

room	tools	you	foods
chew	flew	blue	July
tooth	knew	stew	shoe
crowd	couch	choice	soy
coin	toy	town	loud

Ruth knew Sue was at school.
June threw the glue at you!

crew	food	moose	roof
room	spoons	through	too
igloo	threw	balloon	cool
rejoin	counties	downtown	ploy
noise	joy	cloud	now

Ruth is in my room at school.
Where is the blue broom?
roomful shoeless outgrew clueless

Build Fluency: Connected Text

- Have children reread with a partner *Soon the North Wind Blew* from the **Decodable Reader Library**. Circulate and listen in, providing corrective feedback as needed.
- Comment on children's **speed**, **accuracy**, and **intonation**. Model each as needed. For example, model how your voice rises at the end of a question.

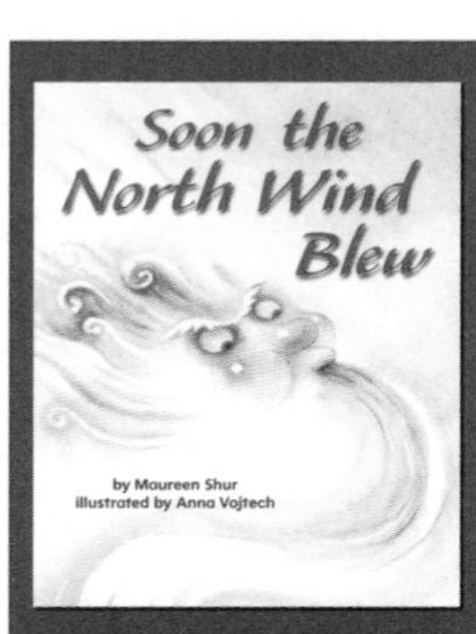

Soon the North Wind Blew

Corrective Feedback

For children needing additional practice reading one-syllable and multisyllabic words with vowel digraphs /ü/, use the Speed Drills in the **Intervention Kit** (**Fluency**).

Objectives

- Spell words with vowel digraphs *oo, ui, ew, ue, oe*
- Spell high-frequency words

Materials

- paper and pencils

5-Day Spelling	
DAY 1	Dictation; Pretest
DAY 2	Teacher-Modeled Word Sort
DAY 3	Student Word Sort
DAY 4	Test Practice
DAY 5	Posttest

Review and Assess

Phonics/Spelling

Words with *oo, ui, ew, ue, oe*

POSTTEST

Use the following procedure to assess children's spelling of the weekly spelling words.

- Pronounce each spelling word and use it in the sentence provided below. Say the word again.
- Have children write the word on a piece of paper. Then continue with the next word.
- When children have finished, collect their papers and analyze their spellings of misspelled words.
- Have children create personal word lists in their Writer's Notebooks that include words they need to continue practicing.

1. **room:** Dad is in the other <u>room</u>.
2. **tool:** Do you need a special <u>tool</u> to fix the car?
3. **suit:** He wore a black striped <u>suit</u>.
4. **fruit:** Oranges are my favorite <u>fruit</u>.
5. **clue:** The detective needed a <u>clue</u>.
6. **glue:** Can you <u>glue</u> the wheel on the model car?
7. **flew:** The plane <u>flew</u> over the ocean.
8. **new:** I gave my mom a <u>new</u> watch.
9. **shoe:** Mark found his <u>shoe</u> under the bed.
10. **canoe:** I took my <u>canoe</u> down the river.
11. **point:** Can you <u>point</u> to the balloon you like the best?
12. **royal:** Jullian is a <u>royal</u> prince.
13. **follow:** Can you <u>follow</u> me to the park?
14. **near:** Are you <u>near</u> a telephone?
15. **paper:** Please write your name on your <u>paper</u>.

Word Wall Use a Word Wall to group words by spelling patterns. Also use it to review previous weeks' spelling words. Remove words from the Word Wall when children have mastered them.

Review and Assess

Vocabulary

Words in Context

REVIEW

Tell children that some words in each sentence mean about the same thing as a vocabulary word. Have children tell which vocabulary word fits into each sentence and reread the sentence substituting the correct vocabulary word for the underlined words.

- A broken leg is an example of an important medical problem. (serious)
- The doctor tells the patient about the operation. (informs)
- Your name and address are your own information. (personal)
- The paramedics came to her rescue. (aid)
- Putting a cast on a broken bone will help it get better. (heal)
- Then have children use each word in a sentence.

Spiral Vocabulary Review

Divide the class into two groups for a word activity. Write vocabulary words from this week and last week (*accident, attention, buddy, enormous, obeys, tip*) on index cards for each group. Have one child pick a card and give clues to help the rest of the group identify the word.

Once groups identify the word, have them write a sentence using that word.

Continue until both groups have identified each word and used it in a sentence.

Write About It

Which hospital worker or emergency worker do you think is most interesting? Write about what this person does and explain why you might want to do this job.

Objectives

- Use context to determine the meaning of unfamiliar words
- Review vocabulary words from this week and last week

Materials

- index cards

Objectives

- Determine when they might use the comprehension strategy again
- Describe the order of events or ideas in a text
- Make comparisons across texts
- Review asking relevant questions and seeking clarification about texts

Materials

- Practice Book for asking relevant questions and seeking clarification about texts, p. 205

Skills Trace

Sequence of Events	
Introduce	U4: 81A–B
Practice/ Apply	U4: 81K–85A; Practice Book: 198–199
Reteach/ Review	U4: 89K, 89V–X, 89BB–DD, 93A–B, 93K–115A, 119G, 119R–T, 119X–Z; Practice Book: 209–210
Assess	Weekly Tests; Unit 4, 5 Tests
Maintain	U4: 155N; U5: 201N, 209J–233A, 239G, 239R–T, 239X–Z, 311N; Practice Book: 243–244

Review and Assess

Comprehension

STRATEGY Analyze Text Structure

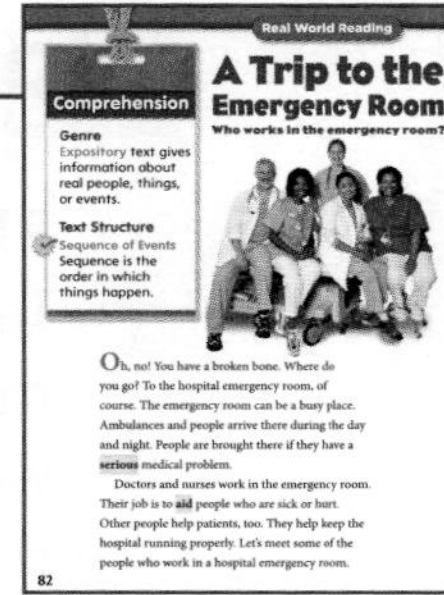

Main Selection

TRANSFER THE STRATEGY Remind children that as they read "A Trip to the Emergency Room" they paid attention to the way the text is organized and how the writer presented the information. Model how using this strategy helped you.

Think Aloud I know that nonfiction texts are organized in different ways. As I was reading, I realized that the author was telling about the people you see in the emergency room in the order that you meet them. The author used special signal words helped me to recognize that the text structure is sequence of events. I used the text structure to figure out and remember the order that things happen on a visit to the emergency room. I paid attention to the events that happened *first*, *next*, and *last* in the article.

Focus Question Ask children to describe how the strategy helped them. Offer these sentence starters and questions:

What kind of signal words did I look for as I read?

This helped me ________.

How might this strategy help me when I read another selection?

SKILL Sequence of Events

READING ACROSS TEXTS Model making a connection between the use of sequence in "Time for an X-Ray" and *A Trip to the Emergency Room*.

Think Aloud I made a connection between the way the information was presented in the article about getting an X-ray and the article about people who work in the emergency room. In both articles, the authors used signal words, such as *first* and *next*, to describe the time order in which events happen.

Provide a sentence starter to help children make their own connections between selections:

I made a connection between ________.

Approaching Level

High-Frequency/Vocabulary

Objective Identify high-frequency words and selection vocabulary

Materials
- **High-Frequency Word Cards**
- **Sound-Spelling WorkBoards**
- **Visual Vocabulary Resources**
- **Vocabulary Cards**
- **Approaching Reproducible**, p. 196

Sound-Spelling WorkBoard

PRETEACH WORDS

- **Introduce High-Frequency Words** Preteach the high-frequency words **follow**, **near**, and **paper** using the **Read/Spell/Write** routine. Display the **High-Frequency Word Cards** and have children write each word on their **WorkBoards**.
- **Introduce Vocabulary Words** Use the **Visual Vocabulary Resources** to preteach the selection words **aid**, **heal**, **personal**, **informs**, and **serious**. Refer to the detailed routine on the cards.
- Have children write each word on their WorkBoards. Use the context sentences on **Approaching Reproducible** page 196.

CUMULATIVE REVIEW

Tier 2

Display the High-Frequency Word Cards for **follow**, **near**, and **paper**. Display one card at a time as children chorally say the word. Then repeat this procedure using the High-Frequency Word Cards from the previous six weeks. Note words needing review.

Then display the **Vocabulary Cards** from the previous four weeks. Say the meaning of each word and have children identify it. Then point to words randomly for children to provide definitions.

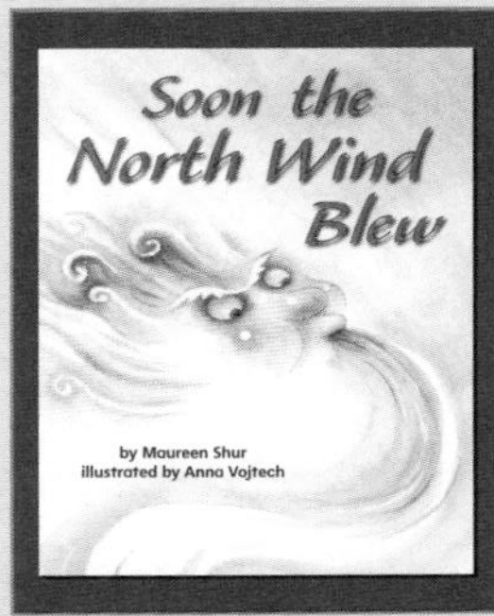

Decodable Reader

Decodable Reader

Objective Read and decode words with vowel digraph /ü/*oo, ui, ew, ue, u, ou, oe*

Materials
- **Decodable Reader:** *Soon the North Wind Blew*

READ THE TEXT

- **Preview and Predict** Point to the book's title and have children sound out each word as you run your finger under it. *I see a wind blowing.* Ask: *How powerful do you think the wind is?*
- **Read the Book** Turn to page 14. Have children point to each word, sounding out decodable words and saying the high-frequency words quickly. If children struggle sounding out words, provide "with you" blending models.
- **Check Comprehension** Ask the following:
  - *What was the Moon's plan?*
  - *Why did the North Wind blow the man's coat away?*

If you wish to preteach the main selection, use StudentWorks Plus for:
- Vocabulary preteaching
- Word-by-word highlighting
- Think Aloud prompts

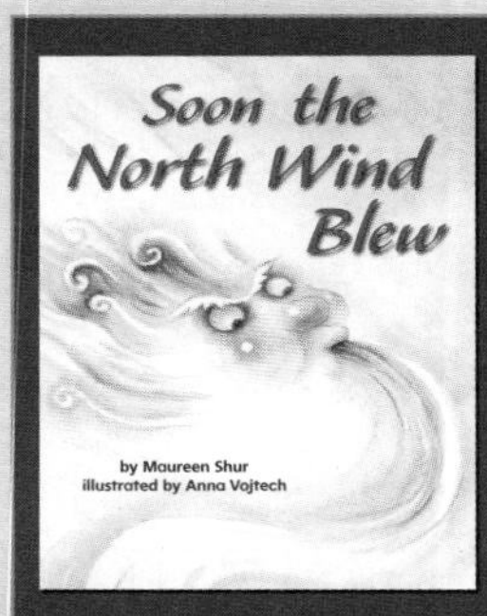
Decodable Reader

On Level

Phonics

Objective Decode words with vowel digraphs /ü/*oo, ui, ew, ue, u, ou, oe*

Materials
- **Sound-Spelling Cards**
- **Word-Building Cards**
- **Decodable Reader**

REVIEW VOWEL DIGRAPH /ü/

- **Review Vowel Digraph /ü/** Display the *Spoon* **Sound-Spelling Card**. Remind children that the sound /ü/ can be spelled with the letters *oo, ui, ew, ue, u, ou,* or *oe.*
- **Blend Words** Write words and sentences from the charts on pages 79D and 85G on the board. Quickly have children chorally read the words. Repeat by pointing to the words in random order. Model blending the sounds in any words children have difficulty reading. Continue with the words below to help children apply their skills to new words. Write each word on the board for children to read.

fruit	suits	flew	foods	rooted
fooling	toolbox	rebooted	drew	soon
new	crewcut	scooted	moon	stewed

- **Build Words** Display **Word-Building Cards** *e, w, u, i, o, s, h, p, n, f, r, l, t, b, d, r, m.* Have partners make as many words as they can. Tell them to write their words in lists based on spelling patterns. For example, words with *oo* go in one list; words with *ui* go in another list; words with *ew* go in a third list, and so on. Provide time for children to share their lists.

Words with *oo*	Words with *ui*	Words with *ew*	Words with *ue*

Words with *u*	Words with *ou*	Words with *oe*

REREAD FOR FLUENCY

- Have partners reread *Soon the North Wind Blew*. Work with children to read at the appropriate rate and pronunciation. Model fluent reading as needed.

ELL

Reread for Fluency Use the Interactive Question-Response Guide Technique to help English Language Learners understand the content of *Soon the North Wind Blew*. As you read the text, make the meaning clear by pointing to the pictures, demonstrating word meaning, paraphrasing text, and asking children questions.

Beyond Level

Phonics

Objective Decode multisyllabic words with vowel digraphs

Materials • **Sound-Spelling Cards** • **Word-Building Cards**

EXTEND/ACCELERATE

- **Vowel Team Syllables** Write the word *soothing* on the board. Underline the letters *oo*. Say: *Sometimes two vowels can stand for one sound. Listen as I blend this word: /süthing/. The two o's are a team. They work together to stand for one sound: /ü/. When two vowels together stand for one sound, they are a vowel team.* The letters in a vowel team appear in the same syllable.
- **Blend Words** Help children read words with vowel teams. Write each word below on the board. Model blending as needed.

cruiser	scooter	loosely	platoon	cooler
noodle	fruitcake	foodstuff	maroon	doodle
cartoon	toolbox	spacesuit	rooster	juicy
	roommate			

- Have children search this week's books for words with vowel teams. Ask children to state the word found and read aloud the sentence. Have children record these words in their Writer's Notebooks. Challenge them to make new words by adding suffixes or inflected endings to the words they listed.

Vocabulary

Objective Alphabetize a series of words to the third letter

REVIEW ORAL VOCABULARY

Gifted Talented

- Write these words and have children read them aloud: *clever, comfort, recuperate, sympathy* and *urgent*. Then add some review words: *succeed, represents, supply, coincidence, soothing.*
  - Say: *Alphabetizing is when you put words in alphabetical order. Today we will learn to alphabetize words to the third letter. Let's look at the list to see if there are any words that begin with the first letter of the alphabet, a.* Continue until the letter *c*.
  - Write the three words that begin with the letter *c*: *comfort, clever* and *coincidence*. Model alphabetizing the words to the third letter.

  - Tell children that they will work with a partner to alphabetize the remaining words. Have them write their words in a list.
  - Afterwards, have volunteers help you finish your list on the board.

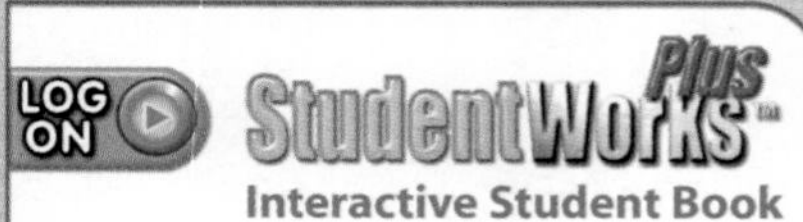

Interactive Student Book

If you wish to preteach the main selection, use StudentWorks Plus for:

- Vocabulary preteaching
- Word-by-word highlighting
- Think Aloud prompts

Cognates

Help children identify similarities and differences in pronunciation and spelling between English words and Spanish cognates.

Cognates

serious *serio*

personal *personal*

inform *informar*

sequence *sequencia*

event *evento*

irregular *irregular*

verb *verbo*

ELL ENGLISH LANGUAGE LEARNERS

Prepare to Read

Content Objective Describe what the workers in an emergency room do

Language Objective Use key words to identify and describe workers in an emergency room

Materials **StudentWorks Plus** (interactive eBook)

BUILD BACKGROUND

All Language Levels

- This version of the **Student Book** contains oral summaries in multiple languages, on-line multilingual glossaries, word-by-word highlighting, and questions that assess and build comprehension.
- Children can build their word reading fluency by reading along as the text is read or by listening during the first reading and, at the end of each paragraph, returning to the beginning of the paragraph and reading along.
- Children can build their comprehension by reviewing the definitions of key words in the on-line glossary and by answering the comprehension questions. When appropriate, the text required to answer the question is highlighted to provide children with additional support and scaffolding.
- Following the reading, ask children to respond in writing to a question that links the story to their personal experiences, such as *Have you ever been to a hospital? If so, what workers did you see? If not, who do you think works in a hospital?*

Academic Language

Language Objective Use academic language in classroom conversations

All Language Levels

- This week's academic words are **boldfaced** throughout the lesson. Define the word in context and provide a clear example from the selection. Then ask children to generate an example or a word with a similar meaning.

Academic Language Used in Whole Group Instruction

Oral Vocabulary Words	Key Selection Words	Strategy and Skill Words
urgent	**serious**	**sequence**
recuperate	**personal**	**events**
clever	**informs**	**summarize**
comfort	**heal**	**irregular verb**
sympathy	**aide**	

ELL ENGLISH LANGUAGE LEARNERS

Vocabulary

Language Objective Demonstrate understanding and use of key words by identifying and describing what emergency workers do

Materials • **Visual Vocabulary Resources** • **ELL Resource Book**, p. 246

PRETEACH KEY VOCABULARY

All Language Levels

Use the **Visual Vocabulary Resources** to preteach the key selection words **aid**, **heal**, **informs**, **personal**, and **serious**. Focus on two words per day. Use the following routine that appears in detail on the cards.

- Define the word in English and provide the example given.
- Define the word in Spanish, if appropriate, and indicate if the word is a cognate.
- Display the picture and explain how it illustrates or demonstrates the word. Engage children in structured partner-talk about the image, using the key word. Ask children to chorally say the word three times. Point out any known sound-spellings or focus on a key aspect of phonemic awareness related to the word. Then distribute copies of the Vocabulary Glossary, **ELL Resource Book** page 246.

PRETEACH FUNCTION WORDS AND PHRASES

All Language Levels

Use the Visual Vocabulary Resources to preteach the function words and phrases *probably*, *properly*, *day and night*, and *as quickly as possible*. Focus on one word per day. Use the detailed routine on the cards.

- Define the word in English and, if appropriate, in Spanish. Point out if the word is a cognate. Then refer to the picture and engage children in talk about the word. For example, children will Partner-Talk using sentence frames or they will listen to sentences and replace a word or phrase with the new function word.
- Ask children to chorally repeat the word three times.

TEACH BASIC WORDS

Beginning/Intermediate

Use the Visual Vocabulary Resources to teach the basic words *paramedic*, *siren*, *ambulance*, *X-ray*, *patients*, and *wheelchair*. Teach these "emergency room sights" using the routine provided on the card.

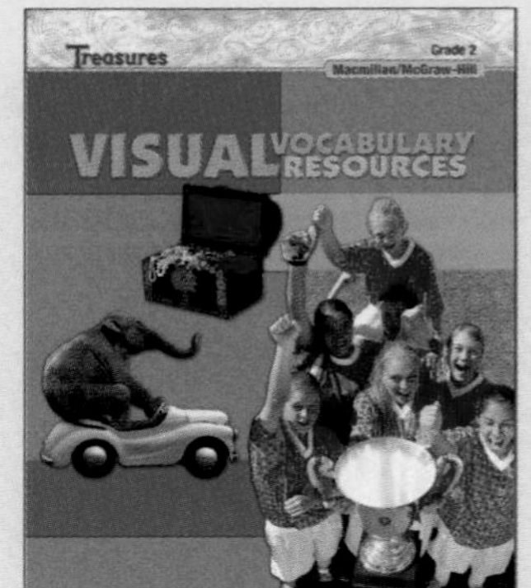

Visual Vocabulary Resources

ELL Resource Book, page 246

Use the word chart to study this week's vocabulary words. Write a sentence using each word in your writer's notebook.

Word	Context Sentence	Illustration
serious	The police officer has a serious look on her face.	When should you act in a serious way?
personal	The doctor was personal. She really cared.	
aid	Nurses give aid to sick people.	
informs	The officer informs us about bicycle safety.	What else might a police officer inform you about?
heal	It took a long time for the cut on my arm to heal.	

Approaching Level

Phonemic Awareness

Objective Recognize the change in a word when a phoneme is changed

Materials
- none

INITIAL SOUND SUBSTITUTION

Tier 2

- Draw a picture of a boot on the board. Say: *Listen as I say the word,* boot. *I'm going to change /b/ to /s/ to make a new word. The new word is* suit.
- Say the following words one at a time. Tell children to change each initial sound to form a new rhyming word:
  Say: root. *Change /r/ to /b/.* (boot)
  Say: flu. *Change /f/ to /b/.* (blue)
  Say: tool. *Change /t/ to /k/.* (cool)
  Say: new. *Change /n/ to /d/.* (do)

Phonics

Objective Decode words with vowel digraph /ü/*oo, ui, ew, ue, u, ou, oe*

Materials
- **Sound-Spelling Cards**
- **Word-Building Cards**
- **Decodable Reader:** *Soon the North Wind Blew*
- pocket chart

Soon the North Wind Blew
by Maureen Shur
illustrated by Anna Vojtech

Decodable Reader

SOUND-SPELLING REVIEW

Tier 2

Display **Word-Building Cards** for the following: *oo, ui, ew, ue, u, ou, oe, oi, oy, ou, ow, are, air, ear, ere, or, ore, oar, ar, gn, kn, wr, mb, eer, ere, ear*. Have children chorally say each sound. Repeat.

RETEACH SKILL

- Display the *Spoon* **Sound-Spelling Card**. Review that the vowel digraph /ü/ can be spelled *oo, ui, ew, ue, u, ou,* or *oe*.
- **Model Blending** Write words and sentences from the chart on page 79D on the board. Model blending using the **Blending Routine**. Have children blend and read the words multiple times.
- **Build Words** Place Word-Building Card *s* in a pocket chart. Ask: *What sound does this stand for?* Place *oo* next to *s*. Ask: *What sound do these letters stand for?* Blend the sounds: /sü/. Say: *Now you say it*. Then place the card for *n* to the right side of *o*. Blend the sounds: /sün/. Say: *Now you blend the sounds. What's the word?* Repeat with the words *cool, suit, shoe, new, flu,* and *fruit*.

REREAD FOR FLUENCY

- Reread *Soon the North Wind Blew* with children. Have them reread the book with the appropriate rate and pronunciation to a partner. Circulate, listen in, and provide corrective feedback.

ELL

Reread for Fluency Use the Interactive Question-Response Guide Technique to help English Language Learners understand the content of *Soon the North Wind Blew*. As you read the text, make the meaning clear by pointing to the pictures, demonstrating word meaning, paraphrasing text, and asking children questions.

Approaching Level

High-Frequency/Vocabulary

Objective Identify high-frequency words and vocabulary words

Materials
- **High-Frequency Word Cards**
- **Vocabulary Cards**

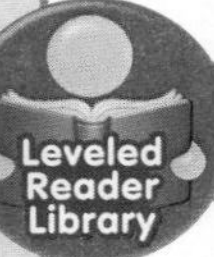

RETEACH WORDS

Tier 2

Display **High-Frequency Word Cards** for **follow, near** and **paper**. Review the words using the **Read/Spell/Write** routine. Display **Vocabulary Cards** for **serious**, **heal**, **informs**, **personal**, and **aid**. Review words using the **Define/Example/Ask** routine.

CUMULATIVE REVIEW

Display the High-Frequency and Vocabulary Cards from the previous six weeks. Display one card at a time as children chorally read the word. Mix and repeat. Note words needing review.

Leveled Reader Library

Leveled Reader Lesson 1

Objectives Describe the order of events; read to apply skills and strategies

Materials
- **Leveled Reader:** *People At Work*
- **Approaching Reproducible**, p. 198

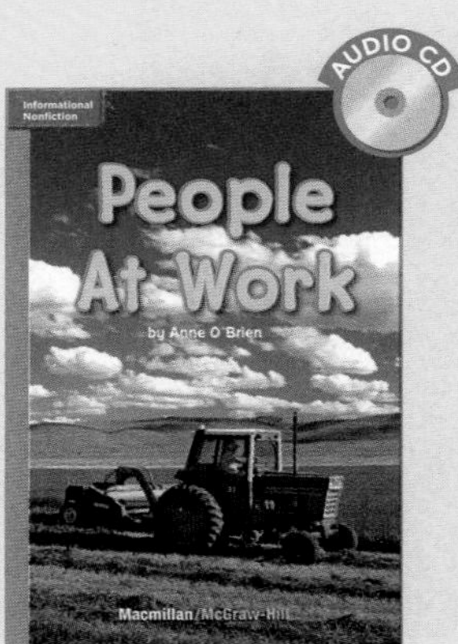

Leveled Reader

BEFORE READING

- **Preview and Predict** Read the title and author name. Ask: *What do you think you will learn about in this book?*
- **Review Skills** Use the inside front cover to review the phonics skill and vocabulary words.
- **Set a Purpose** Say: *Let's read to find out why and how people work.*

DURING READING

- Have children whisper-read each page. Circulate and provide corrective feedback, such as modeling how to blend a word.
- **Sequence of Events** Remind children that authors present facts in a logical order, or sequence of events. Draw a Sequence Chart like the one on the Reproducible. Have children copy it. After children have read a few pages, ask them to describe an important fact. Model how to record the information and have children copy it. Then have them continue identifying the order of events and record the events on their Sequence Chart.

AFTER READING

- Discuss words that gave children difficulty and the decoding strategies they used. Reinforce good reading behaviors you saw.
- **Retell** Have children take turns retelling the selection.

Leveled Reader

On Level

Leveled Reader Lesson 1

Objectives Describe the order of events; read to apply skills and strategies

Materials • **Leveled Reader:** *People At Work* • **Practice Book**, p. 198

BEFORE READING

Preview and Predict Read the title and the name of the author. Ask: *What do you think you will learn about in this book?* Preview the photos throughout the book.

Review Skills Use the inside front cover to review the phonics skill and teach the new vocabulary words.

Set a Purpose Say: *Let's read to find out why and how people work.*

DURING READING

- Have children turn to page 2 and begin by whisper-reading the first two pages.
- Remind children to look for the new vocabulary words. Tell them that you will help them blend sounds in words with variant vowel /ü/.
- Monitor children's reading. Stop periodically and ask open-ended questions to facilitate rich discussion, such as *What is the most important information you have learned so far? What does the author want us to know about why people work?* Build on children's responses to develop deeper understanding of the text.

- **Sequence of Events** Remind children that describing the events in a story or the facts in a selection in order, or sequence, helps a reader to organize and remember what they have read. Draw a Sequence Chart like the one on the **Practice Book** page. Have children copy it. As children reread, ask them for the first important fact in the selection. Model how to record the information and have children copy it. Then have them begin to fill in their Sequence Chart.

AFTER READING

- Discuss words that gave children difficulty and the strategies they used to decode them. Reinforce good reading behaviors you noticed.
- **Retell** Have children take turns retelling the information in *People At Work* in the order in which it was presented. Help them make a real-world connection (Text-to-World) by asking, *Where do you see workers every day in our community?*

ELL

Retell Use the Interactive Question-Response Guide Technique to help English Language Learners understand the content of *People at Work*. As you read the text, make the meaning clear by pointing to the pictures, demonstrating word meaning, paraphrasing text, and asking children questions.

Beyond Level

Leveled Reader Lesson 1

Objective Read to apply skills and strategies

Materials
- **Leveled Reader:** *People At Work*
- **Beyond Reproducible**, p. 198
- self-stick notes

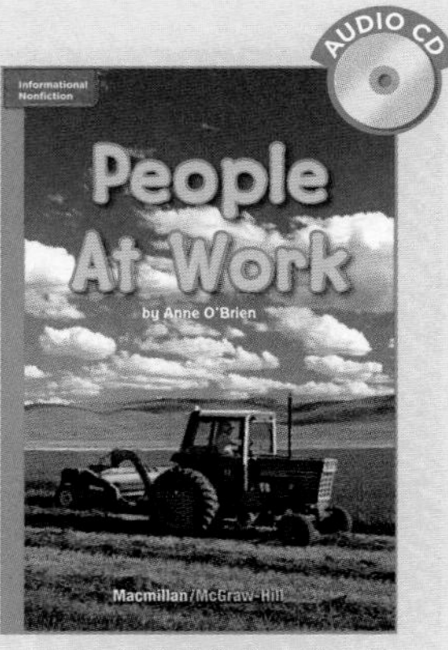

Leveled Reader

BEFORE READING

Preview and Predict Read the title and the name of the author. Preview the photos throughout the book.

Review Skills Use the inside front cover to review the phonics skill and vocabulary words.

Set a Purpose Say: *Let's read to find out how and why people work.*

DURING READING

- Have children turn to page 2 and begin by whisper-reading the first two pages. Guide them to place self-stick notes next to words they have difficulty with.
- Remind children that when they come to an unfamiliar word, they can look for familiar spellings and chunks. For longer words, they will need to break the word into smaller chunks, or syllables, and sound out each part.
- Monitor children's reading. Stop periodically and ask open-ended questions to facilitate rich discussion, such as *What did you learn so far that you did not know before? What does the author want us to know about why work is important?* Have children support their answers with evidence from the text.

- **Sequence of Events** Draw a Sequence Chart like the one on the Reproducible. Stop after a few pages and ask children to tell about the first fact they read. Model how to record the information. Have children continue describing the order of events as they read and fill in their Sequence Charts.

AFTER READING

Gifted Talented

- **Analyze** Review the story with children. Discuss some of the jobs mentioned in the story. Have children describe them, if possible.

- Have children think about a job they would like to have when they get older. Have children pick a partner and discuss the jobs they picked. Ask: *What do you like about this job?*
- Then have children share their jobs with the group. Make a list of jobs children would like to have. After you've created the list, have children identify which jobs are services and which are creating goods.

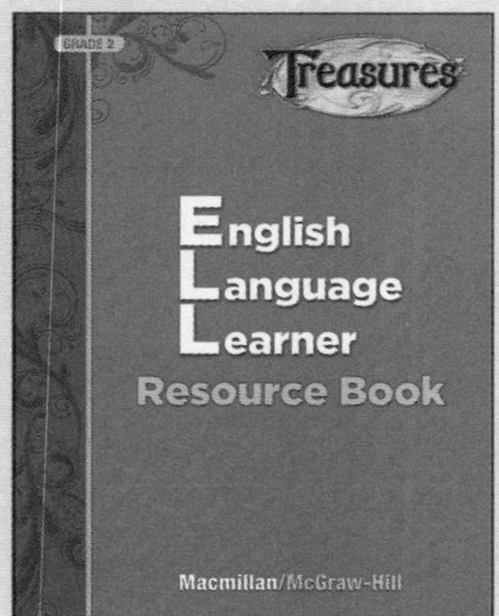

ELL Resource Book

ELL ENGLISH LANGUAGE LEARNERS

Access to Core Content

Content Objective Read grade-level text
Language Objective Discuss text using key words and sentence frames
Materials • **ELL Resource Book**, pp. 244–245

PRETEACH MAIN SELECTION (PAGES 82–85)

All Language Levels

Use the Interactive Question-Response Guide on **ELL Resource Book pages 244–245** to introduce children to *A Trip to the Emergency Room*. Preteach half of the selection on **Day 2** and half on **Day 3**.

- Use the prompts provided in the guide to develop meaning and vocabulary. Use the Partner-Talk and whole-class responses to engage children and increase student talk.
- When completed, have partners reread the story.

Beginning

Use Visuals During the Interactive Reading, select several pictures that show a sequence of events. Describe them and have children summarize what you said.

Intermediate

Summarize During the Interactive Reading, select a few lines of text that show sequence of events. After you read and explain the text, have children tell the sequence of events.

Advanced

Expand During the Interactive Reading, select a larger portion of text that shows a sequence of events. After you read it and explain it, have children tell the sequence of events.

ELL ENGLISH LANGUAGE LEARNERS

Grammar

Content Objective Identify irregular verbs
Language Objective Speak in complete sentences, using sentence frames

STATEMENTS AND QUESTIONS

Beginning/Intermediate

- Review that irregular verbs do not use *-ed* to form the past tense.

All Language Levels

- Review that irregular verbs do not use *-ed* to form the past tense. They have their own special forms. Write these sentences on the board: *We go to school. We do our work. We say new words. We see our friends.* Read the sentences and underline the verb. Then cross out the present tense and write the past tense of each underlined verb. Reread the new sentences: *We went to school. We did our work. We said new words. We saw our friends.*
- Write sentences on the board, such as those provided below. Have children replace the underlined verb with its correct past tense in each sentence, then read the sentence aloud. Have them say: *The past tense of* __________ *is* __________.

  The nurse says to go in here.
  The patient goes to the emergency room.
  He sees the doctor right away.
  The admissions worker does the paper work.

PEER DISCUSSION STARTERS

All Language Levels

- Write the following sentences on the board.

  At the emergency room they saw __________.
  They went to the dentist to __________.
- Pair children and have them complete each sentence frame. Ask them to expand on their sentences by providing as many details as they can from this week's readings. Circulate, listen in, and take note of each child's language use and proficiency.

Beginning

Use Visuals Use irregular verbs as you describe the pictures in *A Trip to the Emergency Room* to children. Ask: *What do you see?* Help children use irregular verbs to describe what is happening.

Intermediate

Describe Ask children to describe the same pictures, adding more irregular verbs to their descriptions. Have them use complete sentences.

Advanced

Narrate Ask children to describe the pictures, adding new irregular verbs to their descriptions.

Transfer Skills

Irregular Verbs In Hmong and Khmer, verbs do not change form to express tense. Children who speak these languages may have found the *-ed* ending confusing. They will most likely need even more practice and reinforcement in identifying and forming past tense of irregular verbs. Give immediate feedback by modeling correct usage and having children repeat. Call attention to irregular past tense verbs in the texts.

Corrective Feedback

During whole group grammar lessons, follow the routine on the **Grammar Transparencies** to provide children with extra support. This routine includes completing the items with English Language Learners while other children work independently, having children reread the sentences with partners to build fluency, and providing a generative task such as writing a new sentence using the skill.

Approaching Level

Phonemic Awareness

Objective Blend phonemes to form words

Materials • none

PHONEME BLENDING

Tier 2

Model how to blend the sounds in a word. Say: *Listen as I say a word in parts: /n/ /ü/. Now listen as I blend the sounds to say the word: /nü/,* new. Have children practice blending the following sounds and then saying the words:

/f/ /l/ /ü/	/f/ /r/ /ü/ /t/	/h/ /ü/ /t/	/k/ /ü/ /l/
/t/ /r/ / ü/	/s/ /ü/ /n/	/b/ /l/ /ü/	/b/ /ü/ /t/

Phonics

Objective Decode words with vowel digraph /ü/*oo, ui, ew, ue, u, ou, oe*

Materials • **Sound-Spelling Cards** • **Word-Building Cards** • **Decodable Reader:** *Soon the North Wind Blew* • pocket chart

Soon the North Wind Blew
by Moureen Shur
illustrated by Anna Vojtech

Decodable Reader

SOUND-SPELLING REVIEW

Tier 2

Display **Word-Building Cards** for the following, one at a time: *oo, ui, ew, ue, u, ou, oe, oi, oy, ou, ow, are, air, ear, ere, or, ore, oar, ar, gn, kn, wr, mb, eer, ere, ear*. Have children chorally say each sound.

RETEACH SKILL

- Display the *Spoon* **Sound-Spelling Card** for vowel digraph /ü/. Review that the /ü/ sound can be spelled with the letters *oo, ui, ew, ue, u, ou,* or *oe*.
- **Model Blending** Write words and sentences from the chart on page 85G on the board. Model how to blend the sounds in each word using the **Blending Routine**. Have children repeat. Then have children read each word multiple times.
- **Build Words** Build vowel digraph /ü/ words with children. Place Word-Building Cards *n, e, w* in a pocket chart. Help children blend the sounds to read the word. Then do the following:

  Change the n *in* new *to* ch. *What word did you make?*
  Change the ch *in* chew *to* fl. *What word did you make?*
  Change the f *in* flew *to* b. *What word did you make?*
  Change the bl *in* blew *to* cr. *What word did you make?*

  Repeat with the word set *fruit, suit, soon, spoon,* and *moon*.
- **Read the Decodable** Reread *Soon the North Wind Blew* with children. Provide blending models as needed. When completed, have children chorally reread the story.

ELL

Demonstrate Comprehension Use the Interactive Question-Response Guide Technique to help English Language Learners understand the content of *Soon the North Wind Blew*. As you read the text, make the meaning clear by pointing to the pictures, demonstrating word meaning, paraphrasing text, and asking children questions.

Approaching Level

High-Frequency/Vocabulary

Objective Identify high-frequency words and vocabulary words

Materials • **High-Frequency Word Cards** • **Vocabulary Cards**

BUILD WORD AUTOMATICITY

Fluency Display **High-Frequency Word Cards** for **follow**, **near**, **paper** and **Vocabulary Cards** for **aid**, **heal**, **informs**, **personal**, and **serious**. Point to the words in random order. Have children chorally read them. Repeat at a faster pace.

CUMULATIVE REVIEW

Display High-Frequency Word Cards and Vocabulary Cards from the past six weeks. Have children chorally read the words. Note words children need to review.

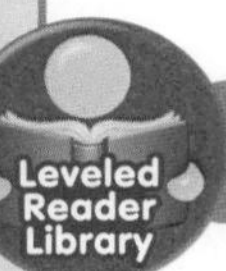

Leveled Reader Lesson 2

Objectives Describe the order of events; read to apply skills and strategies

Materials • **Leveled Reader:** *People At Work* • **Sound-Spelling WorkBoards** • **Approaching Reproducible**, pp. 198–199

BEFORE READING

Review Have children retell *People At Work*. Ask them to look at the pictures page by page and say the facts they learned about work on each page in their own words. Reinforce key vocabulary words by asking questions about the book using the key words.

DURING READING

Sequence of Events As children reread the book, help them finish adding information to their Sequence Charts. Ask them to think of the facts in order.

AFTER READING

- **Retell** Have children use their Sequence Charts to orally retell important facts in the order they read them in *People At Work*.
- **Model Fluency** Read the sentences in the book one at a time. Have children chorally repeat. Point out to children that when you read difficult information, you read at a slower rate.

Book Talk

Bringing Groups Together Children will work with peers of various language and reading abilities to discuss this week's Leveled Readers. Refer to page 179 in the **Teacher's Resource Book** for how to conduct a Book Talk.

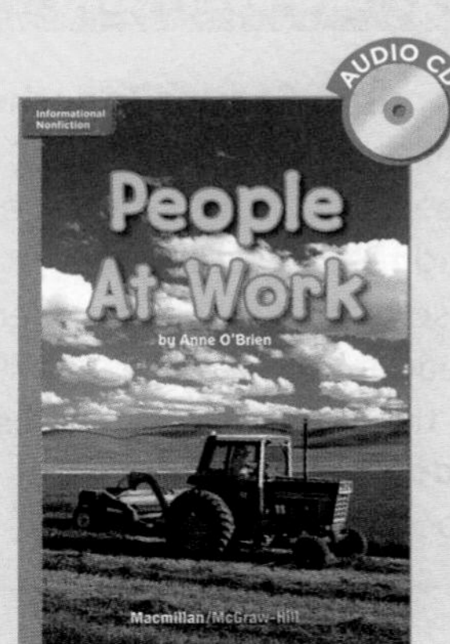

Leveled Reader

Approaching Reproducible, page 199

Sequence is the order that things happen in a story.

Read the story. Then number the pictures to show the order in which things happened in the story.

Sam Gets His Tonsils Out

Sam woke up with a very sore throat. He told his dad. Sam and his mom met with the doctor. "Your tonsils have to come out," the doctor said.

Sam's mom took him to the hospital the next day. When he woke up after the operation, his dad asked, "Are you feeling better?" Sam said his throat was still a bit sore.

The doctor came in with a bowl of ice cream. "This will help you feel better," she said. Sam smiled and began to eat.

1.  4

2.  1

3. 2

4.  3

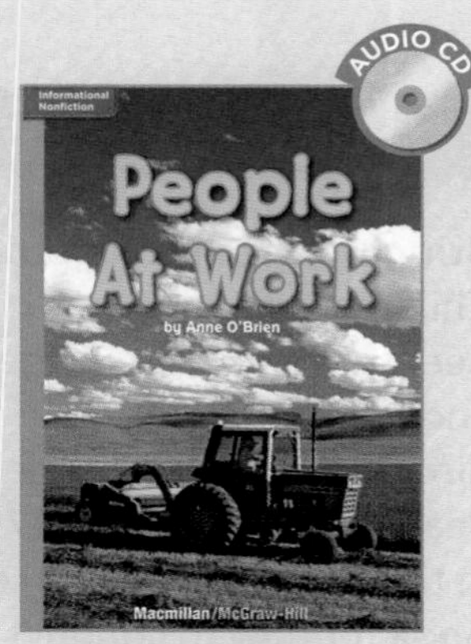

Leveled Reader

On Level

Leveled Reader Lesson 2

Objectives Describe the order of events; read to apply skills and strategies

Materials • **Leveled Reader:** *People At Work* • **Practice Book**, pp. 198, 202

BEFORE READING

- **Review** Have children retell *People At Work*. If children struggle, ask guiding questions about each page to help them recall what they learned. Reinforce vocabulary by having several children answer the same question using different words. For example, *Why do people work?* People work to make money; they work to earn a living.

DURING READING

- **Sequence of Events** Explain to children that good readers should pay attention to the order of the information in nonfiction selections as well as the sequence of events in fiction. *Telling the events in order is a good way to help you remember the facts and check that you understood what you read.* As they reread the book, help children complete their Sequence Charts, one section at a time. Model your thinking to show how you determined which important facts to include.

AFTER READING

- Have children use their Sequence Charts to orally retell the important facts learned in the order in which they appeared in *People At Work*.

REREAD FOR FLUENCY

- Read the sentences in the book one at a time. Have children chorally repeat. Point out to children how you use intonation to make the reading interesting and how your voice goes up at the end of a question.
- Have children read a portion of *People at Work* for fluency.
- Have chidren continue to work on their fluency using **Practice Book** page 202.

Book Talk

Bringing Groups Together Children will work with peers of various language and reading abilities to discuss this week's Leveled Readers. Refer to page 179 in the **Teacher's Resource Book** for how to conduct a Book Talk.

Practice Book, page 202

As I read, I will pay attention to the pronunciation of vocabulary words.

Your body is working even when you are just
9 sitting still. You can see, hear, smell, taste, and feel.
19 Your body knows when it is cold or hot. It can
30 even **heal** itself when a part is broken or you feel
41 sick.
42 Sometimes a doctor can help your body get well.
51 A doctor can also give you a **personal** checkup
60 once a year to be sure you stay healthy.
69 Let's take a look at the human body. Then
78 we will see how a doctor can help you keep it
89 healthy. 90

Comprehension Check

1. Summarize what the author says in the second paragraph. **Sequence of Events** Answers will vary.
2. How do you know that your body is working even when you are still? **Make and Confirm Predictions** You know your body is working because you see, hear, smell, taste, and feel.

	Words Read	–	Number of Errors	=	Words Correct Score
First Read		–		=	
Second Read		–		=	

Beyond Level

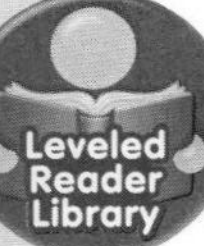

Leveled Reader Lesson 2

Objectives Describe the order of events; read to apply skills and strategies

Materials
- **Leveled Reader:** *People At Work*
- **Beyond Reproducible**, pp. 198, 202

BEFORE READING

- **Review** Have children retell *People At Work* to a partner. Circulate and listen in. Prompt children to use the new words they learned from the book in their retellings.

DURING READING

- **Sequence of Events** As children reread the book, help them complete their Sequence Charts. Guide them by asking who, what, when, where, why and how questions.

AFTER READING

- **Retell** Have children use their Sequence Charts to write the important facts in the order in which they were presented in *People At Work*.

Gifted Talented

- **Review Flow Charts** Have children review the list of jobs showing jobs they would like to have when they grow up.
- **Synthesize** Tell children that they will pretend there is a shortage of workers in the jobs they listed on their chart. To help remedy this, ask children to create an article for a newspaper that will encourage people to want to pursue these jobs.
- Have children work in pairs to pick a job and write an article about it. The article should tell as many details about the job and some of the reasons why it is a good job. Children may include a piece of art or a photograph with the article.
- **Evaluate** Have each pair present their article to the group. Have children respond to each article, telling what they liked about it.

REREAD FOR FLUENCY

- Read the sentences in the book one at a time. Have children chorally repeat. Point out to children how you use intonation to make the reading interesting.

PARTNERS

- Have children practice reading the book to a partner. Say: *Read expressively. Use your voice to show expression. When you see a question read with curiosity by raising your voice at the end.*
- Have children continue to work on their fluency using Practice Book page 202.

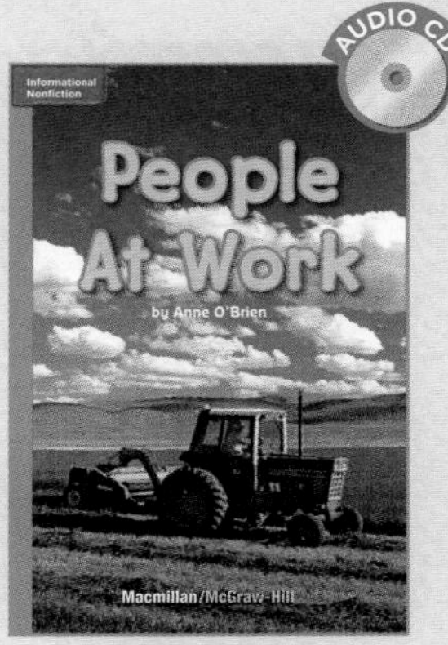

Leveled Reader

Book Talk

Bringing Groups Together Children will work with peers of various language and reading abilities to discuss this week's Leveled Readers. Refer to page 179 in the **Teacher's Resource Book** for how to conduct a Book Talk.

Beyond Reproducible, page 202

As I read, I will pay attention to the pronunciation of the vocabulary words.

Even if you are exercising and eating right, you
9 can still get sick. Germs can make you sick.
18 There are some simple things you can do to get
28 rid of germs. The easiest way is to wash your hands.
39 You should wash your hands after you use the
48 bathroom and before each meal.
53 Take care of your cuts. If the skin is **broken**,
63 germs can get into your blood. Ask an adult to help
74 you clean the cut. Use an antiseptic to kill any
84 germs. Then cover the cut with a bandage. These
93 steps will help the cut **heal**. 99

Comprehension Check

1. When should you wash your hands? **Sequence of Events** Hands should be washed before every meal and after using the bathroom.
2. Should a cut heal if it is properly cleaned, disinfected, and bandaged? **Make and Confirm Predictions** Yes, if a cut is properly treated, it should heal well.

	Words Read	–	Number of Errors	=	Words Correct Score
First Read		–		=	
Second Read		–		=	

Leveled Reader

Vocabulary

Preteach Vocabulary Use the routine in the **Visual Vocabulary Resources**, page 416, to preteach the ELL Vocabulary listed on the inside front cover of the Leveled Reader.

ELL ENGLISH LANGUAGE LEARNERS

Leveled Reader Library

Leveled Reader Lesson 1

Content Objective Read to apply skills and strategies
Language Objective Retell information using complete sentences
Materials • **Leveled Reader:** *People Work* • **Visual Vocabulary Resources**

BEFORE READING

All Language Levels

- **Preview** Read the title *People Work*. Ask: *What's the title? Say it again.* Repeat with the author's name. Then page through the book. Use simple language to tell about each page. Immediately follow up with questions, such as *What are the people doing in this photo? Would you like to have this job? Why or why not?*
- **Review Skills** Use the inside front cover to review the phonics skill and vocabulary words.
- **Set a Purpose** Say: *Let's read to find out about different kinds of work people do and why.*

DURING READING

- Have children read each page aloud using the differentiated suggestions. Provide corrective feedback, such as modeling how to blend a decodable word or clarifying meaning by using techniques from the Interactive Question-Response Guide.
- **Sequence of Events** After every two pages, ask children to state the main ideas they have learned so far. Help them to complete the Sequence of Events Chart. Restate children's comments when they have difficulty using story-specific words. Provide differentiated sentence frames to support children's responses and engage children in partner-talk where appropriate.

Beginning

Echo-Read Have children echo-read.

Check Comprehension Point to pictures and ask questions such as *Look at this picture. Is it a tractor or a bus? Do you see a police officer? Point to the officer.*

Intermediate

Choral-Read Have children choral-read with you.

Check Comprehension Ask questions/prompts such as *What are the people doing in this photo? Why do people work? What jobs did you learn about?*

Advanced

Choral-Read Have children choral-read.

Check Comprehension Ask: *Which jobs did you learn about that you might like to do? Why would you like to do that kind of work?*

ELL ENGLISH LANGUAGE LEARNERS

AFTER READING

Use the chart below and the Think and Compare questions from page 16 of *People Work* to determine children's progress.

Think and Compare	Beginning	Intermediate	Advanced
1 Look at page 10. How does food get from the farm to the table? List the steps.	Responses will vary. Nonverbal response. Farmer. Food.	A farmer grows food. A farmer sells food. A store sells food.	First, a farmer grows food. Then the farmer sells it to a grocer. Then the grocer sells the food.
2 What are three goods you can buy? What are three services you can pay for?	Responses will vary. Nonverbal response. One-word response or gestures to objects.	Responses will vary. ball, apple, pencil a haircut, bus ride, bike fixed.	Responses will vary. You can get your hair cut, your bike fixed. You can ride a bus.
3 What are three things that can make people happy in their work?	Responses will vary. Nonverbal response. Help. Like people.	Responses will vary: They like helping. They like the people. They like the job.	Responses will vary: Some people are happy when they help others and like the people they work with. They like what they do.

Writing/Spelling

Content Objective Spell words correctly

Language Objective Write in complete sentences, using sentence frames

All Language Levels

- Write the key vocabulary words on the board: **aid**, **heal**, **informs**, **personal**, and **serious**. Have children copy each word on their **WorkBoards**. Then help them say, then write sentences for each word.

Beginning/Intermediate

- Help children spell words using their growing knowledge of English sound-spelling relationships. Model how to segment the word children are trying to spell and attach a spelling to each sound (or spellings to each syllable if a multisyllabic word). Use the Sound-Spelling Cards to reinforce the spellings.

Advanced/Advanced High

- Dictate the following words for children to spell: *soon, room, tool, fruit, suit, new, flew, crew*. Guide children using the Sound-Spelling Cards as they spell each word. When completed, review the meanings of words that can be easily demonstrated or explained. Use actions, gestures, and available pictures.

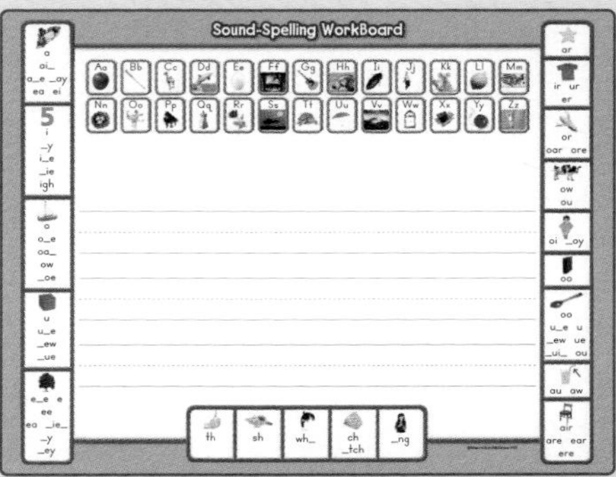

Sound-Spelling WorkBoard

Phonics/Word Study

For English Language Learners who need more practice with this week's phonics/spelling skill, see the **Approaching Level** lesson on page 89Q. Focus on minimal contrasts, articulation, and those sounds that do not transfer from the child's first language to English. For a complete listing of transfers, see pages T16–T31.

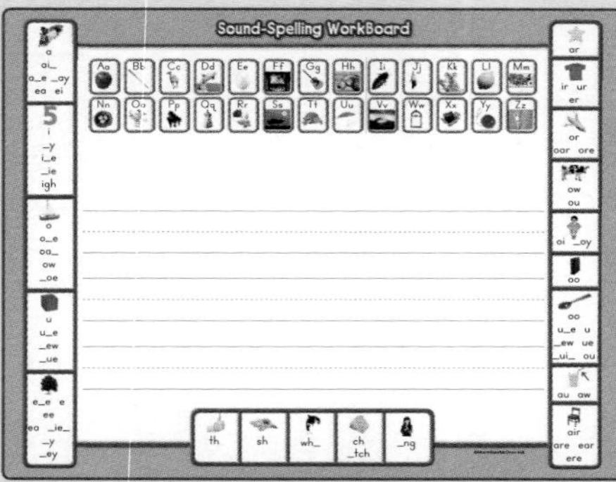
Sound-Spelling WorkBoard

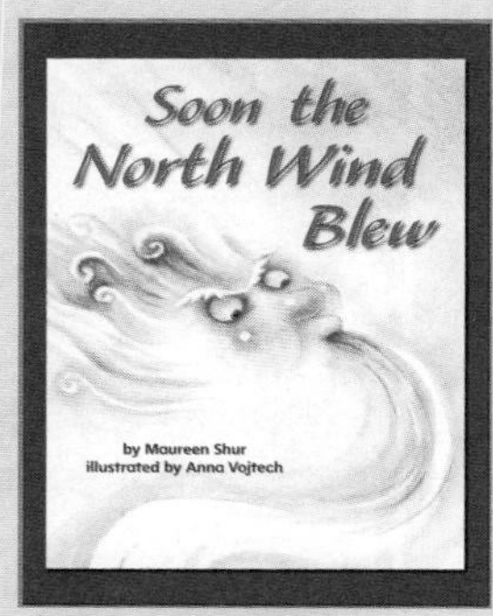

Decodable Reader

Approaching Level

Phonemic Awareness

Objective Segment words into phonemes

Materials
- **Teacher's Resource Book**, p. 143
- markers
- **Sound-Spelling WorkBoards**

PHONEME SEGMENTATION

Tier 2

- Distribute copies of the **WorkBoards** and markers. Say a word, stretching each sound for 1½ seconds. Model for children how to drag one marker onto each box for each sound. Have children repeat and count the number of sounds. Do this for the following words: *shoe, fruit, tool, drew, soon, suit, due, stew, scoot*.
- **Link to Spelling** When completed, segment each word again. Then help children replace each marker with a letter that stands for the sound. Help children read the completed words.

Phonics

Objective Decode words with vowel digraph /ü/*oo, ui, ew, ue, u, ou, oe*

Materials
- **Decodable Reader:** *Soon the North Wind Blew*
- **Word-Building Cards**
- **Sound-Spelling Cards**

SOUND-SPELLING REVIEW

Tier 2

Display **Word-Building Cards** for the following, one at a time: *oo, ui, ew, ue, u, ou, oe, oi, oy, ou, ow, are, air, ear, ere, or, ore, oar, ar, gn, kn, wr, mb, eer, ere, ear*. Have children chorally say each sound.

RETEACH SKILL

- Display the *Spoon* **Sound-Spelling Card**. Review that the /ü/ sound can be spelled with the letters *oo, ui, ew, ue, u, ou,* or *oe*.
- **Model Blending** Write words and sentences from the chart on page 85G on the board. Model how to blend the sounds in each word using the **Blending Routine**. Have children repeat.
- **Read in Context** Write the sentences below on the board. Have children chorally read the sentences. Help children blend sounds in decodable words and read vocabulary words.

  The boy is serious about school.
  The fruit is in a brown bag.
  Soon the moon will be out.
  Your cut will heal with first aid.
  The root is in the soil.
  His tools are on the chair.
  I have a new blue suit.
  Chew your food.

- **Read the Decodable** Reread *Soon the North Wind Blew* with children. Ask children to reread the story to a partner. Give corrective feedback.

ELL

Reread Continue using the Interactive Question-Response Guide Technique to help English Language Learners understand the content of *Soon the North Wind Blew*. As you read the text, make the meaning clear by pointing to the pictures, demonstrating word meaning, paraphrasing text, and asking children questions.

Approaching Level

High-Frequency/Vocabulary

Objective Review high-frequency and vocabulary words

Materials
- **Vocabulary Cards**
- **Sound-Spelling WorkBoards**
- **High-Frequency Word Cards**

REVIEW WORDS

- Display **High-Frequency** for **follow**, **near**, **paper** and **Vocabulary Cards** for **aid**, **heal**, **informs**, **personal**, and **serious**. Have children copy each word on their **WorkBoards**. Then help them write sentences for each word. Provide sentence stems or starters, such as *The nurse* informs *the boy that* ________. *I sometimes need* aid *when* ________.

CUMULATIVE REVIEW

- Display the High-Frequency and Vocabulary Cards from the previous six weeks. Display one card at a time as children chorally read the word. Mix and repeat.

Fluency

Objective Read aloud with fluency and comprehension

Materials
- **Leveled Reader:** *People At Work*
- **Approaching Reproducible**, p. 202

READ FOR FLUENCY

- Tell children that they will be doing a final fluent reading of *People At Work*. Remind them to think about intonation and expression.
- As they read, note words children mispronounce or struggle to read. Also note their overall accuracy and pace. Use this information to determine if additional instruction is needed on this week's phonics skill and vocabulary words. Send the book home for independent reading.

REREAD PREVIOUSLY READ BOOKS

Tier 2

- Tell children that rereading **Leveled Readers** will help them develop their skills. The more times they read the same words, the quicker they will learn these words.
- Circulate and listen in as children read. Stop children periodically and ask them how they are figuring out difficult words or checking their understanding as they read.
- Have children read other Leveled Readers during independent reading time or for homework.

Meet Grade-Level Expectations

As an alternative to this day's lesson, guide children through a reading of the On Level Leveled Reader. See page 89W. Because both books contain the same vocabulary, phonics, and comprehension skills, the scaffolding you provided will help most children gain access to this more challenging text.

Approaching Reproducible, page 202

As I read, I will pay attention to the pronunciation of the vocabulary words.

Hospitals are busy, **serious** places.
5 Doctors and nurses help sick and hurt people.
13 Many people work in a hospital. There are many kinds of
24 jobs. You can meet many helpers at a hospital.
33 Hospitals need to know all about you. A worker puts your
44 **personal** facts into the computer. Then the worker wraps a
54 band on your wrist. It has your name on it. 64

Comprehension Check

1. What does a hospital worker do for you at the hospital? **Sequence of Events** Hospital workers prepare people for stays in the hospital.
2. What sort of people are helped in hospitals? **Main Idea and Details** Hospitals help sick and hurt people.

	Words Read	–	Number of Errors	=	Words Correct Score
First Read		–		=	
Second Read		–		=	

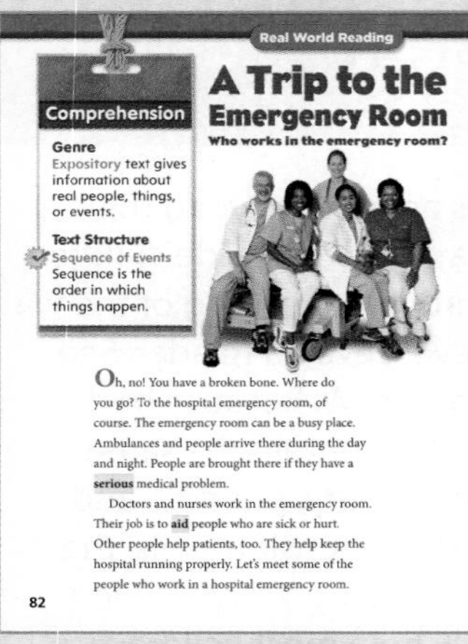
Student Book

On Level

Fluency

Objectives Read aloud with fluency; reread to analyze text structure

Materials • **Student Book:** "A Trip to the Emergency Room"

REREAD FOR FLUENCY

- Have children reread "A Trip to the Emergency Room." Work with children to read with the appropriate pronunciation. Explain that nonfiction selections often have more difficult words. Model fluent reading as needed. Provide time for children to read a section of the text to you. Comment on their accuracy, rate, and pronunciation and provide corrective feedback.

REREAD FOR STRATEGY

- Review that text structure is the way writers organize information. Sequence is one type of text structure that writer use to help reader understand and remember what they read.
- Have children reread the story to look for sequence words such as *first*, *next*, *then*, and *last* to show the time order of events.

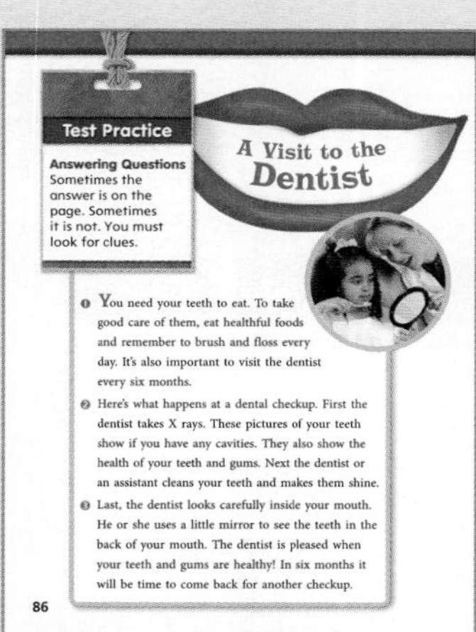
Student Book

Beyond Level

Fluency

Objectives Read aloud with fluency; reread to analyze text structure

Materials • **Student Book:** "A Trip to the Emergency Room," "A Visit to the Dentist"

REREAD FOR FLUENCY

- Have children reread "A Trip to the Emergency Room" and "A Visit to the Dentist." Work with children to read with accuracy and the appropriate pace, pausing when appropriate. Provide time for children to read a section of the text to you. Comment on their rate and pronunciation. Provide corrective feedback.

REREAD FOR STRATEGY

- Review that text structure is the way writers organize information when they write. The different types of text structure are: cause and effect, problem and solution, sequence, compare and contrast and description.
- Have children reread each selection and identify the type of text structure the author used.

ELL ENGLISH LANGUAGE LEARNERS

Leveled Reader Lesson 2

Content Objective Read grade-level text
Language Objective Discuss text using key words and sentence frames
Materials • **ELL Resource Book**, p. 247 • **Leveled Reader:** *People Work*

AFTER READING

All Language Levels

Book Talk Distribute copies of **ELL Resource Book** page 247. Children will work with peers of varying language abilities to discuss them. Help students determine who will be the leader for the discussion.

Develop Listening and Speaking Skills Tell children to remember the following:

- Share information in cooperative learning interactions. Remind children to work with their partners to retell the story and complete any activities. Ask: What happened next in the story?
- Employ self-corrective techniques and monitor their own and other children's language production. Children should ask themselves: What parts of this passage were confusing to me? Can my classmates help me clarify a word or sentence that I don't understand?
- Distinguish between formal and informal English and know when to use each one. Remind children to note whether the selection is written in formal or informal English. Ask: Why do you think it is written in this way? Remind children that they may use informal English when speaking with their classmates, but they should use formal language when they talk to teachers or write essays.
- Use high-frequency English words to describe people, places, and objects.

ELL Resource Book

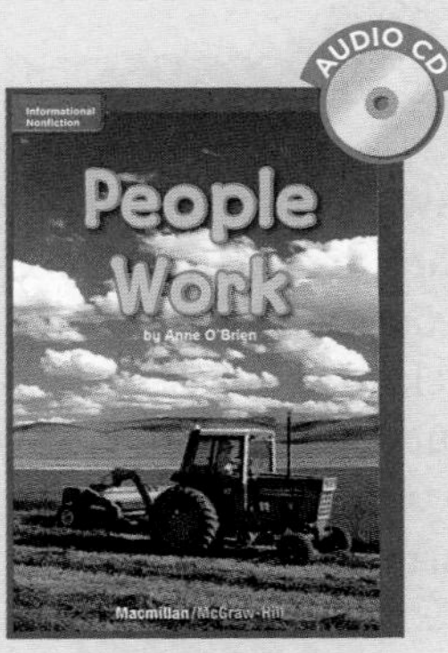

Leveled Reader

Book Talk

Bringing Groups Together
Children will work with peers of varying language abilities to discuss the Book Talk questions. Form groups so that students who read the Beyond Level, On Level, Approaching Level, and English Language Learner readers are in the same group for the activity.

Approaching Level

Oral Language

Objectives Build worker-related vocabulary; review week's oral vocabulary words
Materials • chart paper

EXPAND VOCABULARY

- Draw a one-column chart labeled *Workers Who Help*. Remind children that this week they learned about people at work. One group of people they learned about were workers in an emergency room.
- Write *doctor*, *nurse*, *admissions worker*, and *orderly* on the chart. Point to each word, read it, and have children repeat.

Workers Who Help
doctor
nurse
admissions worker
orderly
paramedic
firefighter
police officer
security guard

- Tell children that many workers have jobs that let them help other people in the community. Ask children to name other workers they know who help people.
- List children's responses on the chart, adding as necessary to provide support. Have children read each word as you write it on the chart. Discuss with children how each of the workers listed help in the community.

REVIEW VOCABULARY

Tier 2

- Use the **Define/Example/Ask** vocabulary routine in the **Instructional Routine Handbook** to review this week's oral vocabulary words: **clever**, **comfort**, **recuperate**, **sympathy**, and **urgent**.
- Tell children you are going to start a sentence using one of the words and you want them to think of an ending. For example, say: *When you have been sick and are trying to* recuperate, *you should* ________. Repeat with remaining words.

ELL

Draw If children are having a hard time naming workers, encourage them to draw quick sketches or act out what the person does. Name the workers and add to the chart.

Approaching Level

Fluency

Objectives Read aloud with fluency; review high-frequency/vocabulary words

Materials
- **Student Book:** "A Trip to the Emergency Room"
- **High-Frequency Word Cards**
- **Vocabulary Cards**

REREAD FOR FLUENCY

- Have children reread a portion of "A Trip to the Emergency Room." Tell them to focus on two to four of their favorite pages from the selection. Work with children to read the pages with accuracy and the appropriate intonation. For example, read each sentence and have children echo. Remind them to read the facts at a slow enough pace to make them clearly understood.
- Provide time to listen as children read their sections of text. Comment on their accuracy and pace and provide corrective feedback by modeling proper fluency.

REVIEW HIGH-FREQUENCY/VOCABULARY WORDS

- Display **High-Frequency Word Cards** for **follow**, **near**, and **paper** and **Vocabulary Words** for **serious**, **heal**, **informs**, **personal**, and **aid**. Model using two or three of the words in a sentence. Then have children come up with their own sentence using two or three of the words.

CUMULATIVE REVIEW

- Display the High-Frequency Word Cards and Vocabulary Cards from the previous four weeks. Display one card at a time as children chorally read the word. Mix and repeat. Note words children need to review.

Self-Selected Reading

Objective Read independently and retell a story read

Materials
- **Leveled Classroom Library**
- other informational books

APPLY SKILLS TO INDEPENDENT READING

- Have each child choose an informational book for independent reading. (See the **Theme Bibliography** on pages T8–T9 for book suggestions.)
- After reading, ask children to use their Sequence Charts to orally retell the events in the order in which the author presented them. Provide time for children to comment on their reactions to the books. Ask: *What is the most important fact you learned? Why is it important?*

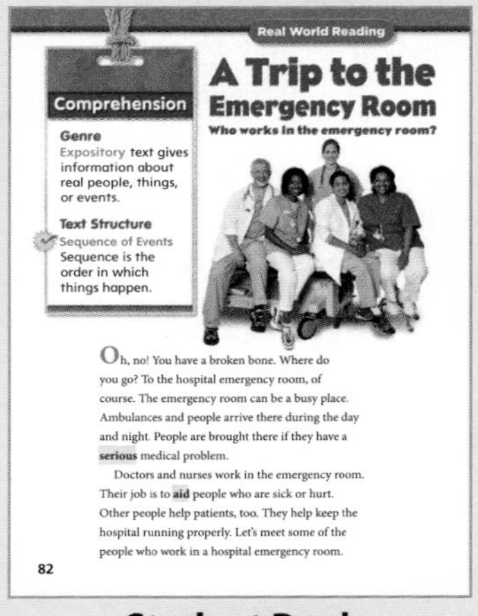

Student Book

Decodable Text

Use the decodable stories in the **Teacher's Resource Book** to help children build fluency with basic decoding patterns.

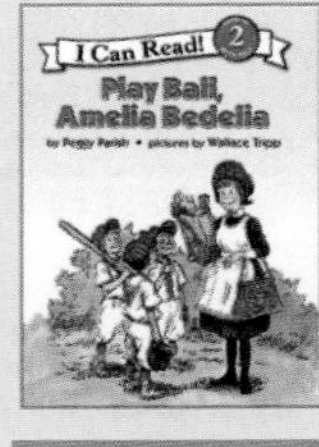

Approaching

Leveled Classroom Library
See Leveled Classroom Library lessons on pages T2–T7.

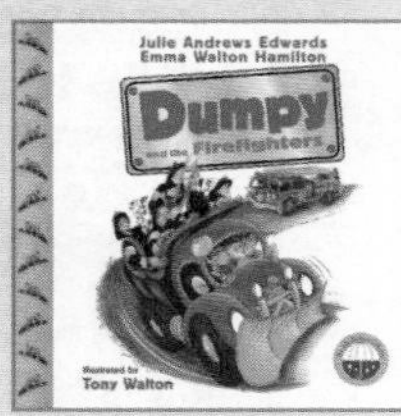

On Level

Leveled Classroom Library

See Leveled Classroom Library lessons on pages T2–T7.

On Level

Self-Selected Reading

Objective Read independently and retell an informational selection

Materials • **Leveled Classroom Library** • other informational books

APPLY SKILLS TO INDEPENDENT READING

- Have each child choose an informational book for independent reading. (See the **Theme Bibliography** on pages T8–T9 for book suggestions.)
- After reading, ask children to use their Sequence Charts to orally retell the books. Provide time for children to comment on their reactions to the books. Ask: *What is the most important information you learned from this book? Why is it important? Why is it helpful to remember the sequence or order of facts in the book?*

ELL

Share Information Pair English Language Learners with fluent speakers. Have them choose the same book and work together on the Retelling Chart.

Beyond

Leveled Classroom Library

See Leveled Classroom Library lessons on pages T2–T7.

Beyond Level

Self-Selected Reading

Objective Read independently and retell information learned

Materials • **Leveled Classroom Library** • other informational books

APPLY SKILLS TO INDEPENDENT READING

- Have each child choose an informational book for independent reading. (See the **Theme Bibliography** on pages T8–T9 for book suggestions.)
- After reading, ask children to use their Sequence Charts to write the important facts in order in their Writer's Notebooks. Provide time for children to comment on the books. Ask: *What did you learn from this book that you did not know before?*

EVALUATE

- Challenge students to discuss how the self-selected books they have chosen relate to the theme of this unit, Better Together. Ask: *How is working as a team better than working alone?* Have children have a debate to discuss their views.

ENGLISH LANGUAGE LEARNERS

Fluency

Content Objectives Reread selections to develop fluency; develop speaking skills

Language Objective Tell a partner what a selection is about

Materials
- **Decodable Reader:** *Soon the North Wind Blew*
- **Student Books:** "A Trip to the Emergency Room", "A Visit to the Dentist"

REREAD FOR FLUENCY

Beginning

Have children read the Decodable Reader.

Intermediate/Advanced

- Have children reread a portion of "A Trip to the Emergency Room." Ask them to focus on two to four of their favorite pages from the selection. Work with children to read the pages with accuracy and the appropriate pace. For example, read each sentence of the first paragraph and have children echo. Remind them to read the facts at a slow enough pace to make them clearly understood.
- Provide time for children to read their sections of text to you. Comment on their expression and provide corrective feedback by modeling proper fluency.

DEVELOP SPEAKING/LISTENING SKILLS

All Language Levels

- Have children practice reading "A Visit to the Dentist." Work with children to read with accuracy and appropriate pacing.
- Provide time for children to read aloud the article to a partner. Ask children to tell what they learned about going to the dentist. Provide the sentence frame *I learned that the dentist* ________.

Self-Selected Reading

Content Objective Read independently

Language Objective Orally retell information learned

Materials
- **Leveled Classroom Library**
- other nonfiction books

APPLY SKILLS AND STRATEGIES TO INDEPENDENT READING

All Language Levels

- Have children choose a nonfiction book for independent reading. (See the **Theme Bibliography** on pages T8–T9.) After reading, ask children to orally summarize the book. Provide time for children to comment on their reactions to the book.

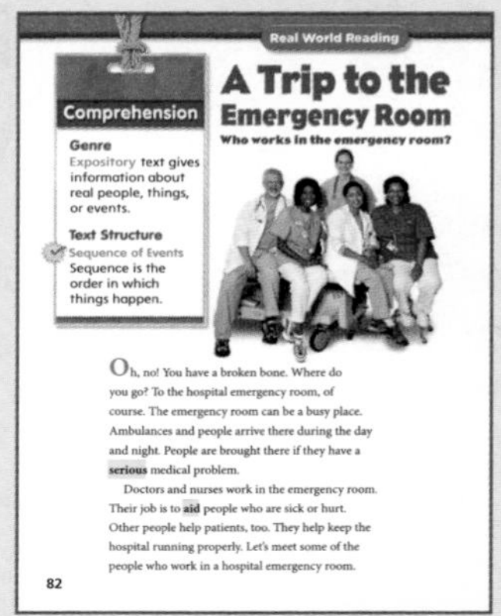

Real World Reading

A Trip to the Emergency Room

Who works in the emergency room?

Comprehension

Genre: Expository text gives information about real people, things, or events.

Text Structure: Sequence of Events. Sequence is the order in which things happen.

Oh, no! You have a broken bone. Where do you go? To the hospital emergency room, of course. The emergency room can be a busy place. Ambulances and people arrive there during the day and night. People are brought there if they have a **serious** medical problem.

Doctors and nurses work in the emergency room. Their job is to **aid** people who are sick or hurt. Other people help patients, too. They help keep the hospital running properly. Let's meet some of the people who work in a hospital emergency room.

82

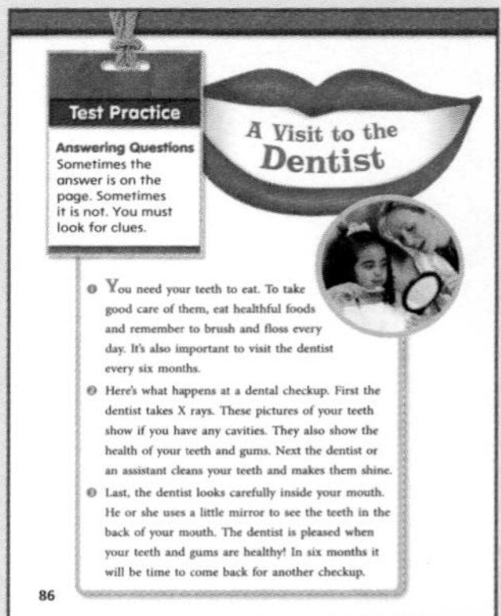

Test Practice

Answering Questions: Sometimes the answer is on the page. Sometimes it is not. You must look for clues.

A Visit to the Dentist

You need your teeth to eat. To take good care of them, eat healthful foods and remember to brush and floss every day. It's also important to visit the dentist every six months.

Here's what happens at a dental checkup. First the dentist takes X rays. These pictures of your teeth show if you have any cavities. They also show the health of your teeth and gums. Next the dentist or an assistant cleans your teeth and makes them shine.

Last, the dentist looks carefully inside your mouth. He or she uses a little mirror to see the teeth in the back of your mouth. The dentist is pleased when your teeth and gums are healthy! In six months it will be time to come back for another checkup.

86

Student Book

End-of-Week Assessment

Progress Monitoring

Weekly Assessment

ASSESSED SKILLS

- Phonics: Vowel Digraphs; Suffixes *-ful*, *-less*
- Selection Vocabulary
- Comprehension: Sequence of Events
- Grammar: Irregular Verbs

Selection Test for* A Trip to the Emergency Room *Also Available.

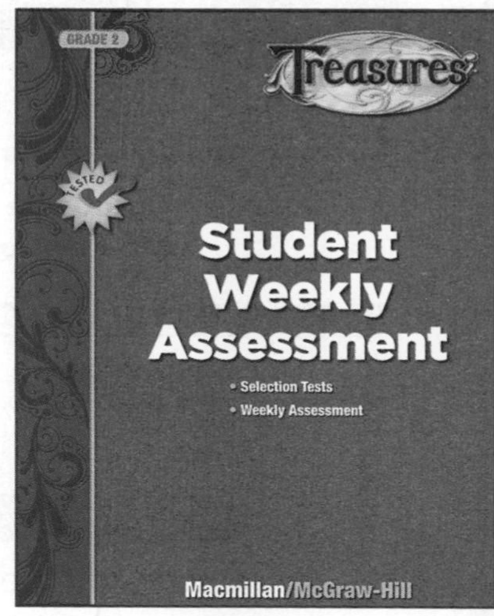

Student Weekly Assessment Unit 4 Week 3

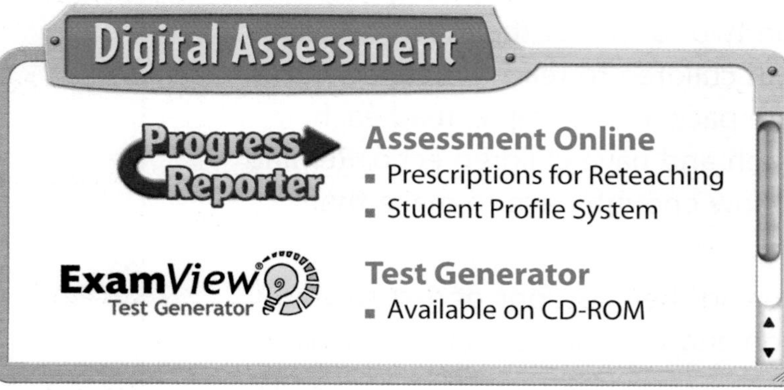

Fluency Assessment

Assess fluency for one group of students per week. Use the Oral Fluency Record Sheet to track the number of words read correctly. Fluency goals for all students:

62–82 words correct per minute (WCPM)

Approaching Level	Weeks 1, 3, 5
On Level	Weeks 2, 4
Beyond Level	Week 6

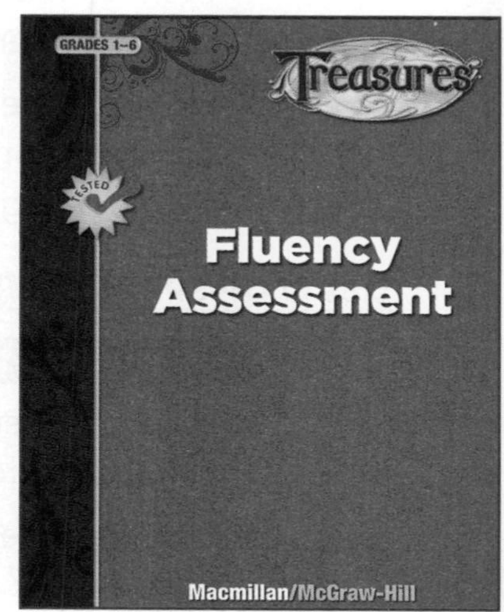

Fluency Assessment

DIBELS LINK

PROGRESS MONITORING

Use your DIBELS results to inform instruction.

IF

DIBELS Oral **R**eading **F**luency (**DORF**) 0–67

THEN

Evaluate for Intervention

TPRI LINK

PROGRESS MONITORING

Use your TPRI scores to inform instruction.

IF

Graphophonemic Knowledge	Still Developing
Reading Fluency/Accuracy	Reading Grade 2, Story 4 Less Than 75 WCPM
Reading Comprehension Questions	0–3 correct

THEN

Evaluate for Intervention

Diagnose		Prescribe
Review the assessment answers with students. Have them correct their errors. Then provide additional instruction as needed.		
	IF...	**THEN...**
PHONICS AND SPELLING Vowel Digraphs *oo, ui, ew, ue, u, ou, oe* Suffixes *-ful, -less*	0–1 items correct . . .	LOG ON Online Practice: Go to **www.macmillanmh.com**. See **Phonics Intervention Teacher's Edition.** See Sound-Spelling Fluency and mixed review blending lines in upcoming lessons.
VOCABULARY WORDS **VOCABULARY STRATEGY** Dictionary: Homophones	0–1 items correct . . .	See **Phonics Intervention Teacher's Edition.** SPIRAL REVIEW See Vocabulary review lessons Unit 4, Week 4.
COMPREHENSION Sequence of Events	0–1 items correct . . .	See **Comprehension Intervention Teacher's Edition.** SPIRAL REVIEW See Sequence of Events lessons Unit 4, Week 5.
GRAMMAR Irregular Verbs	0–1 items correct . . .	See the **Grammar and Writing Handbook.**
FLUENCY	53–61 WCPM	AUDIO CD Fluency Solutions Audio CD
	0–52 WCPM	See **Fluency Intervention Teacher's Edition.**

Response to Intervention

To place students in Tier 2 or Tier 3 Intervention use the *Diagnostic Assessment.*

- Phonemic Awareness
- Phonics
- Vocabulary
- Comprehension
- Fluency

Week 4 ★ At a Glance

Priority Skills and Concepts

Comprehension
- **Genre:** Expository
- **Strategy:** Analyze Text Structure
- **Skill:** Sequence of Events
- **Use Illustrations/Photos**

High-Frequency Words
- ***below, city, own***

Oral Vocabulary
- **Build Robust Vocabulary:** ***baffled, compassion, daring, lunge, survive***

Vocabulary
- ***young, examines, mammal, normal, hunger, rescued***
- **Strategy:** Context Clues/Antonyms

Fluency
- **Phrasing**

Phonemic Awareness
- **Phoneme Segmentation**

Phonics/Spelling
- **Vowel Diagraph** *oo, ou*: ***shook, hook, crook, good, should, brook, foot, soot, could, would, fruit, glue, below, city, own***

Grammar/Mechanics
- **Irregular Verbs**
- **Letter Punctuation**

Writing
- **Friendly Letter**
- **Important Details**
- **Trait:** Ideas

Key

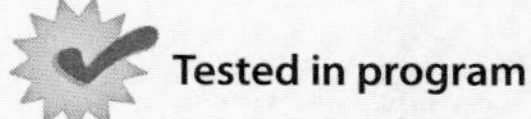

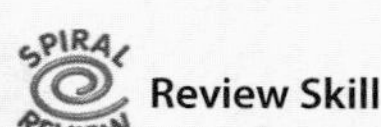

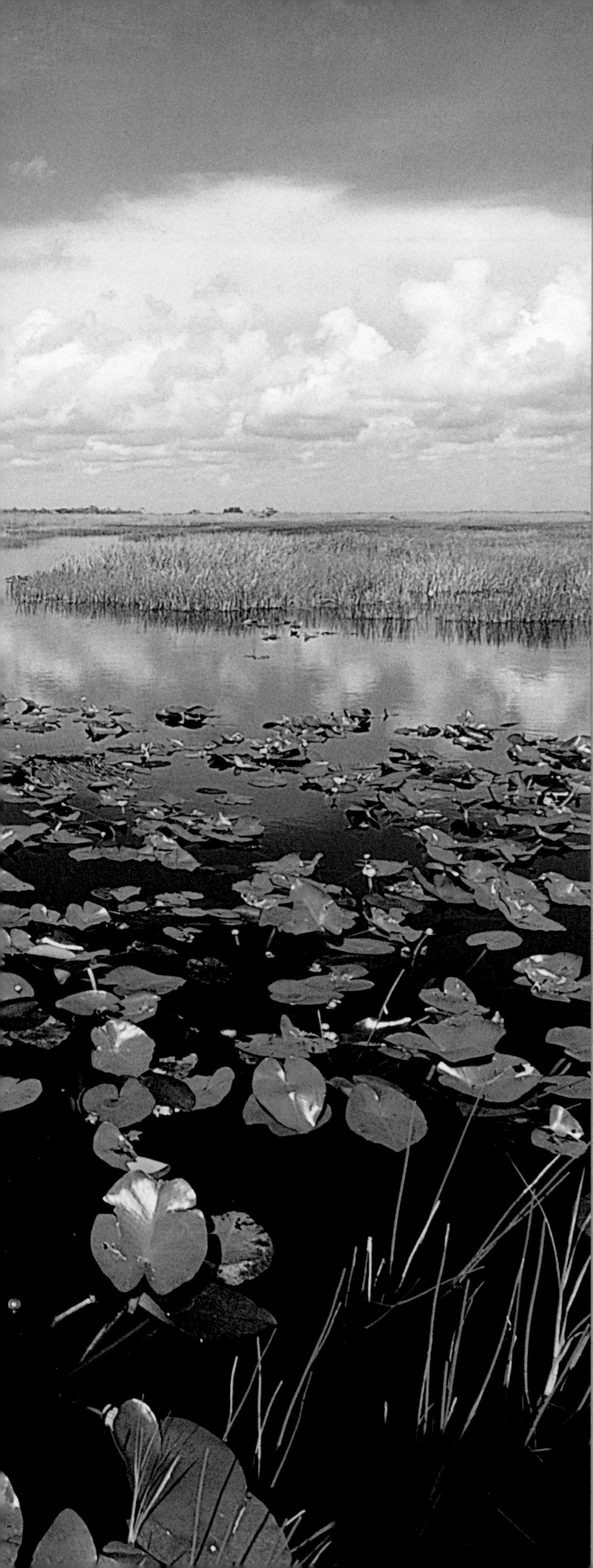

Digital Learning

Digital solutions to help plan and implement instruction.

Teacher Resources

LOG ON

ONLINE www.macmillanmh.com

- **Teacher's Edition**
  - Lesson Planner and Resources also on CD-ROM
- **Formative Assessment**
  - ExamView® on CD-ROM also available
- **Instructional Resources**
  - Unit Videos
  - Classroom Presentation Toolkit

- **Professional Development**
  - Video Library

Student Resources

LOG ON

ONLINE www.macmillanmh.com

- **Interactive Student Book**

- **Leveled Reader Database**
- **Activities**
  - Research Toolkit
  - Oral Language Activities
  - Vocabulary/Spelling Activities

Listening Library

- Recordings of Student Books and Leveled Readers

Fluency Solutions

- Fluency Modeling and Practice

Weekly Literature

Theme: Community Teams

Student Book

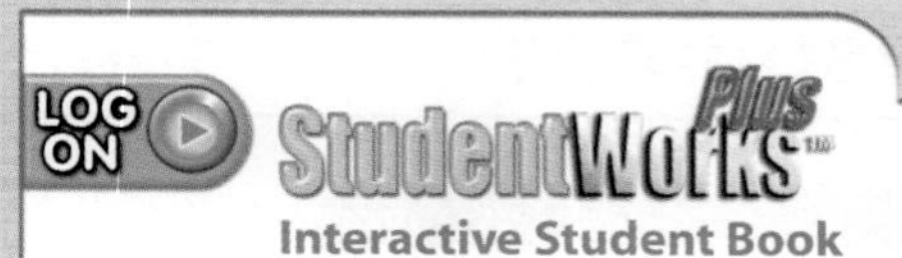

Interactive Student Book

- Word-by-Word Reading
- Summaries in Multiple Languages
- Comprehension Questions

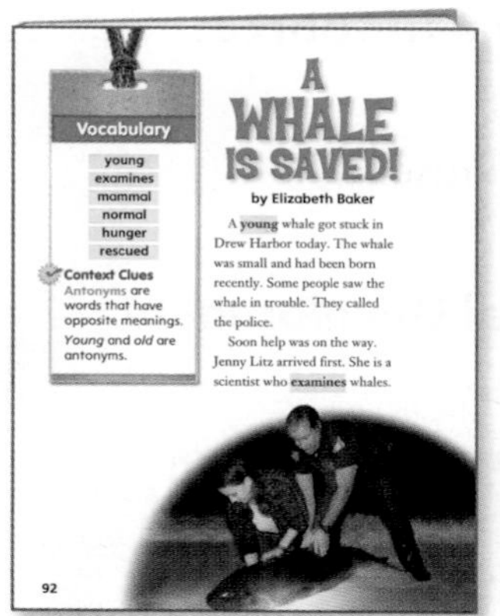

Preteach Vocabulary and Comprehension

Genre Expository

Main Selection

Genre Expository

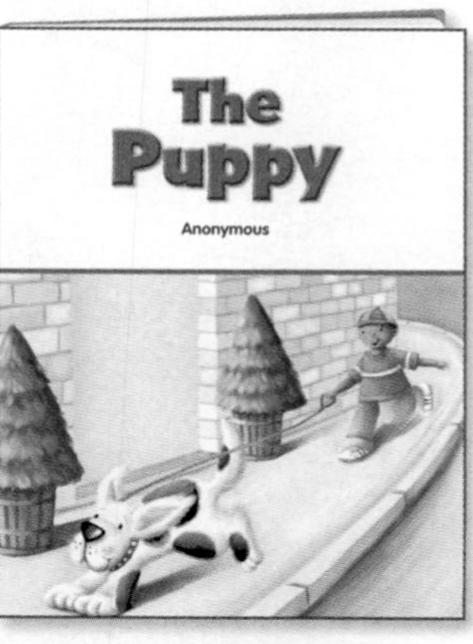

Paired Selection

Genre Poetry

Support Literature

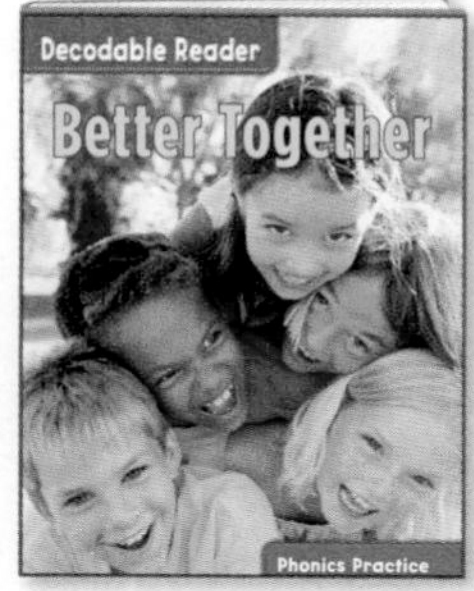

Decodable Reader Library

- One decodable read each week

Oral Vocabulary Cards

- Listening Comprehension
- Build Robust Vocabulary

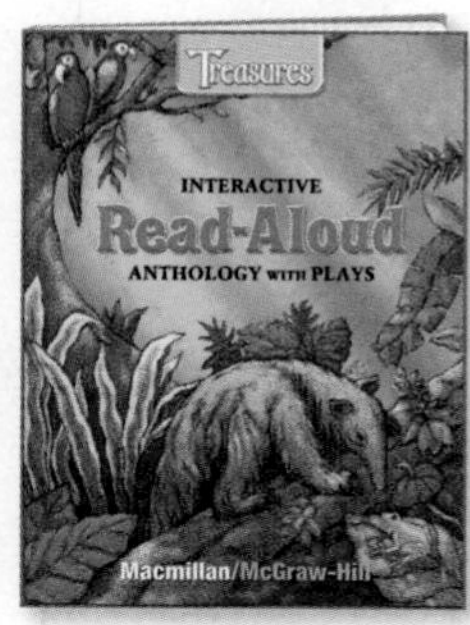

Interactive Read-Aloud Anthology

- Listening Comprehension
- Readers Theater Plays for Fluency

Resources for Differentiated Instruction

Leveled Readers: Science

GR Levels H-O

Genre	Expository

- Same Theme
- Same Vocabulary
- Same Comprehension Skills

Approaching Level

On Level

Beyond Level

ELL

Leveled Reader Database
Go to **www.macmillanmh.com.**

Leveled Practice

Approaching

On Level

Beyond

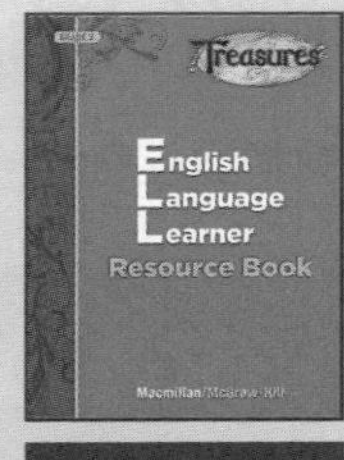

ELL

Leveled Classroom Library

Approaching

On Level

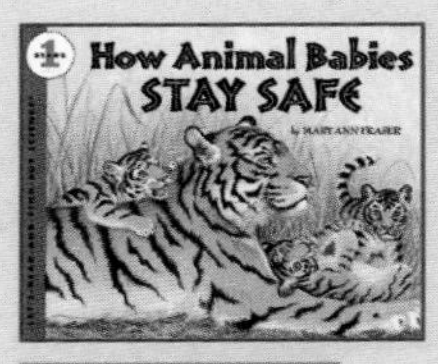

Beyond

Response to Intervention

- Phonemic Awareness
- Phonics
- Vocabulary
- Comprehension
- Fluency

Assessment

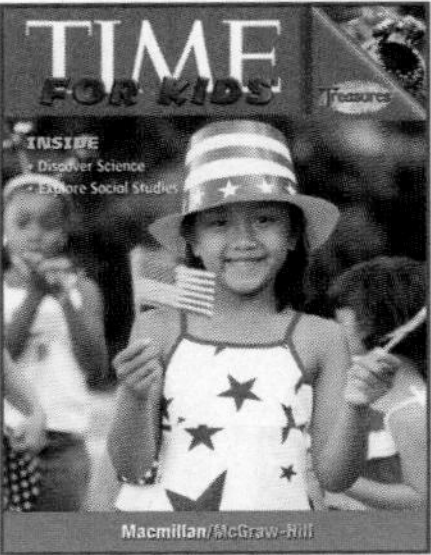

Time For Kids

- Teacher's Edition
- Apply Answering Questions Strategies

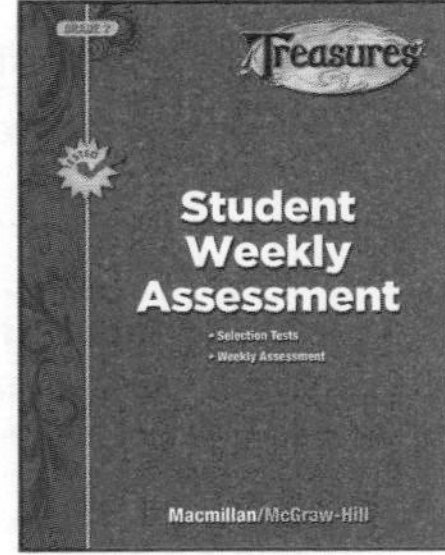

Weekly Assessment

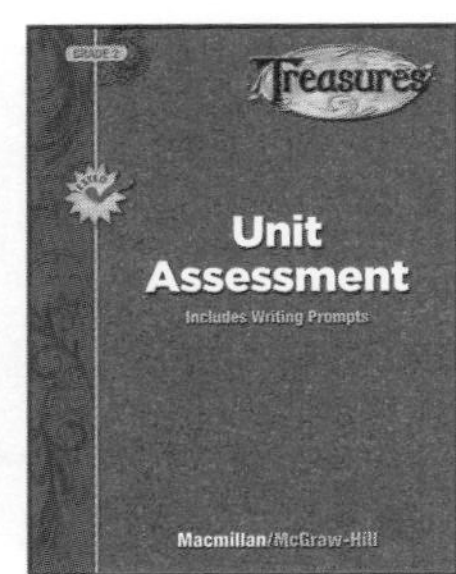

Unit Assessment

Benchmark Assessment

HOME-SCHOOL CONNECTION

- Family letters in English and Spanish
- Take-home stories and activities

Online Homework
www.macmillanmh.com

Suggested Lesson Plan

LOG ON

Go to www.macmillanmh.com for Online Lesson Planner

Professional Development Video Library

A Harbor Seal Pup Grows Up, pp. 94/95–112/113

WHOLE GROUP	DAY 1	DAY 2
ORAL LANGUAGE • Oral Vocabulary • Listening Comprehension • Phonemic Awareness	**Focus Question** How do different people in your town work together to accomplish a goal? Build Background, 90M **Oral Vocabulary** *baffled, compassion, daring, lunge, survive*, 91A Oral Vocabulary Cards "The Woman, the Tiger, and the Jackal" **Phonemic Awareness** Phoneme Segmentation, 91B	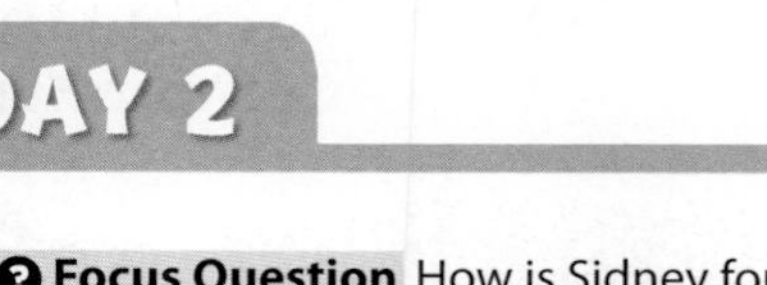 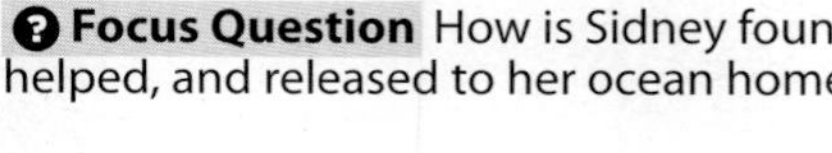 **Focus Question** How is Sidney found, helped, and released to her ocean home? 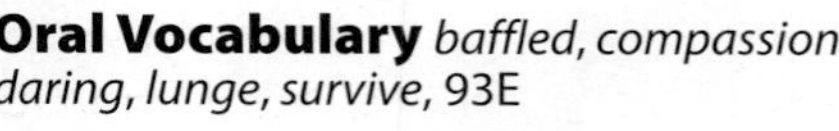 **Oral Vocabulary** *baffled, compassion, daring, lunge, survive*, 93E  **Phonemic Awareness** Phoneme Blending, 93
WORD STUDY • Phonics • Spelling • Vocabulary	**Phonics** Vowel Digraph *oo, ou*, 91C Practice Book, 20 **Spelling** Pretest: Words with Vowel Digraph *oo, ou*, 91E Spelling, 73 **Vocabulary** *examines, hunger, mammal, normal, rescued, young*, 91G **Strategy:** Context Clues/Antonyms Practice Book, 207	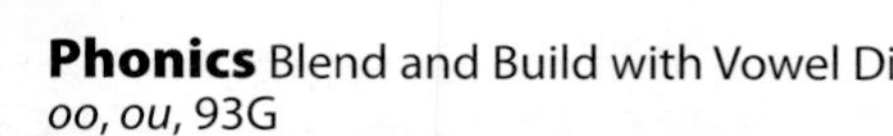 **Phonics** Blend and Build with Vowel Digraph *oo, ou*, 93G **Spelling** Word Sort with *oo, ou*, 93I Spelling, 74 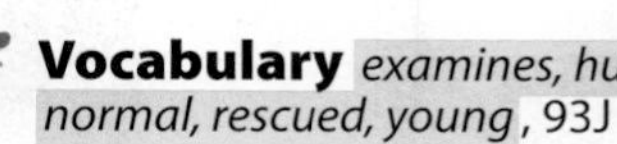 **Vocabulary** *examines, hunger, mammal, normal, rescued, young*, 93J 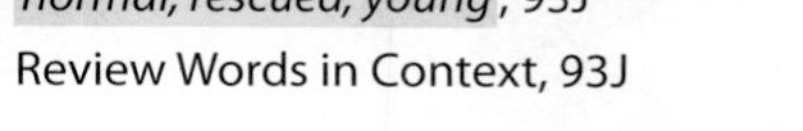 Review Words in Context, 93J
READING • Comprehension • Fluency	**Read** Decodable Reader, *Flip and Spots*, 91F Flip and Spots (Decodable Reader) **Comprehension**, 93A–93B "A Whale Is Saved," 92/93 **Strategy:** Analyze Text Structure **Skill:** Identify Sequence of Events **Fluency** Build Fluency, 91C	**Read** *A Harbor Seal Pup Grows Up*, 94/95–112/113 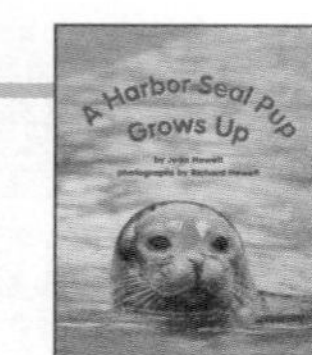 Student Book **Comprehension**, 93K–115A **Strategy:** Analyze Text Structure **Skill:** Identify Sequence of Events Practice Book, 209–210 **Fluency** Build Fluency, 93H
LANGUAGE ARTS • Writing • Grammar	**Writing** **Daily Writing** Look at the picture. Write about what you see, 90M Expository: Friendly Letter, 93D **Grammar** Irregular Verbs, 93C Grammar, 91	**Writing** **Daily Writing** Imagine you are a rescued ocean animal. Write a paragraph or a poem about your experience, 93E Prewrite a Friendly Letter, 115C **Grammar** Irregular Verbs, 115B Grammar, 92
ASSESSMENT • Informal/Formal	**Quick Check** Phonics, 91D Vocabulary, 92/93	**Quick Check** Comprehension, 112/113

SMALL GROUP Lesson Plan — **Differentiated Instruction 90G–90H**

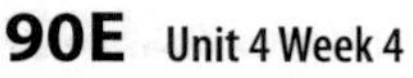

Priority Skills

Phonics	Vocabulary	Comprehension	Writing
Vowel Digraph *oo, ou*	**Words:** *examines, hunger, mammal, normal, rescued, young* **Strategy:** Context Clues/ Antonyms	**Strategy:** Analyze Sentence Structure **Skill:** Identify Sequence of Events	How-to Explanation

DAY 3

Focus Question Did you think the story of a real seal was more interesting than the story of an imaginary seal would have been? Why or why not?

Read Aloud "A Thousand Pails of Water," 115D

Oral Vocabulary *baffled, compassion, daring, lunge, survive*, 115K

Phonemic Awareness Identify Syllables, 115E

Phonics Blend and Build with Vowel Digraph *oo, ou*, 115F
Inflectional Ending *-ing*, 115G
Practice Book, 211

Spelling Word Sort, 115H
Spelling, 75

Vocabulary *examines, hunger, mammal, normal, rescued, young*

Strategy: Context Clues/Antonyms, 115J

Practice Book, 212

Read A *Harbor Seal Pup Grows Up*, 94/95–112/113

Student Book

Comprehension
Review Skill: Illustrations/ Photos, 115N

Fluency Repeated Reading: Prosody/ Phrasing, 115L
Practice Book, 213

Writing

Daily Writing Respond to the Read-Aloud by writing about what you would do if a whale needed help, 115D
Writing Trait: Ideas, 115Q
Important Details, 115P
Draft a Friendly Letter, 115Q

Grammar **Mechanics:** Letter Punctuation, 115O
Grammar, 93

Quick Check Fluency, 115M

DAY 4

Focus Question How is caring for a seal pup like caring for a puppy or a dog?

Oral Vocabulary *baffled, compassion, daring, lunge, survive*, 115R

Phonemic Awareness Phoneme Blending, 115S

Phonics Blend and Build with Vowel Digraph *oo, ou*, 115T

Spelling Practice Words with Vowel Digraph *oo, ou*, 115U

Spelling, 76

Vocabulary *examines, hunger, mammal, normal, rescued, young*

Review Words in Context, 115V

Read "The Puppy," 116/117

Student Book

Comprehension, 115W
Literary Element: Similes

Practice Book, 214

Fluency Build Fluency, 155U

Writing

Daily Writing Imagine you are a lost seal and people are helping to return you to the ocean. Tell how you feel, 115R

Revise and Proofread a Friendly Letter, 117D

Grammar Irregular Verbs, 117B
Grammar, 94

Quick Check Spelling, 115U

DAY 5
Review and Assess

Focus Question How will summarizing help you read and understand another selection?

Oral Vocabulary *baffled, compassion, daring, lunge, survive*, 119A

Phonemic Awareness Identify Syllables, 119C

Phonics Blend and Build with Vowel Digraph *oo, ou*, 119C

Spelling Posttest, 119E

Vocabulary *examines, hunger, mammal, normal, rescued, young*, 119F

Read Self-Selected Reading, 90J

Student Book

Comprehension, 119G
Strategy: Analyze Text Structure
Skill: Identify Sequence of Events

Fluency Repeated Reading: Prosody/ Phrasing, 119B

Writing

Daily Writing Write a journal entry about what you did to help animals during one day on the job, 119F
Publish and Present a Friendly Letter, 119I
Speaking, Listening, and Viewing, 119J

Grammar Letter punctuation, Irregular Verbs, 119H
Grammar, 95

Weekly Assessment, 119KK–119LL

Differentiated Instruction

What do I do in small groups?

Focus on Skills

IF... students need additional instruction, practice, or extension based on your Quick Check observations for the following priority skills

 **Phonics/Word Study**
Variant Vowel *oo*, *ou*; Inflectional Endings *-ing*

 **Vocabulary Words**
examines, hunger, mammal, normal, rescued, young
Strategy: Context Clues: Antonyms

 **Comprehension**
Strategy: Analyze Text Structure
Skill: Identify Sequence of Events

 **Fluency**
Phonics, High-Frequency Words, Phrasing

THEN...

Approaching	Preteach and
English Learners	Reteach Skills
On Level	Practice
Beyond	Enrich and Accelerate Learning

Suggested Small Group Lesson Plan

	DAY 1	DAY 2
Approaching Level • **Preteach/Reteach** Tier 2 **Tier 2 Instruction**	• Phonemic Awareness, 119K • Phonics, 119K ELL • High-Frequency/Vocabulary, 119L • Decodable Reader, *Flip and Spots*, 119L	• Phonemic Awareness, 119Q • Phonics, 119Q ELL • High-Frequency/Vocabulary, 119R • Leveled Reader Lesson 1, 119R
On Level • **Practice**	• Phonics, 119M ELL • Fluency, 119M ELL	• Leveled Reader Lesson 1, 119S ELL
Beyond Level • **Extend/Accelerate** Gifted Talented **Gifted and Talented**	• Phonics, 119N ELL • Vocabulary, 119N	• Leveled Reader Lesson 1, 119T • Analyze, 119T
ELL • **Build English Language Proficiency** • **See ELL in other levels.**	• Prepare to Read, 119O • Academic Language, 119O • Preteach Vocabulary, 119P	• Preteach Main Selection, 119U • Grammar, 119V

Focus on Leveled Readers

Levels H-O

Approaching

On Level

Beyond

ELL

Manipulatives

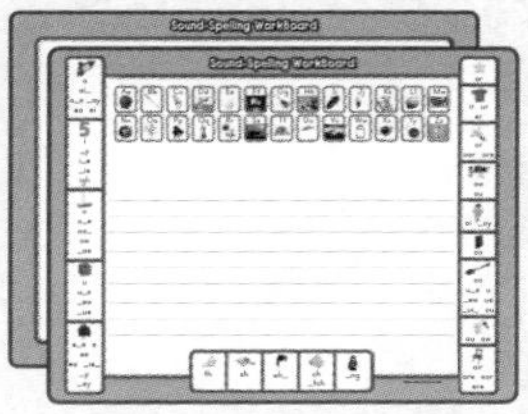

Sound-Spelling WorkBoards

Sound-Spelling Cards

Photo Cards

High-Frequency Word Cards

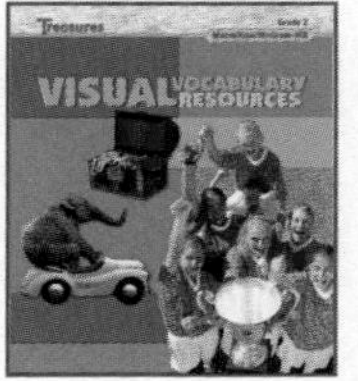
Visual Vocabulary Resources

Science

Teacher's Annotated Edition

Identify external characteristics of plants and animal that allow their needs to be met; compare the ways living organisms depend on each other and on their environments.

Additional Leveled Readers

Leveled Reader Database
www.macmillanmh.com

Search by

- Comprehension Skill
- Content Area
- Genre
- Text Feature
- Guided Reading Level
- Reading Recovery Level
- Lexile Score
- Benchmark Level

Subscription also available.

DAY 3	DAY 4	DAY 5
• Phonemic Awareness, 119W • Phonics, 119W ELL • High-Frequency/Vocabulary, 119X • Leveled Reader Lesson 2, 119X • Book Talk, 119X	• Phonemic Awareness, 119CC • Phonics, 119CC ELL • High-Frequency/Vocabulary, 119DD • Fluency, 119DD • Review Leveled Readers, 119DD	• Oral Language, 119GG ELL • Fluency, 119HH • Self-Selected Independent Reading, 119HH
• Leveled Reader Lesson 2, 119Y • Fluency, 119Y • Book Talk, 119Y	• Fluency, 119EE	• Self-Selected Independent Reading, 119II ELL
• Leveled Reader Lesson 2, 119Z • Synthesize and Evaluate, 119Z • Fluency, 119Z • Book Talk, 119Z	• Fluency, 119EE	• Self-Selected Independent Reading, 119II • Evaluate, 119II
• Leveled Reader Lesson 1, 119AA • Writing/Spelling, 119BB	• Preteach Paired Selection, 119FF • Leveled Reader Lesson 2, 119FF	• Fluency, 119JJ • Self-Selected Independent Reading, 119JJ

What do I do with the rest of my class?

- Literacy Workstations
- Leveled Reader Activities
- Practice Book and Reproducibles
- Online Activities
- English Language Learner Practice Book

Classroom Management Tools

Weekly Contract

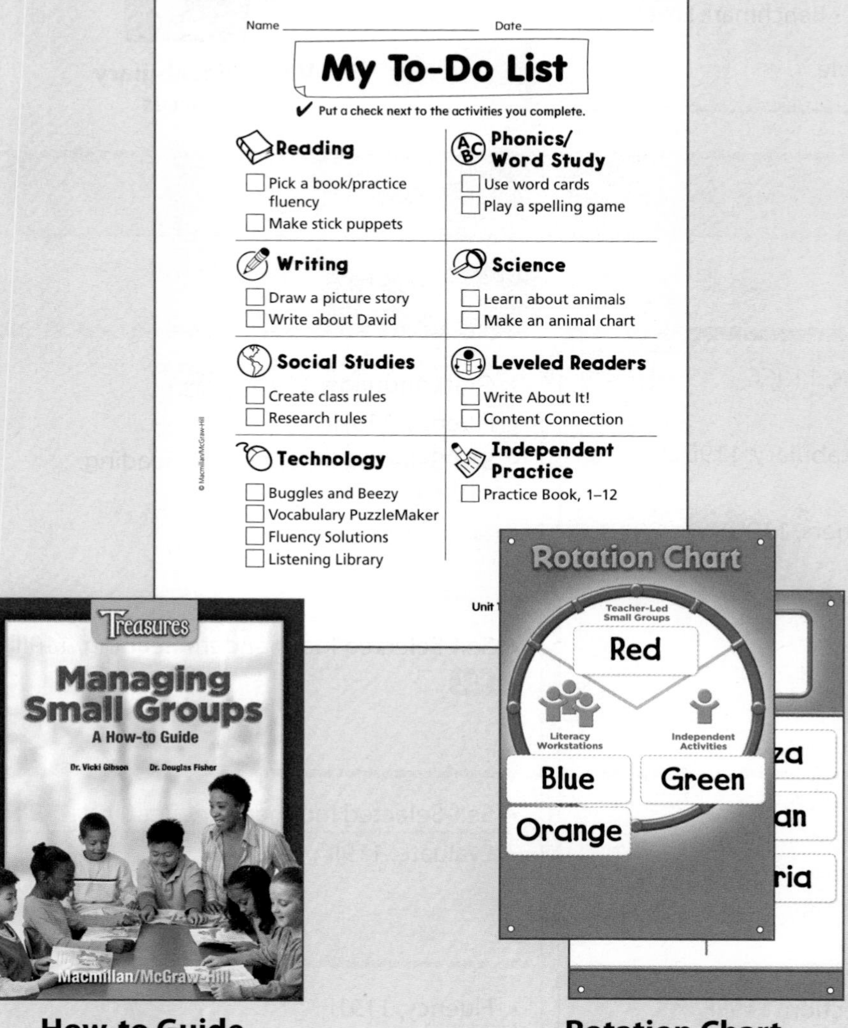

Name ____________ Date ____________

My To-Do List

✔ Put a check next to the activities you complete.

Reading
- ☐ Pick a book/practice fluency
- ☐ Make stick puppets

Phonics/ Word Study
- ☐ Use word cards
- ☐ Play a spelling game

Writing
- ☐ Draw a picture story
- ☐ Write about David

Science
- ☐ Learn about animals
- ☐ Make an animal chart

Social Studies
- ☐ Create class rules
- ☐ Research rules

Leveled Readers
- ☐ Write About It!
- ☐ Content Connection

Technology
- ☐ Buggles and Beezy
- ☐ Vocabulary PuzzleMaker
- ☐ Fluency Solutions
- ☐ Listening Library

Independent Practice
- ☐ Practice Book, 1–12

How-to Guide

Rotation Chart

Digital Learning

StudentWorks Plus
- Summaries in Multiple Languages
- Word-by-Word Reading
- Comprehension Questions

Meet the Author/Illustrator

Joe Cepeda
- Joe remembers having bruises from trying to get the candy that fell out of piñatas at childhood birthday parties.
- Joe has illustrated several books.
- He lives in Southern California with his family.

Other books illustrated by Joe Cepeda
- Herron, Carolivia. *Nappy Hair.* New York: Bantam Doubleday Dell Books for Young Readers, 1999.
- Lester, Julius. *What a Truly Cool World.* New York: Scholastic, Inc., 1999.

- Read Other Books by the Author or Illustrator

Leveled Practice

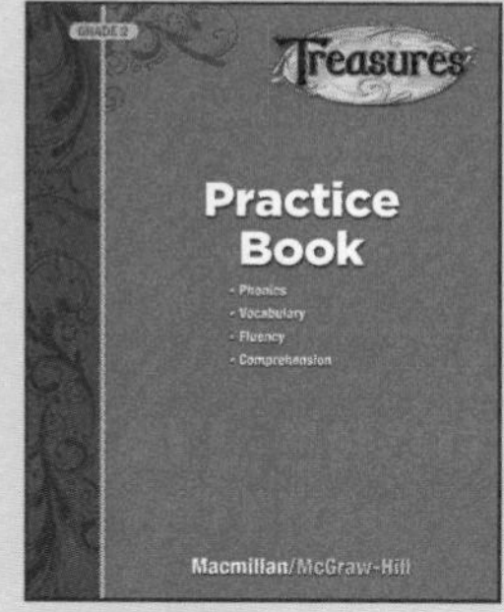

On Level

Treasures
English Language Learner Resource Book
Macmillan/McGraw-Hill

ELL

Also Available:

Approaching Reproducible

Beyond Reproducible

Independent Activities

ONLINE INSTRUCTION www.macmillanmh.com

Oral Language Activities

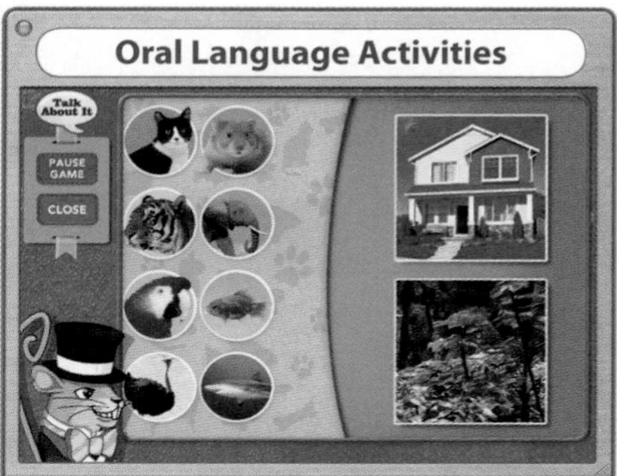

- Focus on Vocabulary and Concepts
- English Language Learner Support

Leveled Reader Database

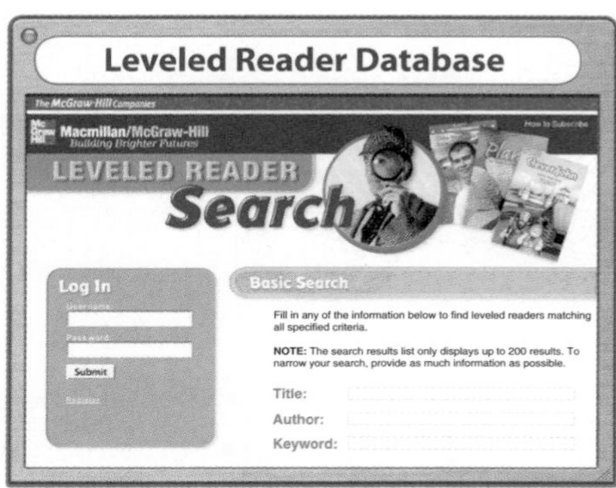

- Leveled Reader Database
- Search titles by level, skill, content area, and more

Vocabulary/Spelling Activities

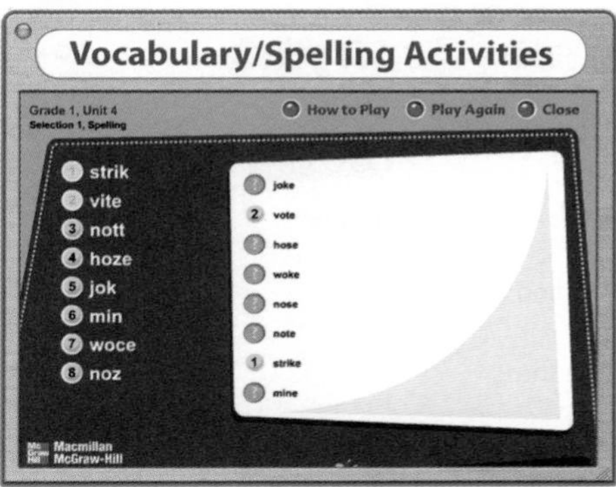

- Differentiated Lists and Activities

Research Toolkit

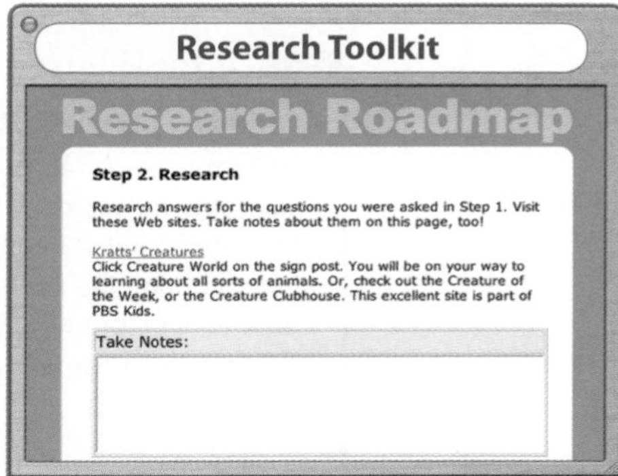

- Research Roadmap
- Research and Presentation Tools
- Theme Launcher Video
- Links to Science and Social Studies

Available on CD

LISTENING LIBRARY
Recordings of selections
- Main Selections
- Paired Selections
- Leveled Readers
- ELL Readers

NEW ADVENTURES WITH BUGGLES AND BEEZY
Phonemic awareness and phonics activities

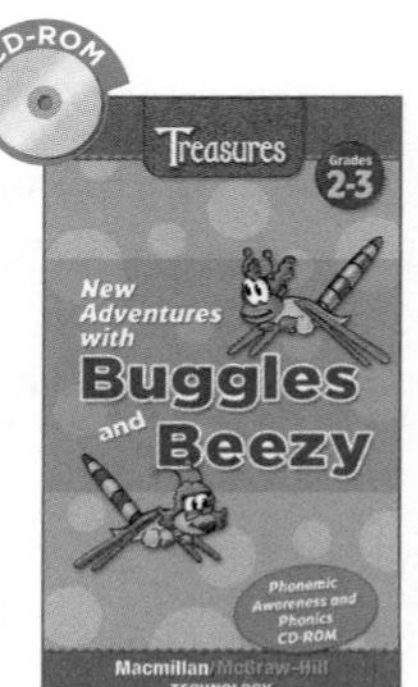

FLUENCY SOLUTIONS
Recorded passages at two speeds for modeling and practicing fluency

Leveled Reader Activities

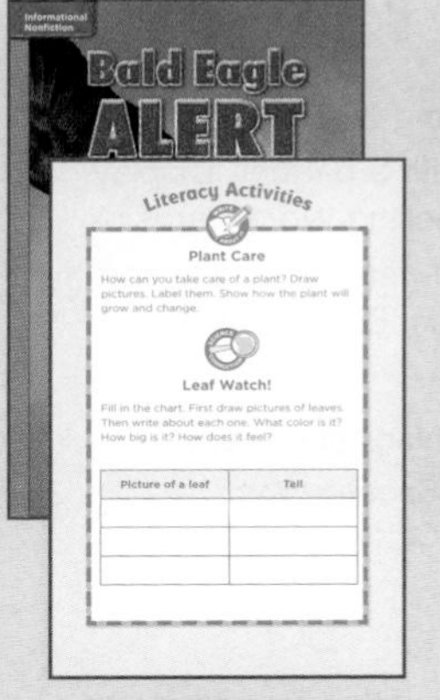

Approaching

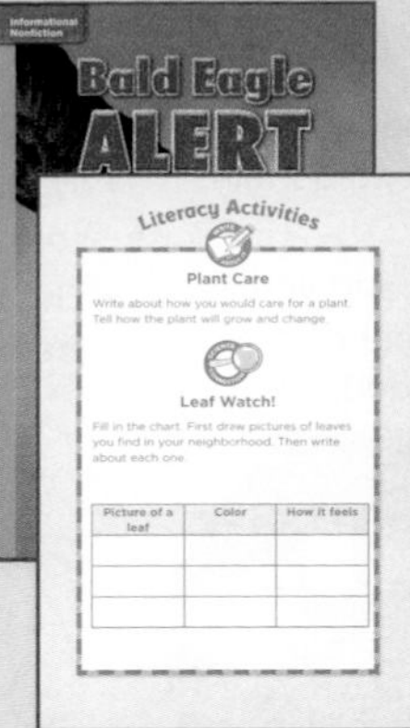

On Level

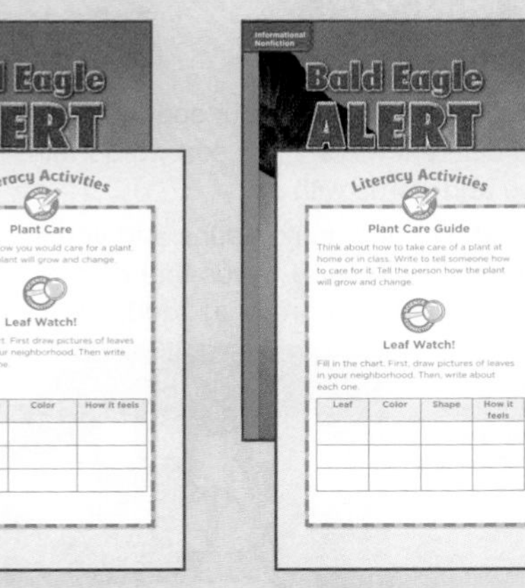

Beyond

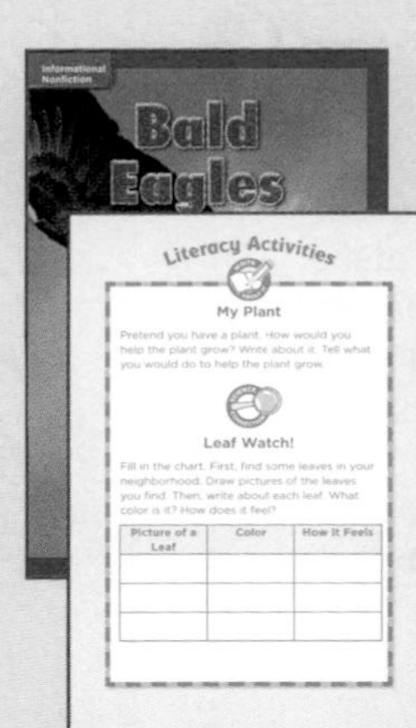

ELL

See inside cover for all Leveled Readers.

Literacy Workstations

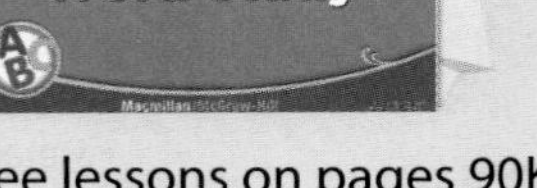

See lessons on pages 90K–90L

What do I do with the rest of my class?

Reading

Objectives

- Read aloud fluently and accurately
- Ask a partner why parts in the story were interesting
- Describe how Sidney changed throughout the story

Phonics/Word Study

Objectives

- Identify and explain common antonyms
- Sort words by vowel sounds

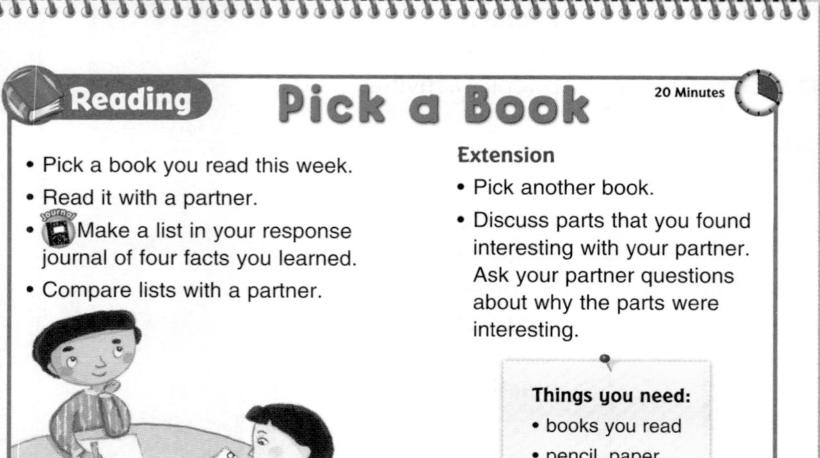

Reading — **Pick a Book** — 20 Minutes

- Pick a book you read this week.
- Read it with a partner.
- Make a list in your response journal of four facts you learned.
- Compare lists with a partner.

Extension

- Pick another book.
- Discuss parts that you found interesting with your partner. Ask your partner questions about why the parts were interesting.

Things you need:

- books you read
- pencil, paper
- response journal

1. A seal is a mammal.

For more book titles, go to the Author/Illustrator section of www.macmillanmh.com

Listening Library

37

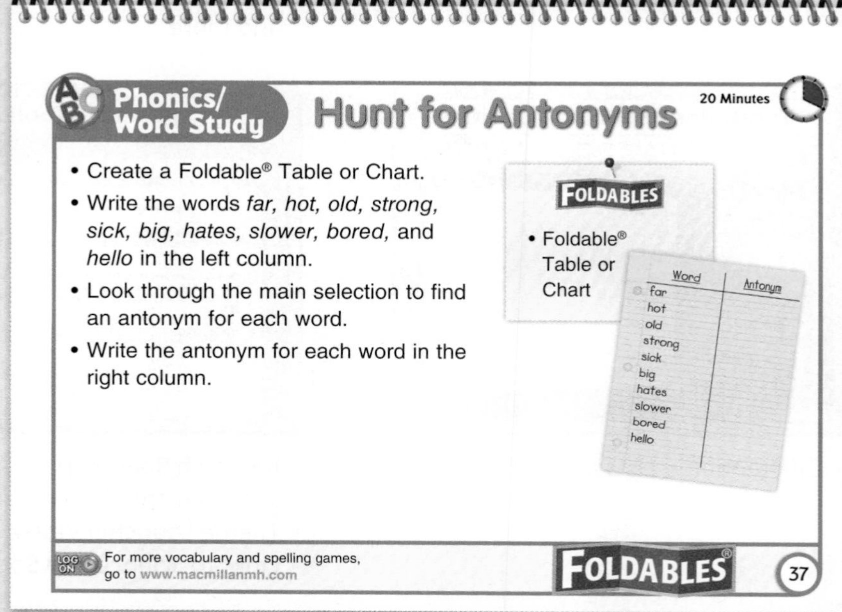

Phonics/Word Study — **Hunt for Antonyms** — 20 Minutes

- Create a Foldable® Table or Chart.
- Write the words *far, hot, old, strong, sick, big, hates, slower, bored,* and *hello* in the left column.
- Look through the main selection to find an antonym for each word.
- Write the antonym for each word in the right column.

FOLDABLES

- Foldable® Table or Chart

Word	Antonym
far	
hot	
old	
strong	
sick	
big	
hates	
slower	
bored	
hello	

For more vocabulary and spelling games, go to www.macmillanmh.com

FOLDABLES®

37

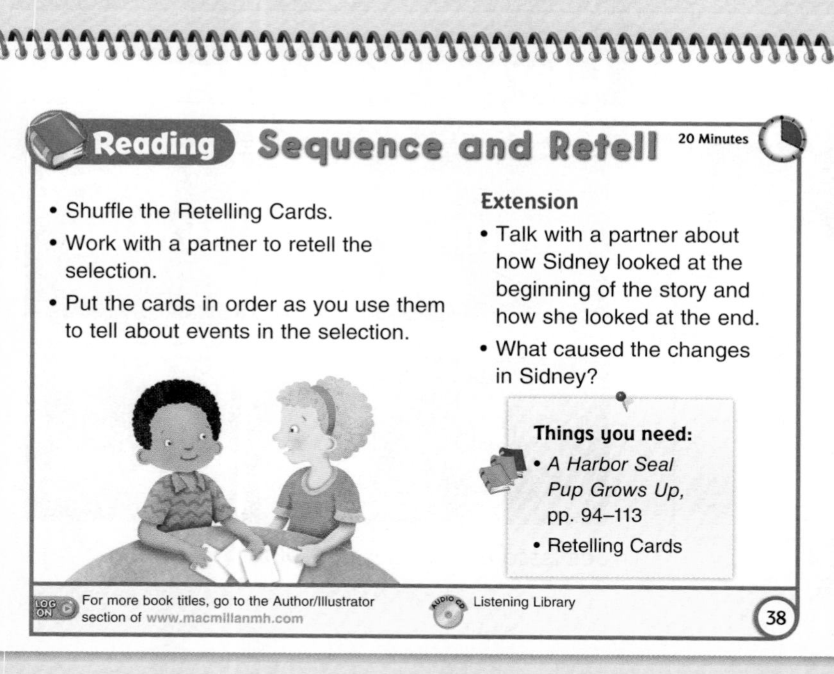

Reading — **Sequence and Retell** — 20 Minutes

- Shuffle the Retelling Cards.
- Work with a partner to retell the selection.
- Put the cards in order as you use them to tell about events in the selection.

Extension

- Talk with a partner about how Sidney looked at the beginning of the story and how she looked at the end.
- What caused the changes in Sidney?

Things you need:

- *A Harbor Seal Pup Grows Up,* pp. 94–113
- Retelling Cards

For more book titles, go to the Author/Illustrator section of www.macmillanmh.com

Listening Library

38

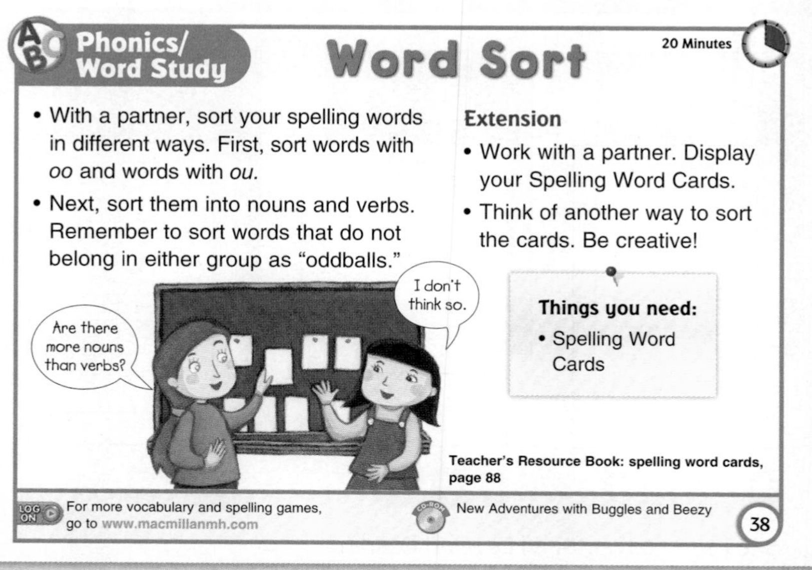

Phonics/Word Study — **Word Sort** — 20 Minutes

- With a partner, sort your spelling words in different ways. First, sort words with *oo* and words with *ou.*
- Next, sort them into nouns and verbs. Remember to sort words that do not belong in either group as "oddballs."

Are there more nouns than verbs?

I don't think so.

Extension

- Work with a partner. Display your Spelling Word Cards.
- Think of another way to sort the cards. Be creative!

Things you need:

- Spelling Word Cards

Teacher's Resource Book: spelling word cards, page 88

For more vocabulary and spelling games, go to www.macmillanmh.com

New Adventures with Buggles and Beezy

38

Literacy Workstation Flip Charts

Writing

Objectives

- Write a brief narrative using a sequence of events
- Write an alternative ending to the selection

Content Literacy

Objectives

- Make a list of jobs that show characteristics of good citizenship in justice, truth, equality, and responsibility
- Compare how different animals are able to meet their needs

Writing — Caring for Sidney

20 Minutes

- Write about how Sidney was cared for at the sea mammal center in your response journal.
- Describe what Peter and Nicole did to make her healthy and strong.
- Share your writing with a classmate.

Sidney was weak and hungry. So Peter put a tube in her mouth.

Extension

- Think about why Peter may have chosen his job. Have you ever seen anyone on television or in the movies with this job?
- Write about a job helping animals or people.

Things you need:
- paper, pencil
- response journal
- crayons

Internet Research and Inquiry Activity
www.macmillanmh.com

37

Social Studies — Meaningful Jobs

20 Minutes

- Work with a partner. Talk about jobs where people work with animals.
- List two jobs. Write what you think people do in each job.
- Which job would you enjoy doing?

Extension

- With a partner, make a list of jobs that show characteristics of good citizenship, such as belief in justice, truth, equality, and responsibility for the common good.

Things you need:
- paper, pencil

37

Writing — Sidney's New Home

20 Minutes

- At the end of the selection, Sidney is in her ocean home. Write a paragraph that tells what you think Sidney's life will be like in her new home.
- Proofread your paragraph. Make sure your sentences are complete and correct.
- You may wish to add this writing to your portfolio.

Extension

- Share your writing with a classmate.
- Talk about other animal rescue stories you have read or heard about.

Things you need:
- pencil, paper

38

Science — All Kinds of Animals

20 Minutes

- Draw the animal web shown below. Add the names of other animals.
- Choose two animals from your web. Make a chart to show how they are alike and different.

dog — animals — gerbil

Extension

- Use the Internet or books. Find out other ways in which the two animals are alike and different.
- Add these facts to your chart.

Things you need:
- paper, pencil
- Internet or books

Internet Research and Inquiry Activity
www.macmillanmh.com

38

Day 1 At a Glance

WHOLE GROUP

Oral Language
- Build Background
- Oral Vocabulary

Phonemic Awareness
- Phoneme Segmentation

Phonics
- Vowel Digraphs *oo, ou*
- Build Fluency
- Spelling: Pretest: Words with *oo, ou*
- Read *Flip and Spots*

Vocabulary
- Teach Words in Context:
- Use Context Clues: Antonyms
- Read "A Whale Is Saved!"

Comprehension
- Strategy: Analyze Text Structure
- Skill: Sequence of Events

Language Arts
- Grammar: Irregular Verbs
- Writing: Expository

SMALL GROUP

- Differentiated Instruction, pages 119K–119JJ

Oral Vocabulary

Week 4

baffled	compassion
daring	lunge
survive	

Oral Language

Build Background

ACCESS PRIOR KNOWLEDGE
Discuss with children the idea of people helping animals in need. Tell them that people can work together to aid animals that are sick, injured, or lost. *Do you know anyone who has helped an animal?*

COMMUNITY TEAMS POEM
Read the poem "'Fire!, Fire!' Cried Mrs. McGuire!" and have children add stanzas and act out ways firefighters work as a team to help animals and people in need.

AUDIO CD

"Fire! Fire!" Cried Mrs. McGuire!

"Fire, Fire!"
Cried Mrs. McGuire.
"Where, Where?"
Asked Mrs. Blair.
"All over town!"
Said Mrs. Brown.
"Save us! Save us!"
Screamed Mrs. Davis.

The fire department
Got the call,
And the firemen saved
them one and all!

FOCUS QUESTION Read the question on **Student Book** page 91. Describe the photograph providing academic language. Point out that the animals are sea turtles. Talk about how the people are showing **compassion**, or caring, by returning the turtles to the wild.

Use the Picture Prompt

BUILD WRITING FLUENCY
Ask children to respond to the picture by writing in their Writer's Notebooks about helping animals in need. Children should write for eight minutes. Meet with children during individual Writing Conference time to provide feedback and revision assignments.

ELL ENGLISH LANGUAGE LEARNERS

Beginning

Respond Tell children about the photograph. *The people are working together. They are helping the turtles.* Then ask children to tell you about the photograph. Give children ample time to respond.

Intermediate

Describe Ask children to describe the photograph. *What are the people doing? How are they helping the turtles?* Elicit details to support children's responses.

Advanced

Expand Ask children to elaborate on the concept. Ask, *How are these people helping the turtles? Do you know people who help animals? Have you ever helped an animal?* Elicit details to support children's responses.

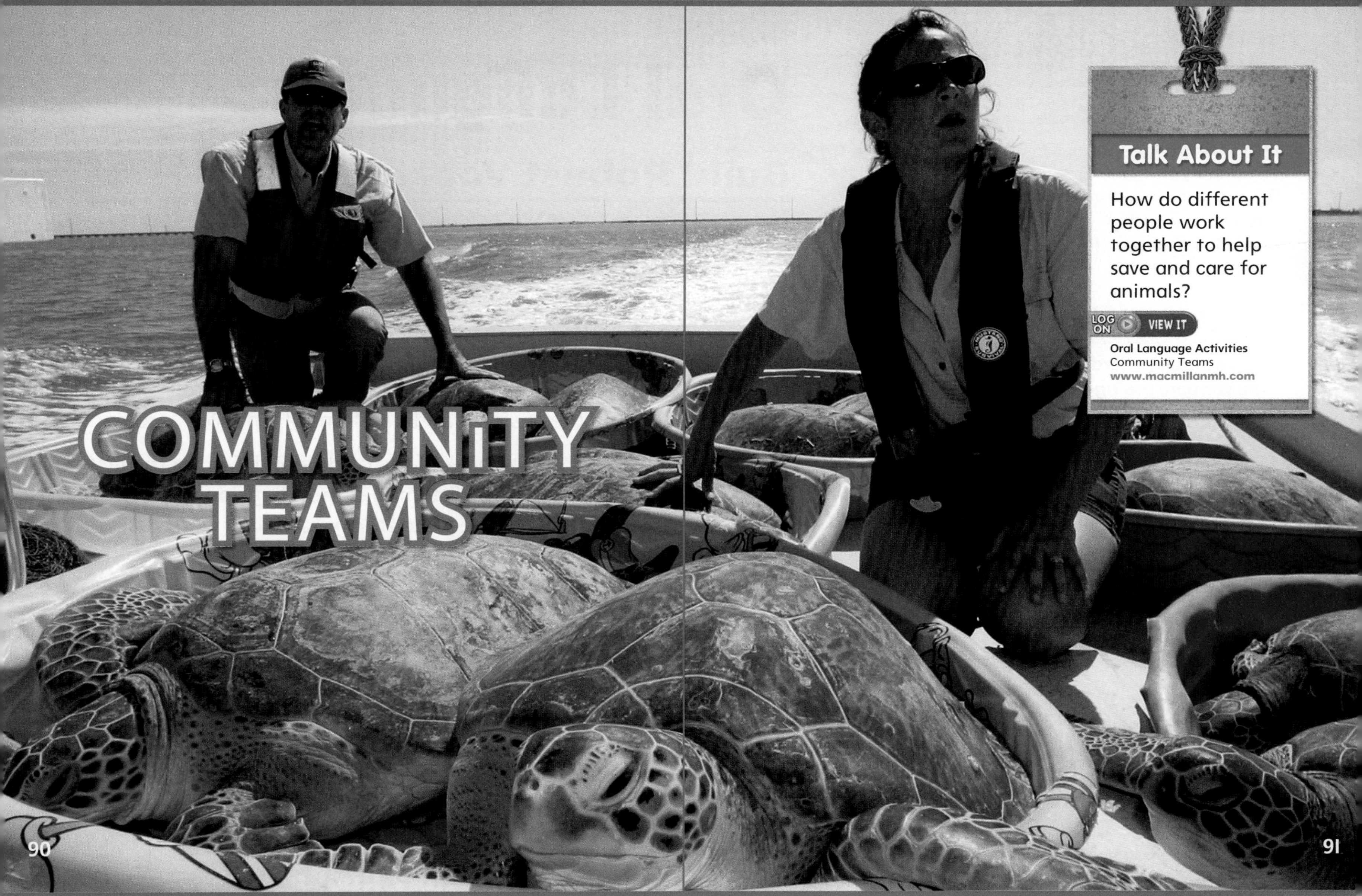
COMMUNITY TEAMS
Talk About It
How do different people work together to help save and care for animals?
LOG ON VIEW IT
Oral Language Activities
Community Teams
www.macmillanmh.com
90
91

Connect to the Unit Theme

People work together to help save animals in need, such as when an animal is sick or needs to be returned to its home in the wild.

CONNECT TO THEME
Ask children what they have learned so far about working together.

USE THEME FOLDABLE
Read aloud the **Big Idea** statement. Write **compassion** on the board. Remind children that *compassion* means "wanting to help people or animals in need." Read it aloud and have children repeat. Ask children to add it to their Unit Theme Foldables. Tell children that they will add pictures of people showing compassion throughout the week.

Dinah Zike's
FOLDABLES®
Study Organizer

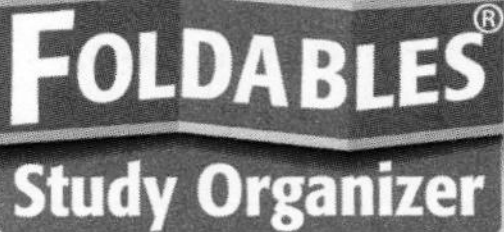

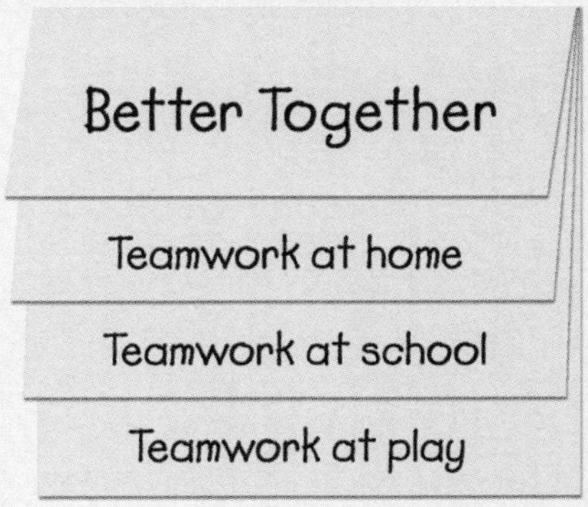
Better Together
Teamwork at home
Teamwork at school
Teamwork at play

Unit 4 Theme Foldable

Objectives

- Introduce oral vocabulary words
- Review last week's oral vocabulary words
- Read "The Woman, the Tiger, and the Jackal"

Materials

- Oral Vocabulary Cards: "The Woman, the Tiger, and the Jackal"

Oral Language

Build Robust Vocabulary

BUILD BACKGROUND Display "The Woman, The Tiger, and the Jackal" **Oral Vocabulary Card** 1 and read the title aloud. *We are going to read a folktale today about a tiger that is trapped in a hole. He promises a kind woman he will not eat her if she rescues him. Can tigers make promises? Why or why not? We will need to read and see if the tiger keeps his promise.* Remind children that a folktale is made-up story based on the customs and traditions of a people or region.

- Read the story on the back of the cards aloud. During the first reading, check children's listening comprehension using the Retell prompts on Card 4. Review the story vocabulary words using the routine below.

Oral Vocabulary Cards

Additional Vocabulary

To provide 15–20 minutes of additional vocabulary instruction, see **Oral Vocabulary Cards** 5-Day Plan. The pre- and post-tests for this week can be found on **Teacher's Resource Book** pages 245–263.

Vocabulary Routine

Use the routine below to discuss the meaning of each story word.

Define: If you are **baffled** by something, you are confused and don't understand it.
Example: *The game had so many rules that I was completely baffled.*
Ask: When have you felt baffled? PRIOR KNOWLEDGE

- When you have **compassion**, you want to help people or animals in need. *I feel compassion for the dogs at the animal shelter, so I volunteer there.* When do you feel compassion? What do you do to help? EXAMPLE
- If you are **daring**, you are not afraid to try something dangerous. *People who go rock climbing are daring.* Have you been daring? How? EXAMPLE
- To **lunge** means "to jump suddenly at someone or something." *My cat likes to lunge at a toy mouse.* What animals can lunge? EXAMPLE
- To **survive** means "to stay alive." *People need food and water to survive.* How can you help animals survive? EXPLANATION

Use the routine to review last week's words: *clever*, *comfort*, *urgent*, *recuperate*, and *sympathy*.

Phonemic Awareness

Phoneme Segmentation

Model

Show children how to segment phonemes in words.

I am going to say a word sound by sound. Listen carefully to all the sounds in the word *look*. The first sound is /l/, the second sound is /ů/, and the third sound is /k/. Now watch as I say each sound in the word *look* again and hold up one finger for each sound: /l/ /ů/ /k/.

How many sounds does *look* have? (3) Now say the word with me sound by sound: /l/ /ů/ /k/, *look*.

Repeat the routine, finding the three sounds in each of the words *book*, *shook*, *good*, *could*, and *would*.

Guided Practice/Practice

Have children practice segmenting phonemes with the examples provided. Do the first row with them.

Now I am going to say a word. I want you to say each sound in the word. Let me try first. The word is *should. Should*, /sh/ /ů/ /d/. *Should* has three sounds.

It's your turn. Listen carefully. How many sounds are in these words?

brook (4)	foot (3)	hoof (3)
wood (3)	would (3)	soot (3)
look (3)	stood (4)	crook (4)

Objective

- Segment phonemes in words with vowel digraphs *oo, ou*

ELL

Minimal Contrasts Focus on articulation. Make the /ů/ sound and point out your mouth position. Have children repeat. Use the articulation photos on the small Sound-Spelling Cards. Repeat for the /ü/ sound. Then have children say each sound together, noticing the slight differences in mouth position. Continue by having children read minimal contrast word pairs, such as *shook/shoe*, *brook/brew*, *took/too*.

Objectives

- Identify letter-sound correspondence for vowel digraphs *oo, ou*
- Blend sounds in words with vowel digraphs *oo, ou*
- Review previously taught phonics skills

Materials

- Sound-Spelling Card: *Book*
- Word-Building Cards; Teacher's Resource Book, p. 66
- pocket chart
- chart paper
- Practice Book, p. 206

Skills Trace

Vowel Digraphs *oo, ou*	
Introduce	91C–D
Practice/ Apply	91F, 93G-H, 115F-G, 115I, 115T; Practice Book: p. 206; Decodable Reader: *Flip and Spots*
Reteach/ Review	119D; 119K-N, 119Q, 119W, 119CC
Assess	Weekly Test; Unit 4 Test
Maintain	Build Fluency: Sound/Spellings

ELL

Variations in Languages
Speakers of Spanish as well as most Asian languages will have difficulty pronouncing and perceiving the variant vowel /ů/. Use the Approaching Level Phonics lessons for additional pronunciation and decoding practice for these children.

Sound Pronunciation

See **Sound Pronunciation CD** for a model of the /ů/ sound. Play this for children needing additional models.

Phonics

Words with *oo, ou*

Model

Teach the sound /ů/ spelled *oo* and *ou*. Show the *Book* **Sound-Spelling Card**. Model writing the letters. Use handwriting models.

This is the *Book* Sound-Spelling Card. The sound is /ů/. The /ů/ sound can be spelled with the letters *oo* or *ou*. Say it with me: /ů/. Watch as I write the letters *oo*. I'll say the sound /ů/ as I write the letters several times. (Repeat with sound-spelling *ou*.)

Guided Practice/Practice

Have children practice connecting the letters and sound through writing.

Now do it with me. Say /ů/ as I write the letters *oo*.

This time, write the letters *oo* five times as you say the /ů/ sound. (Repeat with *ou*.)

Build Fluency: Sound/Spellings

oo ou ui

Display the following **Word-Building Cards:** *oo, ou, oo, ui, ew, ue, u, ou, oe, oi, oy, ou, ow, are, air, ear, ere, or, ore, oar, ar, gn, kn, wr, mb*. Have children chorally say each sound. Repeat and vary the pace.

Blend Vowel Digraphs *oo, ou*

Model

Display Word-Building Cards *f, o, o, t*. Model how to blend sounds as you run your finger under each letter. Repeat with *cook, stood, good, hooded, looking* and *should*.

This is the letter *f*. It stands for /f/. This is the letter *o*. Together the letters *oo* stand for /ů/. This is the letter *t*. It stands for /t/. Listen as I blend all the sounds: /fůt/, *foot*. Say it with me.

Guided Practice/Practice

Write the words below on chart paper. Read each one in the first row, blending the sounds. For example, /g/ /ů/ /d/ /z/, /gůdz/. The word is *goods*. Have children blend the sounds in each word with you. Then use the appropriate blending level to complete the remaining lines chorally. See the **Sound-by-Sound Blending Routine** in the **Instructional Routine Handbook** for support. (Save the chart for use in tomorrow's lesson.)

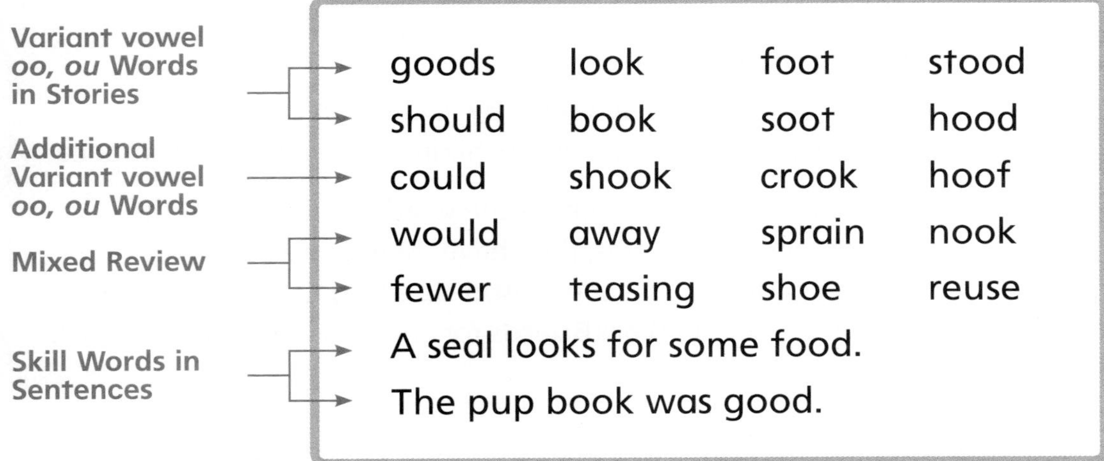

Variant vowel *oo, ou* Words in Stories	goods	look	foot	stood
	should	book	soot	hood
Additional Variant vowel *oo, ou* Words	could	shook	crook	hoof
Mixed Review	would	away	sprain	nook
	fewer	teasing	shoe	reuse
Skill Words in Sentences	A seal looks for some food.			
	The pup book was good.			

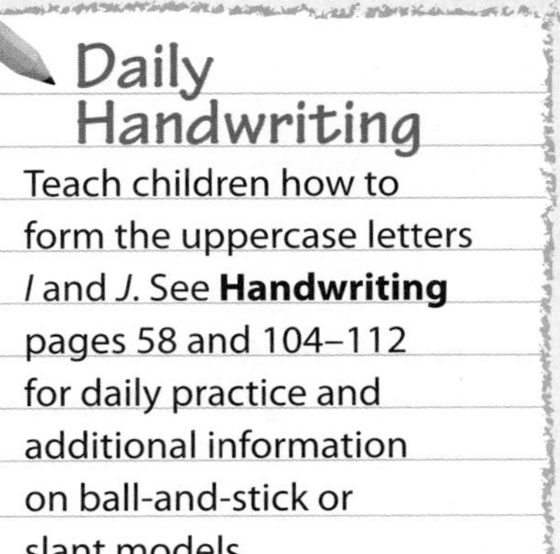

Daily Handwriting

Teach children how to form the uppercase letters *I* and *J*. See **Handwriting** pages 58 and 104–112 for daily practice and additional information on ball-and-stick or slant models.

Corrective Feedback

Blending: Sound Error Model the sound that children missed. Then have them repeat the sound. Say: *My turn.* Tap under the letter and say: *Sound? /ů/. What's the sound?* Then return to the beginning of the word. Say: *Let's start over.* Blend the sounds in the word with children again.

Quick Check

Can children blend sounds in words with vowel digraphs *oo, ou*?

During **Small Group Instruction**

Tier 2

If No → **Approaching Level** Repeat blending using the chart above. Explicitly correct the error and provide more "with me" type practice. Use a lower level of blending to provide support.

If Yes → **On Level** Consolidate the learning by having children read additional words with vowel digraphs *oo, ou*. See page 119M.

Beyond Level Extend the learning by having children read harder words containing vowel digraphs *oo, ou*. See page 119N.

ON YOUR OWN

Practice Book, page 206

The letters ***oo*** and ***ou*** can stand for the vowel sound you hear in ***took*** and ***should***.

A. Read each word. Write a new word that rhymes. Then underline the letters in each word that make the sound you hear in the middle of *took* and *should*. Possible responses provided

1. stood wood
2. looking book
3. soot foot
4. could would
5. cooking hook
6. good hood

B. Write two sentences using two of the words you wrote above. Possible responses provided

7. I will read my favorite book again.
8. You can hang your coat on the hook.

Approaching Reproducible, page 206

Beyond Reproducible, page 206

Objectives

- Spell words with vowel digraphs *oo, ou*
- Identify spelling patterns

Materials

- paper and pencils
- Sound-Spelling Card: *Book*
- Sound-Spelling WorkBoards; Teacher's Resource Book, p. 143
- Phonics/Spelling Practice Book, p. 73

5-Day Spelling	
DAY 1	Dictation; Pretest
DAY 2	Teacher-Modeled Word Sort
DAY 3	Student Word Sort
DAY 4	Test Practice
DAY 5	Posttest

ON YOUR OWN

Spelling, page 73

Using the Word Study Steps

1. LOOK at the word.
2. SAY the word aloud.
3. STUDY the letters in the word.
4. WRITE the word.
5. CHECK the word. Did you spell the word right? If not, go back to step 1.

Find and Circle

Where are the spelling words?

w	o	u	l	d	q	w	s	r	t	y
p	s	d	f	g	h	c	o	u	l	d
j	k	l	z	x	c	v	o	b	n	m
m	s	h	o	o	k	n	t	b	v	c
x	z	o	l	k	j	h	g	f	d	s
r	t	o	z	p	q	w	r	t	y	p
w	q	k	s	d	f	g	s	h	j	k
l	z	x	c	v	b	n	g	m	q	w
r	b	r	o	o	k	t	o	q	y	p
c	s	d	f	g	h	j	o	k	l	z
r	x	s	h	o	u	l	d	c	v	b
o	n	m	q	w	r	t	y	p	s	d
o	f	g	h	j	k	l	z	x	c	v
k	b	n	m	q	w	f	o	o	t	r

would soot shook brook should foot hook crook could good

Phonics/Spelling

Words with *oo, ou*

DICTATION

Use dictation to help children transfer their growing knowledge of sound-spellings to writing. Follow the **Dictation Routine** below with each spelling word.

DICTATION ROUTINE

- Pronounce one word at a time. Have children clearly state the word. Then repeat the word for children and use it in a sentence.
- Ask children to orally segment the word to think about the word's individual sounds, then have them write the word. Prompt children to use the **Sound-Spelling Card** spellings as they write. Provide **WorkBoards** for children who need support.

PRETEST

Pronounce each spelling word. Read the sentence and pronounce the word again. Ask children to say each word softly, stretching the sounds, before writing it. After the pretest, write each word on the board as you say the letter names. Have children check their words.

Spelling Words

Approaching	On Level	Beyond
shook	shook	shook
hook	hook	hooked
cook	crook	crooked
book	good	good-bye
look	should	should
good	brook	brook
hood	foot	soot
foot	soot	wooden
could	could	couldn't
would	would	would
zoo	fruit	glued
new	glue	canoe
below	below	below
city	city	city
own	own	own

1. **shook:** I <u>shook</u> the piggy bank.
2. **hook:** My hat is on the <u>hook</u>.
3. **crook:** The <u>crook</u> tried to run away.
4. **good:** I had a very <u>good</u> day.
5. **should:** We <u>should</u> go to dinner.
6. **brook:** We saw fish in the <u>brook</u>.
7. **foot:** My <u>foot</u> is a size four.
8. **soot:** The fire made a lot of <u>soot</u>.
9. **could:** We <u>could</u> go out later.
10. **would:** <u>Would</u> you like to help us?
11. **fruit:** Apples are my favorite <u>fruit</u>.
12. **glue:** Use <u>glue</u> to stick the glitter on.
13. **below:** Put the box <u>below</u> the chair.
14. **city:** We get to the <u>city</u> by train.
15. **own:** I <u>own</u> two bikes.

Decodable Reader

- **Review High-Frequency Words** Write **follow**, **near**, and **paper** on the board. Review the words with children using the **Read/Spell/Write** routine.

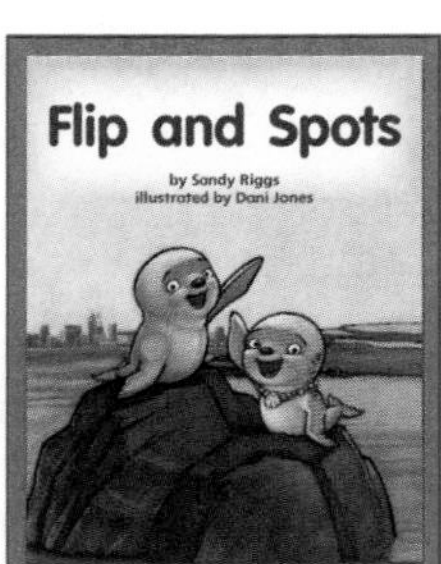

Flip and Spots

- **Preview and Predict** Point to the book's title and have children sound out each word as you run your finger under it. Discuss the cover illustration. Ask:
  - *Where are the seal pups?*
  - *What do they appear to be doing?*
  - *Have you ever seen seals? Where?*
- **First Read** Turn to page 22. Have children point to each word, sounding out decodable words and saying the high-frequency words quickly. Children should chorally read the story the first time through. If children have difficulty, provide corrective feedback page by page as needed. See the **Decodable Text Routine** in the **Instructional Routine Handbook** for correction models.
- **Check Comprehension** Ask the following:
  - *Why did the seal pups get out of the sea?*
  - *What did the seal pups start doing? Why?*
  - *Point to the pup's flippers. What do you think they are used for?*
  - *Turn to your partner and retell the story.*

- **Second Read** Reread the story with children.
  - Approaching Level If children struggle sounding out words, provide "with you" blending models. Then review blending using the words on the Word List at the end of the book during Small Group time. Conclude by guiding children through a rereading of the book.
  - Beyond Level If children can sound out the words, then have them quietly read the text with a partner.

Objectives

- Decode words with variant vowel *oo, ou* in connected text
- Identify and read last week's high-frequency words *follow, near, paper*

Materials

- Decodable Reader Library: *Flip and Spots*

High-Frequency Words

Use the **Read/Spell/Write** routine to teach each high-frequency word.

- **Read** Read the word. Have children repeat.
- **Spell** Chorally spell the word.
- **Write** Have children write the word as they spell it aloud. Then ask children to write a sentence using each word.

SMALL GROUP OPTION

You may wish to read the Decodable Reader during **Small Group** time.

See pages 119K–119JJ

Objectives

- Learn the meanings of vocabulary words by using context
- Review last week's vocabulary words
- Use antonyms to figure out word meanings

Materials

- Student Book: "A Whale Is Saved!"
- Practice Book, p. 207

Vocabulary	
examines	hunger
mammal	normal
rescued	young

ELL

Preteach Vocabulary
See page 119H to preteach the vocabulary words to ELL and Approaching Level children. Use the **Visual Vocabulary Resources** to demonstrate and discuss each word.

Vocabulary

TEACH WORDS
Introduce each word using the **Define/Example/Ask** routine. Model reading each word.

Vocabulary Routine

Use the routine below to discuss the meaning of each word.

Define: When a person **examines** something, she looks at it carefully.
Example: *My mom examines the toy to see if it is broken.*
Ask: Name a job in which the worker examines someone. EXAMPLE

- Someone who feels **hunger** feels a strong need to eat. *The lost dog felt sick from hunger.* When have you felt hunger? PRIOR KNOWLEDGE
- A **mammal** is a warm-blooded animal that drinks its mother's milk and has hair. *A seal is a mammal.* Name another mammal. EXAMPLE
- Something that is **normal** happens in a regular or healthy way. *The doctor checks your heartbeat to make sure it is normal.* Name a word that means the same as *normal*. SYNONYM
- Something that is **rescued** is saved from danger. *I rescued a dog that was caught in a broken fence.* What is a word that means the same as *rescued*? SYNONYM
- When something is **young**, it is at an early time of its life. *The young cat followed its mother.* What word means the opposite of *young*? ANTONYM
- **Word Wall** Add these words to the Word Wall.

Use the vocabulary routine to review last week's words: *serious*, *personal*, *informs*, *heal*, and *aid*.

STRATEGY Use Context Clues: Antonyms

- When you don't know what a word means, identify and use nearby words and sentences for clues to help you understand. An author may use an antonym, or a word that has the opposite meaning, in a way that can help you understand an unknown word.

Have children find the word *hunger* in "A Whale Is Saved!" on page 93 and read the sentence with the word.

Think Aloud I'm not sure what *hunger* means. I notice the word *but*. This tells me that a word or words are coming that might mean the opposite. Then I read that the whale seemed well fed. That tells me that when an animals feels hunger, it is not well fed.

Vocabulary

young
examines
mammal
normal
hunger
rescued

Context Clues
Antonyms are words that have opposite meanings.
Young and *old* are antonyms.

A WHALE IS SAVED!

by Elizabeth Baker

A **young** whale got stuck in Drew Harbor today. The whale was small and had been born recently. Some people saw the whale in trouble. They called the police.

Soon help was on the way. Jenny Litz arrived first. She is a scientist who **examines** whales.

Jenny looks at every part of an animal to see if it is healthy. A whale is a **mammal**. Mammals are warm-blooded animals that have hair and drink their mother's milk. Jenny checked the whale's heartbeat and breathing. She said the whale seemed **normal**. There were no signs of illness.

Next Jenny checked to see if **hunger** was a problem. Going a long time without food can be dangerous for a whale. But this whale seemed healthy and well fed.

The helpers acted fast. They kept the animal wet. The tide slowly came in. The water got deeper. Soon the whale could swim again. At last the whale was **rescued**! Jenny and the other helpers saved the whale's life.

Reread for **Comprehension**

Analyze Text Structure

Sequence of Events Looking at how ideas and information are organized in a text helps to describe the sequence of events. Reread the article and use the chart to help you understand what happens first, next, and last to save the whale.

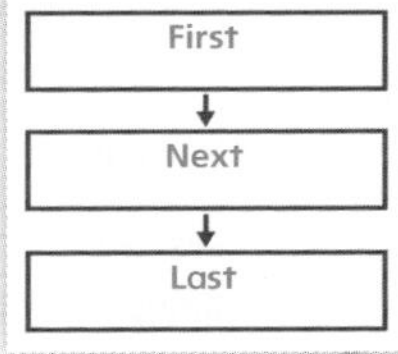

LOG ON LEARN IT Comprehension www.macmillanmh.com

Read "A Whale Is Saved!"

Read "A Whale Is Saved!" with children. Stop at each **highlighted** word. Ask children to identify text clues that reveal the meanings of the highlighted words. Model asking relevant questions to check overall comprehension of the passage and review the meanings of the words to confirm understanding. Tell children that they will read these words again in *A Harbor Seal Pup Grows Up*.

Quick Check

Do children understand word meanings?

During **Small Group Instruction**

If No → Approaching Level Vocabulary pages: 119N, 119P, 119R, 119T.

If Yes → On Level Reread Vocabulary Selection.

Beyond Level Reread Vocabulary Selection.

ON YOUR OWN

Practice Book, page 207

Use what you know about the words in the question to choose the correct word from the box that makes the most sense in the blank. Write the word on the line.

young normal rescued examines mammal hunger

1. What is another word for *saved*? rescued
2. Which word names a kind of animal that drinks its mother's milk and has hair or fur? mammal
3. Which word best tells about someone who is not old? young
4. Which word tells what a doctor does to an animal to see if it is well? examines
5. Which word tells about the feeling an animal has when it needs to eat? hunger
6. Which word tells about something that is not odd? normal

Approaching Reproducible, page 207

Beyond Reproducible, page 207

Objectives

- Summarize
- Identify sequence of events
- Use academic language: *text structure, sequence of events*

Materials

- Transparencies 10, 19a, 19b
- Student Book, pp. 92–93

Skills Trace

Sequence of Events	
Introduce	U4: 81A–B
Practice/ Apply	U4: 81K–85A; Practice Book: 198–199
Reteach/ Review	U4: 89K, 89V–X, 89BB–DD, 93A–B, 93K–115A, 119G, 119R–T, 119X–Z; Practice Book: 209–210
Assess	Weekly Tests; Unit 4, 5 Tests
Maintain	U4: 155N; U5: 201N, 209JA–B, 209J–233A, 239G, 239R–T, 239X–Z, 311N; Practice Book: 243–244

ELL

Academic Language
Preteach the following academic language words to ELL and Approaching Level children during Small Group time: *text structure, sequence of events*. See page 119O.

Comprehension

STRATEGY Analyze Text Structure

EXPLAIN

What Is It? Point out that an author of nonfiction can present information in various ways. **Text structure** is the way writers organize information in nonfiction. Different kinds of text structures include sequence, cause and effect, problem and solution, compare and contrast, and description. Special signal words often help the reader recognize the kind of text structure an author is using.

Why Is It Important? Point out that recognizing the text structure can help readers remember and understand the ideas and events in an expository text.

SKILL Sequence of Events

EXPLAIN

What Is It? Explain that **sequence** is the order of events or ideas in a text. Writers often describe events or ideas in sequence, or in the time order that they happen. Writers may use signal words such as *first*, *next*, *then*, and *last* to help the reader follow the order of events.

Why Is It Important? Understanding and describing the order of events helps readers to identify and remember key events and ideas.

Transparency 19a

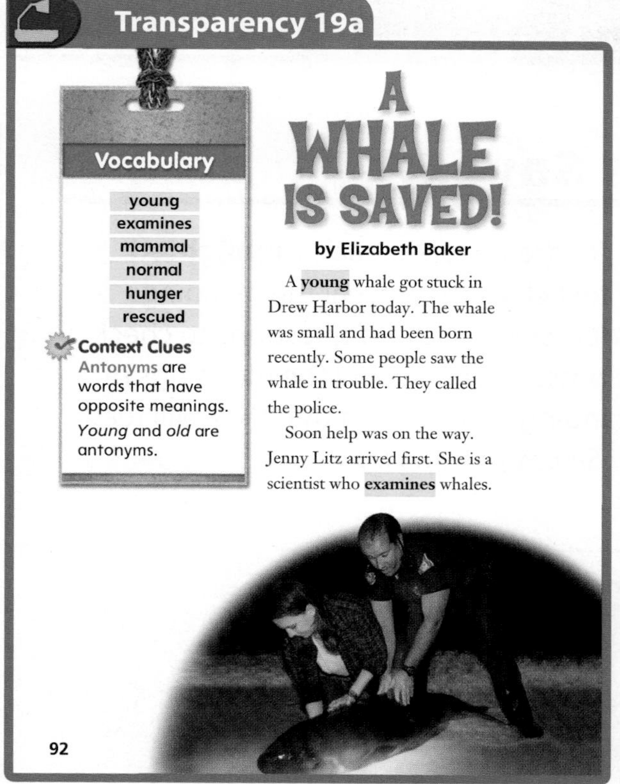

Vocabulary
young
examines
mammal
normal
hunger
rescued

Context Clues
Antonyms are words that have opposite meanings. *Young* and *old* are antonyms.

A WHALE IS SAVED!
by Elizabeth Baker

A **young** whale got stuck in Drew Harbor today. The whale was small and had been born recently. Some people saw the whale in trouble. They called the police.

Soon help was on the way. Jenny Litz arrived first. She is a scientist who **examines** whales.

92

Transparency 19b

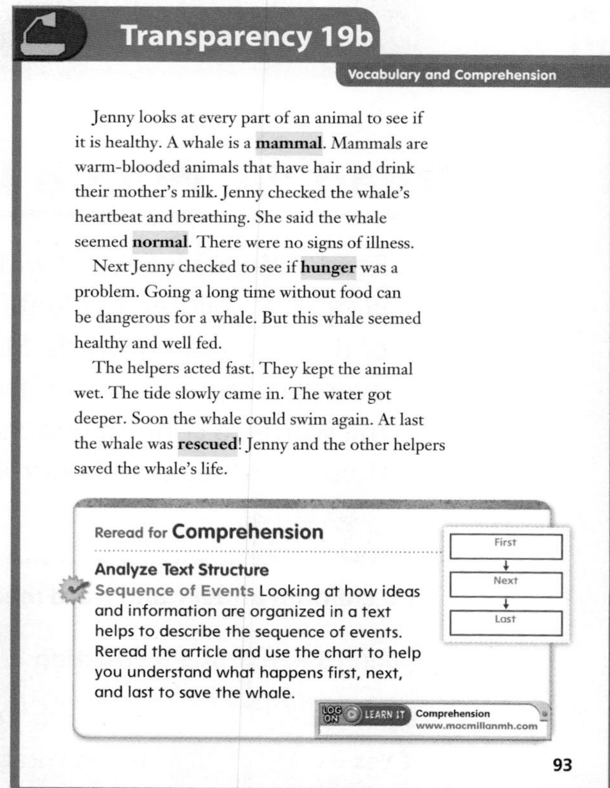

Vocabulary and Comprehension

Jenny looks at every part of an animal to see if it is healthy. A whale is a **mammal**. Mammals are warm-blooded animals that have hair and drink their mother's milk. Jenny checked the whale's heartbeat and breathing. She said the whale seemed **normal**. There were no signs of illness.

Next Jenny checked to see if **hunger** was a problem. Going a long time without food can be dangerous for a whale. But this whale seemed healthy and well fed.

The helpers acted fast. They kept the animal wet. The tide slowly came in. The water got deeper. Soon the whale could swim again. At last the whale was **rescued**! Jenny and the other helpers saved the whale's life.

Reread for **Comprehension**

Analyze Text Structure
Sequence of Events Looking at how ideas and information are organized in a text helps to describe the sequence of events. Reread the article and use the chart to help you understand what happens first, next, and last to save the whale.

First → Next → Last

LOG ON LEARN IT Comprehension www.macmillanmh.com

93

Student Book pages 92–93 are available on Comprehension Transparencies 19a and 19b.

Phonemic Awareness

Phoneme Blending

Model

Use the **WorkBoards** to show children how to orally blend phonemes.

I am going to put one marker in each box as I say each sound. Then I will blend the sounds to form a word.

Listen and watch. /s/ (Place marker in the first box.) /ů/ (Extend the vowel sound and place marker in the second box.) /t/ (Place marker in the third box.)

This word has three sounds: /s/ /ů/ /t/. Listen as I blend the sounds to form the word: /sůt/. (Extend the /ů/ sound.) The word is *soot*.

Repeat using these additional words, each with three phonemes: *wood*, *shook*, *could*, *cook*, and *took*.

Guided Practice/Practice

Help children practice blending. Distribute markers and copies of WorkBoards. Do the first three words together.

Let's do some together. Place a marker for each sound you hear. I will say one sound at a time. Then we will blend the sounds to say the word.

/h/ /ů/ /k/ /w/ /ů/ /d/ /b/ /ů/ /k/

Now it's your turn. Listen carefully.

/sh/ /ů/ /d/ /g/ /ů/ /d/ /sh/ /ů/ /k/
/h/ /ů/ /f/ /w/ /ů/ /l/ /t/ /ů/ /k/

Objectives

- Blend phonemes in words with vowel digraphs *oo*, *ou*
- Review Folktales

Materials

- Sound-Spelling WorkBoards; Teacher's Resource Book, p. 143
- Practice Book for Folktales, p. 208

Objectives

- Blend and build words with vowel digraphs *oo*, *ou*
- Review previously taught phonics skills
- Read multisyllabic words

Materials

- Word-Building Cards; Teacher's Resource Book, p. 66
- pocket chart
- word chart from Day 1
- Decodable Reader Library: *Flip and Spots*

Skills Trace

Vowel Digraphs *oo*, *ou*	
Introduce	91C–D
Practice/ Apply	91F, 93G-H, 115F-G, 115I, 115T; Practice Book: p. 206; Decodable Reader: *Flip and Spots*
Reteach/ Review	119D; 119K-N, 119Q, 119W, 119CC
Assess	Weekly Test; Unit 4 Test
Maintain	Build Fluency: Sound/Spellings

Phonics

Build Fluency: Sound/Spellings

Display the following **Word-Building Cards** one at a time: *oo*, *ou*, *oo*, *ui*, *ew*, *ue*, *u*, *ou*, *oe*, *oi*, *oy*, *ou*, *ow*, *are*, *air*, *ear*, *ere*, *or*, *ore*, *oar*, *ar*, *gn*, *kn*, *wr*, *mb*. Have children chorally say each sound. Repeat and vary the pace. Children should work to say each sound within a two-second pause.

Blend with Vowel Digraphs *oo*, *ou*

Model

Place Word-Building Cards *n*, *o*, *o*, *k* in the pocket chart to form *nook*. Model how to generate and blend the sounds to say the word.

The letter *n* stands for /n/. The letters *oo* together stand for /ů/. The letter *k* stands for /k/. Now listen as I blend all three sounds: /nůk/ (Extend the /ů/ sound.) Now you say it. Let's read the word together: *nook*.

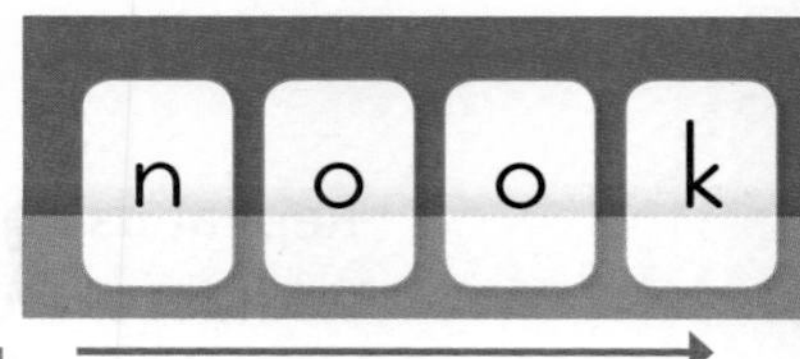

Repeat with *would*, *hood*, *woof*, *foot*, and *good*.

Guided Practice/Practice

Repeat with additional words. Have children blend the sounds in words with you.

soot	could	book	cook
brook	stood	wool	took
took	nook	hook	would
football	relook	wooden	rooftop

Build with Variant Vowel *oo, ou*

Model

Place **Word-Building Cards** *w, o, o, d* in the pocket chart. Blend the phonemes.

Let's blend all the sounds together and read the word: /wůd/, *wood*.

Change *w* to *h* and repeat with *hood*.

Let's blend all the sounds together and read the word: /hůd/, *hood*.

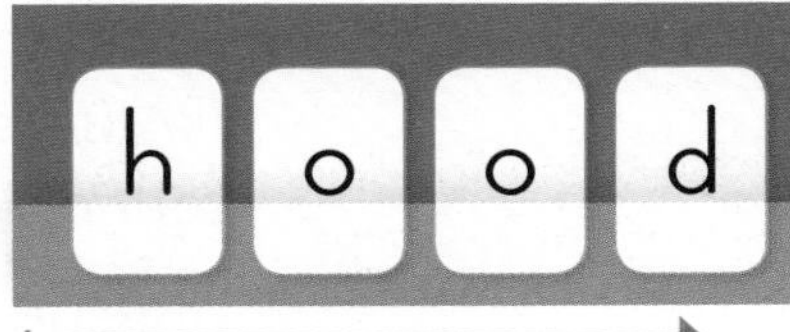

Change *h* to *g* and repeat with *good*.

Let's blend all the sounds together and read the word: /gůd/, *good*.

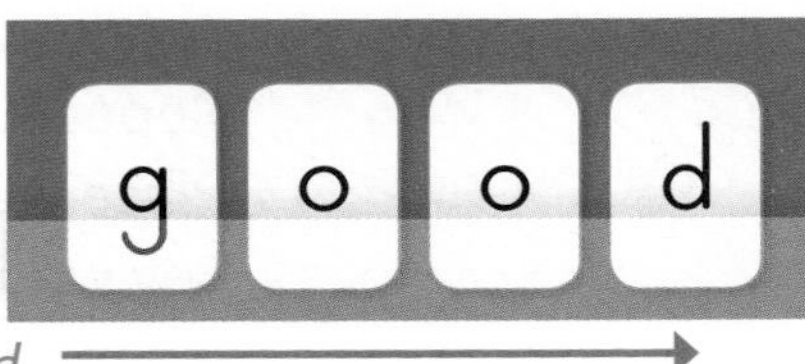

Guided Practice/Practice

Continue to build with additional words.

stood, soot, foot, shook, book, brook, cook, look, wool, would, should, could

Build Fluency: Word Automaticity

Display the word chart from Day 1. Point to each word as children chorally read it. Aim for one word every two seconds. Model blending the sounds in words children miss. Then point to words in random order at varying speeds for children to read.

goods	look	foot	stood
should	book	soot	hood
could	shook	crook	hoof
would	away	sprain	nook
fewer	teasing	shoe	reuse

A seal looks for some food.

The pup book was good.

Build Fluency: Connected Text

Have children independently reread *Flip and Spots* from **Decodable Reader Library**. Circulate and listen in, providing corrective feedback as needed.

- **Approaching Level** Have children read with a more-skilled partner or listen to the text on **Audio CD** and read with the narrator.
- **Beyond Level** While the other children are reading, teach the Accelerate Pacing lesson.

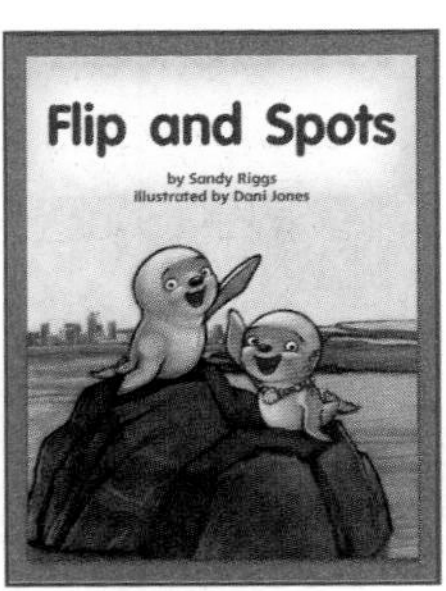

Flip and Spots

Transition to Multisyllabic Words

Consonant + *le* Syllables

- Say the words *poodle* and *noodle*. Point out that the words have two syllables.
- Write *poodle* and *noodle* on the board. Underline the final syllable in each word.
- Explain that when a word ends in *-le*, *-el*, or *-al*, the consonant before those letters teams up with them to form the last syllable. Say: *Listen: /dəl/. This leaves n-o-o, /nů/. When I put the two word parts together, I get the word* noodle.
- Write these words and help children blend them and divide them into syllables: *middle, puddle, apple, struggle, scramble.*

ELL

Build Vocabulary Review meanings of words on your word chart that can be explained or demonstrated in a concrete way. For example, ask children to stand on one *foot*. Explain that *goods* are things that are sold or things that belong to someone. Make up sentence starters for children to complete, such as *I* would *like to learn to* ________.

Objectives

- Spell words with vowel digraphs *oo, ou*
- Sort words with vowel digraphs *oo, ou*
- Build Fluency: Word Automaticity

Materials

- large index cards with spelling words
- pocket chart
- Phonics/Spelling Practice Book, p. 74

5-Day Spelling	
DAY 1	Dictation; Pretest
DAY 2	Teacher-Modeled Word Sort
DAY 3	Student Word Sort
DAY 4	Test Practice
DAY 5	Posttest

ON YOUR OWN **Spelling**, page 74

would	shook	should	hook	could
soot	brook	foot	crook	good

A. Word Sort

Look at the spelling words in the box. Match the spelling word with the spelling pattern and write the word.

oot 1. soot 2. foot

ook 3. shook 4. hook
5. brook 6. crook

ood 7. good

ould 8. would 9. should
10. could

B. Pattern Smart

Write the spelling words that have the same pattern as *book*.

11. shook 12. hook
13. brook 14. crook

Write the spelling word that has the same pattern as *hood*.

15. good

Phonics/Spelling

Word Sort with *oo, ou*

- Display the pocket chart. Place index cards with the key word cards *cook* and *could* to form two columns in the pocket chart. Generate sentences for the key words *cook* and *could*.
- Say each key word and pronounce the sounds: /k/ /ů/ /k/ and /k/ /ů/ /d/. Pronounce each word again, emphasizing the /ů/ sound. Ask children to chorally spell each word.
- Hold up the word card *hook*. Pronounce each sound clearly: /h/ /ů/ /k/. Blend the sounds: /hůk/. Repeat with each *oo* and *ou* word. Place words below the correct key word labels so there is one example of each. Have children read each word, listening for the /ů/ sound. Ask children to chorally spell each word.

- Have children place the remaining cards under the correct key label.
- **Build Fluency: Word Automaticity** Have children chorally read the words several times for fluency.

Analyze Errors — Articulation Support

- Use children's pretest errors to analyze spelling problems and provide corrective feedback. For example, the /ů/ and /ū/ sounds are formed in similar ways. Some children will substitute the letter *u* for the letters *oo* or *ou*.
- Have these children say /ů/, paying attention to how it feels in the mouth. Use hand mirrors, if available. Then have children make the /ū/ sound, noting how the face position changes slightly. Go back and forth between /ů/ and /ū/ to help them feel the difference.
- Then have children orally segment one of the spelling words. When children get to the /ů/ sound, ask: *How does your mouth feel? What letters do we write for that sound?*

Vocabulary

Words in Context

REVIEW

Review the meanings of the vocabulary words. Display **Transparency 37**. Model how to use word meanings and context clues to fill in the first missing word.

Think Aloud The first paragraph tells about the cat: warm-blooded, has hair, and has babies who get milk from her. The missing word must be **mammal**. When I try **mammal** in the sentence, it makes sense.

Transparency 37

rescued mammal young hunger examines normal

Ruby knew her cat was a (1) mammal. It was warm-blooded. It had hair. And it was about to have kittens. They would get their milk from the mother cat.

The kittens' eyes were closed when they were born. "They're so (2) young," Ruby said. Ruby could hear the kittens' (3) hunger in their little kitten noises when it was time to eat.

Ruby's grandmother said that a cat (4) examines its kittens often to make sure they are well. The cat can make sure they are (5) normal and are not getting sick.

Ruby's kittens grew quickly. One got caught in a tree. Ruby (6) rescued it and took it to safety. All the kittens had to stay inside after that day!

Vocabulary Transparency

PRACTICE

Have children use context clues to complete items 2–6. Ask partners to check each other's answers and explain context clues they used to fill in the words. Finally, have children chorally reread the paragraphs on the transparency to build fluency.

During independent work time, have children write sentences in their Writer's Notebooks using their vocabulary words.

Review last week's words *serious*, *personal*, *informs*, *heal*, and *aid* in context.

Objectives

- Apply knowledge of word meanings and context clues
- Review last week's vocabulary words in context

Materials

- Transparency 37

Objectives

- Summarize the story
- Identify sequence of events
- Use a graphic organizer
- Use academic language: *text structure, sequence*

Materials

- Student Book: *A Harbor Seal Pup Grows Up*, pp. 94–113
- Practice Book, p. 209

Skills Trace

Sequence of Events	
Introduce	U4: 81A–B
Practice/ Apply	U4: 81K–85A; Practice Book: 198–199
Reteach/ Review	U4: 89K, 89V–X, 89BB–DD, 93A–B, 93K–115A, 119G, 119R–T, 119X–Z; Practice Book: 209–210
Assess	Weekly Tests; Unit 4, 5 Tests
Maintain	U4: 155N; U5: 201N, 209JA–B, 209J–233A, 239G, 239R–T, 239X–Z, 311N; Practice Book: 243–244

Story Words

Provide these definitions.

harbor (p. 96): a place of shelter near the shore

scientist (p. 100): a person who studies science

Digital Learning

Story available on **Listening Library Audio CD** and **StudentWorks Plus**, the Interactive eBook.

Interactive Student Book

www.macmillanmh.com

Comprehension

STRATEGY Analyze Text Structure

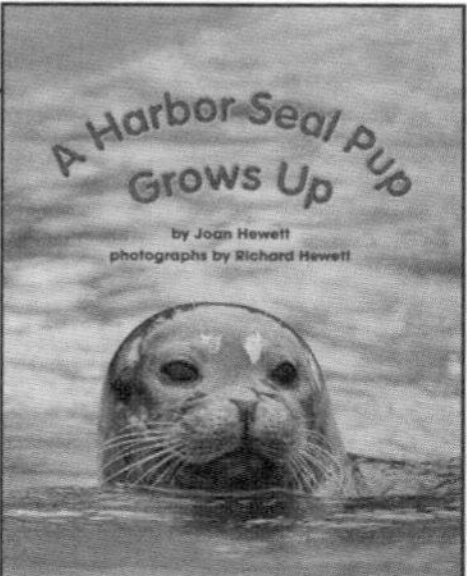

Main Selection

Review that **text structure** is the way writers organize information in nonfiction. Different kinds of text structure include sequence, cause and effect, problem and solution, compare and contrast, and description. Readers who can recognize nonfiction text structures will better understand and remember what they read.

SKILL Sequence of Events

Remind children that writers often describe events or ideas in **sequence**, or the time order in which they happen. Writers may use signal words such as *first*, *next*, *then*, and *last* to show the time order of events. Point out that finding out the correct sequence of events will help children better understand what happens.

Prepare to Read

PREVIEW AND PREDICT

- Ask children to preview the title and cover to make predictions about *A Harbor Seal Pup Grows Up. What does the selection seem to be about? Does it look realistic or unrealistic? Why?*
- **Genre** Have a child read the definition of nonfiction on **Student Book** page 94. Share these features: about real people or things; told by a narrator; events that happened in real life.

SET A PURPOSE FOR READING

- **Focus Question** Discuss the "Read to Find Out" question on Student Book page 94. Remind children to look for the answers as they read.
- Point out the Retelling Chart in the **Student Book**. Remind children that they will use the chart to record the sequence of events in the selection.
- Prompt children to set their own purposes for reading.

Comprehension

Genre
Expository text can be a retelling of a true event.

Analyze Text Structure
Sequence of Events
As you read, use your Sequence Chart.

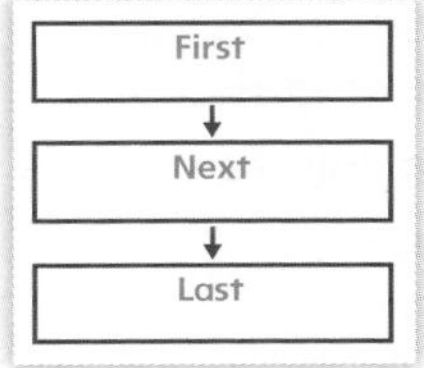

Read to Find Out
How is Sidney found, helped, and released to her ocean home?

A Harbor Seal Pup Grows Up

by Joan Hewett
photographs by Richard Hewett

Read Main Selection

Purpose for Reading Ask children to read the "Read to Find Out" question. Remind them to pay attention to how Sidney is found, helped, and released as they read the selection.

PARTNERS Preteach	Read Together
Have Approaching Level children in English Language Learners listen to the story on **StudentWorks Plus**, the Interactive eBook, before reading with the class.	Use the prompts to guide comprehension and model how to complete the graphic organizer. Have children use **Think/Pair/Share** as they respond to the prompts.

ON YOUR OWN **Practice Book,** page 209

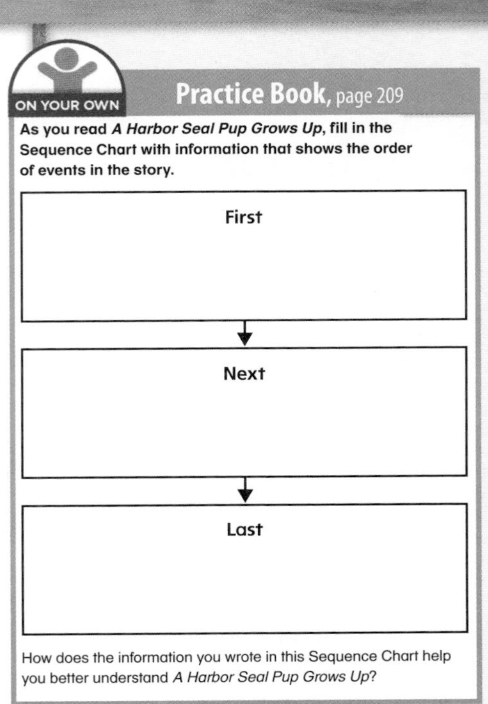
As you read *A Harbor Seal Pup Grows Up*, fill in the Sequence Chart with information that shows the order of events in the story.

First

Next

Last

How does the information you wrote in this Sequence Chart help you better understand *A Harbor Seal Pup Grows Up*?

Approaching Reproducible, page 209

Beyond Reproducible, page 209

By the Ocean

The harbor seal pup is 2 weeks old. Her name is Sidney. Sidney stays close to her mother. She drinks her mother's milk.

Waves crash on the rocky beach. Harbor seal families lie in the warm sun.

Sidney and her mother lie in the sun too.

96

1

Sidney's mother gets hungry. She dives in the water to catch fish. The water is too cold for Sidney. So Sidney stays on the shore.

97

ELL

Preview Text Have children use **StudentWorks Plus**, the interactive eBook, to preview the text. This eBook contains summaries in multiple languages, word-by-word reading support, bilingual glossary, and comprehension questions with corrective feedback. Use the Interactive Question-Response Guide to preteach the content in *A Harbor Seal Pup Grows Up* and develop meaning.

Develop Comprehension

1 GENRE: NONFICTION

How can you tell that this selection is **nonfiction**? (I know that this selection is nonfiction because the photos show real seals. The text explains events that actually happened.) What text features can you expect to find in the selection? (photographs)

2 STRATEGY Analyze Text Structure

Think about how this selection is organized.

Teacher Think Aloud Let's see, I know that this selection is nonfiction. On page 98, I see the signal words *she waits for three days*. These words tell me that the author is using sequence as a text structure, so I know the information will be presented in time order. The signal words help me to understand what happens to Sidney in the order that it takes place.

The seal pup waits for her mother. She waits for 3 days. She is very hungry. **2**

People notice the seal pup. She is alone. Will her mother come back?

The next day, the pup is still alone. The people call for help. Sidney is **rescued**.

3 **Sequence of Events**
Think about what has happened so far. Use details from the text to describe how Sidney ends up alone on the beach.

3 SKILL Sequence of Events

How does Sidney end up alone on the beach? Describe the order of events. (Sidney's mother went into the ocean to find food. This is the first thing that happened. She did not come back.) Let's put this information on our Sequence Chart in the first section and keep reading to find out what happens to Sidney.

Think/Pair/Share Turn to a partner. Discuss how the photographs help you to understand the sequence of events so far.

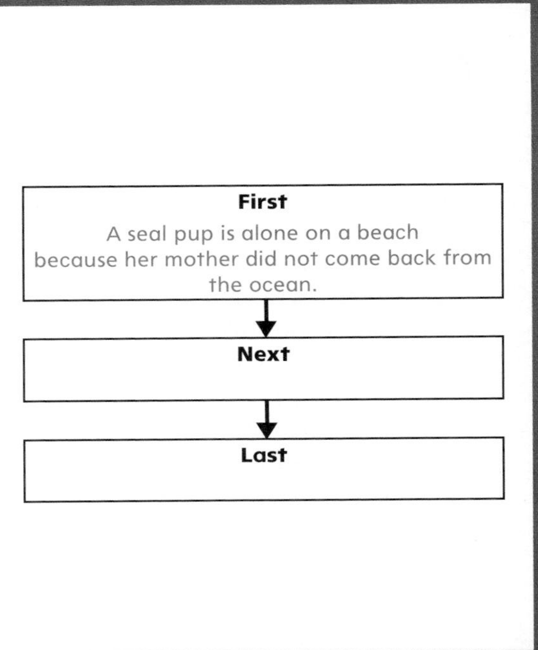

Nursed Back to Health

4 Sidney is brought to a sea **mammal** center.

A scientist named Peter is in charge. Peter takes care of **young** seals. He lifts the thin pup from her cage.

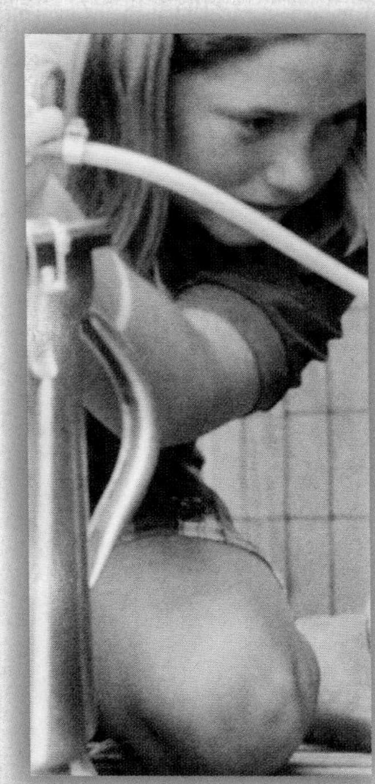

Sidney is weak from **hunger**. Peter knows just what to do. He puts a tube in Sidney's mouth.

Then Nicole pumps 5 a drink into Sidney's stomach. The drink is like a mother seal's milk.

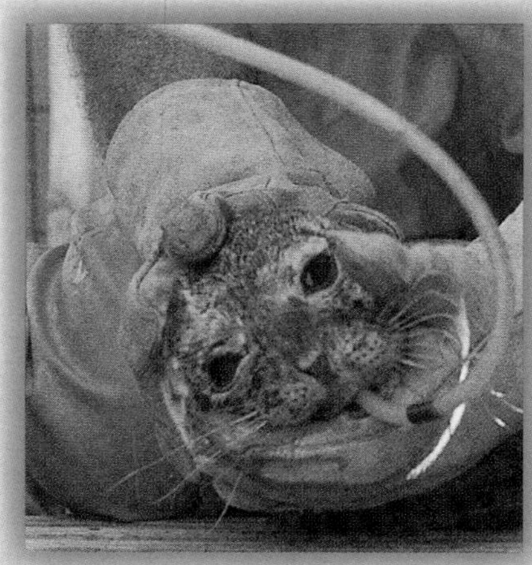

ELL

Use Context Write *weak* and *week* on the board. Discuss the similarity in pronunciation, but differences in meaning and spelling. Guide children in using context to tell that Sidney is thin and hungry, so she has very little energy. She is weak. Explain that this meaning makes sense in the sentence.

Develop Comprehension

4 VOCABULARY: CONTEXT CLUES

Sidney is brought to a sea mammal center. What **context clues** help you figure out the meaning of *center*? (The text says that Sidney is brought to a place with a scientist who will take care of Sidney. These clues help me figure out that a *center* is a place where animals get special care. That meaning makes sense here.)

5 SKILL Sequence of Events

Think about the events that take place in order to feed Sydney. What happens after Peter puts a tube in the pup's mouth? (Nicole pumps a drink into Sidney's stomach. I know this is what happens next because I see the signal word *then*, which helps me figure out the sequence, or order of events.)

Sidney is full. She is also very tired. She falls asleep.

6

When Sidney wakes up, her eyes are bright. She looks around. 7

6 **MAINTAIN** **Use Illustrations/Photographs**

How can you tell by the **photographs** that Sidney will get better in the mammal center? (By looking at the photographs you can tell that these scientists are handling Sidney with care and she seems happy to be there. She looks very comfortable in the photo that shows her sleeping in her dish and she looks healthier in the next photograph.)

7 **SELF-SELECTED STRATEGY USE**

What strategies have you used so far to help you understand the selection? Where did you use them? Why? How did they help?

Text Evidence

Sequence

Reread question 5 aloud to children. Point out the signal word "after" which tells the reader about the sequence of events. Have children find the text evidence on page 101, "He puts a tube in Sidney's mouth." They can look for the events that come after that: "Then Nicole pumps a drink into Sydney's stomach."

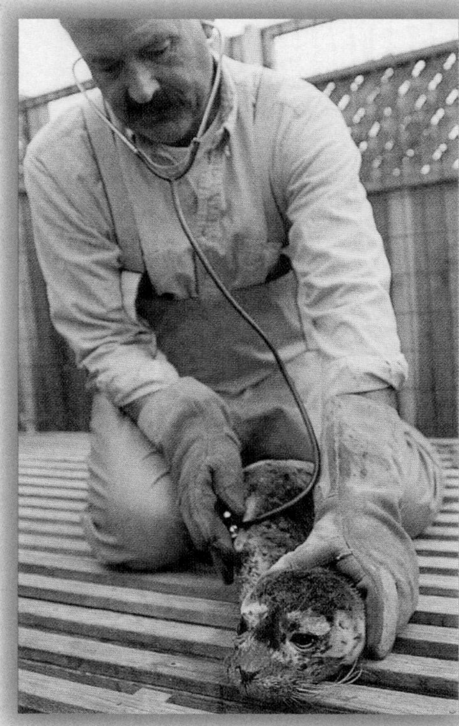

8 9 Peter **examines** the pup. Her heartbeat is **normal**. So is her temperature. She is healthy.

Sidney has a full set of teeth. That means she is at least 3 weeks old. Sidney is small for her age.

104

Sidney gets her drink 3 times a day. She becomes stronger. Using her flippers, she scoots around.

A child's plastic pool becomes Sidney's playpen. She likes the water. She swims faster and faster.

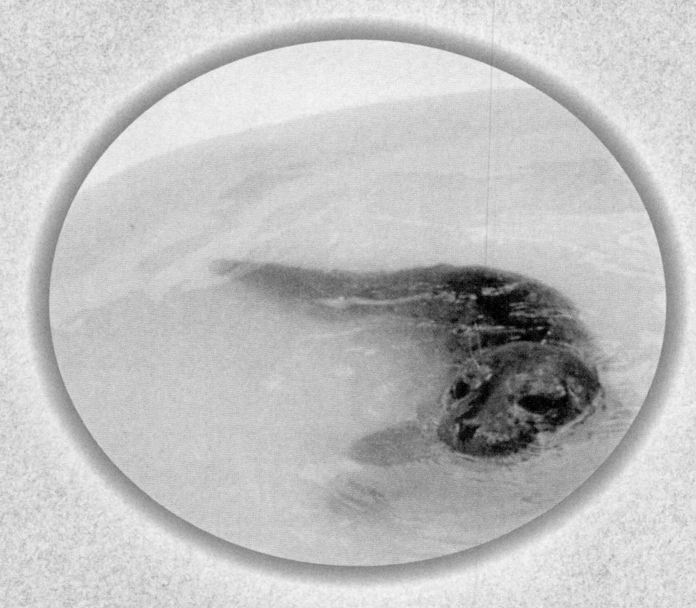

105

Decoding

Apply Phonics Skills While reading, point out words with the sound/spelling patterns children have recently learned. You may focus on variant vowel *oo*, *ou* words such as *looks*, *good*, and *good-bye*.

Model blending each word sound by sound. Then have children repeat.

Develop Comprehension

8 MONITOR AND CLARIFY: REREAD TO CLARIFY

Peter and Nicole are helping Sidney to get better. How can you **clarify** this from the text? (To clarify, I will go back and reread some pages. I find out that Peter and Nicole are giving Sidney food. She is also getting rest and this is helping her to feel better. I also read that her eyes are bright and her heartbeat and temperature are normal.)

9 FLUENCY: PHRASING

Point out the paragraphs on pages 104 and 105 and read them aloud. Ask children to notice when you pause at the commas and stop for a moment at the periods. Guide children to read the paragraphs after you, using the same phrasing.

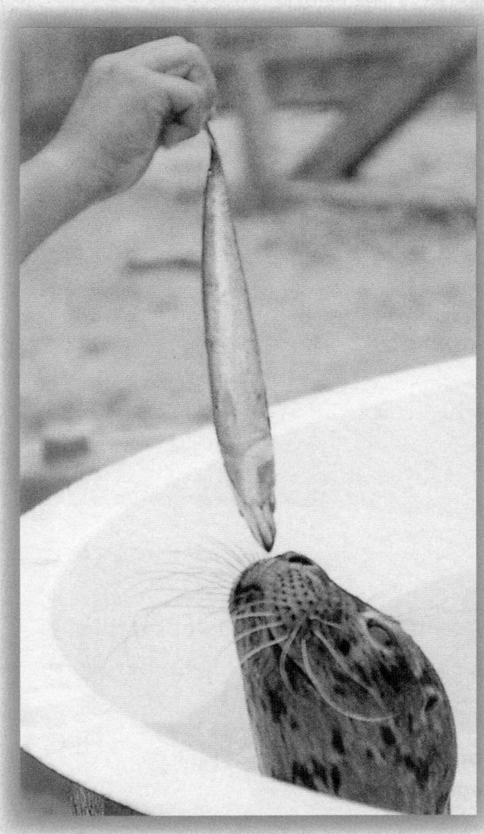

Nicole shows Sidney a fish. Sidney does not want it.

10 Nicole does not give up. Day after day, she wiggles a fish in front of Sidney. Then one day, the pup swallows it.

10 STRATEGY Analyze Text Structure

Teacher Think Aloud I know that text structure is the way authors organize information. One kind of text structure is sequence. Look at page 107. What words does the author use to signal what happens next? What is the sequence of events on this page?

Prompt children to apply the strategy in a Think Aloud.

Student Think Aloud Let's see. The phrase "Then one day" helps me understand what happens after Nicole tries to feed Sidney a fish day after day. First Nicole shows Sidney the fish, but Sidney does not want it. Day after day Nicole wiggles a fish in front of Sidney. *Then* one day, Sidney eats the fish.

Extra Support

Help children retell the events from this page in order. Ask: *What happened when Nicole showed Sidney the fish for the first time?* (Sidney did not want it.) *What did Nicole do day after day?* (She wiggled a fish in front of Sidney.) *What happened in the end?* (Sidney swallowed the fish.)

Before long, Sidney wants to eat fish. She waits for her bucket of fish in the morning.

The pup is gaining weight. She no longer needs her healthy drink.

Sidney is 5 weeks old. She has a thick layer of fat. The fat will keep her warm in cold water. 

Sidney is ready to be on her own.

12 **Sequence of Events**
Describe the order of events that people take to help Sidney at the sea mammal center.

First
A seal pup is alone on a beach because her mother did not come back from the ocean.

Next
Sidney got help at the sea mammal center. People give her food and a place to live, and get her ready to be on her own.

Last

Develop Comprehension

11 MONITOR AND CLARIFY: REREAD TO CLARIFY

Sidney is feeling better and ready to be on her own. What text evidence can you reread to help **clarify** this? (At first Sidney had to be fed milk from a tube, and she didn't want to eat fish. Now, she wants to eat fish. She also has a thick layer of fat.)

12 SKILL Sequence of Events

What steps are taken to help Sidney at the sea mammal center? (Sidney got help at the mammal center. People gave her food, then a place to live, and last they got her ready to be set free and live on her own.) Let's add this information to our Sequence Chart.

Think/Pair/Share Review your Sequence chart. With a partner, retell the sequence of events so far. Remember to use words such as *first*, *next*, and *then*.

Returning to the Ocean 13

Peter puts the pup in a carrying case. Other scientists take over. They carry Sidney onto a boat. Sidney is excited by the ocean's salty smell. She shakes the case.

The boat heads toward an island. When they are almost there, the boat stops. It is time to say good-bye.

A scientist tips the case. "Good luck, little one," she says. 14

13 STRATEGY Analyze Text Structure

How does this section help you understand the text structure?

Student Think Aloud I see the title of this section is *Returning to the Ocean*. It tells me that this section will tell about what happens after Sidney is nursed back to health. In the beginning, Sidney was left alone near the ocean. Next, Sidney was rescued. At the end, Sidney is let free in the ocean to live with other seals.

14 SKILL Sequence of Events

What happens at the end of this selection? (When Sidney is strong enough, the scientists return her to the ocean to live with the other harbor seals.) Add to the last section of our Sequence Chart.

SELF-SELECTED STRATEGY USE

What strategies did you use to make sense of what you read? Where? How were these strategies helpful?

ELL

Question 12

SEQUENCE OF EVENTS

What is the first thing that happens to Sidney? What is the last thing that happens to Sidney?

Provide Sentence Prompts

The first thing that happens to Sidney is that she is __________.

Then some people __________ Sidney. At the end of the story Sidney is __________.

First
A seal pup is alone on a beach because her mother did not come back from the ocean.
Next
People take care of Sidney to help her feel better. They give her food and a place to live. They get her ready to be on her own.
Last
Sidney returns to the ocean.

Develop Comprehension

COMPLETE THE SEQUENCE CHART

Review the information recorded on the sequence Chart. Ask children to add any additional details that they wish.

RETURN TO PREDICTIONS AND PURPOSES

Review and confirm children's predictions and the Focus Question. Have them describe how Sidney is found, helped, and released.

Quick Check

Can children summarize the selection and identify the sequence of events?

During **Small Group Instruction**

If No → **Approaching Level** Apply the skill to a simpler text. See page 119R.

If Yes → **On Level** Apply the skill to another text. See page 119S.

Beyond Level Apply the skill to a harder text. See page 119T.

Joan and Richard Hewett's Animal Adventures

Joan Hewett and her husband, **Richard Hewett**, created their first children's book in 1977. After that, Richard says, "I knew that this was what I wanted to do. Children's books are the best."

Joan and Richard have worked on more than 20 children's books together. Many of these books are about animals. Joan says, "We always enjoy doing books that bring us in close contact with animals. Still, photographing harbor seals and other wild animals takes patience. It's a challenge, and that's part of the fun."

Other books by Joan Hewett and Richard Hewett

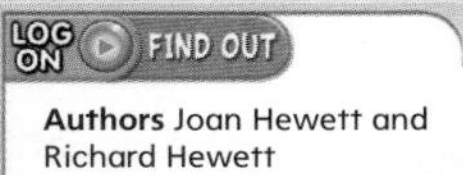

Authors Joan Hewett and Richard Hewett
www.macmillanmh.com

Author's Purpose
The Hewetts like to write about animals. Think about when you helped an animal or a person. Write a paragraph about how you helped.

114

Meet the Author/Photographer

Read aloud page 114 with children. Ask them what made Joan and Robert Hewett want to write a book about harbor seals. Tell children to review the selection and share what they think inspired the authors and what their purpose was in writing *A Harbor Seal Pup Grows Up.*

Author's Purpose

Joan Hewett wrote this book to teach readers about people who help seals. Have children write about how they helped with an animal or pet. Help children organize their thoughts before writing, by having them make a chart with columns titled "Who I Helped," "The Problem," and "How I Helped." Remind children that they need not write about a big problem. They can write about something as simple as feeding a pet.

Author's Craft

Author's Purpose

- Author's purpose is the reason an author writes a selection. An author may tell a story or explain about something. Sometimes, an author does both.
- For example, on the first page we learn that a harbor seal pup stays close to its mother and drinks its mother's milk. However, the author tells this information like a story by giving the seal a name.
- Discuss other places where the author incorporates information about seals into the telling of Sidney's story. (Possible answers: when Sidney learns to eat fish; when Sidney is released into the ocean)

Connect to Content

Animal Needs

Sidney' s body helps her meet her needs. On page 105, it says that she uses her flippers to scoot around and swim. On page 109, we read that Sidney's layer of fat helps keep her warm. Also, she has teeth to help her eat fish. Think of other animals. Which of their external characteristics, or physical traits, help them meet their needs? You can ask yourself, *How does the animal's body help it get food or stay* warm?

Objectives

- Retell a selection to show understanding
- Answer comprehension questions

Materials

- Student Book: *A Harbor Seal Pup Grows Up*, pp. 94–113
- Retelling Cards for *A Harbor Seal Pup Grows Up*
- chart paper
- Practice Book, p. 210

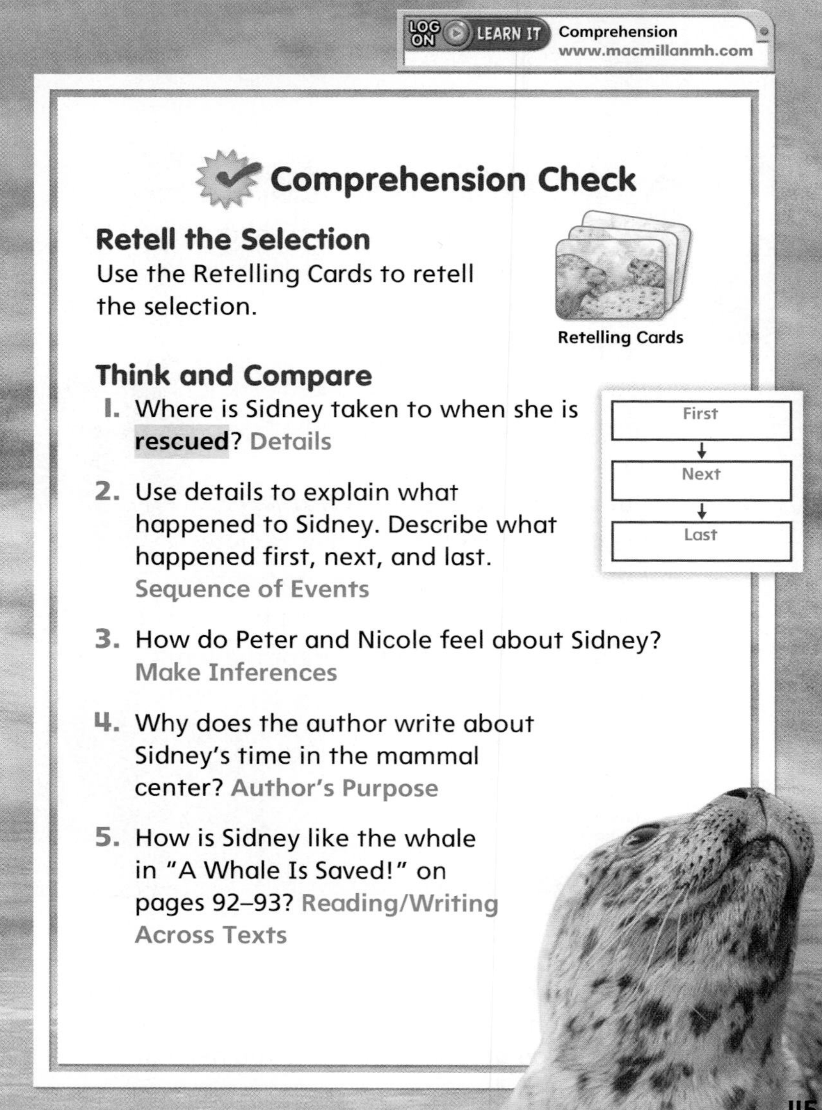
LOG ON LEARN IT Comprehension www.macmillanmh.com

Comprehension Check

Retell the Selection
Use the Retelling Cards to retell the selection.

Retelling Cards

Think and Compare

1. Where is Sidney taken to when she is **rescued**? Details
2. Use details to explain what happened to Sidney. Describe what happened first, next, and last. Sequence of Events
3. How do Peter and Nicole feel about Sidney? Make Inferences
4. Why does the author write about Sidney's time in the mammal center? Author's Purpose
5. How is Sidney like the whale in "A Whale Is Saved!" on pages 92–93? Reading/Writing Across Texts

First
Next
Last

115

Retelling Rubric

4	**Excellent**
	Retells the selection without prompting, using detailed information, and referring to text structure and features. Clearly describes the main idea.
 3	**Good**
	Retells the selection with little guidance, using some details, and occasionally referring to text structure and features. Generally describes the main idea.
 2	**Fair**
	Retells the selection with some guidance, using limited details. Partially describes the main idea.
 1	**Unsatisfactory**
	Retells the selection only when prompted, using limited details. Does not describe the main idea.

Retelling Cards

 Retell the Selection

RETELL *A HARBOR SEAL PUP GROWS UP*

- Remind children that as they read *A Harbor Seal Pup Grows Up* they told about the sequence of events. Now they will use this information to retell the whole selection. You can record children's retelling on chart paper.
- **Model Retelling** Use the prompts on the backs of **Retelling Cards** to model retelling the story.
- ELL **Guide Retelling** Use the leveled language acquisition prompts to guide children's retelling.
- **Discuss the Retelling** *What happens to Sidney first? What happens to her next? What is the last thing that happens to her?*

Phonological Awareness

Identify Syllables

Model

Show children how to identify and work with syllables in spoken words.

A syllable is a word part that has a vowel sound. I can clap the number of syllables in a word. Listen as I clap and say the word *cook*. *Cook* has one vowel sound; therefore it has one syllable. Listen as I clap and say the word *cooking*. *Cooking* has two vowel sounds; therefore, it has two syllables.

Clapping the syllables in a word can help you when you spell a long word. Writing one syllable at a time makes writing a longer word easier.

Guided Practice/Practice

Have children clap syllables with these examples. Guide practice with the first two rows.

Let's do some together. Clap the syllables in each word. How many syllables do you hear in each?

look	could	understood
Brooklyn	textbook	neighborhood

To extend the lesson, have children practice blending vowel digraphs in multisyllabic words.

Now it's your turn. Listen carefully. Tell the number of syllables you hear in each word. Then blend the sounds in each word.

should	shook	understood
good-bye	driftwood	motherhood
likelihood	crooked	checkbook
goodness	underfoot	footnote

Objective

- Identify syllables in spoken words

Objectives

- Identify letter-sound correspondence for vowel digraphs /ů/ spelled *oo*, *ou*
- Blend sounds in words with vowel digraphs *oo*, *ou*
- Review previously taught phonics skills
- Read multisyllabic words

Materials

- Sound-Spelling Card: *Book*
- Word-Building Cards; Teacher's Resource Book, p. 66
- pocket chart
- chart paper
- Practice Book, p. 211

Skills Trace

Vowel Digraphs *oo*, *ou*	
Introduce	91C–D
Practice/ Apply	91F, 93G-H, 115F-G, 115I, 115T; Practice Book: p. 206; Decodable Reader: *Flip and Spots*
Reteach/ Review	119D; 119K-N, 119Q, 119W, 119CC
Assess	Weekly Test; Unit 4 Test
Maintain	Build Fluency: Sound/Spellings

Phonics

Review Vowel Digraphs *oo*, *ou*

Model

Review the vowel digraph sound /ů/ spelled *oo* and *ou*. Show the *Book* **Sound-Spelling Card**.

This is the *Book* Sound-Spelling Card. The sound is /ů/. The /ů/ sound can be spelled with the letters *oo* or *ou*. Say it with me: /ů/. This is the sound in the middle of the word *book*.

We've been reading words with the /ů/ sound all week. Today we will read more.

Guided Practice/Practice

Have children practice connecting the letters and sound.

(Point to the Sound-Spelling Card.) What are these letters? What sound do they stand for?

Build Fluency: Sound/Spellings

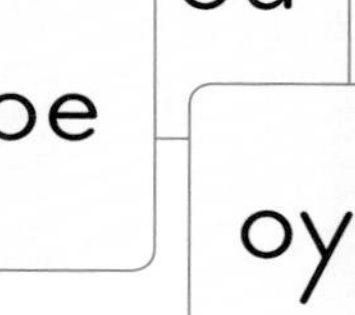

Display the following **Word-Building Cards** one at a time: *oo, ou, oo, ui, ew, ue, u, ou, oe, oi, oy, ou, ow, are, air, ear, ere, or, ore, oar, ar, gn, kn, wr, mb*. Have children chorally say each sound. Repeat and vary the pace.

Blend with Vowel Digraphs *oo*, *ou*

Model

Display Word-Building Cards *l, o, o, k*. Model how to blend the sounds together as you run your finger under each letter.

Continue by modeling the words *good, hood, wooden, would, hooked,* and *rebook*.

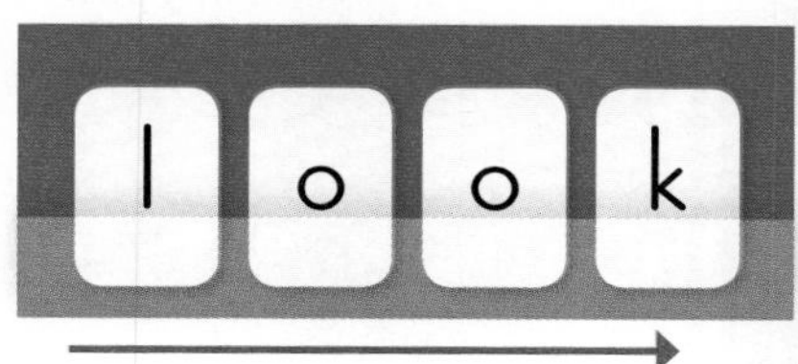

(Point to *l*.) This is the letter *l*. It stands for /l/. (Point to *oo*.) These are the letters *oo*. Together they stand for /ů/. Listen as I blend these sounds together. (Extend the sounds.)

(Point to *k*.) This is the letter *k*. It stands for /k/. Listen as I blend all three sounds together: /lůk/. Say it with me: *look*.

Guided Practice/Practice
Write the words below on chart paper. Read the first line with children. Then have children chorally read the words on the chart. Use the appropriate blending level.

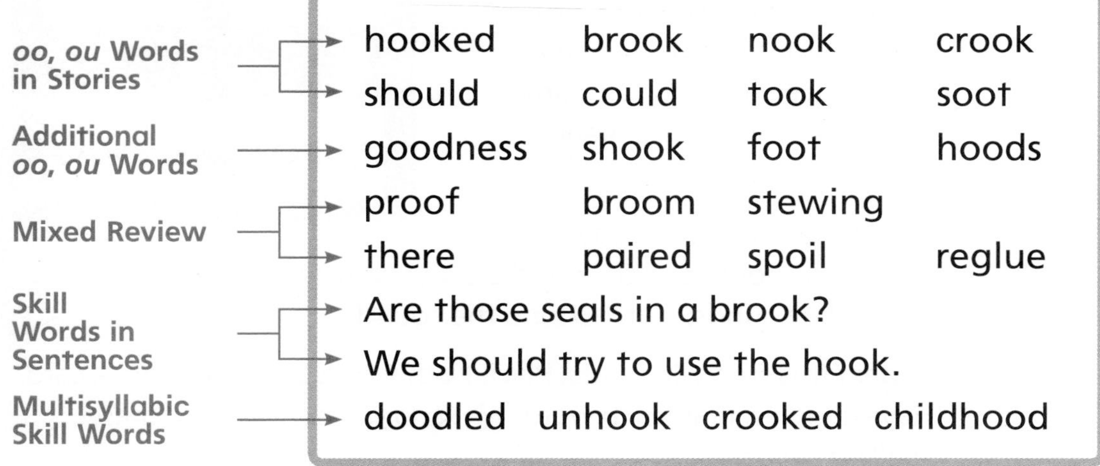

Corrective Feedback

Blending Error Say: *My turn.* Model blending using the appropriate signaling procedures. Then lead children in blending the sounds. Say: *Do it with me.* You will respond with children to offer support. Then say: *Your turn. Blend.* Have children chorally blend. Return to the beginning of the word. Say: *Let's start over.*

Ending *-ing*

Teach
- Say the words *cooking* and *footing*. Ask children to listen closely to hear what is the same in both words.
- Point out the /ing/ sound at the end of the words.
- Write the words *cooking* and *footing* on the board. Underline the letters *-ing*.
- Tell children that the inflectional ending *-ing* in *cooking* and *footing* means action is happening now.

Practice/Apply
- Then write the following words on the board and help children blend them: *hook, hooking; foot, footing; look, looking*. Point out that the letters *-ing* at the end of a word can stand for the /ing/ sound, as in *looking*.
- Ask children to look for words that end in *-ing* and that tell about actions happening now as they read this week's stories. Keep a running list on chart paper.

ON YOUR OWN

Practice Book, page 211

The letters ***-ing*** can be added to the end of a verb to change its tense.
If a word ends in silent ***e***, drop the ***e*** before adding ***-ing***.
smile – e + ing = smiling

Add *-ing* to the end of each word. Write the new word. Then use the word in a sentence. Possible responses provided

1. dive diving
   Shawn is diving into the pool.
2. make making
   What are you making in art class today?
3. snore snoring
   Dad is snoring very loudly.
4. ride riding
   Pam is riding her bike.

Approaching Reproducible, page 211
Beyond Reproducible, page 211

Objectives

- Sort words with vowel digraphs *oo*, *ou*
- Spell words with vowel digraphs *oo*, *ou*
- Build Fluency: Word Automaticity

Materials

- index cards from Day 2
- pocket chart
- Spelling Word Cards BLM; Teacher's Resource Book, p. 70
- Phonics/Spelling Practice Book, p. 75

5-Day Spelling	
DAY 1	Dictation; Pretest
DAY 2	Teacher-Modeled Word Sort
DAY 3	Student Word Sort
DAY 4	Test Practice
DAY 5	Posttest

ON YOUR OWN

Spelling, page 75

hook	brook	would	should	shook
good	crook	foot	could	soot

Sentences to Complete

Write a spelling word on each line to complete the sentence.

1. The crook stole a watch from the shop.
2. An inch is smaller than a foot.
3. Hang your coat up on the hook.
4. We saw ducks swimming in the brook.
5. I am good at standing on one foot.
6. He would not be able to play in the game.
7. The little boy shook with fear.
8. Mom knew I could pick her up at the mall.
9. There was soot in the fireplace.
10. You should know the answer to this question.

Phonics/Spelling

Word Sort with *oo*, *ou*

WORD SORT

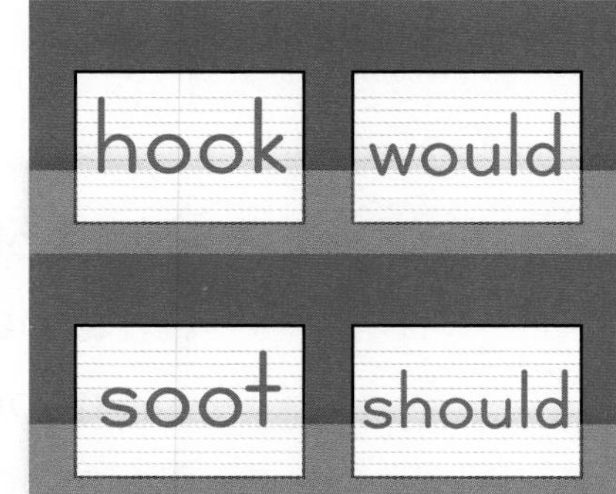

- Use the index cards from Day 2 for each spelling word. Place the *hook* and *would* cards to form two columns in a pocket chart. Pronounce each sound clearly: /h/ /ů/ /k/, /w/ /ů/ /d/. Blend sounds with children.
- Hold up the *soot* card. Say and spell it. Pronounce each sound clearly: /s/ /ů/ /t/. Blend the sounds: /sůt/. Extend the sounds.
- Repeat this step with *good*. Place both words below the *hook* card. Have children read each word. *What do you notice about these spelling words?* (They have the /ů/ sound, and they are spelled *oo*.) Repeat the process with the rest of the spelling words.
- Display the words *below*, *city*, and *own*. Read and spell the words together with children. Point out that these spelling words do not contain the /ů/ sound.
- **Build Fluency: Word Automaticity** Conclude by asking children to chorally read the words to build fluency. Then ask children to orally generate additional words that rhyme with each word.

High-Frequency Words

- **Teach High-Frequency Words** Write the new high-frequency words for the week **below**, **city**, and **own** on the board. Teach the words using the **Read/Spell/Write** routine.
  - **Read** Read the word. Have children repeat.
  - **Spell** Chorally spell the word.
  - **Write** Have children write the word as they spell it aloud. Then ask children to write a sentence using each word.
- **Practice** Write sample cloze sentences for each word on the board.

  I like to ride the subway in the ________.
  My friend Jack has his ________ room.
  I saw a squirrel outside ________ the bushes.
- Have children read the sentences and write the missing word for each one.
- **Additional High-Frequency Words** Introduce an additional six words (Additional Words #219–224: **open**, **read**, **wash**, **gave**, **sleep**, **and**) for more practice. Have children use the **Read/Spell/Write** routine to learn the words. Finish with a speed drill of all the words taught for the day. Display each High-Frequency Word Card quickly and have children identify and read the word aloud. Repeat with any words children have difficulty with.

Decodable Reader

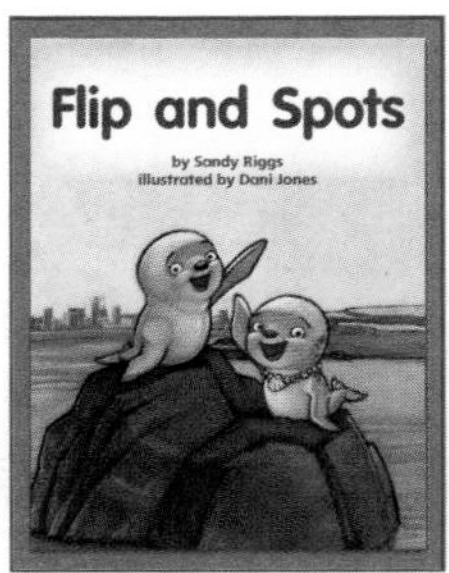

Decodable Reader

- **Review High-Frequency Words** Review the high-frequency words that appear in the book: **follow**, **near**, and **paper**. Have children read each aloud and provide a sentence for each.

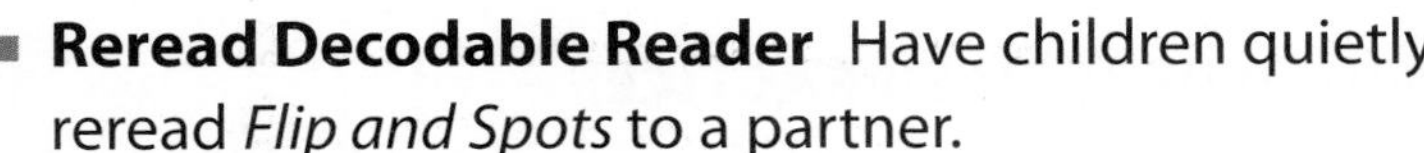

- **Reread Decodable Reader** Have children quietly reread *Flip and Spots* to a partner.

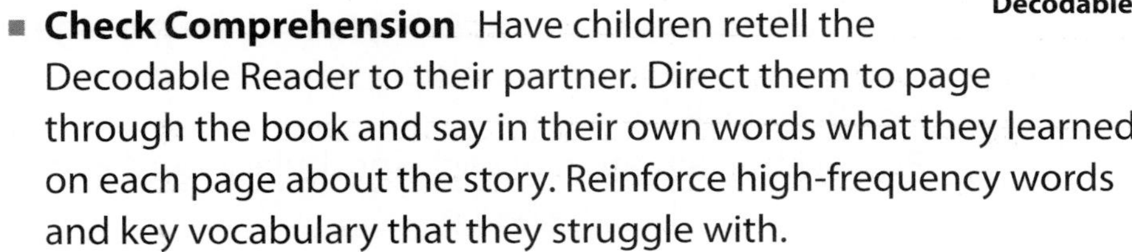

- **Check Comprehension** Have children retell the Decodable Reader to their partner. Direct them to page through the book and say in their own words what they learned on each page about the story. Reinforce high-frequency words and key vocabulary that they struggle with.

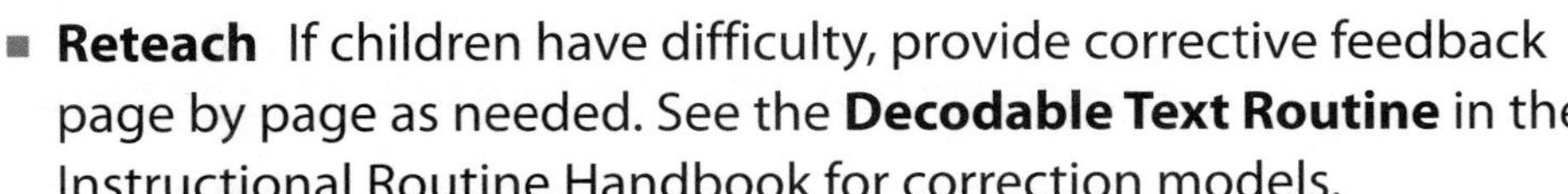

- **Reteach** If children have difficulty, provide corrective feedback page by page as needed. See the **Decodable Text Routine** in the Instructional Routine Handbook for correction models.

Objectives

- Decode multisyllabic words in connected text
- Teach high-frequency words *below, city, own*

Materials

- Decodable Reader Library: *Flip and Spots*

SMALL GROUP OPTION

You may wish to read the Decodable Reader during **Small Group** time.

See pages 119K–119JJ

Objectives

- Use context clues to determine the meaning of words
- Identify and use antonyms
- Review this week's and last week's vocabulary words

Materials

- Transparency 38
- Practice Book, p. 212

Vocabulary

examines	hunger
mammal	normal
rescued	young

ON YOUR OWN **Practice Book,** page 212

Antonyms are words that have opposite or almost opposite meanings.

Circle the antonyms in each pair of sentences. Then write them on the lines.

1. I remember my first animal rescue. first
   I knew it would not be my last. last
2. My neighbor lost her puppy. lost
   I found him the next day. found
3. The puppy did not go very far. far
   He was near the park behind my house. near
4. The puppy was shaking from the cold. cold
   His fur could not keep him warm in all the snow. warm
5. I bent down to see if the puppy was alright. down
   He let me pick him up to carry him home. up

Approaching Reproducible, page 212
Beyond Reproducible, page 212

Vocabulary

STRATEGY Use Context Clues: Antonyms

EXPLAIN

- You can often figure out the meaning of an unfamiliar word by finding clues, such as antonyms, in nearby sentences.

MODEL

Use **Transparency 38** to model how to use antonyms to figure out the meaning of **young**. Read aloud the first paragraph. Underline the antonym for **young**.

Think Aloud I don't know what **young** means, but I read that one place was for young seals and a different place was for older seals. I know that *older* means at a later time in life, so I can tell that **young** means at an early time in life.

Transparency 38

Use Context Clues: Antonyms

Our class visited a research center where scientists rescue and study sea mammals. My favorite sea mammals are seals. First, we saw the nursery. This is where the scientists took care of the young seals. Then, we went to another area where different scientists studied the older seals.

Sometimes the seals that come in are sick. The scientists feed them and give them medicine. Soon most of the seals are healthy again. When they are well enough, scientists bring them back to the ocean.

We saw one seal that was the biggest in the whole center. We were surprised to see a picture of it when it arrived at the center. It was the smallest seal they had ever rescued!

Vocabulary Transparency

GUIDED PRACTICE/PRACTICE

Help children figure out the meaning of *healthy* and use context clues to find the antonyms in the rest of the passage.

REVIEW WORDS

Review the definition of each vocabulary word and write a sentence using the word on the board.

Practice Ask children questions relating each word on their own experience, such as: *When you are* sick, *what do you do to feel better*?

Repeat using last week's words *serious*, *personal*, *informs*, *heal*, *aid*.

Oral Vocabulary

REVIEW WORDS

- Remind children of this week's oral vocabulary words.

If you feel **compassion**, you want to help people or animals in need. *I felt compassion for the cat that was stuck in a tree, so I tried to help get her down.*

Baffled means you are confused or don't understand something. *The jackal was baffled by how the tiger was rescued from the hole.*

Someone who is **daring** is not afraid to try something. *Jeff was daring when he climbed the tall tree.*

Lunging at something means jumping quickly at it. *The lion lunged at the small animal.*

Surviving means "staying alive." *The lady was surviving only on water when she was lost.*

Use the statements and questions below to help reinforce the meanings of the words.

- *Show me how you lunge in a sport you like to play.*
- *How can you show compassion to a friend who is hurt?*
- *Show how you look when you're ready to do something daring.*
- *Which word goes with "breathing air"?* survive
- *If your friend was baffled about how to climb a tree, what could you do to help?*
- Then have a child say what each word means and use it in a sentence.

- Use similar activities to review last week's words: *clever*, *comfort*, *urgent*, *recuperate*, and *sympathy*.

Objectives

- Practice repeated oral reading
- 62–82 WCPM
- Practice fluency prosody

Materials

- Transparency 19
- Fluency Solutions Audio CD
- Practice Book, p. 213

Fluency

Repeated Reading: Prosody

EXPLAIN/MODEL

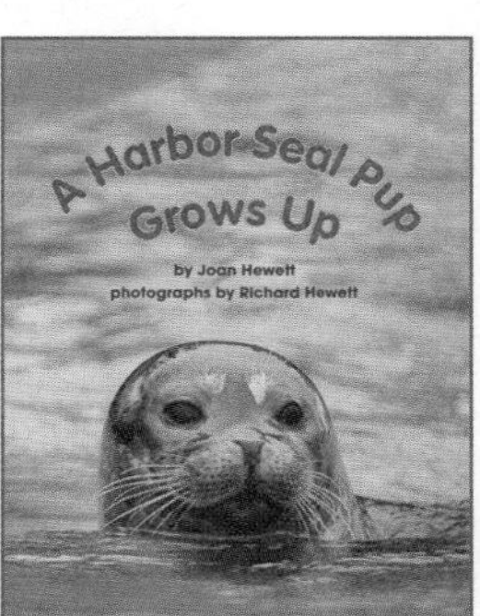

Main Selection

- **Punctuation** Explain that the punctuation in a text helps the reader know when to pause or stop.
- **Phrasing** Display **Transparency 19** and point out the double slashes. Remind children that the double slashes show stops. Explain to children that it is helpful to read sentences in meaningful chunks. In this passage the double slashes point out the meaningful chunks.

Point out the first sentence on Transparency 19. *The first meaningful chunk of text is the sentence* Sidney is brought to a sea mammal center, *so I can read that together.*

- Explain that if children struggle with any word, they should decode it or ask for help, then go back to the beginning of the slash and reread that section of the text.
- Model reading aloud Transparency 19. *When did I stop when I read?*

Transparency 19

Sidney is brought to a sea mammal center. //

A scientist named Peter is in charge. // Peter takes care of young seals. // He lifts the thin pup from her cage. //

Sidney is weak from hunger. // Peter knows just what to do. // He puts a tube in Sidney's mouth. //

Then Nicole pumps a drink into Sidney's stomach. // The drink is like a mother seal's milk. //

—from *A Harbor Seal Pup Grows Up* (pages 100–101)

Fluency Transparency

ELL

Accuracy Read each sentence aloud and explain what each one means. If children have trouble pronouncing a specific word correctly, have them listen as you read it aloud to them. Then choral read the word.

- **Expression** Discuss how your intonation changes depending on the type of material you are reading. Explain that nonfiction text usually contains a great deal of information and should be read slowly and clearly.

Demonstrate how you adjust your reading rate based on the genre and style of the writing. When the author is describing exciting actions, you adjust your reading rate by reading more quickly. Model reading the passage with natural expression.

- **Pronunciation** Model reading the passage. Have children note your pronunciation of *Sidney, mammal*, and *scientist*. Point out that good readers slow down their reading rate when reading longer words or unfamiliar words to make sure they pronounce them correctly.

PRACTICE

- Have children reread the passage chorally, using the slashes to think about their phrasing.

Repeat the reading to give children even more practice with natural phrasing, speed, and prosody.

- **Daily Fluency** Children will practice fluency reading aloud **Practice Book** page 213, then paraphrasing what they have read. Students can also practice using the **Fluency Solutions Audio CD**. The passage is recorded at a slow, practice speed, and a faster, fluent speed.

Quick Check

Can children read the passage fluently and with prosody?

During **Small Group Instruction**

If No → **Approaching Level** See pages: 119DD, 119HH.

If Yes → **On Level** See Fluency 119EE.

Beyond Level See Fluency 119EE.

ON YOUR OWN

Practice Book, page 213

As I read, I will pay attention to my phrasing.

All tigers have stripes. But each tiger has different
9 stripes.
10 Tigers live in jungles and forests. A tiger's coat
19 helps it blend in with long grass, bushes, and trees.
29 This helps keep the tiger safe.
35 Tigers are mammals. A **mammal** feeds its
42 **young** on milk. Tiger cubs live with their mother for
52 two to three years. Adult male tigers live alone.
61 Tigers hunt alone. They hide and then sneak up
70 on their prey. They catch deer, wild pigs, and cattle. 80

Comprehension Check

1. How does a tiger's diet change as it grows up? **Sequence of Events**
   First, tiger cubs drink their mothers' milk. When they are older, they hunt deer, pigs, and cattle.
2. How do stripes help a tiger? **Main Idea and Details**
   Stripes help a tiger blend into the jungle or forest.

	Words Read	–	Number of Errors	=	Words Correct Score
First Read		–		=	
Second Read		–		=	

Approaching Reproducible, page 213

Beyond Reproducible, page 213

Objectives

- Analyze illustrations/photos
- Express personal responses to literature
- Discuss genre characteristics

Materials

- Student Book: *A Harbor Seal Pup Grows Up*, pp. 94–114

Comprehension

REVIEW SKILL **Illustrations/Photos**

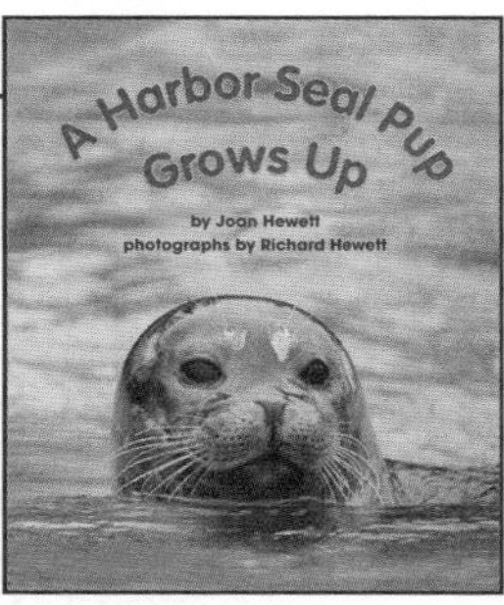

Main Selection

EXPLAIN/MODEL

- Review that an **illustration** is a drawn picture. A **photo** is a photograph and is often used in nonfiction selections. Illustrations and photos can often help you better understand the text of a story or nonfiction selection.
- Remind children that using illustrations and photos can
  1. give you many clues about a story's character and plot.
  2. help you understand something in a nonfiction selection that you don't know about before you read it.

PRACTICE

How does the seal look in the photos in the beginning of A Harbor Seal Pup Grows Up*? How does the seal look at the end?*

Respond to Literature

Personal Response Have children pose relevant questions about *A Harbor Seal Pup Grows Up.* Have them record the responses in their Writer's Notebooks.

- *Summarize the selection. When you began the selection, what did you think would happen to Sidney? Why? What did happen to Sidney first, next, and last?*
- *Compare two of the settings in the selection: the beach where Sidney was found and the sea mammal center. How are they alike? How are they different?*
- *What do you think happened to Sidney after she was set free?*

Focus Question: Nonfiction Remind children that nonfiction is about real people and events.

- *Did you think the story of a real seal was more interesting than the story of an imaginary seal would have been? Why or why not?*
- *Think about what the selection would be like if it was a fiction story. What details in it might be different?*

Skills Trace

Use Illustrations	
Introduce	U4: 45A–B
Practice/ Apply	U4: 45K–71A; Practice Book: 187–188
Reteach/ Review	U4: 77G, 77R–T, 77X–Z
Assess	Weekly Test; Unit 4 Test
Maintain	U4: 115N

Phonemic Awareness

Phoneme Blending

Model

Show children how to orally blend phonemes.

I am going to put one marker in each box as I say each sound. Then I will blend the sounds to form a word.

Listen and watch. /f/ (Place marker in the first box.) /ů/ (Place marker in the second box.) /t/ (Place marker in the third box.)

This word has three sounds: /f/ /ů/ /t/. Listen as I blend the sounds to form the word: /fůt/. (Stretch the vowel sound.) The word is *foot.*

Guided Practice/Practice

Help children practice blending phonemes. Do the first six words together.

Let's do some together. Place a marker for each sound you hear. I will say one sound at a time. Then we will blend the sounds to say the word.

/k/ /ů/ /k/ /sh/ /ů/ /k/ /b/ /r/ /ů/ /k/
/g/ /ů/ /d/ /k/ /r/ /ů/ /k/ /s/ /ů/ /t/

Now it's your turn. Listen carefully. Blend the sounds and say the word.

/n/ /ů/ /k/ /sh/ /ů/ /d/ /w/ /ů/ /d/
/f/ /ů/ /t/ /k/ /ů/ /d/ /h/ /ů/ /d/
/l/ /ů/ /k/ /b/ /ů/ /k/
/u/ /n/ /h/ /ů/ /k/

Objective

- Blend phonemes in words

Materials

- markers
- Sound-Spelling WorkBoards; Teacher's Resource Book, p. 143

Objectives

- Build words with vowel digraphs *oo, ou*
- Read multisyllabic words

Materials

- Word-Building Cards; Teacher's Resource Book, p. 66
- pocket chart

Phonics

Blend with Vowel Digraphs *oo, ou*

Model

Place **Word-Building Cards** *g, o, o, d* in the pocket chart to form *good*. Model how to generate and blend sounds to say the word. Repeat with *could*.

The letter *g* stand for /g/. The letters *oo* together stand for /ů/. The letter *d* stands for /d/. Listen as I blend all three sounds: /gůd/. Let's read the word together: *good*.

Guided Practice/Practice

Repeat with the examples given.

should hook nook wood would
understood looking crooked uncooked

Build with Vowel Digraphs *oo, ou*

Model

Place Word-Building Cards *b, o, o, k* in the pocket chart. Blend the phonemes.

Let's blend all the sounds and read the word: /bůk/, *book*.

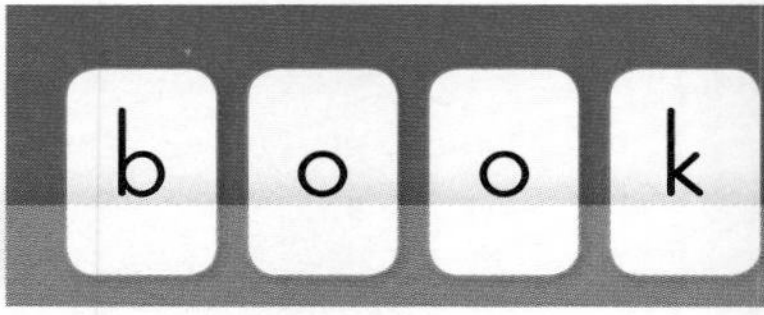

Add *s* and repeat with *books*.

Let's blend all the sounds and read the word: /bůks/, *books*.

Change *b* to *l* and repeat with *looks*.

Let's blend all the sounds and read the word: /lůks/, *looks*.

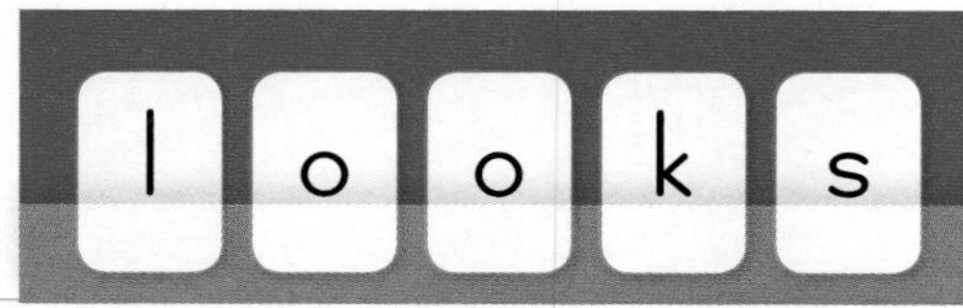

Guided Practice/Practice

Continue building with these examples.

shook, stood, wood, good, cooking, looking, prebook, rebook, rehooked

Skills Trace

Vowel Digraphs *oo, ou*	
Introduce	91C–D
Practice/ Apply	91F, 93G-H, 115F-G, 115I, 115T; Practice Book: p. 206; Decodable Reader: *Flip and Spots*
Reteach/ Review	119D; 119K-N, 119Q, 119W, 119CC
Assess	Weekly Test; Unit 4 Test
Maintain	Build Fluency: Sound/Spellings

Phonics/Spelling

Words with Vowel Digraphs *oo, ou*

- Provide pairs of children with individual copies of the **Spelling Word Cards**.
- While one partner reads the words one at a time, the other partner should orally segment the word (e.g., /f/ /ů/ /t/) and then write the word. Have **WorkBoards** available for children who need hands-on support in segmenting the word and attaching one spelling to each sound.

- After reading all the words, partners should switch roles.
- When both partners have spelled all the words, children should correct their own papers.
- **Build Fluency: Word Automaticity** Partners should use their Spelling Word Cards to practice reading each word quickly to gain fluency.

Quick Check

Can children spell words with vowel digraphs *oo, ou*?

During **Small Group Instruction**

If No → **Approaching Level** Repeat blending using the weekly spelling words. Explicitly correct the error, and provide more "with me" type practice. Use a lower level of blending to provide support.

If Yes → **On Level** Consolidate the learning by having children spell additional words with vowel digraphs *oo, ou*. See page 119M.

Beyond Level Extend the learning by having children spell harder words containing vowel digraphs *oo, ou*. See page 119N.

Objectives

- Spell words with vowel digraphs *oo, ou*
- Build Fluency: Word Automaticity

Materials

- Spelling Word Cards BLM; Teacher's Resource Book, p. 70
- Sound-Spelling WorkBoards; Teacher's Resource Book, p. 143
- paper and pencils
- Phonics/Spelling Practice Book, p. 76

5-Day Spelling	
DAY 1	Dictation; Pretest
DAY 2	Teacher-Modeled Word Sort
DAY 3	Student Word Sort
DAY 4	Test Practice
DAY 5	Posttest

ON YOUR OWN

Spelling, page 76

A. There are six spelling mistakes in the paragraph below. Circle the misspelled words. Write the words correctly on the lines below.

Our class stood by the brouk. It was littered with trash. We knew we shood do something. We got some garbage bags and gloves. We started picking up the trash. Jan's fut almost slipped into the brook. We had to be careful. Someone cuold get hurt. But we knew everyone woold be very happy that we took gud care of the brook.

1. brook 2. should 3. foot
4. could 5. would 6. good

B. Writing

Write about cleaning up something to make Earth a better place. Use four spelling words from your list.

Answers will vary.

DAY 4
WHOLE GROUP

Objectives

- Use vocabulary words from this week in context
- Review this week's and last week's vocabulary words

Vocabulary

Words in Context

REVIEW VOCABULARY
Review this week's vocabulary words (**examines**, **hunger**, **mammal**, **normal**, **rescued**, and **young**) using the questions below.

- *If your brother rescues a cat from a tree, does he get it down or leave it up there?*
- *Who examines you during a physical, the doctor or a mail carrier?*
- *If you feel hunger, do you want food to eat or juice to drink?*
- *Which animal is a mammal? A cat or a fish?*
- *If you have a normal temperature, do you feel fine or are you sick?*
- *If you are in the second grade, are you old or young?*
- Then have children use each word in a sentence.

- Repeat the activity with last week's vocabulary words: *serious*, *personal*, *informs*, *heal*, and *aid*.

EXTEND
Word Relationships Remind children that synonyms are words that have the same or almost the same meaning, while antonyms are words that have opposite meanings. Explain that antonyms and synonyms are types of word relationships. Ask children to think of antonyms for the vocabulary words *normal* and *young*. Then have children think of synonyms for the vocabulary words *examines* and *rescued*. Have children discuss each word pair relationship.

Poetry

Genre

POEM

Tell children that the next selection they will read is a poem. Discuss the features of the genre and the literary element. Explain that a poem can describe things in interesting or unusual ways. Also, tell children that rhyme, rhythm, and repetition in poetry work together to help to create images for the reader.

Paired Selection

Literary Element: Similes

EXPLAIN/MODEL

Explain that a simile is a figure of speech that compares one thing to another. A simile uses the word *like* or *as* to help readers picture what something looks, sounds, or feels like. Words and phrases in similes sometimes have multiple meanings. They have a literal meaning, or what they actually mean or refer to in real life. But they can also have non-literal, or figurative, meanings. Non-literal meanings can help the words create images and make writing interesting to read. Read the poem on Student Book, page 116 to children. Then read it again and have them listen for the simile.

Think Aloud When I read the poem aloud, I notice that the poet writes that the puppy's coat is brushed until it shines like silk. But the topic of this sentence is not silk. The phrase must have a meaning that is not literal, or not directly what it is saying. I know that the word *like* is used in similes to compare things. So, the poet is comparing the puppy's fur to silk. Silk is smooth and shiny. This simile helps me picture what the puppy's fur is like. It must be smooth and shiny, too. This simile makes a comparison and shows the phrase's non-literal meaning. It also makes the poem more interesting to read!

Objectives

- Read a poem
- Understand that similes compare using *like* or *as*

Materials

- Student Book: "The Puppy," pp. 116–117
- Practice Book, p. 214

ELL

Paired Reading Prepare children to read the story prior to the whole-class reading. Use the Interactive Question-Response Guide in the English Language Learners Resource Book, pages 248–257, to preteach the story content, build language, and develop meaning.

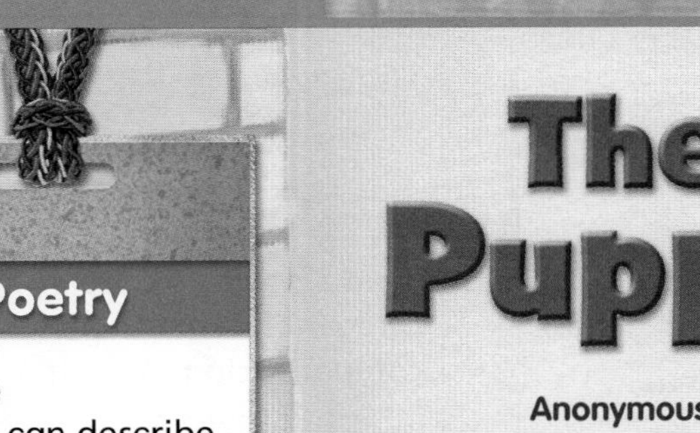

Poetry

Poetry

Genre
Poems can describe things in interesting or unusual ways. Rhyme, rhythm, and repetition help create images in poetry.

Literary Element
Similes compare one thing to another. A simile uses the words *like* or *as*.

The Puppy

Anonymous

Call the puppy,
And give him some milk. **1**
Brush his coat
Till it shines like silk. **2**
Call the dog
And give him a bone.
Go for a walk,
Then take him home.

Connect and Compare

1. What things are compared in the poem? How can you tell that the comparison is a simile? **Simile**
2. Think about how the scientists cared for Sidney in *A Harbor Seal Pup Grows Up*. How is caring for a seal pup like caring for a puppy? How is it different? **Reading/Writing Across Texts**

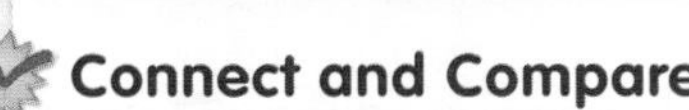

LOG ON FIND OUT **Poetry** Animal care
www.macmillanmh.com

116 117

ON YOUR OWN **Practice Book,** page 214

A **simile** creates a non-literal meaning by comparing one thing to another. Similes use the words ***like*** or ***as***.

Read each question. Answer it with a complete sentence that includes the underlined simile from the question. Then draw a picture to show what is happening in the sentence.

Possible responses provided.

1. When might a person be as hungry as a bear?
   A person might be as hungry as a bear if he or she hasn't eaten in a long time.
2. What might people be doing when they are as busy as bees?
   People might be as busy as bees when they are getting a lot of work done.

Approaching Reproducible, page 214

Beyond Reproducible, page 214

Read Poetry

1 USE LITERARY ELEMENT: RHYME

Say the words *bone* and *cone*. Point out that these words rhyme because they have the same ending sounds. Explain that a rhyming poem has words with the same sounds at the ends of some lines. Remind students that rhyme, rhythmic patterns, and repetition all work to create images in poems. Read the poem and have students identify the rhyming words. (*milk/silk*) Then have them visualize and describe the images the rhyming words create.

2 USE LITERARY ELEMENT: SIMILES

How do you know the puppy's fur is shiny and smooth? (The poet uses a simile to compare the puppy's coat to silk. Since silk is smooth and shiny, the puppy's fur must be smooth and shiny, too.)

Connect and Compare

SUGGESTED ANSWERS

1. The puppy's coat and silk are compared. The comparison uses the word *like* so I know that it is a simile. SIMILE

2. Focus Question: A seal pup and a puppy both need milk. A puppy should also be brushed and walked. You do not need to do this to care for a seal pup. A seal pup needs fish and a place to swim. READING/WRITING ACROSS TEXTS

Write Poetry

REVIEW

Review the features of a rhyming poem and the literary element simile.

- A **rhyming poem** has lines that end with the same rhyming sounds.
- A **simile** is a figure of speech that compares one thing to another. Examples are "sly like a fox" or "the paper was light as a feather."

BRAINSTORM

- Discuss the weekly topic: Community Teams.
- Have children think of an animal in need of help from people. They can write down how they think the animal is feeling in their Writer's Notebooks.

WRITE

Have each child write a poem about being an animal in need and tell what it needs. Challenge children to write rhyming poems that contain sensory details. Tell children to include a simile. Use the sentence starters and examples below if needed.

- I wish I was home on my nice warm ________.
- Happy as a ________, when my owner rubs my ________.
- I hope someone ________ me.
- I'm lost, can't you ________.
- Help me, please. Take care of me like ________.

SHARE

Have children share their poems with the class. Ask them to discuss the words that rhyme in the poem, if appropriate.

Objectives

- Read a poem
- Understand that similes compare using *like* or *as*
- Recognize literal and non-literal meanings of phrases

Materials

- Student Book: "The Puppy," pp. 116–117
- Practice Book, p. 214

Test Practice

Answering Questions

To apply **answering questions strategies** to content-area reading, see pages 23–28 in the *Time for Kids Test Practice Edition.*

Digital Learning

Story available on **Listening Library Audio CD** and **StudentWorks Plus**, the Interactive eBook.

www.macmillanmh.com

Objectives

- Proofread for punctuation and capitalization
- Use irregular verbs in reading, writing, and speaking

Materials

- Transparency 94
- Proofreading Marks BLM; TRB, p. 191
- Grammar Practice Book, p. 94

Future Verbs

Teach/Model
Remind children that verbs can show future actions as well as present and past actions. Tell them that the helping verb *will*, shows that the action is going to happen in the future. Explain that although the verbs *come*, *run*, and *give* are irregular because the past tense does not end in *-ed*, they form the future tense like regular verbs. Write *come*, *run*, and *give* on the board. Then write the future tense for each verb below the present form: *will come*, *will run*, and *will give*. Tell children that adding the helping verb *will* shows that the action is going to happen in the future. Then explain that the verb *is*, does have an irregular future tense. Write the verbs *is* and *will be* on the board and explain that *will be* is the future tense of *is*. Then write the following example, *Kara will be seven years old next year.*

Practice/Apply
Have children practice writing future verbs in sentences. Ask them to read the sentences aloud to a partner.

Grammar

Irregular Verbs

REVIEW

- Remind children that some verbs are **irregular** and do not end with *-ed* in the past tense (e.g., *was*, *were*, *came*, *ran*, *gave*). Some irregular verbs are *is*, *come*, *run*, and *give*.

PRACTICE

Have children work in pairs to write sentences about community teams that have helped an animal or person in need. One partner should write two sentences that include the past-tense form of the verbs *come* and *run*, and the other should write two sentences that include the past-tense form of *is* and *give*.

Have partners exchange papers and check to see that the verb forms are correct. Then have partners read aloud their sentences to each other. Example sentences are:

- The store owners came to rescue the cat. It ran down the gutter in the street.
- What was going on in the mall? The security guards gave a woman help when she fainted.

ELL ENGLISH LANGUAGE LEARNERS

Beginning

Practice To help children practice using the irregular past tense, model actions such as giving a child a pencil, and then saying, *I gave [child's name] a pencil.* Write a sentence frame, *I gave [child's name]* ___________. Have children complete it, and choral read it aloud. Repeat this exercise with the other irregular verbs.

Intermediate

Practice Write simple sentence frames like the following: *Yesterday I [give, gave] my friend a pencil.* Read the sentences aloud and then have children copy the sentences, choosing the correct past tense form of the verb. Invite children to read their sentences aloud. Correct for pronunciation as needed.

Advanced

Write Ask children to rewrite the following sentences using the past tense. *The dog runs to the man. The man is lost. The dog comes to help him.*

Review and Assess
Fluency

Phrasing

MODEL FLUENT READING

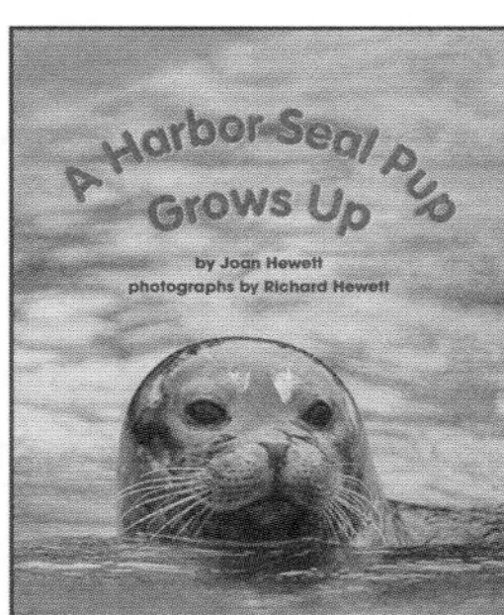

Main Selection

- Read aloud a few pages of *A Harbor Seal Pup Grows Up*. Have children echo each sentence. Model how to pause and stop at commas and punctuation using correct phrasing.

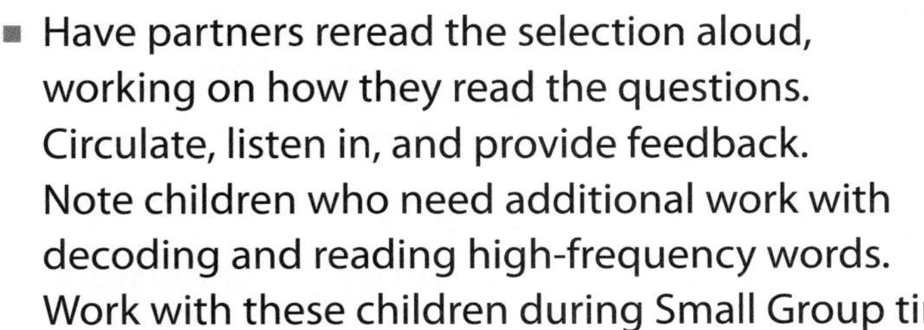

- Have partners reread the selection aloud, working on how they read the questions. Circulate, listen in, and provide feedback. Note children who need additional work with decoding and reading high-frequency words. Work with these children during Small Group time.

REPEATED READINGS

- Have children select a story from the **Student Book** or a book that they have previously read. Tell children that by rereading these books, they can become better readers. *The more practice we have sounding out words and seeing those important high-frequency words in text, the easier it will be for us to read new stories.*
- Provide 15–20 minutes for children to enjoy independent reading. Then have student paraphrase what they read, maintaining meaning. Read with them or use this time for assessment using the Fluency Assessment in the **Diagnostic Assessment Handbook**.

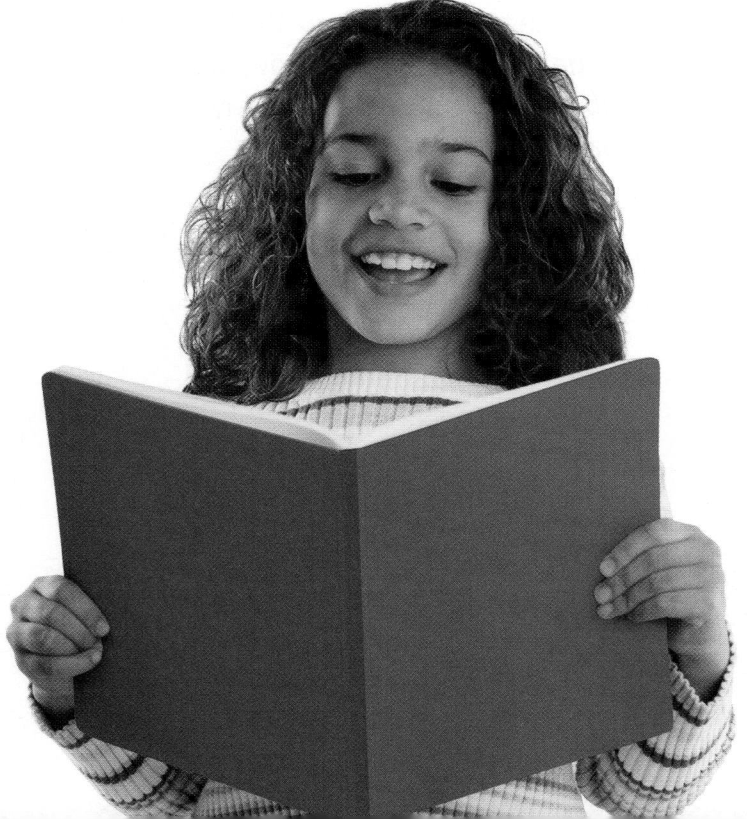

Objectives

- Review and assess vocabulary
- Read with fluency and paraphrase text

Materials

- Student Book

Readers Theater

BUILDING LISTENING AND SPEAKING SKILLS
Distribute copies of "A Whale of a Story" from **Read-Aloud Anthology** pages 179–191. Have children practice reading the play throughout the unit. Assign parts and have children present the play or perform it as a dramatic reading at the end of the unit.

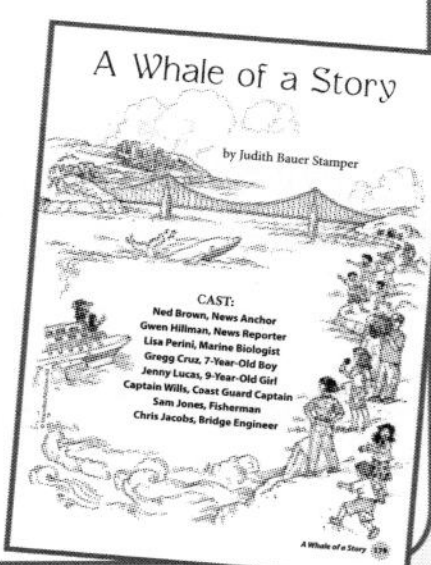

Objectives

- Identify syllables in spoken words with vowel digraphs *oo, ou*
- Blend sounds in words with vowel digraphs *oo, ou*
- Read multisyllabic words
- Review vowel digraphs

Materials

- Word-Building Cards; Teacher's Resource Book, p. 66
- word charts from Days 1, 3
- pocket chart
- Decodable Reader Library: *Flip and Spots*
- Practice Book for vowel digraphs, p. 215

Skills Trace

Vowel Digraphs *oo, ou*	
Introduce	91C–D
Practice/ Apply	91F, 93G-H, 115F-G, 115I, 115T; Practice Book: p. 206; Decodable Reader: *Flip and Spots*
Reteach/ Review	119D; 119K-N, 119Q, 119W, 119CC
Assess	Weekly Test; Unit 4 Test
Maintain	Build Fluency: Sound/Spellings

Review and Assess

Phonological Awareness

Identify Syllables

Guided Practice/Practice

Have children practice counting syllables with the examples provided. Guide practice with the first word.

Remember that a syllable is a word part that has a vowel sound.

As I say a word, listen carefully for the number of vowel sounds. That is the number of syllables the word has. Repeat the word and clap once for each syllable you hear.

looking	brook	wooded
good-bye	understood	cooking
childhood	cookbook	barefoot
underfoot	sisterhood	scrapbook

Review and Assess

Phonics

Build Fluency: Sound/Spellings

Display the following **Word-Building Cards** one at a time: *oo, ou, oo, ui, ew, ue, u, ou, oe, oi, oy, ou, ow, are, air, ear, ere, or, ore, oar, ar, gn, kn, wr, mb*. Have children chorally say each sound. Mix, repeat, and vary the pace.

Blend with Vowel Digraphs *oo, ou*

Guided Practice

Display **Word-Building Cards** *h, o, o, k*. Blend the sounds.

What sounds do each of these letters stand for? Help me blend the sounds: /hůk/. Let's read the word together: *hook*.

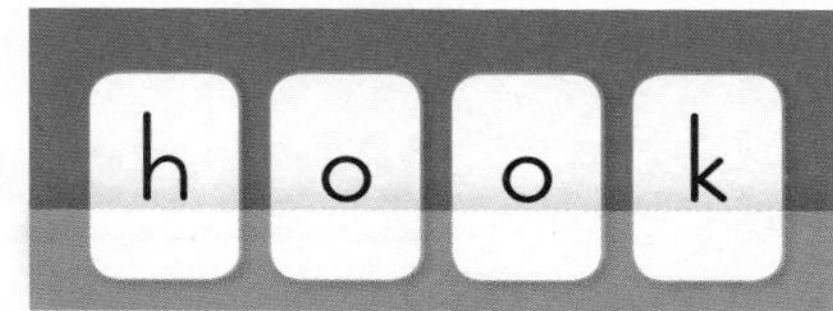

Practice

Have children practice generating and blending sounds to form real words and nonsense words. Write these examples on the board.

nook good could wood stood
shook brook would hood soot
booked looking mistook footing
understood wooden booking relook
zooting vouldness rejooking lood

Build Fluency: Word Automaticity

Use word charts from Days 1 and 3. Point to each word as children chorally read it. Model blending the sounds in any words children miss. Point to words randomly at varying speeds for children to chorally read.

goods	look	foot	stood
should	book	soot	hood
could	shook	crook	hoof
would	away	sprain	nook
fewer	teasing	shoe	reuse

A seal looks for some food.
The pup book was good.

hooked	brook	nook	crook
should	could	took	soot
goodness	shook	foot	hoods
proof	broom	stewing	
there	paired	spoil	reglue

Are those seals in a brook?
We should try to use the hook.
doodled unhook crooked childhood

Build Fluency: Connected Text

- Have children reread with a partner *Flip and Spots* from the **Decodable Reader Library**. Listen in, providing corrective feedback as needed.
- Comment on children's **speed**, **accuracy**, and **intonation**. Model each as needed. For example, model how your voice rises at the end of a question.

Flip and Spots

Ending *-ing*

Teach

- Say the words *cooking* and *footing*. Ask children to listen closely to hear what is the same in both words.
- Point out the /ing/ sound at the end of the words.
- Write the words *cooking* and *footing* on the board. Underline the letters *-ing*.
- Tell children that the inflectional ending *-ing* in *cooking* and *footing* means action is happening now.

Practice/Apply

- Then write the following words on the board and help children blend them: *hook, hooking*; *foot, footing*; *look, looking*. Point out that the letters *-ing* at the end of a word can stand for the /ing/ sound, as in *looking*.
- Ask children to look for words that end in *-ing* and that tell about actions happening now as they read this week's stories. Keep a running list on chart paper.

Corrective Feedback

For children needing additional practice reading words with vowel digraphs *oo, ou*, use the one syllable and multisyllabic Speed Drills in the **Intervention Kit** (**Fluency**).

Objectives

- Spell and assess words with vowel digraphs *oo* and *ou*
- Spell high-frequency words
- Use the Word Wall as a resource to find spellings

Materials

- paper and pencils

5-Day Spelling	
DAY 1	Dictation; Pretest
DAY 2	Teacher-Modeled Word Sort
DAY 3	Student Word Sort
DAY 4	Test Practice
DAY 5	Posttest

Review and Assess

Phonics/Spelling

Words with Vowel Digraphs *oo, ou*

POSTTEST

Use the following procedure to assess children's spelling of the weekly spelling words.

- Say a spelling word and use it in the sentence provided below.
- Have children write the word on a piece of paper. Then continue with the next word.
- When children have finished, collect their papers and analyze their spellings of misspelled words.
- Have children create a personal word list in their Writer's Notebooks that includes words they need to continue practicing.

1. **shook:** Dad shook the bag of popcorn.
2. **hook:** Hang your coat on the hook.
3. **crook:** The police caught the crook.
4. **good:** I think I look good today.
5. **should:** Tamara should study for her test.
6. **brook:** We saw fish in the brook.
7. **foot:** My foot will not fit in this shoe.
8. **soot:** The chimney is covered in black soot.
9. **could:** We could eat a snack before dinner.
10. **would:** Would you like to play a game with me?
11. **fruit:** It is important to eat fruit to stay healthy.
12. **glue:** I love to use glue on my pictures.
13. **below:** Put the toy below the shelf.
14. **city:** In what city do you live?
15. **own:** My family does not own a car.

Word Wall Use a Word Wall to group words by spelling patterns. Also use it to review previous weeks' spelling words. Remove words from the Word Wall when children have mastered them.

Review and Assess
Vocabulary

Words in Context

REVIEW
Review the meaning of each vocabulary word. Have children tell you which vocabulary word matches each definition. Then ask them to generate their own sentences using the vocabulary words.

- at an early time of life (young)
- saved from danger (rescued)
- happening in a regular or healthy way (normal)
- a strong need to eat (hunger)
- a warm-blooded animal that drinks its mother's milk and has hair (mammal)
- looks at carefully (examines)
- Then have children use each word in a sentence.

Spiral Vocabulary Review

- Have small groups participate in a vocabulary activity called Word Home Run! Write the vocabulary words from Unit 4, Weeks 3 (*serious*, *personal*, *informs*, *heal*, and *aid*) and 4 on index cards. Write the definition on the other side of each card. Create a set of cards for each group. For each group, draw a baseball diamond on construction paper, clearly marking each base. Provide buttons for playing pieces.
- One child is the pitcher. Other children are players. The pitcher takes a card and reads the word. If the player defines the word correctly, the player moves to first base. If the player correctly uses the word in a sentence, the player moves to second base. Each child continues to play until reaching home plate and scoring a run or until missing a word. When a player gets to home plate, that player becomes the pitcher and the pitcher becomes a player.

Write About It
Imagine you have the job you chose. Write in your Writer's Notebook an entry about what you did to help animals during one day on the job. Try to use at least one vocabulary word in your writing.

Objectives
- Use vocabulary in context
- Review this week's and last week's vocabulary words

Materials
- index cards

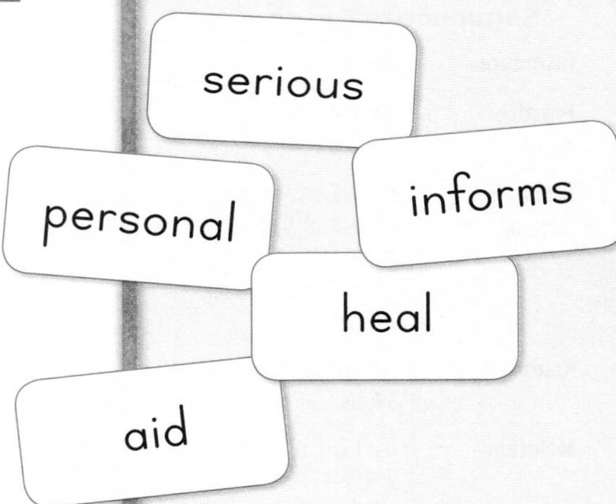

Objectives

- Determine when children may need to analyze text structure again
- Identify the sequence of events in the selections
- Make comparisons across texts
- Review sensory language (literal and non-literal meanings)

Materials

- Practice Book for Sensory Language, p. 216

Skills Trace

Sequence of Events	
Introduce	U4: 81A–B
Practice/ Apply	U4: 81K–85A; Practice Book: 198–199
Reteach/ Review	U4: 89K, 89V–X, 89BB–DD, 93A–B, 93K–115A, 119G, 119R–T, 119X–Z; Practice Book: 209–210
Assess	Weekly Tests; Unit 4, 5 Tests
Maintain	U4: 155N; U5: 201N, 209JA–B, 209J–233A, 239G, 239R–T, 239X–Z, 311N; Practice Book: 243–244

Review and Assess
Comprehension

STRATEGY Analyze Text Structure

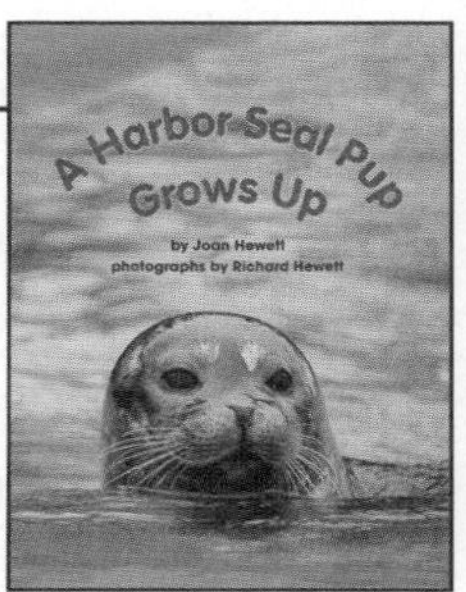

Main Selection

TRANSFER THE STRATEGY Remind children that as they read *A Harbor Seal Pup Grows Up*, they tried to analyze the nonfiction text structure. Model how using this strategy helped you.

Think Aloud I know that nonfiction texts are organized in different ways. As I was reading, I realized that the author was telling about what happened to Sidney in different stages. The selection started with Sidney being left alone on a beach. Then, she is rescued and helped by scientists. Finally, she is returned to the ocean. Paying attention to the text structure helped me remember the order of events.

Focus Question Ask children to describe how the strategy helped them. Offer these sentence starters:

The events that happened to Sidney were ________.

Paying attention to the text structure helped me ________.

How might this strategy help you when you read another selection?

SKILL Identify Sequence of Events

READING ACROSS TEXTS Model making a connection between the sequence of events in *A Harbor Seal Pup Grows Up* and "A Whale Is Saved!"

Think Aloud As I read these selections, I noticed that they had some things in common. Both selections started with an animal that was in trouble. The next thing that happened in both selections is that people noticed the animal and called for help. The last thing that happened in both of the selections was that the animals were released into the ocean.

Provide a sentence starter to help children make their own connections between texts:

I made a connection between ________.

What topic do these two selections have in common?

Additional Review For additional review of sensory language, (literal, non-literal meanings of words) use **Practice Book**, page 216.

Approaching Level

High-Frequency/Vocabulary

Objective Identify high-frequency words and selection vocabulary

Materials
- **High-Frequency Word Cards**
- **Sound-Spelling WorkBoards**
- **Visual Vocabulary Resources**
- **Vocabulary Cards**
- **Approaching Reproducible**, p. 207

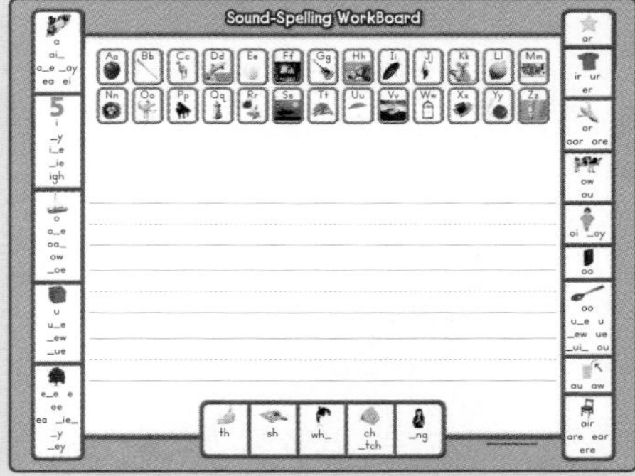
Sound-Spelling WorkBoard

PRETEACH WORDS

- **Introduce High-Frequency Words** Identify the high-frequency words **below**, **city**, and **own** using the **Read/Spell/Write** routine. Display the **High-Frequency Word Cards** and have children write each word on their **WorkBoards**.
- **Introduce Vocabulary Words** Use the **Visual Vocabulary Resources** to preteach the selection words **examines**, **hunger**, **mammal**, **normal**, **rescued**, and **young**. Refer to the detailed routine on the cards.
- Have children write each word on their WorkBoards. Use the context sentences on **Approaching Reproducible** page 207.

CUMULATIVE REVIEW

Tier 2

Display the High-Frequency Word Cards for **below**, **city**, and **own**. Display one card at a time as children chorally say the word. Repeat using the cards from the previous six weeks. Note words needing review. Then display the **Vocabulary Cards** from the previous four weeks. Say the meaning of each word and have children identify it. Point to words randomly for children to provide definitions.

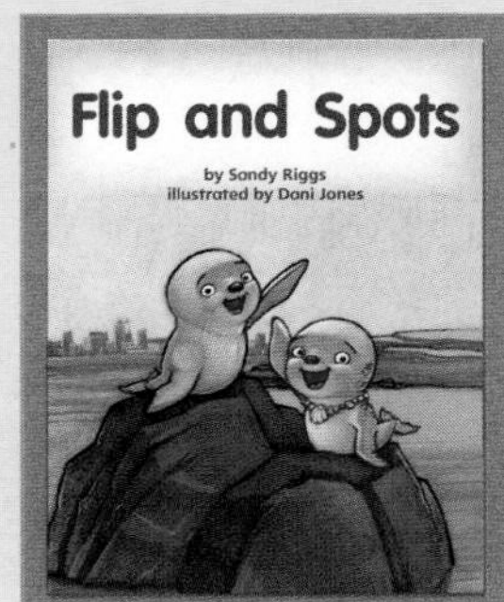

Decodable Reader

Decodable Reader

Objective Read and decode words with digraph /ů/*oo*, *ou* in connected text

Materials
- **Decodable Reader:** *Flip and Spots*

READ THE TEXT

- **Preview and Predict** Point to the book's title and have children sound out each word as you run your finger under it. *I see two seal pups on a rock in a harbor.* Ask: *What will this story be about?*
- **Read the Book** Turn to page 22. Have children point to each word, sounding out decodable words and saying the high-frequency words quickly. If children struggle sounding out words, provide "with you" blending models.
- **Check Comprehension** Ask the following:
  - *What happened in the beginning of the story?*
  - *Why did the pups do tricks?*

Interactive Student Book

If you wish to preteach the main selection, use StudentWorks Plus for:
- Vocabulary preteaching
- Word-by-word highlighting
- Think Aloud prompts

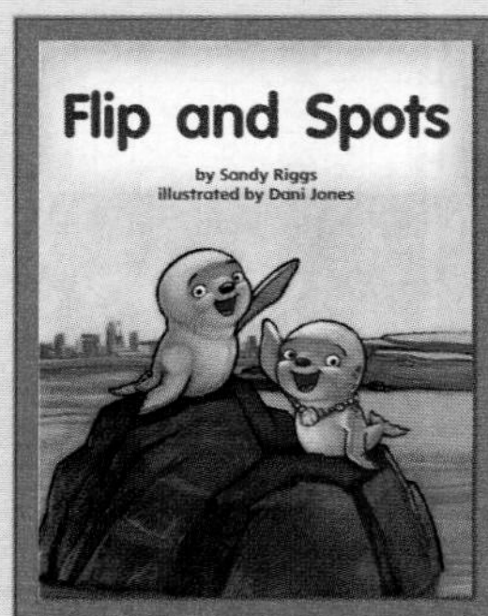

Decodable Reader

On Level

Phonics

Objective Decode words with vowel digraph /ů/ spelled *oo, ou*

Materials
- **Sound-Spelling Cards**
- **Word-Building Cards**
- **Decodable Reader**

REVIEW VOWEL DIGRAPH *oo*

- **Review Vowel Digraph /ů/*oo, ou*** Display the *Book* **Sound-Spelling Card**. Remind children that the sound /ů/ can be spelled with the letters *oo* or *ou*.
- **Blend Words** Write words and sentences from the charts on pages 91D and 115G on the board. Quickly have children chorally read the words. Repeat by pointing to the words in random order. Model blending the sounds in any words children have difficulty reading. Continue with the words below to help children apply their skills to new words. Write each word on the board for children to read.

looked	shook	could	hoods	stood
hook	books	should	wood	wool
cooking	brook	would	good	footed

- **Build Words** Display **Word-Building Cards** *b, c, d, f, g, h, k, l, o, o, r, s, t, u,* and *w*. Have partners make as many words as they can. Instruct them to write their words in lists based on spelling patterns. For example, all the words that end in *-ood* go in one list; the words that end in *-ook* go in another list. Provide time for children to share their lists.

Words with *-ood*	Words with *-ook*	Words with *-ould*	Words with *-ool*

REREAD FOR FLUENCY

- Have partners reread *Flip and Spots*. Work with children to read at the appropriate rate and phrasing. Model fluent reading as needed.

ELL

Reread for Fluency Use the Interactive Question-Response Guide Technique to help English Language Learners understand the content of *Flip and Spots.* As you read the text, make the meaning clear by pointing to the pictures, demonstrating word meaning, paraphrasing text, and asking children questions.

Beyond Level

Phonics

Objective Decode words with vowel digraph /ů/*oo, ou*

Materials • **Sound-Spelling Cards** • **Word-Building Cards**

EXTEND/ACCELERATE

- **Vowel Team Syllables** Tell children that when they see a vowel team in a long word, such as *oo* or *ou*, the letters that make up the team must remain together in the same syllable. This can help children decide how to chunk an unfamiliar word to figure out how to pronounce it. Help children read the words below.

precook	footed	lookout	bookish	bookcase
goodness	football	cookbook	bookmark	hooded
woolen	footstool	cooking	wooded	shouldn't
wooden	woodwind	woodwork	cookie	cookout

- **Find Words in Books** Have children go on a word hunt for words with vowel digraph oo or ou in books they've read this week. Ask children to state each word found, read aloud the sentence, and record these words in their Writer's Notebooks. Challenge them to search other classroom books for oo and ou words, and ask them to think of ways to expand these words.

Vocabulary

Objective Use context to determine the meaning of multiple-meaning words

Gifted Talented

EXPAND ORAL VOCABULARY

- Review the meanings of oral vocabulary words *accomplish*, *arduous*, *labor*, *rejoice*, and *succeed.*
- Say the sentences below. Have children say the vocabulary word that fits in the sentence. Write the missing word in each sentence.
  - She _________ when she won the art contest.
  - The farmer _________ for an hour to get the the seeds planted.
  - Bill _________ at convincing his Mom to let him have a sleepover.
  - After working very hard, Sue _________ her goal.
  - If you're not used to shoveling snow, it can be an _________ task.

- Afterwards, have children each come up with a sentence with one of the vocabulary words missing. Then have children work with a partner to fill in the missing words on each others' papers. Then have children share their sentences aloud.

ELL

Minimal Contrasts Focus on articulation. Make the /ů/ sound and point out your mouth position. Have children repeat. Use the articulation photos on the small Sound-Spelling Cards. Repeat for the /ü/ sound. Then have children say each sound together, noticing the slight differences in mouth position. Continue by having children read minimal-contrast word pairs, such as *shook/shoe*, *brook/brew*, *took/too*.

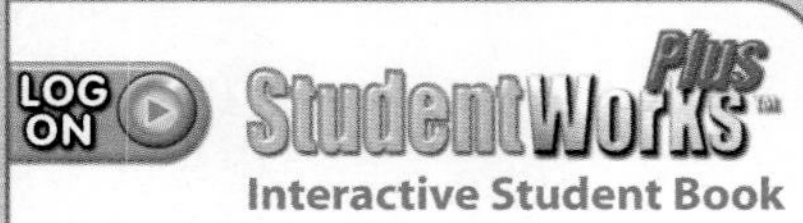

Interactive Student Book

If you wish to preteach the main selection, use StudentWorks Plus for:

- Vocabulary preteaching
- Word-by-word highlighting
- Think Aloud prompts

Cognates

Help children identify similarities and differences in pronunciation and spelling between English words and Spanish cognates:

Cognates

compassion *compasión*

examine *examinar*

seqquence *secuencia*

normal *normal*

event *evento*

ELL ENGLISH LANGUAGE LEARNERS

Prepare to Read

Content Objective Describe how an abandoned harbor seal pup is rescued

Language Objective Use key words to describe what happens to an abandoned harbor seal pup

Materials • **StudentWorks Plus** (interactive eBook)

BUILD BACKGROUND

All Language Levels

- This version of the **Student Book** contains oral summaries in multiple languages, on-line multilingual glossaries, word-by-word highlighting, and questions that assess and build comprehension.
- Children can build their word reading fluency by reading along as the text is read or by listening during the first reading and, at the end of each paragraph, returning to the beginning of the paragraph and reading along.
- Children can build their comprehension by reviewing the definitions of key words in the on-line glossary and by answering the comprehension questions. When appropriate, the text required to answer the question is highlighted to provide children with additional support and scaffolding.
- Following the reading, ask children to respond in writing to a question that links the story to their personal experiences, such as *How have you helped an animal or a person who needed help?*

Academic Language

Language Objective Use academic language in classroom conversations

All Language Levels

- This week's academic words are **boldfaced** throughout the lesson. Define the word in context and provide a clear example from the selection. Then ask children to generate an example or a word with a similar meaning.

Academic Language Used in Whole Group Instruction

Oral Vocabulary Words	Key Selection Words	Strategy and Skill Words
daring	**young**	**sequence**
survive	**examines**	**events**
baffled	**mammal**	**summarize**
compassion	**normal**	**poetry**
lunge	**hunger**	
	rescued	

ENGLISH LANGUAGE LEARNERS

Vocabulary

Language Objective Demonstrate understanding and use of key words by describing what happens to an abandoned harbor seal pup

Materials • **Visual Vocabulary Resources** • **ELL Resource Book**, p. 260

PRETEACH KEY VOCABULARY

All Language Levels

Use the **Visual Vocabulary Resources** to preteach the key selection words **examines**, **hunger**, **mammal**, **normal**, **rescued**, and **young**. Focus on two words per day. Use the following routine that appears in detail on the cards.

- Define the word in English and provide the example given.
- Define the word in Spanish, if appropriate, and indicate if the word is a cognate.
- Display the picture and explain how it illustrates or demonstrates the word. Engage children in structured partner-talk about the image, using the key word.
- Ask children to chorally say the word three times. Point out any known sound-spellings or focus on a key aspect of phonemic awareness related to the word.
- Distribute copies of the Vocabulary Glossary, **ELL Resource Book** page 260.

PRETEACH FUNCTION WORDS AND PHRASES

All Language Levels

Use the Visual Vocabulary Resources to preteach the function words and phrases *become stronger*, *on her own*, *almost there*, and *in front of*. Focus on one word per day. Use the detailed routine on the cards.

- Define the word in English and, if appropriate, in Spanish. Point out if the word is a cognate.
- Refer to the picture and engage children in talk about the word. For example, children will partner-talk using sentence frames or they will listen to sentences and replace a word or phrase with the new function word.
- Ask children to chorally repeat the word three times.

TEACH BASIC WORDS

Beginning/Intermediate

Use the Visual Vocabulary Resources to teach the basic words *height*, *temperature*, *teeth*, *heartbeat*, *eyes*, and *size*.

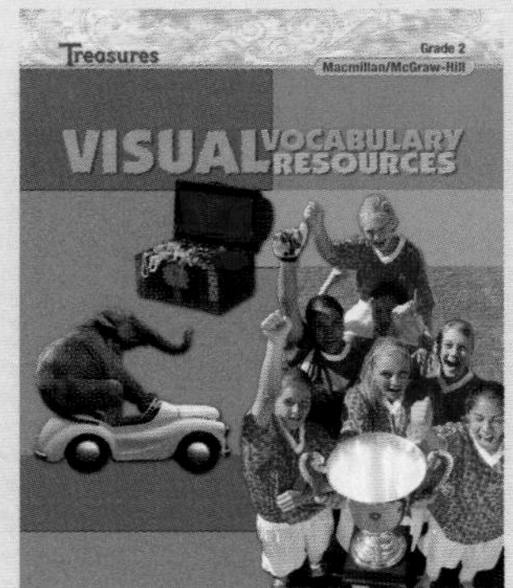

Visual Vocabulary Resources

ELL Resource Book, page 260

Use the word chart to study this week's vocabulary words.
Write a sentence using each word in your writer's notebook.

Word	Context Sentence	Illustration
young	The young bird fell from the nest and needed help.	
examines	The doctor takes her time when she examines her patient.	
mammal	Today in school we learned about mammals.	
normal	It is not normal to see a whale on a beach.	
hunger	An animal will feel hunger if it can not find food.	
rescued	The firefighter rescued the cat from the tree.	Why might someone need to be rescued at the beach?

Approaching Level

Phonemic Awareness

Objective Blend phonemes to form words

Materials • none

PHONEME BLENDING

Tier 2

Have three children stand side by side. Ask the first child to say the sound /l/. Have the next child say the sound /ů/. Have the third child say the sound /k/. Have them say the sounds in order and blend them: /lůk/, stretching the vowel sound. Have children repeat: *look*. Repeat with other sound sets and children.

/b/ /r/ /ů/ /k/	/w/ /ů/ /d/	/sh/ /ů/ /d/	/f/ /ů/ /t/
/w/ /ů/ /l/	/s/ /t/ /ů/ /d/	/h/ /ů/ /f/	/t/ /ů/ /k/

Phonics

Objective Decode words with vowel digraph /ů/*oo, ou*

Materials
- **Sound-Spelling Cards**
- pocket chart
- **Word-Building Cards**
- **Decodable Reader:** *Flip and Spots*

SOUND-SPELLING REVIEW

Tier 2

Display **Word-Building Cards** for the following, one letter or spelling at a time: *oo, ou, oo, ui, ew, ue, u, ou, oe, oi, oy, ou, ow, are, air, ear, ere, or, ore, oar, ar, gn, kn, wr, mb*. Have children chorally say each sound. Repeat and vary the pace.

RETEACH SKILL

- Display the *Book* **Sound-Spelling Card**. Review that the vowel digraph /ů/ can be spelled with the letters *oo* or *ou*.
- **Model Blending** Write words and sentences from the chart on page 91D on the board. Model how to blend the sounds in each word using the **Blending Routine**. Have children repeat.
- **Build Words** Place Word-Building Card *h* in a pocket chart. *What sound does this stand for?* Place two *o* cards next to *h*. *What sound do these letters stand for?* Blend the sounds: /hů/. *Now you say it.* Place the *d* card to the right of *oo*. *What sound?* Blend the sounds: /hůd/. *Now you blend the sounds. What's the word?*

  Repeat with the words *brook*, *should*, *wood*, *hook*, and *could*.

REREAD FOR FLUENCY

- Reread *Flip and Spots* with children. Then have them practice rereading the book with the appropriate rate and phrasing to a partner. Circulate, listen in, and provide corrective feedback.

Flip and Spots
by Sandy Riggs
illustrated by Dani Jones

Decodable Reader

ELL

Reread for Fluency Use the Interactive Question-Response Guide Technique to help English Language Learners understand the content of *Flip and Spots*. As you read the text, make the meaning clear by pointing to the pictures, demonstrating word meaning, paraphrasing text, and asking children questions.

Approaching Level

High-Frequency/Vocabulary

Objective Identify high-frequency words and vocabulary words

Materials • **High-Frequency Word Cards** • **Vocabulary Cards**

RETEACH WORDS

Tier 2

Display High-Frequency Word Cards for **below**, **city**, and **own**. Review each using the **Read/Spell/Write** routine. Display **Vocabulary Cards** for **examines**, **hunger**, **mammal**, **normal**, **rescued**, and **young**. Review each word using the **Define/Example/Ask** routine.

CUMULATIVE REVIEW

Display the High-Frequency and Vocabulary Cards from the previous six weeks. Display one card at a time as children chorally read the word. Mix and repeat. Note words needing review.

Leveled Reader Library

Leveled Reader Lesson 1

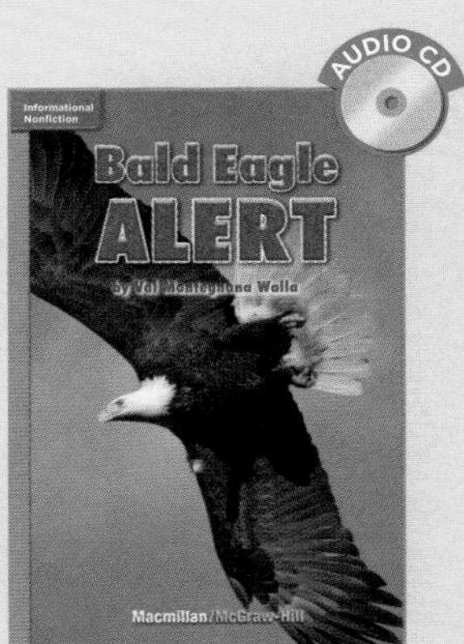

Leveled Reader

Objectives Describe the order of events in a text; read to apply skills and strategies

Materials
- **Leveled Reader:** *Bald Eagle Alert*
- **Approaching Reproducible**, p. 209

BEFORE READING

- **Preview and Predict** Read the title and author name. Have children turn to the title page. Ask: *What do you think you might learn about by reading this book?*
- **Review Skills** Use the inside front cover to review the phonics skill and vocabulary words.
- **Set a Purpose** Say: *Let's read to find out about bald eagles.*

DURING READING

- Have children whisper-read each page. Circulate and give feedback, such as modeling how to blend a decodable word.
- **Sequence of Events** Draw a Sequence of Events Chart like the one on the Reproducible. Have children copy it. After children have read a few pages, ask them to retell in order the information they have read so far. Model how to record the information and have children fill in their charts.

AFTER READING

- Discuss words that gave children difficulty and the strategies they used. Reinforce good reading behaviors you noticed.
- **Retell** Have children take turns retelling the selection.

Leveled Reader

On Level

Leveled Reader Lesson 1

Objectives Describe the order of events in a text; read to apply skills and strategies

Materials • **Leveled Reader:** *Bald Eagle Alert* • **Practice Book**, p. 209

BEFORE READING

Preview and Predict Read the title and look at the illustration on the cover. *What do you see in this photograph?* Read the chapter headings and the table of contents. *What kind of information do you think you might learn about in this book?* Preview the title page and the photos.

Review Skills Use the inside front cover to review the phonics skill and teach the new vocabulary words.

Set a Purpose Say: *Let's read to find out about bald eagles.*

DURING READING

- Have children turn to page 2 and begin by whisper-reading the first two pages.
- Remind children to look for the new vocabulary words. Tell them that you will help them blend sounds in words with *oo* or *ou.*
- Monitor children's reading. Stop periodically and ask open-ended questions to facilitate rich discussion, such as *What have you learned so far about bald eagles? Why are bald eagles important?* Have children support their answers with evidence from the text.
- **Sequence of Events** Remind children that when they read a selection, they need to remember the events or ideas in the order in which they were presented. Draw a Retelling Chart like the one on the **Practice Book** page. Have children copy it. As children reread, ask them what ideas they learned so far. Model how to record the information and have children copy it. Then have them begin to fill in their Sequence of Events Chart.

AFTER READING

- Discuss words that gave children difficulty and the strategies they used to decode them. Reinforce good reading behaviors you noticed.
- **Retell** Have children take turns retelling the selection. Help them make a personal connection (Text-to-Self) by asking: *Have you ever seen a bald eagle? If so, where did you see it? If not, where could you go to see one?*

ELL

Retell Use the Interactive Question-Response Guide Technique to help English Language Learners understand the content of *Bald Eagle Alert.* As you read the text, make the meaning clear by pointing to the pictures, demonstrating word meaning, paraphrasing text, and asking children questions.

Beyond Level

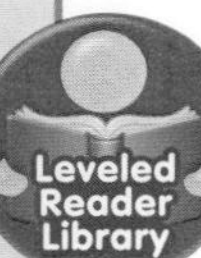

Leveled Reader Lesson 1

Objectives Describe the order of events in a text; read to apply skills and strategies

Materials
- **Leveled Reader:** *Bald Eagle Alert*
- self-stick notes
- **Beyond Reproducible**, p. 209

Leveled Reader

BEFORE READING

Preview and Predict Read the title and look at the picture on the cover. Preview the title page and the photographs. Have children name some clues that help them tell what the book will be about.

Review Skills Use the inside front cover to review the phonics skill and vocabulary.

Set a Purpose Say: *Let's read to find out about bald eagles.*

DURING READING

- Have children turn to page 2, whisper-read the first two pages, and place self-stick notes next to words they have difficulty with.
- Remind children that when they come to an unfamiliar word, they can look for familiar spellings and chunks. For longer words, they will need to break the word into smaller chunks, or syllables, and sound out each part.
- Monitor children's reading. Stop periodically and ask open-ended questions to facilitate rich discussion, such as *What have you learned so far about bald eagles? Where do bald eagles live?* Build on children's responses to develop deeper understanding.

- **Sequence of Events** Remind children to pay attention to the order in which facts are given in a nonfiction selection. Draw a Retelling Chart like the one on the Reproducible. After a few pages, have children tell facts they read about so far. Model recording the information. Have children complete their Retelling Charts as they read. Ask them to explain strategies they used to problem-solve and organize the facts as they read.

AFTER READING

Gifted Talented

- **Analyze** Discuss the story with children. *What has happened to bald eagles over the past 40 years?*

- Ask: *Was it a good idea or bad idea to pass the law saying people could not hurt or kill bald eagles?* Have children choose a partner and share their views with each other. Have children go back to the text as they think about their answers.
- Then have partners share their answers with the class.

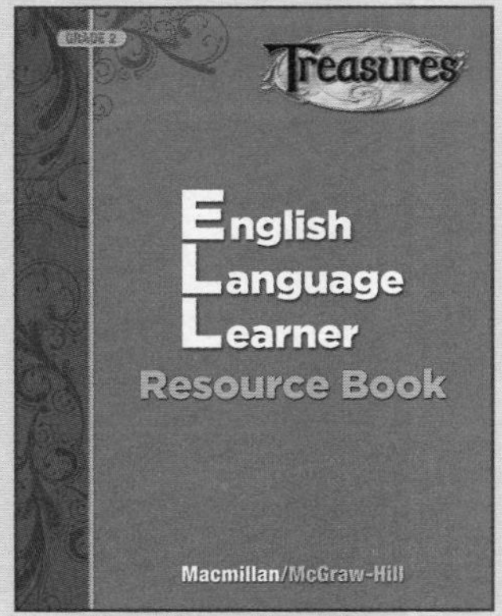

ELL Resource Book

ELL ENGLISH LANGUAGE LEARNERS

Access to Core Content

Content Objective Read grade-level text
Language Objective Discuss text using key words and sentence frames
Materials • **ELL Resource Book**, pp. 248–257

PRETEACH MAIN SELECTION (PAGES 94–113)

All Language Levels

Use the Interactive Question-Response Guide on **ELL Resource Book** pages 248–257 to introduce children to *A Harbor Seal Pup Grows Up*. Preteach half of the selection on **Day 2** and half on **Day 3**.

- Use the prompts provided in the guide to develop meaning and vocabulary. Use the partner-talk and whole-class responses to engage children and increase student talk.
- When completed, have partners reread the story.

Beginning

Use Visuals During the Interactive Reading, select several pictures. Describe them by telling a sequence of events. Ask children sequence of events questions that can be answered in single words or short phrases.

Intermediate

Demonstrate Understanding During the Interactive Reading, select a few lines of text that show a sequence of events. After you read it and explain it, have children tell you the sequence of events.

Advanced

Demonstrate Understanding During the Interactive Reading, select a larger portion of text that shows a sequence of events. After you read it and explain it, have children tell you the sequence of events.

ELL ENGLISH LANGUAGE LEARNERS

Grammar

Content Objective Identify irregular verbs.
Language Objective Speak in complete sentences, using sentence frames.
Materials • none

IRREGULAR VERBS

Beginning/Intermediate

- Review that irregular verbs do not use *-ed* to form the past tense. They have special forms.

All Language Levels

- Review that irregular verbs do not use *-ed* to form the past tense. They have special forms.
- Write these sentences on the board: *The people run to the water. They come to help the seal.* Read each sentence and underline the irregular verb. Cross out the present tense and write the past tense of each. Explain that only one letter changed to make the present-tense verb a past-tense verb. Read the new sentences: Review *sing/sang* and *give/gave* as well.
- Write sentences on the board, such as those provided below. Have children replace the underlined verb with its correct past tense in each sentence, then read the sentence aloud. Have them say: *The past tense of* ________ *is* ________.

People run *to get help.*	*They* give *food to the seal.*
They sing *a quiet song.*	*Scientists* come *to say goodbye.*

PEER DISCUSSION STARTERS

All Language Levels

- Write the following sentences on the board.

  The scientist gave the seal ________.
  Sidney came to the center because ________.
- Pair children and have them complete sentence frames by providing details from this week's readings. Note each child's language use and proficiency.

Beginning

Use Visuals Describe the photographs in *A Harbor Seal Grows Up* to children by using irregular past-tense verbs. Ask: *What do you see?* Help children to use irregular past-tense verbs in their descriptions.

Intermediate

Describe Ask children to describe the same photographs, adding more irregular past-tense verbs to their descriptions. Have them use complete sentences.

Advanced

Describe Ask children to describe the photographs, adding new irregular past-tense verbs to their descriptions.

Transfer Skills

Irregular Verbs Speakers of Spanish and Cantonese may find it surprising and confusing that a simple vowel change in irregular verbs (*come/came; run/ran; give/gave*) can signal a completely different tense. Give immediate feedback by modeling correct usage and having children repeat. Call attention to irregular past tense verbs as children read the sentences in this activity and their selections.

Corrective Feedback

During Whole Group grammar lessons, follow the routine on the **Grammar Transparencies** to provide children with extra support. This routine includes completing the items with English Language Learners while other children work independently, having children reread the sentences with partners to build fluency, and providing a generative task such as writing a new sentence using the skill.

Approaching Level

Phonological Awareness

Objective Identify syllables in spoken words

Materials • none

SYLLABLE IDENTIFICATION

Tier 2

Remind children that a *syllable* is a word part with a vowel sound. Say: *I'm going to say a word*: cookbook. *I will tap out the syllables in* cookbook: cook-book, *two taps for two syllables. Listen to these words and tap out the syllables.*

football	goodness	bookmark	hoodwinked
looking	wooden	footwear	woolen

Phonics

Objective Decode words with vowel digraph /ů/*oo, ou*

Materials
- **Sound-Spelling Cards**
- **Word-Building Cards**
- pocket chart
- **Decodable Reader:** *Flip and Spots*

SOUND-SPELLING REVIEW

Tier 2

Display **Word-Building Cards** for the following, one letter or spelling at a time: *oo, ou, oo, ui, ew, ue, u, ou, oe, oi, oy, ou, ow, are, air, ear, ere, or, ore, oar, ar, gn, kn, wr, mb.* Have children chorally say each sound.

RETEACH SKILL

- Display the *Book* **Sound-Spelling Card**. Review that the vowel digraph /ů/ can be spelled with the letters *oo* or *ou*.
- **Model Blending** Write words and sentences from the chart on page 115G on the board. Model how to blend the sounds in each word using the **Blending Routine**. Have children repeat. Then have children read each word multiple times.
- **Build Words** Build /ů/ words with children. Place Word-Building Cards *l, o, o, k* in a pocket chart. Help children blend the sounds to read the word. Then do the following:

  Change the l *in* look *to* b. *What word did you make?*
  Change the b *in* book *to* h. *What word did you make?*
  Change the k *in* hook *to* f. *What word did you make?*
  Change the f *in* hoof *to* d. *What word did you make?*
  Change the h *in* hood *to* w. *What word did you make?*

  Repeat with the word set *could, would, should.*
- **Read the Decodable** Reread *Flip and Spots* with children. Offer blending models. When completed, chorally reread the story.

Flip and Spots
by Sandy Riggs
illustrated by Dani Jones

Decodable Reader

ELL

Demonstrate Comprehension Use the Interactive Question-Response Guide Technique to help English Language Learners understand the content of *Flip and Spots.* As you read the text, make the meaning clear by pointing to the pictures, demonstrating word meaning, paraphrasing text, and asking children questions.

Approaching Level

High-Frequency/Vocabulary

Objective Identify high-frequency words and vocabulary words

Materials • **High-Frequency Word Cards** • **Vocabulary Cards**

BUILD WORD AUTOMATICITY

Fluency Display **High-Frequency Word Cards** for **below**, **city**, **own** and **Vocabulary Cards** for **examines**, **hunger**, **mammal**, **normal**, **rescued**, and **young**. Point to words in random order. Have children chorally read them. Repeat at a faster pace.

CUMULATIVE REVIEW

Display High-Frequency Word Cards and Vocabulary Cards from the previous four weeks, one at a time. Have children chorally read each word. Mix cards and repeat. Note words needing review.

Leveled Reader Library

Leveled Reader Lesson 2

Objectives Describe the order of events in a text; read to apply skills and strategies

Materials • **Leveled Reader:** *Bald Eagle Alert* • **Sound-Spelling WorkBoards** • **Approaching Reproducible**, pp. 209, 210

BEFORE READING

Review Have children retell *Bald Eagle Alert* by paging through the book and telling in their own words what they learned about eagles. Reinforce key vocabulary words by restating children's responses using key words.

DURING READING

Sequence of Events As children reread the book, help them finish adding information to their Sequence of Events Charts. Review the words first, next and last with children. Ask children to stop reading after a few pages and describe the order of ideas.

AFTER READING

- **Retell** Have children use their Sequence of Events Charts to orally retell in order the important facts and ideas they learned in *Bald Eagle Alert*.
- **Model Fluency** Read the sentences in the book one at a time, paying extra attention to your phrasing. Have children chorally repeat. Point out to children how you pay attention to punctuation to vary your voice and rate.

Book Talk

Bringing Groups Together Children will work with peers of various language and reading abilities to discuss this week's Leveled Readers. Refer to page 179 in the **Teacher's Resource Book** for how to conduct a Book Talk.

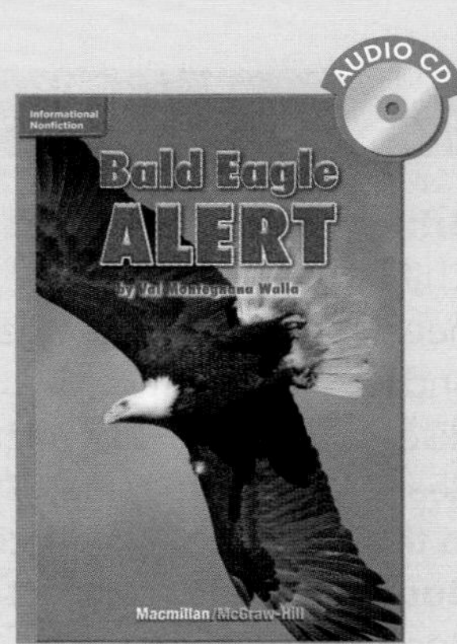

Leveled Reader

Approaching Reproducible, page 210

The **sequence** is the order in which things happen in a story.

Words like ***first***, ***next***, and ***last*** are clue words to help you tell the story order.

First Juan's teacher told the children about their homework.

Next Juan did his homework.

Last Juan gave his homework to his teacher.

A. Read the story. Then write the number 1, 2, or 3 below each picture to tell the sequence of the story.

First the pet pig got lost. It was afraid. Next the people found their pet pig. Last the people took the pig back home.

3

1

2

B. Write a sentence telling what might happen next in the story. Possible response provided

The people played with their pig.

Leveled Reader

On Level

Leveled Reader Lesson 2

Leveled Reader Library

Objectives Describe the order of events in a text; read to apply skills and strategies

Materials • **Leveled Reader:** *Bald Eagle Alert* • **Practice Book**, pp. 209, 213

BEFORE READING

- **Review** Have children retell *Bald Eagle Alert*. If children struggle, have them page through the story and say what they learned about eagles on each page. Reinforce vocabulary by restating children's sentences using more sophisticated language. For example, *You're right. There aren't as many bald eagles in the wild as there used to be. Bald eagles are endangered animals.*

DURING READING

- **Sequence of Events** Explain to children that good readers can retell important facts and ideas from a nonfiction selection in the order they were presented. *Describing the sequence of ideas is a good way to check to make sure you remember the facts from the book. It also gives you a chance to use the new words you have learned.* As children reread the book, help them complete their Sequence of Events Charts.

AFTER READING

- Have children use their Sequence of Events Charts to orally retell the important facts and ideas learned in *Bald Eagle Alert*.

REREAD FOR FLUENCY

- Read the sentences in the book one at a time. Have children chorally repeat. Point out to children how you use expression to make the reading interesting and how your voice goes up at the end of a question.
- Have children read a portion of *Bald Eagle Alert* for fluency.
- Have children continue to work on their fluency using **Practice Book** page 213.

Book Talk

Bringing Groups Together Children will work with peers of various language and reading abilities to discuss this week's Leveled Readers. Refer to page 179 in the **Teacher's Resource Book** for how to conduct a Book Talk.

Practice Book, page 213

As I read, I will pay attention to my phrasing.

All tigers have stripes. But each tiger has different
9 stripes.
10 Tigers live in jungles and forests. A tiger's coat
19 helps it blend in with long grass, bushes, and trees.
29 This helps keep the tiger safe.
35 Tigers are mammals. A **mammal** feeds its
42 **young** on milk. Tiger cubs live with their mother for
52 two to three years. Adult male tigers live alone.
61 Tigers hunt alone. They hide and then sneak up
70 on their prey. They catch deer, wild pigs, and cattle. 80

Comprehension Check

1. How does a tiger's diet change as it grows up? **Sequence of Events**
First, tiger cubs drink their mothers' milk. When they are older, they hunt deer, pigs, and cattle.
2. How do stripes help a tiger? **Main Idea and Details**
Stripes help a tiger blend into the jungle or forest.

	Words Read	–	Number of Errors	=	Words Correct Score
First Read		–		=	
Second Read		–		=	

Beyond Level

Leveled Reader Lesson 2

Objectives Describe the order of events in a text; read to apply skills and strategies

Materials
- **Leveled Reader:** *Bald Eagle Alert*
- **Beyond Reproducible**, pp. 209, 213

BEFORE READING

- **Review** Have children retell *Bald Eagle Alert* to a partner. Circulate and listen in. Prompt children to use the new words they learned from the book in their retellings. Remind them also to retell the parts of the selection in a logical sequence.

DURING READING

- **Sequence of Events** As children reread the book, help them add more details to their Sequence of Events Charts on their reproducible page. Guide them by asking who, what, when, where, why, and how questions. Remind them to describe the order of ideas using the sequence words *first, next,* and *last.*

AFTER READING

- **Retell** Have children use their Retelling Charts to write a summary of the important facts learned in *Bald Eagle Alert*.

Gifted Talented

- **Review** Have children recall their discussion of bald eagles.
- **Synthesize** Tell children that today they will create a learning toy that will teach children about bald eagles. Have children think of examples of learning toys they have at home such as puzzles, board games, electronic toys and so on.
- Have children work with a partner to come up with their idea for a toy. Then have them draw a picture or diagram of it and write about it.
- **Evaluate** Have each pair present their toy to the group. Have children respond to each toy by telling what they like about it.

REREAD FOR FLUENCY

- Read the sentences in the book one at a time. Have children chorally repeat. Then write the following sentence on the board: *If we make less waste, we may have less pollution.* Point out to children how you use pause when you come to the comma.

- Have children practice reading the book to a partner. Say: *Read with phrasing.*
- Have children continue to work on their fluency using Practice Book page 213.

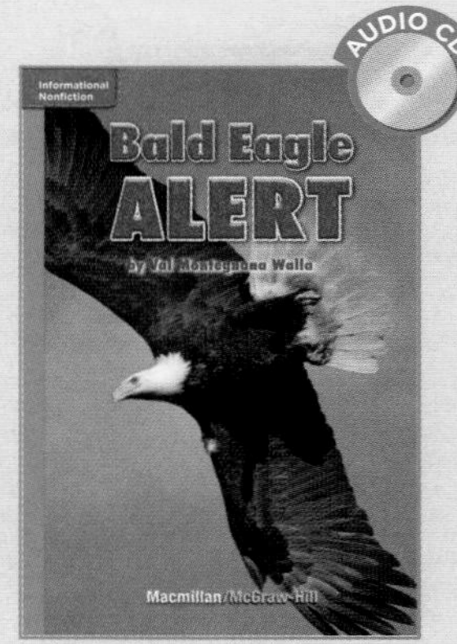

Leveled Reader

Book Talk

Bringing Groups Together Children will work with peers of various language and reading abilities to discuss this week's Leveled Readers. Refer to page 179 in the **Teacher's Resource Book** for how to conduct a Book Talk.

Beyond Reproducible, page 213

As I read, I will pay attention to my phrasing.

Bald eagles were in danger of becoming extinct. Scientists
9 **examined** the problem to find out the reasons why.
18 A bald eagle's habitat is near the sea. But people like to
30 live near the sea, too. Bald eagles can't always find places to
42 build their nests and lay eggs.
48 Bald eagles also have trouble finding food. They eat fish.
58 But people eat fish, too. Sometimes people catch too
67 many of the fish that bald eagles would eat. Then the birds
79 can die of **hunger**.
83 People and bald eagles don't want to eat the same food. Bald
95 eagles only like to eat fish that are sick and dying or already
108 dead. They actually leave the healthy fish for us. 117

Comprehension Check

1. Why is it difficult for bald eagles to find places to build their nests and lay eggs? **Sequence of Events** People now live in areas that were formerly bald eagle habitats.
2. What are two reasons why bald eagles were in danger of becoming extinct? **Identify Main Idea and Details** People have destroyed much of the bald eagles' natural habitat, and people also catch much of the fish that bald eagles would ordinarily eat.

	Words Read	–	Number of Errors	=	Words Correct Score
First Read		–		=	
Second Read		–		=	

Leveled Reader

Vocabulary

Preteach Vocabulary Use the routine in the **Visual Vocabulary Resources**, pages 417–418, to preteach the ELL Vocabulary listed on the inside front cover of the Leveled Reader.

ELL ENGLISH LANGUAGE LEARNERS

Leveled Reader Library

Leveled Reader Lesson 1

Content Objective Read to apply skills and strategies
Language Objective Retell information using complete sentences
Materials • **Leveled Reader:** *Bald Eagles* • **Visual Vocabulary Resources**

BEFORE READING

All Language Levels

- **Preview** Read the title *Bald Eagles*. Ask: *What's the title? Say it again.* Repeat with the author's name. Then page through the book. Use simple language to tell about each page. Immediately follow up with questions, such as *What do bald eagles look like? What does this photo show?*
- **Review Skills** Use the inside front cover to review the phonics skill and the vocabulary words.
- **Set a Purpose** Say: *Let's read to find out about bald eagles and why they need help.*

DURING READING

All Language Levels

- Have children read each page aloud using the differentiated suggestions. Provide corrective feedback, such as modeling how to blend a decodable word or clarifying meaning by using techniques from the Interactive Question-Response Guide.
- **Sequence of Events** After every two pages, ask children to state the main ideas they have learned so far. Help them to complete the Sequence of Events. Restate children's comments when they have difficulty using story-specific words. Provide differentiated sentence frames to support children's responses and engage children in partner-talk where appropriate.

Beginning	Intermediate	Advanced
Echo-Read Have children echo-read after you. **Check Comprehension** Point to pictures and ask questions such as *Do you see the bald eagle? Point to it. Does this photo show the bald eagle standing or flying?*	**Choral-Read** Have children choral-read with you. **Check Comprehension** Ask questions/prompts such as *Describe what you see in this photo. What do the maps show?*	**Choral-Read** Have children choral-read. **Check Comprehension** On the appropriate pages ask questions such as *What did you learn about where bald eagles live? Read sentences that tell facts about where they live. How are bald eagles hurt? Read sentences that tell about this.*

ENGLISH LANGUAGE LEARNERS

AFTER READING

Use the chart below and the Think and Compare questions from page 16 of *Bald Eagles* to determine children's progress.

Think and Compare	Beginning	Intermediate	Advanced
1 Turn to page 10. How did people help eagles? Write the steps in order.	Possible Responses: Nonverbal response. Law. Pass law.	Possible Responses: Eagles need help. People made law. The law helps eagles.	Possible Responses: People saw that bald eagles need to be rescued. They passed a law. The law said said people could not hurt bald eagles.
2 What are some ways you can help bald eagles?	Possible Responses: Nonverbal response. Teach people.	Possible Responses: Stop pollution. Teach people about bald eagles.	Possible Responses: I can help bald eagles by teaching people about them. I can not pollute.
3 Some people think that bald eagles don't need to be helped by people. What do you think?	Possible Responses: Nonverbal response. Help. Need help.	Possible Responses: People should help bald eagles.	Possible Responses: The bald eagles need to be helped. If they are not helped, they might all die.

Writing/Spelling

Content Objective Spell words correctly

Language Objective Write in complete sentences, using sentence frames

All Language Levels

- Write the key vocabulary words on the board: **examines**, **hunger**, **mammal**, **normal**, **rescued**, and **young**. Have children copy each word on their **WorkBoards**. Then help them say each word and write sentences for each word.

Beginning/Intermediate

- Help children spell words using their growing knowledge of English sound-spelling relationships. Model how to segment the word children are trying to spell and attach a spelling to each sound (or spellings to each syllable if a multisyllabic word). Use the **Sound-Spelling Cards** to reinforce the spellings for each English sound.

Advanced/Advanced High

- Dictate the following words for children to spell: *brook, should, good, could, hook, would*. Guide children using the Sound-Spelling Cards as they spell each word.
- When completed, review the meanings of words that can be easily demonstrated or explained. Use actions, gestures, and available pictures.

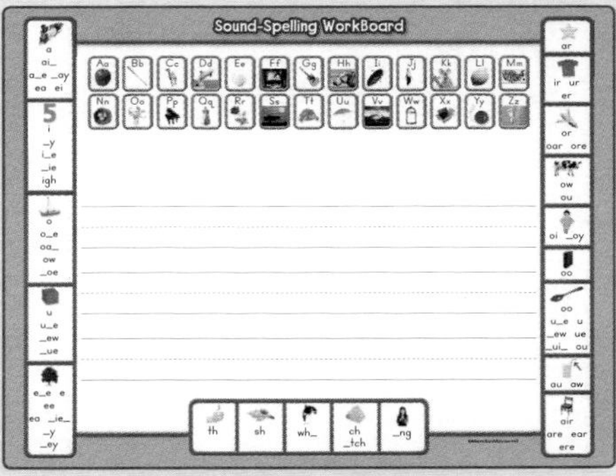

Sound-Spelling WorkBoard

Phonics/Word Study

For English Language Learners who need more practice with this week's phonics/spelling skill, see the Approaching Level lesson on page 119K. Focus on minimal contrasts, articulation, and those sounds that do not transfer from the child's first language to English. For a complete listing of language transfer sounds, see pages T18–T33.

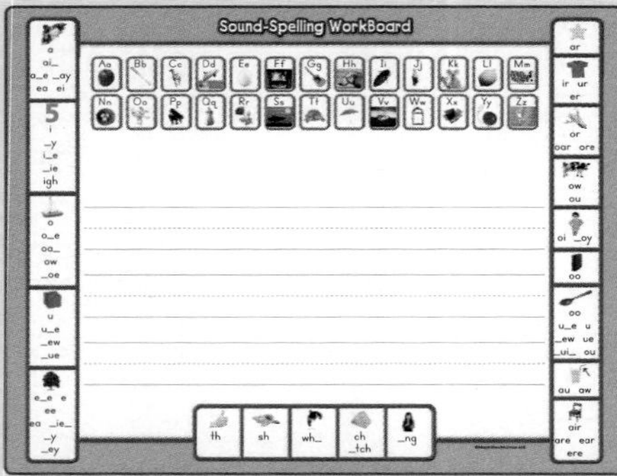

Sound-Spelling WorkBoard

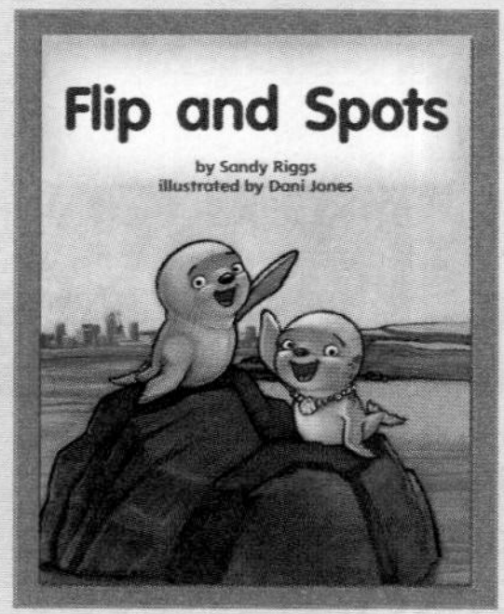

Decodable Reader

ELL

Reread Continue using the Interactive Question-Response Guide Technique to help English Language Learners understand the content of *Flip and Spots.* As you read the text, make the meaning clear by pointing to the pictures, demonstrating word meaning, paraphrasing text, and asking children questions.

Approaching Level

Phonemic Awareness

Objective Segment words into phonemes

Materials
- **Teacher's Resource Book**, p. 143
- **Sound-Spelling WorkBoards**
- markers

PHONEME SEGMENTATION

Tier 2

- Distribute copies of the **WorkBoards** and markers. Say a word, stretching each sound for 1½ seconds. Model for children how to drag one marker onto each box for each sound. Then have children repeat and count the number of sounds. Do this for the words *should*, *could*, *would*, *stood*, *shook*, *look*, *foot*.
- **Link to Spelling** When completed, segment each word again. Then help children replace each marker with a letter that stands for the sound. Help children read the completed words.

Phonics

Objective Decode words with vowel digraph /ů/*oo, ou*

Materials
- **Decodable Reader:** *Flip and Spots*
- **Sound-Spelling Cards**
- **Word-Building Cards**

SOUND-SPELLING REVIEW

Tier 2

Display **Word-Building Cards** one letter or spelling at a time: *oo, ou, oo, ui, ew, ue, u, ou, oe, oi, oy, ou, ow, are, air, ear, ere, or, ore, oar, ar, gn, kn, wr, mb.* Have children chorally say each sound.

RETEACH SKILL

- Display the *Book* **Sound-Spelling Card** /ů/. Review that the /ů/ sound can be spelled with the letters *oo* or *ou.*
- **Model Blending** Write words and sentences from the chart on page 115G on the board. Model how to blend the sounds in each word using the **Blending Routine**. Have children repeat.
- **Read in Context** Write the sentences below on the board. Have children chorally read the sentences. Help children blend sounds in decodable words and read vocabulary words.

  Did you examine the wood?
  I will help you look.
  Can Sam cook?
  Yes. He can cook well.
  I stood right there.
  She rescued the broken toy.
  The book was very good.
  That young dog is cute.

- **Read the Decodable** Reread *Flip and Spots* with children. Then have children practice reading the story to a partner. Circulate, listen in, and provide corrective feedback.

Approaching Level

High-Frequency/Vocabulary

Objective Identify high-frequency and vocabulary words

Materials
- **Vocabulary Cards**
- **Sound-Spelling WorkBoards**
- **High-Frequency Word Cards**

REVIEW WORDS

- Display **High-Frequency Word Cards** for **below**, **city**, **own** and **Vocabulary Cards** for **examines**, **hunger**, **mammal**, **normal**, **rescued**, and **young**. Have children copy each word on their **WorkBoards**. Then help them write sentences for each word. Provide sentence starters, such as *Is your dog _______ or old?*

CUMULATIVE REVIEW

- Display the High-Frequency Word Cards and Vocabulary Cards from the previous six weeks. Display one card at a time as children chorally read the word. Note words needing review.

Fluency

Objective Read aloud with fluency and comprehension

Materials
- **Leveled Reader:** *Bald Eagle Alert*
- **Approaching Reproducible**, p. 213

READ FOR FLUENCY

- Tell children that they will be doing a final fluent reading of *Bald Eagle Alert.*
- As they read, note words children mispronounce or struggle to read. Also note their comprehension and overall intonation and rate. Use this information to determine if additional instruction is needed on this week's phonics skill and vocabulary words. Send the book home for independent reading.

REREAD PREVIOUSLY READ BOOKS

Tier 2

- Distribute copies of the past six **Leveled Readers**. Tell children that rereading these books will help them develop their skills. The more times they read the same words, the quicker they will learn these words. This will make the reading of other books easier.
- Circulate and listen in as children read. Stop children periodically and ask them how they are figuring out difficult words or checking their understanding as they read.
- Ask children to read other previously read Leveled Readers during independent reading time or for homework.

Meet Grade-Level Expectations

As an alternative to this day's lesson, guide children through a reading of the On Level Leveled Reader. See page 119S. Because both books contain the same vocabulary, phonics, and comprehension skills, the scaffolding you provided will help most children gain access to this more challenging text.

Approaching Reproducible, page 213

As I read, I will pay attention to my phrasing.

People have always hunted whales. Hunting
6 whales for food was **normal**. People also made
14 things from whales.
17 There was no electricity long ago. People used oil
26 to light lamps. The oil was often made from whale
36 fat, or blubber.
39 Many whales were killed. There were very few
47 whales left. Today the laws protect whales.
54 Now people go on a whale watch to see whales.
64 They hunt for whales with their cameras. 71

Comprehension Check

1. Why did people hunt whales? **Cause and Effect** People hunted whales for food and to make things.
2. What happened that caused people to pass laws to protect whales? **Sequence of Events** People were hunting whales so much that there were very few whales left.

	Words Read	–	Number of Errors	=	Words Correct Score
First Read		–		=	
Second Read		–		=	

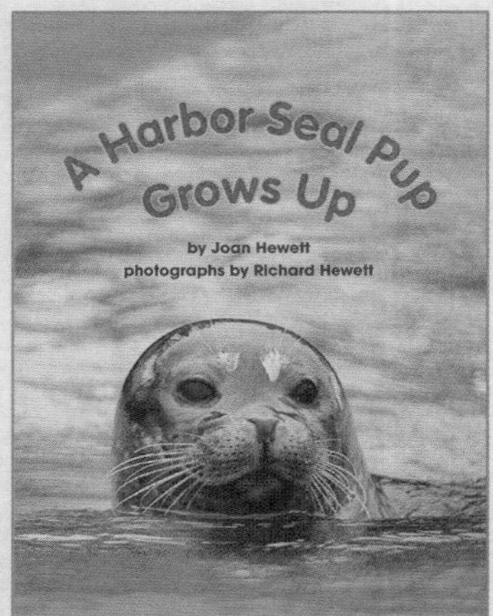

Student Book

On Level

Fluency

Objectives Read aloud with fluency; develop speaking skills

Materials • **Student Book:** *A Harbor Seal Pup Grows Up*

REREAD FOR FLUENCY

- Have children reread *A Harbor Seal Pup Grows Up*. Work with children to read with accuracy and appropriate rate and phrasing. Model fluent reading as needed.
- Provide time for children to read a section of the text to you. Comment on their understanding, rate, and phrasing and provide corrective feedback as needed.

DEVELOP SPEAKING/LISTENING SKILLS

- Provide time for children to read aloud a portion of *A Harbor Seal Pup Grows Up* to the class. Ask children to name ways the reader varied his or her voice and rate because of phrasing.
- Challenge children to memorize a few lines of the text from their favorite part of the selection.

Student Book

Beyond Level

Fluency

Objectives Read aloud with fluency and comprehension; develop speaking skills

Materials • **Student Book:** *A Harbor Seal Pup Grows Up*, "The Puppy"

REREAD FOR FLUENCY

- Have children reread *A Harbor Seal Pup Grows Up* and "The Puppy." Work with children to read with accuracy and appropriate attention to phrasing.
- Provide time for children to read a section of the text to you. Comment on their rate and attention to phrasing and provide corrective feedback. Also check their understanding.

DEVELOP SPEAKING/LISTENING SKILLS

Provide time for children to read aloud *A Harbor Seal Pup Grows Up* or "The Puppy" to the class. Ask children to name ways the reader changed his or her voice or rate because of phrasing.

Challenge children to memorize their favorite page or two of the text and recite it for you.

ELL ENGLISH LANGUAGE LEARNERS

Access to Core Content

Content Objective Read grade-level text
Language Objective Discuss text using key words and sentence frames
Materials • **ELL Resource Book**, pp. 248–257.

PRETEACH PAIRED SELECTION (PAGES 94–114)

Use the Interactive Question-Response Guide on **ELL Resource Book** pages 248–357 to preview the paired selection "The Puppy." Preteach the selection on **Day 4**.

ELL Resource Book

Leveled Reader Lesson 2

Content Objective To apply skills and strategies
Language Objective Tell informaton using complete sentences
Materials • **ELL Resource Book**, pp. 261 • **Leveled Reader:** *Bald Eagles*

AFTER READING

All Language Levels

Book Talk Distribute copies of ELL Resource Book page 261. Children will work with peers of varying language abilities to discuss them. Help students determine who will be the leader for the discussion.

Develop Listening and Speaking Skills Tell children to remember the following while engaged in the Book Talk:

- Share information in cooperative learning interactions. Remind children to work with their partners to retell the story and complete any activities. Ask: *What happened next in the story?*
- Employ self-corrective techniques and monitor their own and other children's language production. Children should ask themselves: *What parts of this passage were confusing to me? Can my classmates help me clarify a word or sentence that I don't understand?*
- Distinguish between formal and informal English and know when to use each one. Remind children to note whether the selection is written in formal or informal English. Ask: *Why do you think it is written in this way?* Remind children that they may use informal English when speaking with their classmates, but they should use formal language when they talk to teachers or write essays.
- Use high-frequency English words to describe people, places, and objects.

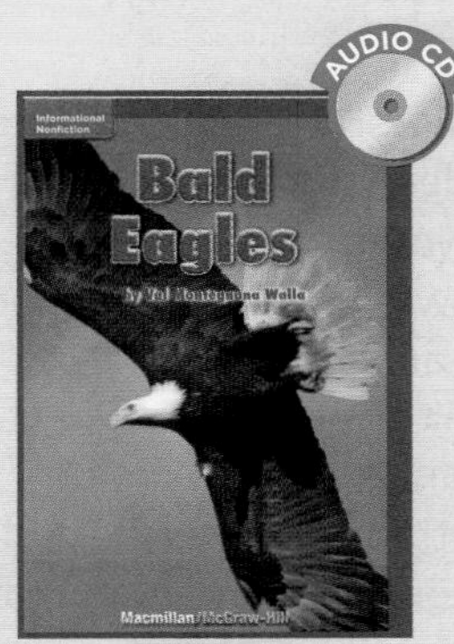

Leveled Reader

Book Talk

Bringing Groups Together
Students will work with peers of varying language abilities to discuss the Book Talk questions. Form groups so that students who read the Beyond Level, On Level, Approaching Level, and English Language Learner readers are in the same group for the activity.

Approaching Level

Oral Language

Objectives Build vocabulary related to animal babies; review oral vocabulary

Materials • chart paper

EXPAND VOCABULARY

- Draw a two-column chart on chart paper. Label the columns *Animals* and *Animal Babies*. Remind children that this week they learned about one kind of animal baby: the harbor seal pup.
- Write *seal* in column 1 of the chart and *pup* in column 2. Point to each word, read it, and have children repeat.

Animals	Animal Babies
seal	pup
eagle	chick
dog	puppy
cat	kitten
horse	foal
cow	calf
whale	calf
shark	pup
lion	cub

- Tell children that there are special names for different kinds of animal babies. For example, baby seals are called *pups* and baby eagles are called *chicks.*
- Ask children to name other animals and the names of their babies, such as *dog/puppy*, *cat/kitten*, *horse/foal*, and so on. Use this information to complete the chart.

REVIEW VOCABULARY

Tier 2

- Use the **Define/Example/Ask** vocabulary routine in the **Instructional Routine Handbook** to review this week's oral vocabulary words: **baffled**, **daring**, **compassion**, **lunge**, and **survive**.
- Tell children you are going to start a sentence using one of the words and you want them to think of an ending. For example, say: *I am a caring person and I have* compassion *for* ________*!* Repeat for remaining words.

ELL

Understand Help children understand the meaning of words on the chart by showing pictures or miming the animals. If children don't know the name of an animal and wish to contribute to the chart, encourage participation by having them sketch a quick drawing, point to a picture, or mime the animal they wish to name.

Approaching Level

Fluency

Objectives Read aloud with fluency; review high-frequency and vocabulary words

Materials
- **Student Book:** *A Harbor Seal Pup Grows Up*
- **High-Frequency Word Cards**
- **Vocabulary Cards**

REREAD FOR FLUENCY

- Have children reread a portion of *A Harbor Seal Pup Grows Up*. Direct them to focus on two to four of their favorite pages from the selection. Work with children to read the pages with the appropriate phrasing and understanding. For example, read each sentence and have children echo. Remind children to pay attention to phrasing.
- Provide time to listen as children read their sections of text. Comment on their phrasing and provide corrective feedback by modeling proper fluency.

REVIEW HIGH-FREQUENCY/VOCABULARY WORDS

- Display **High-Frequency Word Cards** for **below**, **city**, **own** and **Vocabulary Cards** for **baffled**, **daring**, **compassion**, **lunge**, and **survive**. Model using two or three of the words in a sentence. Then have children come up with their own sentence using two or three of the words.

CUMULATIVE REVIEW

- Display the High-Frequency Word Cards and Vocabulary Cards from the previous four weeks. Display one card at a time as children chorally read the word. Mix and repeat. Note words children need to review.

Self-Selected Reading

Objective Read independently and describe the sequence of events

Materials
- **Leveled Classroom Library**
- other fiction books

APPLY SKILLS TO INDEPENDENT READING

- Have each child choose an informational book for independent reading. (See the **Theme Bibliography** on pages T8–T9 for book suggestions.)
- After reading, ask children to use their Sequence of Events Charts to orally retell the sequence of events. Provide time for children to comment on their reactions to the books. Ask: *What happened first? What happened next? What happened last?*

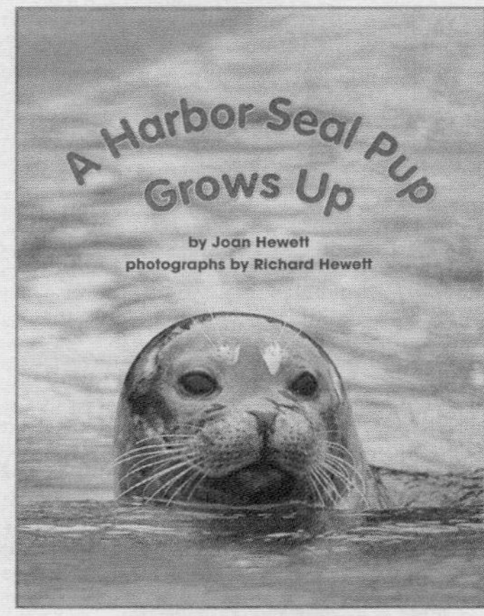

Student Book

Decodable Text

Use the decodable stories in the **Teacher's Resource Book** to help children build fluency with basic decoding patterns.

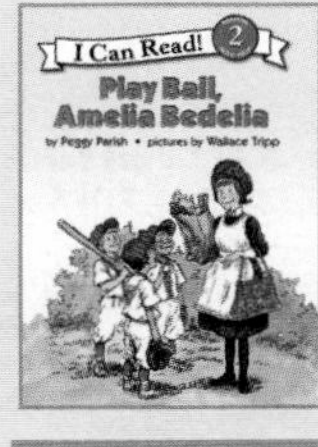

Approaching

Leveled Classroom Library

See Leveled Classroom Library lessons on pages T2–T7.

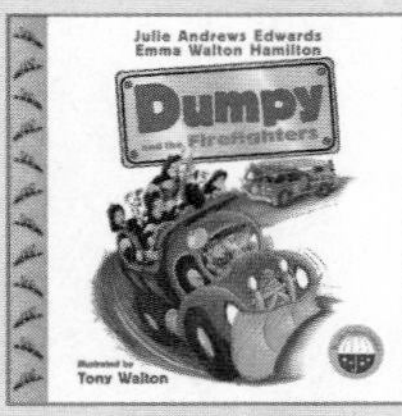

On Level

Leveled Classroom Library

See Leveled Classroom Library lessons on pages T2–T7.

On Level

Self-Selected Reading

Objective Read independently and retell an informational selection

Materials • **Leveled Classroom Library** • other informational books

APPLY SKILLS TO INDEPENDENT READING

- Have each child choose an informational book for independent reading. (See the **Theme Bibliography** on pages T8–T9 for book suggestions.)
- After reading, ask children to use their Sequence of Events Charts to orally retell the books. Provide time for children to comment on their reactions to the books. Ask: *What happened first? What happened next? What happened last?*

ELL

Share Information Pair English Language Learners with fluent speakers. Have them choose the same book and work together on the Retelling Chart.

Beyond Level

Self-Selected Reading

Objective Read independently and retell information learned

Materials • **Leveled Classroom Library** • other informational books

APPLY SKILLS TO INDEPENDENT READING

- Have each child choose an informational book for independent reading. (See the **Theme Bibliography** on pages T8–T9 for book suggestions.)
- After reading, ask children to use their Sequence of Events Charts to write a retelling of the book in their **Writer's Notebooks**. Provide time for children to comment on the books. Ask: *What did you like best about this book? What surprised you?*

EVALUATE

- Challenge students to discuss how the self-selected books they have chosen relate to the theme of this unit, Better Together. Ask: *How can people work together to help animals?* Have children discuss their views.

Beyond

Leveled Classroom Library

See Leveled Classroom Library lessons on pages T2–T7.

ELL ENGLISH LANGUAGE LEARNERS

Fluency

Content Objectives Reread selections to develop fluency; develop speaking skills
Language Objective Tell a partner what a selection is about
Materials
- **Decodable Reader:** *Flip and Spots*
- **Student Book:** *A Harbor Seal Pup Grows Up*, "The Puppy"

REREAD FOR FLUENCY

Beginning

Have children read the Decodable Reader.

Intermediate/Advanced

- Have children reread a portion of *A Harbor Seal Pup Grows Up*. Ask them to focus on two to four of their favorite pages from the selection. Work with children to read the pages with appropriate pace and intonation. For example, read each sentence of the first two pages and have children echo. Then have children choral read the sentences. Remind them to pay attention to punctuation and to vary their voice and pace appropriately.
- Provide time for children to read their sections of text to you. Comment on their expression and provide corrective feedback by modeling proper fluency.

DEVELOP SPEAKING/LISTENING SKILLS

All Language Levels

- Have children practice reading "The Puppy." Work with children to read with appropriate pace and intonation. Then provide time for children to read aloud the poem to a partner. Ask children to tell what they liked about the poem. Provide the sentence frame *I liked this poem because* ______.

Self-Selected Reading

Content Objective Read independently
Language Objective Orally retell information learned
Materials
- **Leveled Classroom Library**
- other nonfiction books

APPLY SKILLS AND STRATEGIES TO INDEPENDENT READING

All Language Levels

- Have each child choose a nonfiction book for independent reading. (See the **Theme Bibliography** on pages T8–T9.) After reading, ask children to orally summarize the book. Provide time for children to comment on their reactions to the book and share them with classmates.

Student Book

Progress Monitoring

Weekly Assessment

ASSESSED SKILLS

- Phonics: Vowel Digraphs *oo*, *ou*; Inflectional Endings *-ing*
- Selection Vocabulary
- Comprehension: Sequence of Events
- Grammar: Irregular Verbs

Selection Test for* A Harbor Seal Pup Grows Up *Also Available.

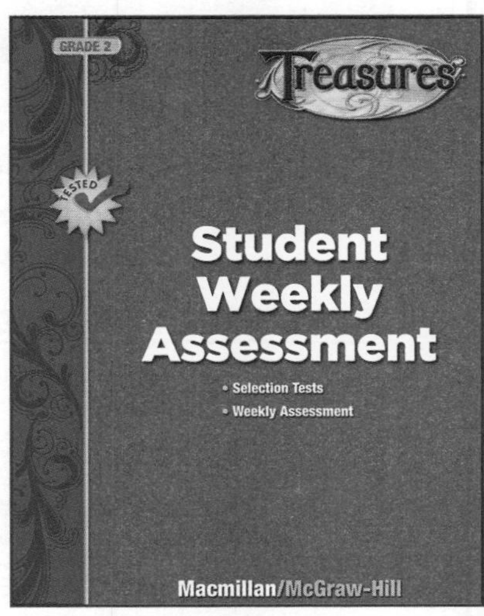

Student Weekly Assessment
Unit 4 Week 4

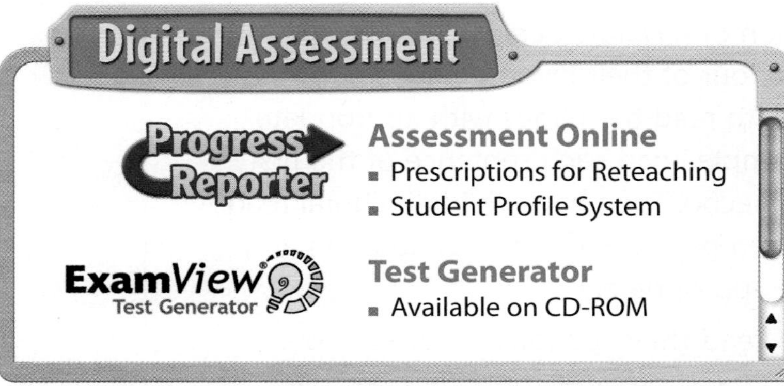

Fluency Assessment

Assess fluency for one group of students per week.
Use the Oral Fluency Record Sheet to track the number of words read correctly. Fluency goals for all students:

62–82 words correct per minute (WCPM)

Approaching Level	Weeks 1, 3, 5
On Level	Weeks 2, 4
Beyond Level	Week 6

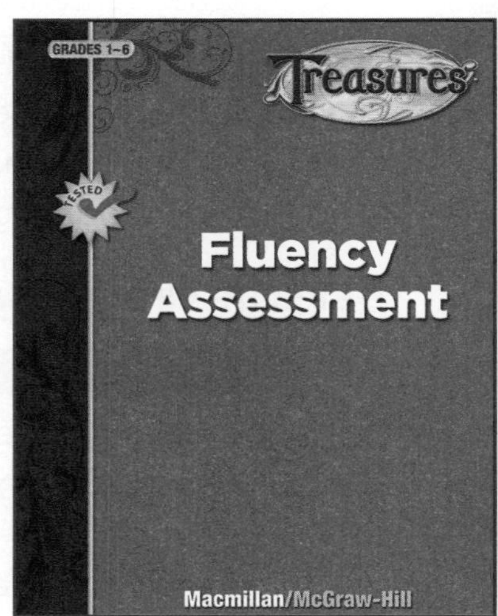

Fluency Assessment

DIBELS LINK

PROGRESS MONITORING

Use your DIBELS results to inform instruction.

IF

DIBELS Oral **R**eading **F**luency (**DORF**) 0–67

THEN

Evaluate for Intervention

TPRI LINK

PROGRESS MONITORING

Use your TPRI scores to inform instruction.

IF

Graphophonemic Knowledge	Still Developing
Reading Fluency/Accuracy	Reading Grade 2, Story 4 Less Than 75 WCPM
Reading Comprehension Questions	0–3 correct

THEN

Evaluate for Intervention

Diagnose		Prescribe
Review the assessment answers with students. Have them correct their errors. Then provide additional instruction as needed.		
	IF...	**THEN...**
PHONICS AND SPELLING Vowel Digraphs *oo*, *ou* Inflectional Endings *–ing*	0–1 items correct . . .	LOG ON Online Practice: Go to **www.macmillanmh.com**. See **Phonics Intervention Teacher's Edition.** See Sound-Spelling Fluency and mixed review blending lines in upcoming lessons.
VOCABULARY WORDS **VOCABULARY STRATEGY** Context Clues: Antonyms	0–1 items correct . . .	See **Phonics Intervention Teacher's Edition.** SPIRAL REVIEW See Vocabulary review lessons Unit 4, Week 5.
COMPREHENSION Sequence of Events	0–1 items correct . . .	See **Comprehension Intervention Teacher's Edition.** SPIRAL REVIEW See Sequence of Events lessons Unit 4, Week 5.
GRAMMAR Irregular Verbs	0–1 items correct . . .	See the **Grammar and Writing Handbook.**
FLUENCY	53–61 WCPM	AUDIO CD Fluency Solutions Audio CD
	0–52 WCPM	See **Fluency Intervention Teacher's Edition.**

Response to Intervention

To place students in Tier 2 or Tier 3 Intervention use the *Diagnostic Assessment.*

- Phonemic Awareness
- Phonics
- Vocabulary
- Comprehension
- Fluency

Week 5 ★ At a Glance

Priority Skills and Concepts

Comprehension

- **Genre:** Fiction
- **Strategy:** Analyze Story Structure
- **Skill:** Fantasy and Reality

- **Sequence of Events**

High-Frequency Words

- ***among, bought, decided***

Oral Vocabulary

- **Build Robust Vocabulary:** ***applause, deceive, display, exquisite, vain***

Vocabulary

- ***menu, fetch, simmered, assembled, devoured***
- **Strategy:** Word Parts/Inflected Verbs

Fluency

- **Expression**

Phonemic Awareness

- **Identify and Work with Syllables**

Phonics/Spelling

- **Vowel Digraph *au*, *aw*, *a*:** ***pause, draw, launch, law, fault, jaw, sauce, hawk, raw, crawl, good, could, among, bought, decided***

Grammar/Mechanics

- **Contractions**
- **Contractions/Apostrophes**

Writing

- **Descriptive Flyer**
- **Vary Words**
- **Trait:** Word Choice

Key

 Tested in program

 Review Skill

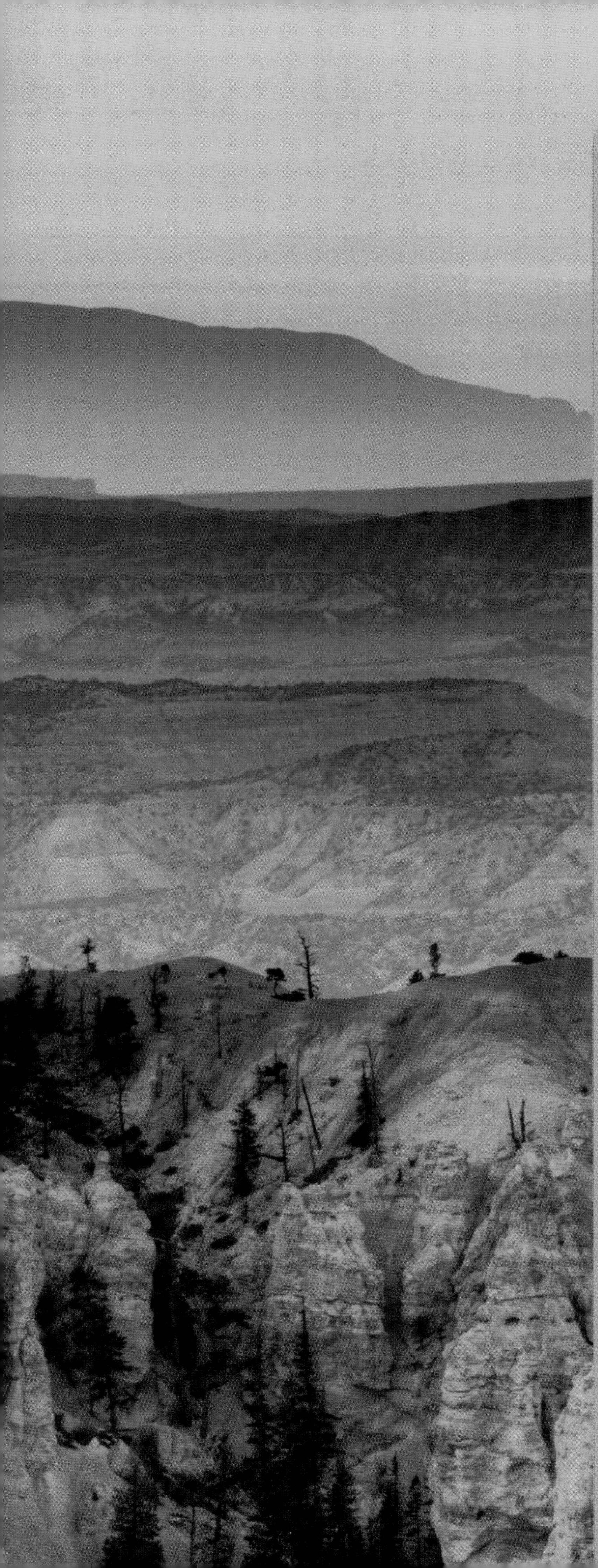

Digital Learning

Digital solutions to help plan and implement instruction.

Teacher Resources

LOG ON

ONLINE
www.macmillanmh.com

- **Teacher's Edition**
  - Lesson Planner and Resources also on CD-ROM
- **Formative Assessment**
  - ExamView® on CD-ROM also available
- **Instructional Resources**
  - Unit Videos
  - Classroom Presentation Toolkit
- **Professional Development**
  - Video Library

TeacherWorks Plus

Progress Reporter

VIDEO

Student Resources

ONLINE
www.macmillanmh.com

- **Interactive Student Book**
- **Leveled Reader Database**
- **Activities**
  - Research Toolkit
  - Oral Language Activities
  - Vocabulary/Spelling Activities

StudentWorks Plus

Listening Library

- Recordings of Student Books and Leveled Readers

Fluency Solutions

- Fluency Modeling and Practice

Weekly Literature

Theme: Surprising Teamwork

Student Book

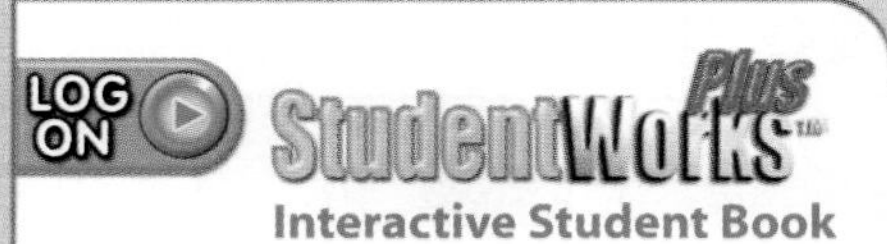

Interactive Student Book

- Word-by-Word Reading
- Summaries in Multiple Languages
- Comprehension Questions

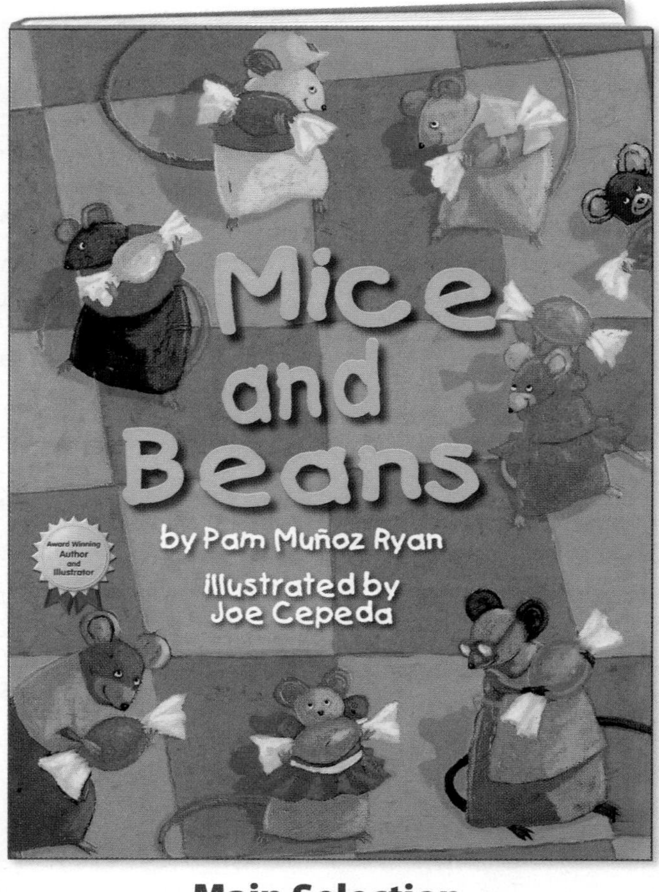

Main Selection

Genre Fiction

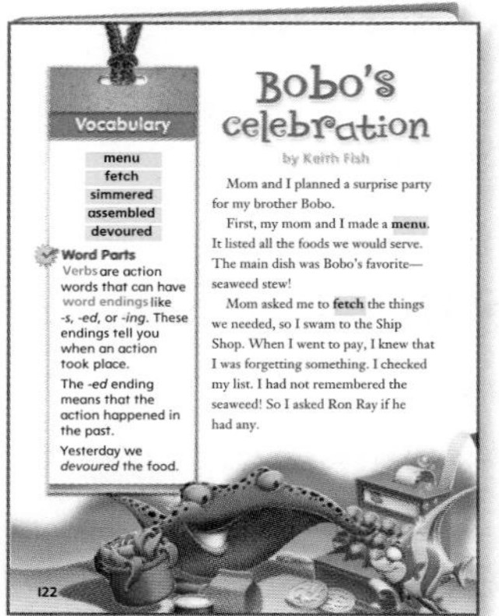

Preteach Vocabulary and Comprehension

Genre Fiction

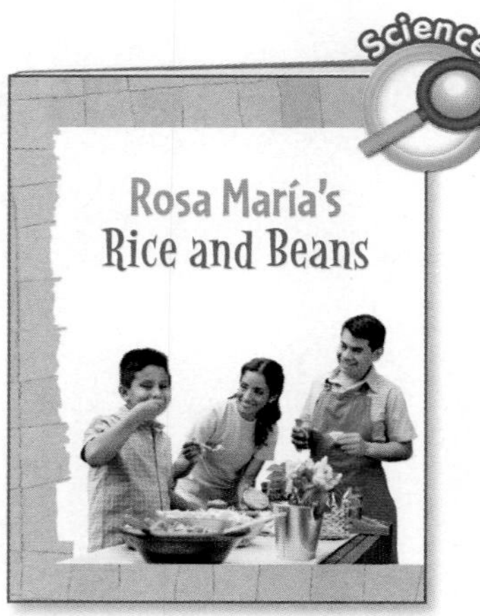

Paired Selection

Genre Expository

Support Literature

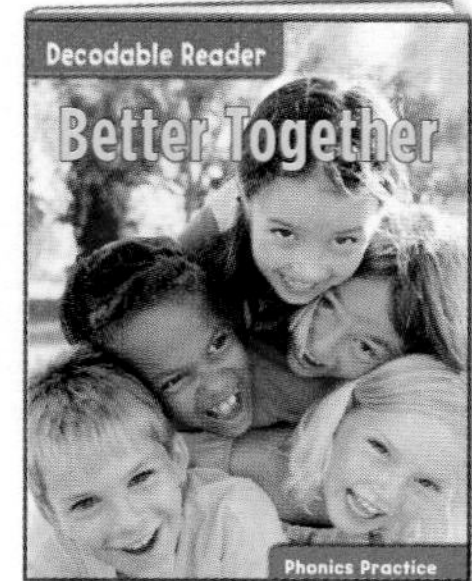

Decodable Reader Library

- One decodable read each week

Oral Vocabulary Cards

- Listening Comprehension
- Build Robust Vocabulary

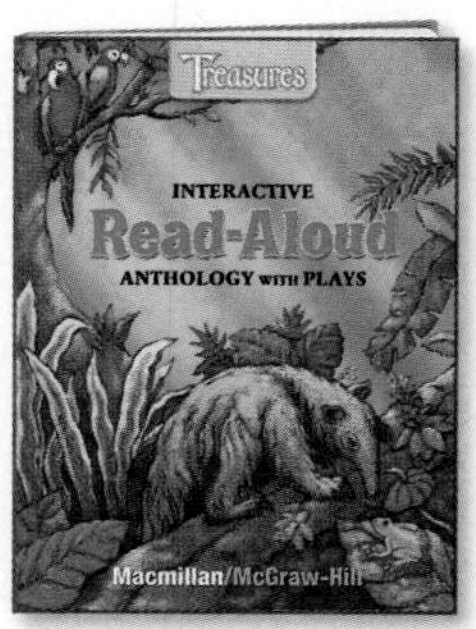

Interactive Read-Aloud Anthology

- Listening Comprehension
- Readers Theater Plays for Fluency

Resources for Differentiated Instruction

Leveled Readers

GR Levels H-O

Genre	Fiction

- Same Theme
- Same Vocabulary
- Same Comprehension Skills

Approaching Level

On Level

Beyond Level

ELL

Leveled Reader Database
Go to www.macmillanmh.com.

Leveled Practice

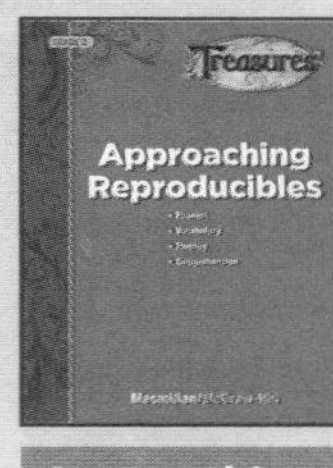
Approaching

On Level

Beyond

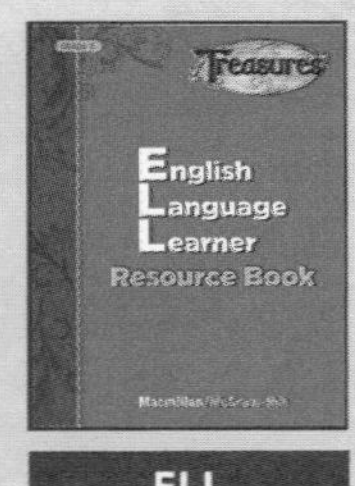
ELL

Leveled Classroom Library

Approaching

On Level

Beyond

Response to Intervention

- Phonemic Awareness
- Phonics
- Vocabulary
- Comprehension
- Fluency

Assessment

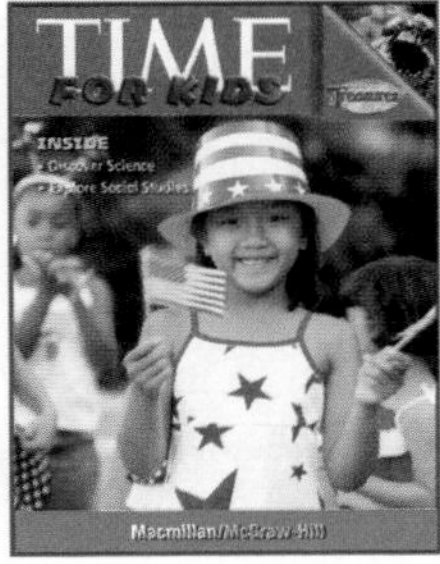

Time For Kids
- Teacher's Edition
- Apply Answering Questions Strategies

Weekly Assessment

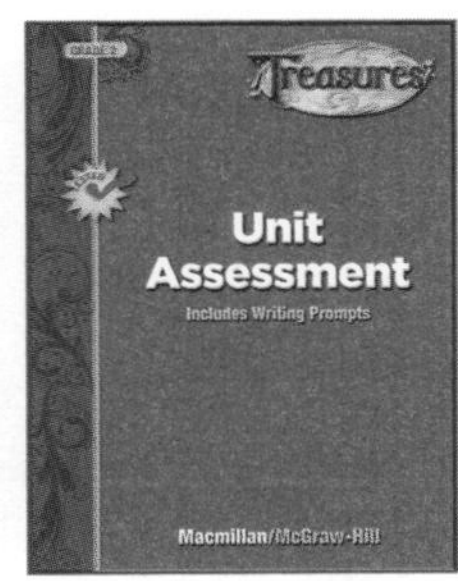
Unit Assessment

Benchmark Assessment

HOME-SCHOOL CONNECTION

- Family letters in English and Spanish
- Take-home stories and activities

Online Homework
www.macmillanmh.com

Suggested Lesson Plan

Go to www.macmillanmh.com for Online Lesson Planner

Mice and Beans, pp. 124/125–152/153

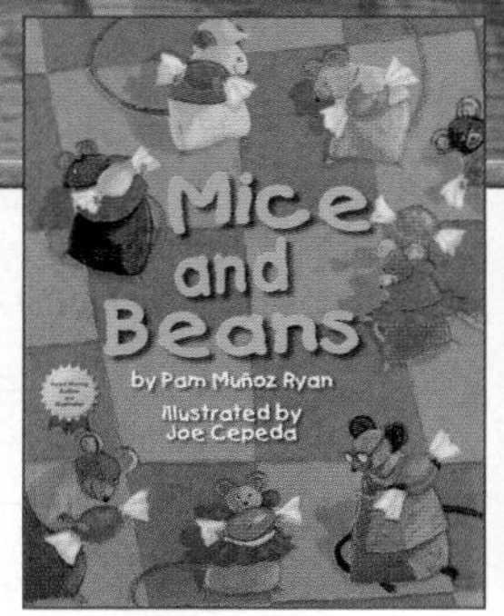

WHOLE GROUP	DAY 1	DAY 2
ORAL LANGUAGE • Oral Vocabulary • Listening Comprehension • Phonemic Awareness	**Focus Question** When have you seen people work together in a surprising or unusual way? Build Background, 120M **Oral Vocabulary** *applause, deceive, display, exquisite, vain*, 121A Oral Vocabulary Cards, "The Emperor's New Clothes," 121A **Phonemic Awareness** Identify and Work with Syllables, 121B	**Focus Question** What do the mice do in this story that they can't do in real life? **Oral Vocabulary** *applause, deceive, display, exquisite, vain*, 123E **Phonemic Awareness** Phoneme Categorization, 123F
WORD STUDY • Phonics • Spelling • Vocabulary	**Phonics** Introduce and Blend with Vowel Digraph *a, au, aw*, 121C Practice Book, 217 **Spelling** Pretest: Words with Vowel Digraph *au, aw*, 121E Spelling, 77 **Vocabulary** *assembled, devoured, fetch, menu, simmered*, 121G **Strategy:** Word Parts/Inflected Verbs Practice Book, 218	**Phonics** Blend and Build with Vowel Digraph *a, au, aw*, 123G **Spelling** Word Sort with *au, aw*, 123H Spelling, 78 **Vocabulary** *assembled, devoured, fetch, menu, simmered* Review Words in Context, 123I
READING • Comprehension • Fluency	**Read** Decodable Reader, *Paul Saw Arctic Foxes*, 121F Decodable Reader **Comprehension**, 123A–123B "Bobo's Celebration," 122/123 **Strategy:** Analyze Story Structure **Skill**: Distinguish Between Fantasy and Reality **Fluency** Build Fluency, 121C	**Read** *Mice and Beans*, 124/125–152/153 Student Book **Comprehension**, 123J–155A **Strategy:** Analyze Story Structure **Skill:** Distinguish Between Fantasy and Reality Practice Book, 220–221 **Fluency** Build Fluency, 123G
LANGUAGE ARTS • Writing • Grammar	**Writing** **Daily Writing** Look at the picture. Write about what you see, 120M Expository: Descriptive Flyer, 123D **Grammar** Contractions, 123C Grammar, 96	**Writing** **Daily Writing** Write an article about a show or a movie you've seen that received a lot of applause. Evaluate what you saw, 123E Prewrite a Descriptive Flyer, 155C **Grammar** Contractions, 155B Grammar, 97
ASSESSMENT • Informal/Formal	**Quick Check** Phonics, 121D Vocabulary, 122/123	**Quick Check** Comprehension, 152/153

SMALL GROUP Lesson Plan — Differentiated Instruction 120G–120H

Priority Skills

Phonics	Vocabulary	Comprehension	Writing
Vowel Digraph *a, au, aw*	**Words:** *assembled, devoured, fetch, menu, simmered* **Strategy:** Inflected Verbs	**Strategy:** Analyze Story Structure **Skill:** Distinguish Between Fantasy and Reality	Descriptive Flyer **Science**

DAY 3

Focus Question What parts of the story could not happen in real life? How do you know this story is a fantasy? How did the illustrations show that this story was a fantasy?

Read Aloud: "When Elephant Goes to a Party," 155D

Oral Vocabulary *applause, deceive, display, exquisite, vain*, 155K

Phonemic Awareness Phoneme Blending, 155E

Phonics Blend words with Vowel Digraph *a, au, aw*, 155F
Inflectional ending *-ed*, 155G
Practice Book, 222

Spelling Word Sort, 155H
Spelling, 79

Vocabulary *assembled, devoured, fetch, menu, simmered*
Strategy: Word Parts/Inflected Verbs, 155J
Practice Book, 223

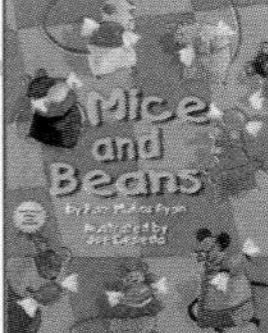

Student Book

Read *Mice and Beans*, 124/125–152/153

Comprehension,
Review Skill: Sequence of Events, 155N

Fluency Repeated Reading: Prosody/ Expression, 155L
Practice Book, 224

Writing

Daily Writing Respond to the Read-Aloud by writing a different version of "When Elephant Goes to a Party," 155D

Vary Words, 155P

Writing Trait: Word Choice, 155Q

Draft a Descriptive Flyer, 155Q

Grammar Mechanics: Contractions, 155O
Grammar, 98

Quick Check Fluency, 155M

DAY 4

Focus Question Think about your favorite recipe. Write about the solids, liquids, and gases in the recipe.

Oral Vocabulary *applause, deceive, display, exquisite, vain*, 155W

Phonemic Awareness Phoneme Categorization, 155S

Phonics Blend and Build Words with Vowel Digraph *a, au, aw*, 155T

Spelling Practice Words with Vowel Digraph *au, aw*, 155V
Spelling, 80

Vocabulary *assembled, devoured, fetch, menu, simmered*
Review Words in Context, 155W

Student Book

Read "Rosa Maria's Rice and Beans," 156/157–158/159

Comprehension, 155X
Text Feature: Written Directions

Content Vocabulary: *liquids, solids, gas*, 155X

Practice Book, 225

Fluency Build Fluency, 155

Writing

Daily Writing Think about wearing an exquisite costume in a school play on stage. Write about how applause would make you feel, 155R

Revise and Proofread a Descriptive Flyer, 159D

Grammar Contractions, 159B
Grammar, 99

Quick Check Spelling, 155V

DAY 5
Review and Assess

Focus Question How will analyzing the story structure help you read and understand another selection?

Oral Vocabulary *applause, deceive, display, exquisite, vain*, 161A

Phonemic Awareness Phoneme Blending, 161C

Phonics Blend and Build with Vowel Digraph *a, au, aw*, 161C

Spelling Posttest, 161E

Vocabulary *assembled, devoured, fetch, menu, simmered*, 161F

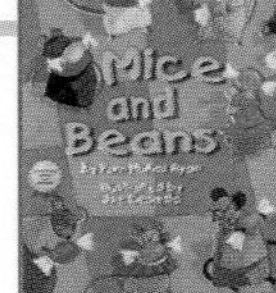

Student Book

Read Self-Selected Reading, 120J

Comprehension, 161G
Strategy: Analyze Story Structure

Skill: Distinguish Between Fantasy and Reality

Fluency Repeated Reading: Prosody/ Expression, 161B

Writing

Daily Writing Think about a time that you worked with people to get something done. Describe what everyone involved did and how teamwork helped with the project. 161F
Publish and Present a Descriptive Flyer, 161I

Speaking, Listening, and Viewing, 161J

Grammar Contractions, Apostrophes, 161H
Grammar, 100

Weekly Assessment, 161KK–161LL

Differentiated Instruction

What do I do in small groups?

Focus on Skills

IF... **students need additional instruction, practice, or extension based on your** 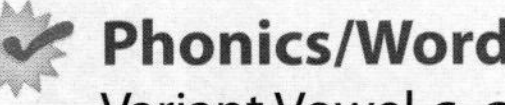 **observations for the following priority skills**

Phonics/Word Study
Variant Vowel *a, au, aw*; Inflectional Endings *-ed*

Vocabulary Words
assembled, devoured, fetch, menu, simmered
Strategy: Word Parts: Endings *-s, -ed, -ing*

Comprehension
Strategy: Analyze Story Structure
Skill: Distinguish Between Fantasy and Reality

Fluency
Phonics, High-Frequency Words, Expression

THEN...

Approaching	Preteach and
English Learners	Reteach Skills
On Level	Practice
Beyond	Enrich and Accelerate Learning

LOG ON Suggested Small Group Lesson Plan

	DAY 1	DAY 2
Approaching Level • **Preteach/Reteach** Tier 2 **Tier 2 Instruction**	• Phonemic Awareness, 161K • Phonics, 161K ELL • High-Frequency/Vocabulary, 161L • Decodable Reader, *Paul Saw Arctic Foxes,* 161L	• Phonemic Awareness, 161Q • Phonics, 161Q ELL • High-Frequency/Vocabulary, 161R • Leveled Reader Lesson 1, 161R
On Level • **Practice**	• Phonics, 161M ELL • Fluency, 161M ELL	• Leveled Reader Lesson 1, 161S ELL
Beyond Level • **Extend/Accelerate** Gifted Talented **Gifted and Talented**	• Phonics, 161N ELL • Vocabulary, 161N	• Leveled Reader Lesson 1, 161T • Analyze, 161T
ELL • **Build English Language Proficiency** • **See ELL in other levels.**	• Prepare to Read, 161O • Academic Language, 161O • Preteach Vocabulary, 161P	• Preteach Main Selection, 161U • Grammar, 161V

Focus on Leveled Readers

Levels H-O

Approaching

On Level

Beyond

ELL

Manipulatives

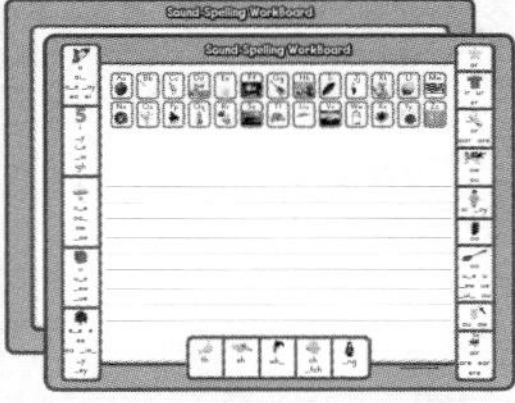
Sound-Spelling WorkBoards

Sound-Spelling Cards

Photo Cards

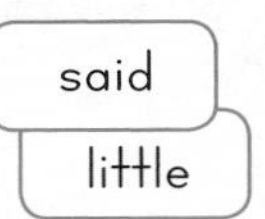

High-Frequency Word Cards

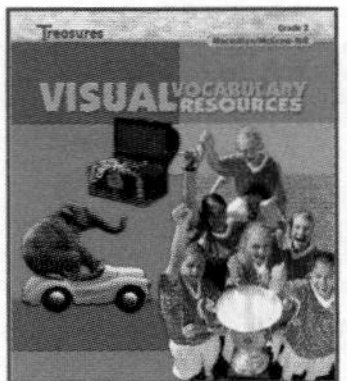

Visual Vocabulary Resources

Additional Leveled Readers

Leveled Reader Database
www.macmillanmh.com

Search by

- Comprehension Skill
- Content Area
- Genre
- Text Feature
- Guided Reading Level
- Reading Recovery Level
- Lexile Score
- Benchmark Level

Subscription also available.

DAY 3

- Phonemic Awareness, 161W
- Phonics, 161W ELL
- High-Frequency/Vocabulary, 161X
- Leveled Reader Lesson 2, 161X
- Book Talk, 161X

- Leveled Reader Lesson 2, 161Y
- Fluency, 161Y
- Book Talk, 161Y

- Leveled Reader Lesson 2, 161Z
- Synthesize and Evaluate, 161Z
- Fluency, 161Z
- Book Talk, 161Z

- Leveled Reader Lesson 1, 161AA
- Writing/Spelling, 161BB

DAY 4

- Phonemic Awareness, 161CC
- Phonics, 161CC ELL
- High-Frequency/Vocabulary, 161DD
- Fluency, 161DD
- Review Leveled Readers, 161DD

- Fluency, 161EE

- Fluency, 161EE

- Preteach Paired Selection, 161FF
- Leveled Reader Lesson 2, 161FF

DAY 5

- Oral Language, 161GG ELL
- Fluency, 161HH
- Self-Selected Independent Reading, 161HH

- Self-Selected Independent Reading, 161II ELL

- Self-Selected Independent Reading, 161II
- Evaluate, 161II

- Fluency, 161JJ
- Self-Selected Independent Reading, 161JJ

What do I do with the rest of my class?

- Literacy Workstations
- Leveled Reader Activities
- Practice Book and Reproducibles
- Online Activities
- English Language Learner Practice Book

Classroom Management Tools

Weekly Contract

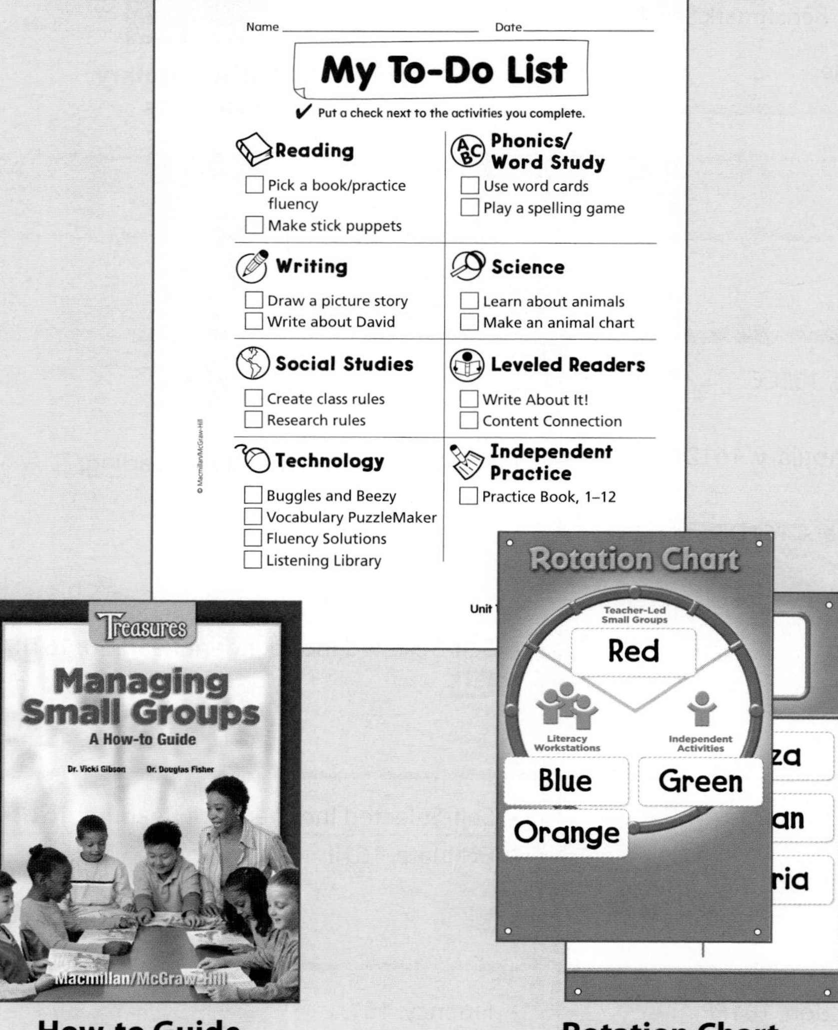

Name ______ Date ______

My To-Do List

✔ Put a check next to the activities you complete.

Reading
- ☐ Pick a book/practice fluency
- ☐ Make stick puppets

Phonics/ Word Study
- ☐ Use word cards
- ☐ Play a spelling game

Writing
- ☐ Draw a picture story
- ☐ Write about David

Science
- ☐ Learn about animals
- ☐ Make an animal chart

Social Studies
- ☐ Create class rules
- ☐ Research rules

Leveled Readers
- ☐ Write About It!
- ☐ Content Connection

Technology
- ☐ Buggles and Beezy
- ☐ Vocabulary PuzzleMaker
- ☐ Fluency Solutions
- ☐ Listening Library

Independent Practice
- ☐ Practice Book, 1–12

How-to Guide

Rotation Chart

Digital Learning

StudentWorks Plus
- Summaries in Multiple Languages
- Word-by-Word Reading
- Comprehension Questions

- Read Other Books by the Author or Illustrator

Leveled Practice

On Level

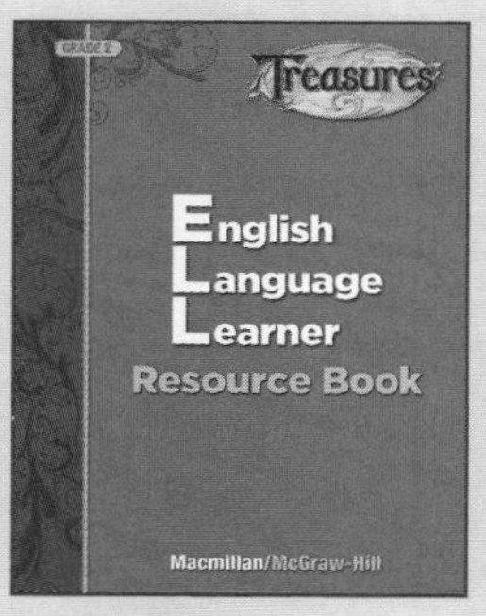

ELL

Also Available:

Approaching Reproducible

Beyond Reproducible

Independent Activities

ONLINE INSTRUCTION www.macmillanmh.com

Oral Language Activities

- Focus on Vocabulary and Concepts
- English Language Learner Support

Leveled Reader Database

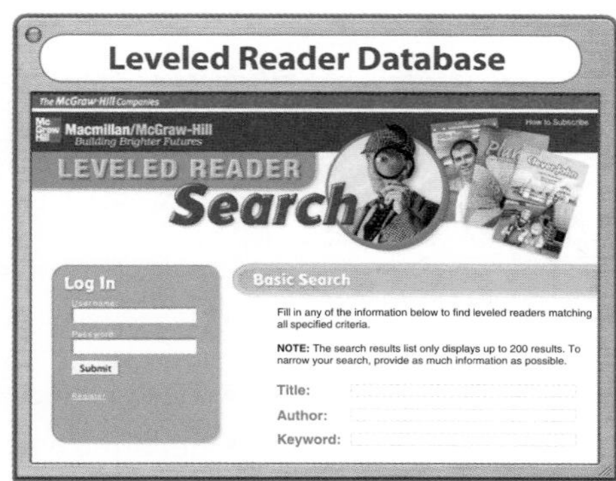

- Leveled Reader Database
- Search titles by level, skill, content area, and more

Vocabulary/Spelling Activities

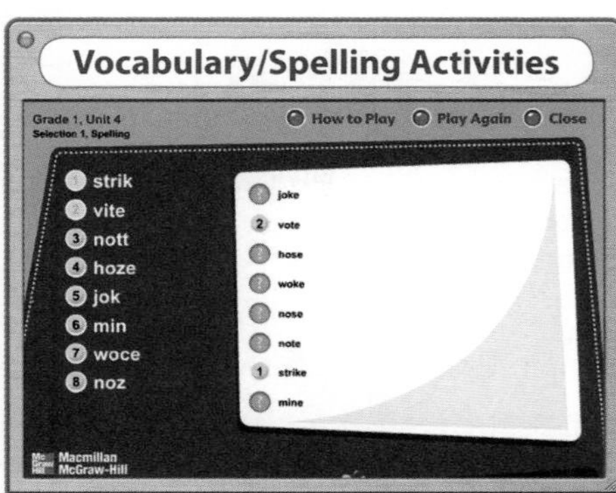

- Differentiated Lists and Activities

Research Toolkit

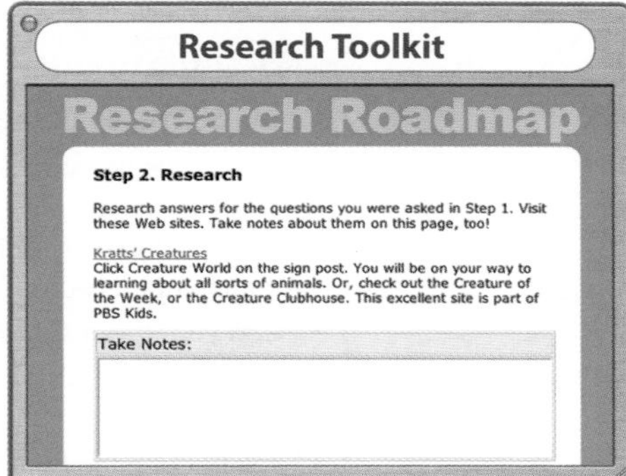

- Research Roadmap
- Research and Presentation Tools
- Theme Launcher Video
- Links to Science and Social Studies

Available on CD

LISTENING LIBRARY
Recordings of selections
- Main Selections
- Paired Selections
- Leveled Readers
- ELL Readers

NEW ADVENTURES WITH BUGGLES AND BEEZY
Phonemic awareness and phonics activities

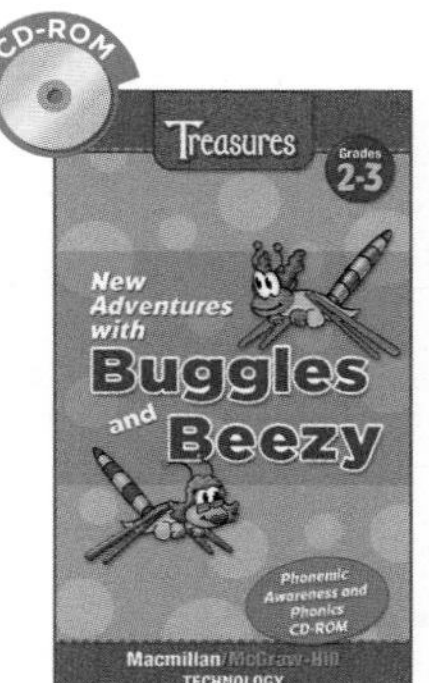

FLUENCY SOLUTIONS
Recorded passages at two speeds for modeling and practicing fluency

Leveled Reader Activities

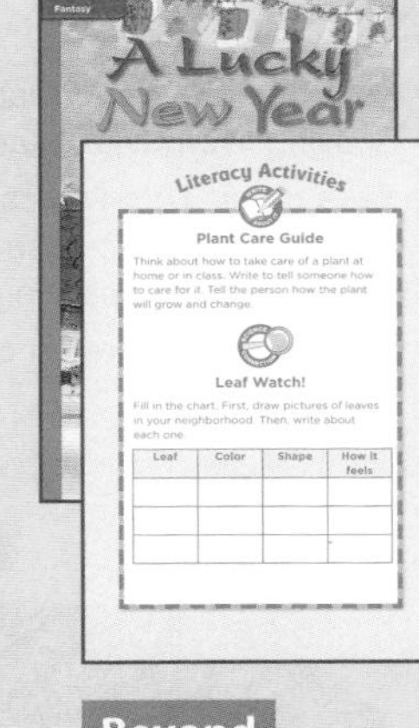

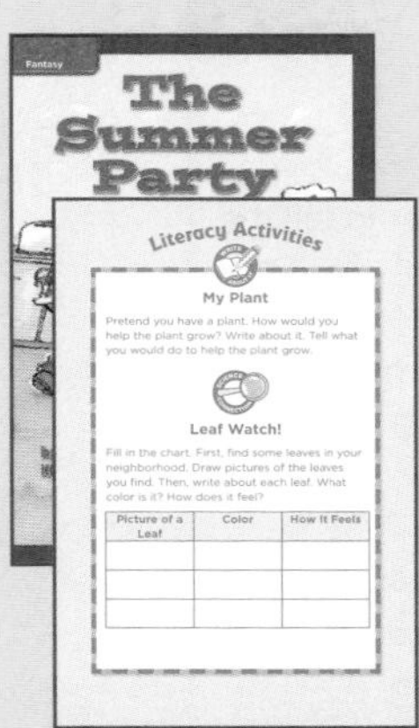

The Summer Party

Approaching | On Level | Beyond | ELL

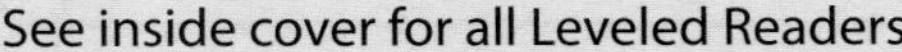

See inside cover for all Leveled Readers.

Literacy Workstations

Writing

See lessons on pages 120K–120L

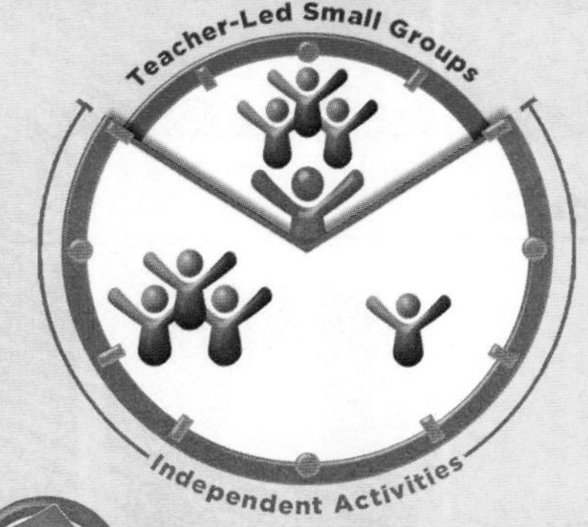

What do I do with the rest of my class?

Reading

Objectives

- Read aloud fluently and accurately
- Retell a story including character, setting, and plot

Phonics/Word Study

Objectives

- Identify and use verbs correctly
- Recognize spelling patterns

Reading — Pick a Book

20 Minutes

- Pick a book you read this week.
- Tell which parts of the story could happen in real life and which parts are fantasy and could not really happen.
- Make a chart that shows this information.

Extension

- Reread the parts that are fantasy in another book you read this week.
- Use the Fluency Solutions CD.

Things you need:

- books you read this week
- pencil, paper
- Fluency Solutions CD

For more book titles, go to the Author/Illustrator section of www.macmillanmh.com

Listening Library
Fluency Solutions

39

Phonics/Word Study — Verbs and Endings

20 Minutes

- Create a Three-Tab Foldable®.
- On the outside tabs, write the words *devoured, assembled,* and *simmered*.
- On the inside tabs, write a sentence for each of the words.
- Read your three sentences to your partner.

Extension

- Look through the books you read this week. Find five other verbs that end with *-ed*.
- Make up a sentence for each one.

FOLDABLES

- Three-Tab Foldable®

devoured | assembled | simmered

For more vocabulary and spelling games, go to www.macmillanmh.com

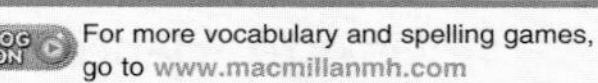

39

Reading — Retell a Fantasy

20 Minutes

- Use the Retelling Cards to retell the story with a partner.
- Retell the story in the order in which things happened.
- Tell what happened first, next, and last.

Extension

- Work with a partner to tell the story from the point of view of the mice.
- Describe what the mice were thinking and feeling during the story.

Things you need:

- *Mice and Beans*, pp. 124–153
- Retelling Cards

For more book titles, go to the Author/Illustrator section of www.macmillanmh.com

Listening Library

40

Phonics/Word Study — Concentration

20 Minutes

- Play with a partner. Place two sets of Spelling Word Cards face down.
- Take turns. Turn two cards face up. If the words match, use the word in a sentence and keep the cards.
- Play until there are no cards left.

Extension

- Play again.Turn two cards face up. If both words contain the same letters *au* or *aw,* then you have a match. The words do not have to be the same.

Things you need:

- two sets of Spelling Word Cards

Teacher's Resource Book: spelling word cards, pages 70–89

For more vocabulary and spelling games, go to www.macmillanmh.com

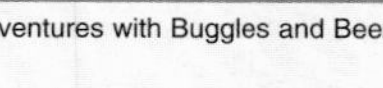
New Adventures with Buggles and Beezy

40

Literacy Workstation Flip Charts

Writing

Objectives

- Write, proofread, and revise a poster
- Write legibly so that it can be easily read
- Rewrite a story with a beginning, middle, and end

Content Literacy

Objectives

- Describe an American or family custom
- Write a list of questions about healthful food
- Conduct research to answer your questions

Writing **Lost and Found** 20 Minutes

- Pretend you have lost something at school. Create a poster or flyer that describes the missing object.
- Use words that describe what the object looks like. You may draw a picture of it, too.

Extension

- Proofread your poster or flyer. Be sure that you used lively words to describe the object. Write cleanly and clearly.
-  Add your poster or flyer to your portfolio.

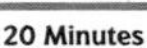

Things you need:
- drawing paper
- crayons or markers

39

Social Studies **Celebrations and Customs** 20 Minutes

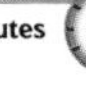

- Explain an American custom or celebration or one practiced by your family.
- With a partner, create a chart to describe the event.

Food	Games	Songs	Other Customs

Extension

- Use the Internet or books to learn about customs and celebrations in other parts of the world.

Things you need:
- pencil, paper
- Internet or books

Internet Research and Inquiry Activity
www.macmillanmh.com

39

Writing **MOUSE TALES** 20 Minutes

- Rewrite *Mice and Beans* from the point of view of a mouse. Include a beginning, middle, and end.
- Explain why the mice decide to help Rosa María by filling the piñata.

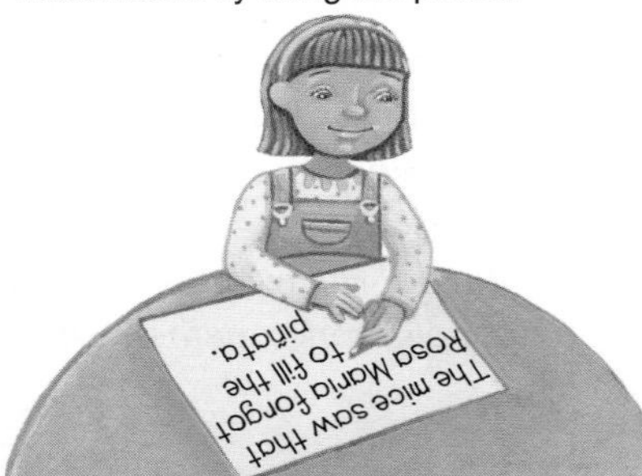

Extension

- Share your story with a partner. Talk about why the mice are good story characters.
- Make a list of other stories or movies that have mice as characters.

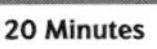

Things you need:
- pencil, paper

40

Science **HEALTHFUL FOODS** 20 Minutes

- Work with a partner. Talk about fruits and vegetables you like to eat.
- Write a recipe for a salad.
- Draw a picture of all the healthful things in your salad.

Extension

- Write a list of questions about whether certain foods are healthful.
- Use books or the Internet to answer your questions.

Things you need:
- Internet or books
- pencil, paper
- crayons

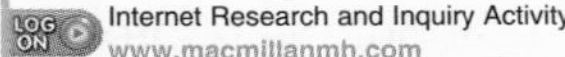

Internet Research and Inquiry Activity
www.macmillanmh.com

40

Day 1 At a Glance

WHOLE GROUP

Oral Language
- Build Background
- Oral Vocabulary

Phonological Awareness
- Identify and Work with Syllables

Phonics
- Vowel Digraph *a, au, aw*
- Read *Paul Saw Arctic Foxes*
- Spelling Pretest: Words with *au, aw*

Vocabulary
- Teach Words in Context
- Word Parts: Endings *-s, -ed, -ing*
- Read "Bobo's Celebration"

Comprehension
- Strategy: Analyze Story Structure
- Skill: Fantasy and Reality

Language Arts
- Grammar: Contractions
- Writing: Expository

SMALL GROUP

- Differentiated Instruction, pages 161K–161JJ

Oral Vocabulary

Week 5

applause
display
vain
deceive
exquisite

Oral Language

Build Background

ACCESS PRIOR KNOWLEDGE
Discuss with children the different ways people can work together. Talk about the importance of playing together on a team, working together to get a job done, and helping classmates complete a project. Ask children to think of ways people work together.

SING ABOUT TEAMWORK
Sing the song "There's a Hole in the Bucket" and have children list the ways people in the song worked together. Have them add a verse and then act it out.

FOCUS QUESTION Chorally read the "Talk About It" question on **Student Book** page 121 with children. Describe the photograph, providing academic language. Talk about the rewards of working together, like satisfaction and **applause**, or clapping. Have them describe some other ways people **display**, or show, how it feels to work together.

There's a Hole in the Bucket

There's a hole in the bucket,
dear Liza,
dear Liza,
There's a hole in the bucket,
dear Liza, a hole.

Mend the hole, then,
dear Georgie, dear Georgie,
dear Georgie,
Mend the hole, then, dear
Georgie, dear Georgie,
the hole.

Use the Picture Prompt

BUILD WRITING FLUENCY
Ask children to respond to the picture by writing in their Writer's Notebooks about a time they saw people working together. Meet with them during Writing Conference time to provide feedback.

ELL ENGLISH LANGUAGE LEARNERS

Beginning

Describe Tell children about the photograph. *The girls are in a race. One girl has to give the other girl the stick. These girls are working together to win the race.* Then ask children to tell you about the photograph.

Intermediate

Describe Ask children to describe the photograph. Ask: *What do you think these children are doing? Are they working together?* Elicit details to support children's responses.

Advanced

Explain Have children talk about working together. Ask: *When have you worked with someone else? What did you do? Have you seen other people work together? Who?*

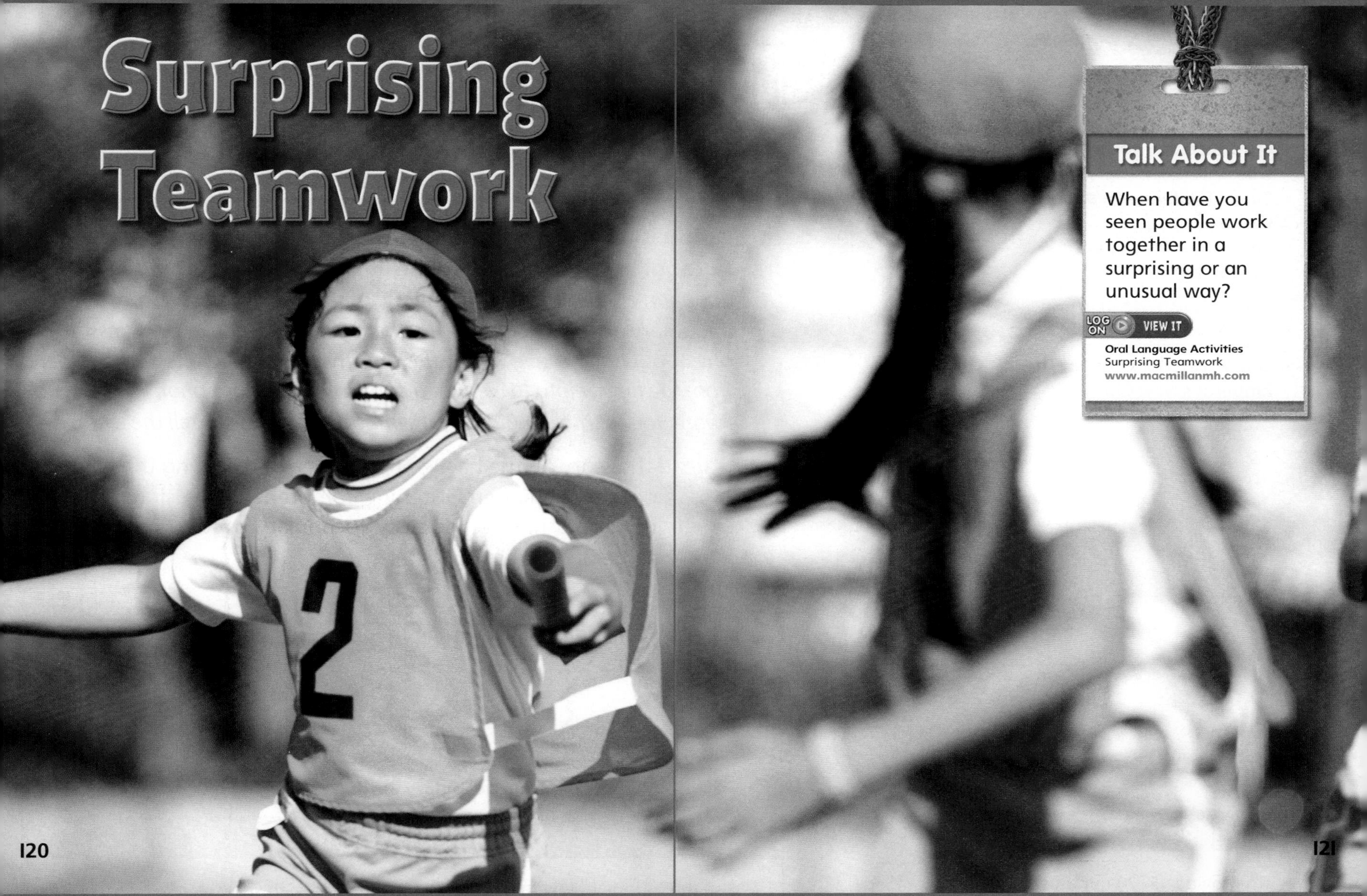
Surprising Teamwork
Talk About It
When have you seen people work together in a surprising or an unusual way?
LOG ON VIEW IT
Oral Language Activities
Surprising Teamwork
www.macmillanmh.com
120
121

Connect to the Unit Theme

Sometimes help can come from surprising and unusual places.

CONNECT TO THEME
Ask children to talk about what they have learned so far about teamwork.

USE THEME FOLDABLE
Read aloud the **Big Idea** statement. Write the word **exquisite** on the board. Remind children that *exquisite* means "very beautiful." Read the word aloud and have children repeat. Ask them to add it to their Unit Theme Foldables. Tell children that they will add pictures of surprising and unusual ways of getting help throughout the week.

Dinah Zike's
FOLDABLES®
Study Organizer

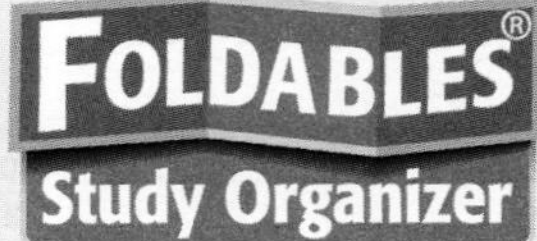

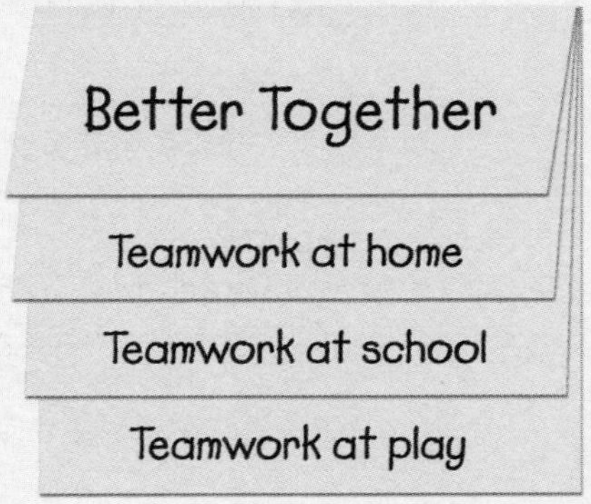
Better Together
Teamwork at home
Teamwork at school
Teamwork at play

Unit 4 Theme Foldable

Objectives

- Introduce oral vocabulary words
- Read "The Emperor's New Clothes"
- Review last week's oral vocabulary words

Materials

- Oral Vocabulary Cards: "The Emperor's New Clothes"

Additional Vocabulary

To provide 15–20 minutes of additional vocabulary instruction, see **Oral Vocabulary Cards** 5-Day Plan. The pre- and post-tests for this week can be found on **Teacher's Resource Book** pages 245–263.

Oral Language

Build Robust Vocabulary

BUILD BACKGROUND Display "The Emperor's New Clothes" **Oral Vocabulary Card** 1 and read the title. *We are going to read a fairy tale about an emperor who loves fancy clothes. A fairy tale is a story about imaginary people or creatures. Fairy tales often teach a moral lesson, or one about how to be good. In this one, the emperor wants a suit made from the finest cloth to wear at a performance in his honor. While I read, I want you to think about why it's important to always tell the truth.*

- Read the story on the back of the cards aloud. During the first reading, check children's listening comprehension using the Retell prompts. Review the story vocabulary words using the routine below.

Oral Vocabulary Cards

Vocabulary Routine

Use the routine below to discuss the meaning of each story word.

Define: **Applause** is the clapping of hands to show that something is well liked.
Example: *There was loud applause at the end of the school play.*
Ask: When have you heard applause? PRIOR KNOWLEDGE

- **Deceive** means to make someone believe something that is not true. *It is hard to deceive a smart person who has all the facts.* How do most people feel when they have been deceived? DESCRIPTION
- When you put something on **display**, you show it. *Our class mural is on display in the lunchroom.* What are some things on display in your home? EXAMPLE
- Something that is **exquisite** is very beautiful. *The red roses in the garden are exquisite.* What exquisite thing have you seen lately? EXAMPLE
- Someone who is **vain** has too much pride in his or her looks. *The vain girl could not pass a mirror without looking at herself.* Would you want a vain person as a friend? Why or why not? PRIOR KNOWLEDGE

Use the routine to review last week's words: *baffled, daring, compassion, lunge,* and *survive.*

Phonological Awareness

Identify and Work with Syllables

Model

Show children how to identify syllables in a word. Remind them that a syllable is a word part with a vowel sound.

Listen to the syllables in the word *because*. The first syllable is /bē/. The second syllable is /côz/. Say *because* with me. I will hold up one finger for each syllable. *Because* has two syllables, so I hold up two fingers.

Guided Practice/Practice

Have children practice identifying syllables by holding up a finger for each syllable in these examples. Do the first two together.

Listen as I read each word. Then repeat the word and hold up a finger for each syllable you hear.

auto	pause	awful
sausage	fault	strawberry

Objective

- Identify and work with syllables in words with variant vowel /ô/

ELL

Minimal Contrasts Focus on articulation. Make the /ô/ sound and point out your mouth position. Have children repeat. Use the articulation photos on the small **Sound-Spelling Cards**. Repeat for the /oi/ sound. Then have children say each sound together, noticing the slight differences in mouth position. Continue by having children read minimal-contrast word pairs, such as *bawl/boil, jaw/joy, pause/poise*.

Objectives

- Identify letter-sound correspondence for vowel digraph /ô/*a, au, aw*
- Blend sounds in words with vowel digraph *a, au, aw*
- Review previously taught phonics skills

Materials

- Sound-Spelling Card: *Straw*
- Word-Building Cards; Teacher's Resource Book, p. 66
- chart paper
- Practice Book, p. 217

Skills Trace

Vowel Digraph *a, au, aw*

Introduce	121C–D
Practice/ Apply	121F, 123G, 155F-G, 155I, 155T-U; Practice Book: p. 217; Decodable Reader: *Paul Saw Arctic Foxes*
Reteach/ Review	161D; 1161K-N, 161Q, 161W, 161CC
Assess	Weekly Test; Unit 4 Test
Maintain	Build Fluency: Sound/Spelling

ELL

Variations in Languages Speakers of Spanish and most Asian languages will have difficulty pronouncing and perceiving the *l*-controlled variant vowel /ô/. Use the Approaching Level Phonics lessons for additional pronunciation and decoding practice.

Sound Pronunciation

See **Sound Pronunciation CD** for a model of the /ô/ sound. Play this for children needing additional models.

Phonics

Introduce *a, au, aw*

Model

Teach the sound /ô/ spelled *au* and *aw*. Show the *Straw* **Sound-Spelling Card**.

Model writing the letters. Use the handwriting models.

This is the *Straw* Sound-Spelling Card. The sound is /ô/. The /ô/ sound is spelled with the letters *aw*. Say it with me: /ô/. This is the sound at the end of the word *straw*. Listen: /s/ /t/ /r/ /ô/, *straw*. Watch as I write the letters *aw*. I will say the sound /ô/ as I write the letters several times.

Guided Practice/Practice

Have children practice connecting the letters and sound through writing.

Now do it with me. Say /ô/ as I write the letters. This time, write the letters *aw* five times as you say the /ô/ sound. (Repeat with *au, alt, alk, all*.)

Build Fluency: Sound/Spellings

Display the following **Word-Building Cards:** *au, aw, oo, ou, oo, ui, ew, ue, u, ou, oe, oi, oy, ou, ow, are, air, ear, ere, or, ore, oar, ar*. Have children chorally say each sound. Repeat and vary the pace.

au aw ou

Blend with Vowel Digraph *a, au, aw*

Model

Display Word-Building Cards *s, a,* w. Model blending the sounds as you run your finger under each letter.

Continue with *claw, fault, brawn, walking, halted, relaunch*.

This is the letter *s*. It stands for /s/. These are the letters *aw*. They stand for /ô/.

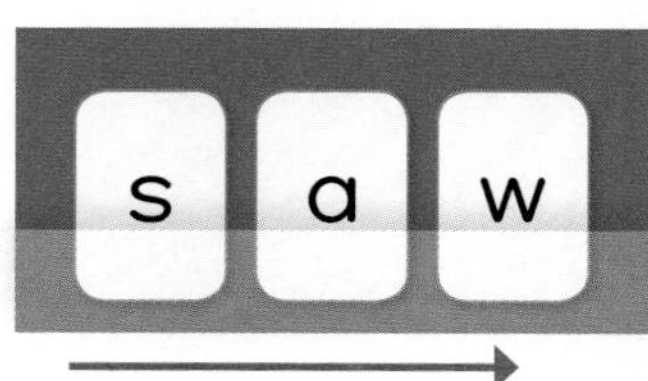

(Stretch the sounds.) Listen as I blend all the sounds together: /sô/. Say it with me.

Guided Practice/Practice
Write the words below on chart paper. Read each one in the first row, blending the sounds; for example, /p/ /ô/. The word is *paw*. Have children blend the sounds in each word with you. Then use the appropriate blending level to complete the remaining lines chorally. See **Sound-by-Sound Blending Routine** in the **Instructional Routine Handbook** for support. (Save the chart for tomorrow's lesson.)

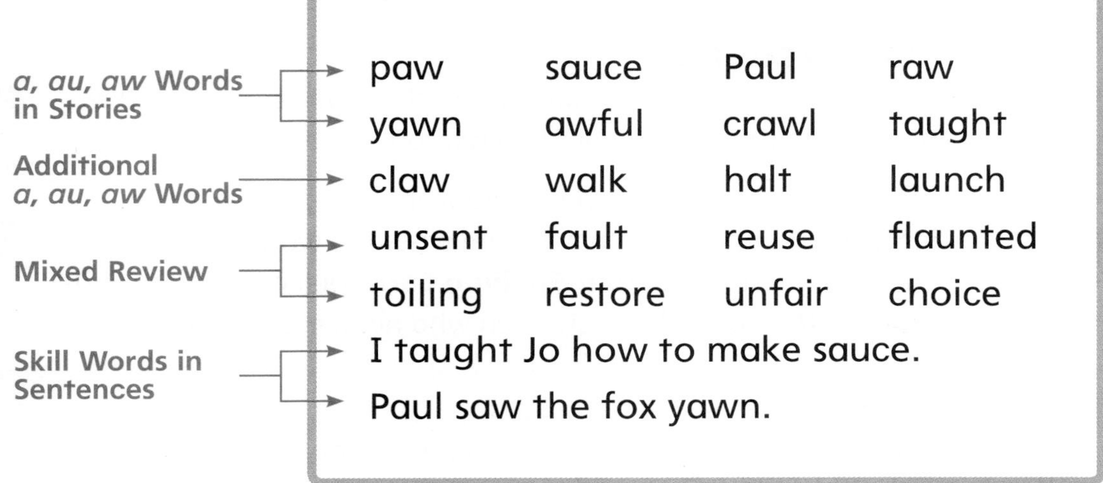

a, au, aw Words in Stories	paw	sauce	Paul	raw
	yawn	awful	crawl	taught
Additional *a, au, aw* Words	claw	walk	halt	launch
Mixed Review	unsent	fault	reuse	flaunted
	toiling	restore	unfair	choice
Skill Words in Sentences	I taught Jo how to make sauce.			
	Paul saw the fox yawn.			

Daily Handwriting
Review with children how to form the uppercase letters. See **Handwriting** pages 59 and 104–112.

Corrective Feedback

Blending: Sound Error Model the sound that the children missed, then have them repeat the sound. Say: *My turn.* Tap under the letters and say: *Sound? /ô/. What's the sound?* Then return to the beginning of the word. Say: *Let's start over.* Blend the sounds in the word with children again.

Quick Check

Can children blend sounds in words with vowel digraph *a, au, aw*?

During **Small Group Instruction**

Tier 2

If No → **Approaching Level** Repeat blending using the words on the chart above. Explicitly correct the error and provide more "with me" type practice. Use a lower level of blending to provide support.

If Yes → **On Level** Consolidate the learning by having children read additional words with variant vowel *a, au, aw*. See page 161M.

Beyond Level Extend the learning by having children read harder words containing variant vowel *a, au, aw*. See page 161N.

ON YOUR OWN

Practice Book, page 217

The letters ***au*** and ***aw*** often stand for the same sounds. You can hear these sounds ***caught*** and ***claw***.

Choose the word from the box that best matches each picture and clue. Then write it on the line below.

sauce yawn laundry straw sausage

1. This is clothing that needs to be washed. laundry
2. This is something that can help you drink. straw
3. This can be good with spaghetti. sauce
4. You may do this when you are tired. yawn
5. You might eat this for breakfast. sausage

Approaching Reproducible, page 217
Beyond Reproducible, page 217

Objectives

- Spell words with variant vowel *au*, *aw*
- Identify spelling patterns
- Sort words with variant vowel *au*, *aw*

Materials

- paper and pencils
- Sound-Spelling WorkBoards; Teacher's Resource Book, p. 143
- Phonics/Spelling Practice Book, p. 77

5-Day Spelling	
DAY 1	Dictation; Pretest
DAY 2	Teacher-Modeled Word Sort
DAY 3	Student Word Sort
DAY 4	Test Practice
DAY 5	Posttest

ON YOUR OWN **Spelling**, page 77

Using the Word Study Steps

1. LOOK at the word.
2. SAY the word aloud.
3. STUDY the letters in the word.
4. WRITE the word.
5. CHECK the word.
   Did you spell the word right?
   If not, go back to step 1.

X the Word

Put an X on the word in each row that has a different vowel sound.

1. crawl lamb law
2. wait pause fault
3. draw sauce bo[illegible]d
4. raw jaw join
5. lunch launch hawk

Phonics/Spelling

Words with Variant Vowel *au*, *aw*

DICTATION

Use dictation to help children transfer their growing knowledge of sound-spellings to writing. Follow the **Dictation Routine** below with each spelling word.

DICTATION ROUTINE

- Pronounce one word at a time. Have children clearly state the word. Then repeat the word for children and use it in a sentence.
- Ask children to orally segment the word to think about the individual sounds, then have them write the word. Prompt children to use the **Sound-Spelling Card** spellings as they write. Provide **Workboards** for children who need more support.

PRETEST

Pronounce each spelling word. Read the sentence and pronounce the word again. Ask children to say each word softly, stretching the sounds, before writing it. After the pretest, write each word on the board as you say the letter names. Have children check their work.

Spelling Words

Approaching	On Level	Beyond
pause	pause	pause
draw	draw	because
saw	launch	launch
law	law	lawn
fault	fault	fault
jaw	jaw	caught
fawn	sauce	sauce
hawk	hawk	laundry
raw	raw	thaw
paw	crawl	crawl
book	good	wooden
could	could	couldn't
among	among	among
bought	bought	bought
decided	decided	decided

1. **pause:** I saw a rabbit pause to eat.
2. **draw:** Can you draw a fox?
3. **launch:** The rocket launch is Monday.
4. **law:** It is against the law to steal.
5. **fault:** It is my fault that the cup broke.
6. **jaw:** A lion has a strong jaw.
7. **sauce:** I learned how to cook sauce.
8. **hawk:** The hawk built a nest.
9. **raw:** Wolves eat raw meat.
10. **crawl:** The bugs crawl on the leaf.
11. **good:** That was a good movie.
12. **could:** Could the bird fly away?
13. **among:** There was one rose growing among the daisies.
14. **bought:** I bought a new notebook.
15. **decided:** We decided to take a hike.

Decodable Reader

- **Review High-Frequency Words** Write **below**, **city**, and **own** on the board. Review the words with children using the **Read/Spell/Write** routine.

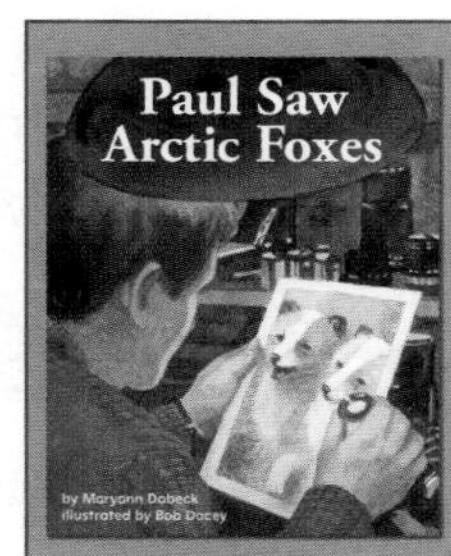

Paul Saw Arctic Foxes

- **Preview and Predict** Point to the book's title and have children sound out each word as you run your finger under it. Then ask:
  - *What is Paul doing?*
  - *Why do you think he is holding the photograph?*
  - *What do you think he is thinking about?*

- **First Read** Turn to page 28. Have children point to each word, sounding out decodable words and saying the high-frequency words quickly. Children should chorally read the story the first time through. If they have difficulty, provide corrective feedback page by page as needed. See the **Decodable Text Routine** in the **Instructional Routine Handbook** for correction models.

- **Check Comprehension** Ask the following:
  - *What made Paul want to study arctic foxes?*
  - *Why did he take pictures of them?*
  - *How far was Paul from the foxes when he took pictures?*
  - PARTNERS *Turn to your partner and retell the story.*

- **Second Read** Reread the story with children.
  - Remind children that an abbreviation is a shorter way to spell a word. Have them identify and read the abbreviation, "TV," on page 29. Have them tell what word the abbreviation is short for.
  - **Approaching Level** If children struggle sounding out words, provide "with you" blending models. Then review blending using the words on the Word List at the end of the story during Small Group time. Conclude by guiding children through a rereading of the book.
  - **Beyond Level** If children can sound out the words, then have them quietly read the text with a partner.

Objectives

- **Decode words with variant vowel *a, au, aw* in connected text**
- **Review last week's high-frequency words *below, city, own***

Materials

- **Decodable Reader Library: *Paul Saw Arctic Foxes***

High-Frequency Words

Use the **Read/Spell/Write** routine to teach each high-frequency word.

- **Read** Read the word. Have children repeat.
- **Spell** Chorally spell the word.
- **Write** Have children write the word as they spell it aloud. Then ask them to write a sentence using each word.

SMALL GROUP OPTION

You may wish to read the Decodable Reader during **Small Group** time.

See pages 161K–161JJ

Objectives

- Introduce the meaning of vocabulary words
- Use word parts: inflected verbs
- Teach words in context
- Review last week's vocabulary words

Materials

- Student Book: "Bobo's Celebration"
- Practice Book, p. 218

Vocabulary

assembled	devoured
fetch	menu
simmered	

ELL

Preteach Vocabulary
See page 161P to preteach the vocabulary words to ELL and Approaching Level children. Use the **Visual Vocabulary Resources** to demonstrate and discuss each word.

Vocabulary

TEACH WORDS
Introduce each word using the **Define/Example/Ask** routine. Model reading each word.

Vocabulary Routine

Use the routine below to discuss the meaning of each word.

Define: If you **assembled** something, you put it together.
Example: *Mom assembled all the parts to build my new bicycle.*
Say: Name something that you have assembled. EXAMPLE

- If you **devoured** food, you ate it greedily. *I was so hungry that I devoured my lunch.* How are the words *devoured* and *nibbled* alike and different? COMPARE AND CONTRAST
- When a dog goes to **fetch** something, it goes after it and brings it back. *Could you fetch me the paints from the art closet?* Name a word that means the same as *fetch*. SYNONYM
- When you plan a **menu**, you write a list of what foods will be served at a meal. *Dad is planning the menu for my birthday dinner.* Describe the menu for your favorite dinner. DESCRIPTION
- If something was **simmered**, it was cooked slowly for a long time. *Grandma simmered the soup for an hour.* What other foods can be simmered? EXAMPLE
- **Word Wall** Add these words to the Word Wall.

Use the vocabulary routine to review last week's words: *young*, *examines*, *mammal*, *normal*, *hunger*, and *rescued*.

STRATEGY Use Word Parts: Inflected Verbs

- Explain that a verb is an action word. Tell children that they can often figure out the meaning of an inflected verb by putting together the meanings of its word parts (its base and inflected ending). Have children find the word *assembled* in "Bobo's Celebration" on page 123 and read the sentence with the word.

Think Aloud I'm not sure what *assembled* means. It has the ending *-ed*, which means "in the past." If I take *-ed* off the word, I see *assemble*. *Assemble* means "to gather together." So *assembled* must mean "gathered together in the past." Also, I know that *assembled* is a multiple-meaning word and can also mean "put together in the past."

Vocabulary

menu
fetch
simmered
assembled
devoured

Word Parts
Verbs are action words that can have word endings like *-s*, *-ed*, or *-ing*. These endings tell you when an action took place.

The *-ed* ending means that the action happened in the past.

Yesterday we *devoured* the food.

Bobo's celebration

by Keith Fish

Mom and I planned a surprise party for my brother Bobo.

First, my mom and I made a **menu**. It listed all the foods we would serve. The main dish was Bobo's favorite—seaweed stew!

Mom asked me to **fetch** the things we needed, so I swam to the Ship Shop. When I went to pay, I knew that I was forgetting something. I checked my list. I had not remembered the seaweed! So I asked Ron Ray if he had any.

Vocabulary and Comprehension

"Yes, I have some seaweed," he said. "That's 20 sand dollars, please." I paid him and swam home.

The day of the party, the stew **simmered** on the stove. I watched it bubble over low heat for hours.

An hour before the party, the guests **assembled** in one spot. The group gathered with Mom and me by the reef. When Bobo came, we yelled "Surprise!"

Bobo's party was fun. We **devoured** all of the stew. We ate until there was nothing left. Bobo said it was the best surprise ever!

Reread for **Comprehension**

Story Structure
Fantasy and Reality A fantasy story could not happen in real life. A reality story could happen. Reread the story and use details to fill in the chart. Based on the details, could "Bobo's Celebration" happen in real life?

Reality What Could Happen?	Fantasy What Could Not Happen?

LOG ON LEARN IT Comprehension www.macmillanmh.com

Read "Bobo's Celebration"

Read "Bobo's Celebration" with children. Stop at each **highlighted** word. Ask children to identify text clues that reveal the meanings of the highlighted words. Have children ask relevant questions to check overall comprehension of the passage and review the meanings to confirm understanding. Tell children that they will read these words again in *Mice and Beans*.

Quick Check

Do children understand word meanings?

During **Small Group Instruction**

If No → Approaching Level Vocabulary pages: 161L, 161R, 161X, 161DD

If Yes → On Level Reread Vocabulary Selection

Beyond Level Reread Vocabulary Selection

ON YOUR OWN **Practice Book**, page 218

A. Use what you know about the definitions to choose the word that makes sense in the blank. Write the word on the line. Then number the words so they are in ABC order.

fetch simmered menu assembled devoured

1. put together assembled 1
2. to go get fetch 3
3. cooked on low heat on a stove simmered 5
4. ate greedily devoured 2
5. foods being served menu 4

B. Write two sentences using words from the box.
Possible responses provided

6. We devoured the food we had ordered from the menu.
7. I simmered the stew for three hours.

Approaching Reproducible, page 218
Beyond Reproducible, page 218

Objectives

- Analyze story structure
- Distinguish between fantasy and reality
- Use academic language: *fantasy, reality, story structure*

Materials

- Transparencies 6, 20a, 20b
- Student Book: "Bobo's Celebration," pp. 122–123

Skills Trace

Distinguish Between Fantasy and Reality

Introduce	U4: 123A–B
Practice/ Apply	U4: 123J–155A; Practice Book: 220–221
Reteach/ Review	U4: 161G, 161R–T, 161X–Z
Assess	Weekly Test, Unit 4 Test
Maintain	U5: 279N

ELL

Academic Language
Preteach the following academic language words to ELL and Approaching Level children during Small Group time: *story structure, fantasy, reality*. See page 161O.

Comprehension

STRATEGY Analyze Story Structure

EXPLAIN

What Is It? Explain to children that when they **analyze story structure** they look at the way the author has organized the events of the plot using story elements such as character and setting. Children should think about how these parts are put together. For example, the setting might influence a character's feelings or have an effect on the problem the character in a story has to solve.

Why Is It Important? Understanding how the events in a story are organized can help children better understand the relationship between characters' actions and events in the story.

SKILL Distinguish Between Fantasy and Reality

EXPLAIN

What Is It? Tell children that a **fantasy** is a story with events or characters that could not happen or exist in real life. A **realistic** story has events and characters that could happen or be found in real life. A **true** story is one that actually happened in real life.

Why Is It Important? Knowing how to determine whether a story is true or a fantasy helps children understand the plot and characters better. It also helps students analyze the different parts of the story.

Transparency 20a

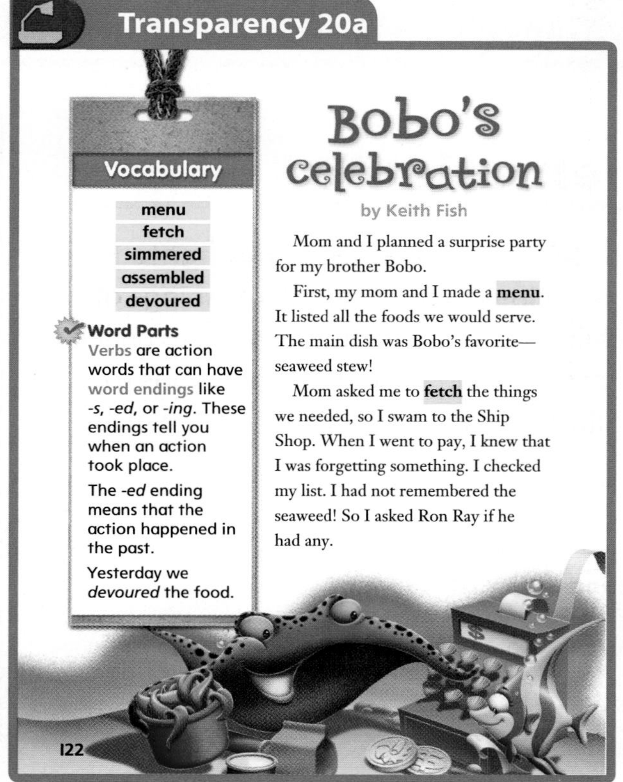

Vocabulary
menu
fetch
simmered
assembled
devoured

Word Parts
Verbs are action words that can have word endings like *-s, -ed,* or *-ing*. These endings tell you when an action took place.
The *-ed* ending means that the action happened in the past.
Yesterday we *devoured* the food.

Bobo's Celebration
by Keith Fish

Mom and I planned a surprise party for my brother Bobo.

First, my mom and I made a **menu**. It listed all the foods we would serve. The main dish was Bobo's favorite—seaweed stew!

Mom asked me to **fetch** the things we needed, so I swam to the Ship Shop. When I went to pay, I knew that I was forgetting something. I checked my list. I had not remembered the seaweed! So I asked Ron Ray if he had any.

122

Transparency 20b

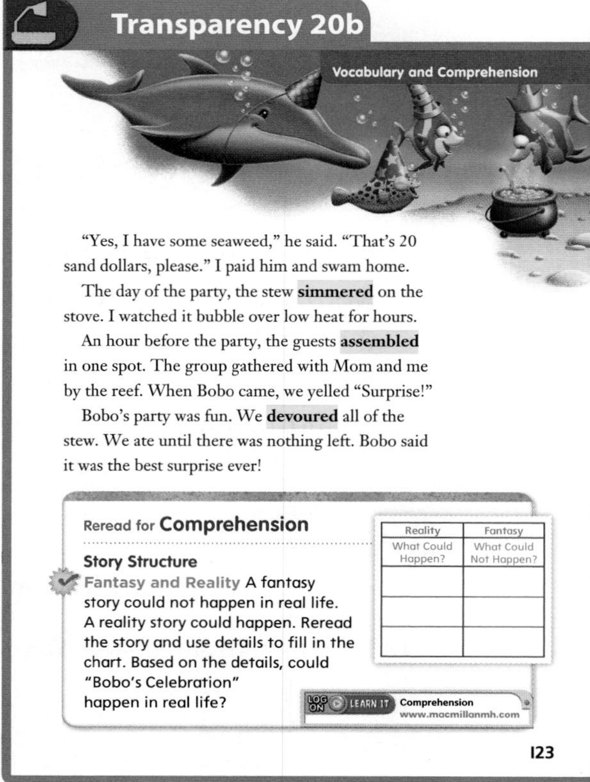

Vocabulary and Comprehension

"Yes, I have some seaweed," he said. "That's 20 sand dollars, please." I paid him and swam home.

The day of the party, the stew **simmered** on the stove. I watched it bubble over low heat for hours.

An hour before the party, the guests **assembled** in one spot. The group gathered with Mom and me by the reef. When Bobo came, we yelled "Surprise!"

Bobo's party was fun. We **devoured** all of the stew. We ate until there was nothing left. Bobo said it was the best surprise ever!

Reread for Comprehension

Story Structure
Fantasy and Reality A fantasy story could not happen in real life. A reality story could happen. Reread the story and use details to fill in the chart. Based on the details, could "Bobo's Celebration" happen in real life?

Reality	Fantasy
What Could Happen?	What Could Not Happen?

LOG ON LEARN IT Comprehension www.macmillanmh.com

123

Student Book pages 122–123 are available on Comprehension Transparencies 20a and 20b.

Phonemic Awareness

Phoneme Categorization

Model

Be sure children can identify and isolate the beginning and final sounds in words. Then show children how to isolate the medial /ô/ sounds.

Repeat with *caught* and *salt*. Then continue modeling with *crawl, launch, straw, chalk,* and *malt*.

I am going to say a word. I will pay attention to the sounds I hear at the beginning, middle, and end of the word. Listen to the word *dawn*: /d/ /ô/ /n/. I hear the /d/ sound at the beginning and the /n/ sound at the end. I hear the vowel sound /ô/ in the middle of the word *dawn*. What vowel sound do you hear in *dawn*? (/ô/) Which letters make the /ô/ sound? (aw)

Now let's listen to the sounds in the word *talk*. *Talk* has the /t/ sound at the beginning and the /k/ sound at the end. It has the /ô/ sound in the middle. What vowel sound do you hear in *talk*?

Guided Practice/Practice

Have children practice medial phoneme isolation with the examples provided. Do the first two words with them.

Let's do some together. I will say the word. Listen for the sound in the middle and say what it is. (Stretch the vowel sound as you say each word.)

walk	launch	fault	yawn	salt
brawl	stalk	drawn	lawn	straws
balls	haunt	caught	balk	cause

Objectives

- Categorize phonemes by medial sound
- Review fairy tale

Materials

- Practice Book for fairy tale, p. 219

Objectives

- Blend and build words with vowel digraph *a, au, aw*
- Read multisyllabic words

Materials

- Word-Building Cards; Teacher's Resource Book, p. 66
- pocket chart

Skills Trace

Vowel Digraph *a, au, aw*	
Introduce	121C–D
Practice/ Apply	121F, 123G, 155F-G, 155I, 155T-U; Practice Book: p. 217; Decodable Reader: *Paul Saw Arctic Foxes*
Reteach/ Review	161D; 1161K-N, 161Q, 161W, 161CC
Assess	Weekly Test; Unit 4 Test
Maintain	Build Fluency: Sound/Spellings

Build Fluency

Connected Text

Have children independently reread *Paul Saw Arctic Foxes* from the **Decodable Reader Library**.

Phonics

Blend with Vowel Digraph *a, au, aw*

Model

Place **Word-Building Cards** *w, a, l, l* in the pocket chart to form *wall*. Model how to generate and blend the sounds to say the word. Repeat with *fault*, *crawl*, *walk*, and *salt*.

The letter *w* stands for /w/. The letter *a* stands for /ô/. The letters *ll* stand for /l/. (Stretch the sounds.) Now listen as I blend all three sounds. Now you say it. Let's read the word together.

Guided Practice/Practice

Repeat with additional words. Have children blend the sounds in the words with you.

talk	mall	caught	flaunt	bald
dawn	taught	flaw	vault	halt
yawn	brawl	launch	fault	chalk

Build Words with *a, au, aw*

Model

Place Word-Building Cards *m, a, l, t* in the pocket chart. Blend the phonemes.

Let's blend all the sounds together and read the word.

Change *m* to *s* and repeat with *salt*.

Let's blend all the sounds together and read the word.

Change *alt* to *aw* and repeat with *saw*.

Let's blend all the sounds together and read the word.

Guided Practice/Practice

Continue to build with additional words.

flaw, flaunt, haunt, halt, hall, ball, wall, tall, talk, walk, balk, drawl, bawling, haunted, redrawn, baseball

Phonics/Spelling

Word Sort with *au, aw*

saw | vault
law | launch
hawk | sauce

- Display the pocket chart. Place index cards with the key words *saw* and *vault* to form two columns in the pocket chart. Generate sentences for the key words *saw* and *vault*.
- Say each key word and pronounce the sounds. Pronounce each word again, emphasizing the /ô/ sound.
- Hold up the word card *law*. Pronounce each sound clearly: /l/ /ô/. Blend the sounds. Repeat with each *au* and *aw* word. Place words below the correct key word labels so there is one example of each. Have children read each word, listening for the sound of /ô/. Ask them to chorally spell each word.

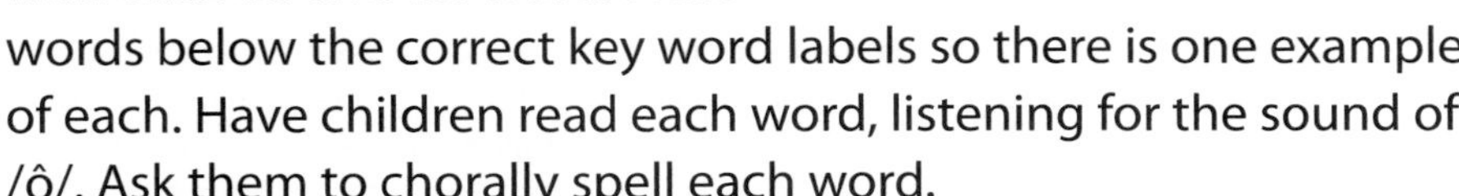

- Have children place remaining cards under the correct key label.
- **Build Fluency: Word Automaticity** Have children chorally read the words several times for fluency.

Analyze Errors — Multiple Spellings

- Use children's pretest errors to analyze spelling problems and provide corrective feedback. For example, children may confuse the various *a*, *au*, and *aw* spellings for /ô/.
- Write *saw*, *vault*, *tall*, *halt*, and *walk* on the board. Point out the different spellings of /ô/. Pronounce each word and have children repeat as you underline the sound-spellings.
- Then provide children with common word families for each spelling, including *-ald*, *-all*, *-alk*, *-alt*, *-auce*, *-aud*, *-aught*, *-aul*, *-ault*, *-aunt*, *-ause*, *-aut*, *-aw*, *-awk*, *-awl*, and *-awn*. Have children generate word lists for each word family. Post these lists on the Big Question Board for children to refer to when writing.

Objectives

- Spell words with variant vowel *au, aw*
- Sort words with variant vowel *au, aw*
- Build Fluency: Word Automaticity

Materials

- pocket chart
- large index cards with spelling words
- Phonics/Spelling Practice Book, p. 78

5-Day Spelling

DAY 1	Dictation; Pretest
DAY 2	Teacher-Modeled Word Sort
DAY 3	Student Word Sort
DAY 4	Test Practice
DAY 5	Posttest

ON YOUR OWN

Spelling, page 78

launch draw hawk sauce pause
law crawl fault raw jaw

A. Word Sort

Look at the spelling words in the box. Write the spelling words that have the *au* pattern.

1. launch 2. sauce 3. pause
4. fault

Write the spelling words that have the *aw* pattern.

5. draw 6. hawk 7. law
8. crawl 9. raw 10. jaw

B. Missing Letter

A letter is missing from each spelling word below. Write the missing letter in the box. Then write the spelling word correctly on the line.

11. pase [u] pause
12. hak [w] hawk
13. lanch [u] launch
14. cral [w] crawl
15. falt [u] fault

Objectives

- Apply knowledge of word meanings and context clues
- Review last week's vocabulary words

Materials

- Transparency 39

Vocabulary

Words in Context

REVIEW

Review the meanings of the vocabulary words. Display **Transparency 39**. Model how to use word meanings and context clues to fill in the first missing word.

Think Aloud I look at the first paragraph and see the word *lunch*. Lunch is a meal. The next sentence says that they will eat rice and beans. These are foods. A **menu** is a list of foods that will be served at a meal, so **menu** must be the missing word.

Transparency 39

menu	fetch	devoured
simmered	assembled	

Mom was planning for my birthday celebration. She decided to make a lunch, so she prepared the (1) menu. She said we will eat my favorite: rice and beans! Mom made the beans and put them in a pot on the stove. The beans (2) simmered for an hour over a low heat.

Mom went to the store to (3) fetch some balloons, party plates, and party favors. She kept thinking that she was forgetting something so she pulled out her shopping list. Good thing she did because she forgot about the cups.

When she got home, she (4) assembled goodie bags by putting favors in separate plastic bags. Finally, guests arrived. Everyone must have been hungry because they (5) devoured the food. I had a wonderful birthday party.

Vocabulary Transparency

GUIDED PRACTICE/PRACTICE

- Help children with the next word. Then have them use context clues to write missing words 3–5. Ask partners to check each other's answers and identify context clues they used to fill in the words.
- Have children write sentences using their vocabulary words from this week and last week.

Review last week's words (*examines*, *hunger*, *mammal*, *normal*, *rescued*, and *young*) in context.

Comprehension

STRATEGY Analyze Story Structure

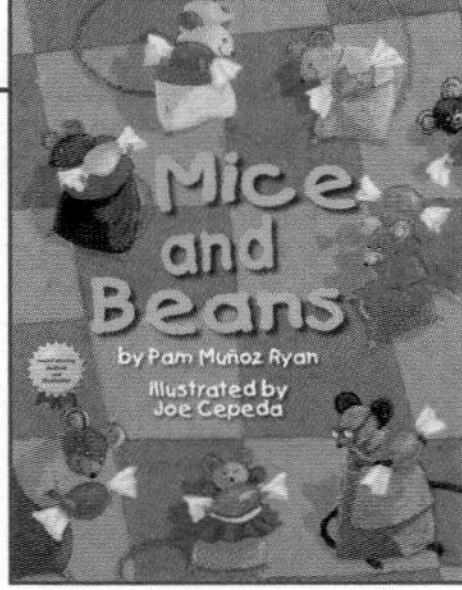

Main Selection

Remind children that **analyzing story structure** means thinking about the way an author has organized the events of the plot, using elements such as character and setting. *When you analyze story structure, you think about how the setting and the actions of the characters affect the events of the plot.*

SKILL Distinguish Between Fantasy and Reality

Review with children that distinguishing between **fantasy and reality** means figuring out which story events could happen in real life and which could not. Children can compare story events and characters to people and events in their own lives to help them distinguish fantasy from what is realistic. Analyzing a story's structure can also help children determine whether a story is a fantasy or contains characters and events that could be found in real life.

Prepare to Read

PREVIEW AND PREDICT

- Ask children to use ideas from the title and illustrations to make predictions about *Mice and Beans. What does the story seem to be about? Do the pictures seem to show things that could happen in real life? Explain why or why not.*
- **Genre** Have a child read the definition of fantasy on **Student Book** page 124. Share these features of a fantasy: made-up characters and settings, could not happen in real life. *How will knowing that this story is a fantasy help you as you read it?*
- **Word Origins** Tell children that there are many Spanish words in the story. Preview the Story Words and ask a Spanish speaker in the class to tell what the words mean. Have the child use the word in a sentence.

SET A PURPOSE FOR READING

- **Focus Question** Discuss the "Read to Find Out" question on Student Book page 124. Tell children to look for the answer as they read.
- Point out the Fantasy and Reality Chart in the Student Book. Tell children to use it to record elements of fantasy and reality in the story.
- Have children set their own purposes for reading.

Objectives

- Analyze story structure
- Read to distinguish between fantasy and reality
- Use academic language: *fantasy, reality, story structure*

Materials

- Transparency 6
- Student Book, pp. 124–153
- Practice Book, p. 220

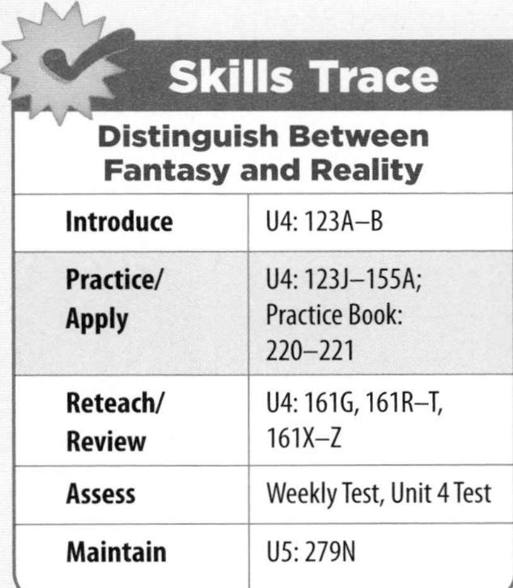

Skills Trace

Distinguish Between Fantasy and Reality	
Introduce	U4: 123A–B
Practice/ Apply	U4: 123J–155A; Practice Book: 220–221
Reteach/ Review	U4: 161G, 161R–T, 161X–Z
Assess	Weekly Test, Unit 4 Test
Maintain	U5: 279N

Story Words

Provide child-friendly definitions for these words.

casita (p. 127): a small house

enchiladas (p. 129): filled tortillas covered with sauce

piñata (p. 129): a hanging container filled with candy

tortillas (p. 133): round, thin cakes of cornmeal

fiesta (p. 149): a party

Digital Learning

Story available on **Listening Library Audio CD** and **StudentWorks Plus**, the Interactive eBook.

www.macmillanmh.com

Comprehension

Genre
Fantasy has made-up characters, settings, or events that could not happen in real life.

Story Structure

Fantasy and Reality
As you read, use your Fantasy and Reality Chart.

Reality	Fantasy
What Could Happen?	What Could Not Happen?

Read to Find Out
What do the mice do in this story that they can't do in real life?

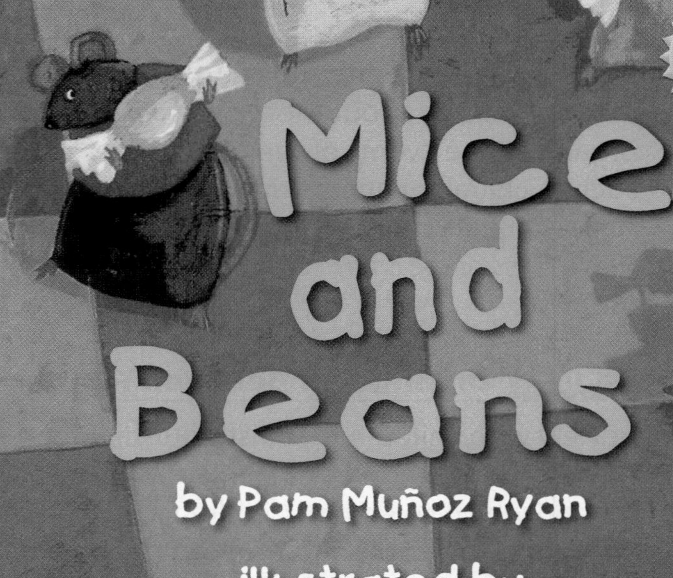

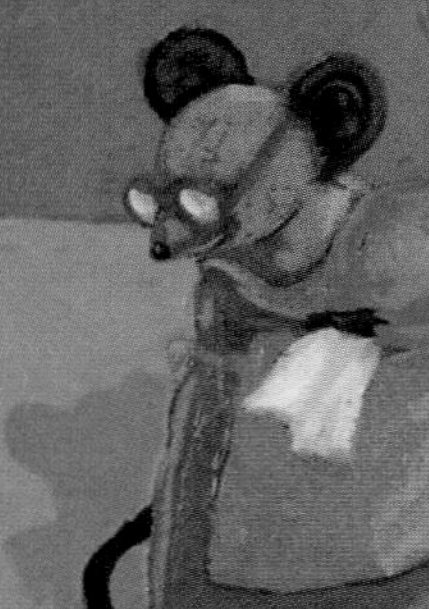

Mice and Beans

by Pam Muñoz Ryan

illustrated by Joe Cepeda

ON YOUR OWN **Practice Book**, page 220

As you read *Mice and Beans*, fill in the Compare and Contrast Chart.

REALITY	FANTASY
What Could Happen?	What Could Not Happen?

How does the information you wrote in this Compare and Contrast Chart help you to better understand *Mice and Beans*?

Approaching Reproducible, page 220

Beyond Reproducible, page 220

Read Main Selection

Purpose for Reading Ask children to read the "Read to Find Out" question. Remind them to pay attention to what the mice do as they read the story.

PARTNERS

Preteach	Read Together
Have Approaching Level children in English Language Learners listen to the story on **StudentWorks Plus**, the Interactive Book before reading with the class.	Use the prompts to guide comprehension and model how to complete the graphic organizer. Have children use **Think/Pair/Share** as they respond to the prompts.

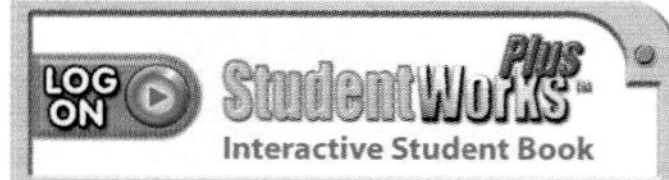

1 **Rosa María** lived in a tiny house with a tiny yard. But she had a big heart, a big family, and more than anything, she loved to cook big meals for them.

In one week, her youngest grandchild, Little Catalina, would be seven years old, and the whole family would squeeze into her *casita* for the party.

Rosa María didn't mind because she believed what her mother had always said: "When there's room in the heart, there's room in the house, **except** for a mouse."

126 127

Develop Comprehension

1 **STRATEGY** **Analyze Story Structure**

From reading the text on page 126 and looking at the illustration how would you describe the characters, setting, and plot so far?

Teacher Think Aloud The main character seems to be Rosa María; most of the text on this page is about her. I read that she is a kind person and has a big family. The picture shows her smiling. The setting is her tiny house. I can see that her house is painted pink. So far I know that Rosa María has invited her family to come to her house and celebrate her youngest grandchild's birthday. Maybe the story's problem will have to do with the birthday party. I will read on to find out more.

ELL

Preview Text Have children use **StudentWorks Plus**, the interactive eBook to preview the text. This eBook contains summaries in multiple languages, word-by-word reading support, bilingual glossary, and comprehension questions with corrective feedback. Use the Interactive Question-Response Guide in the ELL Resource Book to preteach the content in *Mice and Beans* and develop meaning.

2

Sunday, Rosa María planned the **menu**: *enchiladas*, rice and beans (no dinner was complete without rice and beans!), birthday cake, lemonade, and a *piñata* filled with candy. 3

She ordered the birthday present—something Little Catalina had wanted for a long time.

Satisfied with the plans, she wiped down the table so she wouldn't get mice and took out a mousetrap just in case. She was sure she had set one the night before, but now she couldn't find it. Maybe she'd forgotten.

When it was set and ready to **snap,** she turned off the light and went to bed.

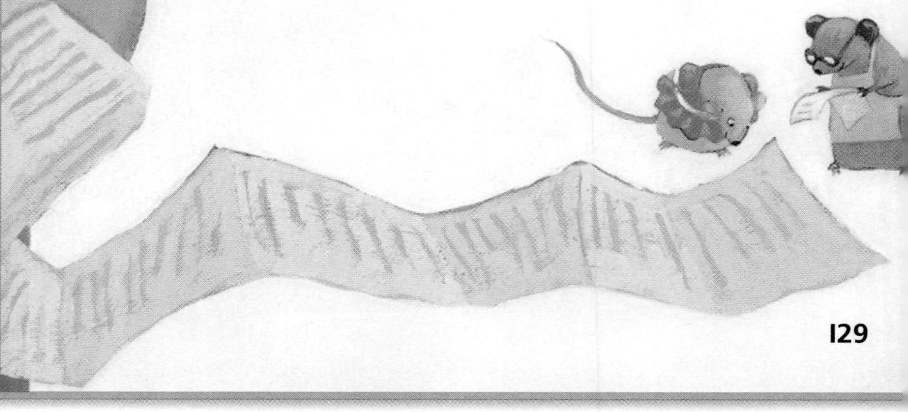

128 129

Reality	Fantasy
What Could Happen?	**What Could Not Happen?**
Rosa María plans for a party	Mice move a mousetrap.
Rosa María makes a list.	Mice read a list.

Develop Comprehension

2 SKILL Distinguish Between Fantasy and Reality

What have we read in the story so far that could happen in real life? (Rosa María is planning a birthday party. She's making a list of the things she needs to do.) Look at the illustrations on pages 128–129. What is happening that could not happen in real life or that makes this story a fantasy? (Mice can't pick up mousetraps in real life or read lists.) Let's add this to the Fantasy and Reality Chart.

3 VOCABULARY: WORD ORIGINS

Remind children that many words in this story are Spanish words. Review the Spanish words in the story so far: *casita, enchiladas, piñata*. What do these words mean in English? (little house, tortilla, and hanging container filled with something, such as small toys or candy)

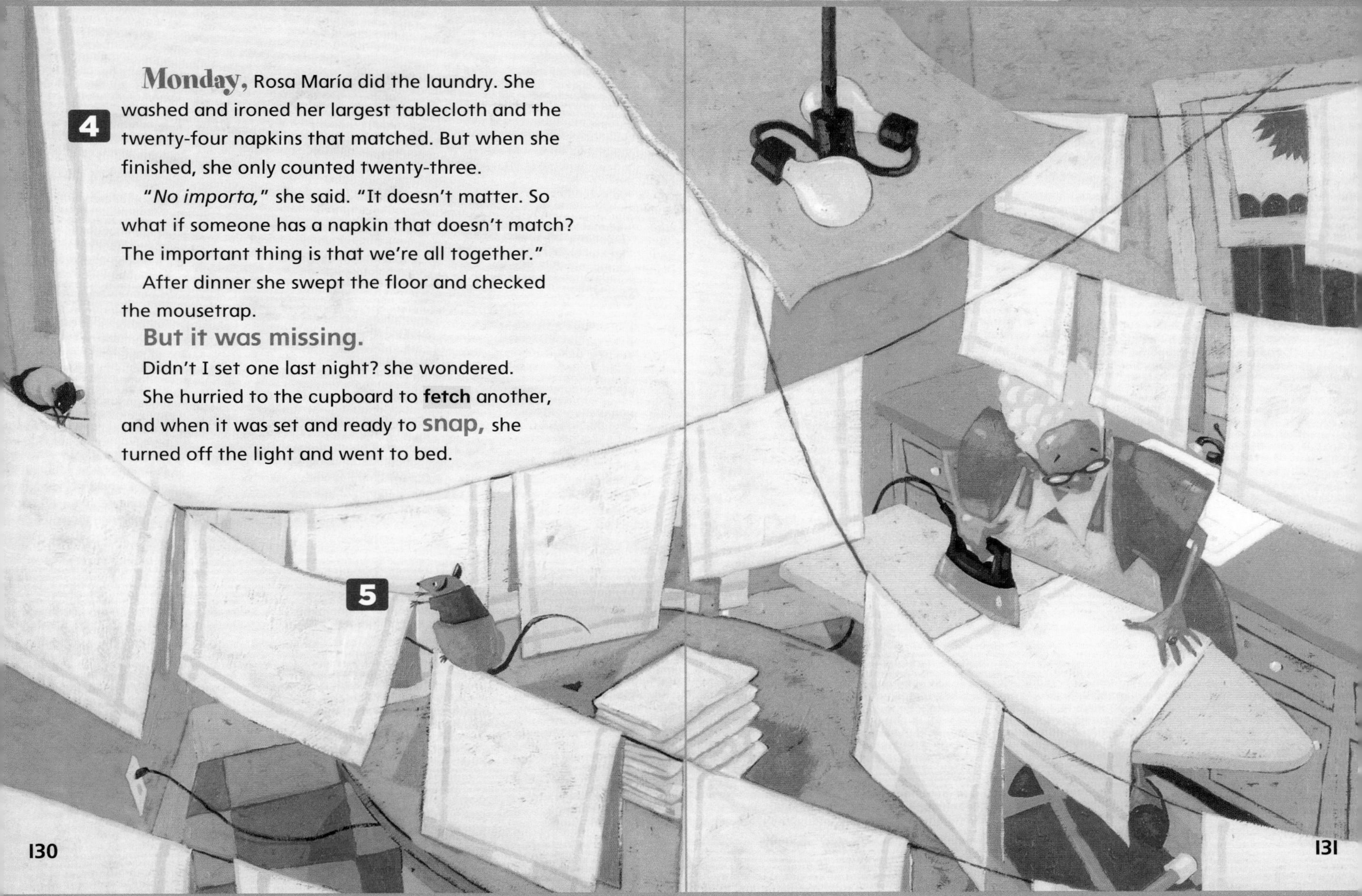

Monday, Rosa María did the laundry. She
4 washed and ironed her largest tablecloth and the twenty-four napkins that matched. But when she finished, she only counted twenty-three.

"*No importa,*" she said. "It doesn't matter. So what if someone has a napkin that doesn't match? The important thing is that we're all together."

After dinner she swept the floor and checked the mousetrap.

But it was missing.

Didn't I set one last night? she wondered.

She hurried to the cupboard to **fetch** another, and when it was set and ready to **snap,** she turned off the light and went to bed.

5

4 VOCABULARY: WORD PARTS: INFLECTED ENDINGS

Look at the word *wondered* on page 130. What could you do if you are not sure what the word means? You could look at the word to see if it has word parts. What is the base word? (*wonder*) What does the word *wonder* mean? ("to want to know or learn") The *-ed* ending changes the word to something that happened in the past. So, *wondered* means "wanted to know or learn."

5 GENRE: FANTASY

What type of characters or events do you expect to see in a **fantasy**? (Characters that could not exist and events that could not happen in real life.) List some things you've read in this story so far that could not happen in real life. (The mice moved the mousetrap. They read Rosa María's list. They took one of her napkins off the clothesline.)

Decoding

Apply Phonics Skills While reading, point out words with the sound-spelling patterns children have recently learned. You may wish to focus on words with *au*, *aw*, *alk*, *alt*, and *all*, such as *laundry*, *all*, and *sauce*.

Model blending each word sound by sound. Then have children repeat.

Tuesday, Rosa María walked to the market. She filled her big *bolsa* with *tortillas,* cheese, red sauce, white rice, pinto beans, and a bag of candy. She bought a *piñata* and on her way home she stopped at the *pastelería* to order the cake.

After dinner, she washed the dishes and checked the mousetrap.

But it had vanished.

"*¡Qué boba soy!* Silly me, I must have forgotten, again!" **6**

She hurried to the cupboard to fetch another and when it was set and ready to **snap,** she turned off the light and went to bed.

Fantasy and Reality **7**
What illustrations so far tell you that this story might be a fantasy?

132 133

ELL

Question 7 FANTASY AND REALITY
Ask children: *What is Rosa María doing? Could someone do this in real life? How do you know? What is the mouse doing? Do you think that a mouse could do that in real life? How do you know?* If children are having trouble answering, have them point to clues in the picture and create sentences for them. Give children ample wait time to respond.

Develop Comprehension

6 STRATEGY Analyze Story Structure

Think about how you can analyze the story structure.

Teacher Think Aloud To analyze the story structure, I will retell the events so far and think about the character's problem. Rosa María is planning for a birthday party. Each day she completes tasks on her list, but then she notices things missing, like the mousetrap. I see the mice doing things in the illustrations, but it looks like Rosa María doesn't know that they are taking things.

7 SKILL Distinguish between Fantasy and Reality

What clues from the illustrations show that this story is not true? (The pictures show the mice doing things that mice can't do in real life, like tagging along with Rosa María on a shopping trip.)

8 FLUENCY: EXPRESSION

Model reading the first two paragraphs on page 135. Ask children to explain how your expression changed when you read the words that Rosa María said. Remind children that paying attention to punctuation is important when reading aloud. Chorally read the page together with good expression.

9 REVIEW Sequence of Events

Think about the order of events so far. What happened at the beginning of the story? (In the beginning of the story, Rosa María decided to plan a birthday party and made a list of all the things she needed to do.) What happened next? (She starts doing the things on her list. She also sets a mousetrap each night before going to sleep. The illustrations show that mice join her as she does her tasks without her knowledge. They also unset the mousetraps.)

Decoding

Word Order/ Context Clues

Explain Good readers use word order and context clues to read an unfamiliar word.

Model Point to the last paragraph on page 135. *At first, I read the word* fetch *as* fear. *From the sentence structure, I know the word is a verb. But it doesn't make sense. Why would Rosa Maria go to the cupboard to* fear *something? I know that you find food or things in a cupboard. So, I look carefully at the word and sound it out. The word* fetch *makes sense in this sentence.*

Thursday, Rosa María simmered the beans. She searched for her favorite wooden spoon, the one she always used to cook *frijoles,* but she couldn't find it.

"*No importa,*" she said. "The beans will taste just as good if I use another spoon."

She added water all day long until the beans were plump and soft. Then she scrubbed the stove and checked the mousetrap.

But it was nowhere in sight!

"*¡Cielos!*" she said. "Heavens! Where is my mind?"

She hurried to the cupboard to fetch another and when it was set and ready to **snap,** she turned off the light and went to bed.

136

Friday, Rosa María picked up the cake and seven candles.

Tomorrow was the big day. Rosa María knew she mustn't forget anything, so she carefully went over the list one last time.

After dinner she wrapped the cake and checked the mousetrap.

She couldn't believe her eyes.

No mousetrap!

"Thank goodness I've got plenty."

She hurried to the cupboard to fetch another and when it was set and ready to **snap,** she turned off the light and went to bed. **10**

11

137

Reality	Fantasy
What Could Happen?	**What Could Not Happen?**
Rosa María plans for a party.	Mice move a mousetrap.
Rosa María makes a list.	Mice read a list.
She cooks and gets everything ready for the party.	Mice wear clothes.

Develop Comprehension

10 **SKILL** **Distinguish Between Fantasy and Reality**

Reread pages 136–137. List the things that could happen in **real life**. (Rosa María cooked the beans and scrubbed the stove. She slept. The next day, she picked up the cake and candles.) Look at the illustrations on these pages. What are the mice in the story doing that real mice cannot do? (They are carrying a candle. They are looking inside a bag. The mice are also wearing clothes.) Let's add this information to the Fantasy and Reality Chart.

Think/Pair/Share Parts of this story are realistic. Discuss with a partner the differences between a realistic story and a true story.

11 **SELF-SELECTED STRATEGY USE**

What strategies did you use to make sense of what you read?

12 MONITOR AND CLARIFY: REREAD

How and when do you know to use rereading as a strategy to seek clarification about what is taking place in the story?

Teacher Think Aloud If I have trouble summarizing what I have read or I do not understand why a character acts in a certain way, these are signals that I may not understand everything I have read. To help me understand the selection better, I can go back and reread to find details or information that I did not notice the first time. I can also ask relevant questions and use evidence from the text to answer them.)

But WAS everything ready?

Fantasy and Reality 13
Is this story a fantasy or a realistic story? Use details to explain.

140 141

ELL

Activate Background Knowledge Explain to children that each page told us what Rosa María did each day to get ready for the party. Point to the words for the days of the week on each page and have children read them with you. Display the classroom calendar frame and help children find each word. Read the words chorally with children.

Develop Comprehension

13 SKILL Distinguish Between Fantasy and Reality

Look carefully at the picture. How do you know that Rosa María forgot to do something? ("Fill Piñata" was not crossed off her list. The other tasks are crossed off.) What clues in the illustration suggest that the mice have noticed what she forgot? (On pages 140 and 141, it looks like the mice have noticed that Rosa María forgot to do something. One points at the piñata, one is reading the list, and one is getting the bag labeled "Dulces," or candy.) Would you expect to find these clues in a fantasy or a realistic story? (in a fantasy, because real mice can't read lists and they couldn't help with tasks)

Think/Pair/Share Think of other parts of the story that show that it is a fantasy. Then share and compare your ideas with a partner.

14 STRATEGY Analyze Story Structure

Pages 142–143 show a new event in the story, but there is no text. Describe the action in the picture.

Teacher Think Aloud In the picture, I see the mice working together to fill Rosa Maria's piñata with the candy. So far in the story, Rosa Maria has been working very hard to complete all the things on her list. But she forgot to do one thing. Do you think the mice will help Rosa Maria with her problem?

Ask children to apply the strategy in the Think Aloud.

Student Think Aloud I know that these mice are not like real mice. They read her list and decide to help her by filling the piñata with candy. I don't know if they will succeed. The tower they are building to reach the piñata looks as if it might fall over any minute. I'll keep reading to see what happens.

Extra Support

Distinguish Between Fantasy and Reality Give each child two index cards. Have them write *fantasy* on one card and *reality* on the other. Ask children to retell the story, using both the pictures and text. As they list events, write them on the board. Reread the list and ask children to hold up the appropriate card to show they know the difference between fantasy and reality.

16 That afternoon Rosa María's family filled her tiny *casita.* They ate the *enchiladas* and rice and beans. They drank the fresh-squeezed lemonade. And they **devoured** the cake.

Little Catalina loved her present—a swing set! And after every cousin had a turn, they chanted, "*¡La piñata! ¡La piñata!*"

They ran to the walnut tree and threw a rope over a high branch.

15

144

145

Reality	Fantasy
What Could Happen?	**What Could Not Happen?**
Rosa María plans for a party.	Mice move a mousetrap.
Rosa María makes a list.	Mice read a list.
She cooks and gets everything ready for the party.	Mice wear clothes.
The family celebrates Catalina's birthday.	

Develop Comprehension

15 SKILL Distinguish Between Fantasy and Reality

Look at the illustration on these pages. Does the picture on pages 144–145 show things that could happen in real life or things that would happen only in a fantasy? (The picture shows Catalina's birthday party. The people in the picture are like real people and the celebration that they are enjoying could happen in real life.) Add details to your chart.

16 REVIEW Sequence of Events

What clue words did the author use to show the sequence of events in the story? (She used the days of the week to show the order of the things Rosa María did each day to get ready for the party. She also uses time-order transition words such as *that* afternoon and *after*.)

17 **Whack! Whack!** Little Catalina swung the *piñata* stick.

"Wait!" cried Rosa María as she remembered what she'd forgotten. But it was too late.

Crack! The *piñata* separated, and the children scrambled to collect the candy.

How could that be? Rosa María puzzled. I must have filled it without even realizing!

She laughed at her own forgetfulness as she hugged her granddaughter and said, "*Feliz cumpleaños,* my Little Catalina. Happy birthday."

146

147

17 **FLUENCY: EXPRESSION**

Read page 146 aloud, modeling for children how to read with good expression. Point out the first two words. What do you notice about them? Why do you think the author wrote them that way? (The first two words are written in larger type than the others and are followed by exclamation marks. They are examples of onomatopoeia, which we learned about when we read the poem "Brush Dance" in Unit 3. Remember, words with onomatopoeia sound like the action or object they refer to. Here, the author wrote these words that way to show the loud sound that Catalina made when she swung the stick at the piñata.) Tell children that when they read onomatopoeia, they can say the word in a way that matches the sound it refers to. Model good expression by saying, "whoosh" and "buzz." Then ask children to read the page chorally, paying attention to punctuation.

Connect to Content

The way in which Rosa María celebrates Little Catalina's birthday teaches us about the cultural heritage of her family. They celebrate with a big party in which they eat certain types of food (*dulces* and *enchiladas*) and play with a piñata. *How do people in your local culture celebrate important events like birthdays and holidays? Are there special types of food, music, events, or art that help you celebrate?* Discuss your traditions as a class.

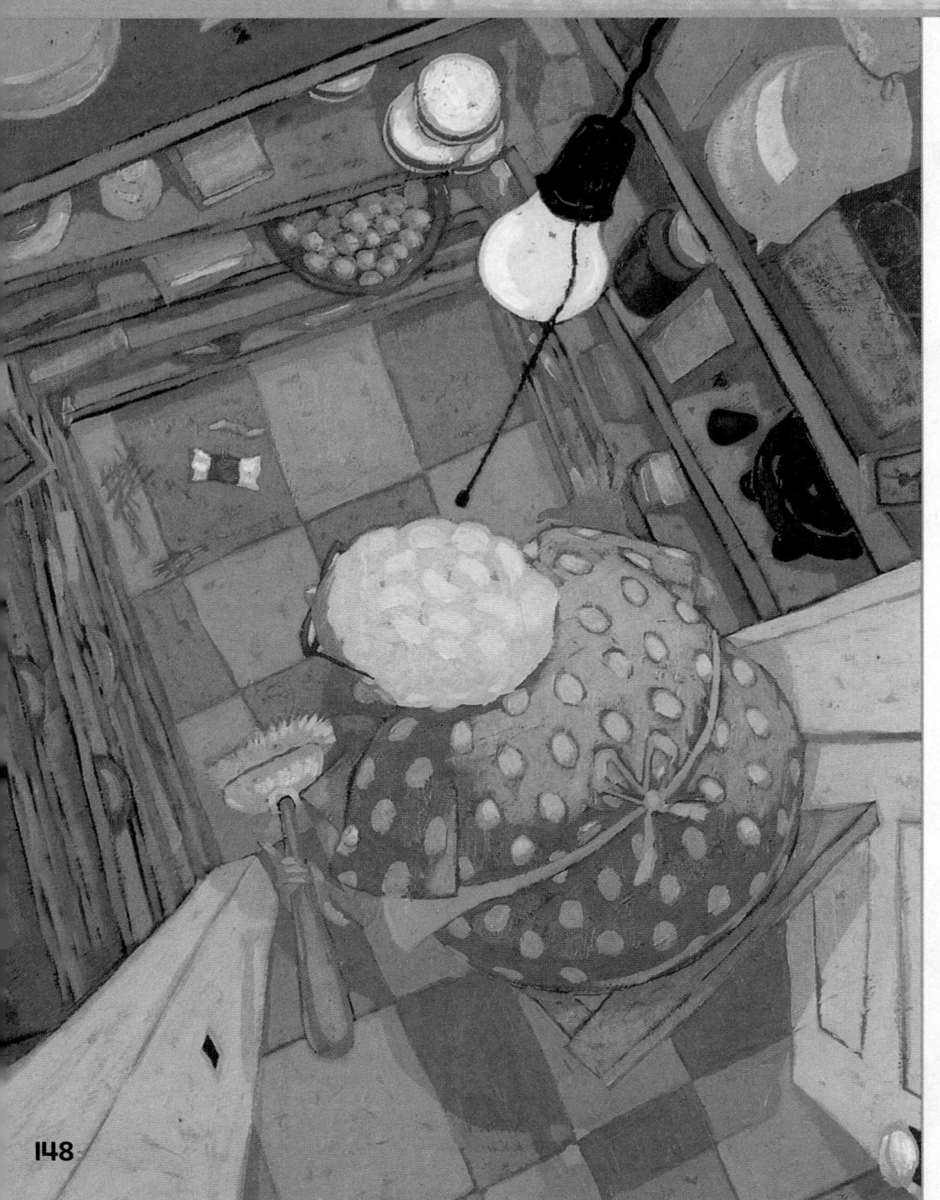

After everyone had gone, Rosa María tidied her kitchen and thought contentedly about the *fiesta.* She pictured the happy look on Little Catalina's face when the candy spilled from the *piñata.* But Rosa María still couldn't remember when she had filled it.

"*No importa,*" she said. "It was a wonderful day."

But as Rosa María swept out the cupboard, she discovered the telltale signs of mice!

"*¡Ratones!*" she cried. "Where are my mousetraps? I will set them all!"

She inched to the floor and when she did, something caught her eye.

She looked closer.

Maybe I **didn't** fill the *piñata,* she thought. 

148

149

Develop Comprehension

18 STRATEGY Analyze Story Structure

The plot events on pages 148 and 149 are a little confusing. How can you analyze the story structure and recognize how a plot event caused Rosa María to change the way she feels?

Student Think Aloud I need to reread to make sure that I understand what is happening on these pages. I know that Rosa María didn't remember filling the piñata. When she sees signs of mice, she starts to wonder how it got filled with candy. Then the text says that something on the floor caught her eye. The illustration on page 148 shows a candy wrapper on the floor, and on page 149 I see that it is next to a mousehole. It says that Rosa María thought she might have had help after all. I will keep reading to see if she finds out that the mice actually helped her.

"Was it possible?" she asked, shaking her head. "Could I have had help?"

19 Rosa María looked at the leftovers. Too much for one person.

And what was it her mother had always said? "When there's room in the heart, there's room in the house . . . **even** for a mouse."

"*¡Fíjate!* Imagine that!" she said. "I remembered the words wrong all these years."

Besides, how many could there be? Two? Four?

"*No importa,*" she said. "It doesn't matter if a few helpful mice live here, too."

Then she turned off the light and went to bed . . .

150

151

19 **SKILL** **Distinguish Between Fantasy and Reality**

List the things that take place on page 151 and determine whether they are fantasy or could really happen. Then read ahead to pages 152 and 153 and list the things that happen on those pages. Could they happen in real life? (On page 151 Rosa María sees that she has too much leftover food and remembers the correct words to the saying her mother used. Those events could happen in real life. Having mice live in her home could happen in real life, too. But on pages 152 and 153, the mice are doing many things that cannot happen in real life. They are wearing birthday hats and clothes and swinging from a swingset made from mousetraps. These pages show things that make the story a fantasy.)

SELF-SELECTED STRATEGY USE

What strategies did you use to make sense of what you read? Where? How are these strategies helpful?

Text Evidence

Fantasy and Reality

Have students reread question 19. *The illustrations in* Mice and Beans *are full of information, and they provide evidence that this is a fantasy. What evidence can you find in these pictures that shows this story is a fantasy?* Students should refer to the mousetrap swingset on pp. 152–153, the mouse in a hammock on p. 152, and the clothes the mice wear.

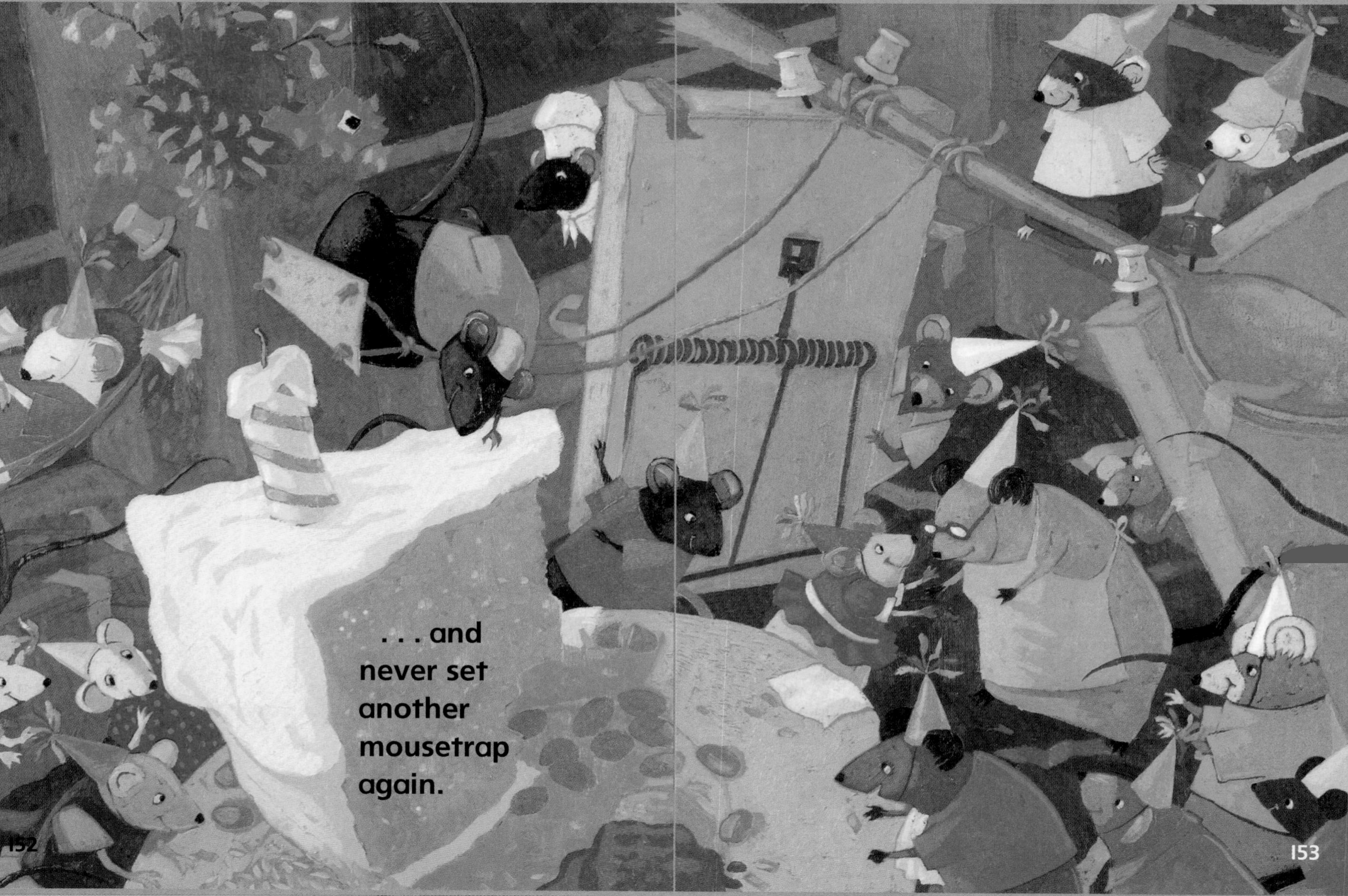

Reality	Fantasy
What Could Happen?	**What Could Not Happen?**
Rosa María plans for a party	Mice move a mousetrap.
Rosa María makes a list.	Mice read a list.
She cooks and gets everything ready for the party.	Mice wear clothes.
The family celebrates Catalina's birthday.	Mouse swings on a swing.
Mice eat cake, rice, and beans.	Mice wear party hats and clothes.

Develop Comprehension

COMPLETE THE FANTASY AND REALITY CHART

Review the Fantasy and Reality Chart. Children may add details.

RETURN TO PREDICTIONS AND PURPOSES

Review children's predictions, purposes, and the Focus Question. Have students use ideas from the story to confirm their predictions.

Quick Check

Can children analyze story structure and compare fantasy and reality?

During **Small Group Instruction**

If No → **Approaching Level** Apply the skill to a simpler text, pp. 161R, 161X.

If Yes → **On Level** Apply the skill to another text, pp. 161S, 161Y.

Beyond Level Apply the skill to a harder text, pp. 161T, 161Z.

Celebrating with Joe Cepeda

Joe Cepeda says that many parties from his childhood looked just like the one in this book. For his son's parties, Joe always finds a special piñata. He has even made a hand-painted piñata stick. He hopes it will become a part of their family traditions.

Joe has received many awards for *Mice and Beans*. He has illustrated more than 15 other children's books. He also does artwork for magazines, newspapers, and businesses.

Other books illustrated by Joe Cepeda

Author's Purpose
Joe Cepeda shares what he knows about parties. What traditions do you share in your family? What are some things your family does together? Write a paragraph about one of them.

154

Meet the Illustrator

Read aloud page 154 with children. Ask them where they think Joe Cepeda got his ideas for the illustrations in the story. Ask how they think details in his illustrations add information to the story and make it more interesting.

Illustrator's Purpose

Discuss what kind of mood Joe Cepeda's art creates in the story. Point out specific parts of the illustrations, such as colors or shapes, that convey this mood. Then have children make a list of different parties they have attended. Help them write about what they enjoy doing at parties, using details and carefully chosen words. Guide them to draw pictures that match the mood or their feelings.

Author's Craft

Word Choice

- Remind children that an author chooses words carefully to show what a story character is like.
- Point out that in *Mice and Beans*, the author chose to include words in Spanish, especially in the words that Rosa María says. Discuss possible reasons for the author's inclusion of Spanish words.
- Ask children to find examples of Spanish words and their meanings in the story. Talk about how these words help show what Rosa María is like.
- Help children recognize that some words from other languages are also commonly used English words.

Genre

Fantasy

Like other types of fiction stories, fantasy stories often contain an overall idea or message about life called a theme. Identifying the theme can help you understand what the author thought was important in telling the story. Suggest that a theme in *Mice and Beans* is teamwork. Ask students to discuss how the story shows that teamwork is important.

Objectives

- Retell a selection in logical order to show understanding
- Answer comprehension questions

Materials

- Student Book: *Mice and Beans*, pp. 124–153
- Retelling Cards for *Mice and Beans*
- chart paper
- Practice Book, p. 221

Retelling Rubric

4 Excellent

Retells the selection without prompting, in sequence, and using supporting details. Clearly describes the setting, main characters, and the complete plot. Describes the problem and its solution.

3 Good

Retells the selection with little guidance, in sequence, and using some details. Generally describes the setting, main characters, and the plot. Recognizes either a problem or a solution.

2 Fair

Retells the selection with some guidance, mostly in sequence, and using limited details. Partially describes the setting, main characters, and plot. Cannot state the problem or solution.

1 Unsatisfactory

Retells the selection only when prompted, out of sequence, and using limited details. Does not describe the main characters or plot.

Retelling Cards

Comprehension Check

Retell the Story

Use the Retelling Cards to retell the story.

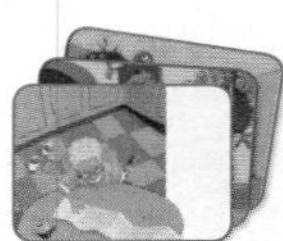

Retelling Cards

Think and Compare

1. On what day did Rosa María go to the market? Details
2. Use details from the story to describe which parts of this story could really happen and which could only happen in a fantasy. Fantasy and Reality

Reality What Could Happen?	Fantasy What Could Not Happen?

3. Why does Rosa María need to **fetch** mousetrap after mousetrap? Make Inferences
4. What does the author want readers to know about the mice that live with Rosa María? Author's Purpose
5. How are "Bobo's Celebration," on pages 122–123, and *Mice and Beans* alike? What do the parties have in common? Reading/Writing Across Texts

155

Retell the Story

RETELL *MICE AND BEANS*

- Remind children that as they read *Mice and Beans* they distinguished between fantasy and reality. Now they will use this information to retell information from the story in logical order. (You can record children's retelling on chart paper.)
- **Model Retelling** Use the prompts provided on the back of the **Retelling Cards** to model retelling the story.
- ELL **Guide Retelling** Use the leveled language acquisition prompts provided to guide children's retelling of the story.
- **Discuss Retelling** Ask children relevant questions: *Who is the main character in the story? Describe the story's plot. How did the illustrations help you understand the story?*

Phonemic Awareness

Phoneme Blending

Model

Place markers in the **Workboard** to show children how to orally blend phonemes.

I am going to put one marker in each box as I say each sound, then I will blend the sounds to form a word.

Listen and watch. /m/ (Place marker in the first box.) /ô/ (Place marker in the second box.) /l/ (Place marker in the third box.) /t/ (Place marker in the fourth box.)

This word has four sounds: /m/ /ô/ /l/ /t/. Listen as I blend the sounds to form the word. (Stretch the sounds.) The word is *malt*.

Guided Practice/Practice

Have children practice blending. Guide practice with the first example.

Say the parts that make up each word. Then blend them together and say the word.

/p /ô/	/k/ /ô/ /t/	/h/ /ô/ /n/ /t/
/d/ /ô/ /n/	/l/ /ô/ /n/ /ch/	/s/ /ô/
/k/ /l/ /ô/	/t/ /ô/ /k/	/j/ /ô/
/f/ /ô/ /n/	/s/ /t/ /r/ /ô/	/d/ /r/ /ô/ /n/

Objectives

- Blend phonemes
- Blend and build words with variant vowel /ô/*au, aw*

Materials

- Sound-Spelling WorkBoard; Teacher's Resource Book, p. 143
- markers

Objectives

- Identify letter-sound correspondence for vowel digraph /ô/ spelled *a, au, aw*
- Blend sounds in words with *a, au, aw*
- Review previously taught phonics skills
- Read multisyllabic words

Materials

- Sound-Spelling Card: *Straw*
- Word-Building Cards; Teacher's Resource Book, p. 66
- chart paper
- Practice Book, p. 222

Phonics

Review *a, au, aw*

Model

Review the vowel digraph sound /ô/ spelled *a*, *au*, and *aw*. Show the *Straw* **Sound-Spelling Card**.

This is the *Straw* Sound-Spelling Card. The sound is /ô/. The /ô/ sound can be spelled with the letters *a*, *au*, or *aw*. Say it with me: /ô/. This is the sound at the end of the word *straw*. We've been reading words with the /ô/ sound all week. Today we will read more.

Guided Practice/Practice

Have children practice connecting the letters and sound.

(Point to the Sound-Spelling Card.) What are these letters? What sound do they stand for?

Build Fluency: Sound/Spellings

au ew ar

Display the following **Word-Building Cards** one at a time: *au, aw, oo, ou, oo, ui, ew, ue, u, ou, oe, oi, oy, ou, ow, are, air, ear, ere, or, ore, oar, ar*. Have children chorally say each sound. Repeat and vary the pace.

Blend with Vowel Digraph *a, au, aw*

Model

Display Word-Building Cards *s, a, l, t*. Model how to blend the sounds together as you run your finger under each letter.

Continue by modeling the words *jaw*, *fawn*, *balking*, *naughty*, and *yawned*.

(Point to *s*.) This is the letter *s*. It stands for /s/. (Point to *a*.) This is the letter *a*. It stands for /ô/. Listen as I blend these sounds together. (Stretch out sounds.)

(Point to *l*.) This is the letter *l*. It stands for /l/. (Point to *t*.) This is the letter *t*. It stands for /t/. Listen as I blend all four sounds together. Say it with me.

Skills Trace

Vowel Digraph *a, au, aw*

Introduce	121C–D
Practice/ Apply	121F, 123G, 155F-G, 155I, 155T-U; Practice Book: p. 217; Decodable Reader: *Paul Saw Arctic Foxes*
Reteach/ Review	161D; 1161K-N, 161Q, 161W, 161CC
Assess	Weekly Test; Unit 4 Test
Maintain	Build Fluency: Sound/Spellings

Guided Practice/Practice

Write the words below on chart paper. Read the first line with children. Then have children chorally read the words on the chart. Use the appropriate blending level.

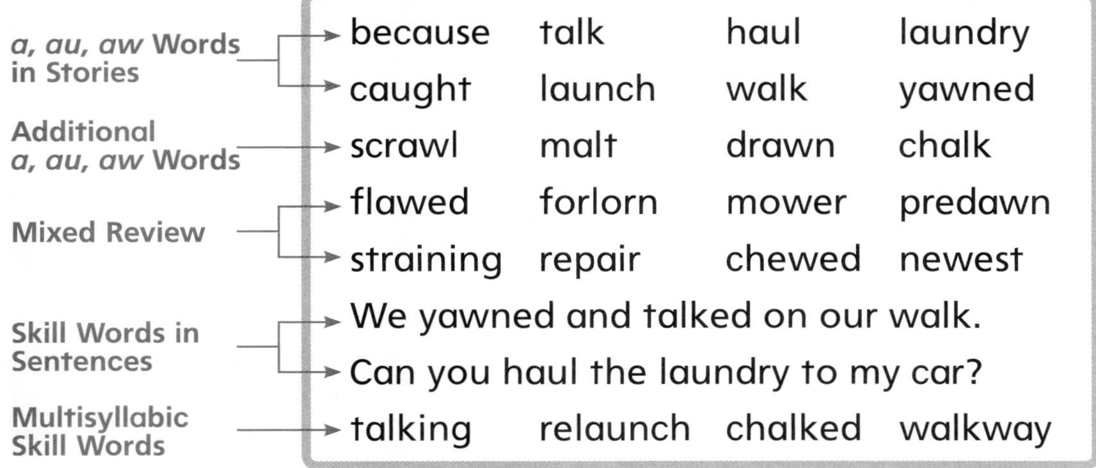

a, au, aw Words in Stories	because	talk	haul	laundry
	caught	launch	walk	yawned
Additional *a, au, aw* Words	scrawl	malt	drawn	chalk
Mixed Review	flawed	forlorn	mower	predawn
	straining	repair	chewed	newest
Skill Words in Sentences	We yawned and talked on our walk.			
	Can you haul the laundry to my car?			
Multisyllabic Skill Words	talking	relaunch	chalked	walkway

Corrective Feedback

Blending Error Say: *My turn*. Model blending using the appropriate signaling procedures. Then lead children in blending the sounds. Say: *Do it with me*. You will respond with children to offer support. Then say: *Your turn. Blend*. Have children chorally blend. Return to the beginning of the word. Say: *Let's start over.*

-ed Ending

Teach

- Say the words *yawn* and *yawned*. Ask children to listen closely to hear what is different.
- Point out the /ed/ sound at the end of *yawned*.
- Write the words *yawn* and *yawned* on the board. Underline the letters *-ed* at the end of *yawned*.
- Tell children that the letters *-ed* at the end of the verb *yawned* mean that it happened in the past.

Practice/Apply

- Help children blend the sounds in the following words: *launched, crawled, halted, talked, walked, haunted*. Point out that the letters *-ed* at the end of a word can stand for the /d/ sound as in *crawled* or the /t/ sound as in *launched*.
- Ask children to look for words that end in *-ed* as they read this week's stories.

ON YOUR OWN

Practice Book, page 222

The letters ***-ed*** can be added to the end of a verb to change its tense.
If a word ends in silent ***e***, drop the ***e*** before adding ***-ed***.
like – e + ed = liked

Add *-ed* to the end of each word. Write the new word. Then use the word in a sentence. Possible sentences provided

1. paste pasted
   I pasted stickers on my card.
2. name named
   The man named his dog Pokey.
3. like liked
   Mitch liked the story very much.
4. close closed
   Betty closed the door.

Approaching Reproducible, page 222

Beyond Reproducible, page 222

Objectives

- Sort words with variant vowel *au, aw*
- Practice spelling words
- Build Fluency: Word Automaticity

Materials

- index cards from Day 2
- pocket chart
- Phonics/Spelling Practice Book, p. 79

5-Day Spelling	
DAY 1	Dictation; Pretest
DAY 2	Teacher-Modeled Word Sort
DAY 3	Student Word Sort
DAY 4	Test Practice
DAY 5	Posttest

ON YOUR OWN **Spelling**, page 79

jaw	crawl	sauce	launch	raw
pause	draw	law	fault	hawk

A. Make a Connection

Write a spelling word to complete each pair of sentences.

1. A child can run. A baby can crawl.
2. I put gravy on my meat. I put sauce on my vegetables.
3. I like to paint. You like to draw.
4. A baby cow is called a calf. A baby deer is called a fawn.
5. Our fingers are part of our hand. Our jaw is part of our mouth.
6. You need to cook the meat. But carrots you can eat raw.

B. Sentences to Complete

Write a spelling word on each line to complete the sentence.

7. They will launch the rocket at noon.
8. Is it your fault that the vase broke?
9. Wearing your seat belt is a law.
10. Stop or pause after you read the first page.

Phonics/Spelling

Word Sort with *au, aw*

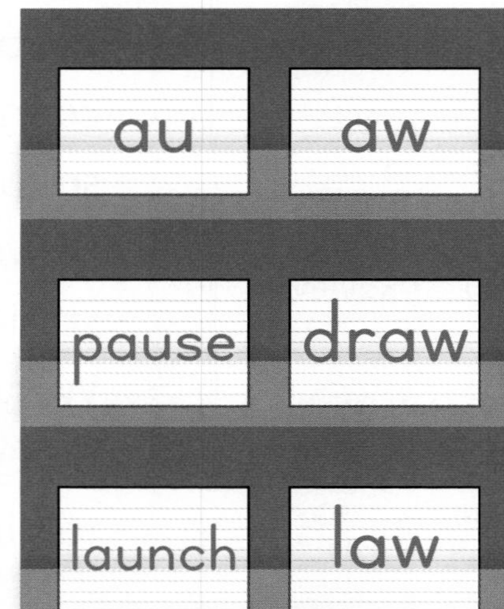

WORD SORT

- Use the index cards from Day 2 for each spelling word, as well as for *au* and *aw*. Place *au* and *aw* cards to form two columns in a pocket chart. Blend sounds with children.
- Hold up the *pause* card. Say and spell it. Pronounce each sound clearly: /p/ /ô/ /z/. Blend the sounds: /pôz/.
- Repeat this step with *launch*. Place both words below the *au* label. Have children read each word. *What do you notice about these spelling words?* (They have the /ô/ sound, and they are spelled with *au*.) Repeat the process with the *aw* words.

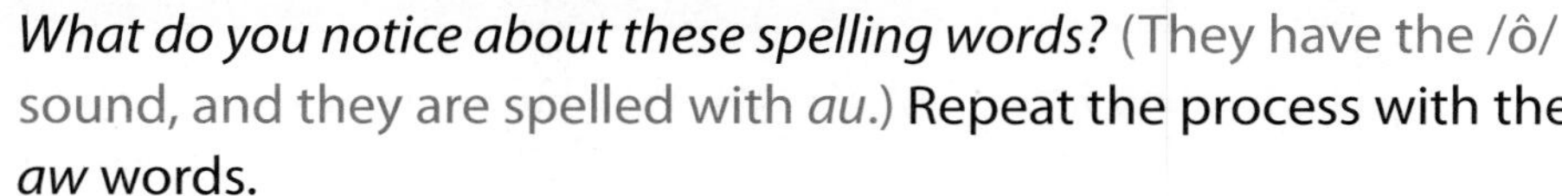

- Display the words *among*, *bought*, and *decided*. Read and spell the words together with children. Point out that these spelling words do not contain the /ô/ sound.

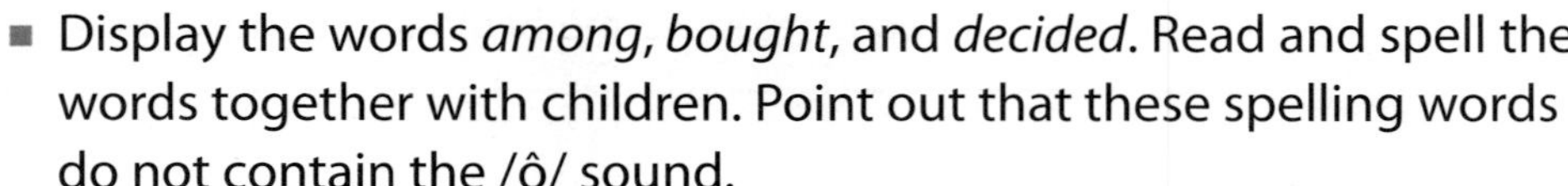

- **Build Fluency: Word Automaticity** Conclude by asking children to chorally read the words to build fluency. Then ask children to orally generate words that rhyme with each word.

High-Frequency Words

- **Teach High-Frequency Words** Write the new high-frequency words for the week **among**, **bought**, and **decided** on the board. Teach the words using the **Read/Spell/Write** routine below.
  - **Read** Read the word. Have children repeat.
  - **Spell** Chorally spell the word.
  - **Write** Have children write the word as they spell it aloud. Then ask children to write a sentence using each word.
- **Practice** Write sample cloze sentences for each word on the board.

  I got to choose __________ several different prizes.
  Beth __________ a pumpkin at the farmer's market.
  Our class __________ to raise money for the library.
- Have children read the sentences and write the missing word for each one.
- **Additional High-Frequency Words** Introduce an additional six words (Additional Words #225–230: **why**, **ride**, **play**, **thought**, **early**, **any**) for more practice. Have children use the **Read/Spell/Write** routine to learn the words. Finish with a speed drill of all the words taught for the day. Display each High-Frequency Word Card quickly and have children identify and read the word aloud. Repeat with any words children have difficulty with.

Decodable Reader

- **Review High-Frequency Words** Review the high-frequency words that appear in the book: **below**, **city**, and **own**. Have children read each one aloud and provide a sentence for it.

Decodable Reader

- **Reread Decodable Reader** Have children quietly reread *Paul Saw Arctic Foxes* to a partner.

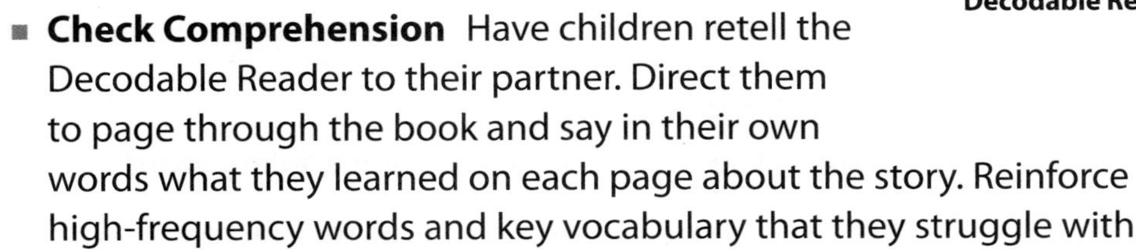
- **Check Comprehension** Have children retell the Decodable Reader to their partner. Direct them to page through the book and say in their own words what they learned on each page about the story. Reinforce high-frequency words and key vocabulary that they struggle with.

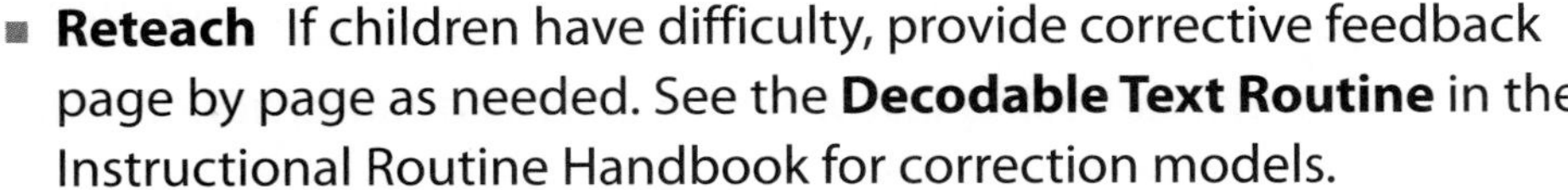
- **Reteach** If children have difficulty, provide corrective feedback page by page as needed. See the **Decodable Text Routine** in the Instructional Routine Handbook for correction models.

Objectives

- Read and decode words with variant vowel *a, au, aw* in connected text
- Teach high-frequency words *among, bought, decided*
- Identify and read last week's high-frequency words

Materials

- Decodable Reader Library: *Paul Saw Arctic Foxes*

SMALL GROUP OPTION

You may wish to read the Decodable Reader during **Small Group** time.

See pages 161K–161JJ

Objectives

- Use word parts to determine meanings of inflected verbs
- Review last week's vocabulary and high-frequency words

Materials

- Transparency 40
- Practice Book, p. 223

Vocabulary

assembled devoured
fetch menu
simmered

ON YOUR OWN

Practice Book, page 223

You can figure out the meaning of an inflected **verb** by putting together the meanings of its **word parts**.

Add the word ending to the verb.
Then write the new word in a sentence.
Possible responses provided

1. wear + ing David is wearing a blue jacket.
2. celebrate + ed We celebrated my birthday at a restaurant.
3. laugh + s My little sister laughs at every joke I tell.
4. confirm + ing Fran is confirming the showtime.
5. giggle + s Stephanie giggles in her sleep.
6. heal + ed Drake quickly healed after his accident.

Approaching Reproducible, page 223
Beyond Reproducible, page 223

Vocabulary

STRATEGY Use Word Parts: Inflected Verbs

EXPLAIN

Tell children that a verb is an action word. To show when action takes place, endings such as *-s*, *-ing*, and *-ed* are added to the verb.

MODEL

Write on the board: *The sauce* **simmered** *for 30 minutes.* Read it aloud and underline **simmered**. Write *simmer* on the board and model how to add *-ed*. Then use **Transparency 40** to model how to figure out the meaning of *simmering*.

Think Aloud I see that **simmered** has *-ed* on the end. *Simmer* is the base word. The *-ed* tells me that an action has happened in the past. By adding *-ed* to *simmer,* I change the word's meaning.

Transparency 40

Use Word Parts

simmer	to cook slowly [The soup should simmer for an hour.]		
simmer + ing	cooking slowly [I am simmering the soup.]		
1. cook	to prepare food		
cook + ing	=	(cooking)	(Example sentences
cook + ed	=	(cooked)	will vary.)
2. play	to take part in a game or sport		
play + ing	=	(playing)	
play + ed	=	(played)	
3. devour	to eat greedily		
devour + ing	=	(devouring)	
devour + ed	=	(devoured)	

Vocabulary Transparency

GUIDED PRACTICE/PRACTICE

Help children identify the meanings of the inflected verbs on the transparency. Have partners create a sentence for each new verb.

REVIEW WORDS

Review the definition of each vocabulary word and write a sentence.

Practice Ask children questions relating each word to their own experience, such as: *What's on the* menu *at your favorite restaurant?*

Repeat using last week's words: *examines*, *hunger*, *mammal*, *normal*, *rescued*, and *young*.

Oral Vocabulary

REVIEW WORDS

Remind children of the week's oral vocabulary words.

- Say the words **applause** and **deceive**. When people clap their hands to show they enjoyed something, that's called applause. *There was lots of applause after the concert.* To deceive means "to not tell the truth." *It's hard to trust someone who likes to deceive others.*
- **Exquisite** means "something very beautiful." *The children wore exquisite costumes in the performance.*
- **Display** means "to show something." *Do you sometimes like to display your school work?*
- A person who is **vain** has too much pride in how he or she looks. *The vain queen spent hours admiring herself in the mirror.*

Use the statements and questions below to help reinforce the meanings of the words.

- *You might give applause after a performance because . . .*
- *How might a magician use a trick to deceive an audience?*
- *Where might you go to see something exquisite on display?*
- *Show how a vain person might act when he or she looks in a mirror.*
- *Talk about why you would want to display something you created.*
- Then have a child say what each word means and use it in a sentence.

- Use similar activities to review last week's words: *baffled*, *daring*, *compassion*, *lunge*, and *survive*.

Objectives

- Practice repeated oral reading
- 62–82 WCPM
- Practice fluency prosody

Materials

- Transparency 20
- Fluency Solutions Audio CD
- Practice Book, p. 224

ELL

Model Reading
Model reading the passage aloud to children. Be sure to emphasize the exclamations and questions in the dialogue. After reading, discuss what each paragraph means so the children understand what is happening in the passage. Finally, have children whisper-read the passage to themselves.

Fluency

Repeated Reading: Prosody

EXPLAIN/MODEL

- **Punctuation** Explain that the punctuation in a text helps readers know when to pause or stop. *Paying close attention to punctuation helps us read the words with expression and the way the speaker would have said them.*

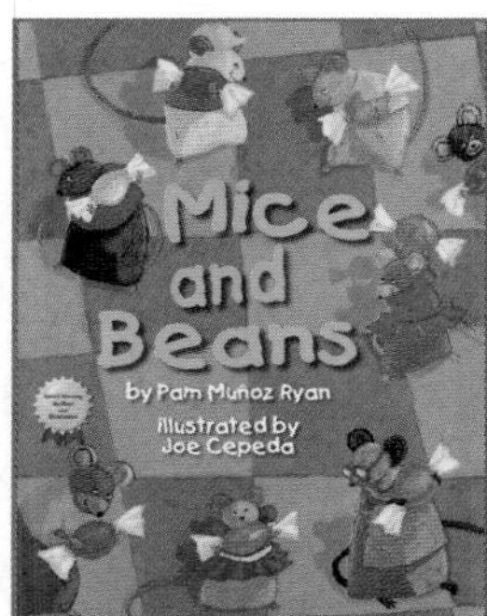

Main Selection

- **Phrasing** Display **Transparency 20** and point out the single and double slashes. Explain that the single slashes show pauses and the double slashes show stops.
- Point out that when the words between slashes are read together, they help us form a mental picture of the text. *If we struggle with any word, we should decode it or ask for help, then go back to the beginning of the slash and reread that section of the text.* Model reading aloud the section on Transparency 20. *When did I pause when I read? When did I stop longer?*

Transparency 20

Thursday, / Rosa María simmered the beans. // She searched for her favorite wooden spoon, / the one she always used to cook *frijoles*, / but she couldn't find it. //

"No importa," / she said. // "The beans will taste just as good if I use another spoon." //

She added water all day long until the beans were plump and soft. // Then she scrubbed the stove and checked the mousetrap. //

But it was nowhere in sight! //

"!Cielos!" / she said. // "Heavens! // Where is my mind?" //

She hurried to the cupboard to fetch another and when it was set and ready to snap, / she turned off the light and went to bed. //

—from *Mice and Beans* (page 136)

Fluency Transparency

- **Expression** Discuss how your intonation changes depending on what activity is being described in each sentence.

Demonstrate how you read with expression based on the style of the writing. *When the author is describing exciting actions and uses exclamation marks, you adjust your reading rate by reading more quickly and with excitement.* Model reading the passage with natural expression.

Point out that you read the text the way the speaker would have said the words, expressing the same emotion and using the same expression.

- **Pronunciation** The selection features many Spanish words, and students might be unfamiliar with proper pronunciation of them. Write *frijoles, no importa,* and *cielos* on the board. Model correct pronunciation for each word for the students. Remind students that they can slow down their reading rate when they encounter unfamiliar words while reading.

PRACTICE

- Have children reread the passage chorally, using the slashes to think about their phrasing. Remind them to read as if the character is speaking.

Repeat the reading to give children even more practice with natural phrasing, speed, and prosody.

- **Daily Fluency** Children will practice fluency by reading aloud **Practice Book** page 224, then paraphrasing what they have read. Students can also listen to the **Fluency Solutions Audio CD**. The passage is recorded at a slow, practice speed, and a faster, fluent speed.

Quick Check

Can children read the passage fluently and with prosody?

During **Small Group Instruction**

If No → **Approaching Level** See pages: 161DD, 161HH.

If Yes → **On Level** See Fluency 161EE.

Beyond Level See Fluency 161EE.

Practice Book, page 224

As I read, I will pay attention to my expression.

Roger woke up with the hot sun already smiling
9 down on him. He felt like it was going to be a
21 special day, but he wasn't sure why.
28 "It's the first day of summer!" said Dad.
36 That was it! Summer was here! It was Roger's
45 favorite time of the year. He thought about the
54 warm sun and the sweet fruits he ate each summer.
64 This year would be no different.
70 Roger and his dad always threw a party to
79 celebrate the new season. This year his dad made
88 the guest list. He said a surprise guest would be the
99 bright spot in the party.
104 Roger got dressed in a hurry. He was so excited to
115 bake with his dad for the party that he almost
125 knocked him over in the hallway. 131

Comprehension Check

1. Could this story be true and happen in real life? Explain why or why not. **Fantasy and Reality** This story is realistic. It could happen in real life.
2. Why did Roger almost knock his dad over in the hallway? **Character** He was so excited about baking with his dad that he was running to the kitchen.

	Words Read	–	Number of Errors	=	Words Correct Score
First Read		–		=	
Second Read		–		=	

Approaching Reproducible, page 224

Beyond Reproducible, page 224

Objectives

- Identify the sequence of events in a story
- Express personal responses to literature
- Discuss genre characteristics

Materials

- Student Book: *Mice and Beans*, pp. 124–153

Comprehension

REVIEW Sequence of Events

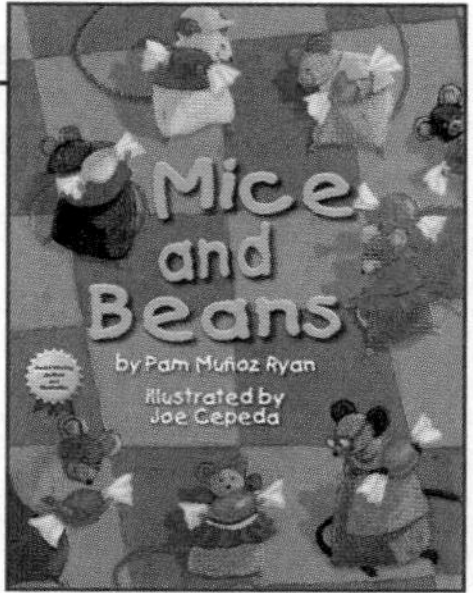

Main Selection

EXPLAIN/MODEL

- Knowing the sequence of events helps students understand what happens in a story, and the relationship between the problem, solution, and the characters' actions.
- Remind children that to identify sequence of events they should do the following:

1. Pay attention to the action in a story, especially as it relates to cause-and-effect relationships.
2. Look for time-order transition, or clue, words such as *first, next, then,* and *last.*

PRACTICE

- *What clue words did you find when reading* Mice and Beans? *What event happened first? Then what happened? How did the clue words help you understand the sequence of the story's events?* Tell children to use details from *Mice and Beans* to support their answers.

Skills Trace

Sequence of Events

Introduce	U4: 81A–B
Practice/ Apply	U4: 81K–85A; Practice Book: 198–199
Reteach/ Review	U4: 89K, 89V–X, 89BB–DD, 93A–B, 93K–115A, 119G, 119R–T, 119X–Z; Practice Book: 209–210
Assess	Weekly Tests; Units 4, 5 Tests
Maintain	U4: 155N; U5: 201N, 209JA–B, 209J–233A, 239G, 239R–T, 239X–Z, 311N; Practice Book: 243–244

Respond to Literature

Personal Response Have children discuss *Mice and Beans*. Have them generate and discuss relevant *how, why,* and *what-if* questions to clarify their understanding of the story. They can record their responses in their Writer's Notebooks.

- *Why do you think the author wrote* Mice and Beans*? Use details from the story to explain the author's purpose.*
- *What is the overall message, or theme, in* Mice and Beans*? Use details from the story to explain how the author developed the theme.*
- *Would you recommend* Mice and Beans *to someone else to read?*

Focus Question: Fantasy Remind children that a fantasy is a story that has events that could not happen in real life.

- *What parts of the story could not happen in real life?*
- *How do you know this story is a fantasy?*
- *How did the illustrations show that the story was a fantasy? How did they add to your enjoyment of this story?*

Expository: Descriptive Flyer

DISCUSS THE MODEL

Display **Writing Transparency 118**. With children, reread the draft and discuss the following points:

- A descriptive flyer should include facts and details to inform the reader about the event.
- A descriptive flyer should include adjectives to give the reader a clear idea of what the event will be like.

WRITE THE DRAFT

Have children draft their own descriptive flyers, keeping in mind their purpose and audience.

ORGANIZATION AND FOCUS

- As they draft, remind children to refer to the Main Idea and Detail Webs that they created yesterday to organize their ideas. Putting their ideas in a logical sequence will help students develop their drafts.
- Direct children to make sure their writing has a consistent focus. Tell children to check their writing to be sure that all of the details describe the event. Instruct children to remove any information that is off-topic.
- Remind children to vary words as they draft their flyers. Have them use classroom resources, such as a dictionary or thesaurus, to select effective vocabulary.

Writing Trait: Word Choice

EXPLAIN/MODEL

Tell children that good writers think about word choice to make sure their writing is clear and easy to understand. Explain that it is important for writers to select words that paint vivid images in readers' minds. Write the following sentence on the board: *My friend is nice.* Ask children whether the example is a strong sentence. Guide children to understand that the word *nice* is not very specific. Ask children to brainstorm precise words to replace *nice*. (sweet, kind, friendly, generous) Point out that words such as *gentle* and *cheerful* can make the sentence more informative and specific.

GUIDED PRACTICE/PRACTICE

Guide practice with this example: *The movie was good.* Children should continue practicing selecting strong, effective vocabulary with these examples: *1. The trip was fun. 2. I like to play games.*

ELL

Beginning

Draw Have children draw flyers showing their events. Ask children about their pictures and have them write labels for things or events shown in their flyers.

Intermediate

Draw Have children draw flyers showing their events and write a couple of sentences about the events on their flyers. If they are having a problem writing about what will be at their events, ask about their drawings to help them come up with appropriate words.

Advanced

Write Have children write four or five sentences for their flyer. Ask them to circle their adjectives, or describing words. If children are having problems formulating sentences, give them sentence frames as needed.

Day 4 At a Glance

WHOLE GROUP

Oral Language
- Build Robust Vocabulary
- Review Oral Vocabulary Words

Phonemic Awareness
- Phoneme Categorization

Phonics
- Build Words with Vowel Digraph *a, au, aw*
- Build Fluency
- Spelling: Test Practice

Vocabulary
- Review Words in Context

Comprehension
- Genre: Nonfiction Recipe
- Text Feature: Written Directions
- Read "Rosa María's Rice and Beans"

Language Arts
- Grammar: Contractions
- Writing: Expository

SMALL GROUP

- Differentiated Instruction, pages 161K–161JJ

Oral Language

Build Robust Vocabulary

REVIEW WORDS

- Use as many oral vocabulary words as possible to lead a class discussion. If possible, connect the discussion to the weekly Big Idea.
- *Name three things that you might see on* **display** *at a museum.*
- *Describe when* **applause** *might happen at a baseball game.*
- *Which word goes with* tricked? **deceived**
- *Describe something you think is* **exquisite**.
- *If any of the things I say are examples of what a* **vain** *person might say, say "vain."*
  - *—I'm so smart that I don't need to study.*
  - *—I will work hard to do better in math.*
  - *—I'm perfect at everything I do.*
  - *—I will try to be kind to my classmates.*
  - *—I'm so great at soccer that I don't need to practice.*
- Have children say what each word means and use it in a sentence.

- Review last week's words: *baffled*, *daring*, *compassion*, *lunge*, and *survive*.

Write About It

Think about wearing an exquisite costume in a school play on stage. If people in the audience were applauding loudly at the end of the play, how do you think they felt about it? Write about how that would make you feel.

Phonemic Awareness

Phoneme Categorization

Model

Show children how to listen for medial /ô/ in words.

Listen as I say each sound in the word *walk*. I hear /w/ at the beginning of *walk*. I hear /ô/ in the middle of *walk*. I hear /k/ at the end of *walk*. Listen: /wôk/, *walk*.

Now I am going to say three words. Two of them have /ô/ in the middle and one does not: *walk, win, taught*. The word *win* does not have /ô/ in the middle.

Repeat the routine with these word sets: *caught, bring, crawl; yawn, malt, tan; claw, spend, scrawl; drop, draw, vault; and launch, salt, lamp.*

Guided Practice/Practice

Have children practice with these examples. Guide practice with the first row.

I am going to say more groups of words. Listen carefully. Tell me which word has a different sound in the middle.

fan, draw, taught dawn, wood, fault

caught, pet, jaw tub, law, pause

launch, hawk, sit drawn, cot, saw

Objective

- Categorize phonemes in words

Objectives

- Blend and build words with vowel digraph *a, au, aw*
- Review previously taught phonics skills
- Read multisyllabic words

Materials

- Word-Building Cards; Teacher's Resource Book, p. 66
- pocket chart
- word chart from Day 3

Skills Trace

Vowel Digraph *a, au, aw*	
Introduce	121C–D
Practice/ Apply	121F, 123G, 155F-G, 155I, 155T-U; Practice Book: 217; Decodable Reader: *Paul Saw Arctic Foxes*
Reteach/ Review	161D; 1161K-N, 161Q, 161W, 161CC
Assess	Weekly Test; Unit 4 Test
Maintain	Build Fluency: Sound/Spellings

Phonics

Build Fluency: Sound/Spellings

Display the following **Word-Building Cards** one at a time: *au, aw, oo, ou, oo, ui, ew, ue, u, ou, oe, oi, oy, ou, ow, are, air, ear, ere, or, ore, oar, ar*. Have children chorally say each sound. Repeat and vary the pace. Children should work to say each sound within a two-second pause.

Blend Words with *au, aw*

Model

Place Word-Building Cards *c, l, a, w* in the pocket chart to form *claw*. Model how to generate and blend the sounds to say the word.

The letter *c* stands for /k/. The letter *l* stands for /l/. The letters *aw* stand for /ô/. Now listen as I blend all three sounds: /klô/. Your turn. Let's read the word together.

Repeat the blending routine for *stalk*, *halt*, *caught*, *drawn*, and *law*.

Guided Practice/Practice

Repeat with additional *a, au, aw* words. Have children blend the sounds in the words "with you."

chalk	straw	taught	vault
malt	pause	fawn	shawl
yawned	calling	relaunch	vaulted
paused	predawn	drawer	haunches

Build with Vowel Digraph *a, au, aw*

Model

Place **Word-Building Cards** *l, a, w* in the pocket chart. Blend the phonemes.

Let's blend all the sounds together and read the word: /lô/, *law*.

Add *n* and repeat with *lawn*.

Let's blend the sounds and read: /lôn/, *lawn*.

Change *aw* to *au,* add *ch* to the end, and repeat with *launch*.

Let's blend all the sounds together and read the word: /lônch/, *launch*.

Guided Practice/ Practice

Give more building practice with this word set: *paw, Paul, haul, hall, tall, talk, chalk, scald.*

Build Fluency: Word Automaticity

Use the word chart from Day 3. Point to each word as children chorally read it. Aim for one word every two seconds. Model blending the sounds in any words children miss. Then point to words in random order at varying speeds for children to read.

because	talk	haul	laundry
caught	launch	walk	yawned
scrawl	malt	drawn	chalk
flawed	forlorn	mower	predawn
straining	repair	chewed	newest
We yawned and talked on our walk.			
Can you haul the laundry to my car?			
talking	relaunch	chalked	walkway

Transition to Multisyllabic Words

Accelerate Pacing: Vowel Team Syllables

- Remind children that *au* and *aw* can stand for /ô/, as in *pause* and *crawl*. Tell them that *walk, halt,* and *ball* also have the /ô/ sound; the sound of *a* changes in these words since it is *l*-controlled.
- Explain that these spellings of /ô/ form vowel teams; in longer words, the vowel teams always appear in the same syllable.
- Help children list on the board words with *au, aw, all, alt, and alk*. Examples: *walk, hall, call, halt, salt, launch, fault, draw, straw, law, yawn.*
- Have children read the words and then use them to make up multisyllabic words. Model using *walk: walking, walkway, sidewalk, sleepwalking.*
- Ask partners to list multisyllabic words using each word on the board. Challenge them to divide the words into syllables and then write sentences for the words.

ELL

Build Vocabulary Review meanings of words on your chart that can be explained or demonstrated in a concrete way. For example, have children use a piece of *chalk* to *scrawl* their name on the board. Model actions for *caught, yawned,* and *haul*. Provide sentence starters for children to complete, such as *I'm happy because* __________.

Objectives

- Practice spelling test
- Build Fluency: Word Automaticity

Materials

- Spelling Word Cards BLM; Teacher's Resource Book, p. 70
- Sound-Spelling WorkBoards; Teacher's Resource Book, p. 143
- paper and pencils
- Phonics/Spelling Practice Book, p. 80

5-Day Spelling	
DAY 1	Dictation; Pretest
DAY 2	Teacher-Modeled Word Sort
DAY 3	Student Word Sort
DAY 4	Test Practice
DAY 5	Posttest

ON YOUR OWN

Spelling, page 80

A. There are five spelling mistakes in the paragraph below. Circle the misspelled words. Write the words correctly on the lines below.

It is very cold and windy in the Arctic. You're likely to see a baby polar bear living there. You might also spot a snowy owl, but not a hauk. But it's not your fawlt. The Arctic is just too cold for some animals! Animals that have a thick coat of fur can crauwl, jump, or play in the snow. You might pawse and watch a reindeer or moose make tracks in the snow.

What other Arctic animals can you think of? Try to drauw them!

1. hawk 2. fault 3. crawl
4. pause 5. draw

B. Writing

Write about one or more animals that can survive in the Arctic. Use five spelling words from your list.

Responses will vary.

Phonics/Spelling

Words with Variant Vowel *au, aw*

PRACTICE

PARTNERS

- Provide pairs of children with individual copies of the **Spelling Word Cards**.
- While one partner reads the words one at a time, the other partner should orally segment the word (e.g., /d/ /r/ /ô/) and then write it. Have **WorkBoards** available for children who need hands-on support in segmenting the word and attaching one spelling to each sound.
- After reading all the words, partners should switch roles.
- When both partners have spelled all the words, children should correct their own papers.
- **Build Fluency: Word Automaticity** Conclude by asking children to read the words chorally to their partner to build fluency.

Quick Check

Can children spell words with variant vowel *a, au, aw*?

During **Small Group Instruction**

If No → **Approaching Level** Repeat blending using the weekly spelling words. Explicitly correct the error, and provide more "with me" type practice. Use a lower level of blending to provide support.

If Yes → **On Level** Consolidate the learning by having children spell additional words with variant vowel *a, au, aw*. See page 161M.

Beyond Level Extend the learning by having children spell harder words containing variant vowel *a, au, aw*. See page 161N.

Vocabulary

Words in Context

REVIEW VOCABULARY

Review this week's vocabulary words **assembled**, **devoured**, **fetch**, **menu**, and **simmered**. Use the sentence stems below. Have children orally complete each one.

- One food that can **simmer** a long time on the stove is _________.
- If a restaurant did not have a **menu**, people would not know _________.
- A kind of toy that needs to be **assembled** is _________.
- If a dog likes to **fetch** it usually runs _________.
- A way to describe the word **devoured** is _________.
- Then have children use each word in a sentence.

- Repeat the activity with last week's vocabulary words: *examines, hunger, mammal, normal, rescued,* and *young*.

Objectives

- Review vocabulary words in context
- Use this week's and last week's vocabulary words in context

Objectives

- Read a procedural text
- Use text feature: written directions

Materials

- Student Book: "Rosa María's Rice and Beans," pp. 156–159
- chart paper

Content Vocabulary

liquids (p. 156): substances that flow easily and take the shape of any container

solids (p. 156): substances that have shape and hardness

gas (p. 156): substance that can move freely and does not have a specific shape

ELL

Paired Reading Prepare children to read the story prior to the whole-class reading. Use the Interactive Question-Response Guide in the **ELL Resource Book**, pages 278–279, to preteach the story content, build language, and develop meaning.

Science Informational Text

Genre

PROCEDURAL: RECIPE

Tell children that the next selection they will read is procedural. It focuses on two recipes. Discuss the format of a recipe, mentioning such features as ingredients list, measurements, and directions. Explain that the number before each ingredient tells the amount, or how much, to use.

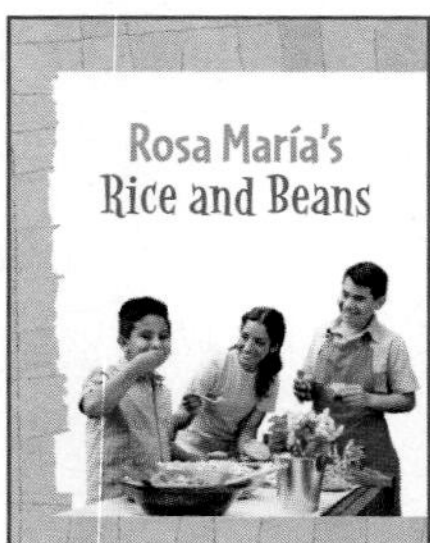

Paired Selection

PREVIEW AND PREDICT

Turn to **Student Book** page 156 and read the title. *What will you learn how to make from these recipes? Why is Rosa María's name in the title? What do you notice about the way the text is presented?*

Text Feature: Written Directions

EXPLAIN/MODEL

Point out the written directions on page 157. **Written directions** are steps that tell you how to make or do something, so they are an example of a procedural text. Recipes have written directions that tell you how to prepare food.

Think Aloud The recipe is organized in a certain way. First, the ingredients are listed. This helps me to know what I will need before I start making the rice. The directions have numbered steps. This helps me follow the directions in the correct order.

Science Content Vocabulary

MEASUREMENT

Discuss the content vocabulary: *liquids, solids, gas*.

- Write the words *liquids*, *solids*, and *gas* on chart paper. Ask children to help you tell what each word means and use it in a sentence.
- Explain to children that these words appear in the next selection.

SCIENCE WORDS

Define the content words using child-friendly definitions and selection visuals.

Science

Genre
Some expository articles give you information about how to make a food or a drink.

Text Feature
Written Directions are steps that tell you how to make or do something.

Content Vocabulary
liquids
solids
gas

Rosa María's Rice and Beans

When you cook, you often mix **liquids** and **solids**, such as when you mix water and flour. These different states of matter can change in different ways as you cook them.

Heating some solids can make them turn brown. Other solids become soft when you heat them. Heating liquids can make them boil. If you boil liquid long enough, it can change its state. It becomes a **gas**, another state of matter.

In the following recipes you will mix solids and liquids to make Rosa María's rice and beans.

Science

Rice

Safety Note Have an adult help you with this recipe.

1 What You Need

- 2 tablespoons vegetable oil
- 1/3 cup minced onion
- 1/3 cup minced bell pepper
- 1 1/2 cups long grain white rice
- 1 14 1/2 -ounce can chicken or vegetable broth
- 1/4 cup tomato sauce stirred into 1 1/2 cups of water

2 What To Do

1. Pour the oil into a large skillet. Oil is a liquid.
2. Add the onion, bell pepper, and rice. These are solids. Sauté (SAW-tay), or fry, these solids over medium heat until rice is lightly toasted, and the vegetables are soft.
3. Add the liquids (broth and tomato sauce water) to the solids. Bring to a boil.
4. Cover, and turn the heat to low.
5. Simmer for 20 to 25 minutes, or until the liquid has been soaked up. Do not stir while simmering or the rice will be mushy.

Read Informational Text

1 GENRE: PROCEDURAL/RECIPE
Remind students that a procedural text gives instructions for how to do something. Procedural texts often share information with a specific audience for a specific purpose. What do you think the purpose is for this recipe? Who might the audience be? (The purpose is to provide instructions for making Rosa María's rice. The audience might be people who like to eat her rice and beans.)

2 USE TEXT FEATURE: WRITTEN DIRECTIONS
Look at the written directions for each recipe. Why is it helpful to number the steps? (The numbers help the person following the recipe to complete each step in the correct order. For a recipe, it is important to do each step in the correct sequence.)

ON YOUR OWN

Practice Book, page 225

Written directions are steps that tell you how to make or do something.

Peanut Butter and Jelly Sandwich
Ingredients: 2 slices of bread; peanut butter; jelly
Directions
1. Spread the peanut butter on one slice of bread.
2. Spread the jelly on the other slice of bread.
3. Put the slices together so the peanut butter and jelly touch.

Write a recipe for something you can make. Then follow the directions to make it. Possible response provided

Turkey Sandwich
Ingredients: 2 slices of bread, sliced turkey, lettuce, tomato slices
Directions
1. Place the turkey on top of one slice of bread.
2. Put the lettuce and tomato on top of the turkey.
3. Put the other slice of bread on top.

Approaching Reproducible, page 225
Beyond Reproducible, page 225

Beans

What You Need

1 16-ounce bag dried pinto beans
1 large onion, chopped
4 cloves garlic, minced
2 14 ½ -ounce cans chicken or vegetable broth
2 14 ½ -ounce soup cans of water
salt and pepper, add to taste

What To Do

1. Follow the directions on the back of the bag for cleaning and soaking the beans.
2. Drain the water (a liquid).
3. Combine the solids (beans, onions, and garlic) with the liquids (broth and water) in a large pot. Bring to a boil. **3**
4. Cover pot. Reduce heat to low and simmer for 2 ½ to 3 hours. Stir often until beans are plump and soft. **4**

Solid, Liquid, or Gas?

The same material can be in three different states—solid, liquid, and gas.

1. A solid has a definite size and shape. Ice is a solid. When water freezes, it becomes ice.
2. Liquid takes up space, but it does not have shape. Liquid in a container takes that container's shape. Water is a liquid.
3. Gas does not take up space or have shape. Steam is a gas. When water boils, it turns to steam.

Connect and Compare

1. What should you do to the beans while they are simmering? **Written Directions**
2. Think about the recipes and the story *Mice and Beans*. Rosa María planned a menu for the party. Write a menu that includes the food you would like to have at a party. **Reading/Writing Across Texts**

Science Activity

Think about your favorite recipe. Write the steps and describe the solids, liquids, and gases.

LOG ON FIND OUT **Science** States of matter www.macmillanmh.com

Vocabulary

Reinforce the content words during reading, using the context sentences and photos. Have children record these sentences, with illustrations, in their Writer's Notebooks.

3 USE TEXT FEATURE: WRITTEN DIRECTIONS

Look at the recipe for beans. What do you do before you reduce the heat to low? (First, bring the beans, onion, garlic, broth, and water to a boil. Then cover the pot before reducing the heat to low.) What do you do after you soak the beans, but before you combine them with onion, garlic, broth, and water? (You drain the water from the soaked beans.)

4 MONITOR AND CLARIFY: REREAD

What could you do if you are cooking and can not remember how long to cook the beans? (I could go back and reread step four of the recipe to find out how long I should cook it.)

Connect and Compare

SUGGESTED ANSWERS

1. Stir the beans often. TEXT FEATURE: WRITTEN DIRECTIONS

2. Focus Question Check children's menus and make sure that they include a variety of types of food. READING/WRITING ACROSS TEXTS

Connect to Content

Science Activity: Create a State of Matter Chart

- Have children look through magazines to find and cut out pictures of solids, liquids, and gases.
- Create a large three-column chart on chart paper. Label one column *Liquid*, the middle column *Solid*, and the last column *Gas*. One at a time, ask children to share their pictures with the class.
- Have children identify the item's state of matter and describe one of its attributes. For example, *This is a liquid. It takes the shape of any container that it is put in.* Then have the child place the picture in the appropriate column on the chart.

Research and Inquiry

RESEARCH: STATES OF MATTER Pair children with partners. Ask partners to do research about a state of matter. Children may choose to research solids, liquids, or gases. Partners should brainstorm together to generate research questions about their topic.

Children should select and use a variety of appropriate reference materials, such as an encyclopedia or the Internet to gather information about their topic. Have each partner report on the topic, including facts and information they learned in their research.

Objectives

- Use written directions
- Connect reading across texts
- Research solids, liquids, and gases

Materials

- Student Book, pp. 156–159
- Practice Book, p. 225

Test Practice

Answering Questions

To apply **answering questions strategies** to content-area reading, see pages 29–34 in the *Time for Kids Test Practice Edition.*

Digital Learning

Story available on **Listening Library Audio CD** and **StudentWorks Plus**, the Interactive eBook.

StudentWorks Plus
Interactive Student Book

www.macmillanmh.com

Objectives

- Proofread for correctly written contractions and book titles
- Use contractions and apostrophes in reading, writing, and speaking

Materials

- paper and pencils
- Transparency 99
- Proofreading Marks BLM; Teacher's Resource Book, p. 191
- Grammar Practice Book, p. 99

5-Day Grammar	
Contractions	
DAY 1	Contractions
DAY 2	Contractions
DAY 3	Mechanics: Contractions/ Apostrophe
DAY 4	Contractions Proofread
DAY 5	Review and Assess Contractions More Contractions

Grammar

Contractions

REVIEW

Remind children of these rules:

- A **contraction** is a short form of two words. (e.g., *do not* = *don't*)
- An **apostrophe** takes the place of the letter or letters left out of a contraction (e.g., *can not* = *can't*)
- The first word and each important word in a book title should begin with a capital letter. Underline all the words in a book title.

PRACTICE

- Have partners write sentences about a time someone helped them. Have each child write two sentences, including at least two contractions, describing what happened and how it made him or her feel. Have partners trade papers and proofread for correct use of apostrophes. Partners should read their sentences to each other. Sample sentences:
- One day I couldn't reach the book *Helping Hands* on the top shelf at the library. "Don't worry, I'll do it," said the school custodian, as she got the book down for me.
- I was upset when I couldn't find my favorite shirt. My brother Nick is the best because he didn't mind helping me look until I found it!

ELL ENGLISH LANGUAGE LEARNERS

Beginning

Practice Provide sentence frames such as the following to help children practice using contractions. *I don't have* __________. *I didn't know* __________. *It isn't easy to* __________. Provide completed examples.Have children work with partners to complete the sentences. Correct for pronunciation as needed.

Intermediate

Practice Give children a list of contractions and make sure they understand the meaning. Then have partners work together to use two of the contractions to write two short sentences. Have children read finished sentences aloud. Correct for form and pronunciation as needed.

Advanced

Write Have partners write three sentences using contractions. Have children read finished sentences aloud. Correct for form and pronunciation as needed.

Proofread

EXPLAIN/MODEL

Explain that good writers always proofread their work. This means they read over their writing to check if the grammar and spelling are correct. Display **Grammar Transparency 99**.

Think Aloud Let's read the first sentence on the transparency. I notice that there is a contraction that is not correct. Let's use the caret mark to show that there should be an apostrophe in the word *havent* between the *n* and *t*.

Transparency 99

Proofread

Devin and his family havent been home in weeks. Their house is'nt safe. After the storm. The town did'nt expect such heavy rains. we do not waste any time in fixing their house! We can'nt wait another day to welcome them back?

Grammar Transparency

GUIDED PRACTICE/PRACTICE

Continue to work with children to identify and correct the errors in each sentence on the transparency. Ask children to point out and fix the errors in the contractions. Remind them that in a contraction, an apostrophe takes the place of a letter in one of the words.

Proofreading Marks

≡	Make a capital letter.
/	Make a small letter.
⊙	Add a period.
sp	Check spelling.
∧	Add.
ℊ	Take out.
¶	New paragraph.

Available on **Teacher's Resource Book** page 191

Grammar, page 99

- A **contraction** is a short form of two words.
- An **apostrophe** (') takes the place of the letters that are left out of a contraction.

Read the paragraph and find the contraction and book punctuation mistakes. Rewrite the paragraph correctly on the lines below.

In the book the lives of arctic animals, I read that Arctic animals dont get cold. It isnt' just a book about animals. I also learned that the sun does'nt come out in the winter at the North Pole. Did you know that there ar'ent any trees in the Arctic?

In the book The Lives of Arctic Animals, I read that Arctic animals don't get cold. It isn't just a book about animals. I also learned that the sun doesn't come out in the winter at the North Pole. Did you know that there aren't any trees in the Arctic?

DAY 5 At a Glance

WHOLE GROUP

Oral Language
- Build Robust Vocabulary

Fluency
- Expression

Phonemic Awareness
- Phoneme Blending

Phonics
- Blend Words with Vowel Digraph *a*, *au*, *aw*
- Spelling: Posttest

Vocabulary
- Words in Context
- Spiral Review

Comprehension
- Strategy: Analyze Story Structure
- Skill: Distinguish Between Fantasy and Reality

Language Arts
- Grammar: Contractions
- Writing: Expository

SMALL GROUP

- Differentiated Instruction, pages 161K–161JJ

Review and Assess

Oral Language

Build Robust Vocabulary

ASSESS WORD KNOWLEDGE

Review the week's oral vocabulary words. Ask children to describe a time when they received **applause** for a show they participated in. *Do you think the audience was trying to* **deceive** *you or do you really think they enjoyed the performance? Why? Sometimes applause can cause a person to act in a* **vain** *way. Why might that happen? Now think about a time when some of your artwork was on* **display**. *Were you proud of it? Name something you've made that was* **exquisite**.

- Read aloud the oral vocabulary words. Have children say a sentence using each word. Provide the following sentence starters:
  - Something I would like to **display** is ________ because ________.
  - I would like **applause** for ________ because ________.
  - Someone who acts **vain** sometimes ________.
  - I would never **deceive** someone because ________.
  - My teacher looks **exquisite** today because ________.
- Review last week's oral vocabulary words *baffled*, *daring*, *compassion*, *lunge*, and *survive.*
- Reread the **Oral Vocabulary Cards** to teach additional vocabulary.

Periodic and Distributed Review You may also wish to use the Posttests in the **Teacher's Resource Book** to check children's mastery of all the words from Unit 4. Continue to use these words during classroom discussions to reinforce their meanings and usage.

ELL ENGLISH LANGUAGE LEARNERS

Beginning

Demonstrate Comprehension Explain meaning using gestures, examples, and pictures when possible. Then use the vocabulary words in statements and questions, such as *I like to display my paintings. What do you like to display?* Restate children's answers in complete sentences as needed.

Intermediate

Demonstrate Comprehension Read the first sentence starter and give an example of a completed sentence. Clarify and discuss meaning as needed. Then have children take turns completing the sentence starter with their own answers. Do the same for all the sentence starters. Help with correct pronunciation.

Advanced

Practice If children are having problems completing the sentences on their own, provide them with sample completed sentences and then have them use their own answers.

Review and Assess
Fluency

Expression

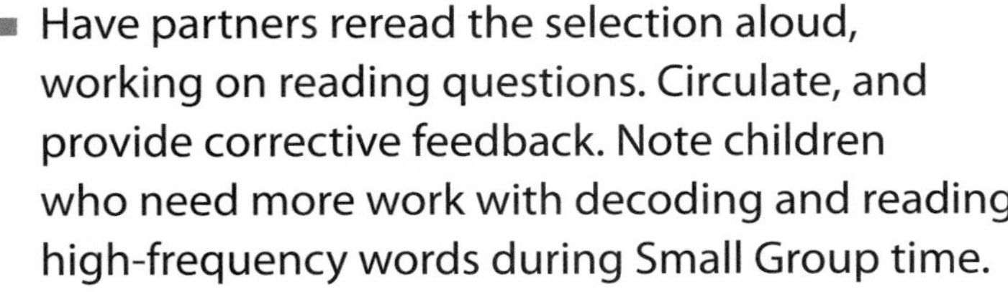

MODEL FLUENT READING

- Read aloud a few pages from *Mice and Beans*, having children echo each sentence. Read dialogue naturally and as if the character was speaking. Point out parts you read with excitement and expression.

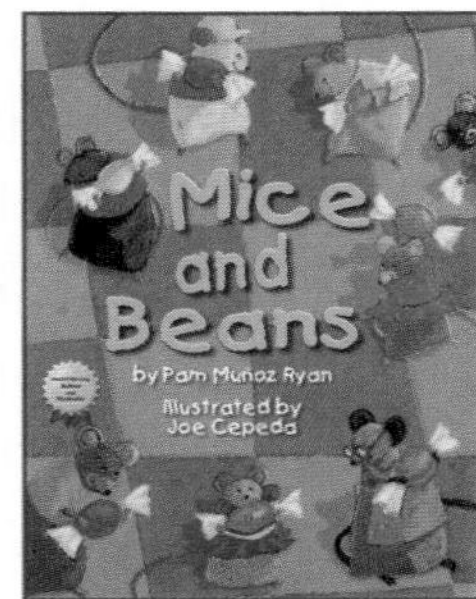

Main Selection

- Have partners reread the selection aloud, working on reading questions. Circulate, and provide corrective feedback. Note children who need more work with decoding and reading high-frequency words during Small Group time.

REPEATED READINGS

- Have children select a story from the **Student Book** or a book that they previously read. Tell them that by rereading, they can become better readers. *The more practice we have sounding out words and seeing high-frequency words, the easier it will be for us to read.*
- Provide 15–20 minutes for children to enjoy independent reading. Then ask students to paraphrase what they have read. Read with children or use this time to assess individuals using the Fluency Assessment in the **Diagnostic Assessment Handbook**.

Objectives

- Review and assess vocabulary
- Build fluency
- Read independently and paraphrase meaning

Materials

- Student Book

Readers Theater

BUILDING LISTENING AND SPEAKING SKILLS
Distribute copies of "A Whale of a Story" from **Read-Aloud Anthology** pages 179–191. Have children practice reading the play throughout the unit. Assign parts and have children present the play or perform it as a dramatic reading at the end of the unit.

A Whale of a Story

Objectives

- Blend phonemes
- Blend sounds in words with variant vowel *a, au, aw*
- Read multisyllabic words
- Review vowel digraph *a, au, aw*

Materials

- Word-Building Cards; Teacher's Resource Book, p. 66
- pocket chart
- word charts from Days 1 and 3
- Decodable Reader Library
- Practice Book for vowel digraph *a, au, aw*, p. 226

Skills Trace

Vowel Digraph *a, au, aw*	
Introduce	121C–D
Practice/ Apply	121F, 123G, 155F-G, 155I, 155T-U; Practice Book: 217; Decodable Reader: *Paul Saw Arctic Foxes*
Reteach/ Review	161D; 1161K-N, 161Q, 161W, 161CC
Assess	Weekly Test; Unit 4 Test
Maintain	Build Fluency: Sound/Spellings

Review and Assess

Phonemic Awareness

Phoneme Blending

Guided Practice/Practice

Have children practice blending sounds to make words. Guide practice with the first one.

I am going to say a word sound by sound. I want you to blend the sounds to form the word. Let me try first. The sounds are /k/ /l/ /ô/. Listen as I blend the sounds: /klô/, *claw*. The word is *claw*.

Your turn.

/s/ /ô/	/t/ /ô/ /t/
/sh/ /ô/ /l/	/s/ /t/ /r/ /ô/
/l/ /ô/ /n/ /ch/	/v/ /ô/ /l/ /t/

Review and Assess

Phonics

Build Fluency: Sound/Spellings

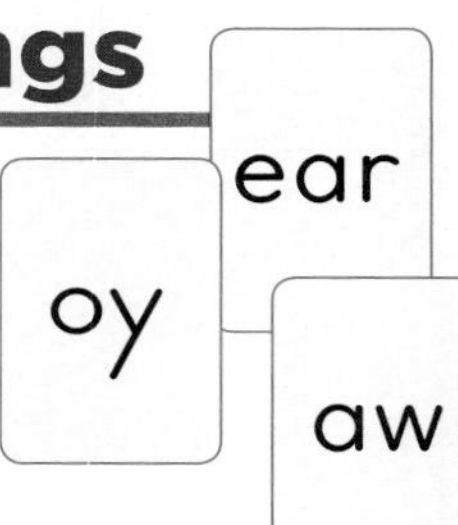

Display the following **Word-Building Cards** one at a time: *au, aw, oo, ou, oo, ui, ew, ue, u, ou, oe, oi, oy, ou, ow, are, air, ear, ere, or, ore, oar, ar*. Have children chorally say each sound. Mix, repeat, and vary the pace.

Blend with Variant Vowel *a, au, aw*

Guided Practice

Display **Word-Building Cards** *d, a, w, n*. Blend.

Repeat using *walk, law, pause, sauce, fawn, walk, salt, straw, yawn.*

What sounds does each of these letters stand for?

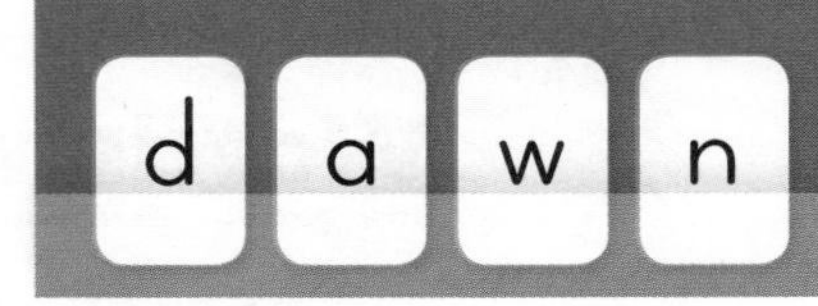

Help me blend the sounds together. Let's read the word together: *dawn*.

Practice

Have children practice generating and blending sounds to form words. Use the examples provided. Write each word on the board.

claw	salt	pawn	crawl
halt	taught	law	tall
malt	pause	stall	launch
falling	jigsaw	stalked	retaught

Have children practice with nonsense words.

dalk	gaught	sawn	flawl

Build Fluency: Word Automaticity

Use word charts from Days 1 and 3. Point to each word as children chorally read it. Model blending sounds in any words children miss. Then point to words in random order at varying speeds for children to chorally read.

paw	sauce	Paul	raw
yawn	awful	crawl	taught
claw	walk	halt	launch
unsent	fault	reuse	flaunted
toiling	restore	unfair	choice

I taught Jo how to make sauce.
Paul saw the fox yawn.

because	talk	haul	laundry
caught	launch	walk	yawned
scrawl	malt	drawn	chalk
flawed	forlorn	mower	predawn
straining	repair	chewed	newest

We yawned and talked on our walk.
Can you haul the laundry to my car?

talking	relaunch	chalked	walkway

Build Fluency: Connected Text

- Have children reread with a partner *Paul Saw Arctic Foxes* from the **Decodable Reader Library**. Circulate and listen in, providing corrective feedback as needed.
- Comment on children's **speed**, **accuracy**, and **intonation**. Model each as needed. For example, model how your voice rises at the end of a question.

Corrective Feedback

For children needing additional practice reading words with vowel digraph *a, au, aw,* use the one-syllable and multisyllabic Speed Drills in the **Intervention Kit** (**Fluency**).

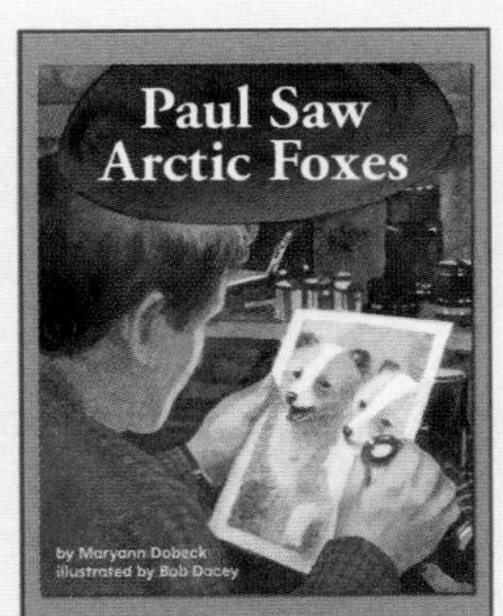

Paul Saw Arctic Foxes

Objectives

- Spell words with vowel digraph *au, aw*
- Spell high-frequency words
- Use the Word Wall as a resource to find spellings

Materials

- paper and pencils

5-Day Spelling	
DAY 1	Dictation; Pretest
DAY 2	Teacher-Modeled Word Sort
DAY 3	Student Word Sort
DAY 4	Test Practice
DAY 5	Posttest

Review and Assess

Phonics/Spelling

Words with Variant Vowel *au, aw*

POSTTEST

Use the following procedure to assess children's spelling of the weekly spelling words.

- Say a spelling word and use it in the sentence provided below.
- Have children write the word on a piece of paper. Then continue with the next word.
- When children have finished, collect their papers and analyze their spellings of misspelled words.
- Have children create personal word lists in their Writer's Notebooks that include words they need to continue practicing.

1. **pause:** Remember to pause when you come to a comma.
2. **draw:** Can you draw a picture to go with your story?
3. **launch:** They will launch the hot air balloons in the morning.
4. **law:** The new traffic law is a good one.
5. **fault:** It is my fault that we missed the bus.
6. **jaw:** A full-grown wolf has a strong jaw.
7. **sauce:** My favorite dinner is pasta and sauce.
8. **hawk:** A hawk circled slowly overhead.
9. **raw:** Chopping raw onions makes my eyes water.
10. **crawl:** The baby learned to crawl on his hands and knees.
11. **good:** The book I am reading is so good!
12. **could:** We could fly kites after school today.
13. **among:** Our teacher was standing among the flowers.
14. **bought:** Mr. Max bought a new pair of shoes.
15. **decided:** I decided to practice my spelling words.

Word Wall Use a Word Wall to group words by spelling patterns. Also use it to review previous weeks' spelling words. Remove words from the Word Wall when children have mastered them.

Review and Assess
Vocabulary

Words in Context

REVIEW

Explain to children that some of the words in each sentence you will read can be replaced with a vocabulary word. Have them tell which vocabulary word fits in each sentence and reread the sentence, substituting the vocabulary word for the boldfaced word or words.

- Chris **gulped down** the entire cake. (devoured)
- I **put together** the toy model car. (assembled)
- Grandma **slowly boiled** the beans. (simmered)
- Ryan created a **list of food choices**. (menu)
- Mom had to **get** the sugar from the cupboard. (fetch)
- Then have children use each word in a sentence.

Spiral Vocabulary Review

Divide the class into two teams for a vocabulary activity. Distribute **Vocabulary Cards** from this week and last week (*examines*, *hunger*, *mammal*, *normal*, *rescued*, and *young*) evenly between the teams. Have a player on Team 1 call out one word, and then have a player on Team 2 give its definition. If the definition is correct, the card is taken out. If not, it is kept in. Have teams take turns reading the words.

Write About It

Think about a time that you worked with people to get something done. Describe what everyone involved did and how teamwork helped with the project. Use lively words in your description. Try to use at least one vocabulary word in your writing.

Objectives

- Apply knowledge of word meanings
- Review this week's and last week's vocabulary words

Materials

- Vocabulary Cards

Objectives

- Determine when children might need to analyze story structure again
- Determine what is fantasy and reality in the selections
- Make comparisons across texts
- Review asking relevant questions and seeking clarification about stories

Materials

- Practice Book for asking relevant questions and seeking clarification about stories, p. 227

Review and Assess
Comprehension

STRATEGY Analyze Story Structure

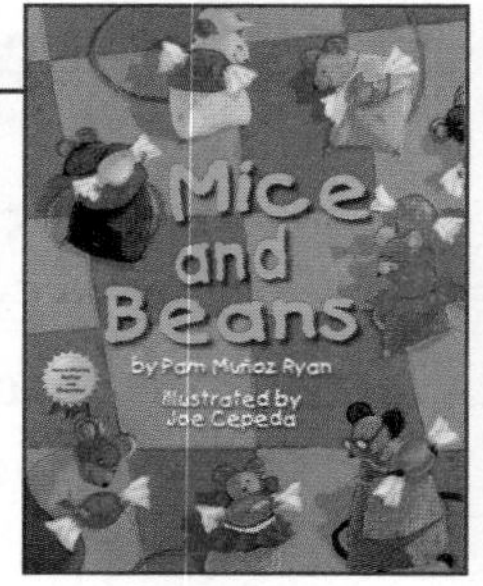

Main Selection

TRANSFER THE STRATEGY Remind children that as they read *Mice and Beans* they paid attention to how the story was organized. Model how using this strategy helped you.

Think Aloud The story was about the character Rosa María and her preparations for a party. Each day, she discovered that something was missing. She thought she was losing things, but it turned out that mice were taking things both to help her and to prepare their own party. Retelling what happened each day in the story helped me understand what the story problem was and how it was solved. I also better understood what Rosa María's character thought, felt, and did.

Focus Question Ask children to describe how analyzing story structure helped them and when they might use the strategy again. Offer these sentence starters:

I noticed that the story was about ________.

This helped me ________.

How might the strategy help you when you read another selection?

SKILL Distinguish Between Fantasy and Reality

READING ACROSS TEXTS Model making a connection between the characters and events in "Bobo's Celebration" and *Mice and Beans*.

Think Aloud I made a connection between *Mice and Beans* and "Bobo's Celebration" because both stories are fantasies. In both stories, animals do things that they could not do in real life. The fish in "Bobo's Celebration" talk and go shopping. The mice in *Mice and Beans* wear clothes and read lists. But both stories are about getting ready for a party, which people can do in real life.

Provide a sentence starter to help children make their own connections between selections:

Both of these stories are ________.

Skills Trace

Distinguish between Fantasy and Reality	
Introduce	U4: 123A–B
Practice/ Apply	U4: 123J–155A; Practice Book: 220–221
Reteach/ Review	U4: 161G, 161R–T, 161X–Z
Assess	Weekly Test, Unit 4 Test
Maintain	U5: 279N

Review and Assess

Grammar

Contractions and Apostrophes

REVIEW

- Remind children that a **contraction** is a short form of two words.
- Remind children that an **apostrophe** takes the place of the letter or letters that are left out.

PRACTICE

- Display **Grammar Transparency 100**. Model how to correct the first sentence. Have children correct items 2–4 to review the appropriate way to form contractions and use apostrophes.

Transparency 100

Review Contractions and Apostrophes

1. This newspaper cannot be right!
   This newspaper can't be right!
2. I did not know that stores gave so much stuff away.
   I didn't know that stores gave so much stuff away.
3. They do not want to waste good food and other items.
   They don't want to waste good food and other items.
4. It is not anything we could have expected.
   It isn't anything we could have expected.

Grammar Transparency

Objectives

- Review contractions
- Proofread sentences for capitalization, punctuation, and spelling of contractions

Materials

- Transparency 100
- Grammar Practice Book, p. 100

5-Day Grammar	
Contractions	
DAY 1	Contractions
DAY 2	Contractions
DAY 3	Mechanics: Contractions/ Apostrophes
DAY 4	Contractions Proofread
DAY 5	Review and Assess Contractions/Apostrophes More Contractions

ON YOUR OWN

Grammar, page 100

Underline two words in each sentence that could be used to form a contraction. Then write the contractions on the lines below.

1. Some animals do not stay awake in cold weather.
2. The bears have not been awake for most of the winter.
3. A bear's heartbeat is not as fast while it sleeps.
4. There are not a lot of things for bears to eat in winter.
5. The bear does not need to eat during this time.
6. It has not used up all the energy stored in its body fat.
7. Other animals can not go so long without food.
8. I did not know that snakes and frogs sleep in winter.

1. don't 2. haven't
3. isn't 4. aren't
5. doesn't 6. hasn't
7. can't 8. didn't

Objective

- Publish and share a descriptive flyer

5-Day Writing	
Descriptive Flyer	
DAY 1	Focus and Plan
DAY 2	Prewrite
DAY 3	Skill: Vary Words; Draft
DAY 4	Revise; Edit/Proofread
DAY 5	Publish and Present

Handwriting

Have children self-check their writing to make sure the heights of their upper- and lowercase letters are equal. For ball-and-stick and slant models, see pages 104–112 in **Handwriting**.

Review and Assess

Writing

Expository: Descriptive Flyer

PUBLISH

- Tell children that to publish their work, they should make a neat final copy. Use the example on **Student Book** page 160 as a model.
- Ask children to read their final writing one more time. Remind them to make sure that they have not left anything out and have made all proofreading changes.
- Tell children to add their flyers to their Writing Portfolios.

EVALUATE

To evaluate children's writing, use the 4-point Scoring Rubric. Consider children's creative efforts, possibly adding a plus (+) for original ideas.

4-POINT SCORING RUBRIC

4 Excellent	3 Good	2 Fair	1 Unsatisfactory
Focus and Coherence Gives interesting and detailed information about a central topic.	**Focus and Coherence** Gives information about a central topic.	**Focus and Coherence** Gives information about a topic, but may stray from focus.	**Focus and Coherence** Does not give information about a central topic.
Organization Presents a main idea that is supported by clear, factual details.	**Organization** Presents a main idea and supports it with details.	**Organization** Omits a main idea or offers few supporting details.	**Organization** Does not present a main idea supported by details.
Development of Ideas/ Word Choice Thoroughly develops ideas. Uses precise word choice to enhance quality of content.	**Development of Ideas/ Word Choice** Attempts to develop ideas. Uses word choice to suit the purpose.	**Development of Ideas/ Word Choice** Attempts to develop ideas, but may be inconsistent. Chooses words that are often ill-suited for the purpose.	**Development of Ideas/ Word Choice** Provides little or no development of ideas. Omits or fails to use chosen words correctly.
Voice Uses a personal voice that adds an inviting, unique tone to the writing.	**Voice** Uses a personal voice that generally expresses an inviting, unique tone.	**Voice** Writer has difficulty expressing an inviting, unique tone.	**Voice** Writer does not express a personal voice.
Conventions/Sentence Fluency Writing is almost entirely free of mechanical, grammatical, and spelling errors. Sentences flow from one to the other.	**Conventions/Sentence Fluency** Spelling, capitalization, punctuation, and usage are mostly correct. Sentences lead naturally to those that follow.	**Conventions/Sentence Fluency** Makes mistakes that can interfere with the reading of the writing. Sentences flow in a somewhat fluid manner.	**Conventions/Sentence Fluency** Makes frequent errors in grammar, spelling, mechanics, and usage. Sentences run together or are confusing.

Speaking, Listening, and Viewing

SPEAKING STRATEGIES

Share the following strategies for presenting a descriptive flyer.

- Plan your presentation beforehand. Organize the information in your presentation to be sure you maintain a clear focus. Only include ideas that relate to your topic.
- Speak loudly and clearly. During the presentation, speak at an appropriate pace for this type of communication. If you are giving lots of specific details, pause frequently so listeners have time to think about the information you are presenting.
- Make eye contact with the audience and speak with expression. Emphasize important parts of your presentation by speaking more slowly and loudly.

LISTENING STRATEGIES

Share the following strategies for listening to a speaker.

- Sit quietly and listen politely to the speaker.
- Determine the purpose of listening to the presentation. Figure out whether you are listening to obtain information, to solve problems, or for enjoyment. For example, if you are listening to obtain information, you might want to take notes to help you remember the information to use at a later time.
- To be sure you understand the speaker's presentation, paraphrase the information that has been shared orally by the speaker.
- After the speaker has finished, ask relevant questions for clarification and explanation of information and ideas that you did not understand.

VIEWING STRATEGIES

Share the following strategies for viewing a descriptive flyer.

- Look at the pictures to see if they match the words.
- Check to see if the pictures help make the descriptive flyer's message clearer.

PRESENT AND EVALUATE

When children are ready, have them present their descriptive flyers.

- Evaluate the speakers: Did they speak loudly and clearly? Did they make eye contact with the audience? Did they speak at an appropriate pace?
- Evaluate the listeners: Did they look at and listen to the speaker? Did they paraphrase to monitor their comprehension?

ELL

Use Visuals Review the names of the objects displayed in the **Reproducible.** Have English Language Learners practice naming the objects.

Approaching Level

Phonological Awareness

Objective Identify and work with syllables in words

Materials • **Photo Cards**

IDENTIFY SYLLABLES

- Remind children that a syllable is a word part with a vowel sound. Show the **Photo Card** for *saw,* say the word, and clap the syllable. *I clapped once because* saw *has one word part, or syllable.*
- Show the Photo Card for *astronaut*. Ask children to listen as you say the word. Have them repeat it and clap the syllables with you. *How many syllables in* astronaut? *How many times did we clap?* Repeat with *raw*, *shawl*, *awful*, *strawberry*, and *sausage*. Ask children to listen to each word, repeat it, and clap the syllables.

Phonics

Objective Decode words with vowel digraph /ô/*a*, *au*, *aw*

Materials • **Sound-Spelling Cards** • **Sound-Spelling WorkBoards** • **Word-Building Cards** • **Approaching Reproducible**, p. 217

SOUND-SPELLING REVIEW

Tier 2

- Display these **Word-Building Cards:** *au, aw, oo, ou, oo, ui, ew, ue, u, ou, oe, oi, oy, ou, ow, are, air, ear, ere, or, ore, oar, ar*. Have children chorally say each sound. Then say a sound. Have children find the corresponding letter(s) on the **WorkBoard** and write the letter(s).

VOWEL DIGRAPH *ô*

- Display the *Straw* **Sound-Spelling Card**. Say: *This is the* Straw *Sound-Spelling Card. The sound is /ô/. The /ô/ sound can be spelled with the letters* aw *as in* straw, au *as in* fault, *and* a *as in* salt. *Say it with me: /ô/. Repeat: /ô/. This is the sound at the end of the word* straw. *What are the letters?* (*a, au, aw*) *What is the sound?* (/ô/)
- **Articulation** Show the back of the small Sound-Spelling Card and discuss how the /ô/ sound is formed. Model correct mouth position, and have children repeat. Compare the /ô/ sound to the /oi/ sound. Point out how different each sound feels.
- **Model Blending** Write words and sentences from the chart on page 121D on the board. Model how to blend using the **Blending Routine**. Have children read the words multiple times.

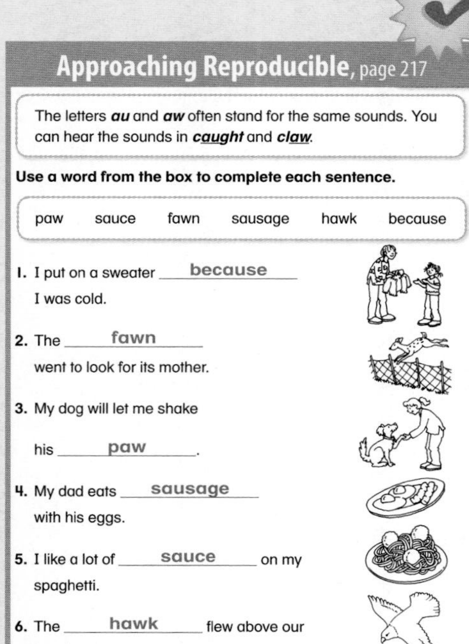
Approaching Reproducible, page 217

The letters ***au*** and ***aw*** often stand for the same sounds. You can hear the sounds in ***caught*** and ***claw***.

Use a word from the box to complete each sentence.

paw sauce fawn sausage hawk because

1. I put on a sweater because I was cold.
2. The fawn went to look for its mother.
3. My dog will let me shake his paw.
4. My dad eats sausage with his eggs.
5. I like a lot of sauce on my spaghetti.
6. The hawk flew above our heads.

Approaching Level

High-Frequency/Vocabulary

Objective Identify high-frequency words and selection vocabulary

Materials
- **High-Frequency Word Cards**
- **Sound-Spelling WorkBoards**
- **Visual Vocabulary Resources**
- **Vocabulary Cards**
- **Approaching Reproducible**, p. 218

PRETEACH WORDS

- **Introduce High-Frequency Words** Preteach the high-frequency words **among**, **bought**, and **decided** using the **Read/Spell/Write** routine. Display the **High-Frequency Word Cards** and have children write each word on their **WorkBoards**.
- **Introduce Vocabulary Words** Use the **Visual Vocabulary Resources** to preteach the selection words **assembled**, **devoured**, **fetch**, **menu**, and **simmered**. Refer to the routine on the cards. Introduce each word using the **Define/Example/Ask** routine. Use the context sentences on **Reproducible** page 218.

CUMULATIVE REVIEW

Tier 2

Display the High-Frequency Word Cards for **among**, **bought**, and **decided**. Display one card at a time as children chorally say the word. Repeat this procedure using the High-Frequency Word Cards from the previous six weeks. Note words needing review.

Then display the **Vocabulary Cards** from the previous four weeks. Say the meaning of each word and have children identify it. Then point to words randomly for children to provide definitions.

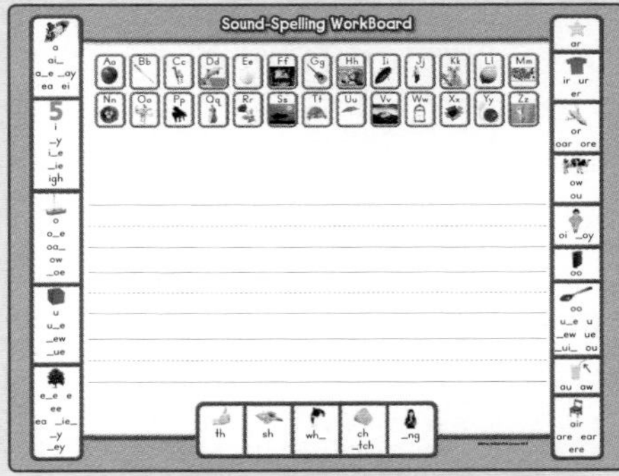

Sound-Spelling WorkBoard

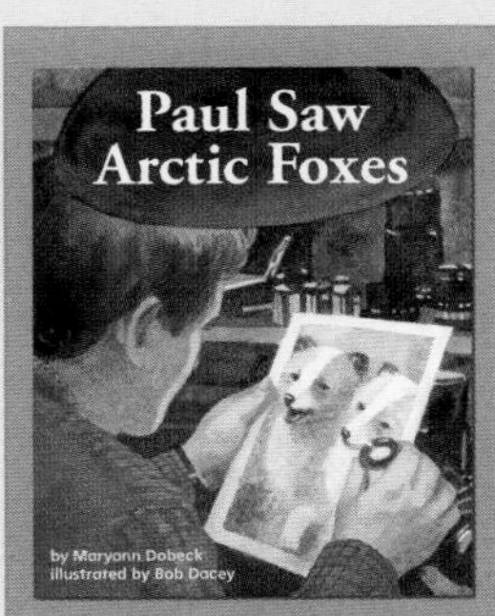

Decodable Reader

Decodable Reader

Objective Read and decode words with vowel digraph /ô/ in connected text

Materials
- **Decodable Reader:** *Paul Saw Arctic Foxes*

READ THE TEXT

- **Preview and Predict** Point to the book's title and have children sound out each word as you run your finger under it. *I see a boy looking at a picture of foxes.* Ask: *What will this story be about?*
- **Read the Book** Turn to page 28. Have children point to each word, sounding out decodable words and saying the high-frequency words quickly. If children struggle sounding out words, provide "with you" blending models.
- **Check Comprehension** Ask the following:
  - *Is this story a fantasy story or could it really have happened?*
  - *How did Paul get interested in foxes?*

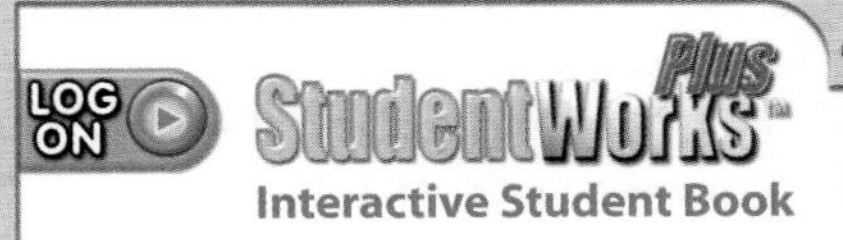

Interactive Student Book

If you wish to preteach the main selection, use StudentWorks Plus for:
- Vocabulary Preteaching
- Word-by-word highlighting
- Think Aloud prompts

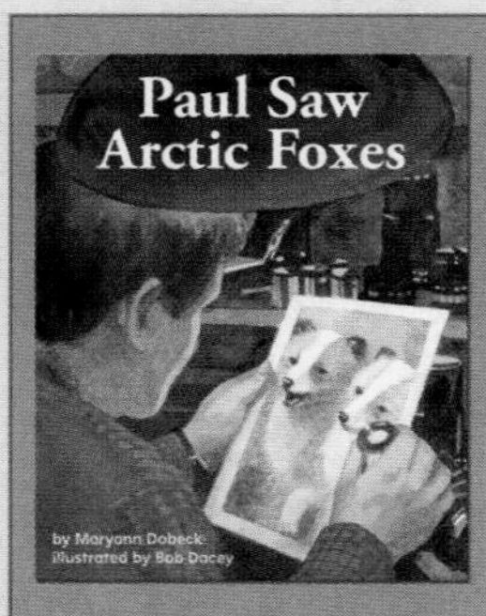

Decodable Reader

On Level

Phonics

Objective Decode words with vowel digraph /ô/ spelled *a, au, aw*

Materials
- **Sound-Spelling Cards**
- **Word-Building Cards**
- **Decodable Reader**

REVIEW VOWEL DIGRAPH *ô*

- **Review Vowel Digraph /ô/*a, au, aw*** Display the *Straw* **Sound-Spelling Card**. Remind children that the vowel digraph /ô/ can be spelled with the letters *au* or *aw* and sometimes with the letter *a*.
- **Blend Words** Write words and sentences from the charts on pages 121D and 155G on the board. Quickly have children chorally read the words. Repeat by pointing to the words in random order. Model blending the sounds in any words children have difficulty reading. Continue with the words below to help children apply their skills to new words. Write each on the board for children to read.

straw	dawn	raw	thaw	draw
claw	yawning	crawl	shawl	drawled
gaunt	cause	launches	flaunt	squall

- **Build Words** Display **Word-Building Cards** *a, au, aw, e, b, c, d, f, g, h, j, k, l, m, n, p, r, s, t,* and *w*. Have partners make as many words as they can. Instruct them to write their words in lists based on spelling patterns. For example, words with *au* go in one list, words with *aw* go in another list, and so on. Provide time for children to share their lists.

Words with *au*	Words with *aw*

REREAD FOR FLUENCY

- Have partners reread *Paul Saw Arctic Foxes*. Work with children to read at the appropriate pace and with expression. Model fluent reading as needed.

ELL

Reread for Fluency Use the Interactive Question-Response Guide Technique to help English Language Learners understand the content of *Paul Saw Artic Foxes*. As you read the text, make the meaning clear by pointing to the pictures, demonstrating word meaning, paraphrasing text, and asking children questions.

Beyond Level

Phonics

Objective Decode words with vowel digraph /ô/*a, au, aw*

Materials • **Sound-Spelling Cards** • **Word-Building Cards**

EXTEND/ACCELERATE

- **Vowel Team Syllables** Tell children that when they see a vowel team in a long word, such as *au* or *aw*, the letters that make up the team must remain together in the same syllable. This can help them decide how to chunk an unfamiliar word to figure out how to pronounce it. Help children read the words below.

freefall	rawhide	jawbone	awesome	awfully
overhauls	hauntingly	applesauce	caught	applause
sleepwalk	talkative	hauled	balked	squawked
unsalted	halter	malted	Walter	washboard
smaller	callback	waterfall	installing	basketball

- **Word Search** Have children search *classroom books* for variant vowel /ô/ words, state the words found, read aloud the sentences, and record these words in their Writer's Notebooks.

Vocabulary

Objective Alphabetize a series of words to the third letter

REVIEW ORAL VOCABULARY

Gifted and Talented

- Write these word on the board and have children read them aloud: *applause, deceive, display, exquisite,* and *vain.* Then add some review words: *annual, anticipate, emotion, vowed, depart, exaggerate.*
- Say: *Alphabetizing is when you put words in alphabetical order. Today we will learn to alphabetize words to the third letter. Let's look at the list to see if there are any words that begin with the first letter of the alphabet, a.*
- Model how to alphabetize words to the third letter with the words *applause, anticipate,* and *annual.*
- PARTNERS Then tell children that they will work with a partner to alphabetize the remaining words. Have them write their words in a list.
- Afterwards, have volunteers help you finish your list on the board.

ELL

Minimal Contrasts Focus on articulation. Make the /ô/ sound and point out your mouth position. Have children repeat. Use the articulation photos on the small Sound-Spelling Cards. Repeat for the /oi/ sound. Then have children say each sound together, noticing the slight differences in mouth position. Continue by having children read minimal contrast word pairs, such as *bawl/boil, jaw/joy, pause/poise.*

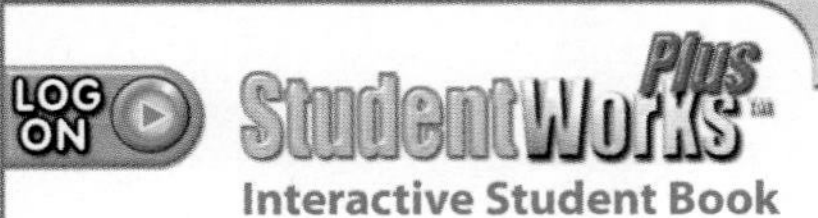

Interactive Student Book

If you wish to preteach the main selection, use StudentWorks Plus for:

- Vocabulary Preteaching
- Word-by-word highlighting
- Think Aloud prompts

Cognates

Help children identify similarities and differences in pronunciation and spelling between English words and Spanish cognates:

Cognates

applause *aplauso*

exquisite *exquisito*

vain *vano*

menu *menú*

devour *devorar*

fantasy *fantasía*

reality *realidad*

structure *estructura*

ELL ENGLISH LANGUAGE LEARNERS

Prepare to Read

Content Objective Learn how mice help Rosa María prepare for her granddaughter's birthday party

Language Objective Use key words to describe what happens as Rosa María prepares for her granddaughter's birthday party

Materials • **StudentWorks Plus** (interactive eBook)

BUILD BACKGROUND

All Language Levels

- This version of the **Student Book** contains oral summaries in multiple languages, on-line multilingual glossaries, word-by-word highlighting, and questions that assess and build comprehension.
- Children can build their word reading fluency by reading along as the text is read or by listening during the first reading and, at the end of each paragraph, returning to the beginning of the paragraph and reading along.
- Children can build their comprehension by reviewing the definitions of key words in the on-line glossary and by answering the comprehension questions. When appropriate, the text required to answer the question is highlighted to provide children with additional support and scaffolding.
- Following the reading, ask children to respond in writing to a question that links the story to their personal experiences, such as *What are some things you do at birthday parties?*

Academic Language

Language Objective Use academic language in classroom conversations

All Language Levels

- This week's academic words are **boldfaced** throughout the lesson. Define the word in context and provide a clear example from the selection. Then ask children to generate an example or a word with a similar meaning.

Academic Language Used in Whole Group Instruction

Oral Vocabulary Words	Key Selection Words	Strategy and Skill Words
applause	**menu**	**fantasy**
deceive	**fetch**	**reality**
display	**simmered**	**analyze**
exquisite	**assembled**	**story structure**
vain	**devoured**	**recipe**

ENGLISH LANGUAGE LEARNERS

Vocabulary

Language Objective Demonstrate understanding and use of key words by describing what happens as Rosa María prepares for her granddaughter's birthday party

Materials • **Visual Vocabulary Resources** • **ELL Resource Book**, p. 280

PRETEACH KEY VOCABULARY

All Language Levels

Use the **Visual Vocabulary Resources 229–232** to preteach the key selection words **assembled**, **devoured**, **fetch**, **menu**, and **simmered**. Focus on two words per day. Use the following routine that appears in detail on the cards.

- Define the word in English and, if appropriate, in Spanish and provide the example given. Indicate if the word is a cognate.
- Display the picture and explain how it illustrates or demonstrates the word. Engage children in structured partner-talk about the image, using the key word. Then ask children to chorally say the word three times.
- Point out any known sound-spellings or focus on a key aspect of phonemic awareness related to the word.
- Distribute copies of the Vocabulary Glossary, **ELL Resource Book** page 280.

PRETEACH FUNCTION WORDS AND PHRASES

All Language Levels

Use the Visual Vocabulary Resources to preteach the function words and phrases *throw over*, *turn off (the light)*, *too late*, and *catch her eye*. Focus on one word per day. Use the detailed routine on the cards.

- Define the word in English and, if appropriate, in Spanish. Point out if the word is a cognate.
- Refer to the picture and engage children in talk about the word. For example, children will Partner-Talk using sentence frames or they will listen to sentences and replace a word or phrase with the new function word. Then ask children to chorally repeat the word three times.

TEACH BASIC WORDS

Beginning/Intermediate

Use the Visual Vocabulary Resources to teach the basic words *birthday*, *cake*, *lemonade*, *candy*, *presents*, and *candles*. Teach these "birthday party" words using the routine provided on the card.

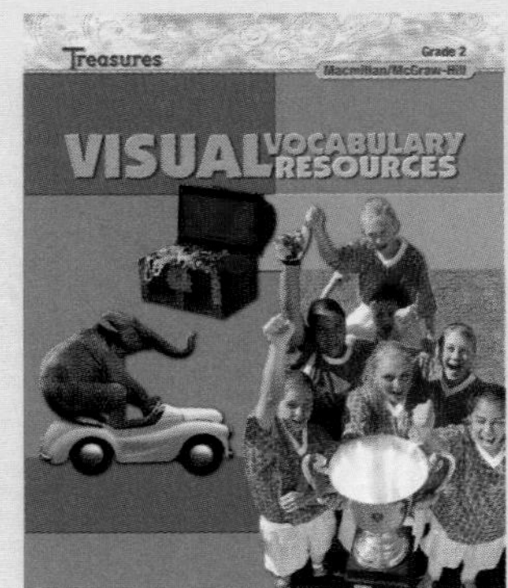

Visual Vocabulary Resources

ELL Resource Book, page 280

Use the word chart to study this week's vocabulary words.
Write a sentence using each word in your writer's notebook.

Word	Context Sentence	Illustration
menu	Yum! The picnic menu listed my favorite foods.	What things might you find on a picnic menu?
fetch	We went to fetch the food from the house.	Does *fetch* mean to catch something or to run and bring it back?
simmered	The soup simmered for an hour before it was done.	
assembled	We assembled all the food for the picnic.	
devoured	Greg devoured his lunch before anyone else.	

Approaching Level

Phonemic Awareness

Objective Identify the same sound in a group of words

Materials • **Photo Cards**

PHONEME CATEGORIZATION

Tier 2

- Display **Photo Cards** for *saw, claws,* and *ant*. Say each picture name. *Listen carefully as I name each picture:* saw, claws, ant. *Saw* and claws *have the same /ô/ sound, but* ant *does not.* Ant *does not belong.*
- Say these word sets: *law, pause, dot; bug, caught, drawl; paw, boy, cause; crawl, taught, loud; talk, shout, salt*. Have children name the word that does not belong. Continue with other word sets.

Phonics

Objective Decode words with vowel digraph /ô/*au, aw, a*

Materials • **Sound-Spelling Cards** • **Word-Building Cards** • pocket chart

SOUND-SPELLING REVIEW

Tier 2

Display these **Word-Building Cards** one at a time: *au, aw, oo, ou, oo, ui, ew, ue, u, ou, oe, oi, oy, ou, ow, are, air, ear, ere, or, ore, oar, ar*. Have children chorally say each sound. Repeat.

RETEACH SKILL

- Display the *Straw* **Sound-Spelling Card**. Review that vowel digraph /ô/ can be spelled *au* or *aw* or sometimes *a*.
- **Model Blending** Write words and sentences from the chart on page 121D on the board. Model how to blend the sounds in each word using the **Blending Routine**. Have children repeat. Have children read each word and sentence multiple times.
- **Build Words** Place Word-Building Card *l* in a pocket chart. Ask: *What sound does this stand for?* Place Word-Building Cards *a, w* next to *l*. Ask: *What sound do these letters together stand for?* Blend the sounds: /lô/. Say: *Now you say it*. Then place the card for *n* to the right of *aw*. Ask: *What sound?* Blend the sounds: /lôn/. Say: *Now you blend the sounds. What's the word?*

  Repeat with the words *haunt*, *dawn*, *washed*, *chalk*, *crawl*, and *vault*.

REREAD FOR FLUENCY

- Reread *Paul Saw Arctic Foxes* with children. Then have them practice rereading the book with the appropriate rate and expression to a partner. Provide corrective feedback.

Paul Saw Arctic Foxes

Decodable Reader

ELL

Reread for Fluency Use the Interactive Question-Response Guide Technique to help English Language Learners understand the content of *Paul Saw Artic Foxes.* As you read the text, make the meaning clear by pointing to the pictures, demonstrating word meaning, paraphrasing text, and asking children questions.

Approaching Level

High-Frequency/Vocabulary

Objective Identify high-frequency words and vocabulary words
Materials • **High-Frequency Word Cards** • **Vocabulary Cards**

RETEACH WORDS

Tier 2

Display **High-Frequency Word Cards** for **among**, **bought**, and **decided.** Review each word using the **Read/Spell/Write** routine. Then display **Vocabulary Cards** for **assembled**, **devoured**, **fetch**, **menu**, and **simmered**. Review each word using the **Define/Example/Ask** routine.

CUMULATIVE REVIEW

Display the High-Frequency and Vocabulary Cards from the previous six weeks. Display one card at a time as children chorally read the word. Mix and repeat. Note words needing review.

Leveled Reader Library

Leveled Reader Lesson 1

Objective Determine whether a story is true or a fantasy
Materials • **Leveled Reader:** *Saving Sofia* • **Approaching Reproducible**, p. 220

BEFORE READING

- **Preview and Predict** Read the title and author name. Then turn to the table of contents and read aloud the chapter titles. Ask: *What do you think will happen in the story?*
- **Review Skills** Use the inside front cover to review the phonics skill and vocabulary words.
- **Set a Purpose** Say: *Let's read to find out what Sofia does.*

DURING READING

- Have children whisper-read each page. Listen in and provide corrective feedback, such as how to blend the sounds in a word.
- **Fantasy and Reality** Draw a Fantasy and Reality Chart like the one on the **Reproducible**. Have children copy it. After children have read a few pages, ask them which story events could and could not happen in real life. Model how to record the information and have children copy it. Then have them finish their Fantasy and Reality Chart.

AFTER READING

- Discuss words that gave children difficulty and the decoding strategies they used. Reinforce good reading behaviors you saw.

Leveled Reader

Leveled Reader

On Level

Leveled Reader Lesson 1

Leveled Reader Library

Objective Determine whether a story is true or a fantasy

Materials • **Leveled Reader:** *A Party and a Half* • **Practice Book**, p. 220

BEFORE READING

Preview and Predict Read the title and look at the cover illustration with children. Ask: *What is happening in this picture? What do you think the title* A Party and a Half *means?*

Review Skills Use the inside front cover to review the phonics skill and teach the new vocabulary words.

Set a Purpose Say: *Let's read to find out about the party. As you read, pay attention to the story events and think about whether the story is real or make-believe.*

DURING READING

- Have children turn to page 2 and begin by whisper-reading the first two pages.
- Remind children to look for the new vocabulary words. Tell them you will help them blend words with /ô/ spelled *a, au,* or *aw*.
- Monitor children's reading. Stop periodically and ask open-ended questions to facilitate rich discussion, such as *What are Roger and his father celebrating? Who do you think the surprise guest will be? Which events in the story are real and which are fantasy?* Build on children's responses to develop deeper understanding of the text.

- **Fantasy and Reality** Remind children that when they read a story, they should consider if the events could or could not actually happen in real life. Draw a Fantasy and Reality Chart like the one on the **Practice Book** page. Have children copy it. As children reread, ask them what events they remember so far. Model how to record the information and have children copy it. Then have them begin to fill in their chart. Help children complete their Fantasy and Reality Chart as they read.

AFTER READING

- Discuss words that gave children difficulty and the strategies they used to decode them. Reinforce good reading behaviors you noticed.
- **Retell** Have children take turns retelling the selection. Help them make a personal connection (Text-to-Self) by asking, *Which events in the story are similar to how you and your family might prepare for a party? Which events are different?*

ELL

Retell Use the Interactive Question-Response Guide Technique to help English Language Learners understand the content of *A Party and a Half.* As you read the text, make the meaning clear by pointing to the pictures, demonstrating word meaning, paraphrasing text, and asking children questions.

Beyond Level

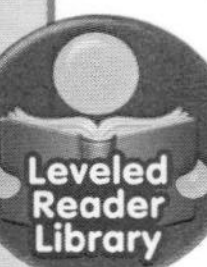

Leveled Reader Lesson 1

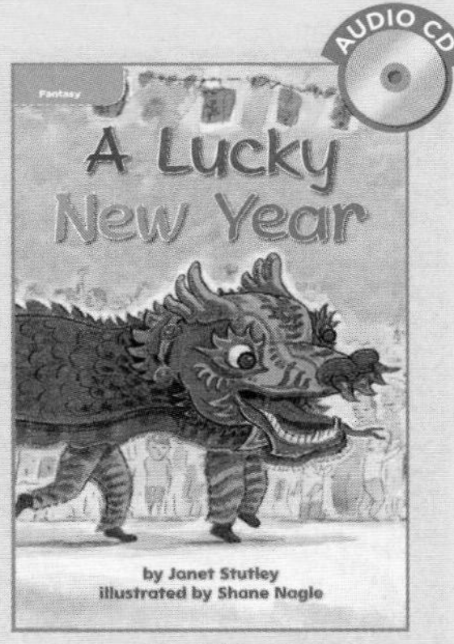

Leveled Reader

Objective Determine whether a story is true or a fantasy

Materials
- **Leveled Reader:** *A Lucky New Year*
- **Beyond Reproducible**, p. 220
- self-stick notes

BEFORE READING

Preview and Predict Show the book cover and read the title aloud. Have children scan the table of contents and the chapter titles in the book. *What do you think will happen in this story?*

Review Skills Use the inside front cover to review the phonics skill and vocabulary words.

Set a Purpose Say: *Let's read to find out how Ling and her family get ready for their Chinese New Year celebration.*

DURING READING

- Have children turn to page 2, whisper-read the first two pages, and place self-stick notes next to words they have difficulty with.
- Remind children that when they come to an unfamiliar word, they can look for familiar spellings and chunks, or syllables. For longer words, they will need to break the word into smaller chunks and sound out each part.
- Monitor children's reading. Stop periodically and ask open-ended questions to facilitate rich discussion, such as *How is the way Ling's family prepares for the holiday different from the way your family prepares for New Year's?* Have children support answers with evidence from the text.

- **Fantasy and Reality** Draw a Fantasy and Reality Chart like the one on the **Reproducible**. After a few pages, have children tell if what they have read could happen in real life. Model recording the information. Have children complete their Fantasy and Reality Charts as they read.

AFTER READING

Gifted and Talented

- **Analyze** Review the story with children. *What are the special events that happen during Chinese New Year?*
- Tell children they will be working with a partner to make a flow chart to show the important events of this family's celebration.

- **Model** Draw a box on the board with a picture of Ling sweeping and her father painting. Then draw an arrow to the right of the box and draw another box. Tell children they will show each stage of the celebration in the boxes of the flow chart. Children may add on as many boxes as they need.

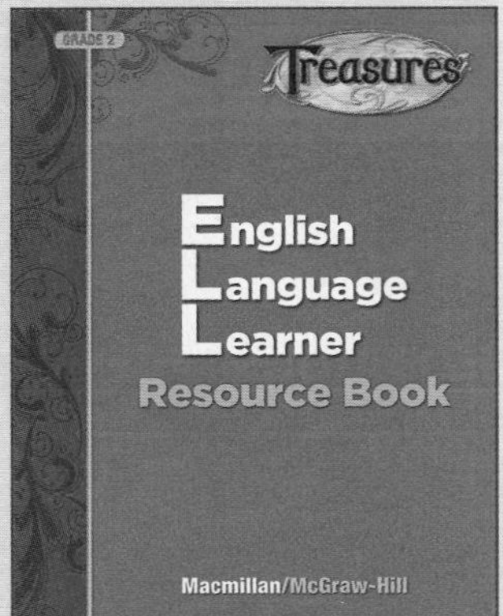

ELL Resource Book

ELL ENGLISH LANGUAGE LEARNERS

Access to Core Content

Content Objective Read grade-level text
Language Objective Discuss text using key words and sentence frames
Materials • **ELL Resource Book**, pp. 262–277

PRETEACH MAIN SELECTION (PAGES 124–155)

All Language Levels

Use the Interactive Question-Response Guide on **ELL Resource Book** pages 262–277 to introduce children to *Mice and Beans*. Preteach half of the selection on **Day 2** and half on **Day 3**.

- Use the prompts provided in the guide to develop meaning and vocabulary. Use the partner-talk and whole-class responses to engage children and increase student talk.
- When completed, have partners reread the story.

Beginning	Intermediate	Advanced
Use Visuals During the Interactive Reading, select several pictures. Describe them and have children point out fantasy elements and then realistic elements. Children can use words or point to images.	**Summarize** During the Interactive Reading, select a few lines of text. After you read it and explain it, have children tell what is realistic and what is fantastical.	**Expand** During the Interactive Reading, select a larger portion of text. After you read it and explain it, have children tell what is realistic and what is fantastical.

ELL ENGLISH LANGUAGE LEARNERS

Grammar

Content Objective Identify contractions

Language Objective Speak in complete sentences, using sentence frames

CONTRACTIONS

Beginning/Intermediate

- Review that a contraction is a short form of two words.

All Language Levels

- Review that a contraction is a short form of two words.
- Write this sentence on the board: *Rosa María did not see the mice.* Read the sentence. Then say: *We can write a contraction to stand for these two words.* Cross out *did not* and write *didn't* above it. *In contractions, an apostrophe takes the place of one or more letters.* Circle the apostrophe. *In the contraction* didn't, *the apostrophe stands for the* o *in* not. Reread the sentence with the contraction.
- Write sentences on the board, such as those provided below. Have children read the sentence and replace the underlined words with a contraction. Have them say *The contraction _________ stands for the words _________.*

  She does not catch the mice.
  She can not find the trap.
  The piñata is not filled.
  The traps are not on the floor.

PEER DISCUSSION STARTERS

All Language Levels

- Write the following sentences on the board.

  Rosa María didn't know _________.
  Rice isn't cooked until _________.
- Pair children and have them complete each sentence frame. Ask them to expand on their sentences with details from this week's readings. Take note of each child's language use and proficiency.

Beginning

Use Visuals Describe the pictures in *Mice and Beans* to children. Ask: *What is happening?* Help them use contractions as they describe what the pictures show.

Intermediate

Describe Ask children to describe the same pictures, adding more contractions to their descriptions. Have them use complete sentences.

Advanced

Narrate Ask children to describe the pictures, adding new contractions to their descriptions.

Transfer Skills

Contractions In Spanish, a double negative is required in many sentence structures. This may cause Spanish-speaking children to make such errors as *She didn't see no mice.* As children read the sentences, have them circle the word *not* before writing the contraction. Reinforce the idea that these contractions state the negative.

Corrective Feedback

During Whole Group grammar lessons, follow the routine on the **Grammar Transparencies** to provide children with extra support. This routine includes completing the items with English Language Learners while other children work independently, having children reread the sentences with partners to build fluency, and providing a generative task such as writing a new sentence using the skill.

Approaching Level

Phonemic Awareness

Objective Blend phonemes to form words

PHONEME BLENDING

Tier 2

Have children listen as you say some sounds. Say: */s/ /ô/ /l/ /t/. Now listen as I blend the sounds together to say the word: /sôlt/*, salt. Repeat, saying the words below sound by sound. Have children blend the sounds to name the word.

/l/ /ô/, law */w/ /ô/ /k/, walk* */p/ /ô/ /z/, pause* */j/ /ô/, jaw*
/r/ /ô/, raw */p/ /ô/ /l/, Paul* */l/ /ô/ /n/ /ch/, launch*

Phonics

Objective Decode words with vowel digraph /ô/*au, aw, a*

Materials
- **Sound-Spelling Cards**
- pocket chart
- **Word-Building Cards**
- **Decodable Reader:** *Paul Saw Arctic Foxes*

SOUND-SPELLING REVIEW

Tier 2

Display the following **Word-Building Cards**, one at a time: *au, aw, oo, ou, oo, ui, ew, ue, u, ou, oe, oi, oy, ou, ow, are, air, ear, ere, or, ore, oar, ar*. Have children chorally say each sound.

RETEACH SKILL

- Display the *Straw* **Sound-Spelling Card**. Review that the /ô/ sound can be spelled with the letters *au* or *aw* and sometimes *a*.
- **Model Blending** Write words and sentences from the chart on page 155G on the board. Model how to blend the sounds in each word using the **Blending Routine**. Have children repeat. Then have children read each word multiple times.
- **Build Words** Build /ô/ words with children. Place Word-Building Cards *s, t, r, a, w* in a pocket chart. Help children blend the sounds to read the word *straw*. Then do the following:

  Change the str *in* straw *to* p. *What word did you make?*
  Change the p *in* paw *to* j. *What word did you make?*
  Change the j *in* jaw *to* r. *What word did you make?*
  Change the r *in* raw *to* l. *What word did you make?*
  Add n *to* law. *What word did you make?* (lawn)

  Repeat with the word sets *Paul, Saul, salt, halt, haul, haunt* and *wall, tall, stall, stalk, walk, chalk*.
- **Read the Decodable** Reread *Paul Saw Arctic Foxes* with children. Provide blending models. When completed, chorally reread the story.

Paul Saw Arctic Foxes

Decodable Reader

ELL

Demonstrate Comprehension Use the Interactive Question-Response Guide Technique o help English Language Learners understand the content of *Paul Saw Artic Foxes*. As you read the text, make the meaning clear by pointing to the pictures, demonstrating word meaning, paraphrasing text, and asking children questions.

Approaching Level

High-Frequency/Vocabulary

Objective Identify high-frequency words and vocabulary words

Materials • **High-Frequency Word Cards** • **Vocabulary Cards**

BUILD WORD AUTOMATICITY

Fluency Display **High-Frequency Word Cards** for **among**, **bought**, and **decided** and **Vocabulary Cards** for **assembled**, **devoured**, **fetch**, **menu**, and **simmered**. Point to the words in random order. Have children chorally read them. Repeat at a faster rate.

CUMULATIVE REVIEW

Display High-Frequency and Vocabulary Cards from the past four weeks. As children chorally read each word, note words they need to review.

Leveled Reader Library

Leveled Reader Lesson 2

Objective Determine whether a story is true or a fantasy

Materials • **Leveled Reader:** *Saving Sofia* • **Sound-Spelling WorkBoards** • **Approaching Reproducible**, pp. 220, 221

BEFORE READING

Review Have children retell *Saving Sofia*. Tell them to page through the book and say in their own words what is happening on each page. Reinforce key vocabulary words by restating children's responses with key words.

DURING READING

Fantasy and Reality As children reread the book, help them finish adding information to their Fantasy and Reality Charts. Ask children to determine whether an event is true or a fantasy.

AFTER READING

- **Retell** Have children use their Fantasy and Reality Charts to orally point out the examples of reality and fantasy in *Saving Sofia*. Review the events on the chart with children.
- **Model Fluency** Read the sentences in the book. Have children chorally repeat. Point out to children how good readers read with expression so that their words sound like a conversation.

Book Talk

Bringing Groups Together Children will work with peers of various language and reading abilities to discuss this week's Leveled Readers. Refer to page 179 in the **Teacher's Resource Book** for how to conduct a Book Talk.

Leveled Reader

Approaching Reproducible, page 221

Fantasy is something that cannot happen in real life.
Reality is something that is true and can happen in real life.
Example: Horses can fly. **fantasy** Dogs can bark. **reality**

Look at each picture below. Decide whether it shows fantasy or reality. Write *fantasy* or *reality* on the line.
Possible responses provided

1. fantasy
2. reality
3. List the clues that tell you which picture is fantasy.
   In the picture on the left, the dog and cat are sitting at a table wearing hats.
4. List the clues that tell you which picture is reality.
   In the picture on the right, the people are putting up decorations and wrapping a present.

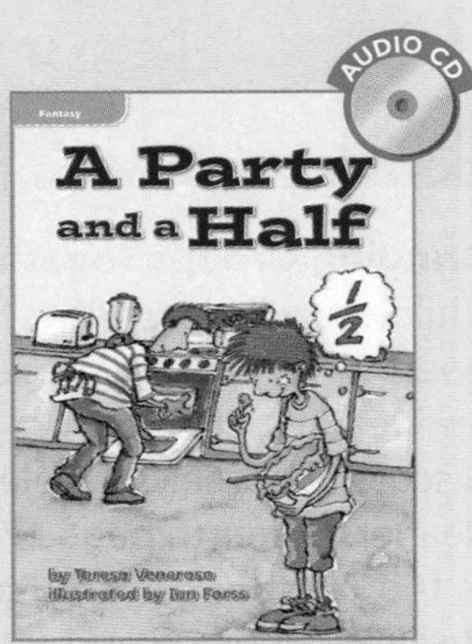

Leveled Reader

Book Talk

Bringing Groups Together Children will work with peers of various language and reading abilities to discuss this week's Leveled Readers. Refer to page 179 in the **Teacher's Resource Book** for how to conduct a Book Talk.

Practice Book, page 224

As I read, I will pay attention to my expression.

Roger woke up with the hot sun already smiling
9 down on him. He felt like it was going to be a
21 special day, but he wasn't sure why.
28 "It's the first day of summer!" said Dad.
36 That was it! Summer was here! It was Roger's
45 favorite time of the year. He thought about the
54 warm sun and the sweet fruits he ate each summer.
64 This year would be no different.
70 Roger and his dad always threw a party to
79 celebrate the new season. This year his dad made
88 the guest list. He said a surprise guest would be the
99 bright spot in the party.
104 Roger got dressed in a hurry. He was so excited to
115 bake with his dad for the party that he almost
125 knocked him over in the hallway. 131

Comprehension Check

1. Could this story be true and happen in real life? Explain why or why not. **Fantasy and Reality** This story is realistic. It could happen in real life.
2. Why did Roger almost knock his dad over in the hallway? **Character** He was so excited about baking with his dad that he was running to the kitchen.

	Words Read	–	Number of Errors	=	Words Correct Score
First Read		–		=	
Second Read		–		=	

On Level

Leveled Reader Lesson 2

Leveled Reader Library

Objective Determine whether a story is true or a fantasy

Materials • **Leveled Reader:** *A Party and a Half* • **Practice Book**, pp. 220, 224

BEFORE READING

- **Retell** Have children retell *A Party and a Half*. If children struggle, have them page through the story and say what is happening on each page. Ask children when they began to notice things in the story that could not really happen. Reinforce vocabulary by restating children's sentences using more sophisticated language. For example: *You're right, it's silly to say that the sun is waving. That's ridiculous!*

DURING READING

- **Fantasy and Reality** Explain to children that good readers can tell which events in a story are real and which are fantasy. Being able to distinguish between fantasy and reality can make reading the story more enjoyable. As children reread the book, help them complete their Fantasy and Reality Charts.

AFTER READING

- Have children use their Fantasy and Reality Charts to orally retell the events in *A Party and a Half*. Have them distinguish reality from fantasy as they retell events.
- **Model Fluency** Read the sentences in the book one at a time. Have children chorally repeat. Point out how you use expression and how you pay attention to punctuation to know where to pause and stop in your reading. Have children continue to work on their fluency using **Practice Book** page 224.

Beyond Level

Leveled Reader Lesson 2

Objective Determine whether a story is true or a fantasy

Materials
- **Leveled Reader:** *A Lucky New Year*
- **Beyond Reproducible**, pp. 220, 224

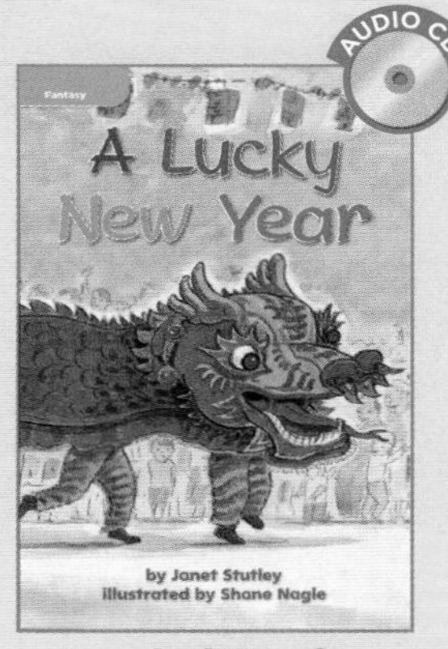

Leveled Reader

BEFORE READING

- **Review** Have children retell *A Lucky New Year* to a partner. Circulate and listen in. Prompt children to use the new words they learned from the book in their retellings.

DURING READING

- **Fantasy and Reality** As children reread the book, help them add more details to their Fantasy and Reality Charts on their **Reproducible** page. Guide them by asking them to explain why something could or could not have happened.

AFTER READING

- **Retell** Have children use their Fantasy and Reality Charts to write a retelling of *A Lucky New Year*.

Gifted Talented

- **Review Flow Charts** Have children review their Flow Charts showing the events of a Chinese New Year celebration.
- **Synthesize** Tell children that today they will work with a partner to design a poster for a Chinese New Year celebration. Be sure to have them include important details and images on the poster. (They may wish to design it on smaller paper in pencil first.)
- Children may wish to use their Flow Charts to help them think of information and images to include in their poster.
- **Evaluate** Have each pair present their poster to the group. Have children respond to each poster by telling why they think it will make people want to attend the celebration.

REREAD FOR FLUENCY

- Read the sentences in the book one at a time. Have children chorally repeat. Point out to children how you use expression to make the reading interesting and how your voice goes up at the end of a question.

- Have children practice reading the book to a partner. Say: *Read expressively. Use your voice to show expression. When you see a question, show curiosity by raising your voice at the end.*
- Have children continue to work on their fluency using **Practice Book** page 224.

Book Talk

Bringing Groups Together Children will work with peers of various language and reading abilities to discuss this week's Leveled Readers. Refer to page 179 in the **Teacher's Resource Book** for how to conduct a Book Talk.

Beyond Reproducible, page 224

As I read, I will pay attention to my expression.

"Can you bring me the ang pow packets, Ling?" her mom asked.
12 Ling picked them up. She loved getting her ang pow on New
24 Year's Day. The packets bulged with a gift of money in them.
36 Ling looked at her bright red piggy bank. She dusted it off
48 and thought about the money she would be adding to it. The
60 pig smiled. He enjoyed this time of year, too!
69 Her aunt and uncle arrived with her two cousins, Betty
79 and Bobby. Everyone was dressed in his or her best clothes.
90 The children were given their ang pow packets. Then they
100 snacked from the Tray of Togetherness.
106 "Ling did all this while I was getting ready," said her mom,
118 giving her a hug.
122 "Lucky for us, Ling has been a big help," said Ling's dad.
134 Everyone was happy to go to the New Year's Day parade. 145

Comprehension Check

1. Where are Ling and her family about to go? **Character and Setting** the New Year's Day parade
2. How do you know that this story could be true? **Fantasy and Reality** Nothing strange happens in this story.

	Words Read	–	Number of Errors	=	Words Correct Score
First Read		–		=	
Second Read		–		=	

ELL ENGLISH LANGUAGE LEARNERS

Leveled Reader Lesson 1

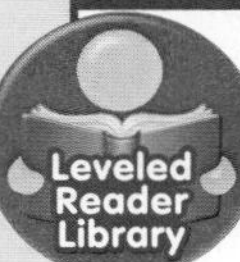

Content Objective Read to apply skills and strategies

Language Objective Retell information using complete sentences

Materials • **Leveled Reader:** *The Summer Party* • **Visual Vocabulary Resources**

BEFORE READING

All Language Levels

- **Preview** Read the title *The Summer Party*. Ask: *What's the title? Say it again.* Repeat with the author's name. Then page through the book. Use simple language to tell about each page. Immediately follow up with questions, such as *Who is coming to the party now? What is Roger thinking about?*
- **Review Skills** Use the inside front cover to review the phonics skill and vocabulary words.
- **Set a Purpose** Say: *Let's read to find out if Roger will have enough food for the party.*

DURING READING

- Have children read each page aloud using the differentiated suggestions. Provide corrective feedback, such as modeling how to blend a decodable word or clarifying meaning by using techniques from the Interactive Question-Response Guide.
- **Retell** After every two pages, ask children to state the main ideas they have learned so far. Help them to complete the Fantasy and Reality Chart. Restate children's comments when they have difficulty using story-specific words. Provide differentiated sentence frames to support children's responses and engage them in partner-talk where appropriate.

Beginning

Echo-Read Have children echo-read after you.

Check Comprehension Point to pictures and ask questions such as *Show me Roger. Is he running or sitting? Look at this picture. Is it the sun?*

Intermediate

Choral-Read Have children choral-read with you.

Check Comprehension Ask questions/prompts such as *Describe what is happening in this picture. What is everyone getting ready for? What is Roger thinking about?*

Advanced

Choral-Read Have children choral-read.

Check Comprehension Ask: *What problem was Roger worried about? How was the problem solved? Do you think it was a good solution? Why or why not?*

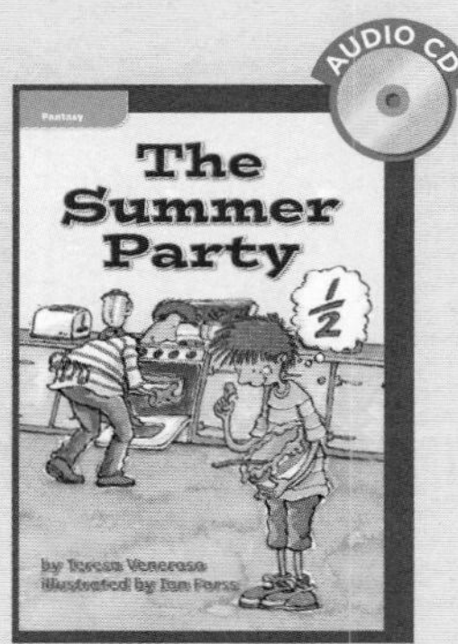

Leveled Reader

Vocabulary

Preteach Vocabulary Use the routine in the **Visual Vocabulary Resources**, pages 419–420, to preteach the ELL Vocabulary listed on the inside front cover of the Leveled Reader.

ELL ENGLISH LANGUAGE LEARNERS

AFTER READING

Use the chart below and the Think and Compare questions from page 16 of *The Summer Party* to determine children's progress.

Think and Compare	Beginning	Intermediate	Advanced
1 Look at pages 12 to 15. Who is the special guest at Roger's party? What does the special guest do?	Possible responses: Nonverbal response. Sun. Smile. Wave.	Possible responses: Sun is guest. Sun eats bread.	Possible responses: The sun is the special guest. The sun waves, smiles, and eats bread.
2 What foods do you like to help cook? How do you help?	Possible Responses: Nonverbal response. One word answers.	Responses will vary. Short phrases or short sentences.	Responses will vary. Children can answer with detailed sentences.
3 Why do you think people like summer?	Possible responses: Nonverbal response. Like sun. Fun	Possible Responses: They like sun. They like fun.	Possible Responses: People like the warm sun. People like to eat fruit and have fun.

Writing/Spelling

Content Objective Spell words correctly

Language Objective Write in complete sentences, using sentence frames

All Language Levels

- Write the key vocabulary words on the board: **assembled**, **devoured**, **fetch**, **menu**, and **simmered**. Have children copy each word on their **WorkBoards**. Help them say and then write sentences for each word.

Beginning/Intermediate

- Help children spell words using their growing knowledge of English sound-spelling relationships. Model how to segment the word children are trying to spell and attach a spelling to each sound (or spellings to each syllable if a multisyllabic word). Use the **Sound-Spelling Cards** to reinforce the spellings for each English sound.

Advanced/Advanced High

- Dictate the following words for children to spell: *vault*, *chalk*, *call*, *walk*, *small*, *haul*. Guide children using the Sound-Spelling Cards as they spell each word. When completed, review the meanings of words that can be easily demonstrated or explained. Use actions, gestures, and available pictures.

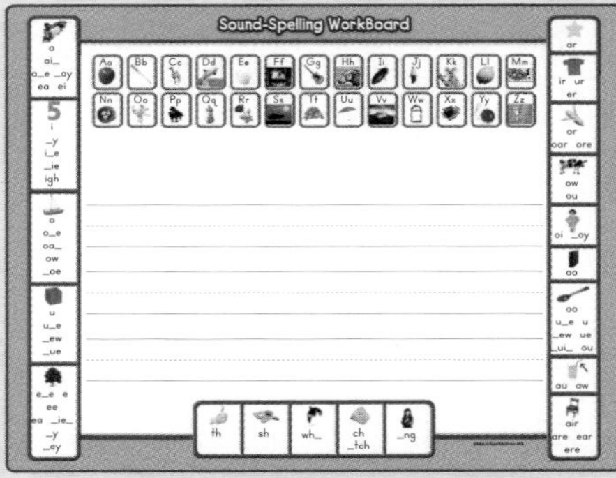

Sound-Spelling WorkBoard

Phonics/Word Study

For English Learners who need more practice with this week's phonics/spelling skill, see the Approaching Level lesson on page 161W. Focus on minimal contrasts, articulation, and those sounds that do not transfer from the child's first language to English. For a complete listing of transfers, see pages T16–T31.

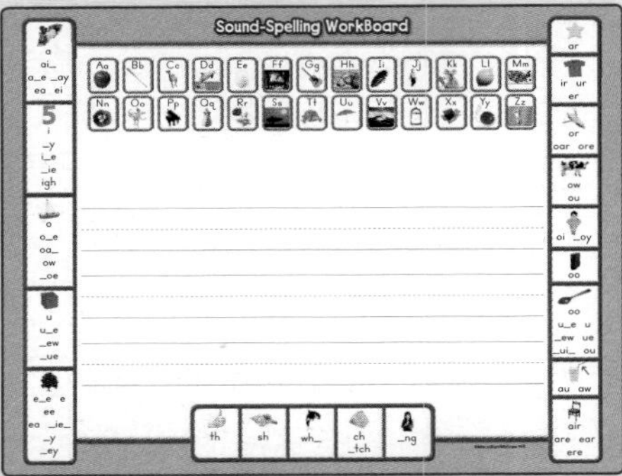
Sound-Spelling WorkBoard

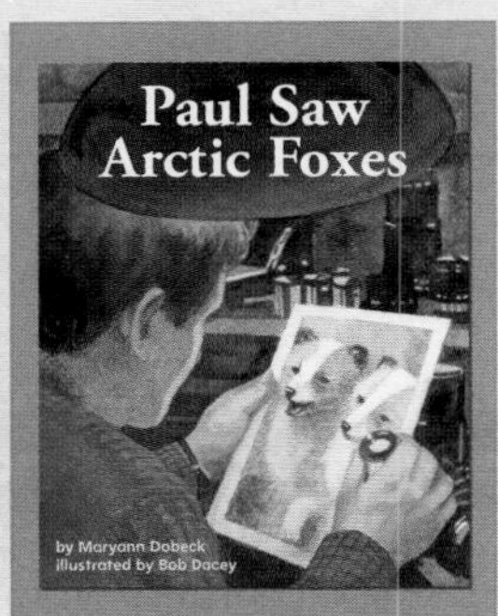
Decodable Reader

ELL

Reread Continue using the Interactive Question-Response Guide Technique to help English Language Learners understand the content of *Paul Saw Artic Foxes*. As you read the text, make the meaning clear by pointing to the pictures, demonstrating word meaning, paraphrasing text, and asking children questions.

Approaching Level

Phonemic Awareness

Objective Segment words into phonemes

Materials
- **Sound Boxes**
- **Teacher's Resource Book**, p. 143
- **Sound-Spelling WorkBoard**
- markers

PHONEME SEGMENTATION

Tier 2

- Distribute copies of the **WorkBoards** and markers. Say a word, stretching each sound for 1½ seconds. Model for children how to drag one marker onto each box for each sound. Then have children repeat and count the number of sounds. Do this for the words *shawl, straw, yawn, flaunt, launch, fault, small, stall, malt*.
- **Link to Spelling** When completed, segment each word again. Then help children replace each marker with the letter or letters that stand for the sound. Help children read the completed words.

Phonics

Objective Decode words with vowel digraph /ô/*a, au, aw*

Materials
- **Decodable Reader:** *Paul Saw Artic Foxes*
- **Sound-Spelling Cards**
- **Word-Building Cards**

SOUND-SPELLING REVIEW

Tier 2

Display the following **Word-Building Cards** one at a time: *au, aw, oo, ou, oo, ui, ew, ue, u, ou, oe, oi, oy, ou, ow, are, air, ear, ere, or, ore, oar, ar*. Have children chorally say each sound.

RETEACH SKILL

- Display the *Straw* **Sound-Spelling Card**. Review that the vowel digraph /ô/ is spelled with the letters *au* or *aw* and sometimes with the letter *a*.
- **Model Blending** Write words and sentences from the chart on page 155G on the board. Model blending using the **Blending Routine**. Have children read each word multiple times.
- **Read in Context** Write the sentences below on the board. Have children chorally read the sentences. Help children blend sounds in decodable words and read vocabulary words.

  Paulie can fetch the ball.
  We saw a deer and its fawn.
  Let's haul and saw the logs.
  Workers assembled the auto.
  Sauce simmered on the stove.
  The hawk's claws held a mouse.
  The astronauts halted on their way to the launch pad.

- **Read the Decodable** Reread *Paul Saw Arctic Foxes* with children. Then have children practice reading the story to a partner.

Approaching Level

High-Frequency/Vocabulary

Objective Read high-frequency and vocabulary words

Materials • **Vocabulary Cards** • **Sound-Spelling WorkBoards** • **High-Frequency Word Cards**

REVIEW WORDS

- Display **High-Frequency Word Cards** for **among**, **bought**, and **decided** and **Vocabulary Cards** for **assembled**, **devoured**, **fetch**, **menu**, and **simmered**. Have children copy each word on their **WorkBoards**. Then help them write sentences for each word. Provide sentence stems or starters, such as *The hot soup* simmered *for* ________ or *Let's play* fetch *with* ________.

CUMULATIVE REVIEW

- Display the High-Frequency and Vocabulary Cards from the previous four to six weeks. Display one card at a time as children chorally read the word. Mix and repeat. Note words children need to review.

Fluency

Objective Read with fluency and comprehension

Materials • **Leveled Reader:** *Saving Sofia* • **Approaching Reproducible**, p. 224

READ FOR FLUENCY

- Tell children that they will be doing a final fluent reading of *Saving Sofia.*
- As they read, note words children mispronounce or struggle to read. Also note their overall use of expression. Use this information to determine if additional instruction is needed on this week's phonics skill and vocabulary words. Send the book home for independent reading.

REREAD PREVIOUSLY READ BOOKS

Tier 2

- Distribute copies of the past six **Leveled Readers**. Tell children that rereading these books will help them develop their skills. The more times they read the same words, the quicker they will learn these words.
- Circulate and listen in as children read. Stop them periodically and ask how they are figuring out difficult words or checking their understanding as they read.
- Have children read other previously read Leveled Readers during independent reading time or for homework.

Meet Grade-Level Expectations

As an alternative to this day's lesson, guide children through a reading of the On Level Leveled Reader. See page 161S. Because both books contain the same vocabulary, phonics, and comprehension skills, the scaffolding you provided will help most children gain access to this more challenging text.

Approaching Reproducible, page 224

As I read, I will pay attention to my expression.

There was something special Sofia wanted to buy.
8 But she needed to earn money fast! So she rushed around
19 doing work.
21 Sofia hung the clothes out to dry. Dad helped, but
31 he paid her a dollar.
36 Sofia washed her brother's car. Her dog Spot helped
45 her. He could **fetch** the hose and spray it, too!
55 Her brother had to help, too. But he still paid her a
67 dollar.
68 Sofia baby-sat for her cousin, Benny. Her aunt was
77 making jam. While it **simmered** on the stove, Sofia helped
87 make a sandwich for Benny. 92

Comprehension Check

1. What can you tell about Sofia's character? **Character** Sofia is clearly determined and hardworking once she sets a goal for herself.
2. Can this story really happen? Explain why or why not. **Fantasy and Reality** Yes, this story can happen. It is very realistic.

	Words Read	–	Number of Errors	=	Words Correct Score
First Read		–		=	
Second Read		–		=	

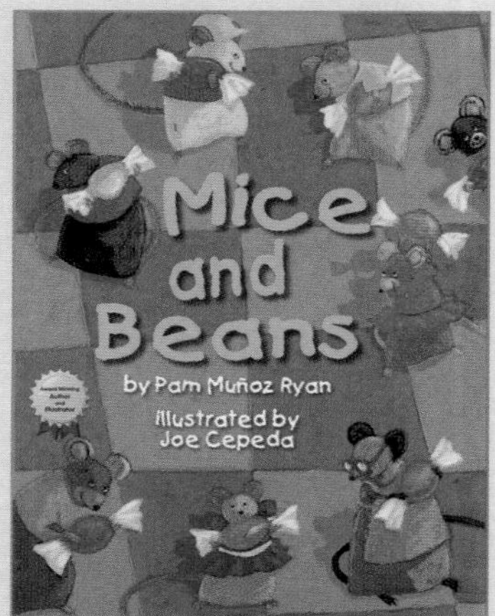

Student Book

On Level

Fluency

Objectives Read aloud with fluency; reread to analyze story structure

Materials • **Student Book:** *Mice and Beans*

REREAD FOR FLUENCY

- Have children reread *Mice and Beans*. Work with children to read with appropriate expression and accuracy. Model fluent reading as needed. Provide time for children to read a section of the text to you. Comment on their accuracy, rate, and expression, and provide corrective feedback.

REREAD FOR STRATEGY

- Review that all stories have characters, a setting, and a beginning, middle, and end. Review that the story structure is how these different parts of the story fit together.
- Have children identify the main character and the setting. Then have them reread the story to tell what this character does in the beginning, middle, and end of the story.

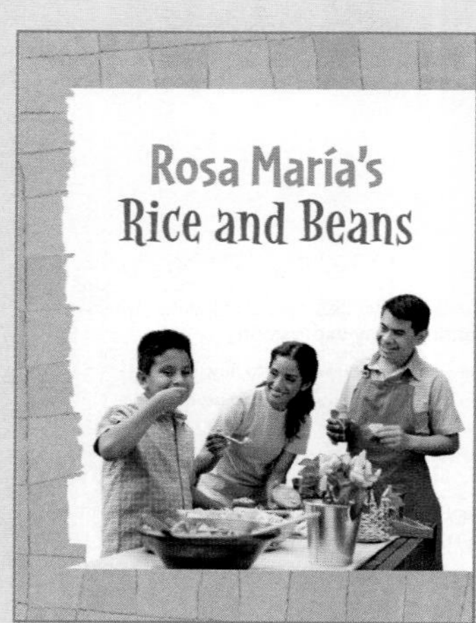

Student Book

Beyond Level

Fluency

Objectives Read aloud with fluency; reread to analyze story structure

Materials • **Student Book:** *Mice and Beans*; "Rosa María's Rice and Beans"

REREAD FOR FLUENCY

- Have children reread *Mice and Beans* and "Rosa María's Rice and Beans." Work with children to read with accuracy and expression.
- Provide time for children to read a section of the text to you. Comment on their expression and provide corrective feedback.

REREAD FOR STRATEGY

- Review that all stories have a structure that includes the characters and setting and a beginning, middle, and end.
- Ask children to work with a partner to determine what happens in the beginning, middle, and end of *Mice and Beans*. Have children create a graphic organizer showing the beginning, middle, and end of the story.

ELL ENGLISH LANGUAGE LEARNERS

Access to Core Content

Content Objective Read grade-level text
Language Objective Discuss text using key words and sentence frames
Materials • **ELL Resource Book**, pp. 262–277

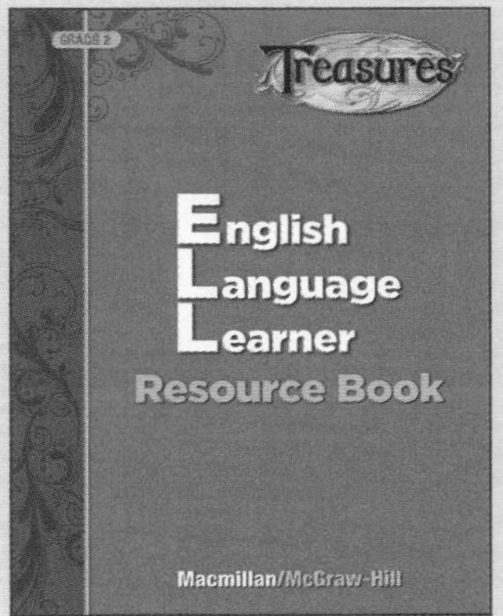

ELL Resource Book

PRETEACH MAIN SELECTION (PAGES 124–153)

All Language Levels

- Use the prompts provided in the guide to develop meaning and vocabulary. Use the partner-talk and whole-class responses to engage children and increase student talk.
- When completed, have partners reread the story.

PRETEACH PAIRED SELECTION (PAGES 156–159)

Use the Interactive Question-Response Guide on **ELL Resource Book** pages 278–279 to preview the paired selection "Rosa María's Rice and Beans." Preteach the selection on **Day 4**.

Leveled Reader Lesson 2

Content Objective Read grade-level text
Language Objective Discuss text using key words and sentence frames
Materials • **ELL Resource Book**, p. 281 • **Leveled Reader:** *The Summer Party*

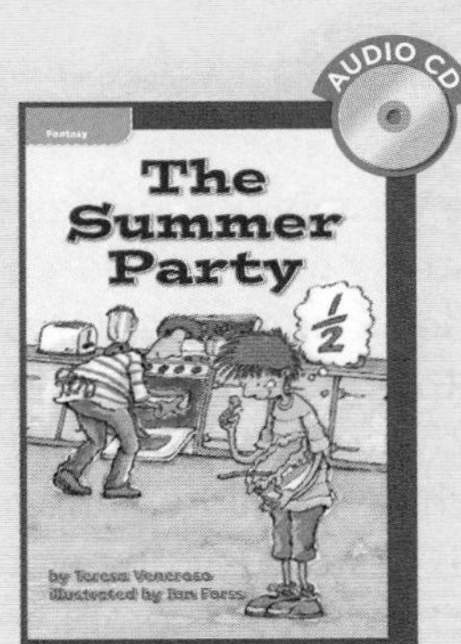

Leveled Reader

AFTER READING

All Language Levels

Book Talk Distribute copies of ELL Resource Book page 271. Children will work with peers of varying language abilities to discuss them. Help students determine who will be the leader for the discussion.

Develop Listening and Speaking Skills

- Share information in cooperative learning interactions. Remind children to work with their partners to retell the story and complete any activities. Ask: *What happened next in the story?*
- Employ self-corrective techniques and monitor their own and other children's language production. Children should ask themselves: What parts of this passage were confusing to me? Can my classmates help me clarify a word or sentence that I don't understand?
- Distinguish between formal and informal English and know when to use each one. Remind children to note whether the selection is written in formal or informal English. Ask: *Why do you think it is written in this way?* Remind children that they may use informal English when speaking with their classmates, but they should use formal language when they talk to teachers or write essays.
- Use high-frequency English words to describe people, places, and objects.

Book Talk

Bringing Groups Together Children will work with peers of varying language abilities to discuss the Book Talk questions. Form groups so that children who read the Beyond Level, On Level, Approaching Level, and English Language Learner readers are in the same group for the activity.

Approaching Level

Oral Language

Objectives Build vocabulary related to food preparation; review oral vocabulary
Materials • chart paper

EXPAND VOCABULARY

- Draw a two-column chart on chart paper. Label the left column *Family Celebration* and the right column *Preparations*. Remind children that this week they read about how Rosa María prepared for her granddaughter's birthday party. They also read about how Ling and her family prepared for the Chinese New Year in *A Lucky New Year.*
- Write *birthday party* in column 1 of the chart and *bake a cake* in column 2. Point to each word, read it, and have children repeat. Ask: *What other celebrations does your family have and how do you prepare for them?*

Family Celebration	Preparations
birthday party	bake a cake, invite guests
Fourth of July	hang streamers, have a BBQ
graduation	plan a party, buy balloons

- Ask children to continue suggesting additional family celebrations and preparations. Add suggestions to the chart.
- Then write the following phrases on the board and read each one aloud: *go shopping, make invitations, clean the house, wrap presents, watch fireworks.* Work with children to determine with which celebration each preparation could belong. Use this information to complete the chart.

REVIEW VOCABULARY

Tier 2

- Use the **Define/Example/Ask** vocabulary routine in the **Instructional Routine Handbook** to review this week's oral vocabulary words: **applause**, **deceive**, **display**, **exquisite**, and **vain**.
- Tell children you are going to start a sentence using one of the words and you want them to think of an ending. For example, say: *The store display showed* ________. Repeat for remaining words.

ELL

Use Visuals Use images and gestures to help children understand the concepts on the board. Encourage all children to contribute to chart. If children answer with gestures or one word, put their words complete sentences, and then rephase for the chart.

Approaching Level

Fluency

Objectives Read aloud with fluency; review high-frequency and vocabulary words

Materials
- **Student Book:** *Mice and Beans*
- **High-Frequency Word Cards**
- **Vocabulary Word Cards**

REREAD FOR FLUENCY

- Have children reread a portion of *Mice and Beans*. Instruct them to focus on two to four of their favorite pages. Work with children to read the pages with accuracy and the appropriate expression and intonation. For example, read each sentence and have children echo. Remind them to read the character's dialogue with expression, the way the character would talk.
- Provide time to listen as children read their sections of text. Comment on their accuracy, expression, and intonation, and provide corrective feedback by modeling proper fluency.

REVIEW HIGH-FREQUENCY/VOCABULARY WORDS

- Display **High-Frequency Word Cards** for **among**, **bought**, and **decided** and **Vocabulary Word Cards** for **assembled**, **devoured**, **fetch**, **menu**, and **simmered**. Model using two or three of the words in a sentence. Then have children come up with their own sentences using two or three of the words.

CUMULATIVE REVIEW

- Display the High-Frequency Word Cards and Vocabulary Word Cards from the previous four weeks. Display one card at a time as children chorally read the word. Mix and repeat. Note words children need to review.

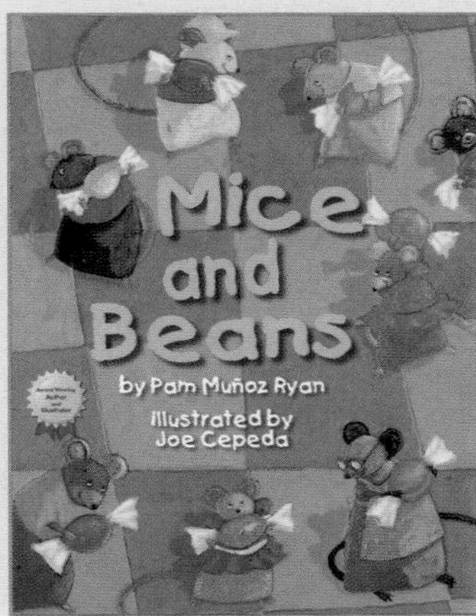

Student Book

Decodable Text

Use the decodable stories in the **Teacher's Resource Book** to help children build fluency with basic decoding patterns.

Self-Selected Reading

Objective Read independently and retell a story read

Materials
- **Leveled Classroom Library**
- other fiction books

APPLY SKILLS TO INDEPENDENT READING

- Have each child to choose a fiction book for independent reading. (See the **Theme Bibliography** on pages T8–T9 for book suggestions.)
- After reading, ask children to use their Fantasy and Reality Charts to orally retell and describe events in the stories. Provide time for children to share their reactions to the books. Ask: *Would you recommend this book to a friend? What do you think your friend would like most about it?*

Approaching

Leveled Classroom Library

See Leveled Classroom Library lessons on pages T2–T7.

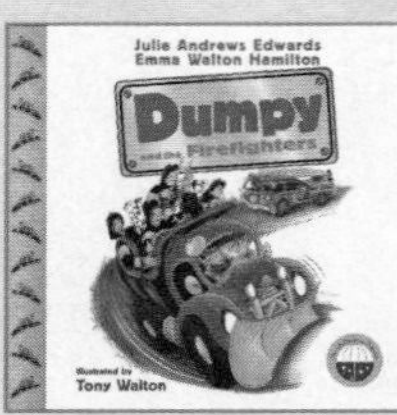

On Level

Leveled Classroom Library

See Leveled Classroom Library lessons on pages T2–T7.

On Level

Self-Selected Reading

Objective Read independently and retell a fiction story

Materials • **Leveled Classroom Library** • other fiction books

APPLY SKILLS TO INDEPENDENT READING

- Have each child choose a fiction book for independent reading. (See the **Theme Bibliography** on pages T8–T9 for book suggestions.)
- After reading, ask children to use their Fantasy and Reality Charts to orally retell the books. Provide time for children to compare their fiction books and to share their reactions to the books. Ask: *Did the story remind you of anything that has happened to you?*

ELL

Share Information Pair English Language Learners with fluent speakers. Have them choose the same book and work together on the Retelling Chart.

Beyond

Leveled Classroom Library

See Leveled Classroom Library lessons on pages T2–T7.

Beyond Level

Self-Selected Reading

Objective Read independently and retell information learned

Materials • **Leveled Classroom Library** • other fiction books

APPLY SKILLS TO INDEPENDENT READING

- Have each child choose a fiction book for independent reading. (See the **Theme Bibliography** on pages T8–T9 for book suggestions.)
- After reading, ask children to use their Fantasy and Reality Charts to write in their Writer's Notebooks about those parts of their selected stories that could be real and those parts that could not. Provide time for children to comment on the books. Ask: *What did you especially like about the story?*

EVALUATE

Gifted and Talented

- Challenge students to discuss how the self-selected books they chose relate to the theme of this unit, Better Together. Ask: *How is it better if we work together?* Have children discuss their views.

ELL ENGLISH LANGUAGE LEARNERS

Fluency

Content Objectives Reread selections to develop fluency; develop speaking skills
Language Objective Tell a partner what a selection is about
Materials • **Decodable Reader:** *Paul Saw Arctic Foxes*
• **Student Book:** *Mice and Beans*, "Rosa María's Rice and Beans"

REREAD FOR FLUENCY

Beginning

Have children read the Decodable Reader.

Intermediate/Advanced

- Have children reread a portion of *Mice and Beans*. Ask them to focus on two to four of their favorite pages from the selection. Work with children to read the pages with accuracy and the appropriate expression. For example, read each sentence of the first three pages and have children echo. Remind them to read the character's words with expression, the way the character would talk.
- Provide time for children to read their sections of text to you. Comment on their expression and provide corrective feedback by modeling proper fluency.

DEVELOP SPEAKING/LISTENING SKILLS

All Language Levels

- Have children practice reading "Rosa María's Rice and Beans." Work with children to read with accuracy and appropriate expression. Provide time for children to read aloud the recipes and directions to a partner. Ask children to tell two things they need to cook rice and beans. Provide the sentence frame *To make rice and beans you need* ________.

Self-Selected Reading

Content Objective Read independently
Language Objective Orally retell information learned
Materials • **Leveled Classroom Library** • other fiction books

APPLY SKILLS AND STRATEGIES TO INDEPENDENT READING

All Language Levels

- Have each child choose a fiction book for independent reading. (See the **Theme Bibliography** on pages T8–T9). After reading, ask children to orally summarize the book. Ask children to share their reactions to the book. Ask: *Would you recommend this book to a classmate? Why or why not?*

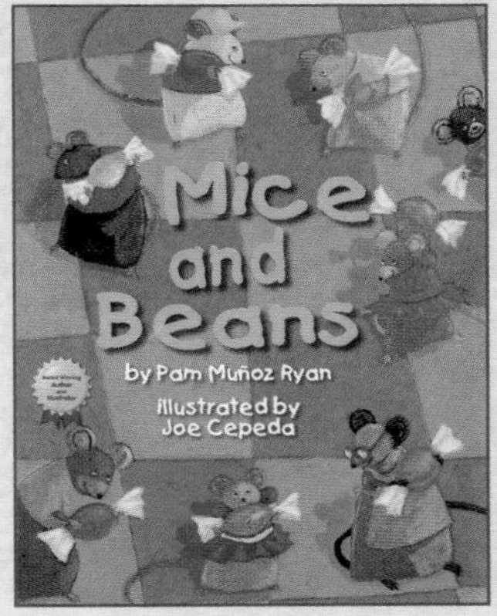

Student Book

Progress Monitoring

Weekly Assessment

ASSESSED SKILLS

- Phonics: Vowel Digraphs *au*, *aw*, *a*; Inflectional Endings *-ed*
- Selection Vocabulary
- Comprehension: Distinguish between Fantasy and Reality
- Grammar: Contractions

Selection Test for* Mice and Beans *Also Available.

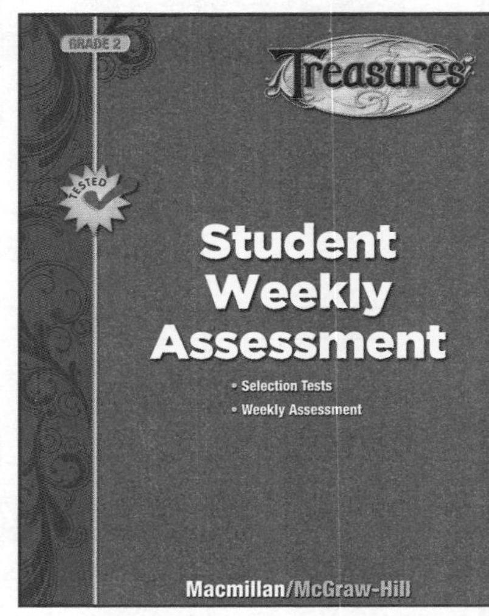

Student Weekly Assessment Unit 4 Week 5

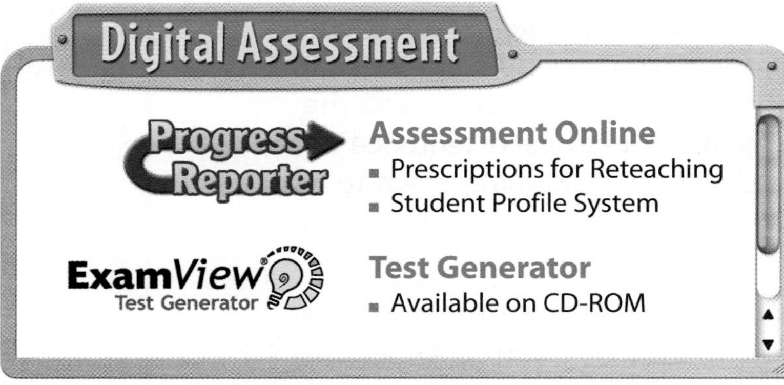

Fluency Assessment

Assess fluency for one group of students per week. Use the Oral Fluency Record Sheet to track the number of words read correctly. Fluency goals for all students:

62–82 words correct per minute (WCPM)

Approaching Level	Weeks 1, 3, 5
On Level	Weeks 2, 4
Beyond Level	Week 6

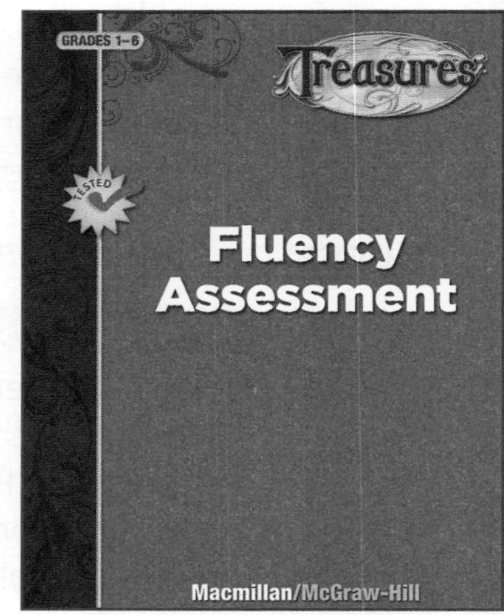

Fluency Assessment

DIBELS LINK

PROGRESS MONITORING

Use your DIBELS results to inform instruction.

IF

DIBELS Oral **R**eading **F**luency (**DORF**) 0–67

THEN

Evaluate for Intervention

TPRI LINK

PROGRESS MONITORING

Use your TPRI scores to inform instruction.

IF

Graphophonemic Knowledge	Still Developing
Reading Fluency/Accuracy	Reading Grade 2, Story 4 Less than 75 WCPM
Reading Comprehension Questions	0–3 correct

THEN

Evaluate for Intervention

Diagnose		Prescribe
Review the assessment answers with students. Have them correct their errors. Then provide additional instruction as needed.		
	IF...	**THEN...**
PHONICS AND SPELLING Vowel Digraphs *au, aw, a* Inflectional Endings *–ed*	0–1 items correct . . .	LOG ON Online Practice: Go to **www.macmillanmh.com.** See **Phonics Intervention Teacher's Edition.** See Sound-Spelling Fluency and mixed review blending lines in upcoming lessons.
VOCABULARY WORDS **VOCABULARY STRATEGY** Word Parts: Inflected Verbs	0–1 items correct . . .	See **Phonics Intervention Teacher's Edition.** SPIRAL REVIEW See Vocabulary review lessons Unit 5, Week 1.
COMPREHENSION Distinguish between Fantasy and Reality	0–1 items correct . . .	See **Comprehension Intervention Teacher's Edition.** SPIRAL REVIEW See Fantasy and Reality lessons Unit 5, Week 4.
GRAMMAR Contractions	0–1 items correct . . .	See the **Grammar and Writing Handbook.**
FLUENCY	53–61 WCPM	AUDIO CD Fluency Solutions Audio CD
	0–52 WCPM	See **Fluency Intervention Teacher's Edition.**

Response to Intervention

To place students in Tier 2 or Tier 3 Intervention use the *Diagnostic Assessment.*

- Phonemic Awareness
- Phonics
- Vocabulary
- Comprehension
- Fluency

Week 6 ★ At a Glance

Review and Assess

Writing Project
- **Expository Writing**
- **Writer's Resources:** Use a Thesaurus

Show What You Know
- **Test Practice**
- **Literacy Activities:** Comprehension, Writing, Word Study

Theme Project
- **Present a Play**
- **Research Strategy:** Use the Library
- **Listening/Speaking**

Computer Literacy
- **Word Processing and Formatting**
- **Importing Text and Graphics**

Media Literacy
- **Exploring E-mail**

Assessment
- **Unit Assessment**

Key

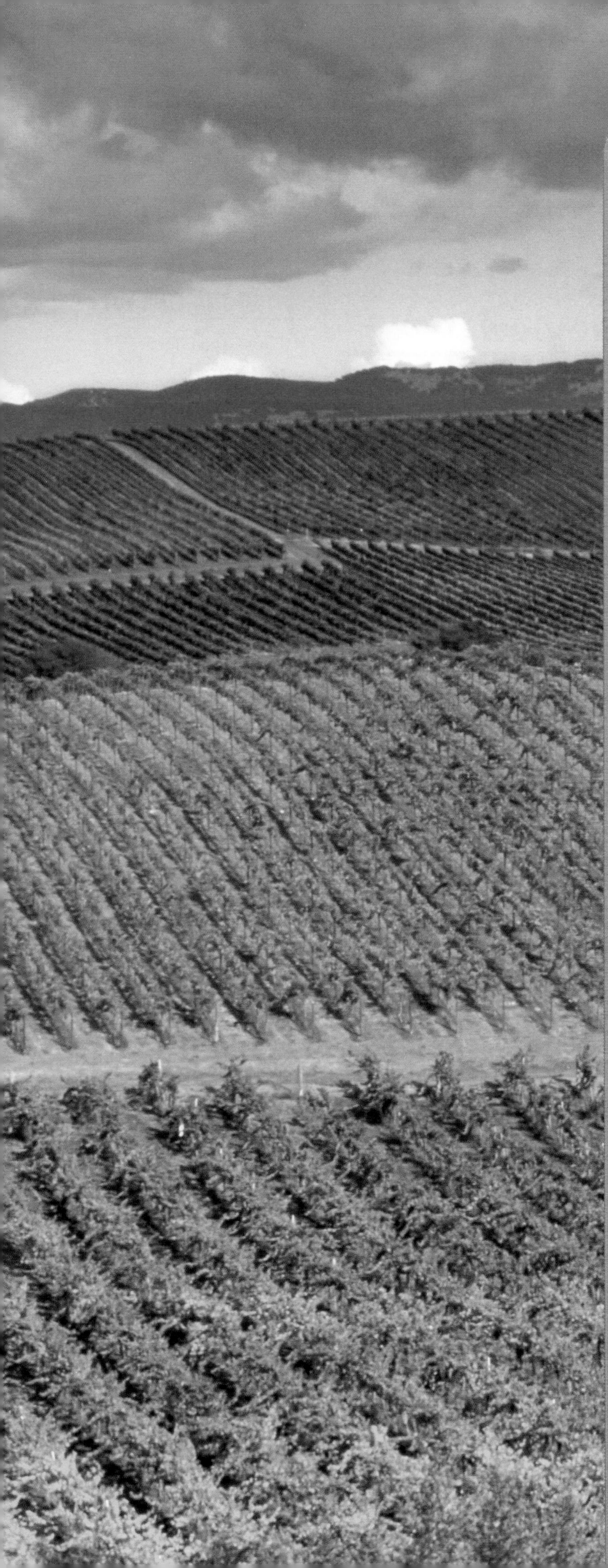

Digital Learning

Digital solutions to help plan and implement instruction.

Teacher Resources

ONLINE www.macmillanmh.com

- **Teacher's Edition**
  - Lesson Planner and Resources also on CD-ROM
- **Formative Assessment**
  - ExamView® on CD-ROM also available
- **Instructional Resources**
  - Unit Videos
  - Classroom Presentation Toolkit
- **Professional Development**
  - Video Library

Student Resources

ONLINE www.macmillanmh.com

- **Interactive Student Book**
- **Leveled Reader Database**
- **Activities**
  - Research Toolkit
  - Oral Language Activities
  - Vocabulary/Spelling Activities

Listening Library

- Recordings of Student Books and Leveled Readers

Fluency Solutions

- Fluency Modeling and Practice

Objectives

- Apply comprehension skills and strategies to new texts
- Apply test-taking strategies to new texts

Materials

- Student Book, pp. 162–165
- Show What You Know, pp. 13–16

Genre

Fiction

Fiction is a made-up story that has characters and events that do not happen in real life.

Setting: is where a story takes place.

Characters: are the people, animals, or things that appear in a story.

Plot: describes the structure of the story. It shows how the events are arranged in a story.

Show What You Know

Spiral Review

Show What You Know provides a spiral review of comprehension and vocabulary skills and strategies previously taught. After reading two selections, children will answer questions that assess reading comprehension and vocabulary.

Skills Review

- Cause and Effect
- Sequence of Events
- Fantasy and Reality
- Character
- Setting
- Synonyms

Read Passage Distribute pages 13–14 from **Show What You Know**. Have children read "Chicken Little" on pages 162 and 163 of the **Student Book**. Once children have completed reading the selection, have them complete the questions. You may wish to read the questions to the children.

Share Your Thinking

After children have completed the assessment, model your own thinking to show them how they can use comprehension strategies and skills, vocabulary strategies and skills, and text features to arrive at correct answers.

Question 1 Character and Setting *Where is Chicken Little at the beginning of the story?* I can locate the stated answer to this question. Chicken little is in the woods at the beginning of this story. (B) RIGHT THERE

Question 2 Cause and Effect *Chicken Little decides to go and see the queen because she—* I can combine the details from different parts of the story to find the stated answer. When Chicken Little sees an acorn fall, she thinks the sky is falling and wants to tell the queen. (A) THINK AND SEARCH

Question 3 Character and Setting *Which word best describes Chicken Little?* I can **connect** the details in this story to the **unstated** answer. Chicken Little thinks the sky is falling and scares many people. This is a silly thing to do. (C) AUTHOR AND ME

Review

Cause and Effect
Sequence of Events
Fantasy and Reality
Character
Setting
Synonyms

Chicken Little

One morning Chicken Little walked through the woods. **PLUNK!** An acorn fell on her head.

Chicken Little clucked, "The sky is falling! I must tell the queen!" She took the acorn with her to prove that the sky was falling.

She had not gone far when—**BUMP!**—she ran into Henny Penny.

Chicken Little clucked, "The sky is falling! We must tell the queen."

Chicken Little and Henny Penny ran. They had not gone far when—**THUMP!**—they bumped into Ducky Lucky.

Chicken Little and Henny Penny clucked, "The sky is falling! We must tell the queen."

Chicken Little, Henny Penny, and Ducky Lucky ran. They had not gone far when—**SCREECH!**—the three friends stopped. Standing before them was Foxy Loxy.

Sly Foxy Loxy smiled, showing his sharp teeth. "Good morning," he said. "What is your hurry?"

Chicken Little clucked, "The sky is falling. We must tell the queen."

Foxy Loxy's smile grew. "I will lead you to the queen," he said.

Chicken Little, Henny Penny, and Ducky Lucky followed Foxy Loxy. That crafty fox led them straight to his den. Before he could eat them, he heard the sounds of the queen coming near. Foxy Loxy was very afraid of the queen. He ran far, far away.

Chicken Little, Henny Penny, and Ducky Lucky told the queen about the sky falling. Chicken Little showed her the acorn.

"Silly animals," said the queen. "The sky is not falling. That acorn simply fell from a tree. Go home and do not worry about the sky anymore."

The three friends marched home and did exactly as the queen said.

Question 4 Synonyms *Sly Foxy Loxy smiled. Which word from the story means the same as* sly? I can **connect** the clues in the story to the **unstated** answer. Foxy Loxy is smart enough to trick the other animals. This means the same as *sly*, or *crafty*. (A) AUTHOR AND ME

Question 5 Sequence of Events *What happens just before the queen comes near? Support your answer with details from the story.* Possible response: Foxy Loxy tells Chicken Little and her friends that he will lead them to the queen, but he leads them to his den instead. THINK AND SEARCH

Use the Short-Answer Reading Rubric on page 198 in the Teacher's Resource Book to score students' written responses.

Pages 13–14

Spiral Review

Read Passage Distribute pages 15–16 from **Show What You Know**. Have children read "Foolish, Timid Rabbit" on pages 164 and 165 of the **Student Book**. Once children have completed reading the selection, have them complete the questions. You may wish to read the questions to the children.

Genre

Fiction

Fiction is a made-up story that has characters and events that do not happen in real life.

Setting: is where a story takes place.

Characters: are the people, animals, or things that appear in a story.

Plot: describes the structure of the story. It shows how the events are arranged in a story.

Share Your Thinking

After children have completed the questions, model your own thinking on how to arrive at correct answers.

Question 1 Sequence of Events *Use the chart to answer the question below. Which idea belongs in the empty box?* This is a chart that tells the important events in the story in the order that they happened. I can **combine** the details in the chart with the details in the story to find the **stated** answer that belongs in the empty box. After a coconut crashes, Rabbit yells and hops away. (C) THINK AND SEARCH

Question 2 Fantasy and Reality *How can you tell that this story is make-believe?* I can **connect** the clues in this story to the **unstated** answer. A rabbit cannot talk in real life, but does in this story, so that is what makes this story make-believe. (C) AUTHOR AND ME

Question 3 Character and Setting *Where does this story take place?* I can **combine** information from different parts of the story to find the **stated** answer. It says Rabbit is sitting under a tree, and that he looks around the forest. This means the story takes place in a forest. (B) THINK AND SEARCH

Question 4 Synonyms *Foolish Rabbit sat under a tree. Which word means the same as foolish?* The answer to this question is **not stated** in the story. I can **connect** the clues in the story to find out which word means *foolish*. Rabbit was frightened by a coconut, and he frightened others as well. This was a *foolish*, or *silly* thing to do. (D) AUTHOR AND ME

Foolish, Timid Rabbit

Foolish, timid Rabbit sat under a coconut tree. He looked around the forest and said, "What will happen to me if the world falls apart?"

KERPLUNK! A coconut crashed behind Rabbit.

Rabbit cried, "The world is falling apart!" He hopped away, yelling loudly.

Soon another rabbit saw him. "What are you yelling about?"

Rabbit cried, "The world is falling apart!" He hopped away, screaming even louder.

Soon the word spread from one rabbit to the next. In no time at all other forest animals heard the scary news. Deer told Buffalo. Buffalo told Rhinoceros. Rhinoceros told Elephant. Now all the animals were running and screaming.

Suddenly Lion stepped quietly from his cave. "Stop a moment, friends. Why are you running so fast?"

"The world is falling apart!" cried Rabbit. "I heard the first piece fall."

Lion nodded wisely. "Show me where it fell," he said.

Rabbit led Lion to the coconut tree.

Lion laughed when he saw the coconut on the ground. "Rabbit," he said. "You only heard a coconut fall. The world is safe and all in one piece. Do not bother the other animals with your nonsense."

"Foolish Rabbit," scolded the other animals. "If not for wise Lion, we would be running away forever."

Question 5 Character and Setting *How are "Chicken Little" and "Foolish, Timid Rabbit" alike? How are they different? Support your answer with details from the stories.* In one story, the main character is a rabbit, and in the other, the main character is a chicken. In both stories, the main character thinks that the world is coming apart because something has fallen from the sky. Both characters tell the other animals what has happened. Both stories take place in the woods or the forest. In "Chicken Little," the Fox lures the other animals into her den to eat them. This does not happen in "Foolish, Timid Rabbit." Both stories end with the lion telling the main character what really fell from a tree. AUTHOR AND ME

Use the Short-Answer Reading Rubric on page 198 in the Teacher's Resource Book to score students' written responses.

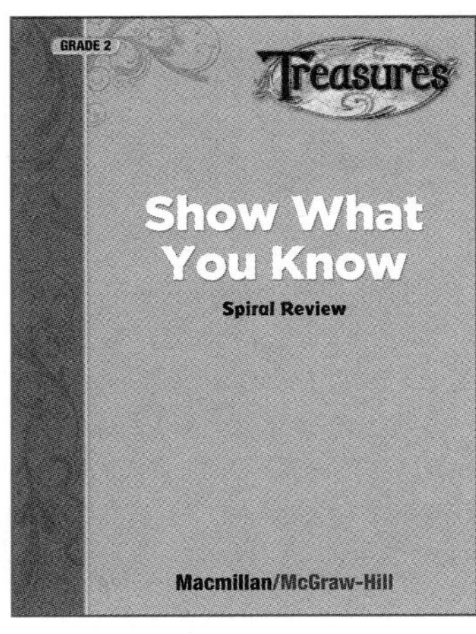

Pages 15–16

Show What You Know

Spiral Review

Show What You Know Unit Review provides a spiral review of the core skill taught in this unit. Children will review by answering questions and completing short, targeted activities.

Have children turn to pages 166 and 167 of the **Student Book**. Have children note their responses on a separate sheet of paper.

Share Your Thinking

Read the questions for each activity in the Student Book with students. If additional review is needed, go back to the lessons in the Teacher's Edition if necessary.

Comprehension: Monitor and Adjust Comprehension Explain to children that when they **monitor** their **comprehension** they make sure they understand what they are reading. If something they are reading does not make sense, they may have missed an important detail. They should make a correction by going back to the text and using background knowledge, creating sensory images, rereading a portion aloud, or generating questions. By doing this, children can make adjustments to their understanding. Read the activity on page 166 of the Student Book. Have children reread parts of the folktale, *Head, Body, Legs*. Then have them write a paragraph about the lesson of the folktale. **To review, see lesson for Monitoring and Adjusting Comprehension on page 8A–8B of the Teacher's Edition.**

Writing: Write a Friendly Letter Have children review the parts of a friendly letter. Read the activity on page 166 of the Student Book. Have children write their letters, paying attention to details and proper conventions. **To review, see lesson for Writing a Friendly Letter on page 83D of the Teacher's Edition.**

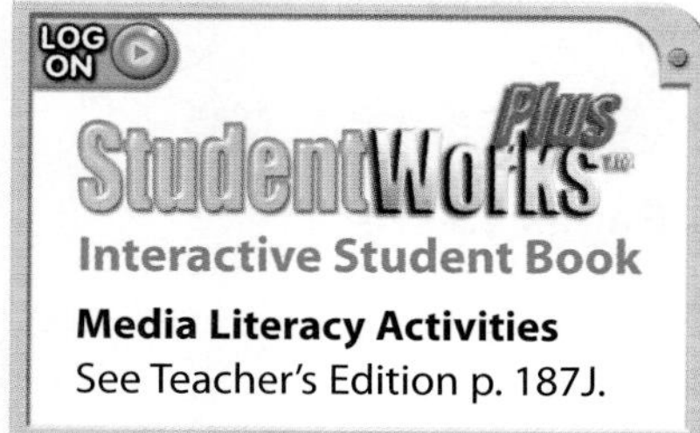

Media Literacy Activities
See Teacher's Edition p. 187J.

Show What You Know ✔ REVIEW

Show What You Know

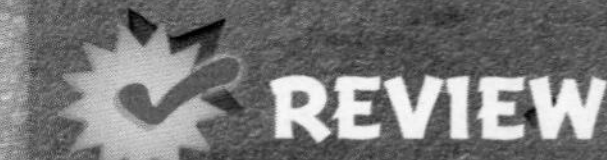

Comprehension

Monitor and Adjust Comprehension

- Good readers monitor and adjust comprehension to better understand text in an article or story. You can monitor comprehension by rereading, using background knowledge, and creating images in your mind.
- With a partner, reread parts of *Head, Body, Legs* on pages 10–35. Discuss with your partner how rereading helps you understand the lesson learned in this folktale.

Writing

Write a Friendly Letter

- Write a letter to a friend or family member about a class project you have worked on. Share details about your story. Be sure to put your ideas in the correct sequence. Include a date, greeting, and closing.

166

REVIEW

Word Study

Phonics

Vowel Digraphs and Diphthongs

- Say each of the following words aloud: *glue, suit, flew, soil, growling, ground, royal,* and *toy*. Review the sound each word makes. Then on a separate piece of paper, list each word. Next to each word write a word that rhymes with it.

Spelling

Words with Vowel Digraphs and Diphthongs

- Review words: *draw, mushroom, crawling, growl, sidewalk, hook, jaw, gnaw, sauce, jigsaw, around, moist,* and *enjoy*. Write each word on a piece of paper.
- On a separate piece of paper, write questions for each word. Then exchange papers with a partner. Ask your partner to answer each question. Have them write and underline the word in their answer.

LOG ON StudentWorks Plus Interactive Student Book Media Literacy Activities www.macmillanmh.com

167

Word Study: Phonics Review vowel digraphs and vowel diphthongs with children. Ask children to name the vowel digraphs and vowel diphthongs they learned. Ask children to explain rhyming words and give examples of some. Read the activity on page 167 of the Student Book. Have children use their knowledge of vowel digraphs and diphthongs to write rhyming words. **To review, see lessons for Phonics on pages 43C–43D and 78C–78D of the Teacher's Edition.**

Word Study: Spelling Ask children to name and spell some spelling words and words with the same spelling patterns they learned in this unit. Read the activity on page 167 of the Student Book. Have children complete the activity independently. Then have a partner check their work. **To review, see lessons for Spelling on pages 43E and 78E of the Teacher's Edition.**

Expository Writing

Read Like a Writer

Read the following excerpt from *Super Storms* by Seymour Simon. Explain that this article is an example of expository writing, and this part of the selection gives information about tornadoes. Ask children to listen for

- the **main idea**
- **facts** and **details** that tell about tornadoes

"Super Storms"

Thunderstorms sometimes give birth to tornadoes. Inside a storm, a funnel-shaped cloud reaches downward. Winds inside a tornado can spin faster than 300 miles per hour. These winds can lift cars off the ground and rip houses apart.

Discuss the Features

After reading, discuss where the writer may have found his information about tornadoes, such as from books, magazines, and encyclopedias. Point out that he summarized the information in his own words. Then discuss the following questions with children:

- **What is the main idea of the paragraph?** (Thunderstorms sometimes create tornadoes.)
- **What important facts and details about tornadoes does the writer give?** (Tornadoes are funnel-shaped. Their winds can spin faster than 300 miles per hour. They can lift cars and rip apart houses.)

Objectives

- Identify features of expository writing
- Prewrite/plan and organize ideas for an expository paragraph
- Draft, revise, edit, proofread, and publish an expository paragraph
- Write brief compositions about topics of interest to the student

Materials

- Transparencies 19–24
- Teacher's Resource Book, pp. 191, 206, 221–224

Features of Expository Writing

- is written using the **writer's own words**
- includes the **main idea** about a topic
- supports the main idea with **facts** and **details**

ELL

Graphic Organizer
Group children together to create a main idea and details graphic organizer about the excerpt from *Super Storms*. Once they have created bubbles for the details, help children add bubbles with other details they know that tell about tornadoes.

Plan/Prewrite

Set a Purpose Remind children that the purpose of expository writing is to give important information about a topic and to support the main idea with facts and details.

Know the Audience Have children think about who will read their expository paragraphs, such as classmates and family members. *What do you want your readers to learn?*

Choose a Topic Help each child choose a science topic, such as rain, earthquakes, the moon, or volcanoes. Children can look at pictures and books to find an idea that interests them. Then have them read about their topics in an encyclopedia or other informational sources from the school or classroom library. As they read, ask: *What do you want to explain about your topic? What questions do you want to answer? What kind of information will you look for?*

Remind children to **focus** and **plan** their expository writing by choosing a main idea and details.

Minilesson Organization

Display **Unit Writing Transparency 19** and tell children they will follow Austin's progress as he writes an expository paragraph about earthquakes. Discuss the following features of Austin's Main Idea and Details Web:

- He gives his **main idea** first.
- He lists **facts** about what causes earthquakes.
- He writes each fact in his own words.

Organize Ideas Have children create a Main Idea and Details Web to plan their expository paragraphs. Use the transparency to demonstrate how to group together related ideas and maintain a consistent focus.

Peer Review

Think, Pair, Share Have partners discuss their Main Idea and Details Webs. Ask them to think about whether or not the details on each web help explain the main idea. Let children share how the discussion helped them.

Flexible Pairing Option Pair children who have written about similar topics.

Writing Topic

We are surrounded by interesting plants, natural formations, and animals. Think about one aspect of nature that interests you. *What would you like to learn about that topic?* Write an expository paragraph about that topic.

Extra Support

For children who need additional support, guide them through the writing process. Use graphic organizers, Teacher Write Alouds, small group work, and Anchor Papers to help scaffold the writing process.

Transparency 19

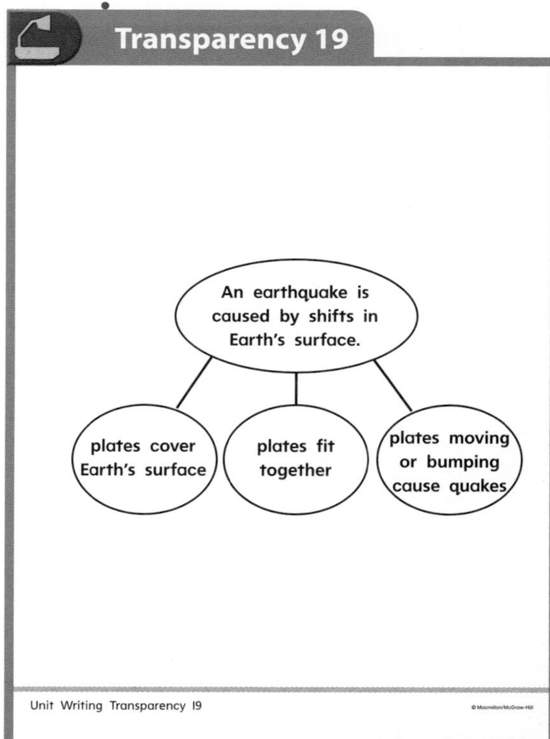

Unit Writing Transparency

ELL

Activate Background Knowledge Have English learners get together in a small group to talk about what they already know or have observed about their topics. As necessary, ask more fluent speakers to help others express their ideas.

Draft

Minilesson **Support Main Ideas with Facts**

Display **Unit Writing Transparency 20** and point out the following details in Austin's first draft:

- Austin maintains a coherent focus by making sure that every sentence in his paragraph is about earthquakes.
- The **facts** help readers understand what causes earthquakes.
- He writes the paragraph in his **own words**.

Tell children that Austin will have the chance to revise and proofread his draft in later stages of the writing process.

Check Your Main Idea and Details Web Have children review their Main Idea and Details Webs. Explain that they should first plan the order in which they want to present the details and facts. They can write one or two sentences about each fact and detail.

Write the Draft Remind children that the purpose of writing a first draft is to get the important information on paper. Share the following tips with children as they begin to write:

- Describe the main topic in the first sentence.
- Include all of the important facts from your web.
- Use your own words to summarize your sources.

Transparency 20

What causes an earthquake?

by Austin C.

An earthquake is caused by shifts in Earth's surface. Earthquakes are scary. Earth's surface made of plates. The plates fit together. When the plates move or bump together they caus an earthquake. Then the ground shakes.

Unit Writing Transparency 20 ©Macmillan/McGraw-Hill

Unit Writing Transparency

Writer's Resources

Use a Thesaurus

Point out that when children write their reports, they will need to change words so they do not copy from a source. Write this sentence on the board: *An earthquake is caused by shifts in the earth's surface*. Point out that Austin wanted to find another word for *shifts*, so he looked it up in a thesaurus. He found these synonyms: *move, swing, stir, budge, movement, relocation, change, step*. He decided that *movement* sounded best. Then he changed the order of words. Now the sentence says: *An earthquake is caused by movements of Earth's surface*.

As children write drafts, have them underline or circle words they want to change in order not to copy from the source. During revision, they can find substitutes in the thesaurus.

Evaluate and Revise

Minilesson Revise

Display **Unit Writing Transparency 21** and point out how Austin revises a good expository paragraph to make it excellent.

- In the first line he changes *shift* to *movement* so as not to copy his source. (Word Choice)
- He takes out the third sentence because it does not support the main idea. (Focus and Coherence)
- He adds a comparison to give the reader a better idea of how the plates fit together. (Development of Ideas)

Tell children that Austin will need to proofread his writing to make final corrections.

Guide children to think about the following writing elements as they evaluate and revise their expository paragraphs.

Development of Ideas Do you pay attention to **details**? Do you offer **facts** that support the **main idea**? Do you remove any sentences that are off topic?

Organization Does your paragraph tell the **main idea** in the first sentence? Do you support the main idea with **details** in the other sentences?

Voice and Word Choice Do you sound sure of your facts? Do you use formal language? Do you use your own words to explain facts?

Sentence Fluency *Do your sentences flow together? Do you use a variety of sentence types?*

Peer Review

Think, Pair, Share Ask each child to read his or her draft aloud to a partner. Then have the listener restate the information. If the listener has difficulty, the writer should read the paragraph again. Tell partners to focus on whether or not the information in the paragraph is easy to understand.

Flexible Pairing Option Group children of similar writing abilities.

ELL

Share Visual Information
Have pairs of English learners draw and share pictures relating to their report topics. Partners can use the pictures to generate specific words and phrases for writers to use in their reports.

TEACHER-DEVELOPED RUBRICS

Use the rubric reproducible found in the **Teacher's Resource Book** on page 206 to create your own rubric. Model for children how to use the rubric as they revise and edit their writing.

Transparency 21

What causes an earthquake?

by Austin C.

An earthquake is caused by ~~shifts in~~ movement of Earth's surface. ~~Earthquakes are scary.~~ Earth's surface made of plates. The plates fit together like very big puzzle pieces. When the plates move or bump together they caus an earthquake. Then the ground shakes.

Unit Writing Transparency 21

Unit Writing Transparency

Speaking and Listening

Share these strategies with the group.

SPEAKING STRATEGIES

- Speak in a loud, clear voice.
- Speak at a good pace, pausing at commas and the end of sentences.
- Make eye contact.

LISTENING STRATEGIES

- Look at the person who is speaking.
- Listen attentively.
- Wait until the speaker is finished to ask questions about anything you don't understand or want to know more about.

Transparency 22

What causes an earthquake?

by Austin C.

An earthquake is caused by [movement of] ~~shifts in~~ Earth's surface. ~~Earthquakes are scary.~~ Earth's surface [is] made of plates. The plates fit together [like very big puzzle pieces]. When the plates move or bump together[,] they caus[e] an earthquake. Then the ground shakes.

Unit Writing Transparency 22 ©Macmillan/McGraw-Hill

Unit Writing Transparency

Edit/Proofread

Minilesson Conventions

Review the proofreading marks on page 191 of the **Teacher's Resource Book** and the rubric you developed with children. Then display **Unit Writing Transparency 22** to discuss Austin's proofreading and editing.

- He capitalizes the important words in the title.
- He corrects the linking verb *is made*.
- He corrects the spelling of *cause*.
- He checks the punctuation of all his sentences.

Have children read and reread their own expository paragraphs to find and correct mistakes.

Peer Review

Think, Pair, Share Ask children to pay particular attention to capital letters and verbs as they look for corrections that need to be made in their partners' edited drafts. Have partners share how they helped one another.

TEACHER CONFERENCE

Use the rubric on page 167G to evaluate children's writing and help you formulate questions to foster self-assessment.

- What is the main idea of your paragraph?
- How does your first sentence introduce the main idea?
- What facts did you include to support the main idea?
- Did you write each fact in your own words?

Publish

Ask children to make final copies of their expository paragraphs to place in a class encyclopedia for use as a reference. Remind them to write legibly and leave space for left and right margins.

PRESENTATION Direct children to make illustrations to support the facts in their paragraphs, which they will share orally.

Author's Chair Have children sit in the Author's Chair and read their expository paragraphs aloud and answer peers' questions.

Using Rubrics

READ AND SCORE

Display **Unit Writing Transparency 23** and ask children to follow along as you read aloud. Ask children to tell what they think or feel about the writing. Then have them use the rubrics they created to assess the writing sample.

Guide children to understand that this report is only a fair writing sample and that they will work together in groups to improve it.

RAISE THE SCORE

Place children in small groups to revise their expository paragraphs. Point out the following problems in the writing sample to help them get started.

Ideas and Content Some of the details are not about the moon or are not facts.

Organization The first sentence does not identify the topic or tell the main idea.

Word Choice and Voice The writing does not sound authoritative; it includes feelings and opinions.

SHARE AND COMPARE

Have groups share their revised expository paragraphs with the class. Let children use their rubrics to assess the improved versions. Then display **Unit Writing Transparency 24** to show the same expository paragraph written at an excellent level. Point out that although paragraphs may vary, different versions could receive an excellent rating. Have children review their own expository paragraphs and raise their scores.

Objective

- **Revise an expository paragraph to raise the writing score from a 2 to a 4**

CREATE A RUBRIC

Review the features of an expository paragraph. Then let children use the blank rubric form (on page 206 in the **Teacher's Resource Book**) to create a rubric for scoring an expository paragraph. Children's rubrics should show the criteria for all four levels.

Transparency 24

The Moon

by Caleb B.

The moon is Earth's closest neighbor. It is the only thing in space that goes around Earth. The moon is the brightest thing in the night sky. It gets its light from the sun. From Earth, the moon seems to change shape. The different shapes that we see are called phases.

Unit Writing Transparency 24

Unit Writing Transparency

4-Point Expository Writing Rubric

Use this four-point rubric to assess children's writing.

4-POINT SCORING RUBRIC			
4 Excellent	3 Good	2 Fair	1 Unsatisfactory
Focus and Coherence Gives interesting and detailed information about a central topic.	**Focus and Coherence** Gives information about a central topic.	**Focus and Coherence** Gives information about a topic, but may stray from focus.	**Focus and Coherence** Does not give information about a central topic.
Organization Presents a main idea that is supported by clear details.	**Organization** Presents a main idea and supports it with details.	**Organization** Omits a main idea or offers few supporting details.	**Organization** Does not present a main idea supported by details.
Development of Ideas/ Word Choice Throughly develops ideas. Uses precise word choice to enhance quality of content.	**Development of Ideas/ Word Choice** Attempts to develop ideas. Uses word choice to suit the purpose.	**Development of Ideas/ Word Choice** Attempts to develop ideas, but may be inconsistent. Chooses words that are often ill-suited for the purpose.	**Development of Ideas/ Word Choice** Provides little or no development of ideas. Omits or fails to use chosen words correctly.
Voice Uses a personal voice that adds an inviting, unique tone to the writing.	**Voice** Uses a personal voice that generally expresses an inviting, unique tone.	**Voice** Writer has difficulty expressing an inviting, unique tone.	**Voice** Writer does not express a personal voice.
Conventions/Sentence Fluency Writing is almost entirely free of mechanical, grammatical, and spelling errors. Sentences flow from one to the other.	**Conventions/Sentence Fluency** Spelling, capitalization, punctuation, and usage are mostly correct. Sentences lead naturally to those that follow.	**Conventions/Sentence Fluency** Makes mistakes that can interfere with the reading of the writing. Sentences flow in a somewhat fluid manner.	**Conventions/Sentence Fluency** Makes frequent errors in grammar, spelling, mechanics, and usage. Sentences run together or are confusing.
Presentation Handwriting or typing is neat, consistent, and error-free.	**Presentation** Handwriting is neat and mostly consistent. Spacing is used between words and at the end of sentences.	**Presentation** Handwriting is difficult to read. Spacing between words is inconsistent	**Presentation** Handwriting is illegible. Spacing is not used correctly.

Portfolio

Instruct children to place their published expository paragraphs in their portfolios. Remind children that portfolios should include more than just finished work. Have children review and evaluate their personal collection of work to determine progress and set goals for improvement. They can also discuss their work with teachers and parents/caregivers. Have them jot down ideas for future writing assignments or tell what they learned about expository writing to include in their portfolios.

Anchor Papers

Use these Anchor Papers in the **Teacher's Resource Book** to evaluate student writing.

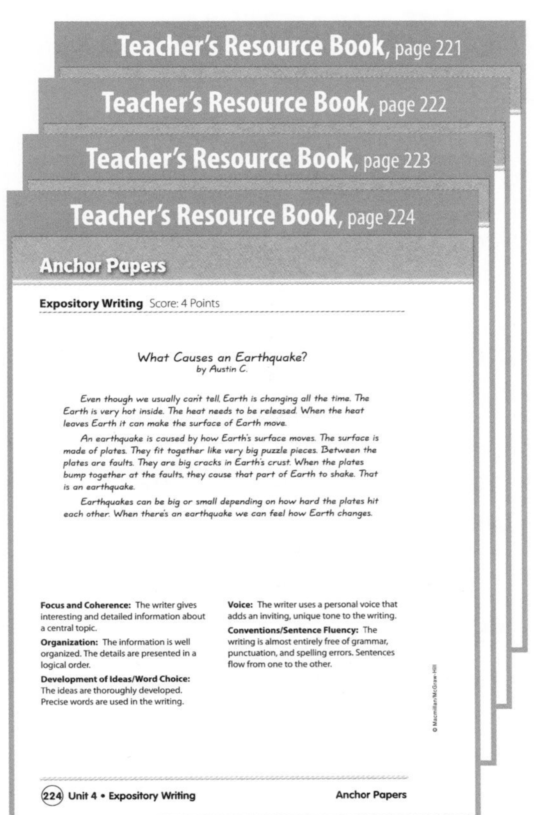

Teacher's Resource Book, page 221

Teacher's Resource Book, page 222

Teacher's Resource Book, page 223

Teacher's Resource Book, page 224

Anchor Papers

Expository Writing Score: 4 Points

What Causes an Earthquake?
by Austin C.

Even though we usually can't tell, Earth is changing all the time. The Earth is very hot inside. The heat needs to be released. When the heat leaves Earth it can make the surface of Earth move.

An earthquake is caused by how Earth's surface moves. The surface is made of plates. They fit together like very big puzzle pieces. Between the plates are faults. They are big cracks in Earth's crust. When the plates bump together at the faults, they cause that part of Earth to shake. That is an earthquake.

Earthquakes can be big or small depending on how hard the plates hit each other. When there's an earthquake we can feel how Earth changes.

Focus and Coherence: The writer gives interesting and detailed information about a central topic.

Organization: The information is well organized. The details are presented in a logical order.

Development of Ideas/Word Choice: The ideas are thoroughly developed. Precise words are used in the writing.

Voice: The writer uses a personal voice that adds an inviting, unique tone to the writing.

Conventions/Sentence Fluency: The writing is almost entirely free of grammar, punctuation, and spelling errors. Sentences flow from one to the other.

224 Unit 4 • Expository Writing　　Anchor Papers

Short-Answer Reading Rubric

Use the Short-Answer Reading Rubric to score students' short-answer responses to the weekly Comprehension Check questions and the short answer questions on weekly and unit assessments.

SHORT-ANSWER READING RUBRIC			
3 Excellent	2 Good	1 Fair	0 Unsatisfactory
Gives an interesting and detailed response strongly supported by text evidence.	Gives a clear and reasonable response supported by text evidence.	Gives a reasonable but vague response weakly connected to text evidence.	Does not respond to the question.

Evidence may be specific words from the story or a retelling.

Computer Literacy

Word Processing and Formatting

Objectives

- Learn about word processing formatting
- Write and edit in a word processing document
- Learn to import text and graphics into a word processing document

Materials

- www.macmillanmh.com
- word processing program

Vocabulary

center button a button on the toolbar that aligns the text to the center of a document

bold button a button in the toolbar that makes selected text darker

highlight to select text by using the mouse

font size the size of the text in a word processing document, indicated by points (12 points, 14 points, etc.)

Computer Literacy
Focus on Keyboard and Internet Skills and Media Literacy
www.macmillanmh.com

Remind children to never change another person's work on the computer without permission.

ACCESS PRIOR KNOWLEDGE

- *How does using a computer make writing easier?* (It makes it easy to create neat, organized documents quickly.)
- *What parts of writing are easier to do with a computer?*

EXPLAIN

Introduce the lesson vocabulary by writing each word on the board and asking for its definition.

- Tell children that when they type on the computer, there are buttons that allow them to change the way the text looks, like the **center button** and the **bold button**.
- When you **highlight** text, you select it so that you can change it using the toolbar and menu bar.
- You can also change **font size**, which is how big (or small) the letters you type will be.

MODEL

- Open a word processing document. Key in your name.
- Show children how to highlight the text and click the bold, italic, and underline buttons on the toolbar.

Technology Makes a Difference

Importing Text and Graphics

- Explain to children that they can add text and graphics from other sources to their word processing documents.
- Open a word processing document and click on "insert" from the menu bar. Insert a piece of clip art into the document.
- Open another document you have created. Highlight a piece of text from the page, copy the text, and paste it into the original document.

Media Literacy

Exploring E-mail

ACCESS PRIOR KNOWLEDGE

Discuss with children:

- *Have you ever sent a letter to someone through the United States Postal Service? If you have, how long did it take your letter to reach its destination?*
- *How many of you have sent a letter on a computer using e-mail?*

EXPLAIN

- Tell students that **e-mail** allows us write and send messages over a computer system or **network**. The term *e-mail* is short for **electronic mail**.
- E-mail is sent over the **Internet**. The computer allows e-mail to be sent very quickly and at no cost to users.
- E-mail is one of the most important communication **inventions** of the 20th century.
- Schools, business, organizations, and Internet companies all provide **e-mail addresses**. The common formula for e-mail addresses is username@emailhost.com.
- The United States Postal Service estimates that it handles 212 billion pieces of mail every year. Nearly that many e-mails are sent *every day*.

MODEL

- With children, compose a letter to your school principal about a subject of your choice. Address the letter, place a stamp on the envelope and place the letter in the mailbox. Ask the principal to reply to the letter via mail.
- Using a classroom or lab computer, write an e-mail to the principal with the children. Point out the to and from fields as well as the subject line and the recipient's e-mail address to children. Send the e-mail. Arrange for your principal to send a prompt response to illustrate how quickly e-mail works.

Objectives

- **Identify written conventions for using digital media**
- **Understand the nature of online interpersonal communication**

Materials

- **Computer with e-mail access**

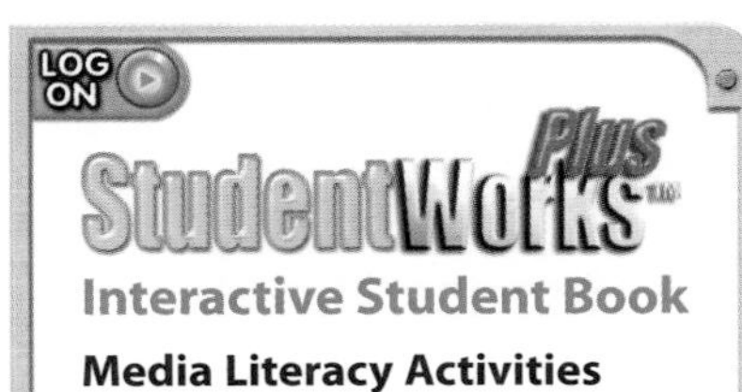

Interactive Student Book

Media Literacy Activities
Lessons that help children to identify various written conventions for using digital media.

Theme Project Wrap-Up

Research and Inquiry

After children complete Steps 1 through 3 of their projects, have them work on the following:

Create the Presentation

Have children give oral presentations about their theme projects. Tell children to explain why they chose their topic and describe the plot of their plays. Remind children to speak clearly and at an appropriate pace. Use the questions below to help you and children evaluate their research and presentations.

Teacher Checklist

Assess the Research Process

Planning the Project

✔ Asked open-ended research questions about teams.

✔ Used books and magazines as informational sources.

Doing the Project

✔ Decided what sources of information could best answer the research question.

✔ Used text features to locate information.

Assess the Presentation

Speaking

✔ Presented information and ideas in a logical sequence.

✔ Spoke clearly at an appropriate pace.

Representing

✔ Created a dramatization to present information.

✔ Used visuals to add details and interest.

Assess the Listener

Listening

✔ Listened attentively to others.

✔ Asked relevant questions to clarify understanding.

Children's Checklist

Research Process

✔ What was the most valuable informational source?

✔ Did you use text features, such as tables of contents, to locate information?

Presenting

Speaking

✔ Did you present information in a logical sequence?

✔ Did you speak in a clear voice?

✔ Did you stay focused on your topic during the presentation?

Representing

✔ Did you pass around your visuals for everyone to see?

✔ Did you give credit for the ideas, images, and information of others?

SCORING RUBRIC FOR THEME PROJECT			
4 Excellent	3 Good	2 Fair	1 Unsatisfactory
The child • presents the information clearly. • includes many details. • may make sophisticated observations.	The child • clearly fulfills all the steps of the project. • provides adequate details. • may make several relevant observations.	The child • attempts to present some of the steps of the project. • may offer few or vague supporting details. • may make few or irrelevant personal observations.	The child • may not grasp the task. • may present incomplete, incorrect, or irrelevant information. • may have extreme difficulty with research or organization.

Home-School Connection

Teamwork Makes It Happen Day provides an excellent opportunity for home and community involvement.

- Invite family members, other children, and members of the community to the presentation of the projects. Have children write thank-you notes, following conventions, to all the guests.
- Children presenting may give the audience instructions to follow, and listeners may need to restate the directions in order to follow them. Remind presenters to allow time for audience involvement.
- Videotape the presentations for family members to borrow or to show at the parent/teacher conferences.
- As part of your character-building feature, have children present their project to younger classes in the school. Be sure to include a question-and-answer period about fairness and responsibility when working together on a team.

Big Question Wrap-Up

Review the Big Question with children. Have them use their Foldables™ and what they learned to help them respond to the following questions: *Why is it sometimes helpful to work in teams? What are some things you can achieve working with other people that you could not achieve alone?*

Monitoring Progress

End-of-Unit Assessment

Administer the Test

Unit 4 TEST
TESTED SKILLS AND STRATEGIES
COMPREHENSION STRATEGIES AND SKILLS
• Strategies: Monitor comprehension: reread, read ahead; analyze text structure
• Skills: Cause and effect; use illustrations; sequence of events; distinguish between fantasy and reality
VOCABULARY STRATEGIES
• Context clues
• Word parts
• Dictionary
PHONICS
• Diphthong *ou, ow, oi, oy*
• Vowel digraph *au, aw, ew, oe, oo, ou, u, ui*
• Inflectional endings *-s, -es, -ing, -ed*
• Prefixes *re-, un-, dis-*
• Suffixes *-ful, -less*
TEXT FEATURES AND STUDY SKILLS
• Drop-down menu
• Floor plan
• Using the Internet
• Written directions
GRAMMAR, MECHANICS, USAGE
• Linking verbs
• Capitalization
• Helping verbs
• Quotation marks
• Irregular verbs
• Book titles
• Letter punctuation
• Contractions
• Apostrophes
WRITING
• Expository: Composition

Use Multiple Assessments for Instructional Planning

To create instructional profiles for your children, look for patterns in the results from any of the following assessments.

Fluency Assessment

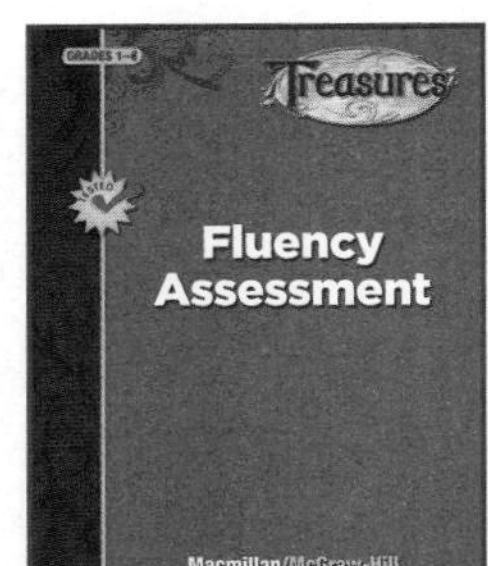

Gather results from the Fluency tests administered throughout the unit to plan appropriate fluency-building activities and practice.

Running Records

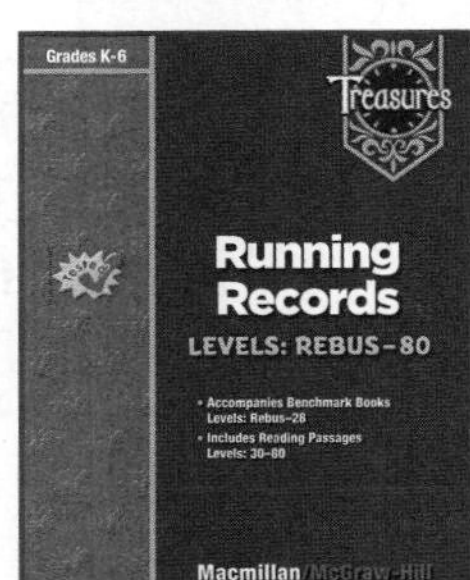

Use the instructional reading level determined by the Running Record calculations for regrouping decisions.

Benchmark Assessment

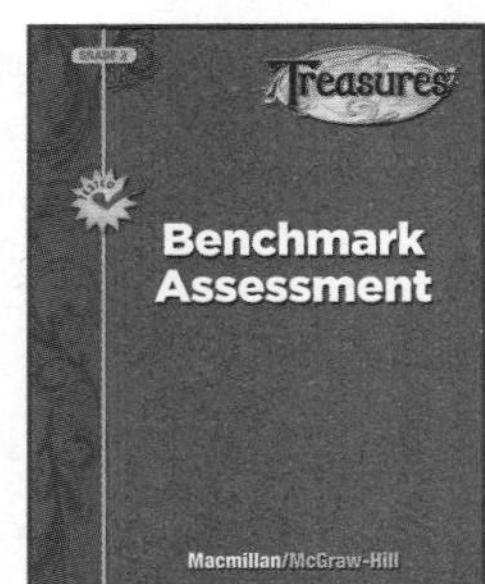

Administer tests three times a year as an additional measure of both children's progress and the effectiveness of the instructional program.

Digital Assessment

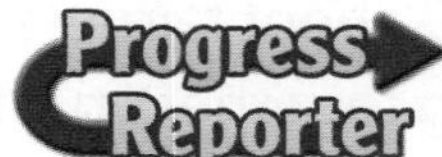

Assessment Online
- Prescriptions for Reteaching
- Student Profile System

Test Generator
- Available on CD-ROM

Analyze the Data

Use information from a variety of informal and formal assessments, as well as your own judgment, to assist in your instructional planning. Children who consistently score at the lowest end of each range should be evaluated for Intervention. Use the **Diagnostic Assessment** for guidelines for decision making.

Diagnose		Prescribe
ASSESSMENTS	**IF...**	**THEN...**
UNIT TEST	0–21 questions correct	Reteach tested skills using the **Intervention Teacher's Edition**.
FLUENCY ASSESSMENT		
Oral Reading Fluency	53–61 WCPM 0–52 WCPM	Fluency Solutions Reteach using the **Fluency Intervention Teacher's Edition**.
RUNNING RECORDS	Level 18 or below	Reteach comprehension and Fluency skills using the **Comprehension Intervention Teacher's Edition**. Provide additional Fluency activities.

DIBELS LINK

PROGRESS MONITORING

Use your DIBELS results to inform instruction.

IF...

DIBELS Oral **R**eading **F**luency (**DORF**) 0–67

THEN...

Evaluate for Intervention

TPRI LINK

PROGRESS MONITORING

Use your TPRI scores to inform instruction.

IF...

Graphophonemic Knowledge	Still Developing
Reading Fluency/Accuracy	Reading Grade 2, Story 4 less than 75 WCPM
Reading Comprehension Questions	0–3 correct

THEN...

Evaluate for Intervention

Response to Intervention

To place children in Tier 2 or Tier 3 Intervention use the *Diagnostic Assessment*.

- Phonemic Awareness
- Phonics
- Vocabulary
- Comprehension
- Fluency

Glossary

Glossary

INTRODUCE
Introduce children to the Glossary by asking them to look through the pages, describing and discussing what they see there.

EXPLAIN
Explain that the Glossary will help them find out the meanings of words. Point out that words in a glossary, like words in a dictionary, are listed in **alphabetical order**. Have children note the order of the pairs of large capital and lowercase letters, and also have them note that all the words listed below a particular letter begin with that letter. Have a child name a letter, then have children turn to that letter in the Glossary. Read aloud with children the words listed under the letter.

Point out the **guide words** at the top of each page and explain that these words tell the first word and the last word that appear on the page.

ENTRIES
Point out the **entry words**. Ask children to note that each entry word is printed in heavy black type and that it appears on a line by itself. Also point out that each entry word is used in a sentence. Some of the entry words have photographs. Mention that there are two sentences for some entry words; in such cases, the second sentence includes a word that has the same meaning as the entry word.

Activity

Have children make a list of entry words that might appear on the pages with the following guide words:

- Airplane/Bear
- Goat/Little
- Tiny/Trucks

Glossary

What Is a Glossary?

A glossary can help you find the **meanings** of words. If you see a word that you don't know, try to find it in the glossary. The words are in **alphabetical order**. **Guide words** at the top of each page tell you the first and last words on the page.

A **definition** is given for each word. An **example** shows the word used in a sentence. Each word is divided into **syllables**. Finally, the **part of speech** is given.

Guide Words

First word on the page — Last word on the page

Sample Entry

Main entry — Definition — Example sentence — Syllable division — Part of speech

burrow A hole dug in the ground by an animal. *A gopher lives in an underground **burrow**.*
bur•row *noun.*

mammal

giggled

desert

Aa

accident A sudden event resulting in loss or injury. *I tripped by **accident** and broke my leg.*
ac·ci·dent *noun.*

adapted Made or became used to. *When he moved to Alaska, he **adapted** to the cold weather.*
a·dapt·ed *verb.* Past tense of **adapt**.

agreed Thought or felt the same way as someone else. *My friends all **agreed** it was a good book.*
a·greed *verb.* Past tense of **agree**.

aid To give help. *I **aid** my grandmother with some household chores.*
aid *verb.*

ancient Having to do with times very long ago. *Scientists found an **ancient** city buried under layers of dirt.*
an·cient *adjective.*

appeal To be attractive or interesting. *Does playing a board game **appeal** to you now?*
ap·peal *verb.*

aroma A pleasant or agreeable smell. *The flowers gave off a wonderful **aroma**.*
a·ro·ma *noun.*

assembled Met together for a purpose. *The crowd **assembled** in the auditorium for the meeting.*
as·sem·bled *verb.* Past tense of **assemble**.

attached Fastened. *Pedro **attached** his poster to the wall with tape.*
at·tached *verb.* Past tense of **attach**.

attention The act of watching or listening carefully. *The clown held the children's **attention** with his balloon shapes.*
at·ten·tion *noun.*

author A person who has written a story, play, article, or poem. *Peggy Rathmann is the **author** of* Officer Buckle and Gloria.
au·thor *noun.*

Bb

beasts Animals that have four feet. *Many **beasts** live at the zoo.*
beasts *plural noun.* Plural of **beast**.

beloved Loved a lot. *The class pet was **beloved** by the students.*
be·lov·ed *adjective.*

beware To be on one's guard; be careful. ***Beware** of speeding cars when crossing the street.*
be·ware *verb.*

beyond Farther on. *Look **beyond** the desert and you'll see the mountains.*
be·yond *preposition, adverb.*

blooming Having flowers. *The rose bushes will be **blooming** in June.*
bloom·ing *adjective.*

buddy A close friend. *His **buddy** goes camping with him.*
bud·dy *noun.*

burrow A hole dug in the ground by an animal. *A gopher lives in an underground **burrow**.*
bur·row *noun.*

Glossary

burst To break open suddenly. *The bag **burst** because I put too much in it.*
burst *verb.*

Cc

calm Not excited or nervous. *Because we stayed **calm** during the fire, we got out safely.*
calm *adjective.*

confirm To show to be true or correct. *Tomorrow's newspaper will **confirm** the report of a fire downtown.*
con·firm *verb.*

condensation The conversion of water from a gas into a liquid. *I saw **condensation** on my glass.*
con·den·sa·tion *noun.*

conservation The wise use of the forests, rivers, minerals, and other natural resources of a country. *Water **conservation** is an important issue in many countries.*
con·ser·va·tion *noun.*

cowboys Those who tend cattle or horses. *The **cowboys** rounded up the cattle.*
cow·boys *plural noun.* Plural of **cowboy**.

Dd

delicious Pleasing or delightful to taste or smell. *The warm apple pie smelled **delicious**.*
de·li·cious *adjective.*

desert A hot, dry, sandy area of land with few or no plants growing on it. *Plants that need a lot of water will not grow in a **desert**.*
des·ert *noun.*

destroy To ruin completely. *A hurricane can **destroy** a building.*
de·stroy *verb.*

devoured Ate or consumed. *The hungry teenager **devoured** the sandwiches.*
de·voured *verb.* Past tense of **devour**.

distant Far away in distance or time; not near. *Some of our **distant** relatives live in Australia.*
dis·tant *adjective.*

drifts Moves because of a current of air or water. *When I stop rowing, my canoe **drifts** along the river.*
drifts *verb.* Present tense of **drift**.

drowns To die by staying underwater and not being able to breathe. *A lifeguard watches the pool carefully to make sure that no one **drowns**.*
drowns *verb.* Present tense of **drown**.

Ee

enormous Much greater than the usual size; very large. *Some dinosaurs were **enormous** compared with animals today.*
e·nor·mous *adjective.*

evaporate The change from a liquid state to a vapor state. *The water began to **evaporate** from the puddles in the street.*
evap·o·rate *verb.*

examines Looks at closely and carefully. *The coach always **examines** the hockey sticks to make sure they are not broken.*
ex·am·ines *verb.* Present tense of **examine**.

extinct When a thing dies out and no more of its kind are living anywhere on Earth. *Dinosaurs are **extinct**.*
ex·tinct *adjective.*

Ff

fetch To go after and bring back; get. *Please **fetch** two more plates from the kitchen.*
fetch *verb.*

fluttered Moved or flew with quick, light, flapping movements. *Moths **fluttered** around the light.*
flut·tered *verb.* Past tense of **flutter**.

force Strength or power. *Wind can have great **force**.*
force *noun.*

frantically Done in a way that is excited by worry or fear. *Maria searched **frantically** for her keys.*
fran·tic·al·ly *adverb.*

friction A rubbing that can slow things. *When I use my feet to stop my bike, I use **friction**.*
fric·tion *noun.*

Gg

gas A substance that spreads to fill a space. *Balloons are filled with air, which is a kind of **gas**.*
gas *noun.*

gasped Said while breathing in suddenly or with effort. *"Help!" **gasped** the struggling child.*
gasped *verb.* Past tense of **gasp**.

gathered Brought together. *Carol **gathered** her favorite books to read on vacation.*
gath·ered *verb.* Past tense of **gather**.

gently Done carefully not to hurt someone or something. *Christopher **gently** stroked the kitten.*
gen·tly *adverb.*

giggled Laughed in a silly or nervous way. *I **giggled** at my mom's funny joke.*
gig·gled *verb.* Past tense of **giggle**.

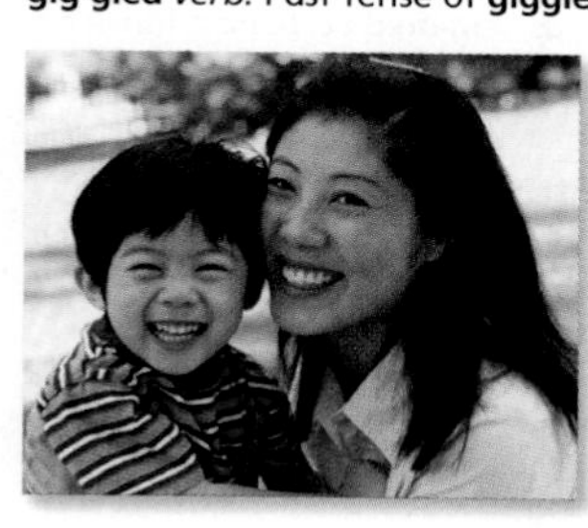

glanced Took a quick look. *The driver **glanced** behind her before safely changing lanes.*
glanced *verb.* Past tense of **glance**.

gleamed Glowed or shone. *The new bike **gleamed** in the sunlight.*
gleamed *verb.* Past tense of **gleam**.

grasslands Lands covered mainly with grass, where animals feed. *Scientists are trying to protect U.S. **grasslands**.*
grass·lands *plural noun.* Plural of **grassland**.

gravity The force that pulls things to Earth and keeps them from floating off into space. ***Gravity** keeps our feet on the ground.*
grav·i·ty *noun.*

Hh

habitats Places where plants and animals live. *Some of the animals' **habitats** are warm and humid while others are cold and dry.*
hab·i·tats *plural noun.* Plural of **habitat.**

handy Within reach. *Dad keeps his car keys **handy** in his front pocket.*
han·dy *adjective.*

hardest Needing or using a lot of work. *My **hardest** chore is cleaning out the garage.*
har·dest *adjective.* Superlative of **hard**.

hatches Comes from an egg. *The baby bird **hatches** from its egg when it is ready.*
hatches *verb.* Present tense of **hatch**.

hazards Things that can cause harm or injury. *Ice, snow, rain, and fog are **hazards** to drivers.*
haz·ards *plural noun.* Plural of **hazard**.

heal To become well or healthy again. *My cut will **heal** after I put a bandage on it.*
heal *verb.*

hopeful Wanting or believing that something wished for will happen. *We are **hopeful** that the rain will stop before the field hockey game starts.*
hope·ful *adjective.*

hunger Pain or weakness caused by not eating enough food. *Some wild animals die from **hunger**.*
hun·ger *noun.*

Ii

informs Gives information to. *The firefighter **informs** the class about fire safety.*
in·forms *verb.* Present tense of **inform**.

interviewed Asked questions to get information. *I **interviewed** the principal for the school newspaper.*
in·ter·viewed *verb.* Past tense of **interview**.

itches Tickling or stinging feelings in the skin. *Kim rubbed her back to scratch her **itches**.*
itch·es *plural noun.* Plural of **itch**.

Jj

jabbing Poking with something pointed. *Jason moved his books so they weren't **jabbing** into his side.*
jab·bing *verb.* Inflected form of **jab**.

Ll

lengthy Being very long in distance or time. *The kangaroo made **lengthy** leaps to cross the field quickly.*
length·y *adjective.*

liquids Materials that are wet and flow. *Water and juice are examples of **liquids.***
liq·uids *plural noun.* Plural of **liquid**.

Mm

mammal A kind of animal that is warm-blooded and has a backbone. Female mammals make milk to feed their young. Most mammals are covered with fur or have some hair. *My teacher told me that a whale is a **mammal**, but a fish is not.*
mam·mal *noun.*

menu A list of food offered in a restaurant. *Patricia likes to read the whole **menu** before choosing what to eat.*
men·u *noun.*

minerals Something found in nature that is not an animal or a plant. *Salt, coal, and gold are **minerals**.*
min·er·als *plural noun.* Plural of **mineral**.

muscles Bundles of tissue that move certain parts of the body. *My aunt goes to the gym every day to keep her **muscles** strong.*
mu·scles *plural noun.* Plural of **muscle**.

Nn

neighbor A person, place, or thing that is near another. *A new **neighbor** moved in next door.*
neigh·bor *noun.*

nibble To eat quickly and with small bites. *A mouse will **nibble** cheese.*
nib·ble *verb.*

noble Impressive looking. *The **noble** lion stood proudly at the opening to the cave.*
no·ble *adjective.*

nocturnal Being seen or happening at night. *Owls are **nocturnal** animals.*
noc·tur·nal *adjective.*

normal Having or showing average health and growth. *The doctor said that it is **normal** for a baby to cry.*
nor·mal *adjective.*

Oo

obeys Does what one is told to do. *The dog **obeys** me when I tell him to stop running.*
o·beys *verb.* Present tense of **obey**.

Pp

patterns The way colors, shapes, and lines are placed. *I like **patterns** with dots and stripes.*
pat·terns *plural noun.* Plural of **pattern**.

peered Looked at closely to see clearly. *Carlos **peered** through a telescope to study the stars.*
peered *verb.* Past tense of **peer**.

personal Having to do with a person. *Denise kept her voice low so no one could hear her **personal** information when she talked on the phone.*
per·son·al *adjective.*

plant To put or set in the ground. *I wanted to **plant** the daffodils in my garden.*
plant *noun.*

preen To make oneself smooth or sleek. *Birds **preen** by washing and smoothing their feathers.*
preen *verb.*

prevent To keep something from happening. *A seat belt will help **prevent** an injury in a car accident.*
prevent *verb.*

prey An animal that is hunted by another animal for food. *Rabbits, birds, and snakes are the **prey** of foxes.*
prey *noun.*

prickly Having small, sharp thorns or points. *The cactus plants are **prickly**.*
prick·ly *adjective.*

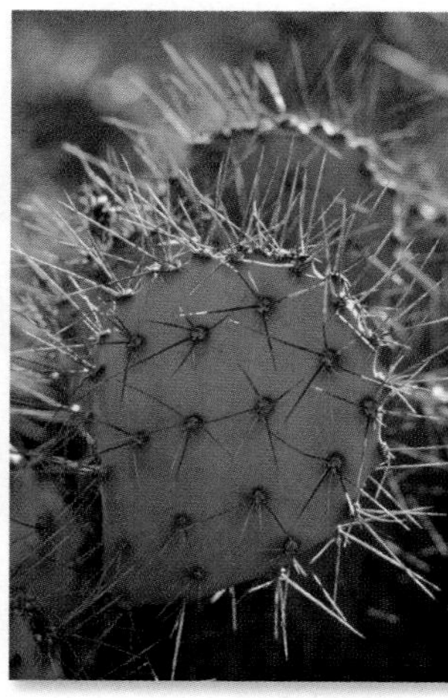

promised Said that something will or will not happen. *I **promised** that I would clean my room.*
prom·ised *verb.* Past tense of **promise**.

puddles Small, shallow pools of water or other liquids. *Our driveway has many **puddles** after a storm.*
pud·dles *plural noun.* Plural of **puddle**.

Rr

randomly Made or done by chance, with no clear pattern. *The teacher **randomly** called three students to the front of the room.*
ran·dom·ly *adverb.*

recognized Knew and remembered from before. *I **recognized** my teacher standing in line at the movies.*
rec·og·nized *verb.* Past tense of **recognize**.

remains Things that are left. *The explorers found the **remains** of an ancient building.*
re·mains *noun.*

rescued Saved or freed. *The firefighter **rescued** the cat that had been stuck in the tree.*
res·cued *verb.* Past tense of **rescue**.

roam To move from place to place without somewhere special to go. *The cows **roam** all over the fields as they eat.*
roam *verb.*

route A road or other course used for traveling. *We took a different **route** to the beach because of the traffic.*
route *noun.*

Ss

scent A smell. *The **scent** of roses filled the air.*
scent *noun.*

seed The part of a plant from which a new plant will grow. *We planted a pumpkin **seed** in the garden to try to grow pumpkins next year.*
seed *noun.*

serious Dangerous. *The doctor told us that cancer is a **serious** illness.*
se·ri·ous *adjective.*

signal A way of showing people to do something. *A red traffic light is a **signal** to stop.*
sig·nal *noun.*

simmered Cooked at or just below the boiling point. *The soup **simmered** on the stove all day.*
sim·mered *verb.* Past tense of **simmer**.

site A place where something has happened or will happen. *The battle **site** is just outside the castle's wall.*
site *noun.*

snuggled Lay close together or held closely for warmth or protection, or to show love. *I **snuggled** up against my mom during the thunderstorm.*
snug·gled *verb.* Past tense of **snuggle**.

solids Firm materials with definite shape. *Rocks are examples of **solids**.*
solids *plural noun.* Plural of **solid**.

stages The different steps or times in a process. *During all **stages** of growth, a flower needs water.*
stag·es *plural noun.* Plural of **stage**.

sunlight The light of the sun. *We enjoyed the bright **sunlight** at the beach.*
sun·light *noun.*

swung Moved back and forth. *We **swung** back and forth on the monkey bars.*
swung *verb.* Past tense of **swing**.